Prentice Hall Realidades 1

Peggy Palo Boyles

OKLAHOMA CITY, OK

Myriam Met

ROCKVILLE, MD

Richard S. Sayers

LONGMONT, CO

Carol Eubanks Wargin

PEARSON

Boston, Massachusetts | Chandler, Arizona
Glenview, Illinois | Upper Saddle River, New Jersey

WE DEDICATE THIS BOOK TO THE
MEMORY OF OUR ESTEEMED COLLEAGUE,
Carol Eubanks Wargin.

Acknowledgments appear on pages 511–513,
which constitute an extension of this
copyright page.

ISBN-13: 978-0-13-369172-6
ISBN-10: 0-13-369172-1
ISBN-NY: 0-13-253514-9

4 5 6 7 8 9 10 11 V052 14 13 12 11 10

Prentice Hall

Realidades 1

"¡Bienvenidos a *Realidades 1* y a

realidades.com ➤ !"

Realidades Authors

Peggy Palo Boyles

During her foreign language career of over thirty years, Peggy Palo Boyles has taught elementary, secondary, and university students in both private and public schools. She is currently an independent consultant who provides assistance to schools, districts, universities, state departments of education, and other organizations of foreign language education in the areas of curriculum, assessment, cultural instruction, professional development, and program evaluation. She was a member of the ACTFL Performance Guidelines for the K–12 Learners task force and served as a Senior Editor for the project. She currently serves on the Advisory Committee for the ACTFL Assessment for Performance and Proficiency of Languages (AAPPL). Peggy is a Past-President of the National Association of District Supervisors of Foreign Language (NADSFL) and was a recipient of ACTFL's K–12 Steiner Award for Leadership in K–12 Foreign Language Education. Peggy lives in Oklahoma City, OK with her husband, Del. Their son, Ryan, works at the University of Texas at Arlington.

Myriam Met

For most of her professional life, Myriam (Mimi) Met has worked in the public schools, first as a high school teacher in New York, then as K–12 supervisor of language programs in the Cincinnati Public Schools, and finally as a Coordinator of Foreign Language in Montgomery County (MD) Public Schools. She is currently a Senior Research Associate at the National Foreign Language Center, University of Maryland, where she works on K–12 language policy and infrastructure development. Mimi Met has served on the Advisory Board for the National Standards for Foreign Language Learning, on the Executive Council of ACTFL, and as President of the National Association of District Supervisors of Foreign Languages (NADSFL). She has been honored by ACTFL with the Steiner Award for Leadership in K–12 Foreign Language Education and the Papalia Award for Excellence in Teacher Education.

Richard S. Sayers

Rich Sayers has been an educator in world languages since 1978. He taught Spanish at Niwot High School in Longmont, CO for 18 years, where he taught levels 1 through AP Spanish. While at Niwot High School, Rich served as department chair, district foreign language coordinator, and board member of the Colorado Congress of Foreign Language Teachers. Rich has also served on the Board of the Southwest Conference on Language Teaching. In 1991, Rich was selected as one of the Disney Company's Foreign Language Teacher Honorees for the American Teacher Awards. Rich has served as a world languages consultant for Pearson since 1996. He is currently the Curriculum Specialist Manager for Pearson in the Mountain Region.

Carol Eubanks Wargin

Carol Eubanks Wargin taught Spanish for 20 years at Glen Crest Middle School, Glen Ellyn, IL, and also served as Foreign Languages department chair. In 1997, Ms. Wargin's presentation "From Text to Test: How to Land Where You Planned" was honored as the best presentation at the Illinois Conference on the Teaching of Foreign Languages (ICTFL) and at the Central States Conference on the Teaching of Foreign Languages (CSC). She was twice named Outstanding Young Educator by the Jaycees. Ms. Wargin passed away in 2004.

Contributing Writers

Eduardo Aparicio
Chicago, IL

Daniel J. Bender
New Trier High School
Winnetka, IL

Marie Deer
Bloomington, IN

Leslie M. Grahn
Howard County Public Schools
Ellicott City, MD

Thomasina Hannum
Albuquerque, NM

Nancy S. Hernández
World Languages Supervisor
Simsbury (CT) Public Schools

Patricia J. Kule
Fountain Valley School
   of Colorado
Colorado Springs, CO

Jacqueline Hall Minet
Upper Montclair, NJ

Alex Paredes
Simi Valley, CA

Martha Singer Semmer
Breckenridge, CO

Dee Dee Drisdale Stafford
Putnam City Schools
Oklahoma City, OK

Christine S. Wells
Cheyenne Mountain
   Junior High School
Colorado Springs, CO

Michael Werner
University of Chicago
Chicago, IL

National Consultants

Lucy Amarillo
Yorktown, VA

María R. Hubbard
Braintree, MA

Patrick T. Raven
Milwaukee, WI

Tabla de materias

Para empezar   **xxxii**

- Greet people at different times of the day
- Introduce yourself to others
- Respond to classroom directions
- Begin using numbers
- Tell time
- Identify parts of the body

- Talk about things in the classroom
- Ask questions about new words and phrases
- Use the Spanish alphabet to spell words
- Talk about things related to the calendar
- Learn about the Aztec calendar

- Describe weather conditions
- Identify the seasons
- Compare weather in the Northern and Southern Hemispheres

realidades.com

eBook, pp. xxxii–23
eBook activities, pp. xxxii–23
Leveled Vocabulary and Grammar Workbook
Audio activities
Puzzles
Self-test

Online Table of Contents, Web Code: jck-0001

Tema 1 Mis amigos y yo

 ¿Qué te gusta hacer? **24**

 Y tú, ¿cómo eres? **48**

Video

Videocultura
Mis amigos y yo
Videohistoria
1A *¿Qué te gusta hacer?*, pp. 28–29
1B *Amigos por Internet*, pp. 52–53
GramActiva
1A Infinitives, p. 32
1A Making negative statements, p. 36

1B Adjectives, p. 55
1B Definite and indefinite articles, p. 60
1B Word order: Placement of adjectives, p. 62

realidades.com

eBook, pp. 24–71
eBook activities, pp. 24–71
Leveled Vocabulary and Grammar Workbook
Audio and Video activities
Canciones de hip hop:
Mambo, ¿Cómo soy yo?
Tutorials: Affirmative and negative;

Conjunction & infinitive; Making a sentence negative; Formation of negative sentences; Definite and indefinite articles; Position of Adjectives; Adjective clauses; Adjectives
Flashcards: Ch. 1A and 1B
Puzzles
Self-test

Tema 2 La escuela

realidades.com ✓

eBook, pp. 72–121
eBook activities, pp. 72–121
Leveled Vocabulary and Grammar Workbook
Audio and Video activities
Canciones de hip hop:
En la clase, ¿Qué hay?
Tutorials: Ordinal Numbers; Present indicative; Pronouns; Subject pronouns,
Subject & verb agreement; Subjects; Verbs; -ar verbs; Singular and plural; Definite and indefinite articles; *Estar;* Noun-adjective agreement; Singular and plural formation

Verb conjugator: *estar, hablar*

Flashcards: Ch. 2A and 2B

Puzzles

Self-test

Video

Videocultura
La escuela
Videohistoria
2A *El primer día de clases*, pp. 76–77
2B *Un ratón en la clase*, pp. 102–103
GramActiva
2A Subject pronouns, p. 82

2A Present tense of -ar verbs, p. 84
2B The verb *estar*, p. 107
2B The plural of nouns and articles, p. 110

Tema 3 **La comida**

realidades.com ⊘

eBook, pp. 122–169
eBook activities, pp. 122–169
Leveled Vocabulary and Grammar Workbook
Audio and Video activities
Canciones de hip hop:
¿Qué comes?,

¿Sabroso o malo?
Tutorials: -er verbs; -ir verbs; Regular verbs; Stem-endings; ser
Verb conjugator: comer, compartir, ser
Flashcards: Ch. 3A and 3B
Puzzles
Self-test

Video 🖥

Videocultura
La comida
Videohistoria
3A *El desayuno,* pp. 126–127
3B *Para mantener la salud,* pp. 150–151
GramActiva
3A Present tense of

-er and -ir verbs, p. 132
3A *Me gustan, me encantan,* p. 135
3B The plurals of adjectives, p. 156
3B The verb *ser,* p. 158

Tema 4 Los pasatiempos

eBook, pp. 170–219
eBook activities, pp. 170–219
Leveled Vocabulary and Grammar Workbook
Audio and Video activities
Canciones de hip hop: ¿Adónde vas?, ¿Qué vas a hacer?
Tutorials: Question words; Questions;

Formation of yes-no questions; Questions with interrogative words; Future with *ir + a +* infinitive; *Vamos a +* infinitive
Verb conjugator: *ir, jugar*
Flashcards: Ch. 4A and 4B
Puzzles
Self-test

Video

Videocultura
Los pasatiempos
Videohistoria
4A *Un chico reservado,* pp. 174–175
4B *¡A jugar!,* pp. 200–201

GramActiva
4A The verb *ir,* p. 180
4A Asking questions, p. 184
4B *Ir + a +* infinitive, p. 206
4B The verb *jugar,* p. 208

Tema 5 Fiesta en familia

Video

Videocultura
Fiesta en familia
Videohistoria
5A *¡Feliz
cumpleaños!*,
pp. 224–225
5B *En el restaurante
Casa Río*, pp. 250–251
GramActiva
5A The verb *tener*,
p. 228

5A Possessive
adjectives, p. 232
5B The verb *venir*,
p. 256
5B The verbs *ser* and
estar, p. 258
Videomisterio
¿Eres tú, María?
Episodios 1 y 2

realidades.com

eBook, pp. 220–269
eBook activities,
pp. 220–269
**Leveled Vocabulary
and Grammar
Workbook**
**Audio and Video
activities**
*Canciones de
hip hop:*
*Fiesta de cumpleaños,
Camarero*

Tutorials: Possessive
adjectives; Possessive
adjectives (Long
form); Irregular verbs;
Possessive with *de* +
pronoun; *Tener; Tener
que; Ser* and *estar*

Verb conjugator:
estar, ser, tener, venir

Flashcards: Ch. 5A
and 5B

Puzzles

Self-test

Tema 6 La casa

Video

Videocultura
La casa
Videohistoria
6A *El cuarto de Ignacio*, pp. 274–275
6B *Los quehaceres de Elena*, pp. 300–301
GramActiva
6A Making comparisons, p. 278
6A The superlative, p. 280

6A Stem-changing verbs: *poder* and *dormir*, p. 284
6B Affirmative *tú* commands, p. 305
6B The present progressive tense, p. 308
Videomisterio
¿Eres tú, María?, Episodios 3 y 4

realidades.com

eBook, pp. 270–319
eBook activities, pp. 270–319
Leveled Vocabulary and Grammar Workbook
Audio and Video activities
Canciones de hip hop:
No podemos dormir, Cenicienta

Tutorials: Comparing things that are equal; Comparing things that are not equal; Superlatives
Verb conjugator: *dormir, poder*
Flashcards: Ch. 6A and 6B
Puzzles
Self-test

Tema 7 De compras

Video

Videocultura
De compras
Videohistoria
7A *Una noche
especial,* pp. 324–325
7B *Un regalo especial,*
pp. 348–349
GramActiva
7A Stem-changing
verbs: *pensar, querer,*
and *preferir,* p. 330

7A Demonstrative
adjectives, p. 332
7B The preterite of *-ar*
verbs, p. 354
7B The preterite of
verbs ending in *-car*
and *-gar,* p. 356
7B Direct object
pronouns, p. 360
Videomisterio
¿Eres tú, María?,
Episodios 5 y 6

 **realidades.com**

eBook, pp. 320–371
eBook activities,
pp. 320–371
**Leveled Vocabulary
and Grammar
Workbook**
**Audio and Video
activities**
*Canciones de
hip hop:*
*¿Quieres ir de
compras?, ¿Qué
compraste ayer?*
Tutorials:
Demonstrative

adjectives; *Querer;*
Past tense; Tense;
Hacer in time
expressions; Preterit
Verb conjugator:
*buscar, comprar, jugar,
pagar, pensar,
practicar, preferir,
querer, sacar, tocar*
Flashcards: Ch. 7A
and 7B
Puzzles
Self-test

Tema 8 Experiencias

Video

Videocultura
Experiencias
Videohistoria
8A *¿Qué te pasó?*,
pp. 376–377
8B *Cómo ayudamos
a los demás*,
pp. 402–403
GramActiva
8A The preterite of *-er*
and *-ir* verbs, p. 383

8A Preterite of *ir*, p. 385
8A The personal *a*, p. 387
8B The present tense of
decir, p. 408
8B Indirect object
pronouns, p. 410
8B The preterite of
hacer and *dar*, p. 412
Videomisterio
¿Eres tú, María?,
Episodios 7 y 8

realidades.com

eBook, pp. 372–423
eBook activities,
pp. 372–423
**Leveled Vocabulary
and Grammar
Workbook**
**Audio and Video
activities**
*Canciones de
hip hop:*
*¿Adónde fuiste?,
Experiencia
inolvidable*

Tutorials: Personal *a*;
Indirect object
pronouns; Indirect
objects; *Decir*

Verb conjugator:
*aprender, dar, decir,
hacer, ir, salir, ver*

Flashcards: Ch. 8A
and 8B

Puzzles

Self-test

Tema 9 Medios de comunicación

Video

Videocultura
Medios de comunicación
Videohistoria
9A *¿Qué dan en la tele?*, pp. 428–429
9B *¿Cómo se comunica?*, pp. 452–453
GramActiva
9A *Acabar de* + infinitive, p. 434

9A *Gustar* and similar verbs, p. 436
9B The present tense of *pedir* and *servir*, p. 458
9B *Saber* and *conocer*, p. 460
Videomisterio
¿Eres tú, María?, Episodios 9 y 10

 **realidades.com**

eBook, pp. 424–471
eBook activities, pp. 424–471
Leveled Vocabulary and Grammar Workbook
Audio and Video activities
Canciones de hip hop:
¿Qué te interesa?, Tecnología
Tutorials: *Acabar de* + infinitive; *Gustar* and

similar verbs; Adverbs; Adverbial clause; *Pedir;*
Verb conjugator: *aburrir, acabar, conocer, doler, encantar, faltar, gustar, interesar, pedir, quedar, saber, servir*
Flashcards: Ch. 9A and 9B
Puzzles
Self-test

México

Ciudad de Guanajuato, México

El Zócalo, México, D.F.

México

Capital: México, D.F.

Population: 110 million

Area: 761,606 sq mi / 1,972,550 sq km

Languages: Spanish (official), Nahuatl, various Mayan and other indigenous languages

Religions: Roman Catholic, Protestant

Government: federal republic

Currency: *peso mexicano*

Exports: manufactured products, oil and oil products, silver, coffee, cotton

Tijuana

Estados Unidos

realidades.com
- Online Atlas
- Web Code: jce-0002

Ciudad
Juárez

Chihuahua

SIERRA MADRE OCCIDENTAL

SIERRA MADRE ORIENTAL

Nuevo
Laredo

Monterrey

Golfo de México

México

OCÉANO PACÍFICO

Guadalajara

Querétaro

Mérida

Paracutín ▲ Ciudad
de
México

Iztaccíhuatl
★ Popócatépetl ▲
Puebla

Veracruz

SIERRA MADRE DEL SUR

Oaxaca

ISTMO DE
TEHUANTEPEC

Belice

Acapulco

Guatemala

Metros		Pies
Más de 3,000		Más de 9,840
2,000–3,000		6,560–9,840
1,000–2,000		3,280–6,560
500–1,000		1,640–3,280
200–500		656–1,640
0–200		0–656

–·–·– Frontera nacional
★ Capital
● Ciudad
▲ Volcán o montaña

norte
oeste ✺ este
sur

0   200   400 millas
0   200   400 kilómetros

Sierra Tarahumara

México **xvii**

América Central

Guatemala

Capital: Ciudad de Guatemala

Population: 13 million

Area: 42,043 sq mi / 108,890 sq km

Languages: Spanish (official), Quiche, Cakchiquel, Kekchi, Mam, Garifuna, Xinca, and other indigenous languages

Religions: Roman Catholic, Protestant, traditional Mayan beliefs

Government: constitutional democratic republic

Currency: *quetzal*, U.S. dollar *(dólar)*

Exports: coffee, sugar, petroleum, clothing, textiles, bananas, vegetables

Honduras

Capital: Tegucigalpa

Population: 7.6 million

Area: 43,278 sq mi / 112,090 sq km

Languages: Spanish (official), indigenous languages

Religions: Roman Catholic, Protestant

Government: democratic constitutional republic

Currency: *lempira*

Exports: coffee, bananas, shrimp, lobster, meat, zinc, wood

El Salvador

Capital: San Salvador

Population: 7.1 million

Area: 8,124 sq mi / 21,040 sq km

Languages: Spanish (official), Nahua

Religions: Roman Catholic, Protestant

Government: republic

Currency: U.S. dollar *(dólar)*

Exports: offshore assembly parts, equipment, coffee, sugar, shrimp, textiles, chemicals, electricity

El Canal de Panamá

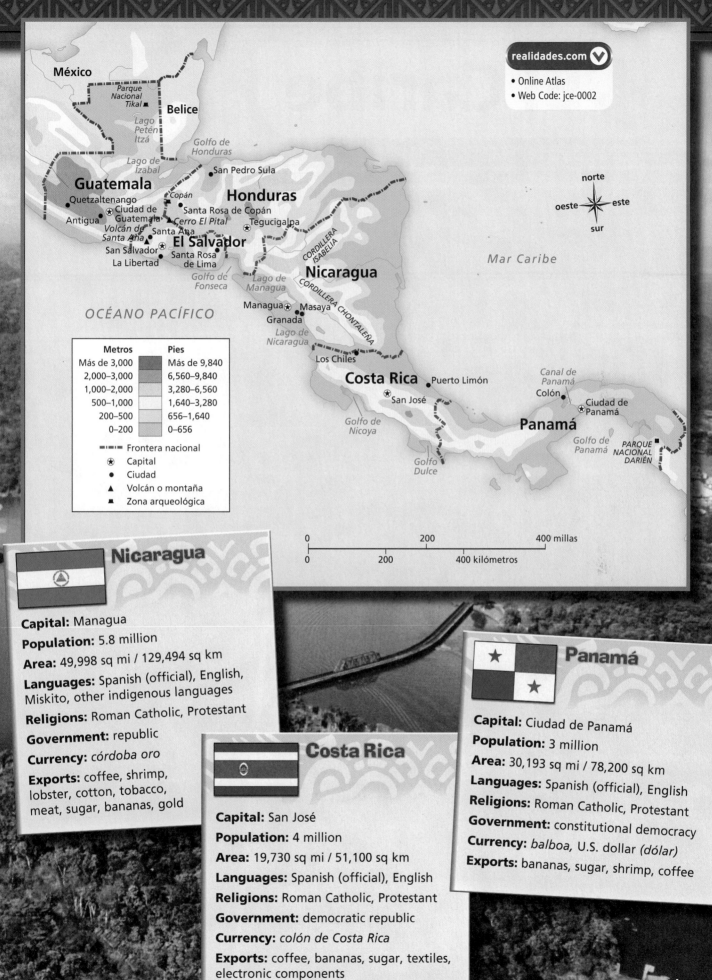

México

Parque Nacional Tikal ▪

Belice

Lago Petén Itzá

Golfo de Honduras

Guatemala

San Pedro Sula

Quetzaltenango

Copán

Honduras

Ciudad de Guatemala ⊛

Santa Rosa de Copán

Antigua

Cerro El Pital ▲

Tegucigalpa ⊛

Volcán de Santa Ana ▲

Santa Ana

El Salvador

San Salvador ⊛

Santa Rosa de Lima

CORDILLERA ISABELIA

La Libertad

Golfo de Fonseca

Nicaragua

Lago de Managua

Managua ⊛ Masaya

Granada

Lago de Nicaragua

CORDILLERA CHONTALEÑA

Mar Caribe

OCÉANO PACÍFICO

Los Chiles

Costa Rica

Puerto Limón

Canal de Panamá

San José ⊛

Colón

Ciudad de Panamá

Golfo de Nicoya

Panamá

Golfo de Panamá

PARQUE NACIONAL DARIÉN ▪

Golfo Dulce

norte

oeste ⊹ este

sur

realidades.com ⓥ
• Online Atlas
• Web Code: jce-0002

Metros

Más de 3,000	Más de 9,840
2,000–3,000	6,560–9,840
1,000–2,000	3,280–6,560
500–1,000	1,640–3,280
200–500	656–1,640
0–200	0–656

Pies

—▪—▪— Frontera nacional
⊛ Capital
● Ciudad
▲ Volcán o montaña
▪ Zona arqueológica

| 0 | 200 | 400 millas |
| 0 | 200 | 400 kilómetros |

Nicaragua

Capital: Managua

Population: 5.8 million

Area: 49,998 sq mi / 129,494 sq km

Languages: Spanish (official), English, Miskito, other indigenous languages

Religions: Roman Catholic, Protestant

Government: republic

Currency: *córdoba oro*

Exports: coffee, shrimp, lobster, cotton, tobacco, meat, sugar, bananas, gold

Costa Rica

Capital: San José

Population: 4 million

Area: 19,730 sq mi / 51,100 sq km

Languages: Spanish (official), English

Religions: Roman Catholic, Protestant

Government: democratic republic

Currency: *colón de Costa Rica*

Exports: coffee, bananas, sugar, textiles, electronic components

Panamá

Capital: Ciudad de Panamá

Population: 3 million

Area: 30,193 sq mi / 78,200 sq km

Languages: Spanish (official), English

Religions: Roman Catholic, Protestant

Government: constitutional democracy

Currency: *balboa*, U.S. dollar (*dólar*)

Exports: bananas, sugar, shrimp, coffee

El Caribe

El Morro, San Juan,
Puerto Rico

El arrecife de coral, República Dominicana

Estados Unidos

Golfo de México

Islas Bahamas

OCÉANO ATLÁNTICO

Estrecho de la Florida

norte
oeste · este
sur

La Habana

Cuba

Isla de la Juventud

Guantánamo

Santiago de Cuba

República Dominicana

Bahía de Samaná

Puerto Rico

Vieques

San Juan

El Yunque

Ponce

Haití

Santo Domingo

Jamaica

Mar Caribe

Metros	Pies
Más de 3,000	Más de 9,840
2,000–3,000	6,560–9,840
1,000–2,000	3,280–6,560
500–1,000	1,640–3,280
200–500	656–1,640
0–200	0–656

0   150   300 millas
0   150   300 kilómetros

Frontera nacional
⊛ Capital
● Ciudad
▲ Volcán o montaña

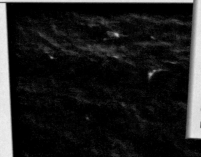

República Dominicana

Capital: Santo Domingo

Population: 9.5 million

Area: 18,815 sq mi / 48,730 sq km

Languages: Spanish (official)

Religions: Roman Catholic, Protestant

Government: representative democracy

Currency: *peso dominicano*

Exports: ferronickel, sugar, gold, silver, cocoa, tobacco, meat

Puerto Rico

Capital: San Juan

Population: 3.9 million

Area: 3,515 sq mi / 9,104 sq km

Languages: Spanish and English (both official)

Religions: Roman Catholic, Protestant

Government: commonwealth of the United States

Currency: U.S. dollar

Exports: chemicals, electronics, apparel, canned tuna, beverage concentrates, medical equipment

Cuba

Capital: La Habana

Population: 11.3 million

Area: 42,803 sq mi / 110,860 sq km

Languages: Spanish (official)

Religions: Roman Catholic, Protestant, and other religions

Government: Communist state

Currency: *peso cubano*

Exports: sugar, nickel, tobacco, shellfish, medical products, citrus, coffee

América del Sur
(Parte norte)

Colombia

Capital: Bogotá

Population: 45 million

Area: 439,736 sq mi / 1,138,910 sq km

Languages: Spanish (official)

Religion: Roman Catholic

Government: republic

Currency: *peso colombiano*

Exports: textiles, petroleum, coal, coffee, gold, emeralds, bananas, flowers, pharmaceuticals, sugar

Ecuador

Capital: Quito

Population: 13.9 million

Area: 109,483 sq mi / 283,560 sq km

Languages: Spanish (official), Quechua, other indigenous languages

Religion: Roman Catholic

Government: republic

Currency: U.S. dollar *(dólar)*

Exports: oil, bananas, tuna, shrimp, cocoa, gold, tropical wood

Perú

Capital: Lima

Population: 27.9 million

Area: 496,226 sq mi / 1,285,220 sq km

Languages: Spanish (official), Quechua (official), Aymara, and other indigenous languages

Religion: Roman Catholic and other religions

Government: constitutional republic

Currency: *nuevo sol*

Exports: gold, zinc, copper, fish and fish products, textiles

Las ruinas de Machu Picchu, Pe

Mar Caribe

Maracaíbo
Cartagena
Caracas
Rio Orinoco

Venezuela

Medellín
Bogotá
Cali

Colombia

Ecuador

realidades.com
• Online Atlas
• Web Code: jce-0002

Ecuador
Quito
Chimborazo
Guayaquil
ISLAS GALÁPAGOS (Ecuador)
Golfo de Guayaquil

CORDILLERA DE LOS ANDES

Perú

Brasil

Huascarán

Machu Picchu
Callao
Cuzco
Lima
Bolivia

OCÉANO PACÍFICO

La Paz
Cochabamba
Sucre
Nevado Sajama
Potosí

Lago Titicaca

Trópico de Capricornio

Chile

Paraguay

Trópico de Capricornio

Argentina

OCÉANO ATLÁNTICO

Uruguay

Metros	Pies
Más de 3,000	Más de 9,840
2,000–3,000	6,560–9,840
1,000–2,000	3,280–6,560
500–1,000	1,640–3,280
200–500	656–1,640
0–200	0–656

━·━·━ Frontera nacional
⭐ Capital
● Ciudad
▲ Volcán o montaña
■ Zona arqueológica

0   400   800 millas
0   400   800 kilómetros

norte
oeste ✦ este
sur

Bolivia

Capital: La Paz, Sucre
Population: 9.2 million
Area: 424,164 sq mi / 1,098,580 sq km
Languages: Spanish, Quechua, Aymara (all official)
Religions: Roman Catholic, Protestant
Government: republic
Currency: *boliviano*
Exports: soy, natural gas, zinc, wood, gold

Venezuela

Capital: Caracas
Population: 26.4 million
Area: 352,144 sq mi / 912,050 sq km
Languages: Spanish (official), various indigenous languages
Religions: Roman Catholic, Protestant
Government: federal republic
Currency: *bolívar*
Exports: oil and oil products, bananas, steel, aluminum, hydroelectricity

América del Sur
(Parte sur)

El Monte Fitz Roy, Patagonia, Argentina

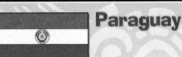
Paraguay

Capital: Asunción

Population: 6.8 million

Area: 157,047 sq mi / 406,750 sq km

Languages: Spanish and Guaraní (both official)

Religions: Roman Catholic, Protestant

Government: constitutional republic

Currency: *Guaraní*

Exports: sugar, meat, tapioca, hydroelectricity

Chile

Capital: Santiago

Population: 16 million

Area: 292,260 sq mi / 756,950 sq km

Languages: Spanish (official)

Religions: Roman Catholic, Protestant

Government: republic

Currency: *peso chileno*

Exports: copper, fish, iron, iodine, fruit, wood, paper and pulp, chemicals

Argentina

Capital: Buenos Aires

Population: 39.5 million

Area: 1,068,302 sq mi / 2,766,890 sq km

Languages: Spanish (official), English, French, Italian, German

Religions: Roman Catholic, Protestant, Jewish

Government: republic

Currency: *peso argentino*

Exports: meat, edible oils, fuels and energy, cereals, feed, motor vehicles

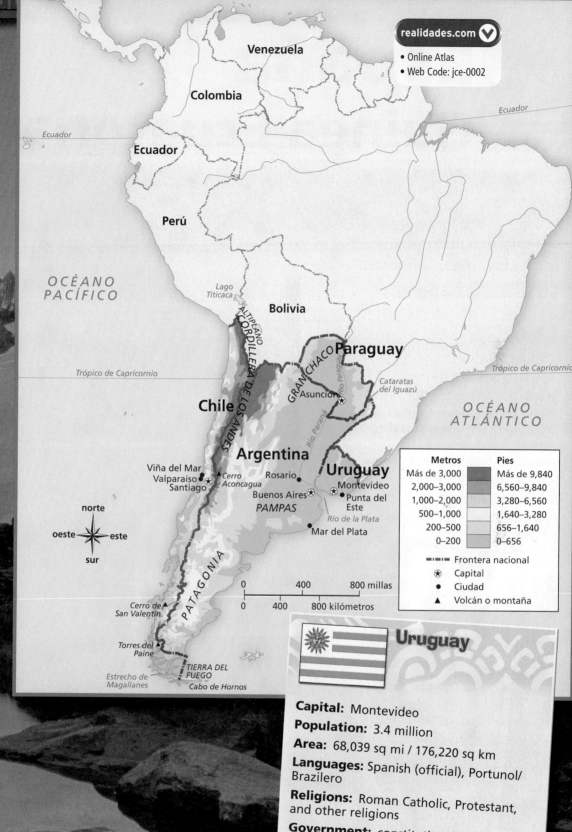

Venezuela

Colombia

Ecuador

Ecuador

Ecuador

Perú

OCÉANO
PACÍFICO

Lago
Titicaca

Bolivia

ALTIPLANO

CORDILLERA DE LOS ANDES

Trópico de Capricornio

Paraguay

GRAN CHACO

Río Paraguay

Cataratas
del Iguazú

Asunción ⊛

Chile

Río Paraná

OCÉANO
ATLÁNTICO

Trópico de Capricornio

Argentina

Viña del Mar
Valparaíso ●
Santiago ⊛

▲ Cerro
Aconcagua

Rosario ●

Uruguay

Montevideo
⊛ ● Punta del
Este

Buenos Aires ⊛
PAMPAS

Río de la Plata

Mar del Plata ●

Metros	Pies
Más de 3,000	Más de 9,840
2,000–3,000	6,560–9,840
1,000–2,000	3,280–6,560
500–1,000	1,640–3,280
200–500	656–1,640
0–200	0–656

norte
oeste ✶ este
sur

PATAGONIA

Cerro de ▲
San Valentín

----- Frontera nacional
⊛ Capital
● Ciudad
▲ Volcán o montaña

0   400   800 millas
0   400   800 kilómetros

Torres del ▲
Paine

TIERRA DEL
FUEGO

Estrecho de
Magallanes

Cabo de Hornos

Uruguay

Capital: Montevideo

Population: 3.4 million

Area: 68,039 sq mi / 176,220 sq km

Languages: Spanish (official), Portunol/
Brazilero

Religions: Roman Catholic, Protestant,
and other religions

Government: constitutional republic

Currency: peso uruguayo

Exports: foods, vehicles, meat, rice, timber

España
Guinea Ecuatorial

España

Capital: Madrid

Population: 40.3 million

Area: 194,897 sq mi / 504,782 sq km

Official Language: Castilian Spanish;
Regional Languages: Catalan, Galician, Basque, Valencian

Religion: Roman Catholic

Government: parliamentary monarchy

Currency: *euro*

Exports: food, machinery, motor vehicles

El Alcázar de Segovia, Segovia, España

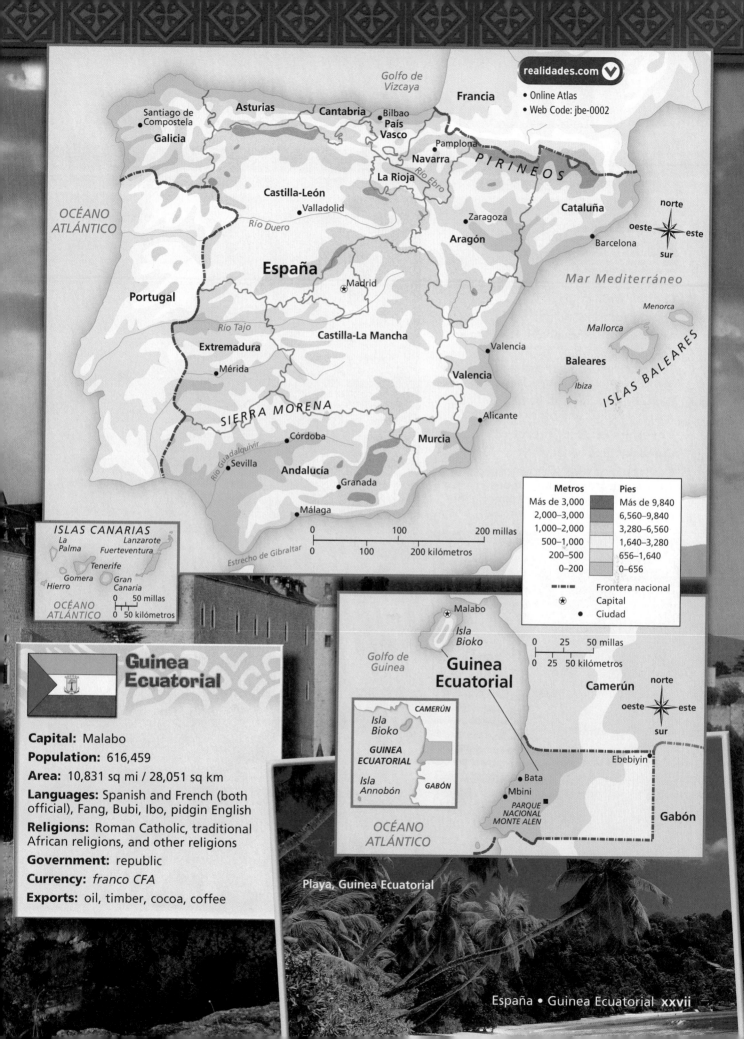

Golfo de Vizcaya

Francia

Santiago de Compostela

Asturias

Cantabria

Bilbao
País Vasco

Galicia

Pamplona

Navarra

P I R I N E O S

OCÉANO ATLÁNTICO

La Rioja

Río Ebro

Castilla-León

Valladolid

Zaragoza

Cataluña

norte
oeste · este
sur

España

Madrid

Aragón

Barcelona

Portugal

Río Duero

Mar Mediterráneo

Río Tajo

Menorca

Mallorca

Extremadura

Castilla-La Mancha

Valencia

Baleares

Mérida

Ibiza

ISLAS BALEARES

Valencia

SIERRA MORENA

Alicante

Córdoba

Río Guadalquivir

Sevilla

Murcia

Andalucía

Granada

Málaga

0   100   200 millas
0   100   200 kilómetros

Estrecho de Gibraltar

ISLAS CANARIAS
La Palma   Lanzarote
Fuerteventura
Tenerife
Gomera   Gran Canaria
Hierro

OCÉANO ATLÁNTICO

0   50 millas
0   50 kilómetros

Metros	Pies
Más de 3,000	Más de 9,840
2,000–3,000	6,560–9,840
1,000–2,000	3,280–6,560
500–1,000	1,640–3,280
200–500	656–1,640
0–200	0–656

– – – Frontera nacional
⊛ Capital
● Ciudad

Guinea Ecuatorial

Capital: Malabo

Population: 616,459

Area: 10,831 sq mi / 28,051 sq km

Languages: Spanish and French (both official), Fang, Bubi, Ibo, pidgin English

Religions: Roman Catholic, traditional African religions, and other religions

Government: republic

Currency: *franco CFA*

Exports: oil, timber, cocoa, coffee

Malabo

Isla Bioko

Golfo de Guinea

Guinea Ecuatorial

Camerún

0   25   50 millas
0   25   50 kilómetros

norte
oeste · este
sur

CAMERÚN

Isla Bioko

GUINEA ECUATORIAL

GABÓN

Isla Annobón

Ebebiyin

Bata
Mbini

PARQUE NACIONAL MONTE ALEN

Gabón

OCÉANO ATLÁNTICO

Playa, Guinea Ecuatorial

España · Guinea Ecuatorial **xxvii**

Estados Unidos

Estados Unidos

Capital: Washington, D.C.

Population: 296 million

Area: 3,717,813 sq mi / 9,631,418 sq km

Languages: English, Spanish, other Indo-European languages, Asian and Pacific Islander languages, other languages

Religions: Protestant, Roman Catholic, Jewish, Muslim, and other religions

Government: federal republic

Currency: U.S. dollar

Exports: motor vehicles, aerospace equipment, telecommunications equipment, electronics, consumer goods, chemicals, food, wheat, corn

Las grandes llanuras

Caras estadounidenses

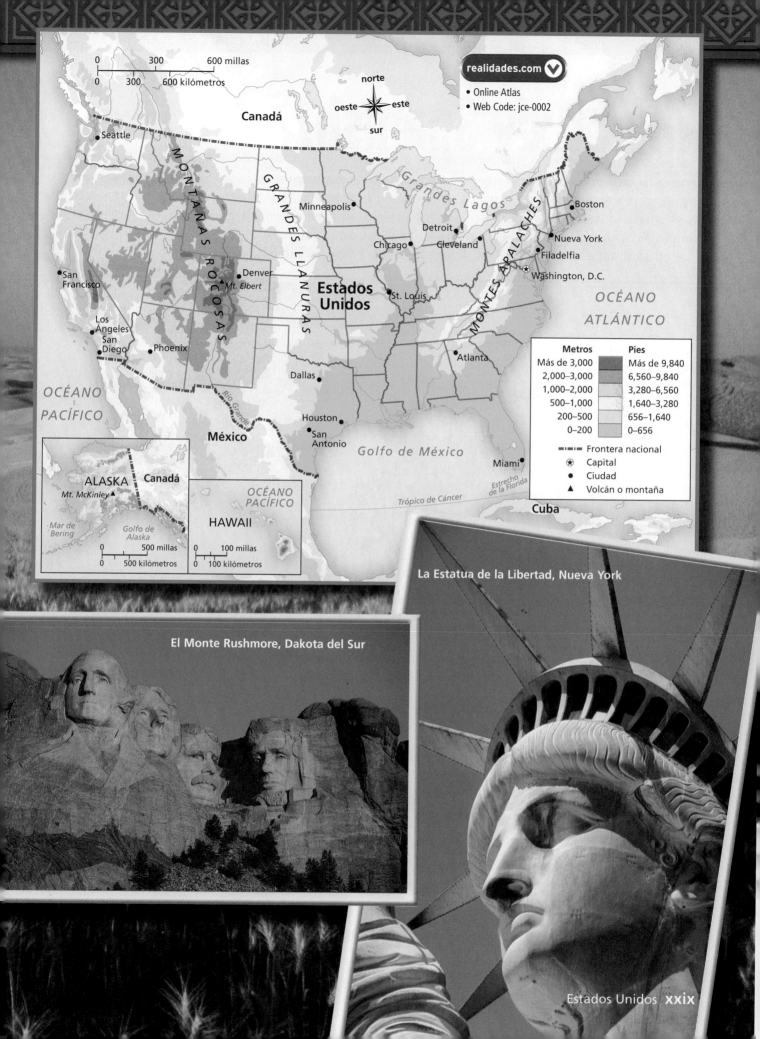

Canadá

norte
oeste · este
sur

0   300   600 millas
0   300   600 kilómetros

realidades.com
• Online Atlas
• Web Code: jce-0002

Seattle

MONTAÑAS ROCOSAS

GRANDES LLANURAS

Grandes Lagos

MONTES APALACHES

Minneapolis

Detroit

Boston

San Francisco

Denver
Mt. Elbert

Chicago

Cleveland

Nueva York

Filadelfia

Washington, D.C.

Estados Unidos

St. Louis

OCÉANO ATLÁNTICO

Los Ángeles
San Diego

Phoenix

Atlanta

Dallas

OCÉANO PACÍFICO

Río Grande

Houston
San Antonio

México

Golfo de México

Miami

Estrecho de la Florida

Trópico de Cáncer

Cuba

Metros	Pies
Más de 3,000	Más de 9,840
2,000–3,000	6,560–9,840
1,000–2,000	3,280–6,560
500–1,000	1,640–3,280
200–500	656–1,640
0–200	0–656

–·–·– Frontera nacional
✪ Capital
● Ciudad
▲ Volcán o montaña

ALASKA   **Canadá**

Mt. McKinley ▲

Mar de Bering

Golfo de Alaska

OCÉANO PACÍFICO

HAWAII

0   500 millas
0   500 kilómetros

0   100 millas
0   100 kilómetros

La Estatua de la Libertad, Nueva York

El Monte Rushmore, Dakota del Sur

Why Study Spanish?

Over 425 million people who live in Spain, 18 Latin American countries, Puerto Rico, Equatorial Guinea, the Philippines, and the United States speak Spanish. It is the second most common language in the United States and the third most commonly spoken language in the world. Studying Spanish helps you to:

Understand Culture The Spanish-speaking world is rich in music, food, art, literature, history, and everyday traditions. Learning about culture helps you understand other people's perspectives, patterns of behavior, and contributions to the world at large. ▶

▲ Expand Career Opportunities
Your career options expand as businesses in the twenty-first century look for employees who can communicate in Spanish.

Enjoy Your Spanish Experiences Climb the Incan ruins of Machu Picchu. Volunteer to build a school in Mexico. Enjoy a meal at a Mexican restaurant. Speaking Spanish enriches your experience whether at home or in another country. ▶

Improve Your Language Skills Studying Spanish improves your first-language skills: vocabulary, grammar, reading, and writing. Research shows your test scores may improve!

Study Tips

realidades.com ✔
- More Tips for Studying Spanish
- Web Code: jce-0003

Take risks, relax, and be patient. The goal of studying Spanish is to communicate! So don't wait until you get it perfect. Just start talking, and you'll get better and better! You'll make some mistakes, but the longer you practice, the more improvement you'll see.

Here are some easy tips to help you learn Spanish!

Use what you already know. You already know lots of Spanish words such as *rodeo, hasta la vista, tacos, armadillo, sombrero, piñata, mesa,* and *tango.* Use your knowledge of English to help you figure out new words such as *comunicación, delicioso, limón,* and *oficina.* You'll find Spanish is easier if you use what you already know.

You don't need to understand everything. As you hear or read Spanish, you'll come across words or expressions you don't know. Try to figure out what the meaning might be. Above all, don't stop! Keep on listening or reading. You'll be surprised how much you can understand without knowing every word.

Look for Strategy and ¿Recuerdas? boxes. Throughout **Realidades**, you'll see boxes that provide strategies or remind you of something you've already learned. The information in the boxes will help you learn.

Make flashcards. One way to learn a new word is to make a flashcard. Create a picture of the word on an index card. On the back, write the word in Spanish. Then use the card to study: look at the picture and say the word or look at the picture and write the word.

Have fun! You'll find lots of activities that allow you to work with other students, play games, act out skits, explore the Internet, create projects, and use technology. Try out all of the activities and you'll have fun.

> ### Strategy
>
> **Using graphic organizers**
> Drawing diagrams can help you understand how things are related.
>
> ¿ ?
> madre
> yo

> ### ¿Recuerdas?
>
> In Capítulo 2B you learned that *de* shows possession and is the equivalent of *-'s* and *-s':*
> - el regalo **de** Esteban
>   You also learned *mi(s)* and *tu(s).*

Fondo cultural

**El mundo hispano •
Estados Unidos**

Greetings Social relations are somewhat more formal in Spanish-speaking countries than in the United States, since new acquaintances usually greet one another with a handshake. Friends, however, greet each other with a hug or a kiss on the cheek.

• How does this compare with the way you greet people in the United States?

Para empezar

Objectives

1 En la escuela

- Greet people at different times of the day
- Introduce yourself to others
- Respond to classroom directions
- Begin using numbers
- Tell time
- Identify parts of the body

2 En la clase

- Talk about things in the classroom
- Ask questions about new words and phrases
- Use the Spanish alphabet to spell words
- Talk about things related to the calendar
- Learn about the Aztec calendar

3 El tiempo

- Describe weather conditions
- Identify the seasons
- Compare weather in the Northern and Southern Hemispheres

Más práctica

- *Real.* para hispanohablantes pp. x–1

 realidades.com
- Fondo cultural Activity

1 En la escuela

¡Hola! ¿Cómo te llamas?

jcd-0099

Objectives
- Greet people at different times of the day
- Introduce yourself to others
- Respond to classroom directions
- Begin using numbers
- Tell time
- Identify parts of the body

—**¡Buenos días, señor!**
—¡Buenos días! **¿Cómo te llamas?**
—**Me llamo** Felipe.

—**¡Buenas tardes, señora!**
—¡Buenas tardes! ¿Cómo te llamas?
—Me llamo Beatriz.
—**Mucho gusto.**
—**Encantada.**

Nota
A woman or girl says *encantada.*
A man or boy says *encantado.*

—**¡Buenas noches!** ¿Cómo te llamas?
—**¡Hola!** Me llamo Graciela. **¿Y tú?**
—Me llamo Lorenzo.
—Mucho gusto.
—**Igualmente.**

Exploración del lenguaje

Señor, señora, señorita

The words *señor, señora,* and *señorita* mean "sir," "madam," and "miss" when used alone. When they are used with people's last names they mean "Mr.," "Mrs.," and "Miss," and are abbreviated *Sr., Sra.,* and *Srta.* Note that the abbreviations are capitalized.

In Spanish you should address adults as *señor, señora,* or *señorita,* or use the titles *Sr., Sra.,* and *Srta.* with their last names.

1 Buenos días

jcd-0099

Escuchar

Listen as people greet each other. Then point to the clock that indicates the time of day when the greetings are probably taking place.

a.
8:00 AM

b.
4:00 PM

c.
10:00 PM

2 ¿Cómo te llamas?

Hablar

Your teacher will divide the class in half. Students in one half of the class will introduce themselves and shake hands, and students in the other half will say they are pleased to meet the others. Move quickly from person to person until time is called. Then switch roles.

Modelo

A —¡Hola! ¿Cómo te llamas?
B —Me llamo David. ¿Y tú?
A —Me llamo Antonio. Mucho gusto.
o: Encantado.
B —Igualmente.

¿Recuerdas?

If you are a girl, you say *encantada*.

3 ¡Hola!

Hablar

Work with a partner. Choose a clock from Actividad 1 and greet each other appropriately for the time of day. Then find out your partner's name. Follow the model. Change partners and repeat.

Modelo

A —Buenas tardes.
B —Buenas tardes. ¿Cómo te llamas?
A —Me llamo Paco. ¿Y tú?
B —Me llamo Lourdes. Mucho gusto.
A —Encantado.

Más práctica

• **Core** Vocab. Practice p. 1

realidades.com ✔
• Audio Activities
• Leveled Workbook
• Web Code: jcd-0001

Los nombres

Chicas
Alicia
Ana
Beatriz
Carmen
Cristina
Dolores (Lola)
Elena
Gloria
Inés
Isabel (Isa)
Juana
Luisa
Luz María (Luzma)
Margarita
María
María Eugenia (Maru)
Marta
Teresa (Tere)

Chicos
Alejandro
Antonio (Toño)
Carlos (Chacho, Cacho)
Diego
Eduardo (Edu)
Federico (Kiko)
Francisco (Paco)
Guillermo (Guille)
Jorge
José (Pepe)
Juan
Manuel (Manolo)
Miguel
Pablo
Pedro
Ricardo
Roberto
Tomás

¡Hola! ¿Cómo estás?

jcd-0099

—Buenos días, Adela.
¿Cómo estás?

—**Bien, gracias,** Sr. Ruiz.
¿Y usted?

—Bien, gracias.

—Buenas tardes, Sr. Ruiz.
¿Cómo está Ud.?

—**Muy** bien, gracias. ¿Y tú?

—Bien, gracias.

—Buenas noches, Miguel.
¿Qué tal?

—**Regular.** ¿Y tú, Carlos?
¿Qué pasa?

—**Nada.**

—**¡Adiós, Srta.** Moreno!
¡Hasta luego!

—**¡Hasta mañana!**

—¡Hasta luego, Juan!

—**¡Nos vemos!**

¿Recuerdas?

Señor, señora, and *señorita* are abbreviated to **Sr., Sra.,** and **Srta.** before a person's last name.

Exploración del lenguaje

Tú vs. *usted*

For most Spanish speakers there are two ways to say "you": *tú* and *usted*. Use *tú* when speaking to friends, family, people your own age, children, and pets. *Usted* is formal. Use it to show respect and when talking to people you don't know well, older people, and people in positions of authority. In writing, *usted* is almost always abbreviated *Ud.*, with a capital *U*.

Would you say *tú* or *Ud.* when talking to the following people?
• your brother
• your teacher
• your best friend
• your friend's mother
• your cat
• your principal
• a new acquaintance who is your age

4 ¿Hola o adiós? 🔊
jcd-0099

Escuchar

Make a chart on your paper with two columns. Label one *Greeting*, the other *Leaving*. Number your paper from 1–8. As you hear each greeting or leave-taking, place a check mark in the appropriate column next to the number.

	Greeting	Leaving
1.		
2.		
3.		

5 ¡Hola! ¿Qué tal?

Hablar

Work with a partner. Greet each other and ask how your partner is. Say good-bye. Then change partners and repeat.

Modelo
A —*Hola, Luisa. ¿Qué tal?*
B —*Bien, Lupe. ¿Y tú?*
A —*Regular. ¡Hasta luego!*
B —*¡Adiós!*

6 Mucho gusto

Leer

Read the conversation and then reply *sí* or *no* to the statements.

Profesor: Buenos días. Me llamo José Guzmán. ¿Y tú?
Estudiante: Me llamo María Hernández. Mucho gusto.
Profesor: Igualmente. ¿Cómo estás, María?
Estudiante: Bien, gracias. ¿Y Ud.?
Profesor: Muy bien, gracias. Hasta luego.
Estudiante: Adiós, señor.

1. The people knew each other.
2. The teacher is a man.
3. We know the last names of both people.
4. The student talks to the teacher in a formal tone.
5. Neither person is feeling well today.

Más práctica
● **Core** Vocab. Practice p. 2

 realidades.com ✔
• Audio Activities
• Speak & Record
• Leveled Workbook

¡Atención, por favor!

jcd-0099

—¡Silencio, **por favor!** Abran el libro en la página 10.

—¡Atención! Cierren el libro.

—Repitan, por favor:
Buenos días.
—Buenos días.

—Levántense, por favor.

—Siéntense, por favor.

—Saquen una hoja de papel. Escriban los números.

—Entreguen sus hojas de papel.

7 ¡Siéntense!

jcd-0099

Escuchar

You will hear some classroom commands. Listen carefully and act them out.

Los números jcd-0099

0 cero	1 uno	2 dos	3 tres	4 cuatro
5 cinco	6 seis	7 siete	8 ocho	9 nueve

10 diez	
11 once	21 veintiuno, . . .
12 doce	30 treinta
13 trece	31 treinta y uno, . . .
14 catorce	40 cuarenta
15 quince	50 cincuenta
16 dieciséis	60 sesenta
17 diecisiete	70 setenta
18 dieciocho	80 ochenta
19 diecinueve	90 noventa
20 veinte	100 cien

8 Los números

Hablar

Supply the missing number. Then read the sequence in Spanish.

1. 1, ___, 3
2. 6, ___, 8
3. 7, ___, 9
4. 10, ___, 12

5. 14, ___, 16
6. 17, ___, 19
7. 23, ___, 25
8. 29, ___, 31

9 Más números

Pensar · Hablar

With a partner, provide the missing numbers in each sequence. Then say the number sequence aloud in Spanish.

1. 1, 2, 3, . . . 10
2. 2, 4, 6, . . . 20
3. 1, 3, 5, . . . 19

4. 5, 10, 15, . . . 60
5. 3, 6, 9, . . . 39
6. 10, 20, 30, . . . 100

Más práctica

● **Core** Vocab. Practice p. 3

realidades.com ✓
- Audio Activities
- Speak & Record
- Leveled Workbook
- Web Code: jcd-0002

10 Números y más números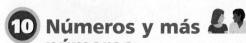

Hablar · Escuchar · Escribir

Tell your partner these numbers in Spanish. He or she will write them using numerals, not words. Then check your partner's work.

1. the phone numbers used to dial for information and emergencies
2. the bar code number on the back of your Spanish book
3. your house or apartment number
4. number of minutes it takes you to get from your home to school
5. number of months until your next birthday

Azulejo *(tile)* de cerámica

¿Qué hora es?

In Spanish, to ask what time it is, you say *¿Qué hora es?* Here are some answers:

Es la una.

Son las dos.

Son las tres y cinco.

Son las cuatro y diez.

Son las cinco y cuarto.

Son las seis y media.

Son las siete menos veinte.

Son las ocho y cincuenta y dos.

11 ¿Qué hora es?

Hablar

Work with a partner to ask and answer questions about the time. Use these clocks.

> **Modelo**
>
> A —*¿Qué hora es?*
> B —*Son las diez.*

1.

2.

3.

4.

5.

6.

12 La hora

jcd-0099

Escuchar

Write the numbers 1–8 on a sheet of paper. Write the times you hear with numerals—1:00, 2:15, and so on.

Más práctica

- **Core** Vocab. Practice p. 4

realidades.com

- Audio Activities
- Leveled Workbook

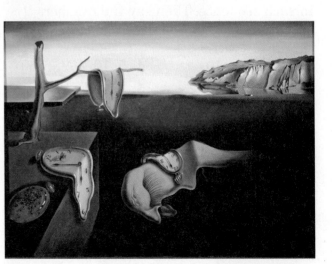

"La persistencia de la memoria / The Persistence of Memory" (1931), Salvador Dalí

Oil on canvas, 9 1/2 x 13 in. (24.1 x 33 cm). Given anonymously. © 2009 Salvador Dalí, Gala-Salvador Dalí Foundation/Artists Rights Society (ARS), New York./A.K.G., Berlin. Photo: Superstock.

El cuerpo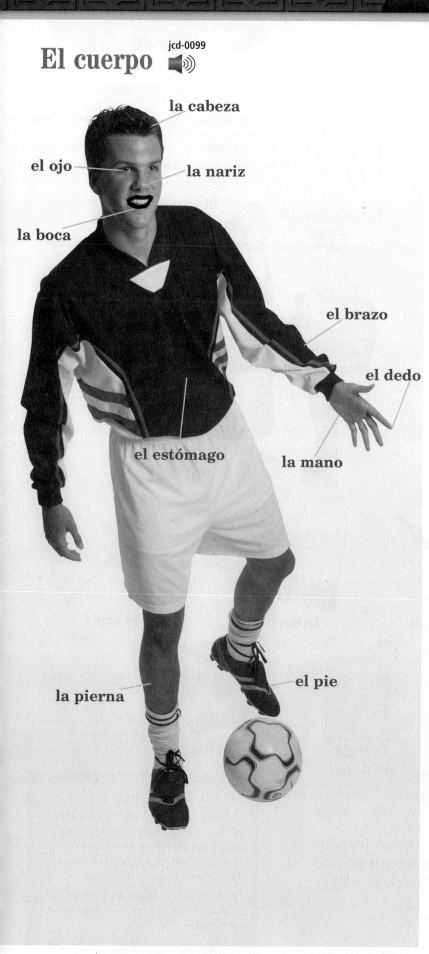

jcd-0099

la cabeza

el ojo

la nariz

la boca

el brazo

el dedo

el estómago

la mano

la pierna

el pie

 ¡Ay! Me duele el pie

13 Señalen

jcd-0099

Escuchar

You will hear some commands. Listen carefully and act out the commands. When you hear the word *señalen,* you should point to that part of the body.

14 Juego

Escuchar

Play the game *Simón dice . . .* (Simon Says). Listen and follow the leader's directions. Remember that if the leader does not say *"Simón dice,"* you should not do the action.

Más práctica

- **Guided** Vocab. Flash Cards, Vocab. Check, Gram. Practice pp. 1–10
- **Core** Vocab. Practice p. 5
- **Communication** Writing p. 4
- *Real.* **para hispanohablantes** pp. 2–3

 realidades.com

- Audio Activities
- Leveled Workbook
- Flashcards
- Web Code: jcd-0003

2 En la clase

La sala de clases jcd-0099

Objectives

- Talk about things in the classroom
- Ask questions about new words and phrases
- Use the Spanish alphabet to spell words
- Talk about things related to the calendar
- Learn about the Aztec calendar

el estudiante

el profesor

—¿Qué quiere decir *lápiz*?
—Quiere decir *pencil*.

la estudiante

la profesora

—¿Cómo se dice *book* en español?
—Se dice *libro*.

el pupitre

el bolígrafo

la carpeta

el lápiz

el cuaderno

la hoja de papel

el libro

jcd-0099

1 El libro, el lápiz, . . .

Escuchar

You will hear the names of classroom objects. After you hear each word, hold up the object if you have it on your desk or point to it if it is somewhere in the classroom.

También se dice . . .

In many Spanish-speaking countries or regions, you will hear different words for the same thing. Words like these are highlighted in the *También se dice . . .* sections.

For example, in Spain a classroom is *el aula*, while in Mexico, it is *el salón de clases*.

2 ¿Cómo se dice . . . ?

Hablar

Talk with a partner about items and people in your classroom.

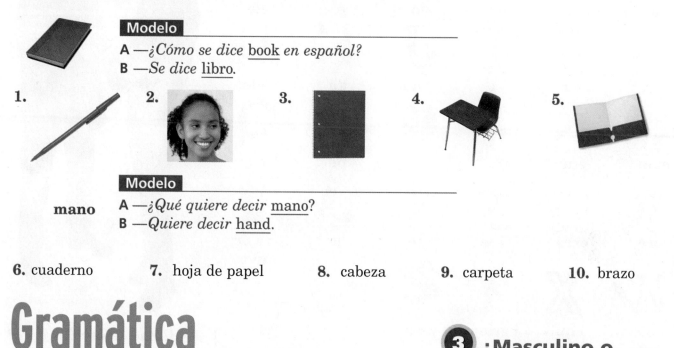

Modelo

A —*¿Cómo se dice* <u>book</u> *en español?*
B —*Se dice* <u>libro</u>.

1. 2. 3. 4. 5.

Modelo

mano

A —*¿Qué quiere decir* <u>mano</u>?
B —*Quiere decir* <u>hand</u>.

6. cuaderno **7.** hoja de papel **8.** cabeza **9.** carpeta **10.** brazo

Gramática

Nouns

Nouns refer to people, animals, places, things, and ideas. In Spanish, nouns have gender. They are either masculine or feminine.

Most nouns that end in -*o* are masculine. Most nouns that end in -*a* are feminine.

Masculine	Feminine
el libro	la carpeta
el bolígrafo	la hoja de papel

The definite articles *el* and *la* also point out if a word is masculine or feminine. They both mean "the."

Spanish nouns that end in -*e* or a consonant must be learned as masculine or feminine. You should practice them with their definite articles, *el* or *la*.

Masculine	Feminine
el profesor	la noche
el lápiz	la conversación

3 ¿Masculino o femenino?

Pensar · Escribir

Look at these words and decide whether each one is masculine or feminine. Rewrite each word and add the appropriate definite article (*el* or *la*).

1. pierna
2. nariz
3. cuaderno
4. hora
5. pupitre
6. pie
7. profesora
8. estudiante

Más práctica

● **Core** Vocab. Practice, Gram. Practice p. 6

realidades.com

• Audio Activities
• Speak & Record
• Canción de hip hop
• Tutorial
• Leveled Workbook
• Web Code: jcd-0004

El alfabeto jcd-0099 🔊

A	B	C	D	E	F
a	be	ce	de	e	efe
G	H	I	J	K	L
ge	hache	i	jota	ka	ele
M	N	Ñ	O	P	Q
eme	ene	eñe	o	pe	cu
R	rr	S	T	U	V
ere	erre	ese	te	u	ve *or* uve
W	X	Y	Z		
doble ve *or* doble u	equis	i griega *or* ye	zeta		

—¿Cómo se escribe *libro*?

—Se escribe ele-i-be-ere-o.

---

4 Escucha y escribe jcd-0099 🔊

Escuchar · Escribir

On a sheet of paper, write the numbers 1–8. You will hear several words you know spelled aloud. Listen carefully and write the letters as you hear them.

---

5 Pregunta y contesta 👥

Hablar · Escribir

Work with a partner. Use the pictures to ask and answer according to the model. As Student B spells the words, Student A should write them out. When you are finished, check your spelling by looking at p. 10.

1. 2. 3.

4. 5.

Modelo

A —¿*Cómo se escribe* <u>lápiz</u>?

B —*Se escribe* <u>ele-a acento-pe-i-zeta</u>.

6 ¿Cómo te llamas?

Hablar

Work with a partner. Follow the model to find out each other's names and how they are spelled. Then change partners and repeat.

Modelo

A —*¿Cómo te llamas?*
B —*Me llamo María.*
A —*¿Cómo se escribe María?*
B —*Se escribe eme-a-ere-i acento-a.*

Strategy

Sustaining a conversation
If you need your partner to spell a word again, say *Repite, por favor.*

Exploración del lenguaje

Punctuation and accent marks

You have probably noticed that in Spanish, questions begin with an upside-down question mark (*¿*) and exclamations with an upside-down exclamation point (*¡*). This lets you know at the beginning of a sentence what kind of sentence you are reading.

You have probably also noticed the accent mark (*el acento*) on words like *días* and *estás*. When you write in Spanish, you must include these accents and punctuation marks.

Try it out! Rewrite these sentences and insert the correct punctuation and accents.

Como estas   Que tal   Hasta luego   Y tu

Fondo cultural

El mundo hispano

Los maya were among the early civilizations in the Western Hemisphere to develop a form of writing with symbols, known as hieroglyphics *(los jeroglíficos)*. Each symbol, or glyph, represents a word or an idea.

• With what other hieroglyphic writing are you familiar?

Jeroglíficos mayas

7 Juego

Escribir • Hablar • Escuchar

❶ Play this game in pairs. Each player makes a list of five Spanish words that you have learned. Don't let your partner see your words.

❷ Spell your first word aloud in Spanish. Don't forget any accent marks. Your partner will write the word as you spell it. Then your partner will spell a word for you to write. Take turns until you have spelled all the words on your lists.

❸ Check each other's papers. The winner is the player with the most words spelled correctly.

El calendario y la fecha

jcd-0099

	AGOSTO					el mes
lunes	martes	miércoles	jueves	viernes	sábado	domingo
				1	2	3
4	5	6	7	8	9	10
11	12	13	14	15	16	17
18	19	20	21	22	23	24
25	26	27	28	29	30	31

el día

la semana

Los meses del año

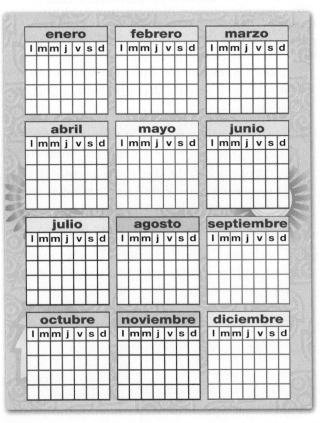

enero	febrero	marzo
l m m j v s d	l m m j v s d	l m m j v s d

abril	mayo	junio
l m m j v s d	l m m j v s d	l m m j v s d

julio	agosto	septiembre
l m m j v s d	l m m j v s d	l m m j v s d

octubre	noviembre	diciembre
l m m j v s d	l m m j v s d	l m m j v s d

—¿**Qué día es hoy?**

—**Hoy** es lunes. **Mañana** es martes.

—¿**Cuántos** días **hay en** el mes de agosto?

—Hay treinta y un días.

Nota

Notice that the days of the week and the months of the year are not capitalized in Spanish, except at the beginning of sentences.

The first day of the week in a Spanish-language calendar is *lunes*.

—**¿Cuál es la fecha?**
—**Es el** 22 **de** agosto.

—**¿Cuál es la fecha?**
—**Es el primero de** agosto.

Nota

To say the first day of the month, use *el primero*. For the other days, use the numbers *dos, tres,* and so on.

8 Hoy y mañana

Hablar

Ask and answer according to the model.

Modelo

lunes
A —*¿Qué día es hoy?*
B —*Hoy es lunes. Mañana es martes.*

1. martes
2. sábado
3. jueves
4. miércoles
5. viernes
6. domingo

El Cinco de Mayo es un día festivo en México.

9 Días de fiesta

Leer • Escribir

Read the following sentences and rewrite them, making the necessary corrections.

1. El Día de San Patricio es el 14 de enero.
2. El Día de San Valentín es en junio.
3. Januká es en febrero.
4. La Navidad (*Christmas*) es el 25 de noviembre.
5. El Día de la Independencia de los Estados Unidos (*United States*) es el 4 de junio.
6. El Año Nuevo (*New Year's Day*) es en diciembre.
7. Hoy es el 3 de agosto.

Escribir

lunes	martes	miércoles	jueves	viernes	sábado	domingo
	1	*2*	*3*	*4*	*5*	*6*
7	*8*	*9*	*10*	*11*	*12*	*13*
14	*15*	*16*	*17*	*18*	*19*	*20*
21	*22*	*23*	*24*	*25*	*26*	*27*
28	*29*	*30*	*31*			

hoy —

Answer the questions based on the calendar page above.

1. ¿Cuál es la fecha hoy?
2. ¿Qué día de la semana es?
3. ¿Qué día es mañana?
4. ¿Cuál es la fecha de mañana?
5. ¿Cuántos días hay en este *(this)* mes?
6. ¿Cuántos días hay en una semana?

Más práctica

- **Guided** Vocab. Flash Cards, Vocab. Check, Gram. Practice pp. 11–18
- **Core** Vocab. Practice, Gram. Practice pp. 7–8
- **Communication** Writing p. 5
- *Real.* **para hispanohablantes** pp. 4–5

realidades.com
- Audio Activities
- Leveled Workbook
- Flashcards
- Web Code: jcd-0005

Fondo cultural
España

Los sanfermines, or the "Running of the Bulls," is a popular two-week festival in Pamplona, Spain, named for the town's patron saint, San Fermín, who is commemorated on July 7 each year. The celebration includes daily bullfights, but before they begin the real fun starts! As the bulls are released from their pens and run through the streets, many people run ahead or alongside them to the bullring.

- What festivals are you familiar with in which animals play a role?

La Fiesta de San Fermín, en Pamplona, España

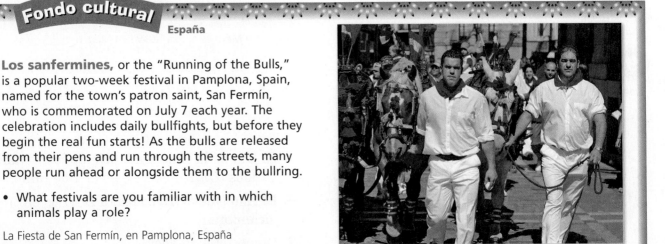

11 El calendario azteca

Leer

The Aztecs were a nomadic tribe that finally settled in the valley of central Mexico in 1325. They established their capital, Tenochtitlán, on a swampy lake and built a mighty empire that dominated most of Mexico. The Aztec empire flourished until 1521, when it was defeated by the Spaniards, led by Hernán Cortés.

México

Conexiones **La historia**

One of the most famous symbols of Mexico is the monolith, or huge stone, carved by the Aztecs in 1479. Known today as the Aztec calendar or the Sun Stone, the carving weighs almost 24 tons and is approximately 12 feet in diameter. The Aztecs dedicated it to the sun, represented by the face in the center. The calendar represents a 260-day year.

Representation of the sun, or Tonatiuh

One of the previous four world creations

This band shows the 20 days of the month.

12 Los símbolos aztecas

Pensar

Here are several glyphs representing days found on the Sun Stone. Match the glyph with the Spanish word. What do you think each of the glyphs represents? Why do you think the Aztecs included those symbols on their calendar?

1.

2.

3.

a. Jaguar
b. Perro
c. Movimiento
d. Serpiente
e. Cráneo
f. Agua

4.

5.

6.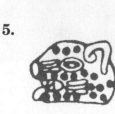

3 El tiempo

¿Qué tiempo hace? jcd-0099

Objectives

- Describe weather conditions
- Identify the seasons
- Compare weather in the Northern and Southern Hemispheres

Hace sol.

Hace calor.

Hace frío.

Hace viento.

Llueve.

Nieva.

Las estaciones

la primavera

el verano

el otoño

el invierno

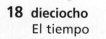

1 El tiempo jcd-0099

Escuchar

You will hear six descriptions of different weather conditions. Write the numbers 1–6 on a sheet of paper. Then, next to each number, write the letter of the photo for which the weather is being described.

a.    b.    c.    d.

2 ¿Qué tiempo hace?

Hablar

Work with a partner. Ask and answer the questions based on the city and weather information for each item.

Modelo

Miami / julio /

A —¿Qué tiempo hace en <u>Miami</u> en <u>julio</u>?
B —<u>Hace sol</u>.

1. Denver / enero /

2. Chicago / octubre /

3. San Francisco / noviembre /

4. Washington, D.C. / junio /

5. Minneapolis / diciembre /

6. Dallas / agosto /

3 Las estaciones

Hablar · Escribir

Answer the questions based on where you live.

1. ¿Qué tiempo hace en la primavera? ¿En el otoño? ¿En el verano? ¿En el invierno?

2. ¿En qué estación hace frío? ¿Calor? ¿Sol? ¿Viento?

3. ¿En qué estación llueve?

4. ¿En qué estación nieva?

Más práctica

- **Guided** Vocab. Flash Cards, Vocab. Check, Gram. Practice pp. 19–24
- **Core** Vocab. Practice, Gram. Practice p. 9
- **Communication** Writing p. 6
- **Real. para hispanohablantes** p. 6

realidades.com
- Audio Activities
- Canción de hip hop
- Leveled Workbook
- Flashcards
- Web Code: jcd-0006

④ Dos hemisferios

Leer · Pensar · Escribir · Hablar

Read about the seasons in the Northern and Southern Hemispheres and then answer the questions.

Conexiones La geografía

Did you know that the seasons for the Northern and Southern Hemispheres are reversed? When it's winter in the Northern Hemisphere, it's summer in the Southern Hemisphere and vice versa. So if you want to ski all year round, go from the slopes of the Rockies in Colorado in December to those of the Andes in Bariloche, Argentina in July. Or for a December getaway to a warmer climate, go to one of the coastal resorts at Viña del Mar, Chile.

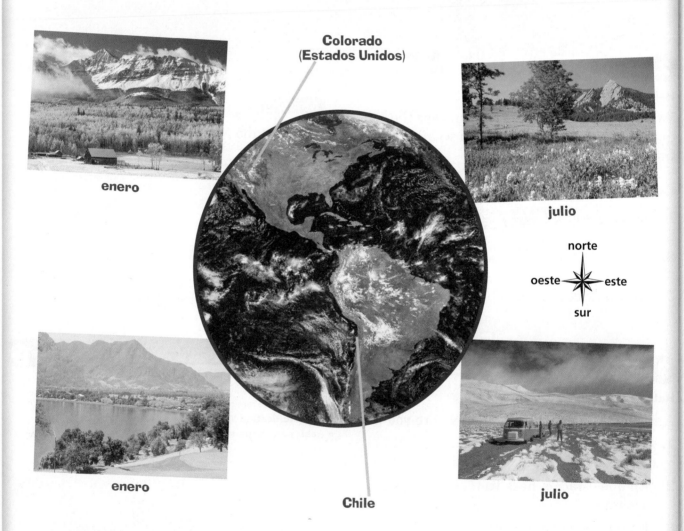

Colorado
(Estados Unidos)

enero

julio

norte

oeste — este

sur

enero

Chile

julio

1. En febrero, ¿qué tiempo hace en Chile?

2. En junio, ¿qué tiempo hace en Colorado?

3. En tu comunidad, ¿qué tiempo hace en diciembre? ¿Y en agosto?

ciudad	diciembre	julio
Asunción, Paraguay	85°F / 29°C	75°F / 24°C
Bogotá, Colombia	66°F / 19°C	64°F / 17°C
Buenos Aires, Argentina	78°F / 26°C	50°F / 10°C
Caracas, Venezuela	80°F / 27°C	80°F / 27°C
Chicago	36°F / 2°C	75°F / 24°C
Ciudad de México, México	70°F / 21°C	74°F / 23°C
Guatemala, Guatemala	72°F / 22°C	74°F / 23°C
La Habana, Cuba	76°F / 24°C	82°F / 28°C
La Paz, Bolivia	58°F / 15°C	55°F / 13°C
Lima, Perú	76°F / 24°C	76°F / 24°C
Los Ángeles	67°F / 19°C	88°F / 31°C
Miami	76°F / 24°C	97°F / 36°C
Nueva York	41°F / 5°C	74°F / 23°C
Quito, Ecuador	65°F / 18°C	67°F / 19°C
San José, Costa Rica	78°F / 26°C	78°F / 26°C
San Juan, Puerto Rico	74°F / 23°C	80°F / 27°C
Santiago, Chile	82°F / 28°C	50°F / 10°C
Seattle	41°F / 5°C	66°F / 19°C
St. Louis	36°F / 2°C	81°F / 27°C
Tegucigalpa, Honduras	70°F / 21°C	81°F / 27°C

Los Ángeles

Tegucigalpa, Honduras

Asunción, Paraguay

°F	°C
110	43.3
100	37.7
90	32.2
80	26.6
70	21.1
60	15.5
50	10
40	4.44
30	-1.11
20	-6.6
10	-12.2
-10	-23.3
-20	-28.8
-30	-34.4

5 ¿Hace calor o hace frío?

Hablar · Escribir

Work with a partner. Discuss the weather in six different places on the chart.

> **Modelo**
>
> A —¿Qué tiempo hace en <u>Chicago</u> en <u>diciembre</u>?
> B —Hace <u>frío</u>.

Nota

In most parts of the world, people express temperatures in Celsius. A simple way to convert from Celsius to Fahrenheit is to multiply the temperature by $\frac{9}{5}$, then add 32.

$$30°C = \underline{\,?\,}\ F$$
$$30 \times \tfrac{9}{5} = 54 + 32$$
$$30°C = 86°F$$

6 ¿Y qué tiempo hace en . . . ?

Hablar

Work with a partner. Ask about the temperature in six different places on the chart.

> **Modelo**
>
> A —¿Cuál es la temperatura en <u>Quito</u> en <u>diciembre</u>?
> B —<u>Sesenta y cinco grados</u>.
> o: —<u>Dieciocho grados</u>.

Para decir más . . .

la temperatura temperature
grados degrees

Repaso del capítulo

Vocabulario jcd-0099 🔊))

Chapter Review

To prepare for the test, check to see if you . . .

- **recognize the vocabulary**
- **can perform the tasks on p. 23**

En la escuela

to greet someone

Buenos días.	Good morning.
Buenas noches.	Good evening.
Buenas tardes.	Good afternoon.
¡Hola!	Hello!
¿Cómo te llamas?	What is your name?
Me llamo . . .	My name is . . .
Encantado, -a.	Delighted.
Igualmente.	Likewise.
Mucho gusto.	Pleased to meet you.
señor, Sr.	sir, Mr.
señora, Sra.	madam, Mrs.
señorita, Srta.	miss, Miss

to ask and tell how someone is

¿Cómo está Ud.? *(formal)*	How are you?
¿Cómo estás? *(familiar)*	How are you?
¿Qué pasa?	What's happening?
¿Qué tal?	How are you?
¿Y tú? / ¿Y usted (Ud.)?	And you?
(muy) bien	(very) well
nada	nothing
regular	okay, so-so
gracias	thank you

to say good-bye

¡Adiós!	Good-bye!
Hasta luego.	See you later.
Hasta mañana.	See you tomorrow.
¡Nos vemos!	See you!

to tell time

¿Qué hora es?	What time is it?
Es la una.	It's one o'clock.
Son las . . . y / menos . . .	It's . . . *(time)*.
y cuarto / menos cuarto	quarter past / quarter to
y media	thirty, half-past

to count up to 100 (Turn to p. 7.)

to talk about the body (Turn to p. 9.)

En la clase

to talk about the classroom

el bolígrafo	pen
la carpeta	folder
el cuaderno	notebook
el estudiante, la estudiante	student
la hoja de papel	sheet of paper
el lápiz	pencil
el libro	book
el profesor, la profesora	teacher
el pupitre	(student) desk
la sala de clases	classroom

to say the date

el año	year
el día	day
el mes	month
la semana	week
¿Qué día es hoy?	What day is today?
¿Cuál es la fecha?	What is the date?
Es el *(number)* de *(month)*.	It's the . . . of . . .
Es el primero de *(month)*.	It's the first of . . .
hoy	today
mañana	tomorrow

to say the days of the week and the months of the year (Turn to p. 14.)

other useful words

¿cuántos, -as?	how many?
en	in
hay	there is / there are
por favor	please

to ask for help

¿Cómo se dice . . . ?	How do you say . . . ?
Se dice . . .	You say . . .
¿Cómo se escribe . . . ?	How is . . . spelled?
Se escribe . . .	It's spelled . . .
¿Qué quiere decir . . . ?	What does . . . mean?
Quiere decir . . .	It means . . .

Más práctica

- **Core** Puzzle p. 10, Organizer p. 11
- **Communication** Integrated Performance Assessment p. 226

realidades.com
- Tutorial
- Puzzles
- Self-test
- Web Code: jcd-0007

El tiempo

to talk about the weather

¿Qué tiempo hace?	What's the weather like?
Hace calor.	It's hot.
Hace frío.	It's cold.
Hace sol.	It's sunny.
Hace viento.	It's windy.
Llueve.	It's raining.
Nieva.	It's snowing.

to talk about the seasons

la estación	season
el invierno	winter
el otoño	fall, autumn
la primavera	spring
el verano	summer

Preparación para el examen

Interpretive

jcd-0099 **1 Escuchar** On the exam you will be asked to listen to and understand people as they greet each other and introduce themselves. To practice, listen to some students greet people in the school halls. Answer these questions about each greeting: Is it morning or afternoon? Was the greeting directed to an adult? How did that person respond?

To review, see pp. 2–5 and Actividades 1, 4.

Interpretive

jcd-0099 **2 Escuchar** You will be asked to listen to and understand someone announcing the current date and time. To practice, listen to the message and answer the questions: What is the time of day? What is the date?

To review, see pp. 7–8 and Actividad 12; pp. 14–16 and Actividad 10.

Interpretive

3 Leer You will be asked to read and understand a description of the weather for a given day. To practice, read the weather forecast below. Answer the questions: What is the date? What are the high and low temperatures? What is the weather like?

> *El dos de septiembre*
> *Hoy en San Antonio hace sol. La temperatura máxima es 75 grados y la mínima es 54. No llueve.*

To review, see pp. 18–21 and Actividades 2–6.

Interpretive

4 Leer You will be asked to read a list of school supplies and identify them. To practice, copy the school supply list below onto a sheet of paper. Please note: *un, una* mean "a" or "an." Then look to see whether you have any of the items on your desk right now. Make a check mark next to each item you have.

un cuaderno	un lápiz	una hoja de papel
un bolígrafo	una carpeta	un libro

To review, see p. 10.

Fondo cultural

España

Pablo Picasso (1881–1973), one of the best-known Spanish artists of the twentieth century, had a long, productive career creating art in a wide range of styles and forms. He showed remarkable artistic talent as a child and had his first exhibition when he was 13 years old. "Three Musicians" is an example of Picasso's cubist painting style.

• Study this painting and list some characteristics that show why this style is known as "cubism."

"Musiciens aux masques / Three Musicians" ▶
(1921), Pablo Picasso

Oil on canvas, 6' 7" X 7' 3 3/4". Mrs. Simon Guggenheim Fund, #55.1949. © 2009 Estate of Pablo Picasso/Artists Rights Society (ARS), New York. Photo: © The Museum of Modern Art/Scala/Art Resource, NY.

¿Qué te gusta hacer?

Chapter Objectives

- Talk about activities you like and don't like to do
- Ask others what they like to do
- Understand cultural perspectives on favorite activities

Video Highlights

Videocultura: *Mis amigos y yo*

A primera vista: *¿Qué te gusta hacer?*

GramActiva Videos: infinitives; making negative statements

Country Connection

As you learn to talk about what you and your friends like to do, you will make connections to these countries and places:

Texas
España
Cuba
México
Costa Rica
República Dominicana
Colombia
Argentina
Guinea Ecuatorial

Más práctica

- *Real.* para hispanohablantes pp. 10–11

realidades.com ✓

- Fondo cultural Activity
- Video Activities
- Online Atlas
- Web Code: jce-0002

ncierto de
rlos Santana

Vocabulario en contexto

jcd-0187

bailar

escuchar música

practicar deportes

nadar

correr

esquiar

—¡Me gusta mucho bailar!

—A mí también. Y también me gusta escuchar música.

—¡Hola, Beatriz! ¿Qué te gusta hacer? ¿Te gusta practicar deportes?

—¡Sí! Me gusta mucho practicar deportes. Me gusta correr, nadar y esquiar. ¿Y a ti? ¿Qué te gusta hacer?

escribir cuentos

montar en monopatín

ver la tele

usar la computadora

dibujar

cantar

montar en bicicleta

jugar videojuegos

—A mí me gusta mucho escribir cuentos y dibujar. **¡No me gusta nada** cantar!

—¡Uy! **A mí tampoco.**

—**¿Qué te gusta más,** ver la tele **o** montar en bicicleta?

—**Pues, no me gusta ni** ver la tele **ni** montar en bicicleta. Me gusta usar la computadora y jugar videojuegos. Y a ti, ¿qué te gusta más?

jcd-0187

1 **¿Te gusta o no te gusta?**

Escuchar

You will hear Rosa say what she likes to do and doesn't like to do. Give a "thumbs-up" sign when you hear her say something she likes to do and a "thumbs-down" sign when she says something she doesn't like to do.

jcd-0187

2 **Me gusta . . .**

Escuchar

Listen to what some people like to do. Point to the picture of the activity each describes.

Más práctica

- **Guided** Vocab. Flash Cards pp. 25–28
- **Core** Vocab. Practice pp. 13–14
- **Communication** Writing p. 14
- *Real.* **para hispanohablantes** p. 12

realidades.com

- Audio Activities
- Leveled Workbook
- Flashcards
- Web Code: jcd-0101

¿Qué te gusta hacer?

You're going to meet eight students from around the Spanish-speaking world and find out what they like and don't like to do. You'll be able to figure out where they live by looking at the globes on the page.

Strategy

Using visuals
Look at the pictures with each postcard to help you understand the meaning of the new words.

• Can you predict what each student likes to do?

Saludos desde Madrid

Y yo me llamo Ana. A mí me gusta **hablar por teléfono**.

Soy Ignacio. Me gusta mucho **tocar la guitarra**.

Ciudad de México

¡Hola! Me llamo Claudia y me gusta usar la computadora y **pasar tiempo con mis amigos**.

Yo soy Teresa. También me gusta usar la computadora, pero **me gusta más** jugar videojuegos.

Recuerdos de San Antonio

❝ Yo soy Esteban. A mí me gusta **patinar** ❞.

❝ ¡Hola, amigos! Me llamo Angélica y me gusta mucho **montar en bicicleta** ❞.

Saludos desde Costa Rica

❝ ¿Qué tal, amigos? Soy Gloria. A mí me gusta **ir a la escuela,** y también me gusta **trabajar** ❞.

❝ Me llamo Raúl. Me gusta ir a la escuela . . . más o menos . . ., pero me gusta más **leer revistas** ❞.

3 ¿Comprendes?

Leer

On a sheet of paper, write the numbers 1–6. Read the following statements by the characters in the *Videohistoria* and write *C (cierto)* if the statement is true, or *F (falso)* if it is false.

1. **Angélica:** No me gusta montar en bicicleta.
2. **Raúl:** Me gusta mucho leer revistas.
3. **Esteban:** Me gusta patinar.
4. **Claudia:** Me gusta pasar tiempo con mis amigos.
5. **Teresa:** No me gusta usar la computadora.
6. **Gloria:** Me gusta trabajar.

4 Y tú, ¿qué dices?

Escribir · Hablar

Write your answers to these questions.

1. ¿Qué te gusta más, leer revistas o montar en monopatín?
2. ¿Qué te gusta más, jugar videojuegos o bailar?
3. ¿Qué te gusta hacer en junio? ¿Y en diciembre?

Más práctica

- **Guided** Vocab. Check pp. 29–32
- **Core** Vocab. Practice pp. 15–16
- **Communication** Video pp. 7–9
- *Real.* para hispanohablantes p. 13

 realidades.com

- Audio Activities
- Video Activities
- Leveled Workbook
- Flashcards
- Web Code: jcd-0102

Vocabulario en uso

Objectives

- Talk about activities
- Say what you like and don't like to do
- Ask others what they like to do
- Learn about infinitives and negative statements

5 ¿Te gusta o no te gusta?

Escribir

Complete the following sentences with one of the activities shown, or with any of the other activities shown on pp. 26–29.

1. Me gusta ___.
2. No me gusta ___.
3. Me gusta mucho ___.
4. No me gusta nada ___.
5. Me gusta ___.
6. No me gusta ni ___ ni ___.

Modelo

Me gusta practicar deportes.

¡Respuesta personal!

6 Me gusta o no me gusta

Escribir

Find four activities on pp. 26–29 that you like to do and four that you don't like to do. Copy this chart on your paper and write the activities in the corresponding columns.

Modelo

Me gusta	No me gusta
correr	cantar

7 ¡A mí también!

Hablar

Using the information from Actividad 6, tell your partner three activities that you like to do. Your partner will agree or disagree with you. Follow the model. Then switch roles and repeat the activity.

Modelo

A —*Me gusta correr.*
B —*¡A mí también!*
o: —*¡A mí no me gusta!*

8 ¿Qué te gusta hacer?

Hablar

Ask your partner whether he or she likes doing the activities below. Your partner will answer using one of the two responses shown. Then switch roles and answer your partner's questions.

Estudiante A
¿Te gusta . . . ?

1.
2.
3.
4.
5.
6.
7.
8.

Estudiante B

¡Respuesta personal!

Fondo cultural

El mundo hispano

Outdoor cafés are popular gathering places throughout the Spanish-speaking world. Friends go there to enjoy a snack or light meal, catch up with one another, or just watch people go by.

• Where do you go to spend time with friends or to meet new ones? How does your experience compare with that of the Spanish teens shown here at a café in Madrid's Plaza Mayor?

En el verano, me gusta pasar tiempo con mis amigos en la Plaza Mayor de Madrid, España.

También se dice . . .

No me gusta nada = No me gusta para nada
(muchos países)

Gramática

Infinitives

Verbs are words that are most often used to name actions. Verbs in English have different forms depending on who is doing the action or when the action is occurring:

I **walk,** she **walks,** we walk**ed,** etc.

The most basic form of a verb is called the infinitive. In English, you can spot infinitives because they usually have the word "to" in front of them:

to swim, **to** read, **to** write

Infinitives in Spanish, though, don't have a separate word like "to" in front of them. Spanish infinitives are only one word, and always end in *-ar, -er,* or *-ir:*

nadar, leer, escribir

GramActiva VIDEO

To learn more about infinitives, watch the **GramActiva** video.

hablar

9 **¿Cuál es?**

Escribir

On a sheet of paper, make a chart with three columns for the headings *-ar, -er,* and *-ir.* Then look at these pictures of activities. Write the infinitive for each activity under the corresponding head. Save your chart to use in Actividad 11.

Modelo

-ar	-er	-ir
nadar		

jcd-0188

10 **Tres papeles** 🔊

Escuchar · GramActiva

Tear a sheet of paper into three equal parts. Write *-ar* on one piece, *-er* on another piece, and *-ir* on the third piece. You will hear several infinitives. Listen carefully to the endings. Hold up the paper with the ending that you hear.

11 El verbo es . . .

Escribir

Here are some verbs in English. Look them up in the English-Spanish glossary at the back of the book and write down the Spanish infinitives on the chart you made in Actividad 9.

to walk   to live   to eat   to study   to have

It's easy to talk about the things you like to do once you know the infinitive, because you just add the infinitive to *Me gusta*. Try writing this sentence in Spanish: *I like to sleep.*

> **Strategy**
>
> **Using a dictionary or glossary**
> When you need to look up a verb, always look under the infinitive form.

12 Encuesta: ¿Qué te gusta hacer?

Escribir · Hablar

1 Ask four classmates to tell you two things they like to do (*¿Qué te gusta hacer?*) and two things they don't like to do (*¿Qué no te gusta hacer?*). Record their names and responses on a chart like this one.

2 Work in groups of four. Add up the results of your interviews to see which activities are the most popular and which ones are the least popular.

3 Share your results with the class.

    1. Las actividades más (*most*) populares:

    2. Las actividades menos (*least*) populares:

Modelo

Nombre	Me gusta	No me gusta
Beto	nadar ir a la escuela	patinar usar la computadora

Actividad	Me gusta	No me gusta
tocar la guitarra	|||		
cantar			|||
trabajar	||	||

13 Escucha y escribe 🔊

jcd-0188

Escuchar · Escribir

Write the numbers 1–7 on a sheet of paper. You will hear Raúl say seven things that he likes to do. Write them down as he says them. Spelling counts!

> **¿Recuerdas?**
>
> Remember to include any accent marks when you spell a word.

Más práctica

- **Guided** Gram. Practice p. 33
- **Core** Gram. Practice p. 17
- **Communication** Writing p. 15
- *Real.* para hispanohablantes
  pp. 14–17

realidades.com ✓

- Audio Activities
- Video Activities
- Speak & Record
- Tutorial
- Leveled Workbook
- Web Code: jcd-0103

Exploración del lenguaje

Cognates

Words that look alike and have similar meanings in English and Spanish are called **cognates** (*cognados*). Here are examples from this chapter:

Spanish	English
popular	popular
usar	to use
guitarra	guitar
computadora	computer

Try it out! Look at pp. 26–29 and make a list of seven cognates from the vocabulary on those pages.

Look at pp. 26–29

Strategy

Recognizing cognates
Becoming skilled at recognizing cognates will help you understand what you read and will increase your vocabulary.

Fondo cultural

República Dominicana

Jaime Antonio González Colson (1901–1975) was an artist from the Dominican Republic. His works usually focused on the people and culture of his homeland.

The *merengue*, the dance shown in this painting, originated in the Dominican Republic in the nineteenth century. One of the instruments used to accompany it is the *güiro* (shown at the top right), made from a gourd and played by scraping it with a stick.

• What instruments set the rhythms in the music that you listen to?

"Merengue" (1937), Jaime Antonio González Colson ▶
Courtesy of Museo Bellapart, Dominican Republic.

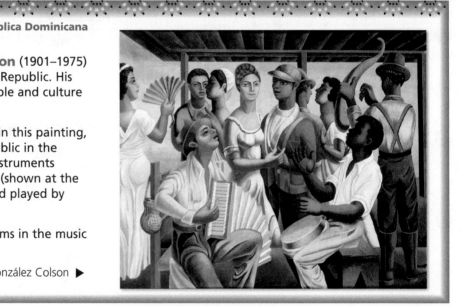

Las maracas, el güiro, la cabassa y las claves son instrumentos típicos de la música del Caribe.

14 **El baile y la música del mundo hispano** 🔊
jcd-0188

Leer • Escuchar • Escribir

Each country in the Spanish-speaking world has distinct musical styles and traditions. Many of the unique rhythms and dances of Spanish-speaking countries are now popular in the United States. This music features instruments such as guitars, violins, accordions, and various types of percussion such as *güiros,* sticks, cymbals, cow bells, and drums. As you read the captions, see how many words you can understand due to their similarity to English words. After you read, your teacher will play examples of each type of music. Listen for the different instruments used.

Conexiones **La música**

El flamenco es un baile típico de España. El instrumento más importante en el flamenco es la guitarra.

En Argentina, el tango es muy popular. Es un baile romántico.

En la República Dominicana, el baile tradicional es el merengue. El merengue tiene muchos ritmos africanos.

En Puerto Rico, la salsa es el baile preferido. El ritmo de la salsa es popular en la música de los Estados Unidos también.

La cumbia es el baile más famoso de Colombia.

- Reread each of the captions and make a list of seven cognates.

- Make a list of instruments you heard in the different songs. You might need to listen to the music again.

Gramática

Negatives

To make a sentence negative in Spanish, you usually put *no* in front of the verb or expression. In English you usually use the word "not."

No me gusta cantar.   *I do not like to sing.*

To answer a question negatively in Spanish you often use *no* twice. The first *no* answers the question. The second *no* says, "I do *not . . . (don't)*." This is similar to the way you answer a question in English.

¿Te gusta escribir cuentos?   *Do you like to write stories?*

No, no me gusta.   *No, I don't.*

In Spanish, you might use one or more negatives after answering "*no.*"

¿Te gusta cantar?   *Do you like to sing?*

No, no me gusta **nada**.   *No, I don't like it **at all**.*

If you want to say that you do not like either of two choices, use *ni . . . ni:*

No me gusta **ni** nadar **ni** dibujar.   *I don't like **either** swimming **or** drawing.*

                                     *I like **neither** swimming **nor** drawing.*

¿Recuerdas?

Did you remember that *nada* has another meaning?

• ¿Qué pasa? **Nada.**

In this case, *nada* means "nothing."

GramActiva VIDEO

To learn more about negatives, watch the **GramActiva** video.

ni bailar ni nadar

---

15 Una persona muy negativa

Leer • Escribir

Fill in the blanks in the dialogue with one of these expressions:
no, nada, tampoco, ni . . . ni.

Tomás es un nuevo estudiante en la clase y es una persona muy negativa.

Ana: Hola, Tomás. ¿Te gusta escuchar música?

Tomás: No, __1.__ me gusta.

Ana: Pues, ¿qué te gusta más, jugar videojuegos o usar la computadora?

Tomás: No me gusta __2.__ jugar videojuegos __3.__ usar la computadora.

Ana: ¿Te gusta practicar deportes?

Tomás: No, no me gusta __4.__ practicar deportes.

Ana: Pues, Tomás, no me gusta pasar tiempo con personas negativas.

Tomás: ¡A mí __5.__ !

16 ¡No, no me gusta!

Hablar

Today you feel as negative as Tomás. With a partner, respond to each question saying that you don't like to do any of these activities.

Modelo

A —¿Te gusta _ver la tele_?
B —No, no me gusta _ver la tele_.

Estudiante A

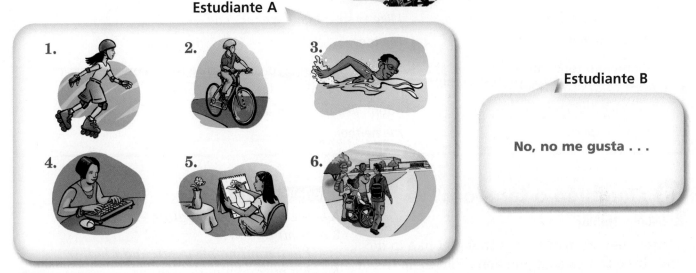

1.
2.
3.
4.
5.
6.

Estudiante B

No, no me gusta . . .

17 ¿Qué te gusta más?

Hablar

Find out what your partner likes more. Then switch roles.

Modelo

A —¿Qué te gusta más, _nadar_ o _esquiar_?
B —Pues, me gusta más _nadar_.
o:—Pues, no me gusta ni _nadar_ ni _esquiar_.

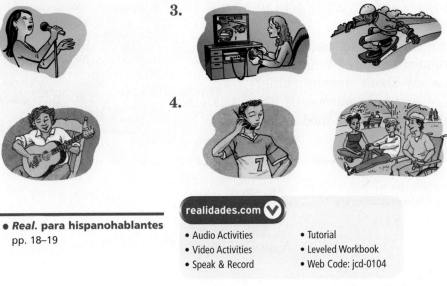

1.
2.
3.
4.

Más práctica

- **Guided** Gram. Practice pp. 34–35
- **Core** Gram. Practice p. 18
- **Communication** Writing p. 16, Test Prep p. 227
- **Real. para hispanohablantes** pp. 18–19

realidades.com

- Audio Activities
- Video Activities
- Speak & Record
- Tutorial
- Leveled Workbook
- Web Code: jcd-0104

Gramática

Expressing agreement or disagreement

To agree with what a person likes, you use *"a mí también."*
It's like saying "me too" in English.

Me gusta pasar tiempo con amigos.	*I like to spend time with friends.*
A mí también.	*Me too.*

If someone tells you that he or she dislikes something, you can agree by saying *"a mí tampoco."* It's like saying "me neither" or "neither do I" in English.

No me gusta nada cantar.	*I don't like to sing at all.*
A mí tampoco.	*Me neither.*

---

18 ¿También o tampoco?

Escribir • Hablar

Write a list of three things that you like to do and three things that you don't like to do. Tell your partner the activities on your list. Your partner will agree or disagree based upon his or her personal preferences. Follow the model.

Modelo

A —*Me gusta mucho bailar.*
B —*A mí también.*
o: —*Pues, a mí no me gusta nada bailar.*
A —*No me gusta nada cantar.*
B —*A mí tampoco.*
o: —*Pues, a mí me gusta cantar.*

---

19 Opiniones

Leer • Escribir

Read the opinions of two students on snowboarding. Then answer the questions.

1. Who thinks that snowboarding is "neither a fad nor a sport"? What does he or she consider it to be?
2. What does the other person consider snowboarding to be? What else does this person say about snowboarding?
3. ¿A ti te gusta el *snowboard?* En tu opinión, ¿es un deporte o una moda?

EL "SNOWBOARD" ¿DEPORTE O MODA?

Ni lo uno ni lo otro
"El snowboard no es ni moda[1] ni deporte. Lo practico como hobby".
Rafael

¿Moda?
"El snowboard es un deporte de invierno como el esquí. A mí me gusta mucho y lo practico mucho. ¡No es una simple moda, es todo un deporte! Y es buen ejercicio[2]".
Alicia

[1] fad [2] good exercise

Más práctica

- **Guided** Gram. Practice p. 36
- **Core** Gram. Practice p. 19
- *Real.* **para hispanohablantes** pp. 19–21

realidades.com ▼

- Audio Activities
- Video Activities
- Speak & Record
- Canción de hip hop
- Leveled Workbook
- Web Code: jcd-0105

Pronunciación

The vowels *a*, *e*, and *i* 🔊

jcd-0188

The vowel sounds in Spanish are different from those in English. In Spanish, each vowel has just one sound. Spanish vowels are also quicker and shorter than those in English.

The letter *a* is similar to the sound in the English word *pop*. Listen to and say these words:

andar	cantar	trabajar
hablar	nadar	pasar

The letter *e* is similar to the sound in the English word *met*. Listen to and say these words:

tele   me   es   Elena   deportes

The letter *i* is similar to the sound in the English word *see*. As you have already seen, the letter *y* sometimes has the same sound as *i*. Listen to and say these words:

sí   escribir   patinar   lápiz   ti   mí

Try it out! Listen to and say this rhyme:

A-E-I   El perro canta para ti.
A-E-I   El tigre baila para mí.

Try it again, substituting *el gato* for *el perro* and *la cebra* for *el tigre*.

El español en la comunidad

Hispanics in the United States make up approximately 13 percent of the total population and are the fastest-growing minority group. By the year 2050, the Hispanic population is expected to be almost 25 percent of the total United States population. Because of this, many Spanish-language media sources—magazines, newspapers, television, radio, and Internet—are available throughout the country.

• Make a list of Spanish-language media sources in your community. Try to find local, regional, national, or even international sources. If possible, bring in examples. How much can you understand?

These sources will help you improve your Spanish, and you'll learn about Spanish-speaking cultures as well.

Lectura
¿Qué te gusta hacer?

Here are some notes that four students have written to a popular teen magazine. All four are looking for e-pals. As you read their notes, think about how their likes and interests compare to yours.

Strategy

Using cognates
Use what you already know about cognates to figure out what new words mean.

Puerto Rico
Marisol, 14 años

"¿Te gusta practicar deportes y escuchar música? ¡A mí me gusta mucho! También me gusta jugar al básquetbol. ¡Hasta luego!".

Colombia
Daniel, 13 años

"Me gusta mucho ver la tele y escuchar música clásica. También me gusta tocar el piano y pasar tiempo con amigos en un café o en una fiesta. ¿Y a ti?".

España
Silvia, 17 años

"Me gusta leer revistas, bailar y cantar. Soy fanática de la música alternativa. También me gusta hablar por teléfono con amigos. ¿Y a ti? ¿Qué te gusta hacer?".

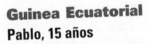

Guinea Ecuatorial
Pablo, 15 años

"Me gusta mucho jugar al vóleibol y al tenis. Me gusta escribir cuentos y también me gusta organizar fiestas con amigos. No me gusta ni jugar videojuegos ni ver la tele. ¡Hasta pronto!".

¿Comprendes?

1. Draw a bar graph. Indicate on the graph how many of the four young people like each of these types of activities: *televisión, música, deportes, pasar tiempo con amigos.* Which are the most popular?

2. Of the four students, with whom do you have the most in common?

3. Write a personal message similar to those in the magazine. Use one of them as a model.

Más práctica

- **Guided** Reading Support p. 37
- **Communication** Writing p. 17, Test Prep p. 228
- *Real.* **para hispanohablantes** pp. 22–23

 realidades.com

- Internet Activity
- Leveled Workbook
- Web Code: jcd-0106

La cultura en vivo
¿Te gusta bailar?

Thanks to the worldwide popularity of Latin music, Latin dances have captured the attention of people of all ages. As a result, people all around the United States are learning dances such as the merengue, tango, and salsa. Here is a dance you can learn. It is called the mambo, and it originated in Cuba in the 1940s.

Bailando el mambo

El mambo

Directions

Beat 1 (of the music): Step forward with the left foot and slightly raise the right foot in a rocking motion.

Beat 2: Step back down on the right foot.

Beat 3: Place the left foot next to the right foot.

Beat 4: Hold both feet in place with the left and right feet next to each other.

Repeat the same motion, now moving backwards.

Beat 5: Step backward with the right foot and slightly raise the left foot in a rocking motion.

Beat 6: Step back down on the left foot.

Beat 7: Place the right foot next to the left foot.

Beat 8: Hold both feet in place with the left and right feet next to each other.

These steps are repeated throughout the music. If partners dance together, then the male should start with his left foot going forward and the female should start with her right foot going backward.

Think about it! How is doing the mambo with a partner different from dances you might do? What dances do you know from the United States that are danced with a partner?

Presentación oral
A mí me gusta mucho . . .

Task
You are a new student at school and have been asked to tell the class a little bit about your likes and dislikes.

❶ **Prepare** Copy this diagram on a sheet of paper. Write a list of at least five activities that you can include in the three different ovals.

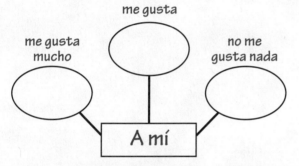

me gusta

me gusta mucho

no me gusta nada

A mí

Using your list, create a poster or other visual aid to illustrate the three categories and at least five activities. To illustrate the activities, you can make drawings, cut pictures out of magazines, or show photos of yourself doing the activity. Make sure that each activity is easy to identify. You will use this visual as part of your presentation.

Strategy
Creating visuals
Making a diagram can help you organize a presentation.

❷ **Practice** Go through your presentation with a few class members. You can use your notes the first time or two, but then practice using only the visuals.

Modelo
Me gusta mucho . . .
Me gusta . . .
No me gusta nada . . .

❸ **Present** Talk about yourself using the visual you have created. Remember to look at the Evaluation list below so you know what you need to emphasize in your presentation. Be sure to begin the presentation with your name. During the presentation, try to:
• use complete sentences
• speak clearly
• use the visuals to keep yourself focused

❹ **Evaluation** Your teacher may give you a rubric explaining how your presentation will be graded. You might be graded on:
• how much information you communicate
• how easy it is to understand you
• how clearly and neatly your visuals match what you are saying

realidades.com
Speak & Record

España

The Spanish empire once included parts of Italy and the Netherlands, much of the Americas and the Caribbean, the Philippines, and colonies in Africa. Today, Spain is a country of rich regional and cultural traditions with a population of more than 40 million people.

Spain was one of the most important provinces of the ancient Roman empire. The Spanish language is very closely related to Latin, the language of that empire. Roman engineering also left its mark on the Spanish landscape, and some Roman bridges are still in use after almost 2,000 years! This photo shows the Roman aqueduct in Segovia, which was constructed entirely without mortar or clamps.

¿Sabes que . . . ?

Spain has five official languages: Spanish, Catalan, Basque, Galician, and Valencian. Originally the language of Castile in central Spain, Spanish is the primary national language and is also spoken in most of Spain's former empire in North, Central, and South America.

Para pensar

Spain has been influenced by many civilizations, including those of the ancient Greeks, Romans, and Moors. What civilizations have most affected the language, culture, and customs of the United States?

Francia

OCÉANO ATLÁNTICO

España

Mar Mediterráneo

Portugal

realidades.com
- Online Atlas
- Web Code: jce-0002

Originally a royal retreat, the Parque del Buen Retiro is now a favorite place for the traditional Sunday-afternoon *paseo* (stroll). Throngs of people come to enjoy the Retiro's lakes, gardens, and museums, or simply to spend time with friends or family. What are your favorite places to go walking with friends? Why? ▼

▲ Arabic-speaking Moors from North Africa ruled much of Spain for nearly 800 years. Córdoba in southern Spain became one of the most important cities in Islam, and its mosque, the Mezquita, was one of the largest in the world. The Alhambra in Granada (shown above) is a strongly fortified and beautiful complex of palaces and gardens. It was also the last stronghold of the Moors in Spain, falling to Spain's Catholic monarchs in 1492.

The Bilbao Guggenheim Museum opened in October 1997 and houses a collection of modern and contemporary art. The building's titanium-paneled curves and concrete blocks imitate the harbor of Bilbao, a principal seaport and former shipbuilding center in the heart of the Basque country in the north.

Repaso del capítulo

Vocabulario y gramática 🔊

jcd-0189

Chapter Review

To prepare for the test, check to see if you . . .
- know the new vocabulary and grammar
- can perform the tasks on p. 47

to talk about activities

bailar	to dance
cantar	to sing
correr	to run
dibujar	to draw
escribir cuentos	to write stories
escuchar música	to listen to music
esquiar	to ski
hablar por teléfono	to talk on the phone
ir a la escuela	to go to school
jugar videojuegos	to play video games
leer revistas	to read magazines
montar en bicicleta	to ride a bicycle
montar en monopatín	to skateboard
nadar	to swim
pasar tiempo con amigos	to spend time with friends
patinar	to skate
practicar deportes	to play sports
tocar la guitarra	to play the guitar
trabajar	to work
usar la computadora	to use the computer
ver la tele	to watch television

to say what you like to do

(A mí) me gusta ___.	I like to ___.
(A mí) me gusta más ___.	I like to ___ better. (I prefer to ___.)
(A mí) me gusta mucho ___.	I like to ___ a lot.
A mí también.	I do too.

to say what you don't like to do

(A mí) no me gusta ___.	I don't like to ___.
(A mí) no me gusta nada ___.	I don't like to ___ at all.
A mí tampoco.	I don't (like to) either.

For *Vocabulario adicional*, see pp. 472–473.

to ask others what they like to do

¿Qué te gusta hacer?	What do you like to do?
¿Qué te gusta más?	What do you like better (prefer)?
¿Te gusta ___?	Do you like to ___?
¿Y a ti?	And you?

other useful words and expressions

ni . . . ni	neither . . . nor, not . . . or
o	or
pues . . .	well . . .
sí	yes
también	also, too
y	and

Más práctica

- **Core** Puzzle p. 20, Organizer p. 21
- **Communication** Practice Test pp. 230–232, Integrated Performance Assessment p. 229

realidades.com ✓

- Tutorial
- Flashcards
- Puzzles
- Self-test
- Web Code: jcd-0107

Preparación para el examen

On the exam you will be asked to . . .	Here are practice tasks similar to those you will find on the exam . . .	If you need review . . .

Interpretive

jcd-0189
🔊

1 Escuchar Listen to and understand a description of what someone likes to do

Listen to a voice mail from a student looking for a "match-up" to the homecoming dance. a) What are two things this person likes doing? b) What is one thing this person dislikes doing?

pp. 26–29 *Vocabulario en contexto*
p. 27 Actividades 1–2
p. 33 Actividad 13

Interpersonal

2 Hablar Talk about yourself and what you like and don't like to do and ask the same of others

You agreed to host a student from the Dominican Republic for a week. What can you tell him or her about yourself in a taped message? Include a brief description of what you like to do. How would you ask the student to tell you something about himself or herself?

p. 30 Actividad 7
p. 31 Actividad 8
p. 33 Actividad 12
p. 37 Actividades 16–17
p. 43 *Presentación oral*

Interpretive

3 Leer Read and understand someone's description of himself or herself

Read this pen pal e-mail from a Spanish-language magazine. What types of things does the person like to do? Does this person have anything in common with you? What is it?

¡Hola! A mí me gusta mucho usar la computadora y tocar la guitarra. No me gusta ni ir a la escuela ni leer. En el verano me gusta nadar y en el invierno me gusta esquiar. ¿Y a ti? ¿Qué te gusta hacer?

pp. 26–29 *Vocabulario en contexto*
p. 29 Actividad 3
p. 36 Actividad 15
p. 38 Actividad 19
pp. 40–41 *Lectura*, no. 3

Presentational

4 Escribir Write about yourself with a description of things you like and don't like to do

A school in the Dominican Republic wants to exchange e-mails with your school. Tell your e-pal your name and what you like to do and don't like to do.

p. 30 Actividades 5–6
p. 33 Actividad 12
p. 38 Actividad 18
p. 41 *¿Comprendes?*

Cultures

5 Pensar Demonstrate an understanding of cultural differences regarding dancing

How would you describe the Latin dances that have become popular in the United States? With what countries do you associate each dance? With what type of music or rhythms do you associate each dance?

p. 34 *Fondo cultural*
p. 35 Actividad 14
p. 42 *La cultura en vivo*

Frida Kahlo (1907–1954) is one of the best-known Mexican painters. In spite of a childhood illness, a crippling traffic accident, and many hospital stays throughout her life, Kahlo was a successful painter and led a very active social life. She used her artwork as an outlet for her physical and emotional suffering.

• Frida Kahlo painted over fifty self-portraits. What is she saying about herself through this painting?

"Autorretrato con mono" (1938), Frida Kahlo ▶

Oil on masonite, 16 X 12 inches. Courtesy of Albright-Knox Art Gallery, Buffalo, NY. Bequest of A. Conger Goodyear, 1966. © 2009 Banco de México, Diego Rivera & Frida Kahlo Museums Trust, México, D.F./Artists Rights Society (ARS), New York.

Y tú, ¿cómo eres?

Chapter Objectives

- Talk about personality traits
- Ask and tell what people are like
- Use adjectives to describe people
- Understand cultural perspectives on friendship

Video Highlights

Videocultura: *Mis amigos y yo*

A primera vista: *Amigos por Internet*

GramActiva Videos: adjectives; definite and indefinite articles; word order: placement of adjectives

Country Connection

As you learn how to describe yourself and your friends, you will make connections to these countries and places:

Más práctica

- *Real.* para hispanohablantes pp. 30–31

realidades.com

- Fondo cultural Activity
- Video Activities
- Online Atlas
- Web Code: jce-0002

Un grupo de amigos, Mercedes, Texas

Vocabulario en contexto

jcd-0197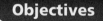

Objectives

Read, listen to, and understand information about
- personality traits

❝¿El chico? **Es mi amigo. ¿Cómo se llama?** Se llama Marcos. **¿Cómo es?** Pues . . .

. . . **él es deportista. Le gusta** mucho practicar deportes.

la chica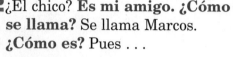

Pero a veces es impaciente . . .

. . . también es **un chico desordenado** ❞.

❝Mi amiga Sarita es **una buena** amiga. **Ella** no es **muy** deportista . . .

. . . pero es una chica **artística** . . .

el chico

. . . y muy **ordenada**.

Es una chica muy **inteligente** ❞.

Hola, me llamo Luz. ¿Yo? ¿Cómo **soy?** Pues . . .

. . . soy **estudiosa** . . .

. . . y **trabajadora** . . .

. . . y también **graciosa** . . .

. . . pero **según mi familia** ¡a veces soy **perezosa!** Y tú, ¿cómo eres?

---

1 **¿Marcos o Sarita?**

jcd-0197

Escuchar

Look at the pictures of Marcos and Sarita. Listen to the descriptions. If a word describes Marcos, point to his picture. If a word describes Sarita, point to her picture.

2 **¿Cierto o falso?**

jcd-0197

Escuchar

You will hear some statements about Luz. Give a "thumbs-up" sign if the statement is true, or a "thumbs-down" sign if it is false.

Más práctica

- **Guided** Vocab. Flash Cards, pp. 39–42
- **Core** Vocab. Practice pp. 22–23
- **Communication** Writing p. 25
- *Real.* **para hispanohablantes** p. 32

realidades.com ⓥ

- Audio Activities
- Flashcards
- Leveled Workbook
- Web Code: jcd-0111

Amigos por Internet

See what happens when *Chica sociable* sends an e-mail message to Esteban.

Strategy

Using cognates
You will see some unfamiliar words in this story. Many of these are cognates. Use their similarity to English words to determine their meaning.

- What does *sociable* mean?
- What does *ideal* mean?

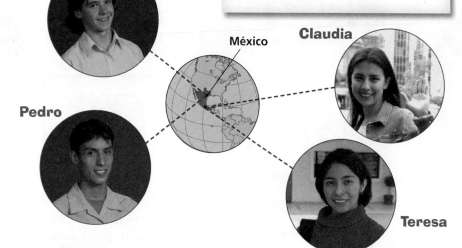

Esteban

México

Claudia

Pedro

Teresa

1 **Pedro:** Esteban, escucha: "Hola, ¿cómo eres? ¿Qué te gusta hacer? Me gusta mucho hablar con mis amigos. Me llamo *Chica sociable.* Escríbeme."

Esteban: ¡Ja! *Chica sociable.* A responder. Escribe, Pedro. . . .

5 **Teresa:** "Soy muy desordenada. Me gusta hablar por teléfono. Y no me gusta ir a la escuela. Escríbeme. *Chica sociable*".

6 **Claudia:** Un momento . . . uno más de mí. Escribe. . . "Yo soy *Chica misteriosa.* Soy amiga de *Chica sociable.* Soy muy simpática".

7 **Claudia:** "Y me gusta ir a la escuela. Soy estudiosa y trabajadora. Yo no soy tu chica ideal. *Chica misteriosa*".

2 Pedro: "Hola. Me llamo *Chico sociable*. ¡Qué coincidencia!".

3 Pedro: "Me gusta pasar tiempo con mis amigos. **No soy** muy **serio**. Según mis amigos, soy gracioso".

4 Claudia: ¡*Chica sociable*! ¡Ja!

Teresa: Yo soy *Chica sociable*.

Claudia: ¡No! ¿Tú **eres** *Chica sociable*? ¡¿Mi buena amiga . . . ?!

3 ¿Comprendes?

Escribir · Hablar

Read each of the sentences below and indicate which character is being described: *Chica sociable* or *Chica misteriosa*.

1. Me gusta hablar por teléfono.

2. Me gusta ir a la escuela.

3. Soy simpática.

4. No soy muy ordenada.

5. Soy trabajadora.

Más práctica

- **Guided** Vocab. Check, pp. 43–46
- **Core** Vocab. Practice pp. 24–25
- **Communication** Video pp. 18–20
- *Real.* **para hispanohablantes** p. 33

realidades.com V

- Audio Activities
- Video Activities
- Leveled Workbook
- Flashcards
- Web Code: jcd-0112

8 Esteban: Pues, Pedro. ¿*Chica sociable* o *Chica misteriosa*?

Pedro: *Chica misteriosa*. Me gusta la escuela y a ella le gusta la escuela también.

Esteban: Perfecto. A mí me gusta más *Chica sociable*.

4 Y tú, ¿qué dices?

Escribir · Hablar

1. Find five cognates in the *Videohistoria* and write what you think they mean in English.

2. Write an activity that goes with each of these characteristics.

    sociable   estudioso   trabajador

3. ¿Qué te gusta más, usar la computadora o hablar por teléfono?

Vocabulario en uso

5 **¿Cómo es el chico o la chica?**

Escribir

Choose the correct word to describe each of the people in the pictures.

Modelo

El chico es
(*impaciente* / *estudioso*).

1. La chica es
(*reservada* / *artística*).

2. La chica es
(*graciosa* / *perezosa*).

3. El chico es
(*reservado* / *deportista*).

4. El chico es
(*desordenado* / *atrevido*).

5. La chica es
(*artística* / *atrevida*).

6. El chico es
(*estudioso* / *desordenado*).

6 **Mi amigo José**

Escribir

Maritza is talking about her friend José. Read the sentences, then choose the appropriate word to fill in each blank.

Modelo

No es un chico impaciente. Es muy __paciente__.

1. Le gusta mucho practicar deportes.
Es ___.

2. A veces no es serio. Es un chico ___.

3. Le gusta pasar tiempo con amigos.
Es muy ___.

4. No es un chico ordenado. Es ___.

5. Le gusta ir a la escuela. Es ___.

6. No es perezoso. Es un chico muy ___.

7. Es simpático. Es un amigo muy ___.

trabajador	deportista	bueno
paciente	estudioso	sociable
gracioso	desordenado	

Manos a la obra

Gramática

Adjectives

Words that describe people and things are called adjectives (*adjetivos*).

- In Spanish, most adjectives have both masculine and feminine forms. The masculine form usually ends in the letter *-o* and the feminine form usually ends in the letter *-a*.

- Masculine adjectives are used to describe masculine nouns.

  Marcos es ordenado y simpático.   *Marcos is organized and nice.*

- Feminine adjectives are used to describe feminine nouns.

  Marta es ordenada y simpática.   *Marta is organized and nice.*

- Adjectives that end in *-e* describe both masculine and feminine nouns.

  Anita es inteligente.   *Anita is smart.*

  Pedro es inteligente también.   *Pedro is also smart.*

Masculine	Feminine
ordenado	ordenada
trabajador	trabajadora
paciente	paciente
deportista	deportista

- Adjectives whose masculine form ends in *-dor* have a feminine form that ends in *-dora*.

  Juan es trabajador.   *Juan is hardworking.*

  Luz es trabajadora.   *Luz is hardworking.*

- Some adjectives that end in *-a*, such as *deportista*, describe both masculine and feminine nouns. You will need to learn which adjectives follow this pattern.

  Tomás es deportista.   *Tomás is sports-minded.*

  Marta es deportista también.   *Marta is also sports-minded.*

GramActiva VIDEO

Want more help with adjectives? Watch the **GramActiva** video.

7 Roberto y Yolanda

Escribir

Copy the Venn diagram on a sheet of paper. Which words from the list below could only describe Roberto? Write them in the oval below his name. Which words could only describe Yolanda? Write them in the oval below her name. Which words could describe either Roberto or Yolanda? Write them in the overlapping area.

Modelo

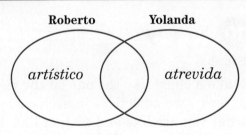

artístico	atrevida	deportista	estudiosa
graciosa	impaciente	simpático	inteligente
ordenada	paciente	perezosa	reservado
serio	sociable	talentosa	trabajador

8 ¿Cómo es Paloma?

Hablar

Work with a partner to ask and answer
questions about the people shown below.

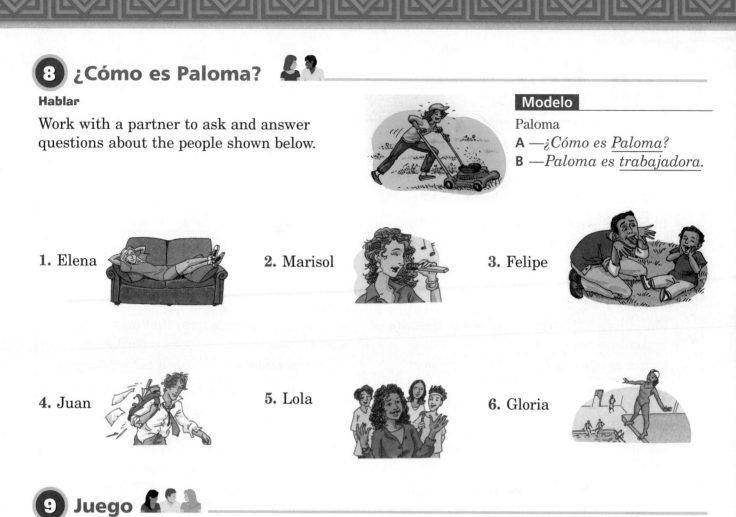

Modelo

Paloma

A —¿Cómo es _Paloma_?

B —_Paloma es trabajadora._

1. Elena

2. Marisol

3. Felipe

4. Juan

5. Lola

6. Gloria

9 Juego

Hablar

Choose an adjective and act it out for a small group or the class. The other
students take turns asking you questions. The first to ask a question with
the correct adjective (in the correct form) gets to do the next charade.

Modelo

A —_¿Eres ordenada?_

B —_Sí, soy ordenada._

o: —_No, no soy ordenada._

10 Yo soy . . .

Escribir

Make a chart like the one on the right. Write
at least two adjectives in each column to say
what you are like and are not like. Include
muy and _a veces_ when they are appropriate.
Save your work to use in later activities.

Modelo

Soy	No soy
estudiosa	perezosa
muy trabajadora	impaciente
deportista	

11 ¿Eres estudioso(a)?

Hablar • Escribir

Use your chart from Actividad 10. Talk with your partner about your personality traits. Take notes on what your partner tells you. Make another two-column chart, but with the headings *Es* and *No es*. Fill it in with information about your partner. You will use this chart in the next activity.

Modelo

A —*¿Cómo eres?*
B —*Soy estudiosa y muy trabajadora. También soy deportista. ¿Y tú?*
A —*Soy artístico. Según mis amigos, soy talentoso. No soy perezoso.*

12 Mi amigo(a)

Escribir • Hablar

Use the information from the previous activity to write a short description of yourself and your partner. Read your description to a small group or the class.

Modelo

Me llamo Luisa. Soy estudiosa y trabajadora. Y soy deportista. Mi amiga se llama Susana. Ella es simpática. También es deportista y trabajadora.

Exploración del lenguaje

Cognates that begin with *es* + consonant

Many words in Spanish that begin with *es* + consonant are easy to understand because they have the same meaning as English words. Knowing this pattern helps you recognize the meaning of new Spanish words and learn them quickly.

Try it out! Look at these words, then cover up the *e* at the beginning. Name the English words that come from the same root word.

estudiante	**es**tudioso	**es**cuela	**es**tómago
esquiar	**es**pecial	**es**tricto	**es**cena

Es muy deportista. Le encanta esquiar.

13 ¿Qué te gusta hacer?

Hablar

Trabaja con otro(a) estudiante. Pregunta y contesta según el modelo.

Modelo

A —¿Te gusta *correr*?

B —Sí, soy *deportista*.

o: —No, no soy *deportista*.

o: —Sí, pero no soy muy *deportista*.

Estudiante A

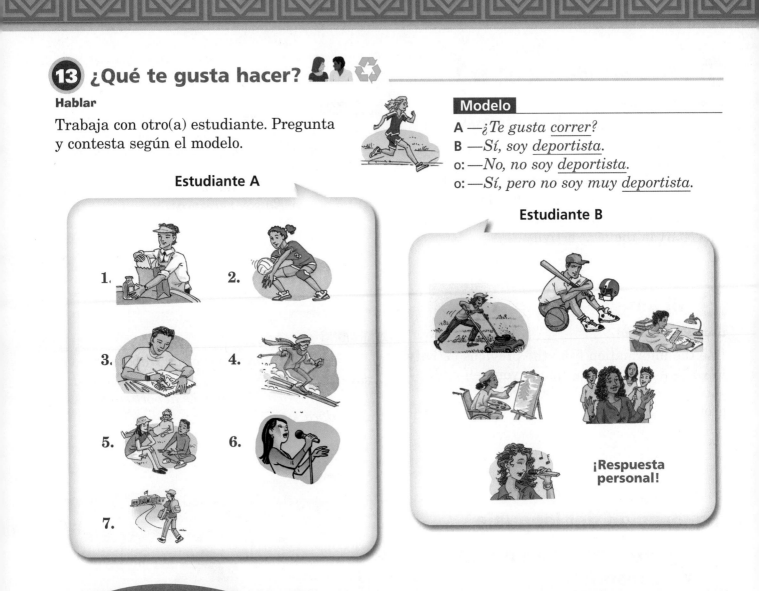

Estudiante B

¡Respuesta personal!

Fondo cultural

El mundo hispano

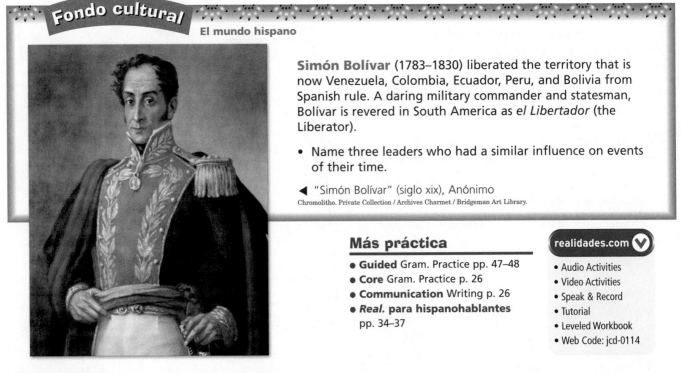

Simón Bolívar (1783–1830) liberated the territory that is now Venezuela, Colombia, Ecuador, Peru, and Bolivia from Spanish rule. A daring military commander and statesman, Bolívar is revered in South America as *el Libertador* (the Liberator).

• Name three leaders who had a similar influence on events of their time.

◀ "Simón Bolívar" (siglo xix), Anónimo
Chromolitho. Private Collection / Archives Charmet / Bridgeman Art Library.

Más práctica

● **Guided** Gram. Practice pp. 47–48
● **Core** Gram. Practice p. 26
● **Communication** Writing p. 26
● *Real.* **para hispanohablantes** pp. 34–37

realidades.com
• Audio Activities
• Video Activities
• Speak & Record
• Tutorial
• Leveled Workbook
• Web Code: jcd-0114

 **El poema "Soy Elena"**

Leer • Escribir

The following poem is called a *poema en diamante*. Can you guess why?
After you've read the poem, answer the questions.

Conexiones **La literatura**

Soy Elena

En general, soy
reservada y ordenada.
A veces, soy atrevida,
graciosa o impaciente.
No soy ni deportista
ni artística.
¡Yo soy yo!

1. Which activity would you invite Elena to do based on
   what she has told you about herself?

   dibujar   montar en monopatín   escuchar música

2. Rewrite the poem replacing *Soy Elena* with *Soy Tomás.*

 **Y tú, ¿qué dices?**

Escribir

Write *un poema en diamante* about yourself.
Choose adjectives that best describe you.
Look back at Actividad 10 for some ideas.
Substitute your adjectives in the poem above.
Be sure to write the poem in the form of a
diamond. You might want to use calligraphy or
an appropriate font on the computer and add
pictures to illustrate your work.

Gramática

Definite and indefinite articles

El and *la* are called definite articles and are the equivalent of "the" in English. *El* is used with masculine nouns; *la* is used with feminine nouns. You've already seen words with definite articles:

el libro   *the book*   la carpeta   *the folder*

Un and *una* are called indefinite articles and are the equivalent of "a" and "an" in English. *Un* is used with masculine nouns; *una* is used with feminine nouns:

un libro   *a book*   una carpeta   *a folder*

el	the
la	the

un	a, an
una	a, an

Strategy

Learning by repetition
When you learn a new noun, say it aloud, along with its definite article, as often as you get a chance. Eventually, you will find that words just "sound right" with the correct definite article and you will know whether nouns are masculine or feminine.

GramActiva VIDEO

Want more help with definite and indefinite articles? Watch the **GramActiva** video.

jcd-0198

16 ¿El o la? 🔊

Escuchar • GramActiva

Write the word *el* in large letters on a sheet of paper or an index card. Write *la* in large letters on another sheet. You will hear eight words you already know. When you hear a masculine word, hold up the paper with *el*. When you hear a feminine word, hold up the paper with the word *la* on it.

17 ¿Qué es?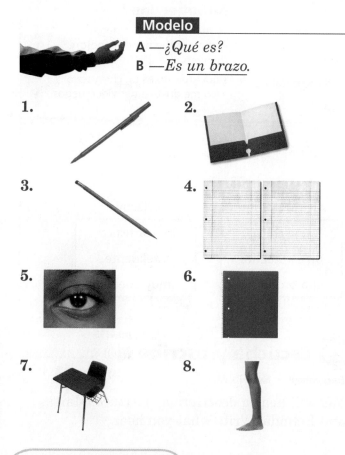

Hablar

Tell your partner the names of the things pictured below.

Modelo

A —¿Qué es?
B —Es un brazo.

1.

2.

3.

4.

5.

6.

7.

8.

18 La escuela de Diego

Escribir

Diego is talking about people at his school. Read the sentences and complete each one with *un* or *una*.

1. La Sra. Secada es ___ profesora simpática.

2. Alicia es ___ estudiante trabajadora.

3. Juan Carlos es ___ chico perezoso.

4. Germán es ___ chico sociable.

5. El Sr. Guzmán es ___ profesor gracioso.

6. Adriana es ___ chica muy seria.

7. La Srta. Cifuentes es ___ profesora paciente.

8. Arturo es ___ estudiante talentoso.

Más práctica

- **Guided** Gram. Practice p. 49
- **Core** Gram. Practice p. 27
- **Communication** Writing p. 27, Test Prep p. 233
- *Real.* **para hispanohablantes** pp. 37–38

realidades.com ▼

- Audio Activities
- Video Activities
- Speak & Record
- Tutorial
- Leveled Workbook
- Web Code: jcd-0113

Pronunciación

jcd-0198

The vowels *o* and *u* 🔊

In Spanish, the pronunciation of the letter *o* is similar to the vowel sound in the English word "boat" but is always cut very short. Say these words, concentrating on making a short *o* sound.

bolígrafo	gracioso	cómo
teléfono	tampoco	otoño

In Spanish, the pronunciation of the letter *u* is similar to the vowel sound in the English word "zoo." Say these words.

mucho	lunes	usted
octubre	estudioso	según

¡Ojo! Careful! Sometimes the words we mispronounce most are the ones that remind us of English words.

Try it out! Pronounce these words, concentrating on the Spanish vowel sounds:

agosto	regular	tropical	música
gusto	universidad	Uruguay	Cuba

El mundo

Gramática

Word order: Placement of adjectives

In Spanish, adjectives usually come after the noun they describe. Notice how *artística* follows *chica* in the Spanish sentence.

Margarita es **una chica artística**.   *Margarita is an artistic girl.*

Did you notice that in the English sentence the adjective comes before the noun?

Here's a simple pattern you can follow when writing a sentence in Spanish.

Subject	Verb	Indefinite Article + Noun	Adjective
Margarita	es	una chica	muy artística.
Pablo	es	un estudiante	inteligente.
La Sra. Ortiz	es	una profesora	muy buena.

19 Frases desordenadas

Escribir

Rewrite these scrambled words to create a sentence. Follow the "building-blocks" pattern above and be sure to add a period at the end of each sentence.

Modelo

perezoso Antonio es chico un
Antonio es un chico perezoso.

1. artística es una chica Marina
2. es un Tito perezoso chico
3. deportista chica una es Paquita
4. Marcos chico un es reservado no
5. chico no Rafael es estudioso un
6. no una Teresa chica es inteligente

20 Escucha y escribe 🔊

jcd-0198

Escuchar · Escribir

You will hear a description of Arturo, Marta, and Belinda. Write what you hear.

21 ¿Cómo es . . . ?

Escribir

You are sitting in your school cafeteria with a new exchange student from Costa Rica. Describe the other students based on their activities.

Modelo

Emilia es una chica talentosa.

22 Y tú, ¿qué dices?

Escribir · Hablar

1. Según tu familia, ¿cómo eres?
2. Según tu mejor *(best)* amigo(a), ¿cómo eres?
3. Y tú, ¿cómo eres?

Más práctica

- **Guided** Gram. Practice p. 50
- **Core** Gram. Practice p. 28
- *Real.* **para hispanohablantes** pp. 39–41

 realidades.com

- Audio Activities
- Video Activities
- Speak & Record
- Canción de hip hop
- Tutorial
- Leveled Workbook
- Web Code: jcd-0115

El español en el mundo del trabajo

Paciente, inteligente, trabajador, ordenado . . . These four qualities will make you a good candidate for any job. And if you add *bilingüe* to the list, your job qualifications will be enhanced.

Make a list of careers in which your knowledge of Spanish would be an asset. Which of these careers are of interest to you?

Lectura

Un *self-quiz*

¿Hay una relación entre los colores y la personalidad? Según un *self-quiz* de la revista *Amigos,* tus colores favoritos revelan perfectamente cómo eres.

Objectives

- **Read and understand an article about personality traits**
- **Understand cultural perspectives on friendship**
- **Write a letter to a pen pal**
- **Learn facts about the Caribbean**

Strategy

Using visual clues to get meaning

You have not yet learned the Spanish words for colors, but see if you can figure out what they are from the visual clues in the article.

¿Cómo eres tú?
¡Los colores revelan tu personalidad!

¿Eres una chica? ¿Te gusta el rojo? ¿Eres un chico? ¿Te gusta el rojo?	Eres muy apasionada. Eres atrevido.
¿Eres una chica? ¿Te gusta el verde? ¿Eres un chico? ¿Te gusta el verde?	Eres una chica natural. Eres muy generoso.
¿Eres una chica? ¿Te gusta el azul? ¿Eres un chico? ¿Te gusta el azul?	Eres muy talentosa. Eres un chico sociable.
¿Eres una chica? ¿Te gusta el anaranjado? ¿Eres un chico? ¿Te gusta el anaranjado?	Eres una chica artística. Eres gracioso.
¿Eres una chica? ¿Te gusta el violeta? ¿Eres un chico? ¿Te gusta el violeta?	Eres una chica muy independiente. Eres un chico romántico.
¿Eres una chica? ¿Te gusta el amarillo? ¿Eres un chico? ¿Te gusta el amarillo?	Eres una chica muy trabajadora. Eres muy serio.

¿Comprendes?

1. You probably were able to understand most of the words in the quiz. Write the English meaning for these Spanish cognates from the reading:

- revelan
- natural
- independiente
- generoso
- apasionada
- romántico

2. According to the "self-quiz," what should be the favorite colors of these teenagers?

a. A Beto le gusta estar con amigos.

b. A Margarita le gusta dibujar.

c. A Lorenzo le gusta el trabajo voluntario.

d. A Lupe le gusta estudiar. Es muy seria.

e. A Isabel le gusta estar con amigos, pero también le gusta estar sola *(alone)*.

3. Which of the colors in this reading best matches your personality? Why?

Modelo

Amarillo: *Soy una chica trabajadora. Me gusta ir a la escuela.*

Fondo cultural
Guatemala • México

Huipil is the word for the colorful, hand-woven blouse worn by female descendants of the Maya. The color, design, and style of weaving are unique to each *huipil* and identify the background and specific village of the weaver. Hundreds of designs and styles of weaving have been identified in the Mayan regions, which are located principally in Guatemala and parts of Mexico.

- What do you wear that might represent your personality or likes and dislikes?

Una niña con huipil

Más práctica

- **Guided** Reading Support p. 51
- **Communication** Writing p. 28, Test Prep p. 234
- *Real.* **para hispanohablantes** pp. 42–45

realidades.com Ⓥ

- Internet Activity
- Leveled Workbook
- Web Code: jcd-0116

Perspectivas del mundo hispano
¿Qué es un amigo?

Marcos, a Costa Rican student on an exchange program in the United States writes:

❝When I arrived in the United States, I was amazed at all the friends my host brother and sister had. They knew a lot of people. These friends came to the house frequently, and we went out in groups. People were very open when meeting me. We'd spend some time together and get to know each other in a short amount of time. And once you got to know them, you ended up talking about everything!❞.

Brianna, a United States student on an exchange program in Colombia writes:

❝After I spent my year in Colombia, I learned that the concept of friendship is a little different than in the United States. My host brother and sisters spent a lot of time with their family. They knew people at school and from after-school activities, but they had just a few close friends and we'd do things with them. It was definitely a smaller group than I was used to. It seems that it took longer to become close friends with people too❞.

In Spanish, two expressions are used frequently to describe friendly relationships: *un amigo,* which means "friend," and *un conocido,* which means "acquaintance." You already know the word *amigo. Conocido* comes from the verb *conocer,* which means "to meet." Each expression implies a different type of relationship.

Dos amigas estudiando en Cozumel, México

Check it out! In many Spanish-speaking countries you'll find lots of expressions for someone who is your friend: *hermano, cuate (México), amigote (España),* and *compinche (Uruguay, Argentina, España).* Make a list of the expressions for "a friend" that are popular in your community. How would you explain them to someone from a Spanish-speaking country?

Think about it! Compare how the United States perspective on friendship is different from that of a Spanish-speaking country. Use the terms *amigo* and *conocido* as you make the comparison.

Amigos en una fiesta en España

Presentación escrita
Amigo por correspondencia

Task
Write an e-mail in which you introduce yourself to a prospective pen pal.

1 Prewrite Think about information you want to give. Answer these questions to help you organize your e-mail message.
- ¿Cómo te llamas?
- ¿Cómo eres?
- ¿Qué te gusta hacer?
- ¿Qué no te gusta hacer?

Strategy

Using the writing process
To create your best work, follow each step in the writing process.

2 Draft Write a first draft of your e-mail message using the answers to the questions above. Begin by introducing yourself: ¡Hola! Me llamo . . . . When you are finished, end with Escríbeme pronto. ("Write to me soon.")

¡Hola! Me llamo Pati. Soy atrevida y muy deportista. Me gusta mucho nadar y correr, pero me gusta más esquiar. ¡No me gusta nada jugar videojuegos! Escríbeme pronto.

3 Revise Review the first draft of your e-mail and share it with a partner. Here are some things to look for:
- Is it well organized?
- Does it include all the information from the Prewrite questions?
- Is the spelling accurate? Did you use the correct form of the adjectives to describe yourself?
- Did you include the opening and the closing?

Decide whether or not you want to use your partner's suggestions. Rewrite your draft.

4 Publish Type up your e-mail. You might want to send it to a pen pal in another class or school, send it to your teacher, or print it and give it to someone else in the class to answer.

5 Evaluation Your teacher may give you a rubric for grading your e-mail. You probably will be graded on:
- completion of task
- following the writing process by turning in the Prewrite and first draft
- using adjectives correctly

El Caribe

A chain of islands extending from the Bahamas in the north to Trinidad in the south, the Caribbean or West Indies is a region of extraordinary cultural and linguistic diversity. The Spanish-speaking countries are Cuba, Puerto Rico, and the Dominican Republic, which occupies the eastern portion of the island of Hispaniola.

Christopher Columbus first landed on the island of Hispaniola in 1492. He returned the following year with 1,000 colonists and founded Isabela, the first European colony in America, on the northern coast of Hispaniola.

¿Sabes que . . . ?

Most Cubans are descendants of people who originally came to the island from Spain and Africa. Although almost all Cubans speak Spanish as their first language, some also speak Lucumi, which is closely related to West African languages. Many people in other parts of the Caribbean speak creole languages, which combine elements of African and European tongues.

Para pensar

African traditions have inspired reggae, calypso, salsa, merengue, and many other musical styles in the Caribbean. What are some of the musical styles from the United States that have been influenced by African traditions?

Estados Unidos
Islas Bahamas
Cuba
República Dominicana
Haití
Puerto Rico
Mar Caribe
OCÉANO ATLÁNTICO

realidades.com
• Online Atlas
• Web Code: jce-0002

The Universidad Autónoma de Santo Domingo, located in the capital of the Dominican Republic, Santo Domingo, is the oldest university in the Americas. It was founded in 1538—almost 100 years before Harvard—and continues to be one of the most important in the Caribbean.

Opened in 1963, the Arecibo Observatory in Puerto Rico has the largest single-dish radio telescope in the world. Some 200 scientists from around the world conduct research at Arecibo every year. In the early 1990s astronomers at Arecibo discovered the first planets outside our solar system.

The Caribbean is famous for its diverse musical styles that fuse African and European influences. Some groups even combine salsa, rumba, cha-cha-cha, and other Caribbean musical styles with jazz, hip-hop, and rock and roll.

Repaso del capítulo

Vocabulario y gramática 🔊

jcd-0199

Chapter Review

To prepare for the test, check to see if you . . .
- know the new vocabulary and grammar
- can answer the questions on p. 71

to talk about what you and others are like

artístico, -a	artistic
atrevido, -a	daring
bueno, -a	good
deportista	sports-minded
desordenado, -a	messy
estudioso, -a	studious
gracioso, -a	funny
impaciente	impatient
inteligente	intelligent
ordenado, -a	neat
paciente	patient
perezoso, -a	lazy
reservado, -a	reserved, shy
serio, -a	serious
simpático, -a	nice, friendly
sociable	sociable
talentoso, -a	talented
trabajador, -ora	hardworking

to ask people about themselves or others

¿Cómo eres?	What are you like?
¿Cómo es?	What is he / she like?
¿Cómo se llama?	What's his / her name?
¿Eres . . . ?	Are you . . . ?

to talk about what someone likes or doesn't like

le gusta . . .	he / she likes . . .
no le gusta . . .	he / she doesn't like . . .

to describe someone

soy	I am
no soy	I am not
es	he / she is

For *Vocabulario adicional*, see pp. 472–473.

to tell whom you are talking about

el amigo	male friend
la amiga	female friend
el chico	boy
la chica	girl
él	he
ella	she
yo	I

other useful words

a veces	sometimes
muy	very
pero	but
según	according to
según mi familia	according to my family

adjectives

Masculine	Feminine
ordenado	ordenada
trabajador	trabajadora
paciente	paciente
deportista	deportista

definite articles

el	the
la	the

indefinite articles

un	a, an
una	a, an

Más práctica

- **Core** Puzzle p. 29, Organizer p. 30
- **Communication** Practice Test pp. 236–238, Integrated Performance Assessment p. 235

realidades.com

- Tutorial
- Flashcards
- Puzzles
- Self-test
- Web Code: jcd-0117

Preparación para el examen

On the exam you will be asked to . . .	Here are practice tasks similar to those you will find on the exam . . .	If you need review . . .

Interpretive

jcd-0199

1 Escuchar Listen to and understand a description of a friend

Listen as a character in a Spanish soap opera describes his ex-girlfriend. What does he think her good qualities are? What does he think her shortcomings are? Can you understand why he broke up with her?

pp. 50–53 *Vocabulario en contexto*
p. 57 Actividades 11–12
p. 62 Actividad 20

Interpersonal

2 Hablar Talk about yourself in terms of how you see yourself

While you're talking to your Spanish teacher, you realize that she doesn't know the "real you." Tell her some things about yourself that would help her understand you.

pp. 50–53 *Vocabulario en contexto*
p. 56 Actividad 9
p. 57 Actividad 11
p. 58 Actividad 13
p. 63 Actividad 22

Interpretive

3 Leer Read and understand a description of someone

In a popular Spanish magazine, you see an interview with the actor who plays the part of a teenager, Carlos, in a TV show you have been watching. See if you can understand what he is saying about the character he plays:

¡No me gusta nada el chico! Él es muy inteligente, pero le gusta hablar y hablar de NADA. Es ridículo. Es muy impaciente y perezoso. Él no es ni simpático ni gracioso. Yo soy un actor . . . ¡no soy como Carlos!

pp. 50–53 *Vocabulario en contexto*
p. 59 Actividad 14
pp. 64–65 *Lectura*

Presentational

4 Escribir Write a short paragraph describing yourself

The first issue of your school's online newspaper is called "Getting to Know You." Submit a brief profile of yourself. Mention what your family thinks of you and list some things you like to do. For example:

Yo soy una chica deportista y muy sociable. Según mi familia, soy graciosa. Me gusta patinar y hablar por teléfono.

pp. 56–57 Actividades 10–12
p. 59 Actividad 15
p. 63 Actividad 22
p. 67 *Presentación escrita*

Cultures • Comparisons

5 Pensar Demonstrate an understanding of cultural perspectives on friendship

Explain the differences between the terms *amigo* and *conocido* in Spanish-speaking cultures. How does this compare to words that we use in the United States?

p. 66 *Perspectivas del mundo hispano*

Fondo cultural

Colombia

Colombian artist Fernando Botero (1932–) is among the best known and most respected Latin American artists. His works have been exhibited around the world in prestigious museums, galleries, and open-air places. Botero's style is unique and recognizable. Pedrito Botero, shown in the painting, was the artist's son. He died in a car accident when he was four years old.

• Based upon the painting, how could you describe Botero's style?

"Pedrito" (1997), Fernando Botero ▶
©Fernando Botero, courtesy of the Marlborough Gallery, New York.

Capítulo 2A

Tu día en la escuela

Chapter Objectives

- Talk about school schedules and subjects
- Discuss what students do during the day
- Ask and tell who is doing an action
- Compare your school with that of a student in a Spanish-speaking country

Video Highlights

Videocultura: *La escuela*

A primera vista: *El primer día de clases*

GramActiva Videos: subject pronouns; present tense of *-ar* verbs

Country Connection

As you learn about the school day in Spanish-speaking countries, you will make connections to these countries and places:

- España
- México
- Venezuela
- Costa Rica
- Colombia

Más práctica

- *Real.* para hispanohablantes pp. 50–51

realidades.com ✔

- Fondo cultural Activity
- Video Activities
- Online Atlas
- Web Code: jce-0002

Vocabulario en contexto

jcd-0287

El horario de Alicia

❝Me gusta mucho mi **horario.** En la **primera hora,** tengo la clase de tecnología . . . ¡es mi clase **favorita!** Es **interesante** y **práctica.** Pero a veces es **difícil**❞.

primera hora — tecnología

segunda hora — arte

tercera hora — ciencias sociales

cuarta hora — ciencias naturales

quinta hora — el almuerzo

sexta hora — español

séptima hora — matemáticas

octava hora — inglés

novena hora — educación física

Más vocabulario
décimo, -a   tenth

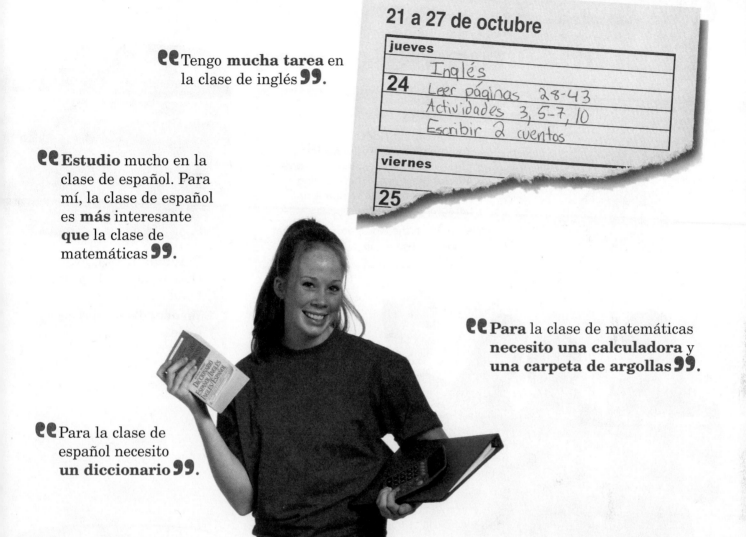

❝Tengo **mucha tarea** en la clase de inglés ❞.

21 a 27 de octubre

jueves	
24	Inglés Leer páginas 28-43 Actividades 3, 5-7, 10 Escribir 2 cuentos

viernes	
25	

❝**Estudio** mucho en la clase de español. Para mí, la clase de español es **más** interesante **que** la clase de matemáticas ❞.

❝**Para** la clase de matemáticas **necesito una calculadora** y **una carpeta de argollas** ❞.

❝Para la clase de español necesito **un diccionario** ❞.

---

1 **¿Sí o no?** 🔊   jcd-0287

Escuchar

You will hear Alicia make several statements about her school day and schedule. Give a "thumbs-up" sign if what she says is true or a "thumbs-down" sign if what she says is false.

2 **El horario de Alicia** 🔊   jcd-0287

Escuchar

Listen to Alicia as she describes her class schedule. Touch the picture of each class as you hear it.

Más práctica

- **Guided** Vocab. Flash Cards pp. 53–58
- **Core** Vocab. Practice pp. 31–32
- **Communication** Writing p. 35
- *Real.* **para hispanohablantes** p. 52

realidades.com Ⓥ

- Audio Activities
- Leveled Workbook
- Flashcards
- Web Code: jcd-0201

El primer día de clases

Es el primer día de clases en la Escuela Bilingüe en la Ciudad de México.

México

Strategy

Using context clues
You can often guess the meaning of new words by reading the words around them and understanding what the rest of the sentence or paragraph is about.

• Based on the words around it, what does *enseña* mean in Panel 2?

1 Claudia: Teresa, ¿qué clase **tienes** en la primera hora?

Teresa: Tengo la clase de inglés.

Srta. Santoro   Teresa   Claudia   Sr. Treviño

5 Teresa: Necesitas hablar con el señor Treviño, en la oficina.

Claudia: Buena idea.

6 Claudia: Buenos días, señor Treviño. Necesito hablar con Ud. Tengo la clase de matemáticas . . .

Sr. Treviño: Sí, sí, Claudia, pero ahora no es posible. Mañana.

7 Srta. Santoro: Buenos días, estudiantes. Las matemáticas son muy interesantes y prácticas, ¿verdad?

Estudiantes: Sí, profesora.

Srta. Santoro: Y es muy importante **estudiar** y trabajar mucho . . .

2 **Claudia:** ¿Quién enseña la clase de inglés?

Teresa: El señor Marín. Es un profesor muy **divertido.** ¿Y tú? ¿Qué clase tienes en la primera hora?

3 **Claudia:** Tengo la clase de matemáticas. Me gusta mucho. Para mí es muy **fácil.** Y, ¿qué tienes en la segunda hora?

Teresa: La clase de educación física.

4 **Teresa:** Y en la segunda hora, ¿qué clase tienes, Claudia?

Claudia: A ver . . . En la segunda hora, tengo la clase de matemáticas. ¡Y también tengo la clase de matemáticas en la tercera, en la cuarta, en la quinta y en la sexta hora!

8 **Srta. Santoro:** ¿Claudia?

Claudia: ¡Tengo seis clases de matemáticas hoy!

Srta. Santoro: ¡Seis! Es **aburrido,** ¿no? . . .

3 **¿Comprendes?**

Leer · Escribir

Read each sentence. Write *sí* if it is correct or *no* if it is incorrect.

1. Es el primer día de clases.

2. A Teresa le gusta la clase de inglés.

3. Para Claudia, la clase de matemáticas es difícil.

4. Claudia tiene la clase de educación física en la segunda hora.

5. Según la profesora, la clase de matemáticas es muy práctica.

6. En la sexta hora la clase de matemáticas es interesante.

Más práctica

● **Guided** Vocab. Check pp. 59–62
● **Core** Vocab. Practice pp. 33–34
● **Communication** Video pp. 29–30
● *Real.* **para hispanohablantes** p. 53

realidades.com

● Audio Activities
● Video Activities
● Leveled Workbook
● Flashcards
● Web Code: jcd-0202

Vocabulario en uso

4 Un horario

Leer · Escribir

Read the list of classes offered at a high school in Querétaro, Mexico. This school has a special focus on the arts. Answer the questions about the schedule.

México

CENTRO DE EDUCACIÓN ARTÍSTICA

"IGNACIO MARIANO DE LAS CASAS"

PRIMER SEMESTRE

Español	5 h semanales
Matemáticas	5 h semanales
Historia universal	3 h semanales
Educación cívica y ética	3 h semanales
Biología	3 h semanales
Introducción a la física	3 h semanales
Inglés	3 h semanales
Danza	3 h semanales
Teatro	3 h semanales
Artes plásticas	3 h semanales
Música	3 h semanales

Total 37 h semanales

1. ¿Cuántas clases hay cada (each) semana?
2. ¿Cuántas horas de inglés hay?
3. ¿Cuántas clases de ciencias sociales hay?
4. ¿Cuántas clases de ciencias naturales hay?
5. Escribe los nombres de las diferentes clases de arte.

5 Mi horario

Escribir

Write out your class schedule. Copy the chart and provide the information for each class.

Modelo

Hora	Clase	Profesor(a)
la primera hora	la clase de inglés	la Sra. Sánchez

¿Recuerdas?

Use *señor*, *señora*, and *señorita* when talking **to** adults. Use *el* in front of *señor* and *la* in front of *señora* or *señorita* when talking **about** adults.

6 Mucha tarea

Hablar

With a partner, ask and tell if you have a lot of homework in each class.

Modelo

A —¿*Tienes mucha tarea en la clase de matemáticas?*
B —*Sí, tengo mucha tarea.*
o: —*No, no tengo mucha tarea.*
o: —*No estudio matemáticas.*

Estudiante A

1. Español
2. ENGLISH LITERATURE
3.
4.
5.
6.
7. El mundo

Estudiante B

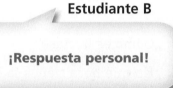

¡Respuesta personal!

7 Me gusta más . . .

Escribir

Write sentences stating which of the two classes you like better and why. Use the list of adjectives to help with your response. Save your paper for Actividad 8.

aburrida	divertida	interesante
difícil	fácil	práctica

Modelo

inglés/español
Me gusta más la clase de español. Es divertida.
o: *Me gusta más la clase de español. No es aburrida.*
o: *No me gusta ni la clase de español ni la clase de inglés.*

1. inglés / español
2. arte / educación física
3. inglés / matemáticas
4. ciencias sociales / ciencias naturales
5. tecnología / música
6. matemáticas / ciencias sociales

8 **¿Qué te gusta más?**

Hablar

With a partner, ask and tell which classes from Actividad 7 you like best
and why.

Modelo

A —*¿Te gusta más la clase de inglés o la clase de español?*
B —*A ver . . . Para mí, la clase de español es más divertida*
que la clase de inglés.

9 **Y tú, ¿qué dices?**

Escribir · Hablar

1. ¿Qué clase te gusta más?

2. ¿Cómo es la clase?

3. ¿En qué hora tienes la clase?

4. ¿Quién enseña la clase?

5. ¿Tienes mucha tarea en la clase?

Fondo cultural

El mundo hispano

Studying English While you're in Spanish
class at your school, large numbers of Spanish-
speaking students are studying to learn the
most popular foreign language worldwide:
English. Many children begin to study English in
grade school and continue through high school.
They often attend special language school
for additional English classes. When visiting a
Spanish-speaking country, you might easily
find someone who is eager to practice his
or her English skills with you in exchange for
helping you improve your Spanish.

• Why do you think English is so popular in
other countries? Are you studying Spanish
for similar reasons?

Estudiantes mexicanos en una clase de inglés

Exploración del lenguaje

Connections between Latin, English, and Spanish

Many words in English and Spanish are based on Latin. Seeing the relationship between these words will help expand your English or Spanish vocabulary. Look at the list of Latin root forms for the numbers 1 to 10.

Try it out! For each Roman numeral listed, choose one of the root forms (if more than one is listed) and write down a Spanish or English word you know that is based on that root.

Try it out! The Roman year used to begin with the month of March. Knowing that, can you explain why *septiembre, octubre, noviembre,* and *diciembre* use the Latin root forms for seven, eight, nine, and ten?

I	uni- prim-	VI	sext-
II	du- bi- second-	VII	sept-
III	tri-	VIII	oct- octav-
IV	quadr- quart-	IX	novem-
V	quint-	X	dec- decim-

Fondo cultural

España

Many Spanish words are derived from Latin because Spain was once part of the Roman Empire. Rome occupied most of Spain from about 209 B.C. to 586 A.D. During that time, massive public structures, including aqueducts and theaters, were built. Some of these, such as the aqueduct that towers over the modern city of Segovia, are still standing. The Latin name for Spain was *Hispania.*

• Can you see the similarity between *Hispania* and the country's name in Spanish, *España?*

El Acueducto de Segovia

Gramática

Subject pronouns

The subject of a sentence tells who is doing the action.
You often use people's names as the subject:

Gregorio escucha música.   ***Gregory*** *listens to music.*

Ana canta y baila.   ***Ana*** *sings and dances.*

You also use subject pronouns (*I, you, he, she, we, they*) to tell
who is doing an action. The subject pronouns replace people's names:

Él escucha música.   ***He*** *listens to music.*

Ella canta y baila.   ***She*** *sings and dances.*

Here are all the subject pronouns in Spanish:

yo	I	nosotros	we *(masc., masc./fem.)*
		nosotras	we *(fem.)*
tú	you *(familiar)*	vosotros	you *(masc., masc./fem.)*
		vosotras	you *(fem.)*
usted (Ud.)	you *(formal)*	ustedes (Uds.)	you *(formal)*
él	he	ellos	they *(masc., masc./fem.)*
ella	she	ellas	they *(fem.)*

Tú, usted, ustedes, and *vosotros(as)* all mean "you."

- Use *tú* with family, friends, people your age or younger, and anyone
  you call by his or her first name.

- Use *usted* with adults you address with a title, such as *señor, señora,
  profesor(a),* etc. *Usted* is usually written as *Ud.*

- In Latin America, use *ustedes* when speaking to two or more people,
  regardless of age. *Ustedes* is usually written as *Uds.*

- In Spain, use *vosotros(as)* when speaking to two or more people you
  call *tú* individually: *tú* + *tú* = *vosotros(as).* Use *ustedes* when talking
  to two or more people you call *usted* individually.

If a group is made up of males only or of both males and females
together, use the masculine forms: *nosotros, vosotros, ellos.*

If a group is all females, use the feminine forms:
nosotras, vosotras, ellas.

You can combine a subject pronoun and a name
to form a subject.

Alejandro y yo = **nosotros**   Pepe y tú = **ustedes**

Carlos y ella = **ellos**   Lola y ella = **ellas**

GramActiva VIDEO

Want more help with
subject pronouns?
Watch the
GramActiva video.

yo

10 ¡Señala!

Escuchar • Hablar • GramActiva

Your teacher will name several subject pronouns. Point to people in the classroom who represent the pronoun you hear. After you have practiced with your teacher, practice with a partner.

11 ¿Es ella?

Escribir

What subject pronouns would you use to talk about these people?

Modelo
Gloria
Ella.

1. Carlos
2. Felipe y yo
3. María y Sarita
4. Pablo, Tomás y Anita
5. el señor Treviño
6. tú y Esteban

12 ¿Tú, Ud. o Uds.?

Hablar

Tell whether you would use *tú*, *Ud.*, or *Uds.* with these people.

Más práctica

- **Guided** Gram. Practice pp. 63–64
- **Core** Gram. Practice p. 35
- **Communication** Writing p. 36, Test Prep p. 239
- ***Real.* para hispanohablantes** pp. 54–57

realidades.com ✔
- Audio Activities
- Video Activities
- Speak & Record
- Tutorial
- Leveled Workbook
- Web Code: jcd-0203

Gramática

Present tense of -ar verbs

You already know that the infinitive forms of Spanish verbs always end in -ar, -er, or -ir.

The largest group of verbs end in -ar. Hablar is one of these -ar verbs.

You will want to use verbs in ways other than in the infinitive form. To do this, you will drop the -ar ending and make changes.

To create the forms of most -ar verbs, you first drop the -ar from the infinitive, leaving the stem:

hablar → habl-

Then you add the verb endings -o, -as, -a, -amos, -áis, or -an to the stem.

Here are the forms of hablar:

(yo)	hablo	(nosotros) (nosotras)	hablamos
(tú)	hablas	(vosotros) (vosotras)	habláis
Ud. (él) (ella)	habla	Uds. (ellos) (ellas)	hablan

In Spanish, the present tense form of a verb can be translated into English in two ways:

Hablo español.   *I speak Spanish.*
                   I am speaking Spanish.

¿Recuerdas?

You already know many -ar verbs, such as *cantar* and *bailar*.

The verb endings always indicate who is doing the action. In this case, they tell *who* is speaking. Because of this, you can often use the verb without a subject:

Hablo inglés.   **¿Hablas** español?

Subject pronouns are often used for emphasis or clarification.

Ella habla inglés pero **él** habla español.

GramActiva VIDEO

Want more help with verbs that end in -ar? Watch the **GramActiva** video.

hablo

---

jcd-0288

13 ¿Una mano o dos? 🔊

Escuchar • Pensar • GramActiva

You will hear eight -ar verbs. If the ending tells you one person is performing the action, raise one hand. If the ending tells you more than one person is doing something, raise both hands.

Strategy

Listening for information
Always listen carefully for the endings on verbs to know who is doing the action.

14 ¿Qué estudian?

Escribir · Hablar

Look at the pictures and tell what these people are studying.

Modelo

Tomás
Tomás estudia música.

1. Laura

2. Josefina, Elena y yo

3. tú

4. Catalina y José

5. Joaquín y tú

6. yo

15 Juego

Escuchar · Hablar · GramActiva

❶ Work with a partner and tear a sheet of paper into eight pieces of equal size. Write a different subject pronoun on each piece (*yo, tú, él, ella, Ud., nosotros, ellas, Uds.*). Place the subject pronouns face down in a pile.

❷ Your teacher will say an infinitive. One partner will select the top piece of paper from the pile, read the subject pronoun, and say the correct verb form. A correct answer earns one point. Place the "used" subject pronouns in a separate pile. Take turns selecting from the pile and answering.

❸ When your teacher tells you to stop, shuffle the pieces of paper with subject pronouns and place them in a new pile face down. When the next verb is read aloud, continue play. The partner with the most correct answers is the winner.

En una escuela en México

Más práctica

- **Guided** Gram. Practice pp. 65–66
- **Core** Gram. Practice pp. 36–37
- **Communication** Writing p. 37
- *Real.* **para hispanohablantes** pp. 58–60

realidades.com ✓

- Audio Activities
- Video Activities
- Speak & Record
- Canción de hip hop
- Animated Verbs
- Tutorial
- Leveled Workbook
- Web Code: jcd-0204

16 En la escuela

Escribir

Use the verbs in the list to complete the sentences about what different activities take place during school.

Modelo

Yo estudio mucho en la clase de español

necesitar	hablar	dibujar
usar	practicar	enseñar
patinar	bailar	

1. Lupe y Guillermo ___ mucho en la clase de arte.
2. Tú ___ la computadora en la clase de tecnología.
3. Yo ___ una calculadora y una carpeta para la clase de matemáticas.
4. Tomás y yo ___ deportes en la clase de educación física.
5. ¿Quién ___ la clase de ciencias naturales?
6. Marta ___ mucho en la clase de español.

17 Escucha y escribe ◀))

jcd-0288

Escuchar • Escribir

Listen to a student describe this picture of himself and other students during their *recreo*. Write what you hear.

Fondo cultural

El mundo hispano

El recreo In Spanish-speaking countries, students usually have *el recreo* (recess or break) in the school *patio*. Students take time to relax and spend time with friends, eat a snack, or participate in activities such as a quick game of basketball, soccer, or volleyball.

• How is this similar to your school? How is it different?

El recreo ▶

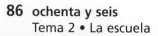

18 **Actividades y más actividades**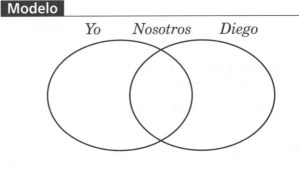

Escribir · Hablar

❶ Work with a partner. Copy the Venn diagram on a sheet of paper. Label the oval on the left *Yo.* Label the oval on the right with the name of your partner. Label the overlapping area *Nosotros* or *Nosotras.*

Modelo

Yo   Nosotros   Diego

❷ From the list below, choose five activities you do a lot. Write your activities in the oval labeled *Yo.* Be sure to conjugate the verb in the *yo* form.

montar en bicicleta	pasar tiempo con amigos	trabajar
hablar por teléfono	practicar deportes	cantar
escuchar música	hablar español	bailar
dibujar	nadar	
estudiar	usar la computadora	

❸ Interview your partner. Ask questions to find out the five activities your partner wrote in his or her diagram. When you find out an activity, write it in the right oval of your diagram. Be sure to conjugate the verb in the *él / ella* form. Save your diagram for Actividad 19.

¿Recuerdas?

When you answer in the negative, you often use *no* twice. The first *no* answers the question. The second *no* goes before the verb and means "not."

Modelo

A —*¿Dibujas mucho?*
B —*A ver . . . No, no dibujo mucho.*
A —*Pues, ¿trabajas mucho?*
B —*Sí, trabajo mucho.*

19 **Nosotros(as) . . .**

Escribir

Compare the two sides of your diagram. Write the activities you and your partner both do in the center. Be sure to use the *nosotros(as)* form. Then use your completed diagram from Actividad 18 to write about what you and/or your partner do. Write at least five complete sentences.

Modelo

Diego y yo trabajamos.
Yo dibujo.

20 Y tú, ¿qué dices?

Escribir · Hablar

1. En tu escuela, ¿quién enseña la clase de arte? ¿Quién enseña la clase de educación física?

2. En tu escuela, ¿quién canta muy bien (*well*)? ¿Quién dibuja muy bien?

3. ¿Escuchan tus amigos(as) mucha música? ¿Bailan bien tú y tus amigos(as)?

4. ¿Qué estudias en la primera hora?

5. ¿Qué clase tienes en la tercera hora?

Una estudiante en la clase de español

21 Los números mayas

Leer · Pensar

Long before the Spaniards set foot in the Americas, many different civilizations already existed here. One of these, the Maya, lived in southern Mexico and Central America, where their decendants still make their home. One of the accomplishments of the ancient Maya was the development of a system of mathematics.

Conexiones Las matemáticas

The Maya used three symbols to write numbers: a dot •, a bar —, and a drawing of a shell. The dot equals 1, the bar equals 5, and the shell equals 0. Mayan numbers were written from bottom to top, not from left to right. Look at the Mayan numbers below.

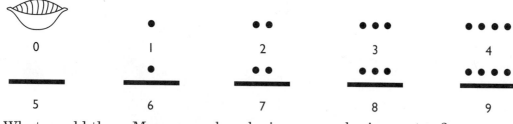

What would these Mayan numbers be in our numbering system?

1. 2. 3.

Now write these numbers in the Mayan system.

4. 13   5. 16   6. 19

Are you familiar with any other numbering systems that remind you of the Mayan system?

Pronunciación

The letter c

jcd-0288

In Spanish the pronunciation of the letter *c* depends on the letter that follows it.

When the letter *c* comes before *a, o, u,* or another consonant, it is pronounced like the *c* in "cat." Listen to and say these words:

computadora	cantar	escuela
tampoco	cómo	tocar
correr	practicar	Carlos

When the letter *c* comes before *e* or *i*, most Spanish speakers pronounce it like the *s* in "Sally." Listen to and say these words:

veces	sociable	gracioso	gracias
hacer	once	doce	trece

Try it out! Listen to this rhyme. Listen particularly for the sound of the letter *c*. Then repeat the rhyme.

$$0 + 4 = 4$$
$$4 + 0 = 4$$

Cero más cuatro,
o cuatro más cero,
siempre° son cuatro.   *always*
¿No es verdadero°?   *true*

Say the rhyme again, first replacing *cuatro* with *doce*, then replacing *cuatro* with *trece*. Then say the rhyme quickly several times.

El español en la comunidad

Do you know about opportunities to learn Spanish in your community outside of your school? Do some research using the Internet, college brochures, and the Yellow Pages about Spanish classes or private lessons offered in your community. Make a list of your findings. Why do you think people in your community want to study Spanish?

Lectura

¡Adelante!

Objectives

- Read a brochure about a school in Costa Rica
- Learn soccer fan chants
- Talk about some of your classes
- Learn facts about Mexico

Consider what an immersion experience in Spanish would be like for you as you read this brochure from a Spanish language school in Costa Rica.

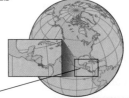

Costa Rica

Strategy

Using photos
Look at the photos to help you understand the contents of a brochure or advertisement.

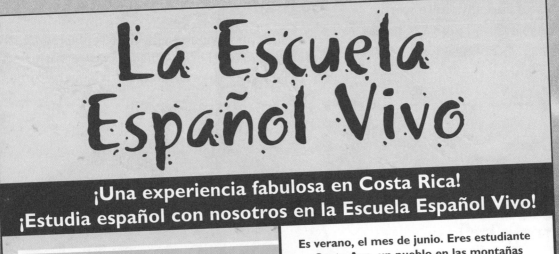

La Escuela Español Vivo

¡Una experiencia fabulosa en Costa Rica!
¡Estudia español con nosotros en la Escuela Español Vivo!

Es verano, el mes de junio. Eres estudiante en Santa Ana, un pueblo en las montañas de Costa Rica.

¿Y cómo es una clase? Hay cinco estudiantes en tu clase. Uds. escuchan, hablan y practican el español todo el día. También usan la computadora.

En la escuela hay estudiantes de muchos países: Estados Unidos, Inglaterra, Francia, Brasil, Canadá, Japón, India, Sudáfrica y otros. ¡Todos estudian español!

Los sábados y los domingos hay actividades muy interesantes: visitar un volcán o un parque nacional, nadar en el océano Pacífico . . . ¡y más!

sábados/domingos
- visitar un volcán
- visitar un parque nacional
- nadar en el océano Pacífico

El horario de clases en la escuela es:

hora	lunes a viernes
08:00–10:30	Clases de español
10:30–11:00	Recreo
11:00–13:00	Clases de español
13:00–14:00	Almuerzo
14:00–15:30	Conversaciones
15:30–16:30	Clase de música y baile

¿Por qué la Escuela Español Vivo?

- La naturaleza de Costa Rica en el pueblo de Santa Ana
- Amigos de muchos países
- Mucha práctica y conversación en español
- Clases de música y baile
- Excursiones los sábados y domingos

¿Comprendes?

1. When does the program take place?
2. Describe what a class is like.
3. What activities are offered on the weekends?
4. How many hours are spent on learning and using Spanish each week?
5. Would you like to study Spanish in Costa Rica? Why or why not?

Más práctica

- **Guided** Reading Support p. 67
- **Communication** Writing p. 38, Test Prep p. 240
- *Real.* **para hispanohablantes** pp. 62–63

realidades.com
- Internet Activity
- Leveled Workbook
- Web Code: jcd-0205

Fondo cultural
El mundo hispano

La hora in Spanish-speaking countries is usually shown using the 24-hour clock on official schedules and timetables. Times in the morning are shown as 00:00 (midnight) through 11:59 (11:59 A.M.), 1:00 P.M. is shown as 13:00, 2:00 P.M. is 14:00, and so on.

- Look at the times in the *horario* from the train station. At what time does the train from Alicante arrive?

En una estación de trenes de Madrid ▶

Próximas Llegadas
Regionales y Nacionales
H. Prev.

13:46	TOLEDO	
13:49	CARTAGENA	
14:15	SANTANDER	5
15:20	ALICANTE	5
15:30	BARCELONA	6
15:46	TOLEDO	4

La cultura en vivo
Aficionados al fútbol

El fútbol (soccer) is the favorite sport in most Spanish-speaking countries. In fact, it is the most popular sport in the entire world. It has grown in popularity in the United States over the past years. As with other sports you are familiar with, *fútbol* has loyal fans, cheers, team songs, and sometimes cheerleaders. If you attended a game in Venezuela at the Escuela Secundaria Bolívar you might hear the following chant:

Chiquitibúm a la bim bom bam
A la bío
A la bao
A la bim bom bam
¡Bolívar! ¡Bolívar!
¡Ra, ra, ra!

Jugando al fútbol en la Ciudad Universitaria, Madrid, España

Except for the school name, the words of this chant do not have any meaning.

Here's another cheer:

¡Se ve! ¡Se siente!	**You see it, you feel it!**
¡Bolívar está presente!	**Bolívar is here!**
¡Que sí, que no!	**Oh, yes, oh, no!**
¡Bolívar ya ganó!	**Bolívar has already won!**
¡A la bío, a la bao!	**¡A la bío! ¡A la bao!**
¡El otro está cansao!	**The other team is tired!**

Try it out! In groups of five, select one of the chants and use it for a model to create a chant for one of your school teams. Present it to the class.

Think about it! How are these cheers and fan enthusiasm similar to or different from the cheers at your school?

Aficionados al fútbol

Presentación oral
Mis clases

Task
Imagine that a student from Costa Rica has just
arrived at your school. Tell the student about some
of your classes.

① **Prepare** Make a chart similar to the one below and fill in
information for three of your classes. You will use this chart to
think through what you may want to say about these classes.

Hora	Clase	Comentarios	Profesor(a)
primera	la clase de español	me gusta hablar español	la Sra. Salinas
cuarta	la clase de arte	difícil	el Sr. Highsmith
octava	la clase de ciencias naturales	divertida	la Srta. Huerta

Strategy

Using graphic organizers
Simple charts can help you
organize your thoughts for a
presentation.

② **Practice** Go through your presentation several times. You
can use your notes in practice, but your teacher may not want
you to use them when you present. Try to:

- mention the information about your classes and your teachers
- use complete sentences
- speak clearly

Modelo

*En la primera hora tengo la clase de español. Me gusta
hablar español. La clase es muy divertida. La Sra. Salinas
es la profesora.*

③ **Present** Describe the three classes you selected.

④ **Evaluation** Your teacher may give you a rubric for how your
presentation will be graded. You probably will be graded on:

- how complete your preparation is
- how much information you communicate
- how easy it is to understand you

realidades.com
- Speak & Record

México

With a population of more than 100 million people, Mexico is the most populous Spanish-speaking country. It has been shaped by ancient indigenous civilizations, European colonialism, and immigration, as well as by its proximity to the United States.

The Mayan city of Tulum, situated on a cliff overlooking the Caribbean, was a major port from about 1200 until the Spaniards arrived in the early 1500s. The Mayan civilization dates from 750 B.C., and includes ancient cities throughout southern Mexico, including the Yucatan Peninsula, and parts of Central America. Today many people in these areas speak one of approximately 30 languages and dialects that developed from ancient Maya.

¿Sabes que . . . ?

The butterfly reserve at El Rosario, Michoacán, lies in the mountains not far from Mexico City. From November through February every year, millions of monarch butterflies migrate to this area from the north, covering the branches of the area's tall pine trees.

Para pensar

These two pages show a brief overview of Mexico. If you were asked to create a similar overview of the United States, what would you highlight? Select five photographs and write a brief caption for each one. Share your results with a small group or the whole class.

Estados Unidos

México

Golfo de México

OCÉANO PACÍFICO

Belice

Guatemala

El Salvador

realidades.com
- Online Atlas
- Web Code: jce-0002

Mexico's most famous dance company, el Ballet Folklórico de México, is a world-class troupe of more than 75 dancers and musicians. For more than five decades, this company has been touring the globe and performing traditional Mexican dances, such as the *jarabe tapatío*, (better known in the United States as the Mexican hat dance), *la culebra*, and the *tilingo lingo*. ▶

Mexico's capital is one of the largest cities in the world. It is also one of the oldest, dating back to 1500 B.C. It was here that the Aztecs built their capital, Tenochtitlán, in the 1300s. When the Spaniards arrived in 1519, Tenochtitlán had a population of more than 100,000—making it larger than most European cities.

▲ Many families in Mexico spend Sundays together. A popular spot for families in Mexico City is Xochimilco, where they can relax on colorful boats while enjoying a meal and music. The canals of Xochimilco are remnants of *chinampas*, the "floating gardens" that helped feed Tenochtitlán and other ancient cities in the valley of Mexico.

Repaso del capítulo

Vocabulario y gramática 🔊

jcd-0289

Chapter Review

To prepare for the test, check to see if you . . .
- **know the new vocabulary and grammar**
- **can perform the tasks on p. 97**

to talk about your school day

el almuerzo	lunch
la clase	class
la clase de . . .	. . . class
arte	art
español	Spanish
ciencias naturales	science
ciencias sociales	social studies
educación física	physical education
inglés	English
matemáticas	mathematics
tecnología	technology/computers
el horario	schedule
en la . . . hora	in the . . . hour (class period)
la tarea	homework

to describe school activities

enseñar	to teach
estudiar	to study
hablar	to talk

to talk about the order of things

primero*, -a	first
segundo, -a	second
tercero*, -a	third
cuarto, -a	fourth
quinto, -a	fifth
sexto, -a	sixth
séptimo, -a	seventh
octavo, -a	eighth
noveno, -a	ninth
décimo, -a	tenth

*Changes to *primer, tercer* before a masculine singular noun.

For *Vocabulario adicional,* see pp. 472–473.

to talk about things you need for school

la calculadora	calculator
la carpeta de argollas	three-ring binder
el diccionario	dictionary
necesito	I need
necesitas	you need

to describe your classes

aburrido, -a	boring
difícil	difficult
divertido, -a	amusing, fun
fácil	easy
favorito, -a	favorite
interesante	interesting
más . . . que	more . . . than
práctico, -a	practical

other useful words

a ver . . .	Let's see
mucho	a lot
para	for
¿Quién?	Who?
(yo) tengo	I have
(tú) tienes	you have

subject pronouns

yo	I	nosotros	we (*masc.,* *masc./fem.*)
		nosotras	we (*fem.*)
tú	you (*fam.*)	vosotros	you (*masc.,* *masc./fem.*)
usted (Ud.)	you (*form.*)	vosotras	you (*fem.*)
		ustedes (Uds.)	you (*form.*)
él	he	ellos	they (*masc.,* *masc./fem.*)
ella	she	ellas	they (*fem.*)

hablar *to talk*

hablo	hablamos
hablas	habláis
habla	hablan

Más práctica

- **Core** Puzzle p. 38, Organizer p. 39
- **Communication** Practice Test pp. 242–244, Integrated Performance Assessment p. 241

realidades.com ⊙

- Tutorial
- Flashcards
- Puzzles
- Self-test
- Web Code: jcd-0206

Preparación para el examen

On the exam you will be asked to . . .	Here are practice tasks similar to those you will find on the exam . . .	If you need review . . .

Interpretive

jcd-0289

1 Escuchar Listen and understand as people talk about their new schedules and what they think of their classes

Listen to two students who have just attended some of the classes on their new schedules. a) Which class does each one like? Why? b) Which class does each one dislike? Why?

pp. 74–77 *Vocabulario en contexto*
p. 75 Actividades 1–2
p. 79 Actividad 7
p. 80 Actividades 8–9

Interpersonal

2 Hablar Talk about activities you and your friends have in common

To get to know you, your homeroom advisor asks you to talk or write about what you and your friends have in common, such as school subjects that you all study and music or activities that you all like. For example, *cantamos.* You might also tell how you and your friends are different. For example, *Yo toco la guitarra y ellos practican deportes.*

p. 80 Actividad 8
p. 86 Actividad 16
p. 87 Actividades 18–19
p. 93 *Presentación oral*

Interpretive

3 Leer Read and understand someone's e-mail description of his or her classes

Read this e-mail that your friend received from his e-pal. What does the e-pal study in school? What does he think of his classes? Do you agree or disagree? Why?

¿Cómo son mis clases? A ver . . . Yo tengo ocho clases. Estudio ciencias naturales, inglés, español, educación física, geografía, matemáticas, tecnología y ciencias sociales. ¡Me gusta más la clase de inglés! Necesito hablar inglés aquí en Ecuador, pero es MUY difícil. Mi clase de geografía es muy aburrida y mi clase de educación física es muy divertida. Y, ¿cómo son tus clases?

pp. 74–77 *Vocabulario en contexto*
p. 78 Actividad 4
pp. 90–91 *Lectura*

Presentational

4 Escribir Write your schedule including hour, class, and teacher's name, and give opinions about the classes

Write a note to a counselor listing reasons why you want to drop two of the classes on your schedule. What might be some reasons for wanting to change classes? You might say that your first hour class is boring and that your second hour class is difficult for you.

p. 78 Actividad 5
p. 79 Actividades 6–7
p. 93 *Presentación oral*

Cultures • Comparisons

5 Pensar Demonstrate an understanding of cultural practices concerning sports

Think about the sports at your school that attract the most fans to their games or competitions. Are these the same sports that are most popular in Spanish-speaking countries? How do spectators show their enthusiasm? How is this similar to or different from the United States?

p. 92 *La cultura en vivo*

Fondo cultural

México

Sor Juana Inés de la Cruz (1648–1695), born near Mexico City, was one of the greatest intellectuals of her time. She wrote poetry, essays, music, and plays. Sor Juana also defended a woman's right to an education at a time when few women had access to it. She entered a convent at the age of 19 and over the years built a library of several thousand books. Sor Juana's living quarters in the convent became a meeting place for other writers and intellectuals, who were drawn to her because of her intelligence and knowledge.

• How are various aspects of Sor Juana's life represented in this painting? If you were to pose for a portrait, what objects would you include that represent you and your interests?

Sor Juana Inés de la Cruz, arte mexicano del siglo xvii ▶
Institut Amatller d'Art Hispànic-Arxiu Mas.

Tu sala de clases

Chapter Objectives

- Describe a classroom
- Indicate where things are located
- Talk about more than one object or person
- Understand cultural perspectives on school

Video Highlights

Videocultura: *La escuela*

A primera vista: *Un ratón en la clase*

GramActiva Videos: the verb *estar;* plurals of nouns and articles

Country Connection

As you learn how to describe your classroom, you will make connections to these countries and places:

México
España
Guatemala
Puerto Rico
El Salvador
Honduras
Nicaragua
Panamá
Costa Rica
Colombia
Perú
Chile
Argentina

Más práctica

- *Real.* para hispanohablantes pp. 70–71

realidades.com

- Fondo cultural Activity
- Video Activities
- Online Atlas
- Web Code: jce-0002

diantes mexicanos

Vocabulario en contexto

jcd-0297

Objectives

Read, listen to, and understand information about
- the classroom
- where objects are located

la bandera

el cartel

las ventanas

el reloj

la puerta

el sacapuntas

la computadora

la papelera

el escritorio

la silla

"¡Hola! Me llamo Enrique. **Aquí está mi** sala de clases. Son las nueve y **los** estudiantes **están en** la clase de español. **Hay** muchos estudiantes en mi clase. ¿Cuántos estudiantes hay en **tu** clase?**"**

la pantalla

el disquete

el ratón

el teclado

la mesa

—Elena, ¿es tu disquete?
—No, es el disquete **de** David.

La hoja de papel está **debajo del** bolígrafo.
El bolígrafo está **encima de la** hoja de papel.
El ratón está **al lado del** teclado.
La bandera está **detrás de la** computadora.
La silla está **delante de la** mesa.

1 ¿Qué hay en la sala de clases?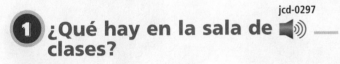

jcd-0297

Escuchar

Look at Enrique's classroom. You will be asked if certain things are there. If you see the item mentioned, raise your hand and give a "thumbs-up" sign. If you don't see it, give a "thumbs-down" sign.

2 En la sala de clases

jcd-0297

Escuchar

Look at the picture of Enrique's classroom again. Listen to where various items are located. If the description is correct, raise one hand, but if the description is not correct, raise both hands.

Más práctica

- **Guided** Vocab. Flash Cards pp. 69–72
- **Core** Vocab. Practice pp. 40–41
- **Communication** Writing p. 45
- *Real.* **para hispanohablantes** p. 72

realidades.com ✔

- Audio Activities
- Leveled Workbook
- Flashcards
- Web Code: jcd-0211

Un ratón en la clase

¿Qué pasa en la clase de
ciencias sociales?
Lee la historia.

México

Strategy

Predicting the outcome
Look at the pictures before
you read to help you predict
what will happen.

• Will Manolo get away
  with his prank?

Manolo

Teresa

Carlos

Claudia

1 **Claudia:** ¿Qué es esto?

Teresa: Es mi hámster.
Es para la clase de ciencias
naturales.

Claudia: ¿Cómo se llama?

Teresa: Paquito.

5 **Claudia:** ¡Está **allí,** delante
de la mesa!

Teresa: ¡Ay, mi Paquito!

Manolo: Pues, ahora está
detrás de la computadora,
encima de los disquetes.

Teresa: ¡Manolo! Es el
ratón de la computadora.
No es mi Paquito.

6 *El director de la escuela,
el Sr. Treviño, entra en
la clase.*

Carlos: ¡Ay! ¡Aquí está!
Está en mi **mochila.**

Sr. Treviño: ¡Silencio, por
favor!

7 **Sr. Treviño:** Teresa,
hablamos en mi oficina.

Teresa: Sí, señor.

2 **Manolo:** ¡Carlos! No tengo mi tarea.

Carlos: ¿Qué?

Manolo: Tengo una idea . . .

3 **Carlos:** ¡Un ratón! Profesora, ¡hay un ratón debajo del escritorio!

Profesora: ¿Un ratón en la clase de ciencias sociales? **¿Dónde** está? ¿Dónde?

4 **Estudiante:** Ahora está debajo de la silla.

Manolo: Y ahora está al lado de la puerta. **Es un** ratón muy impaciente.

Teresa: ¡No es un ratón! Es mi hámster, y se llama Paquito.

8 **Profesora:** Y ahora, Manolo, ¿tu tarea?

Manolo: Pues, profesora . . .

3 **¿Comprendes?**

Leer

Answer *cierto* or *falso* to the following statements.

1. El hámster es para la clase de inglés.
2. Manolo no tiene la tarea.
3. Paquito está al lado de la puerta.
4. Paquito está encima de los disquetes.
5. Paquito está detrás de la mochila.
6. El director está muy serio.

Más práctica

- **Guided** Vocab. Check pp. 73–76
- **Core** Vocab. Practice pp. 42–43
- **Communication** Video pp. 39–40
- *Real.* **para hispanohablantes** p. 73

realidades.com

- Audio Activities
- Video Activities
- Leveled Workbook
- Flashcards
- Web Code: jcd-0212

Vocabulario en uso

4 ¿Qué hay?

Escribir

Write the names of the things you see.

Modelo
Hay una bandera.

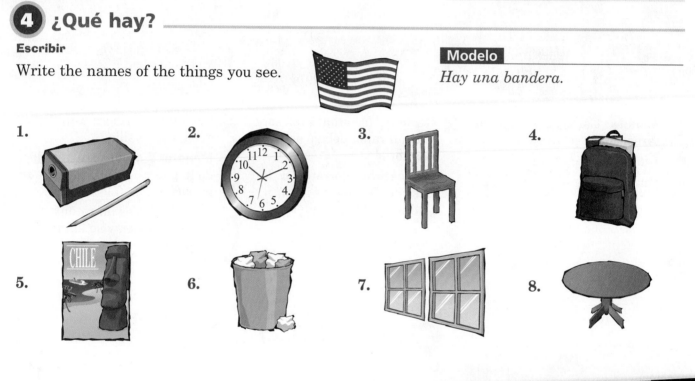

1.
2.
3.
4.
5.
6.
7.
8.

5 ¿Es lógico o no?

Pensar · Escribir

Write the word that doesn't belong in each group.
Then supply a word that logically belongs.

Modelo
el disquete   el teclado   la pantalla   la ventana
La ventana: ¡No! La computadora: ¡Sí!

1. una mesa   una silla   una mochila   un escritorio
2. la sala de clases   al lado de   detrás de   encima de
3. un diccionario   una calculadora   un reloj   una computadora
4. leer   estudiar   escribir   bailar
5. está   habla   necesitan   trabaja
6. el profesor   la chica   el estudiante   el señor

Los estudiantes y la tarea

6 **¿Dónde está?**

Hablar

Take turns with a partner to ask and tell where various items in Beto's bedroom are located.

| Modelo |

A —*¿Dónde está el escritorio?*
B —*Está debajo de la ventana.*

Nota

When the preposition *de* is followed by the masculine definite article *el*, the contraction *del* must be used.

• La papelera está al lado del escritorio.

Estudiante A

¿Dónde está . . . ?

Estudiante B

al lado de	detrás de
delante de	encima de
debajo de	

7 **Juego**

Hablar · Escuchar

❶ Work with a partner. Your partner will face away from you and have a blank piece of paper and a pen or a pencil.

❷ Choose four classroom items and arrange them on your desk, putting objects on top of others, next to each other, and so forth.

❸ Your partner will ask you questions about what is on your desk and how the items are positioned. Based on your answers, he or she will try to draw the arrangement on your desk.

❹ When your teacher tells you to stop, see how closely the picture matches the actual arrangement. Then switch roles.

| Modelo |

A —*¿Tienes un disquete?*
B —*No, no tengo un disquete.*
A —*¿Tienes una calculadora?*
B —*Sí, tengo una calculadora.*
A —*¿Dónde está?*
B —*Está encima de la carpeta.*

Para decir más . . .

a la izquierda de to the left of
a la derecha de to the right of

Exploración del lenguaje

Language through gestures

In Spanish, just as in English, nonverbal body language in the form of gestures, or *gestos,* is very important to communication.

You saw the expression *¡Ojo!* in the video *Un ratón en la clase.* The word literally means "eye," but it is used to mean "be careful" or "pay attention." It is usually accompanied by a gesture, and often people use the *¡Ojo!* gesture without saying the word.

El mundo hispano

School uniforms Many schools in Spanish-speaking countries require their students to wear uniforms. Often students wear a full uniform, like the ones you see in the photo. Sometimes the uniform consists of something more like a smock that is worn over a student's regular clothes and helps protect them from becoming dirty or torn during the school day.

• How are these uniforms similar to or different from those worn by high school students in the United States?

Estudiantes mexicanas

8 Y tú, ¿qué dices?

Escribir · Hablar

Describe your classroom.

1. ¿Dónde está la puerta?
2. ¿Qué está al lado de la puerta?
3. ¿Hay ventanas en la clase? ¿Cuántas?
4. ¿Hay un reloj en la clase? ¿Dónde está?
5. ¿Cuántos escritorios y sillas hay?
6. ¿Qué más *(What else)* hay?

Gramática

The verb *estar*

The *-ar* verbs you have used until now are called **regular verbs** because they follow a regular pattern. Verbs that do not follow a regular pattern are called **irregular verbs.**

Estar is irregular because the *yo* form doesn't follow a regular pattern and because the forms *estás, está,* and *están* require accent marks.

Use *estar* to tell how someone feels or where someone or something is located.

(yo)	estoy	(nosotros) (nosotras)	estamos
(tú)	estás	(vosotros) (vosotras)	estáis
Ud. (él) (ella)	está	Uds. (ellos) (ellas)	están

¿Recuerdas?

You have used the verb *estar* to ask how someone is.

• ¿Cómo **estás?**

• ¿Cómo **está** Ud.?

GramActiva VIDEO

Want more practice with the verb *estar?* Watch the **GramActiva** video.

están debajo de . . .

---

9 ¡Hola! ¿Cómo estás?

Escribir

Write the correct forms of *estar* on a separate sheet of paper.

Marcos: ¡Buenos días! ¿Cómo __1.__ Uds.?

Paula y Roberta: ¡Hola, Marcos! Nosotras __2.__ bien, gracias. ¿Y tú?

Marcos: __3.__ muy bien. ¿Dónde __4.__ Pedro y Juana?

Roberta: Pedro __5.__ en la sala de clases. Juana __6.__ en la oficina.

---

10 ¿En qué clase están?

Hablar

Take turns with a partner to give the correct forms of *estar* as you tell what class each person is in.

ella

Modelo

Ella está en la clase de tecnología.

1. yo

2. los profesores

3. la profesora

2A+B=6

4. nosotros

ENGLISH LITERATURE

5. ella

6. tú

jcd-0298

11 ¿Cierto o falso? 🔊

Escuchar

Write the numbers 1–6 on a sheet of paper. Listen to the statements about Javier's Spanish club photo and write *cierto* or *falso* based on the information provided as you view the photograph from *your* perspective.

12 ¿Y dónde están todos? 👥

Hablar

Work with a partner. Using the club picture above, find out where the various students are located from *Javier's* perspective. Follow the model.

A —¿Y dónde está <u>Lucita</u>?
B —<u>Lucita</u> está <u>encima del escritorio</u>.

1. Julián y Mateo
2. Rosa
3. Sara
4. yo
5. el Sr. Salas
6. Lucita y José
7. Benito
8. Sara y yo

En la clase de ciencias naturales

13 Juego

Escribir • Hablar

Work with a partner. Write down the name of someone in the classroom. Your partner can ask only *sí / no* questions to find out the name. When your partner has guessed the mystery student's identity, change roles.

Modelo

A —*¿Es una estudiante?*

B —*Sí.*

A —*¿Está al lado de Tomás?*

B —*No.*

A —*¿Está detrás de mí?*

B —*Sí.*

A —*¿Es Patricia?*

B —*Sí.*

Para decir más . . .

detrás de mí   behind me

detrás de ti   behind you

14 Leer • Pensar

Conexiones Las matemáticas

Los precios de mochilas en el mundo hispano

Most countries have their own currencies. In Mexico, people pay for their purchases in *pesos,* in Peru they use *nuevos soles,* and so on. The value of each currency can go up or down daily in relation to other countries' currencies. For example, a dollar might be worth 10 Mexican *pesos* one day and 9.5 *pesos* the following day. Read the prices for *una mochila* in six different countries.

España
20 euros

México
250 pesos

Perú
100 nuevos soles

Venezuela
21.000 bolívares

Puerto Rico
25 dólares

Guatemala
180 quetzales

1. How much does a typical *mochila* cost in your community?

2. Convert the prices for *una mochila* into dollars. You can find a currency converter on the Internet.

3. How do these prices compare to those in your community? Why might the same item have different values in different countries?

Más práctica

- **Guided** Gram. Practice pp. 77–78
- **Core** Gram. Practice p. 44
- **Communication** Writing p. 46
- *Real.* **para hispanohablantes** pp. 74–77

realidades.com

- Audio Activities
- Video Activities
- Speak & Record
- Animated Verbs
- Tutorial
- Leveled Workbook
- Web Code: jcd-0214

Gramática

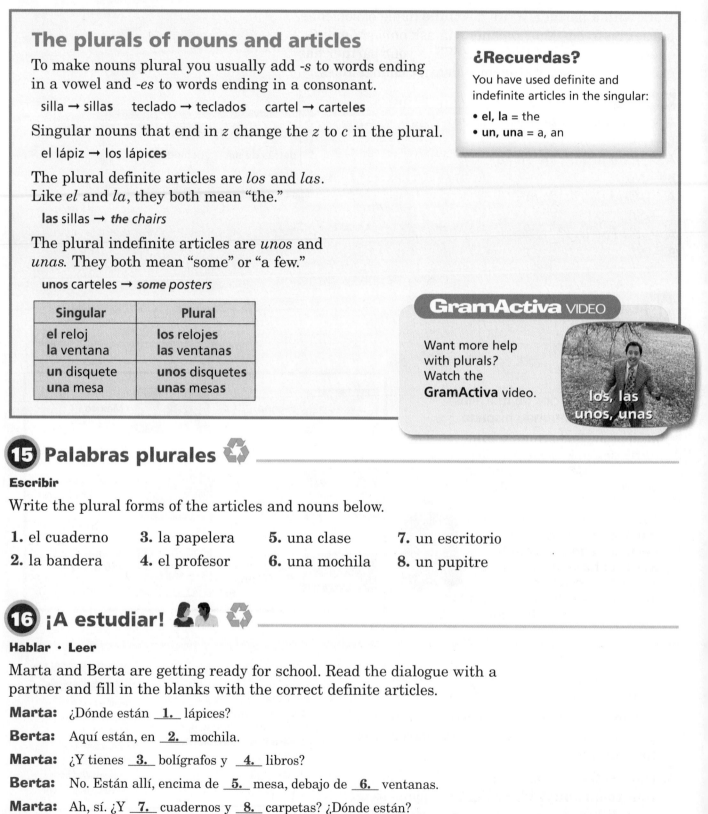

The plurals of nouns and articles

To make nouns plural you usually add -s to words ending in a vowel and -es to words ending in a consonant.

silla → sillas   teclado → teclados   cartel → carteles

Singular nouns that end in z change the z to c in the plural.

el lápiz → los lápices

The plural definite articles are *los* and *las*.
Like *el* and *la*, they both mean "the."

las sillas → *the chairs*

The plural indefinite articles are *unos* and *unas*. They both mean "some" or "a few."

unos carteles → *some posters*

Singular	Plural
el reloj la ventana	los relojes las ventanas
un disquete una mesa	unos disquetes unas mesas

¿Recuerdas?

You have used definite and indefinite articles in the singular:

- **el, la** = the
- **un, una** = a, an

GramActiva VIDEO

Want more help with plurals? Watch the **GramActiva** video.

los, las
unos, unas

15 Palabras plurales ♻

Escribir

Write the plural forms of the articles and nouns below.

1. el cuaderno
2. la bandera
3. la papelera
4. el profesor
5. una clase
6. una mochila
7. un escritorio
8. un pupitre

16 ¡A estudiar! ♻

Hablar · Leer

Marta and Berta are getting ready for school. Read the dialogue with a partner and fill in the blanks with the correct definite articles.

Marta: ¿Dónde están __1.__ lápices?

Berta: Aquí están, en __2.__ mochila.

Marta: ¿Y tienes __3.__ bolígrafos y __4.__ libros?

Berta: No. Están allí, encima de __5.__ mesa, debajo de __6.__ ventanas.

Marta: Ah, sí. ¿Y __7.__ cuadernos y __8.__ carpetas? ¿Dónde están?

Berta: Están encima de __9.__ mesa, detrás de __10.__ computadoras.

jcd-0298

17 **Más palabras plurales**

Escuchar • Hablar

You will hear eight words. Say the plural form of each word as you hear it.

You will hear: *el libro*
You will say: *los libros*

18 **Es el cuaderno de . . .**

Hablar

Work in groups of four. Each of you should choose a classroom object you have brought to class. Show your group what you have chosen. Your teacher will collect all the items, then place them in view in different parts of the classroom. Ask your group where your object is. Take turns until all members of your group have asked their question.

Nota

In Spanish, you express possession by using *de* and the name of the owner of the item.

• el escritorio **de** la profesora
the teacher's desk

Modelo

A —*¿Dónde está mi calculadora?*
B —*Tu calculadora está debajo de la silla de Margarita.*

El español en el mundo del trabajo

School districts in the United States have many positions in which employees need to speak Spanish. For example, school counselors work with new students and parents from Spanish-speaking countries. Counselors help them set up schedules, talk about school policies, and answer questions. Both the parents and the new students feel much more comfortable when the counselor can communicate with them in Spanish.

• Does your district need employees who speak Spanish? In what other jobs within a school system would speaking Spanish be helpful?

19 Una clase de inglés

Hablar • Escribir

Look at this picture of a high school class in Cuba.

① Study the photograph and make a list in Spanish of items you can name.

② Write two questions about the photograph, then ask your partner the questions. Use the models below.

Modelo

A —¿Cuántos estudiantes hay en la clase?
B —Hay seis estudiantes.
A —¿Hay banderas en la clase?
B —No, no hay banderas.

¿Qué es esto?	¿Quién está . . . ?
¿Cuántos(as) . . . hay?	¿Hay . . . ?
¿Dónde está(n) . . . ?	¿Qué hay?

20 Y tú, ¿qué dices?

Escribir

Look around your classroom and write five sentences about it.

Modelo

En mi clase de español hay 33 estudiantes. Hay 35 pupitres y un escritorio. El escritorio está delante de los pupitres. La computadora está encima del escritorio. No hay bandera en mi clase.

Más práctica

● **Guided** Gram. Practice pp. 79–80
● **Core** Gram. Practice pp. 45–46
● **Communication** Writing p. 47
● *Real.* **para hispanohablantes** pp. 78–81

 realidades.com

• Audio Activities
• Video Activities
• Speak & Record
• Canción de hip hop
• Tutorial
• Leveled Workbook
• Web Code: jcd-0213

Pronunciación

The letter *g*

jcd-0298

In Spanish, the letter *g* sounds like *g* in "go" when it is followed by *a*, *o*, or *u*, although it often has a slightly softer sound than in English. Listen to and say the following words and sentences:

Gustavo	domin**go**	ten**go**
a**go**sto	pre**gu**nta	lue**go**
ami**go**	ar**go**llas	**ga**to

In Spanish, the letter *g* sounds like the letter *h* in "hot" when it is followed by *e* or *i*. Listen to and say the following words. Some of these words you have not yet heard or seen. Can you guess the meanings of the cognates?

inteli**ge**nte	**ge**neroso	**ge**neral
gimnasio	tecnolo**gí**a	biolo**gí**a

Try it out! See if you can guess how to pronounce the following Spanish first names. Keep in mind the pronunciation rules for the *g* sound.

Gabriela	Ángela	Gerardo
Gilberto	Gustavo	Rodrigo
Olga	Rogelio	Gregorio

Estudiantes en un gimnasio

Fondo cultural

El mundo hispano

School gyms are rare in Spanish-speaking countries. Students usually have physical education classes in the school's *patio*. High school students usually have P.E. one or two times a week, sometimes before or after regular school hours. School sports teams are also less common than in the United States.

• What are some reasons that schools in Spanish-speaking countries might place less emphasis on physical education, sports, and gymnasiums?

En la clase de educación física ▶

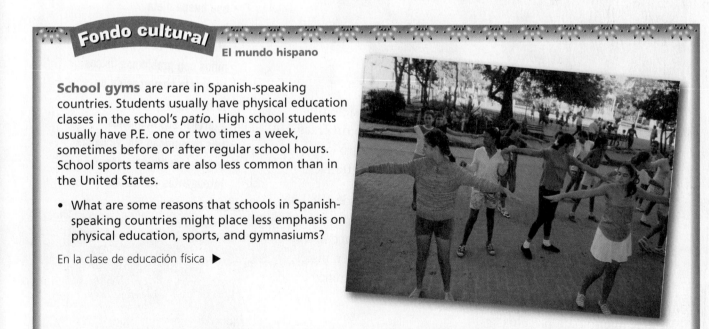

Lectura

El UNICEF y una convención para los niños[1]

¿Sabes que es un privilegio estar en una escuela, tener una mochila con libros, unos lápices, una calculadora, unas hojas de papel y un profesor bueno? En ciertas[2] naciones, ir a la escuela es difícil o no es posible.

El UNICEF es la organización internacional de las Naciones Unidas que trabaja para los niños. UNICEF es una sigla[3] inglesa que significa "Fondo Internacional de Emergencia de las Naciones Unidas para los Niños". Tiene siete oficinas regionales en diversas naciones y un Centro de Investigaciones en Italia.

El 20 de noviembre de 1989, la Organización de las Naciones Unidas escribió[4] "una convención para los niños" en inglés, árabe, chino, ruso y francés.

Esta convención dice que[5] los niños de todas[6] las naciones necesitan:

- dignidad
- una casa
- protección
- una buena dieta
- la práctica de deportes
- atención especial para los niños con problemas físicos
- amor y la comprensión de la familia
- expresar sus opiniones
- una comunidad sin[7] violencia
- ir a la escuela para ser inteligentes y sociables

[5]says that [6]all [7]without

[1]children [2]certain
[3]acronym [4]wrote

¿Comprendes?

1. Para los estudiantes de todas las naciones es fácil estar en una escuela y tener una mochila. ¿Cierto o falso?

2. ¿Cuántas oficinas regionales tiene UNICEF?

3. ¿Qué significa la sigla UNICEF?

4. ¿Dónde está el Centro de Investigaciones?

5. La convención es para los niños de todas las naciones. ¿Cierto o falso?

6. Según la convención para los niños, ¿cuáles *(what)* son cuatro cosas que necesitan los niños?

Más práctica

- **Guided** Reading Support p. 81
- **Communication** Writing p. 48, Test Prep pp. 245, 246
- *Real.* **para hispanohablantes** pp. 82–83

- Internet Activity
- Leveled Workbook
- Web Code: jcd-0215

Perspectivas del mundo hispano
¿Cómo es la escuela?

Did you know that students in many Spanish-speaking countries spend more time in school than you do? The graph to the right shows the length of the school year in various countries.

Here are some other facts you may not know:

- In many schools, when a teacher enters the classroom, the students stand.
- The teacher may call the students by their last name.
- The students, on the other hand, are more likely to address their teacher simply as *maestro(a), profesor(a),* or just *profe,* without a last name.
- Class time is generally spent with the teacher lecturing rather than with class discussion.
- Many public and private schools require uniforms.

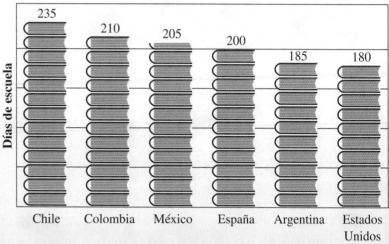

País	Días de escuela
Chile	235
Colombia	210
México	205
España	200
Argentina	185
Estados Unidos	180

Check it out! How are other schools in your area similar to or different from yours? How are they similar to or different from those in Spanish-speaking countries? Make a list of schools in your area and describe these similarities and differences. Are some schools more formal? Do students take classes that are different from the ones you take?

Think about it! Based on the information above, what might you assume are the attitudes toward school in Spanish-speaking cultures? How are these the same as or different from attitudes in your community? List five suggestions that might help an exchange student from Mexico City adjust to your school.

Presentación escrita
Tu sala de clases

Strategy

Creating visuals
Creating a sketch or a drawing can help you remember the things you want to write about in a description.

Task
Your pen pal from Mexico is coming to visit your school next semester and would like to know what to expect. Write her a note describing your Spanish classroom.

❶ **Prewrite** Draw a simple sketch of your classroom, showing the classroom items you intend to describe in your note. Label the items.

❷ **Draft** Write the first draft of your note. Your sketch will help you remember which items you want to describe and where they are located. Use the model to help you organize your writing.

Modelo

En mi sala de clases hay cuatro ventanas. Mi pupitre está delante del escritorio de la profesora. La bandera está al lado de la puerta. Las computadoras están encima de la mesa.

❸ **Revise** Read through your paragraph and check for correct spelling as well as for the criteria under Evaluation.

Share your work with a partner. Your partner should check the following:

• Is your paragraph easy to understand?

• Is there other information you could add?

• Are there any errors?

Rewrite your paragraph making any necessary changes.

❹ **Publish** Make a final copy of your note. You may exhibit it in the classroom or add it to your portfolio.

❺ **Evaluation** Your teacher may give you a rubric for how your paragraph will be graded. You probably will be graded on:

• use of vocabulary

• correct use of the verb *estar*

• amount of information provided

América Central

Central America is made up of seven countries: Belize, Guatemala, El Salvador, Honduras, Nicaragua, Costa Rica, and Panama. Spanish is the official language in all of these countries except Belize, which was colonized by the British.

Costa Rica has set aside large tracts of land for conservation, helping to preserve fragile ecosystems. The oldest park in Costa Rica, Santa Rosa, protects endangered sea turtle nesting sites and the last dry tropical forest in Central America.

¿Sabes que . . . ?

Carlos V of Spain first proposed a canal across the Isthmus of Panama in 1524. In the 1880s, French efforts to build a canal across the isthmus were hindered in large part by diseases. When Panama won its independence from Colombia in 1903, it signed a treaty with the United States granting it rights to the Canal Zone. The United States completed the canal in 1914, and it was turned over to Panama in 1999.

Para pensar

In the early nineteenth century some people imagined that the United States would extend south to Panama. How do you think the United States would be different today if their predictions had come true? How do you think Mexico and Central America would be different?

México
Belice
Guatemala
Honduras
El Salvador
Nicaragua
Mar Caribe
Costa Rica
Panamá
OCÉANO PACÍFICO

realidades.com
• Online Atlas
• Web Code: jce-0002

Founded by the Spanish in 1524, the Nicaraguan city of Granada became an important trading center. The town enjoys easy access to the Caribbean, yet is located less than 100 miles from the Pacific. In the nineteenth and twentieth centuries Nicaragua was proposed as an alternate site for a canal linking the Atlantic and Pacific oceans.

Guatemala has a large indigenous population, many descended from the Maya. These women are wearing the traditional hand-woven *huipil*, which is a very "communicative" part of their clothing. The *huipil* identifies the wearer's village, her marital status, her religious beliefs, wealth, and personality. A well-woven *huipil* may last 20 to 30 years.

From the 1500s to the end of the 1700s, the coasts of Spanish America were plagued by pirates. Panamanian ports were perfect targets, since the silver and gold mined in Peru were loaded on Panama's Pacific coast and carried overland to the Atlantic, where they were put on ships bound for Spain. Fuerte San Lorenzo, on Panama's Atlantic coast, was part of a network of forts that were meant to protect ships and their precious cargo. ▶

Repaso del capítulo

Vocabulario y gramática

jcd-0299

---

to talk about classroom items

la bandera	flag
el cartel	poster
la computadora	computer
el disquete	diskette
la mochila	bookbag, backpack
la pantalla	(computer) screen
la papelera	wastepaper basket
el ratón	(computer) mouse
el reloj	clock
el sacapuntas	pencil sharpener
el teclado	(computer) keyboard

to talk about classroom furniture

el escritorio	desk
la mesa	table
la silla	chair

to talk about parts of a classroom

la puerta	door
la ventana	window

to indicate location

al lado de la / del	next to, beside
allí	there
aquí	here
debajo de la / del	underneath
delante de la / del	in front of
detrás de la / del	behind
¿Dónde?	Where?
en	in, on
encima de la / del	on top of

For *Vocabulario adicional,* see pp. 472–473.

to indicate possession

de	of
mi	my
tu	your

to identify (description, quantity)

Es un(a) . . .	It's a . . .
Hay	There is, There are
¿Qué es esto?	What is this?

estar *to be*

estoy	estamos
estás	estáis
está	están

to identify gender and quantity of nouns

los, las	the
unos, unas	some

Más práctica

- **Core** Puzzle p. 47, Organizer p. 48
- **Communication** Practice Test pp. 248–250, Integrated Performance Assessment p. 247

realidades.com

- Tutorial
- Flashcards
- Puzzles
- Self-test
- Web Code: jcd-0216

Preparación para el examen

On the exam you will be asked to . . .	Here are practice tasks similar to those you will find on the exam . . .	If you need review . . .

Interpretive

jcd-0299

1 Escuchar Listen to identify classrooms and locations

Listen as a student frantically asks some of his friends where he left his homework. Can you identify all of the classrooms and places they suggest that he look?

pp. 100–103 *Vocabulario en contexto*
p. 105 Actividades 6–7
p. 111 Actividad 18

Interpersonal

2 Hablar • Escribir Talk or write about where someone is located by describing where that person is in relation to objects in the classroom

You are trying to find out the name of someone in your class. You ask the person next to you, but he doesn't understand whom you are talking about. Give at least three statements that would help him identify the person. You might include where he or she is in relation to the teacher's desk, the window, someone else's desk, and so on.

pp. 100–103 *Vocabulario en contexto*
p. 105 Actividades 6–7
p. 108 Actividades 11–12
p. 109 Actividad 13
p. 111 Actividad 18

Interpretive

3 Leer Read and understand a letter that contains questions and concerns about school issues

The school counselor has asked you to help him read a note written by a new Spanish-speaking student at school. After reading it, tell the counselor what the problem is and the kinds of questions the student asks.

pp. 100–103 *Vocabulario en contexto*
p. 112 Actividad 19
p. 114 *Lectura*

Necesito una clase para la primera hora. ¿Cómo es la clase de tecnología, fácil o difícil? ¿Qué necesito para la clase? ¿Cuántos estudiantes hay en la clase? ¿Hay mucha tarea?

Presentational

4 Escribir Write an email to a friend about one of her classes

You have just moved to a new town and are sending an e-mail to a friend from your old school. You have lots of questions about her classes. Write at least three questions about one of her classes: whether she likes it, how many students are in it, where her desk is in the room, what else is in the room, etc.

pp. 100–103 *Vocabulario en contexto*
p. 112 Actividad 19

Cultures • Comparisons

5 Pensar Demonstrate an understanding of cultural differences in schools

Think about how students and teachers interact within a typical classroom in a Spanish-speaking country. What are at least four things you might find different from most schools in the United States?

p. 106 *Fondo cultural*
p. 113 *Fondo cultural*
p. 116 *Perspectivas del mundo hispano*

Fondo cultural

España

Bartolomé Murillo (1617–1682) was the first Spanish painter to become famous throughout Europe. Several of his early paintings featured children from his native Sevilla. Murillo used color, light, and a natural portrayal of his subjects to create memorable masterpieces.

• Study the painting and come up with three adjectives that describe it. Would you say the impression Murillo gives of the boys is positive or negative? Why?

"Niños comiendo fruta" (ca. 1650), Bartolomé Murillo ▶
© ARS, NY. Copyright Scala/Art Resource, NY. Alte Pinakothek, Munich, Germany.

¿Desayuno o almuerzo?

Chapter Objectives

- Talk about foods and beverages for breakfast and lunch
- Talk about likes and dislikes
- Express how often something is done
- Understand cultural perspectives on meals

Video Highlights

Videocultura: *La comida*

A primera vista: *El desayuno*

GramActiva Videos: present tense of *-er* and *-ir* verbs; *me gustan, me encantan*

Country Connection

As you learn about foods and meals, you will make connections to these countries and places:

España
Venezuela
Costa Rica
Colombia
Ecuador
Perú
Bolivia
Chile

Más práctica

- *Real.* para hispanohablantes pp. 90–91

realidades.com

- Fondo cultural Activity
- Video Activities
- Online Atlas
- Web Code: jce-0002

Vocabulario en contexto

jcd-0387 🔊

Objectives

Read, listen to, and understand information about
- foods and beverages for breakfast and lunch

El Supermercado de la Plaza

¡Abierto las 24 horas!

¡Ofertas de hoy!

¡Toda la comida que necesitas!

$2.29 las salchichas	$2.45 el tocino	$2.35 el jamón
$3.25 el queso	$.79 el yogur de fresa	$1.29 los huevos
$1.80 el jugo de manzana	$2.50 el jugo de naranja	$1.39 la limonada
$2.40 el té	$1.89 el pan	$2.29 las galletas

el cereal $3.59

los plátanos $.69

la leche $1.75

el agua* $1.09

*Note that *agua* is a feminine noun. However, you use the masculine article *el* to make it easier to say.

❝**El desayuno** es mi **comida** favorita. **En el desayuno,** yo **como** cereal **con** leche, tocino y **pan tostado.** Todos los días **bebo** jugo de naranja. **Nunca** bebo té **sin** leche. Y tú, ¿qué **comes** en el desayuno?❞

El Restaurante de la Plaza

¡Para un almuerzo **rápido!**

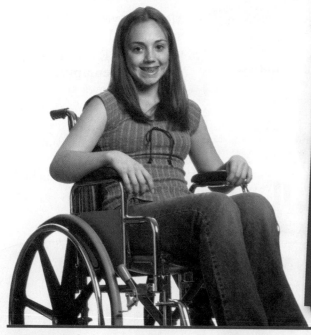

la ensalada de frutas — $3.25

el sándwich de jamón y queso — $3.50

la pizza — $1.75

la hamburguesa — $3.75

el café — $1.00

el perrito caliente — $1.50

los refrescos — $1.00

las papas fritas — $1.25

los jugos — $1.35

la sopa de verduras — $1.80

el té helado — $1.00

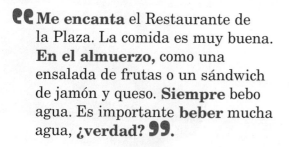

❝ **Me encanta** el Restaurante de la Plaza. La comida es muy buena. **En el almuerzo,** como una ensalada de frutas o un sándwich de jamón y queso. **Siempre** bebo agua. Es importante **beber** mucha agua, ¿verdad? ❞

---

1 **¿Beber o comer?**
jcd-0387

Escuchar

Listen to the names of ten foods and beverages. If an item is a food, pantomime eating. If it's a beverage, pantomime drinking.

2 **¿El desayuno o el almuerzo?**
jcd-0387

Escuchar

Listen as different people tell what they are eating. Hold up one hand if the meal is *el desayuno* and hold up both hands if it is *el almuerzo*.

Más práctica

- **Guided** Vocab. Flash Cards pp. 83–88
- **Core** Vocab. Practice pp. 49–50
- **Communication** Writing p. 56
- *Real.* **para hispanohablantes** p. 92

realidades.com

- Audio Activities
- Leveled Workbook
- Flashcards
- Web Code: jcd-0301

El desayuno

Tomás es de los Estados Unidos. Está en Costa Rica para estudiar. ¿Qué come el primer día? Lee la historia.

Strategy

Using prior experience
Think about breakfast. Do you like a big breakfast? A small one? No breakfast at all? Look at the pictures and see if you can figure out how Tomás feels about breakfast.

Papá

Mamá

Tomás

Raúl

Gloria

Costa Rica

1 **Mamá:** A ver . . . tocino, salchichas, huevos . . .

Papá: ¡Uy! Es mucha comida. No **comprendo.** Tú nunca comes el desayuno.

Mamá: No es mi desayuno. Es para Tomás, **por supuesto.** Los americanos comen mucho en el desayuno.

5 **Tomás:** **Comparto** los huevos, el tocino y las salchichas.

Raúl: ¿**Compartes** tu desayuno? Muchas gracias, Tomás.

6 **Raúl:** ¿Y qué **bebes?**

Tomás: Jugo de naranja, por favor.

Raúl: Te gusta la leche, ¿no?

Tomás: **Más o menos.**

7 **Raúl:** Papá, ¿unos huevos?

Papá: No, gracias. ¡La comida es para Uds.!

2 Raúl: No comes mucho en el desayuno, ¿verdad?

Tomás: ¡No! **¡Qué asco!**

3 Tomás: No me gusta nada el desayuno. A veces bebo jugo de naranja y como pan tostado.

Raúl: Yo tampoco como mucho.

4 Mamá: Buenos días, Tomás. Aquí tienes tu desayuno. Huevos, tocino, salchichas, pan tostado, cereal con leche . . .

Tomás: Gracias. Es un desayuno muy bueno. **Me encantan** los huevos y el tocino.

8 Mamá: ¿Cuál es tu almuerzo favorito, Tomás?

Tomás: Me gustan las hamburguesas, la pizza, **la ensalada** . . .

Mamá: Bueno . . . ¡pizza, hamburguesas y ensalada para el almuerzo!

③ ¿Comprendes?

Escribir

Lee las frases. Escribe los números del 1 al 6 en una hoja de papel y escribe *C (cierto)* si la frase es correcta y *F (falso)* si es incorrecta.

1. Tomás está en Costa Rica.
2. La mamá de Rául siempre come mucho en el desayuno.
3. A Tomás le gusta comer mucho en el desayuno.
4. Hoy Tomás no come mucho en el desayuno.
5. Tomás comparte el desayuno con Raúl.
6. A Tomás le gustan las hamburguesas y la pizza.

Más práctica

- **Guided** Vocab. Check pp. 89–92
- **Core** Vocab. Practice pp. 51–52
- **Communication** Video pp. 49–50
- *Real.* para hispanohablantes p. 93

realidades.com ⓥ

- Audio Activities
- Video Activities
- Leveled Workbook
- Flashcards
- Web Code: jcd-0302

Vocabulario en uso

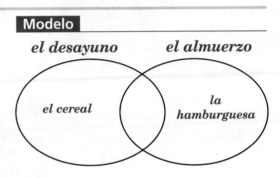

Objectives

- Talk about foods and beverages for breakfast and lunch
- Ask and tell what people eat and drink for breakfast and lunch
- Express likes and dislikes
- Learn to use the present tense of *-er* and *-ir* verbs and *me gustan / me encantan*

4 **¿El desayuno o el almuerzo?**

Pensar • Escribir

Think about what people usually eat for breakfast and lunch. Copy the Venn diagram on a sheet of paper. Which foods pictured below would usually be eaten for breakfast, and which for lunch? Write the Spanish words in the appropriate oval for *el desayuno* or *el almuerzo*. Which items could be eaten for either breakfast or lunch? Write them in the overlapping area.

Modelo

el desayuno   *el almuerzo*

el cereal   *la hamburguesa*

5 **¿Dónde están?** jcd-0388

Escuchar • Escribir

Vas a escuchar ocho descripciones sobre el dibujo de esta página. Escribe los números del 1 al 8 en una hoja de papel y escribe *C* si la descripción es cierta y *F* si es falsa.

6 ¿Qué bebes?

Escribir

❶ On a sheet of paper, make three columns with these headings: *Todos los días, A veces, Nunca.* Write the names of these beverages under the appropriate heading based on how often you drink them.

❷ Write complete sentences telling how often you drink these beverages.

Modelo

Bebo limonada todos los días.
Bebo leche a veces.
Nunca bebo café.

También se dice . . .

beber = tomar *(México)*
el jugo = el zumo *(España)*
la naranja = la china *(Puerto Rico)*
las papas = las patatas *(España)*
el plátano = la banana,
                 el guineo *(Puerto Rico)*
el sándwich = el bocadillo *(España)*,
                 la torta *(México)*

7 ¿Qué comes?

Hablar

Trabaja con otro(a) estudiante y habla de lo que comes.

Modelo

A —¿*Comes cereal?*
B —*Sí, como cereal todos los días.*
o: *No, nunca como cereal.*

Estudiante A

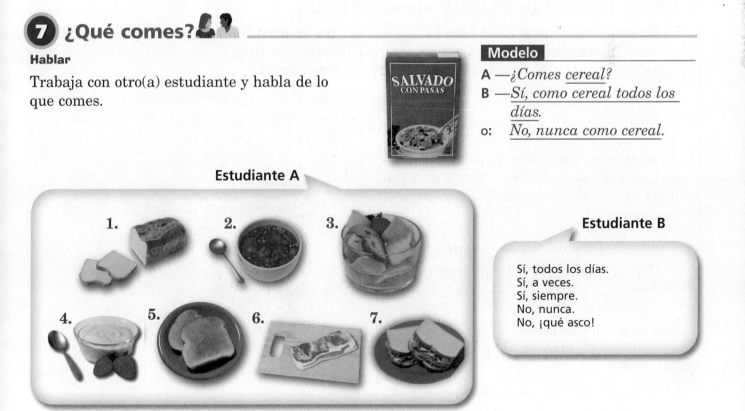

1. 2. 3.

4. 5. 6. 7.

Estudiante B

Sí, todos los días.
Sí, a veces.
Sí, siempre.
No, nunca.
No, ¡qué asco!

8 Mis comidas favoritas

Hablar

Trabaja con otro(a) estudiante y habla de las comidas que te gustan y que no te gustan.

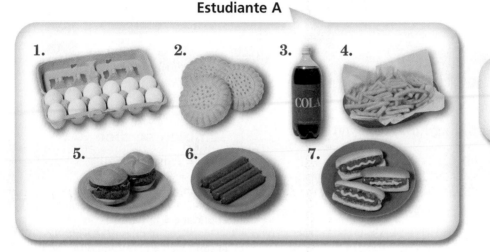

Modelo
A —*Te gustan los plátanos, ¿verdad?*
B —*Sí, ¡por supuesto! Me encantan.*

Estudiante A

1. 2. 3. 4.

5. 6. 7.

Estudiante B

Sí, ¡por supuesto! Me encantan.
Sí, más o menos.
No, no me gustan.
No, ¡qué asco!

Exploración del lenguaje

Using a noun to modify another noun

In English, one noun is often used to describe another noun: *vegetable soup, strawberry yogurt.* Notice that the noun that is being described comes second.

In Spanish, however, the noun that is being described comes first and is followed by *de* + the describing noun: *la sopa de verduras, el yogur de fresa.* Notice that you don't use a definite article in front of the second noun.

The form of the noun following *de* does not change even when the first noun becomes plural.

    el sándwich de **jamón**

    los sándwiches de **jamón**

Try it out! Name five examples of foods or beverages from this chapter that follow this pattern.

Now that you know the pattern, say what these foods and beverages are called in Spanish:

el tomate

la lechuga

la piña

el pollo

El intercambio entre dos mundos

Leer

Conexiones La historia

Think about how your meals would be different without corn, beans, squash, tomatoes, avocados, chiles, peanuts, cashews, turkey, pineapples, potatoes, vanilla, and chocolate. What do these foods have in common? They all had their origin in the Americas and were unknown in Europe until Columbus brought them there from his voyages in the fifteenth century. Today these foods are found in dishes in many countries.

The product exchange benefited both sides of the Atlantic Ocean. The Europeans brought to the Americas a wide range of foods including chicken, pork, beef, milk, cheese, sugar, grapes, and grains such as wheat and barley.

10 Las enchiladas

Leer • Escribir

Read the list of ingredients for a traditional Mexican dish of *enchiladas*. Based upon the information you just read and saw on the map, write which ingredients had their origins in the Americas and which came from Europe.

Enchiladas de pollo[1] con salsa de tomate

Ingredientes:

12 tortillas de maíz[2]
1 taza[3] de pollo
1 taza de queso fresco[4]
6 tomates grandes[5]
2 cebollas[6] no muy grandes
crema
aceite[7] de maíz

[1]chicken [2]corn [3]cup [4]fresh [5]large [6]onions [7]oil

11 Y tú, ¿qué dices?

Escribir • Hablar

1. ¿Cuál es tu comida favorita, el desayuno o el almuerzo?
2. ¿Cuál es tu almuerzo favorito? ¿Y tu desayuno favorito?
3. ¿Qué frutas te gustan más?

Gramática

Present tense of *-er* and *-ir* verbs

To create the present-tense forms of *-er* and *-ir* verbs, drop the endings from the infinitives, then add the verb endings *-o, -es, -e, -emos / -imos, -éis / -ís,* or *-en* to the stem.

Here are the present-tense forms of *-er* and *-ir* verbs using *comer* and *compartir:*

¿Recuerdas?

The pattern of present-tense *-ar* verbs is:

toco	tocamos
tocas	tocáis
toca	tocan

(yo)	com**o**	(nosotros) (nosotras)	com**emos**
(tú)	com**es**	(vosotros) (vosotras)	com**éis**
Ud. (él) (ella)	come	Uds. (ellos) (ellas)	com**en**

(yo)	compart**o**	(nosotros) (nosotras)	compart**imos**
(tú)	compart**es**	(vosotros) (vosotras)	compart**ís**
Ud. (él) (ella)	comparte	Uds. (ellos) (ellas)	compart**en**

- Regular *-er* verbs that you know are *beber, comer, comprender, correr,* and *leer.*
- Regular *-ir* verbs that you know are *compartir* and *escribir.*
- You also know the verb *ver.* It is regular except in the *yo* form, which is *veo.*

GramActiva VIDEO

Want more practice with *-er* and *-ir* verbs? Watch the **GramActiva** video.

comen

12 ¿Quiénes comparten el almuerzo?

Escribir

On a sheet of paper, write complete sentences saying what each person is sharing and with whom. Follow the model.

Modelo

Elena / una manzana / Raúl
Elena comparte una manzana con Raúl.

1. Tomás / una pizza / María
2. tú / unos sándwiches / Ramón
3. nosotros / unas papas fritas / los estudiantes
4. Uds. / unas galletas / el profesor
5. ellas / unos perritos calientes / nosotros
6. tú y yo / unos plátanos / Luis y Roberta
7. yo / ¿-? / mi amigo

Una familia come el almuerzo

13 ¿Qué beben y qué comen?

Hablar

Work with a partner. Use the verbs *comer* and *beber* to ask questions.

Juan / desayuno

> **Modelo**
> A —*¿Qué come Juan en el desayuno?*
> B —*Juan come pan tostado.*

Miguel y Carlos / almuerzo

> **Modelo**
> A —*¿Qué beben Miguel y Carlos en el almuerzo?*
> B —*Miguel y Carlos beben limonada.*

1. Raúl y Gloria / desayuno

2. tú / almuerzo

3. Graciela y Carlos / desayuno

4. Carolina / almuerzo

5. tu familia y tú / desayuno

6. tú / almuerzo   **¡Respuesta personal!**

14 Una tarjeta postal

Leer • Escribir

Lee la tarjeta postal *(post card)* de una amiga de Venezuela. En una hoja de papel, escribe la forma correcta del verbo apropiado que está entre paréntesis.

Querida Amalia:

Elena y yo estamos en Caracas. Nosotras __1.__ (comprender / correr) todos los días y __2.__ (comer / ver) muy bien.

Los estudiantes aquí __3.__ (comer / leer) mucha pizza y __4.__ (ver / beber) mucho café. Ellos __5.__ (leer / beber) muchos libros y __6.__ (escribir / ver) mucho también para las clases. Las clases son difíciles pero me encantan.

En la clase de español nosotros __7.__ (correr / leer) revistas y cuentos en español. Elena __8.__ (comprender / beber) muy bien pero para mí es un poco difícil.

Tengo que estudiar. ¡Hasta luego!
Tu amiga,
Carolina

Más práctica

- **Guided** Gram. Practice pp. 93–94
- **Core** Gram. Practice p. 53
- **Communication** Writing p. 57
- *Real.* para hispanohablantes pp. 94–97

realidades.com

- Audio Activities
- Video Activities
- Speak & Record
- Canción de hip hop
- Animated Verbs
- Tutorial
- Leveled Workbook
- Web Code: jcd-0303

15 Los sábados y la comida

Escribir • Hablar

What do you and your classmates eat and drink for breakfast and lunch on Saturdays? Make a chart like the one below on a sheet of paper and complete each box with information about yourself. Then survey two classmates to find out what their habits are. Record the information in the chart.

Para decir más . . .

la crema de cacahuates	peanut butter
el pan dulce	breakfast pastry
el panqueque	pancake
el pollo	chicken

	¿Qué comes?	¿Qué bebes?
el desayuno	**yo:** huevos, pan tostado, tocino **Sandra:** cereal, plátanos, pan tostado	
el almuerzo		

Modelo

Los sábados, ¿qué comes en el desayuno? ¿Qué bebes?
¿Qué comes en el almuerzo? ¿Qué bebes?

16 Los hábitos de la clase

Escribir • Hablar

Use your completed chart from Actividad 15 to write summary statements based on your survey. Be prepared to read your sentences to the class.

Modelo

Sandra y yo comemos huevos y cereal en el desayuno.
Gregorio no bebe jugo de naranja en el desayuno y le gusta mucho la leche.
Sofía come cereal y bebe leche en el desayuno.

Fondo cultural
El mundo hispano

El desayuno From the popular *churros* and hot chocolate in Spain to the *pan dulce* served in many countries, a wide variety of foods can be found on the breakfast table in the Spanish-speaking world. Most often, people prefer a light breakfast of bread or a roll, coffee or tea, and possibly juice. Items such as cereal, eggs, ham, or sausage are less common.

• In Spain you can ask for a *desayuno americano.* What do you think you would be served?

¿Qué comen en el desayuno?

Gramática

Me gustan, me encantan

Use *me gusta* and *me encanta* to talk about a singular noun.

Me gusta **el té** pero me encanta **el té helado.**

Use *me gustan* and *me encantan* to talk about plural nouns.

Me encantan **las fresas** pero no me gustan mucho **los plátanos.**

When you use *me gusta(n)* and *me encanta(n)* to talk about a noun, include *el, la, los,* or *las.*

Me encanta **el jugo de naranja** pero no me gusta **la leche.**

¿Qué te gustan más, **las hamburguesas** o **los perritos calientes?**

GramActiva VIDEO

Want more help with *me gustan / me encantan?* Watch the **GramActiva** video.

---

jcd-0388

17 ¿Gusta o gustan? 🔊

Escuchar · GramActiva

❶ Tear a sheet of paper in thirds. On the first piece, write *No.* On the second piece write *me gusta.* On the third piece, write *n.*

❷ You will hear eight food items. Indicate whether you like each item by holding up one, two, or all three pieces of paper. Remember to use *me gustan* when the item you hear is plural!

---

18 ¿Qué te gusta?

Escribir

Indicate how much you *do* or *do not* like the foods pictured below.

Modelo

Me gustan las manzanas.

o: *No me gustan nada las manzanas.*

o: *Me encantan las manzanas.*

1.

2.

3.

4.

5.

6.

19 ¿Qué te gusta más?

Escribir • Hablar

❶ A popular magazine has provided this survey to see how much you and a friend have in common. On a sheet of paper, write the numbers 1–7 and then write your preferences.

❷ Take turns asking your partner about the survey items. Keep track of your similarities and differences. See how the magazine rates you.

Modelo

¿La comida mexicana o la comida italiana?

A —¿Qué te gusta más, la comida mexicana o la comida italiana?

B —Me gusta más la comida italiana.

o: —No me gusta ni la comida mexicana ni la comida italiana.

A —A mí también.

o: —A mí me gusta la comida mexicana.

o: —A mí tampoco.

¿Qué te gusta más?

¿Tu amigo(a) y tú son muy similares o muy diferentes? Completa este *quiz* y compara tus respuestas con las de un(a) amigo(a).

1	la comida mexicana	**o**	la comida italiana
2	el desayuno	**o**	el almuerzo
3	el cereal con fruta	**o**	el cereal sin fruta
4	las revistas	**o**	los libros
5	la música rock	**o**	la música rap
6	los amigos graciosos	**o**	los amigos serios
7	las hamburguesas con queso	**o**	las hamburguesas sin queso

Respuestas similares:

7–6 ¡Uds. son gemelos![1]
5–4 Tienen mucho en común, ¿verdad?
3–2 ¡Un poco similares / un poco diferentes!
1–0 ¿Los opuestos[2] se atraen?[3] ¡Por supuesto!

[1]twins [2]opposites [3]attract

Pronunciación

The letters *h* and *j* 🔊

jcd-0388

In Spanish, the letter *h* is never pronounced. Listen to and say these words:

hora	hablar	hasta	hola
hoy	hace	hacer	hotel

The letter *j* is pronounced like the letter *h* in "hat" but with more of a breathy sound. It is made far back in the mouth—almost in the throat. Listen to and say these words:

trabajar	dibujar	jugar	videojuegos
hoja	jueves	junio	julio

Try it out! Find and say five examples of foods or beverages from this chapter that have *h* or *j* in their spelling.

Try it out! Say this *trabalenguas* three times as fast as you can:

Debajo del puente de Guadalajara había un conejo debajo del agua.

20 ¿Qué comida hay en el Ciberc@fé @rrob@?

Leer • Escribir • Hablar

Lee el menú y contesta las preguntas.

Strategy

Skimming
Look quickly through the menu. What meal is it for? Find three dishes you recognize and two that are new to you.

Menú del Ciberc@fé @rrob@

Desayunos

No. 1 Huevos: *(jamón, tocino, chorizo[1])* $18.00
Con cóctel de fruta $20.00

No. 2 Sincronizadas: *(tortilla de harina,[2]* $22.00
queso amarillo, jamón)
Con cóctel de fruta $24.00

No. 3 Cuernitos: *(jamón, queso, tomate* $20.00
y lechuga)
Con cóctel de fruta $22.00

No. 4 Chilaquiles: *verdes o rojos* $14.00
Con cóctel de fruta $16.00

No. 5 Omelet: *(con pollo, jamón, tomate,* $18.00
cebolla, champiñones[3] o queso)

No. 6 Crepas *(champiñones, jamón, pollo)* $12.50

Refrescos $5.00   Café $4.00   Jugos $7.50   Té o té helado $4.00

Tel.: 212 03 95

16 de septiembre #65
Col. Centro

[1]spicy sausage   [2]flour   [3]mushrooms

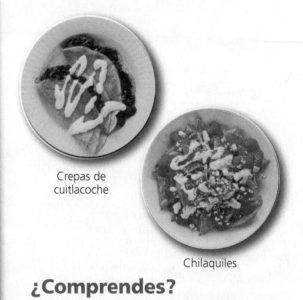

Crepas de cuitlacoche

Chilaquiles

¿Comprendes?

1. Comes el desayuno No. 1, con un jugo de naranja. ¿Cuál es el precio *(price)* del desayuno?

2. Comes un omelet con un café. ¿Cuál es el precio?

3. No te gustan nada los huevos. ¿Qué comes del menú?

4. No te gusta ni el café ni el té helado. ¿Qué bebes?

Más práctica

- **Guided** Gram. Practice pp. 95–96
- **Core** Gram. Practice pp. 54–55
- **Communication** Writing p. 58, Test Prep p. 251
- *Real.* **para hispanohablantes** pp. 98–101

realidades.com
- Audio Activities
- Video Activities
- Speak & Record
- Leveled Workbook
- Web Code: jcd-0304

El español en la comunidad

Foods from different Spanish-speaking countries have become very popular in the United States. Visit a local grocery store and make a list of different types of foods that come from Spanish-speaking countries. Which of these foods have you tried?

Lectura

Objectives

- Read about fruits that are native to the Americas
- Learn about a snack in Spanish-speaking countries, *churros y chocolate*
- Maintain a conversation about what you like, including your food preferences
- Learn facts about the northern part of South America

Frutas y verduras de las Américas

Hay muchas frutas y verduras que son originalmente de las Américas que hoy se comen en todos los países. Las verduras más populares son la papa, el maíz, los frijoles y muchas variedades de chiles. También hay una gran variedad de frutas como la papaya, la piña y el aguacate. Estas frutas y verduras son muy nutritivas, se pueden preparar fácilmente y son muy sabrosas. La papaya y la piña son frutas que se comen en el desayuno o de postre. ¿Cuáles de estas frutas comes?

Strategy

Making guesses
When you find an unknown word, try to guess the meaning. Is it a cognate? What might it mean within the context of the reading and other words around it? Keep reading and the meaning may become clear.

la papaya

Es una fruta con mucha agua. Es perfecta para el verano. Tiene más vitamina C que la naranja.

el aguacate

La pulpa del aguacate es una fuente de energía, proteínas, vitaminas y minerales. Tiene vitaminas A y B.

el mango

Aunque[1] el mango es originalmente del Asia, se cultiva en las regiones tropicales de muchos países de las Américas. Tiene calcio y vitaminas A y C, como la naranja.

[1]Although

Licuado de plátano

El licuado es una bebida muy popular en los países tropicales. ¡Es delicioso y muy nutritivo!

Ingredientes:
–1 plátano
–2 vasos de leche
–1 cucharadita de azúcar
–hielo

Preparación:
1. Cortar el plátano.
2. Colocar los ingredientes en la licuadora.
3. Licuar por unos 5 ó 10 segundos.

¿Comprendes?

1. ¿Qué vitaminas tienen las frutas en la página anterior?

2. De las frutas y verduras en el artículo, ¿cuáles *(which ones)* te gustan? ¿Cuáles no te gustan?

3. ¿Qué otras frutas te gustan? ¿Comes estas frutas en el desayuno o en el almuerzo?

4. ¿Qué fruta no es originalmente de las Américas?

Más práctica

- **Guided** Reading Support p. 97
- **Communication** Writing p. 59, Test Prep p. 252
- **Real. para hispanohablantes** pp. 102–103

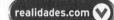 realidades.com

- Internet Activity
- Leveled Workbook
- Web Code: jcd-0305

Fondo cultural

Chile

Frutas y verduras During winter, the United States imports a wide range of fruits from Chile such as cherries, peaches, and grapes. When you purchase grapes from a supermarket in January, look to see if they have a label that says *Producto de Chile* or *Importado de Chile.*

- What are some other fruits and vegetables in your local market that are products of other countries?

La cultura en vivo
Churros y chocolate

In many Spanish-speaking countries, a popular snack is the combination of *churros y chocolate*. Churros are long, slender doughnut-like pastries fried in hot oil. Small restaurants called *churrerías* specialize in churros and cups of delicious hot chocolate. You can also find churros being sold in stands on the street.

Chocolate y churros

Try it out! Here's the recipe to try. Churros are high in fat and calories, so you won't want to sample too many of them!

Churros

1 cup water	$\frac{1}{2}$ cup unsalted butter *(= 1 stick)*
$\frac{1}{4}$ teaspoon salt	1 cup all-purpose flour
4 large eggs	oil for deep frying
1 cup sugar	

Un molinillo

In a heavy saucepan, bring water, butter, and salt to a full boil. Remove from heat. Add the flour all at once, stirring briskly. Stir until the mixture pulls away from the side of the pan and forms a ball. Put the mixture in a bowl. With an electric mixer on medium speed, add one egg at a time. After adding the last egg, beat the mixture for one more minute.

With adult supervision, heat 2–3 inches of oil to 375° F in a deep, heavy pan. Fit a pastry bag or cookie press with a $\frac{1}{2}$ inch star tip. Pipe out 6 inch-long tubes of dough into the oil. ***Be extremely cautious adding dough to the oil, because the oil may spatter and burn you!*** Fry, turning a few times, for 3–5 minutes or until golden brown. Place the sugar on a plate. Drain the churros well on paper towels and then roll them in the sugar.

Chocolate caliente

To make hot chocolate in Mexico, cacao beans are ground to a powder. Cinnamon, powdered almonds, and sugar are then added, and hot milk is poured in. The mixture is whipped with a wooden whisk called *un molinillo* or *un batidor*. You can find Mexican-style chocolate for making *chocolate caliente* in many supermarkets.

Think about it! What kinds of food and drink do you and your friends like? Is chocolate among the popular choices? Can you think of combinations of food and drink that are popular with many people in the United States? Are these combinations popular elsewhere?

Presentación oral
¿Y qué te gusta comer?

Task
An exchange student from the United States is going to Uruguay. You and a partner will role-play a telephone conversation in which you each take one of the roles and gather information about the other person.

1 Prepare You will role-play this conversation with a partner. Be sure to prepare for both roles. Here's how to prepare:

Host student: Make a list of at least four questions that you might ask the exchange student. Find out what he or she likes to study, his or her favorite activities, and what he or she likes to eat and drink for breakfast and lunch.

Exchange student: Jot down some possible answers to questions that the host student might ask and be prepared to provide information about yourself.

2 Practice Work in groups of four in which there are two exchange students and two host students. Work together to practice different questions and different responses. Here's how you might start your phone conversation:

HOST STUDENT:	¡Hola, Pablo! Soy Rosa.
EXCHANGE STUDENT:	¡Hola, Rosa! ¿Cómo estás?
HOST STUDENT:	Bien, gracias. Pues Pablo, ¿te gusta . . . ?

Continue the conversation using your notes. You can use your notes in practice, but not during the role-play.

3 Present You will be paired with another student, and your teacher will tell you which role to play. The host student begins the conversation. Listen to your partner's questions and responses and keep the conversation going.

4 Evaluation Your teacher may give you a rubric for how the presentation will be graded. You probably will be graded on:

- completion of task
- how well you were understood
- your ability to keep the conversation going

Strategy

Making lists
Making lists of questions can help you in conversations where you need to find out specific information.

realidades.com
• Speak & Record

América del Sur

Parte norte

Venezuela, Colombia, Ecuador, Peru, and Bolivia form a region of contrasts, with mountains and lowlands, rain forests and deserts, immense wealth and extreme poverty, remote villages and modern cities. A rugged geography, ancient indigenous civilizations, and abundant natural resources have made this one of the most culturally diverse regions in the world.

Constructed more than 500 years ago, the terraced fields in the highlands of Bolivia were a sophisticated system for conserving soil and water, and some remain in use today. In the 1980s archaeologists reconstructing ancient agricultural systems on the shore of Lake Titicaca (at 12,500 feet the highest navigable body of water in the world) found that these ancient systems worked better in this difficult environment than many modern agricultural techniques.

¿Sabes que . . . ?

The term *America* first appeared on a German map in 1507. The Americas are named for the Italian navigator Amerigo Vespucci, who produced the first European charts of mainland South America in 1497.

Para pensar

The countries of northern South America are lands of varied geography. Think about the North American continent. It is also a land of geographical contrasts. In what ways are both regions rich in natural resources, environmentally protected areas, and ancient civilizations?

realidades.com

- Online Atlas
- Web Code: jce-0002

"Rediscovered" in 1911, the mountaintop city of Machu Picchu in Peru was part of the Incan empire, which in the sixteenth century extended from present-day Ecuador to Chile. Machu Picchu's buildings were made of huge, precisely carved stone blocks that were hauled into place without wheels or heavy draft animals. ▶

◀ Venezuela is one of the most important sources of oil consumed in the United States. Other important Latin American oil producers include Mexico, Colombia, and Ecuador, with new deposits being found every year. Latin America and Canada account for approximately 46 percent of oil imports to the United States. In contrast, the Middle East accounts for approximately 23 percent.

The Galapagos Islands, also called *las islas encantadas* (the enchanted islands), lie 600 miles off the coast of Ecuador. It is believed that the Incas may have traveled to the islands in large ocean-going rafts. In 1835, the naturalist Charles Darwin spent weeks there studying the islands' unique animal life. *Galápagos* are giant tortoises that are native to these islands, which are now a national park and wildlife sanctuary.

Repaso del capítulo

Vocabulario y gramática

jcd-0389

Chapter Review

To prepare for the test, check to see if you . . .
- **know the new vocabulary and grammar**
- **can perform the tasks on p. 145**

to talk about breakfast

en el desayuno	for breakfast
el cereal	cereal
el desayuno	breakfast
los huevos	eggs
el pan	bread
el pan tostado	toast
el plátano	banana
la salchicha	sausage
el tocino	bacon
el yogur	yogurt

to talk about lunch

en el almuerzo	for lunch
la ensalada	salad
la ensalada de frutas	fruit salad
las fresas	strawberries
la galleta	cookie
la hamburguesa	hamburger
el jamón	ham
la manzana	apple
la naranja	orange
las papas fritas	French fries
el perrito caliente	hot dog
la pizza	pizza
el queso	cheese
el sándwich de jamón y queso	ham and cheese sandwich
la sopa de verduras	vegetable soup

to talk about beverages

el agua *f.*	water
el café	coffee
el jugo de manzana	apple juice
el jugo de naranja	orange juice
la leche	milk
la limonada	lemonade
el refresco	soft drink
el té	tea
el té helado	iced tea

to talk about eating and drinking

beber	to drink
comer	to eat
la comida	food, meal
compartir	to share

to indicate how often

nunca	never
siempre	always
todos los días	every day

to say that you like / love something

Me / te encanta(n) ___.	I / you love (___).
Me / te gusta(n) ___.	I / you like (___).

other useful words

comprender	to understand
con	with
¿Cuál?	Which? What?
más o menos	more or less
por supuesto	of course
¡Qué asco!	How awful!
sin	without
¿Verdad?	Right?

present tense of *-er* verbs

como	comemos
comes	coméis
come	comen

present tense of *-ir* verbs

comparto	compartimos
compartes	compartís
comparte	comparten

For *Vocabulario adicional*, see pp. 472–473.

Más práctica

- **Core** Puzzle p. 56, Organizer p. 57
- **Communication** Practice Test pp. 254–256, Integrated Performance Assessment p. 253

realidades.com

- Tutorial
- Flashcards
- Puzzles
- Self-test
- Web Code: jcd-0306

Preparación para el examen

On the exam you will be asked to . . .	Here are practice tasks similar to those you will find on the exam . . .	If you need review . . .

Interpretive

jcd-0389 **1 Escuchar** Listen and understand as people describe what they eat and drink for lunch

Listen as three students describe what they typically eat and drink for lunch. Which is most like the kind of lunch you eat? Did they mention anything you could not buy in your school cafeteria?

pp. 124–127 *Vocabulario en contexto*
p. 125 Actividades 1–2
p. 128 Actividad 5

Interpersonal

2 Hablar Tell someone what you typically eat for breakfast and ask the same of others

Your Spanish club is meeting for breakfast before school next week. Find out what other people in your class typically eat for breakfast. After you tell at least two people what you eat for breakfast, ask what they like to eat. Does everyone eat the same kind of breakfast or do you all like to eat different things?

p. 129 Actividad 7
p. 130 Actividad 8
p. 131 Actividad 11
p. 133 Actividad 13
p. 134 Actividades 15–16
p. 141 *Presentación oral*

Interpretive

3 Leer Read and understand words that are typically found on menus

You are trying to help a child order from the lunch menu below, but he is very difficult to please. He doesn't like anything white. And he refuses to eat anything that grows on trees. Which items from the menu do you think he would refuse to eat or drink?

pp. 124–127 *Vocabulario en contexto*
p. 131 Actividad 10
p. 137 Actividad 20
pp. 138–139 *Lectura*

ALMUERZO

hamburguesa	plátanos
pizza	manzana
ensalada	leche

Presentational

4 Escribir Write a list of foods that you like and others that you dislike

Your Spanish club is sponsoring a "Super Spanish Saturday." Your teacher wants to know what foods the class likes and dislikes so that the club can buy what most people like. Write the headings *Me gusta(n)* and *No me gusta(n)* in two columns. List at least four items that you like to eat and drink for breakfast and four items for lunch. Then list what you don't like to eat and drink for these same meals.

p. 128 Actividad 4
p. 129 Actividad 6
p. 131 Actividad 11
p. 134 Actividad 16
p. 135 Actividad 18
p. 137 Actividad 20

Comparisons

5 Pensar Demonstrate an understanding of cultural differences regarding snacks

Think about popular food combinations in the United States, such as a cup of coffee and a doughnut. What is a similar combination that is popular in many Spanish-speaking countries, and where are you able to buy it?

p. 140 *La cultura en vivo*

Diego Rivera (1886–1957) This detail of a mural entitled "La Gran Tenochtitlán" by Mexican artist Diego Rivera is located in the Palacio Nacional in Mexico City. It shows *el tianguis,* the bustling marketplace at Tenochtitlán, capital of the Aztec Empire. In the foreground there are many kinds of merchandise being traded, including corn and different varieties of beans. This mural is one of many by Rivera that focus on pre-Columbian life and civilizations.

- What impression do you think Rivera is giving about life in the pre-Columbian civilizations?

Detalle de *"La Gran Tenochtitlán"* (1945), Diego Rivera ▶

Para mantener la salud

Chapter Objectives

- **Talk about foods and beverages for dinner**
- **Describe what people or things are like**
- **Discuss food, health, and exercise choices**
- **Understand cultural perspectives on diet and health**

Video Highlights

Videocultura: *La comida*

A primera vista: *Para mantener la salud*

GramActiva Videos: the plurals of adjectives; the verb *ser*

Country Connection

As you learn about foods and health, you will make connections to these countries and places:

España

México

Guatemala

Costa Rica

Ecuador

Paraguay

Uruguay

Chile

Argentina

Más práctica

- *Real.* para hispanohablantes pp. 110–111

realidades.com

- Fondo cultural Activity
- Video Activities
- Online Atlas
- Web Code: jce-0002

Mercado al aire libre en España

Vocabulario en contexto

jcd-0397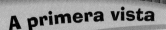

La pirámide nutritiva es la forma más práctica de indicar la comida que **debes** comer **cada día. Para mantener la salud,** es importante comer de **todos** los grupos.

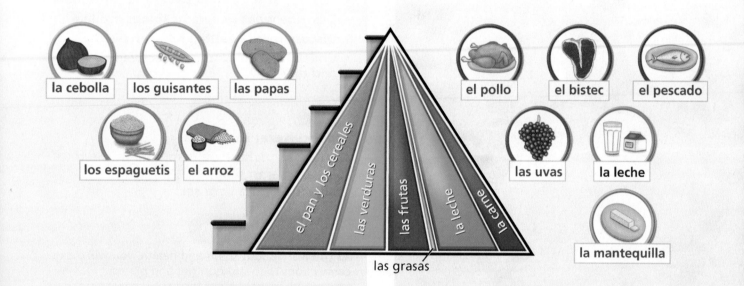

la cebolla | los guisantes | las papas

los espaguetis | el arroz

el pan y los cereales | las verduras | las frutas | la leche | la carne

las grasas

el pollo | el bistec | el pescado

las uvas | la leche

la mantequilla

¡Me encantan las verduras! Como **muchas** ensaladas con lechuga y tomates **.**

También me gustan las zanahorias y las judías verdes **.**

la lechuga

los tomates

las zanahorias

las judías verdes

¡Mi amiga Claudia no come comida buena **para la salud!** Come **muchos** pasteles y helado. **Son horribles .**

los pasteles

el helado

caminar

levantar pesas

—¿Qué **haces** para mantener la salud?

—Pues, cada día **hago ejercicio.** Camino, monto en bicicleta y practico deportes.

—¡Uf! **Tengo hambre. ¿Por qué** no comemos **algo** en el restaurante "A tu salud"? Los sándwiches son muy **sabrosos.**

—¡Por supuesto!

jcd-0397

1 **¿Qué debes comer?**

Escuchar

Your teacher is giving a lecture on foods that you should eat from the Food Guide Pyramid. Touch each item as it is mentioned. Listen carefully for the names of the foods.

jcd-0397

2 **Para mantener la salud**

Escuchar

Listen to students talk about things they do. Give a "thumbs-up" sign if they are describing things that are healthy and a "thumbs-down" sign if the things are unhealthy.

Más práctica

- **Guided** Vocab. Flash Cards pp. 99–104
- **Core** Vocab. Practice pp. 58–59
- **Communication** Writing p. 66
- *Real.* **para hispanohablantes** p. 112

realidades.com

- Audio Activities
- Leveled Workbook
- Flashcards
- Web Code: jcd-0311

Para mantener la salud

¿Qué hacen Raúl, Tomás y Gloria para mantener la salud? Lee la historia.

Strategy

Using visuals to make predictions
Before you read the story, use the pictures to predict what will happen. This will help you understand the story better as you read.

• How did your predictions compare with what you read?

Raúl **Gloria** **Tomás**

Costa Rica

1 **Tomás:** Tengo sed . . .

Raúl: ¿Qué **prefieres**? ¿Te gusta el café? El café de Costa Rica es muy bueno.

Tomás: ¡Pero el café es **malo** para la salud! **Prefiero una bebida** como . . . un jugo de fruta.

5 **Tomás:** ¡Me gusta hacer algo cada día! Hago ejercicio, levanto pesas o camino todos los días.

6 **Tomás:** Tengo hambre.

Raúl: ¿Por qué no comemos en la soda?*

7 **Tomás:** La comida aquí es muy buena. Ahora no tengo hambre. ¿Y tú?

Raúl: ¡**Creo que** no!

Gloria: Pues, **creo que** debemos ir a casa.

La soda is the word for a casual restaurant in Costa Rica.

2 **Raúl:** ¡Ah! **Estoy de acuerdo,** un refresco.

Tomás: Raúl, ¿por qué hablas de *refrescos?* A mí me gustan los jugos de fruta.

Gloria: Porque, Tomás, ¡un *refresco* en Costa Rica *es* un jugo de fruta!

3 **Raúl:** Dos refrescos de mango con leche.

Gloria: Y un refresco de mango con agua, por favor.

4 **Tomás:** ¡Es *muuuy* sabroso!

Gloria y Raúl: Sí, sí . . . ¡y todos los refrescos aquí son buenos para la salud!

Gloria: Tomás, ¿qué haces para mantener la salud?

8 **Mamá:** ¡A comer la cena!
Los jóvenes: *¡Uf!*

③ ¿Comprendes?

Escribir • Hablar

1. ¿Por qué no bebe café Tomás?
2. En Costa Rica, ¿qué es *un refresco?*
3. ¿Los refrescos en Costa Rica son buenos o malos para la salud?
4. Según Tomás, ¿cómo es la comida en la soda?
5. En casa, ¿qué está en la mesa?

Más práctica

- **Guided** Vocab. Check pp. 105–108
- **Core** Vocab. Practice pp. 60–61
- **Communication** Video pp. 60–62
- *Real.* **para hispanohablantes** p. 113

realidades.com ▼

- Audio Activities
- Video Activities
- Leveled Workbook
- Flashcards
- Web Code: jcd-0312

ciento cincuenta y uno 151
Capítulo 3B

Vocabulario en uso

Objectives

- Talk about dinner foods
- Express food preferences
- Describe people and foods
- Talk about healthy and unhealthy lifestyles
- Learn to use the plurals of adjectives and the verb *ser*

4 ¡Claro que no!

Leer · Escribir

For each group of words, choose the word or expression that doesn't belong and write it down on a sheet of paper. Then think of one more word or expression that does fit with the group and write it down beside the first word you wrote.

Modelo		
la *cebolla*	la *lechuga*	la *uva*
la uva	. . .	*la zanahoria*

1.	el pollo	el pescado	el arroz
2.	las zanahorias	los pasteles	las judías verdes
3.	caminar	correr	ver la televisión
4.	malo	horrible	sabroso
5.	comer mucho	levantar pesas	hacer ejercicio
6.	los tomates	el pan	los espaguetis
7.	cada día	un día	todos los días
8.	el bistec	las papas	el pollo
9.	la mantequilla	el helado	el pescado

5 ¿En el refrigerador o no?

Pensar · Escribir

Escribe dos listas. En la primera lista, escribe las comidas y bebidas que deben estar en el refrigerador. En la segunda lista, escribe las comidas y bebidas que no necesitan estar en el refrigerador.

Fondo cultural

Argentina • Paraguay • Uruguay

El mate is the national beverage of Argentina, Paraguay, and Uruguay. This herbal tea is shared among family and friends. It is served hot in a hollow gourd, also called *un mate,* with a straw called *una bombilla.*

- What national beverage does the United States have that compares to *mate?*

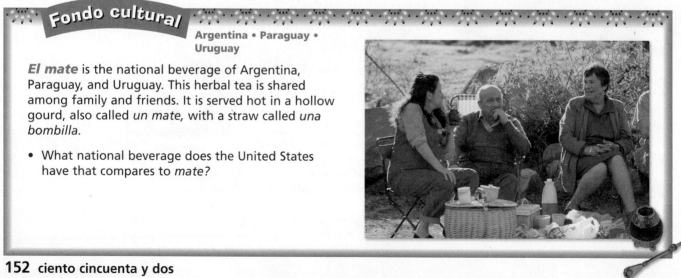

6 **¿Qué prefieres?**

Hablar

Ask your partner which of two foods he or she prefers. Your partner will answer and ask you which one you prefer.

Modelo

A —¿Qué prefieres, _carne o pescado?_
B —Prefiero _carne._ Y tú, ¿qué prefieres?
o: —No como ni _carne_ ni _pescado._ Y tú, ¿qué prefieres?
A —Prefiero _pescado._

Estudiante A

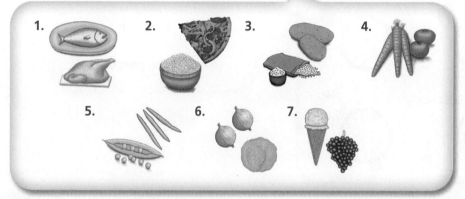

1. 2. 3. 4.

5. 6. 7.

Estudiante B

¡Respuesta personal!

7 **¿Sí o no?**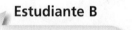

Hablar · Pensar

Habla de lo que debes comer y beber para mantener la salud.

Modelo

A —¿Debo _beber leche_ cada día para mantener la salud?
B —Creo que sí.
o: —Creo que no.

Estudiante A

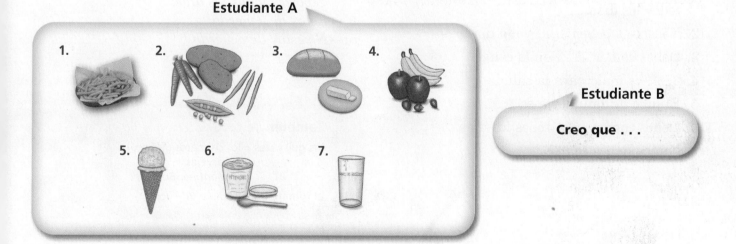

1. 2. 3. 4.

5. 6. 7.

Estudiante B

Creo que . . .

8 **¿Hay algo para comer?**

Hablar

Habla de lo que debes comer y beber a las horas indicadas.

Modelo

A —*Son las ocho de la mañana y tengo hambre y sed. ¿Qué debo comer y beber?*
B —*Debes comer cereal y pan tostado, y debes beber jugo de manzana.*

Para decir más . . .

de la mañana	in the morning
de la tarde	in the afternoon
de la noche	in the evening

Estudiante A

1.
2.
3.
4.
5.
6.

Estudiante B

¡Respuesta personal!

---

9 **Los buenos consejos** _____

Leer • Escribir

Da consejos (*Give advice*) sobre lo que es bueno o malo para la salud. Copia y completa las frases. Necesitas tus frases para la Actividad 10.

1. Para mantener la salud, debes _____ todos los días.

2. Necesitas beber _____ cada día.

3. Debes comer _____ en la cena.

4. _____ es malo para la salud.

5. El jugo de zanahoria es _____.

6. Debes comer _____ todos los días.

7. Nunca debes comer _____.

10 **¿Estás de acuerdo?**

Hablar

Lee tus consejos de la Actividad 9 a otro(a) estudiante. ¿Está de acuerdo con tus consejos?

Modelo

A —*Para mantener la salud, debes practicar deportes todos los días.*
B —*Estoy de acuerdo.*
o:—*No estoy de acuerdo.*

También se dice . . .

los guisantes = los chícharos (*México*),
las arvejas
(*Argentina, Bolivia*)

el tomate = el jitomate (*México*)

11 ¿Qué haces . . .?

Leer • Escribir • Hablar

Take this test on healthy activities to see how you rate.

1 Write your answers in complete sentences on a sheet of paper.

2 Ask a partner each question. Tally your partner's *sí* and *no* answers.

3 Write three recommendations so your partner can have a healthier lifestyle.

Modelo

Debes caminar o correr todos los días.

¿Qué haces para mantener la salud?

Contesta las preguntas según las actividades que haces cada día. Cada "sí" = 1 punto.

- ❏ 1. ¿Haces ejercicio?
- ❏ 2. ¿Practicas deportes?
- ❏ 3. ¿Comes verduras?
- ❏ 4. ¿Comes frutas?
- ❏ 5. ¿Caminas o corres?
- ❏ 6. ¿Comes un buen desayuno?
- ❏ 7. ¿Comes comida que es buena para la salud?
- ❏ 8. ¿Bebes cinco vasos* de agua?
- ❏ 9. ¿Pasas tiempo con amigos?
- ❏ 10.¿Ves tres horas o menos de televisión?

9–10 puntos *¡Felicidades! ¡Haces mucho para mantener la salud!*

6–8 puntos *Bueno, pero debes hacer más para mantener la salud.*

0–5 puntos *¡Ay, ay, ay! Necesitas hacer algo para mantener la salud.*

*glasses

Pronunciación

The letters *l* and *ll* 🔊

jcd-0398

In Spanish, the letter *l* is pronounced much like the letter *l* in the English word "leaf." Listen to and say these words:

lechuga	lunes	pasteles	helado
almuerzo	sol	abril	difícil

For most Spanish speakers, the letter combination *ll* is similar to the sound of the letter *y* in "yes." Listen to and say these words:

llamo	silla	allí	llueve
cebolla	pollo	ella	mantequilla

Try it out! Listen to this song and then sing it.

**Canta el gallo, canta el gallo
con el kiri, kiri, kiri, kiri, kiri;
La gallina, la gallina
con el cara, cara, cara, cara, cara;
Los polluelos, los polluelos
con el pío, pío, pío, pío, pío, pío, pí.**

Gramática

The plurals of adjectives

Just as adjectives agree with a noun depending on whether it's masculine or feminine, they also agree according to whether the noun is singular or plural. To make adjectives plural, just add an *-s* after the vowel at the end of the adjective. If the adjective ends in a consonant, add *-es*.

La hamburguesa es sabrosa. Las hamburguesas son sabrosas.

El pastel es muy popular. Los pasteles son muy populares.

When an adjective describes a group including both masculine and feminine nouns, use the masculine plural form.

La lechuga, las zanahorias y los tomates son buenos para la salud.

Don't forget that the singular form of *mucho* means "much" or "a lot of," but that the plural form, *muchos(as)*, means "many."

No como mucha carne, pero como muchas verduras.

¿Recuerdas?

Adjectives agree in gender with the masculine or feminine nouns they describe.

• **El bistec** es sabros**o**.

• **La ensalada** es sabros**a**.

GramActiva VIDEO

Want more help with the plurals of adjectives? Watch the **GramActiva** video.

---

12 **¿Sabroso o sabrosa?** ♻

Pensar • Leer • GramActiva

Your teacher will give you a GramActiva worksheet. Tear or cut apart the different adjective stems and endings that are printed on the sheet. Then your teacher will show you pictures of several foods. Show how you feel about each food item by holding up the appropriate adjective stem and the appropriate ending.

buen   sabros   mal

-o   -a   -os   -as

Fondo cultural

España

La Tomatina How would you like to attend a festival where a gigantic food fight with tomatoes is the highlight of the day? That's what happens at the annual *Fiesta de la Tomatina* in Buñol, Spain. After the town council distributes more than 130 tons of ripe tomatoes to participants, the hour-long tomato-throwing festival begins.

• Describe any food festivals unique to your community or your state. How do they compare to *La Tomatina*?

La Tomatina, en Buñol, España

---

13 ¿Cómo son?

Escribir • Hablar

1 For each of these adjectives, name two famous people, cartoon characters, or people in your school whom the adjective fits. Then write a sentence that describes both of them.

Modelo

A —*Creo que Cameron Diaz y Antonio Banderas son talentosos.*

1. artístico, -a   **3.** atrevido, -a   **5.** serio, -a   **7.** divertido, -a
2. deportista   **4.** gracioso, -a   **6.** talentoso, -a   **8.** trabajador, -a

2 Now read your sentences to a partner. Does your partner agree? Who fits the adjectives in your partner's opinion?

Modelo

B —*Estoy de acuerdo. Julia Roberts y Tom Cruise son talentosos también.*

o: —*Sí, pero Julia Roberts y Tom Cruise son más talentosos que Cameron Diaz y Antonio Banderas.*

14 ¿Qué prefieres?

Escribir • Hablar

Your class will be divided into groups of five to see what your favorite foods and beverages are.

Más práctica

- **Guided** Gram. Practice pp. 109–110
- **Core** Gram. Practice p. 62
- **Communication** Writing p. 67, Test Prep p. 257
- *Real.* **para hispanohablantes** pp. 114–117

realidades.com

- Audio Activities
- Video Activities
- Speak & Record
- Tutorial
- Leveled Workbook
- Web Code: jcd-0313

Conexiones | Las matemáticas

1 Ask your group members what their favorites are from each of the following groups: *frutas, verduras, carnes,* and *bebidas.* Write the answers on a sheet of paper.

Modelo

A —*¿Qué verduras prefieres?*
B —*Prefiero las zanahorias.*

2 Tally the results to see which foods and beverages are the most popular in each group. Indicate these favorites on a bar graph as shown. As a group, write four sentences that summarize your results. Compare your group's preferences to those of the other groups.

Modelo

Del grupo de las verduras, cuatro estudiantes prefieren las papas.

Prefieren . . .

	1	2	3	4	5
frutas	manzanas				
verduras	papas				
carnes	bístec				
bebidas	refrescos				

Número de estudiantes

Gramática

The verb *ser*

Ser, which means "to be," is an irregular verb.
Use *ser* to describe what a person or thing is like.
Here are the present-tense forms:

(yo)	soy	(nosotros) (nosotras)	somos
(tú)	eres	(vosotros) (vosotras)	sois
Ud. (él) (ella)	es	Uds. (ellos) (ellas)	son

¿Recuerdas?

In previous chapters, you learned how to talk about what a person is like.

—Tú **eres** muy deportista, ¿no?

—Sí, **soy** deportista.

—Mi amigo Pablo **es** deportista también.

GramActiva VIDEO

Want more help with the verb *ser*? Watch the **GramActiva** video.

---

15 **Línea romántica**

Leer • Escribir

Rafa has to tell his father why the cell phone bill was so high. Complete his explanations by using the correct form of the verb *ser*.

¡Ay, Papá, tú __1.__ muy estricto! ¡Yo __2.__ un chico *muuuy* sociable! Hablo con mis amigas porque todas __3.__ muy simpáticas. Hablo con Lidia porque nosotros __4.__ muy deportistas. Mis conversaciones con ella siempre __5.__ muy interesantes. Fátima __6.__ muy estudiosa. Hablamos mucho porque ella y yo __7.__ inteligentes y hablamos de las clases. Y hablo con Lorena porque __8.__ muy graciosa y nosotros __9.__ muy buenos amigos.

16 **Escucha y escribe** jcd-0398

Escuchar • Escribir

You will hear comments from five customers about the food being sold in a market. On a sheet of paper, write the numbers 1–5. As you listen, write the comments next to the numbers.

17 En tu escuela ♻

Hablar · Escribir

Describe the people and places in your school.

Modelo

el / la profesor(a) de tu clase de español
La profesora de mi clase de español es muy simpática.

1. tu clase de español
2. las chicas en tu clase de español
3. los chicos en tu clase de español
4. el / la director(a) de tu escuela
5. la comida de la cafetería
6. tú y tus amigos

18 ¿Sabroso o malo? 👥 ♻

Hablar

En tu opinión, ¿cómo son las comidas y las bebidas? Habla con un(a) compañero(a).
Usa los verbos *comer* o *beber*.

Modelo

A —*¿Comes zanahorias en la cena?*
B —*No, no como zanahorias en la cena porque son horribles.*
o:—*Sí, como zanahorias en la cena porque son buenas para la salud.*

Estudiante A

Estudiante B

(muy) sabroso
bueno para la salud
malo para la salud
horrible
¡Respuesta personal!

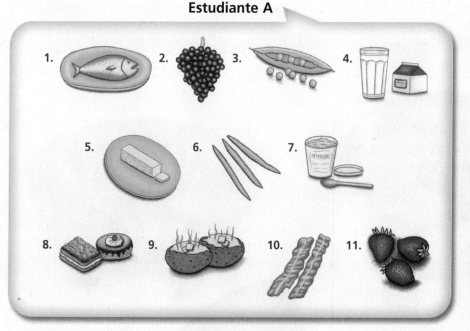

1. 2. 3. 4. 5. 6. 7. 8. 9. 10. 11.

Más práctica

- **Guided** Gram. Practice pp. 111–112
- **Core** Gram. Practice pp. 63–64
- **Communication** Writing p. 68
- *Real.* **para hispanohablantes** pp. 118–121

realidades.com ✓

- Audio Activities
- Video Activities
- Speak & Record
- Canción de hip hop
- Animated Verbs
- Tutorial
- Leveled Workbook
- Web Code: jcd-0314

Los mercados, or open-air markets, are common throughout Latin America. Many towns have a central market, held on a given day of the week, where people come from all around to buy and sell food, as well as flowers, crafts, and clothing.

• How does this market compare with the ways in which fruits and vegetables are bought and sold in your community?

Un mercado guatemalteco

Exploración del lenguaje

Where did it come from?

The names of many foods in Spanish come from Latin as well as from other languages as diverse as Arabic, Italian, Greek, Turkish, and English. While it's clear that the word *espaguetis* comes from the Italian word *spaghetti*, it's not obvious that the word *zanahoria* comes from the Arabic word *safunariya*.

Try it out! Read the Spanish words in the first column and match them up to their counterparts in their language of origin.

agua	*piscatu* (latín)
arroz	*aqua* (latín)
pan	*beefsteak* (inglés)
bistec	*panis* (latín)
salchichas	*pullu* (latín)
pescado	*kahvé* (turco)
café	*salciccia* (italiano)
pollo	*óryza* (griego)

El español en el mundo del trabajo

Rick Bayless's career as a world-class Mexican chef began at the age of 14, when he visited Mexico and decided to study Spanish. Since 1987, Rick has opened gourmet Mexican restaurants, created and starred in cooking shows, written cookbooks, and won many awards.

• How would Rick's Spanish skills be helpful in his career?

Un molcajete *(mortar and pestle)* de México

19 Una pizza para la buena salud ♻

Leer · Escribir

Lee este anuncio *(ad)* de una pizzería y contesta las preguntas.

Pizzería Lilia
¡Pizzas saludables!

A veces la pizza tiene muchas calorías y grasas que no son buenas para la salud.

La Pizzería Lilia tiene una variedad de pizzas con ingredientes que son buenos y saludables.

◆ Menos queso
◆ Usamos ingredientes nutritivos
  • Más verduras (tienen pocas calorías y son muy nutritivas)
◆ Evita[1] la combinación de carnes
  • Las carnes tienen mucho sodio y grasas
  • El pollo o el jamón son mejores[2] que las salchichas

¡Llámanos!

¡Estamos aquí para servirte!

372 42 89

Calle Independencia 28

[1]Avoid [2]better

1. Find and list three cognates in this ad.
2. Write three recommendations in Spanish for a healthier pizza.

20 Y tú, ¿qué dices?

Escribir · Hablar

1. Describe tu pizza favorita.
2. ¿Crees que la pizza es buena o mala para la salud? ¿Por qué?
3. ¿Qué verduras prefieres? ¿Qué verduras no te gustan?
4. ¿Qué ejercicio haces con los brazos? ¿Qué ejercicio haces con las piernas?

En un café en Murcia, España

Lectura

La comida de los atletas

Lee este artículo (*article*) de una revista deportiva. ¿Qué comen y qué beben los atletas profesionales para mantener la salud y estar en buena forma?

Objectives

- Read about a sports diet and learn some facts about an athlete
- Understand cultural perspectives on healthcare
- Make a poster about good health habits
- Learn facts about the southern part of South America

Strategy

Skimming

List three things that you would expect to find in an article about athletes' eating habits. Skim the article to find the information.

¿Qué come un jugador de fútbol?

Los jugadores[1] de fútbol comen comidas equilibradas con muchos carbohidratos, minerales y vitaminas. Ellos consumen cerca de 5.000 calorías en total todos los días.

17% Proteínas

13% Grasas

70% Carbohidratos

Para el desayuno el día de un partido[2], un jugador típico come mucho pan con mantequilla y jalea[3], yogur y té.

Para el almuerzo antes del[4] partido, come pan, pasta, pollo sin grasa, verduras, frutas y una ensalada.

Para la cena después del[5] partido, el atleta come papas, carne sin grasa y más verduras y frutas.

También es muy importante beber muchos líquidos. La noche antes del partido, el jugador bebe un litro de jugo de naranja y durante el partido bebe hasta[6] dos litros de agua y bebidas deportivas.

[1]players [2]game [3]jam [4]before the [5]after the [6]up to

Nombre: Carlos Tévez
Fecha de nacimiento: 2/5/84
Lugar de nacimiento: Capital Federal
País de nacimiento: Argentina
Nacionalidad: argentino
Equipo[7]: Manchester United
Función: Ofensa

Carlos Tévez es jugador del equipo Manchester United, un equipo de fútbol profesional en Inglaterra.

[7]team

¿Comprendes?

1. ¿Qué debe comer Carlos Tévez antes de un partido de fútbol?

2. ¿Qué debe beber?

3. ¿Qué comida no debe comer Carlos?

4. ¿Es tu dieta diferente de la dieta de un jugador de fútbol profesional? ¿Cómo?

5. ¿Cuál es la fecha de nacimiento *(birth date)* de Carlos? Escribe tu fecha de nacimiento cómo lo hacen en los países hispanohablantes.

Más práctica

- **Guided** Reading Support p. 113
- **Communication** Writing p. 69, Test Prep p. 258
- *Real.* **para hispanohablantes** pp. 122–123

realidades.com ✓

- Internet Activity
- Leveled Workbook
- Web Code: jcd-0315

Fondo cultural
El mundo hispano

¡Goooooooooooool! Scoring the winning *gol* in soccer is the most exciting moment of the game. *El fútbol* is the most popular sport in the world, and it has many *fanáticos* (fans) in every Spanish-speaking country. Every four years, teams throughout the world compete regionally in order to become one of the 32 teams to advance to the World Cup *(la Copa Mundial)* competition. Many Spanish-speaking countries compete in what has become the most widely watched sporting event in the world. Since the competition began in 1930, two Spanish-speaking countries have won the World Cup competition: Uruguay in 1930 and 1950 and Argentina in 1978 and 1986.

- How does the enthusiasm for soccer in the United States compare with the rest of the world's view of this sport? Why do you think this is so?

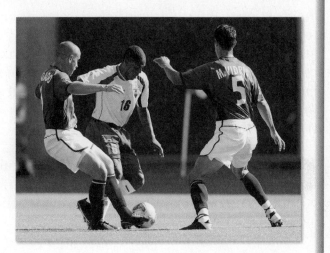

Jugadores de fútbol

Perspectivas del mundo hispano
¿Qué haces para mantener la salud?

Have you ever eaten chicken soup when you have a cold? How about putting aloe on a sunburn? In many countries, including those in the Spanish-speaking world, traditional remedies consisting of medicinal herbs have been used for centuries to treat common medical problems. In Mexico, a mint known as *yerbabuena* may be made into tea and given to someone with a stomachache. Remedies such as these may not be prescribed by licensed physicians, but people have confidence in them because they have been passed down through the generations. Many of those herbs are very safe, though some may have harmful side effects.

En la selva amazónica[1], Perú

Researchers are studying traditional herbal remedies to find modern-day medical solutions. In the Amazon rainforest in South America, an amazing abundance of plant life may hold the key to treating a wide variety of common ailments and diseases. Drug companies are looking for cures found in these plants and herbs that could be reproduced in today's modern drugs.

Increasingly, medicinal herbs are accepted not only as the basis for pharmaceutical drugs, but also for their own inherent healing qualities. In many countries, including the United States, herbal remedies are sometimes used in combination with conventional health care.

Check it out! What alternatives to conventional medical care are available in your community? Make a list of all the health care services you can think of that are not provided by traditional physicians. Are there health stores that sell herbal medicines? What types of herbal medicines are being sold and what remedies are attributed to these medicines?

En un mercado de la Ciudad de México

Think about it! In many Spanish-speaking cultures, herbal remedies have been accepted for centuries. Do you think that medicinal herbs can provide relief and cures? Why or why not?

[1]Amazon rainforest

Presentación escrita
Para mantener la salud

Task
You are doing some research for your health class on good eating and exercise habits. Make a poster in Spanish with five suggestions for better health.

1 **Prewrite** Talk to classmates, teachers, the school nurse, and your parents about good eating and exercise habits, especially for teens. Then list their ideas under the following headings to help you organize your information:

- *Debes comer . . .*
- *Debes beber . . .*
- *Debes . . . para mantener la salud.*
- *No debes comer mucho(a) . . .*
- *No debes beber mucho(a) . . .*

Strategy
Gathering information
Use information from a variety of sources to help you create a more complete presentation on a topic.

2 **Draft** Write the first draft. Decide how to present the information in a logical way. Think about using visuals for clarity. Sketch them on your draft. Give the poster a title.

3 **Revise** Share your draft with a partner. Your partner should check the following:

- Have you communicated the five suggestions well?
- Do the visuals help convey meaning and make the poster attractive?
- Are the vocabulary and grammar correct?

Decide whether to use your partner's suggestions, and then rewrite your poster.

4 **Publish** Make a final copy, adding attractive illustrations or designs and making necessary changes. You might want to:

- post it in the nurse's office, at a local community center, or in your classroom
- include it in your portfolio

5 **Evaluation** Your teacher may give you a rubric for how your poster will be graded. You probably will be graded on:

- completion of task
- accuracy of vocabulary and grammar
- effective use of visuals

América del Sur

Parte sur

A large proportion of the people of Argentina, Uruguay, and Chile live in cities. As in the United States, these cities have been shaped by mass immigration from southern and eastern Europe during the nineteenth and twentieth centuries. Many more Paraguayans, in contrast, live in the countryside.

In the early 1900s, the area of *las cataratas de Iguazú* was made an Argentine national park. Three countries—Brazil, Argentina, and Paraguay—meet at these spectacular falls, which are four times the width of Niagara Falls and 50 percent higher. Hundreds of species of insects, birds, and mammals are found in the area, and at least 500 species of butterflies. As many as 4,000 tourists a day visit the falls, a worrisome number for environmental groups, who continue to lobby against nearby hotel construction projects.

¿Sabes que . . . ?

At 22,840 feet (6,962 meters), Argentina's Cerro Aconcagua is the highest point in the Western Hemisphere, but it is considered a relatively easy climb. Chile's Torres del Paine, consisting of three granite towers, are nearly 6,000 feet lower, but their sheer cliffs, high winds, and extreme cold make them some of the most challenging climbs in the world. Both mountains are part of the Andes, a range that extends from Colombia to the southern tip of South America.

Para pensar

Think about what it would be like to be an immigrant arriving in one of the countries of southern South America. Would you prefer the city life of Buenos Aires, Argentina, Montevideo, Uruguay, or Santiago, Chile? Or would the countryside of Paraguay be more appealing? Why?

realidades.com

- Online Atlas
- Web Code: jce-0002

The Spanish were able to topple large, centralized empires such as those of the Aztecs and Incas quickly, but they were never able to conquer the smaller indigenous groups in the more remote regions. Chile's Pehuenche suffered defeats in the nineteenth century, but they still struggle to maintain their lands and culture. ▶

◀ Spain introduced horses, cows, sheep, and pigs to the Americas in the sixteenth century, transforming the ecology, culture, and economy of the region. In the nineteenth century, the growth of cities, the expansion of railways, and improvements in shipping created a worldwide market for South American meat and hides—and helped spur the development of the cowboy culture throughout the Americas. As on ranches in the western United States and northern Mexico, the main house of an Argentine or Uruguayan *estancia* served as a residence, office, and military stronghold.

With its wide boulevards, parks, museums, and diverse cultural life, Buenos Aires is considered one of the most cosmopolitan cities in the world. Argentina has produced world-class writers such as Jorge Luis Borges, Julio Cortázar, and José Hernández, who wrote a classic about the life of the *gauchos*. The tango, the first dance from Latin America to gain international popularity, is a favorite of the *porteños*—the residents of Buenos Aires.

Repaso del capítulo
Vocabulario y gramática   jcd-0399

Chapter Review

To prepare for the test, check to see if you . . .
- **know the new vocabulary and grammar**
- **can perform the tasks on p. 169**

to talk about food and beverages

la cena	dinner
el bistec	beefsteak
la carne	meat
el pescado	fish
el pollo	chicken
la cebolla	onion
los guisantes	peas
las judías verdes	green beans
la lechuga	lettuce
las papas	potatoes
los tomates	tomatoes
las uvas	grapes
las zanahorias	carrots
el arroz	rice
los cereales	grains
los espaguetis	spaghetti
las grasas	fats
la mantequilla	butter
el helado	ice cream
los pasteles	pastries
las bebidas	beverages

to talk about being hungry and thirsty

Tengo hambre.	I'm hungry.
Tengo sed.	I'm thirsty.

to discuss health

caminar	to walk
hacer ejercicio	to exercise
(yo) hago	I do
(tú) haces	you do
levantar pesas	to lift weights
para la salud	for one's health
para mantener la salud	to maintain one's health

to indicate a preference

(yo) prefiero	I prefer
(tú) prefieres	you prefer
deber	should, must

to indicate agreement or disagreement

creer	to think
Creo que . . .	I think . . .
Creo que sí / no.	I (don't) think so.
(No) estoy de acuerdo.	I (don't) agree.

to ask a question or give an answer

¿Por qué?	Why?
porque	because

to express quantity

algo	something
muchos, -as	many
todos, -as	all

to describe something

horrible	horrible
malo, -a	bad
sabroso, -a	tasty, flavorful

other useful words

cada día	every day

plurals of adjectives

MASCULINE	FEMININE
SINGULAR / PLURAL	SINGULAR / PLURAL
sabroso / sabrosos	sabrosa / sabrosas
popular / populares	popular / populares

ser *to be*

soy	somos
eres	sois
es	son

For *Vocabulario adicional,* see pp. 472–473.

Más práctica

- **Core** Puzzle p. 65, Organizer p. 66
- **Communication** Practice Test pp. 260–262, Integrated Performance Assessment p. 259

realidades.com
- Tutorial
- Flashcards
- Puzzles
- Self-test
- Web Code: jcd-0316

Preparación para el examen

On the exam you will be asked to . . .	Here are practice tasks similar to those you will find on the exam . . .	If you need review . . .

Interpretive

jcd-0399

1 Escuchar Listen and understand as people describe a healthy or unhealthy lifestyle

Listen as two people are interviewed about their habits. See if you can tell which one is an Olympic skier and which one is a drummer. Be prepared to explain your "educated guesses."

pp. 148–151 *Vocabulario en contexto*
p. 149 Actividad 2

Interpersonal

2 Hablar Express your opinion about food preferences

During a telephone survey, you are asked some questions in Spanish about your food preferences. Say whether you think each food choice is good or bad for your health.

p. 153 Actividades 6–7
p. 154 Actividades 8, 10
p. 157 Actividad 14
p. 159 Actividad 18

Interpretive

3 Leer Read and compare what people do and eat in order to determine whether they lead a healthy or unhealthy lifestyle

Read the online conversation that you have just joined in a chat room. Decide whether each person has a healthy or unhealthy lifestyle, based on what they tell each other.

Chato: *¿Qué hago yo? Cuando hace buen tiempo, corro por treinta minutos. Cuando llueve, levanto pesas.*

Chispa: *No me gusta hacer ejercicio. Prefiero comer papas fritas. Son muy sabrosas.*

Andrés: *¿Papas fritas? Son horribles para la salud. Para mantener la salud, nunca debes comer papas fritas.*

pp. 148–151 *Vocabulario en contexto*
p. 154 Actividad 9
p. 155 Actividad 11
p. 161 Actividad 19
pp. 162–163 *Lectura*

Presentational

4 Escribir Write a list of things a person should do to maintain a healthy lifestyle

Many people think that teens don't know anything about a healthy lifestyle. You and your friends are compiling a top-ten list of ways to improve teens' health. Write at least three suggestions for the list.

p. 154 Actividad 9
p. 155 Actividad 11
p. 161 Actividad 19
p. 165 *Presentación escrita*

Cultures • Comparisons

5 Pensar Demonstrate an understanding of cultural perspectives regarding health care

Give an example of an herbal remedy that is accepted in a Spanish-speaking country as a remedy for a common ailment. Compare this with a similar herbal/natural remedy believed by many in the United States to be a cure for a common ailment.

p. 164 *Perspectivas del mundo hispano*

Fondo cultural

España

"El quitasol" is a work by Spanish painter Francisco de Goya (1746–1828). He made this painting in 1777 as a design to be used in the manufacture of a royal tapestry. At that time Goya was already famous for the elegance of his artwork and his ability to capture ordinary events in realistic detail. The brilliant colors of this painting suggest a happy moment of relaxation for two young people.

• Why do people who live in the city go out to the country to relax?

"El quitasol" (1777), Francisco de Goya ▶

Oil on canvas, 104 x 152 cm. Museo Nacional del Prado, Madrid, Spain.
Photo credit: Scala / Art Resource, NY.

¿Adónde vas?

Chapter Objectives

- Talk about locations in your community
- Discuss leisure activities
- Talk about where you go and with whom
- Learn how to ask questions
- Understand cultural perspectives on leisure activities

Video Highlights

Videocultura: *Los pasatiempos*

A primera vista: *Un chico reservado*

GramActiva Videos: the verb *ir;* asking questions

Country Connection

As you learn about leisure activities, you will make connections to these countries and places:

California, Texas, España, Illinois, Arizona, Luisiana, Florida, México, Puerto Rico, Nuevo México, Honduras, Ecuador, Venezuela, Perú, Colombia, Bolivia, Chile, Argentina

Más práctica

- *Real.* para hispanohablantes pp. 130–131

realidades.com ✓

- Fondo cultural Activity
- Online Atlas
- Video Activities
- Web Code: jce-0002

El Parque del Buen Retiro,
Madrid, España

Vocabulario en contexto

jcd-0487

Objectives

Read, listen to, and understand information about

- places to go to when you're not in school

el gimnasio

el parque

el centro comercial

ir de compras

el trabajo

la lección de piano

el cine

ver una película

la biblioteca

la piscina

—En tu **tiempo libre después de** las clases, ¿qué haces?

> —**Voy al** gimnasio **para** levantar pesas y al parque para correr. ¿Y tú?

—Hoy voy **a** mi trabajo. No voy a mi lección de piano.

—¿**Con quién** vas al centro comercial?

> —Voy con Guillermo, y **después vamos** al cine. ¿Y tú?

—Voy a la biblioteca para estudiar. Después voy al **Café** del Mundo con Lucila.

la playa

el restaurante

el campo

las montañas

—¿Qué haces **los** domingos?

— Voy **con mis amigos** a la playa.
Allí comemos el almuerzo.
Hay un restaurante muy bueno.
¿Y tú?

— **Generalmente** voy al campo o
a las montañas.

Más vocabulario

la iglesia	church
la mezquita	mosque
la sinagoga	synagogue
el templo	temple; Protestant church

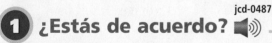

1 **¿Estás de acuerdo?** 🔊   jcd-0487

Escuchar

You will hear Elena describe where
she does seven activities. If a statement
is logical, give a "thumbs-up" sign.
If it is not logical, make a "thumbs-
down" sign.

2 **¡Muchas actividades!** 🔊   jcd-0487

Escuchar

Listen to Antonio describe his weekly list
of after-school activities. As he names his
activities, touch the corresponding picture(s).

Más práctica

- **Guided** Vocab. Flash Cards
  pp. 115–120
- **Core** Vocab. Practice pp. 67–68
- **Communication** Writing p. 75
- *Real.* **para hispanohablantes**
  p. 132

realidades.com ✔

- Audio Activities
- Leveled Workbook
- Flashcards
- Web Code: jcd-0401

Un chico reservado

¿Qué pasa cuando Ignacio, Elena y Ana hablan con el estudiante nuevo *(new)*? Lee la historia.

España

Ignacio

Ana

Elena

Javier

1 **Ignacio:** Mira, el estudiante nuevo es un poco reservado, ¿verdad?

Elena: Ah, sí . . . Está allí **solo.** ¿Por qué no hablamos con él?

Ignacio: Sí, ¡vamos!

5 **Ana:** Los lunes voy a mi lección de piano y los martes, miércoles y jueves voy a la biblioteca para estudiar. Y Javier, ¿qué haces **los fines de semana?**

6 **Javier:** ¿Los fines de semana? **Me quedo en casa.** No tengo muchos amigos aquí.

Ignacio: ¿Qué te gusta hacer?

Javier: ¡Me gusta el fútbol!

7 **Ana:** ¡No me digas! Pues, nosotros vamos al parque para practicar fútbol.

Javier: ¿Cuándo?

Ana: El sábado.

Javier: Está bien.

2 **Elena:** Hola. Me llamo Elena. Él es Ignacio, y ella es Ana.

Javier: Mucho gusto. Me llamo Javier.

Elena: Encantada . . . ¿De dónde eres?

Javier: Soy de Salamanca.

3 **Ana:** Pues, Javier, ¿vas después de las clases **con tus amigos?**

Javier: No, voy **a casa.**

4 **Javier:** ¿**Adónde** vais* vosotros después de las clases?

Elena: Los lunes, miércoles y viernes voy a mi trabajo en el centro comercial.

Ignacio: Generalmente voy al gimnasio. Me gusta levantar pesas.

3 **¿Comprendes?**

Leer • Escribir • Hablar

En una hoja de papel completa las frases según la *Videohistoria*.

1. Javier es de . . .
2. Después de las clases Javier va . . .
3. Después de las clases Ignacio va al . . .
4. El jueves Ana va a la . . .
5. A Javier le gusta practicar . . .
6. Todos van al parque el . . .

8 **Elena:** Pero Ana, ¿fútbol?

Ana: ¿Por qué no? ¡No tiene muchos amigos y le gusta el fútbol!

Más práctica

- **Guided** Vocab. Check pp. 121–124
- **Core** Vocab. Practice pp. 69–70
- **Communication** Video pp. 70–71
- *Real.* **para hispanohablantes** p. 133

realidades.com V

- Audio Activities
- Video Activities
- Leveled Workbook
- Flashcards
- Web Code: jcd-0402

*Remember that in Spain, the *vosotros(as)* form of verbs is used when speaking to a group of people you would address individually with *tú*.

Vocabulario en uso

Objectives

• Communicate about leisure activities
• Tell where you go and with whom
• Learn to use the verb *ir* and how to ask questions

4 ¿Qué haces en . . . ?

Escribir • Hablar

Completa las frases lógicamente.

1. Hago ejercicio en . . .
2. Nado en . . .
3. Veo películas en . . .
4. Leo libros y revistas en . . .
5. Voy de compras en . . .
6. Esquío en . . .
7. Como el desayuno en . . .

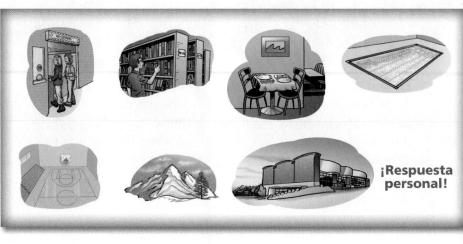

¡Respuesta personal!

5 ¿Vas mucho a . . . ?

Escribir

On a sheet of paper, copy the diagram below and write the names of the places you go under the appropriate expression of frequency.

todos los días   mucho   a veces   nunca

la playa

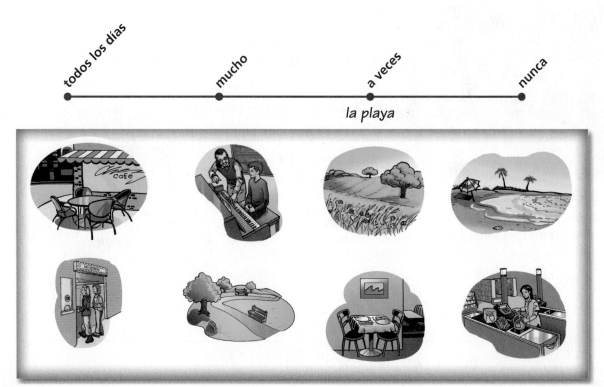

6 ¡No me digas!

Hablar

Work with a partner. Using what you wrote for Actividad 5, take turns saying where you go and how often. React to your partner's statements. Follow the model.

Modelo

A —*Voy a la playa a veces.*
B —*¡No me digas! Yo voy a la playa a veces también.*
o:—*¡No me digas! Yo nunca voy a la playa.*
o:—*Pues, yo voy a la playa todos los días.*

Nota

When *a* is used before *el,* the two words form the contraction *al (to the):*

a + el = al

• Voy **al** centro comercial a veces, pero voy **a la** piscina mucho.

También se dice . . .

la piscina = la alberca *(México);* la pileta *(América del Sur)*

el restaurante = el restaurán *(América del Sur)*

7 Escucha y escribe 🔊

jcd-0488

Escuchar • Escribir

Look at the painting of Plaza Morazán in Tegucigalpa, Honduras. On a sheet of paper, write the numbers 1–6. You will hear six statements about the painting. Write what you hear.

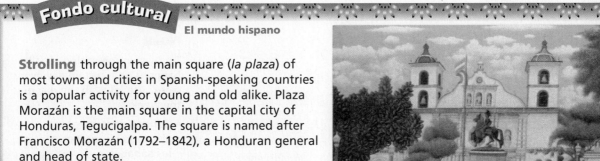

Fondo cultural

El mundo hispano

Strolling through the main square (*la plaza*) of most towns and cities in Spanish-speaking countries is a popular activity for young and old alike. Plaza Morazán is the main square in the capital city of Honduras, Tegucigalpa. The square is named after Francisco Morazán (1792–1842), a Honduran general and head of state.

• What social gathering place in your community is similar to *la plaza*?

"Plaza Morazán en Tegucigalpa" (1969), José Antonio ▶ Velásquez

Origins of the Spanish days of the week

The word *sábado*, like many Spanish words, is based on Latin. The Spanish days of the week come from the Latin names for the gods, planets, sun, and moon, all of which were important in Roman daily life.

Try it out! Match the Spanish days of the week with their Latin origins.

1. lunes	**a.** *dies Mercurii:* named after Mercury, the god of commerce and travelers
2. martes	**b.** *dies Veneris:* named after Venus, the goddess of beauty and love
3. miércoles	**c.** *dies lunae:* the day dedicated to the moon *(luna)*
4. jueves	**d.** *dies solis:* named after the sun *(sol)*, but later changed to *dies Dominicus,* which means "the Lord's day"
5. viernes	**e.** *dies Martis:* dedicated to Mars, the god of war
6. sábado	**f.** *dies Saturni:* named after Saturn; also called *dies Sabbati,* based on the Hebrew word *shabbath,* or "day of rest"
7. domingo	**g.** *dies Jovis:* named after Jove, or Jupiter, the ruler of the gods

- Since you know *día* means "day" in Spanish, what is the word for "day" in Latin?

8 ¿Adónde vas?

Hablar

Habla con otro(a) estudiante sobre los lugares *(about the places)* adónde vas y cuándo vas allí.

Modelo

los lunes
A —¿Adónde vas <u>los lunes</u>?
B —Generalmente voy <u>a mi lección de piano</u>.
o:—Generalmente <u>me quedo en casa</u>.

Nota

To say that something usually happens on a certain day every week, use *los* with the day of the week:

- Generalmente ellos van al campo **los viernes** o **los sábados.**

Estudiante A

1. los miércoles
2. los viernes
3. los sábados
4. los domingos
5. los fines de semana
6. después de las clases

Estudiante B

¡Respuesta personal!

9 Cuando no estamos en la escuela . . .

Hablar • Pensar • Escribir

¿Cómo pasan el tiempo tus compañeros de clase cuando no están en la escuela? Sigue *(follow)* los pasos.

Perú

Conexiones **Las matemáticas**

Muchos jóvenes pasan el día en la playa en Perú.

❶ Working in groups of four, take turns asking each person how often he or she does the activities listed below. Answer using *mucho*, *a veces*, or *nunca*. Keep a group tally of the responses.

❷ Get together with another group of four and combine the results of your tally sheets. Prepare summary statements to report to the class.

❸ Report your summary statements to the class and make a class total. Convert each total to a percentage.

❹ Create a bar graph like the one below for each activity that shows the class's frequency of participation.

| ver películas | usar la computadora | ir a un trabajo |
| correr | ir de compras | ir a la biblioteca |

Modelo

A —*¿Con qué frecuencia* (How often) *usas la computadora?*

B —*Uso la computadora mucho.*

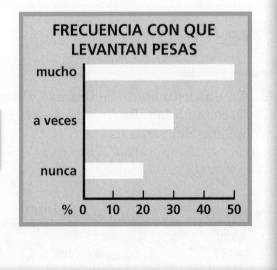

10 Y tú, ¿qué dices?

Escribir • Hablar

1. ¿Dónde ves más películas, en casa o en el cine?

2. Cuando vas de compras, ¿adónde vas?

3. ¿Adónde vas los fines de semana? ¿Vas solo(a) o con tus amigos?

Gramática

The verb *ir*

To say where someone is going, use the verb *ir*.
Here are its present-tense forms:

(yo)	**voy**	(nosotros) (nosotras)	**vamos**
(tú)	**vas**	(vosotros) (vosotras)	**vais**
Ud. (él) (ella)	**va**	Uds. (ellos) (ellas)	**van**

The verb *ir* is almost always followed by *a*.
To ask where someone is going, use *¿Adónde?*

¿Adónde vas?   **Where are you going (to)?**

• You will often hear people say ¡*Vamos!*
This means, "Let's go!"

GramActiva VIDEO

Want more help
with the verb *ir*?
Watch the
GramActiva video.

Voy al cine.

---

11 **Un invierno en Chile**

Leer • Escribir

María, una estudiante de Chicago, Illinois, pasa un año en Santiago,
Chile, con una familia chilena. Lee la carta *(letter)* y escribe las formas
apropiadas del verbo *ir*.

17 de julio

Querida Sonia:
¿Cómo estás? Yo, bien. Generalmente paso tiempo
en casa los fines de semana, pero a veces yo __1.__ a
Portillo con la familia para esquiar. Hace mucho frío
allí y por eso mi "mamá" chilena no __2.__ siempre con
nosotros. En Portillo hay una escuela para los esquiadores
y muchos chicos simpáticos __3.__ a las lecciones.
También hay un cibercafé con computadoras. Muchas
personas __4.__ allí para pasar tiempo con los amigos.
Nosotros __5.__ el domingo. Y tú, ¿ __6.__ a la playa
todos los días con tus amigos?

Hasta luego,

María

Esquiadores en Portillo, Chile

Chile

⓬ La carta

Leer • Hablar

Lee la carta de María en la Actividad 11 y contesta
las preguntas.

1. ¿Quién no va a veces con la familia a Portillo?
2. ¿Por qué a María le gusta ir a las lecciones de esquí?
3. ¿Adónde van para usar las computadoras?
4. ¿Cuándo van al cibercafé?
5. ¿Adónde van muchas personas para pasar tiempo con los amigos?

⓭ ¿Adónde van todos?

Leer • Hablar • Escribir

❶ Read the sentence and determine who does the activity.
Using the correct form of *ir*, ask where they go to do the
activity. Your partner will answer with the most logical place.

Modelo

A —Te gusta esquiar. *(tú) ¿Adónde vas?*
B —*Voy a las montañas para esquiar.*

1. Te gusta levantar pesas.
2. Tú y tu amigo corren mucho.
3. Tus amigos y tú ven muchas películas.
4. A tu amigo le gusta comer bistec.
5. Tus amigas nadan muy bien.
6. Tus amigos hacen ejercicio todos los días.

❷ Now write four sentences about yourself and your friends,
saying where you go and for what purpose.

Modelo

Vamos a . . . para . . .

Fondo cultural
El mundo hispano

Sports clubs and gyms are very popular in
Spanish-speaking countries. Since there are few
school-based sports teams, many young people
join private gyms for individual exercise or
play for privately sponsored teams in order to
compete in their favorite sports.

• What do you think students would do if your
school did not offer opportunities for playing
and competing in sports?

Estudiantes en el gimnasio

14 Juego

Escribir · Hablar

Play this game in teams of two.

1 With a partner, write five sentences saying what the two of you like to do in your free time and when. Also write sentences saying where you go for these activities.

Modelo

Nosotros corremos después de las clases. (Vamos al gimnasio.)

2 Read one of your statements about activities to another team of classmates, but don't read the part that tells where you go. Then have one person try to guess where you go to do this activity. If the student answers correctly, his or her team wins a point. The team that earns the most points wins.

Modelo

A —*Nosotros corremos después de las clases.*
B —*Uds. van al gimnasio, ¿verdad?*
A —*Sí, vamos al gimnasio para correr.*
o: —*No, no vamos al gimnasio para correr. Vamos al parque.*

El español en la comunidad

In many businesses and neighborhoods in the United States, you can hear Spanish being spoken. For example, the Pilsen neighborhood in Chicago, Illinois, is home to one of the nation's largest Mexican communities. The colorful murals, thriving businesses, and popular restaurants give Pilsen its own character.

• Are there areas near you where you can see expressions of community for Spanish speakers? What are they?

En la comunidad de Pilsen, en Chicago

Pronunciación

Stress and accents
jcd-0488

How can you tell which syllable to stress, or emphasize, when you see words written in Spanish? Here are some general rules.

1. When words end in a vowel, *n*, or *s*, place the stress on the **next-to-last syllable.** Copy each of these words and draw a line under the next-to-last syllable. Then listen to and say these words, making sure you stress the underlined syllable:

centro	pasteles	piscina
computadora	trabajo	parque
mantequilla	escriben	generalmente

2. When words end in a consonant (except *n* or *s*), place the stress on the **last syllable.** Listen to and say these words, making sure you stress the last syllable:

señor	nariz	escribir
profesor	reloj	arroz
trabajador	comer	español

3. When a word has a written accent, place the stress on the **accented syllable.** One reason for written accents is to indicate exceptions to the first two rules. Listen to and say these words. Be sure to emphasize the accented syllable.

café	número	teléfono
difícil	película	lápiz
fácil	plátano	artístico

Try it out! Listen to the first verse of the song "La Bamba" and say each word with the stress on the correct syllable. Then listen to the recording again and see if you can sing along with the first verse.

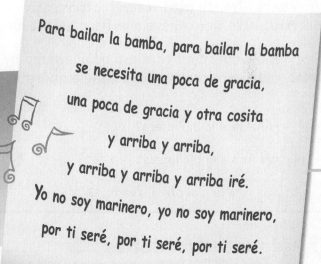

Para bailar la bamba, para bailar la bamba
se necesita una poca de gracia,
una poca de gracia y otra cosita
y arriba y arriba,
y arriba y arriba y arriba iré.
Yo no soy marinero, yo no soy marinero,
por ti seré, por ti seré, por ti seré.

Más práctica

- **Guided** Gram. Practice pp. 125–126
- **Core** Gram. Practice p. 71
- **Communication** Writing p. 76
- *Real.* para hispanohablantes pp. 134–137

realidades.com

- Audio Activities
- Video Activities
- Speak & Record
- Canción de hip hop
- Animated Verbs
- Leveled Workbook
- Web Code: jcd-0403

Gramática

Asking questions

You use interrogative words *(who, what, where,* and so on) to ask questions.

¿Qué?	*What?*	**¿Adónde?**	*(To) Where?*
¿Cómo?	*How?, What?*	**¿De dónde?**	*From where?*
¿Quién?	*Who?*	**¿Cuál?**	*Which?, What?*
¿Con quién?	*With whom?*	**¿Por qué?**	*Why?*
¿Dónde?	*Where?*	**¿Cuándo?**	*When?*
¿Cuántos, -as?	*How many?*		

In Spanish, when you ask a question with an interrogative word you put the verb before the subject.

¿Qué **come Elena** en el restaurante?   *What **does Elena eat** at the restaurant?*

¿Adónde **van Uds.** después de las clases?   *Where **do you go** after classes?*

¿Por qué **va Ignacio** a la playa todos los días?   *Why **does Ignacio go** to the beach every day?*

You have already used several interrogative words. Notice that all interrogative words have a written accent mark.

For simple questions that can be answered by *sí* or *no,* you can indicate with your voice that you're asking a question:

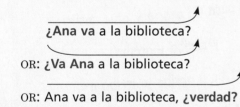

¿Ana va a la biblioteca?

OR: ¿Va Ana a la biblioteca?

OR: Ana va a la biblioteca, ¿verdad?

GramActiva VIDEO

Use the **GramActiva** video to help you learn more about asking questions.

¿Por qué?

15 Preguntas revueltas

Pensar • Escribir

Your new pen pal from Bolivia has sent you an e-mail, but all his questions are scrambled. Unscramble them and write them in the correct order. Then answer his questions.

1. ¿ / eres / de dónde / tú / ?
2. ¿ / Uds. / adónde / van / los fines de semana / ?
3. ¿ / al centro comercial / cuándo / van / Uds. / ?
4. ¿ / clases / tienes / cuántas / ?
5. ¿ / tú / qué / después de las clases / haces / ?
6. ¿ / vas / tú / con quién / al centro comercial / ?

16 ¿Cómo es el cine?

Leer • Pensar • Escribir

Lee este anuncio del cine.

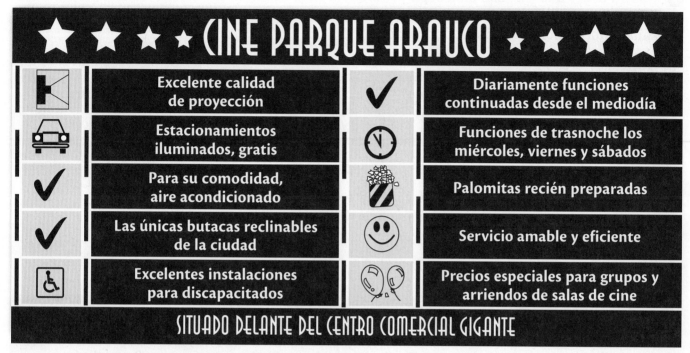

★ ★ ★ ★ **CINE PARQUE ARAUCO** ★ ★ ★ ★

Excelente calidad de proyección	✓ **Diariamente funciones continuadas desde el mediodía**
🚗 **Estacionamientos iluminados, gratis**	🕐 **Funciones de trasnoche los miércoles, viernes y sábados**
✓ **Para su comodidad, aire acondicionado**	🍿 **Palomitas recién preparadas**
✓ **Las únicas butacas reclinables de la ciudad**	☺ **Servicio amable y eficiente**
♿ **Excelentes instalaciones para discapacitados**	🎈 **Precios especiales para grupos y arriendos de salas de cine**

SITUADO DELANTE DEL CENTRO COMERCIAL GIGANTE

Según el anuncio del Cine Parque Arauco, escribe la palabra apropiada para cada pregunta.

1. ¿_____ es la calidad de la proyección en el cine? *Excelente.*

2. ¿_____ comen muchas personas allí? *Palomitas.*

3. ¿_____ es el nombre del cine? *Cine Parque Arauco.*

4. ¿_____ van las personas a ver películas muy tarde *(late)* por la noche? *Los miércoles, viernes y sábados.*

5. ¿_____ está el cine? *Delante del Centro Comercial Gigante.*

Cuándo	Por qué
Cómo	Cuál
Dónde	Qué

Fondo cultural

El mundo hispano

Movies are a popular form of entertainment for teenagers in Spanish-speaking countries. Spain, Mexico, Argentina, Colombia, and Venezuela have important film industries, but movies from the United States are also popular. Spanish-speaking teens tend to go to the movies in groups.

- How do your movie-going habits compare with those of teens in Spanish-speaking countries?

- Are movies from Spanish-speaking countries popular in your community? Why or why not?

Los actores latinoamericanos Mía Maestro, Rodrigo de la Serna y Gael García Bernal

17 Los fines de semana

Escribir • Hablar

1 Copy a chart like this one on a separate sheet of paper and fill in information about one activity you do on the weekends. Then find out the same information from three classmates.

Modelo

A —*¿Adónde vas los fines de semana?*
B —*Voy al centro comercial.*
A —*¿Con quién vas?*
B —*Voy con Selena.*
o:—*Voy solo(a).*

Nombre	¿Adónde vas?	¿Con quién?
yo	a mi lección de guitarra	solo(a)
Laura	al centro comercial	con Selena

2 Tell the class or a classmate where you and each of the three people you interviewed are going and with whom.

Modelo

Yo voy a mi lección de guitarra solo(a).
Laura va al centro comercial con Selena.

18 Y tú, ¿qué preguntas?

Escribir • Hablar

Habla con otro(a) estudiante sobre *(about)* la foto.

1 Mira la foto y escribe cuatro preguntas sobre el parque, las personas y las actividades.

2 Haz tus preguntas *(ask your questions)* a otro(a) estudiante.

Más práctica

- **Guided** Gram. Practice pp. 127–129
- **Core** Gram. Practice pp. 72–73
- **Communication** Writing p. 77
- *Real.* **para hispanohablantes** pp. 138–141

realidades.com Ⓥ

- Audio Activities
- Video Activities
- Speak & Record
- Tutorial
- Leveled Workbook
- Web Code: jcd-0404

Fondo cultural

Puerto Rico

Old San Juan is a popular and lively part of Puerto Rico's capital, San Juan. Puerto Rican authorities are making great efforts to preserve colonial houses and other buildings and restore them to their original beauty.

- Are there historic areas near your community that have been or that are being restored? How do they compare with those in Old San Juan?

Parque de las Palomas, San Juan, Puerto Rico

19 ¡Vamos al Viejo San Juan!

Leer • Escribir

Puerto Rico has been a commonwealth of the United States since 1952. It is an island with a fascinating past. Look at the photos and read about a historic section of Puerto Rico's capital. Then answer the questions below.

Conexiones La historia

El Viejo[1] San Juan es una zona histórica, pintoresca, colonial y muy popular en la capital de Puerto Rico. Los jóvenes[2] pasan el tiempo con sus amigos en los parques, cafés y plazas. Allí cantan, bailan y comen en los restaurantes típicos.

El Morro Construido en el siglo[5] XVI para combatir los ataques de los piratas ingleses y franceses[6]

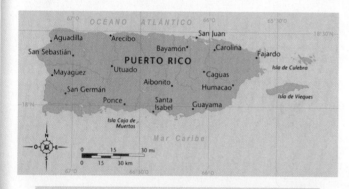

Datos importantes:

• Cristóbal Colón llega[3] aquí durante su segunda visita a las Américas en 1493

• El Viejo San Juan llega a ser[4] la capital de Puerto Rico en 1521

La Catedral de San Juan tiene muchas obras de arte[7]. Allí descansan[8] los restos[9] de Juan Ponce de Léon, famoso explorador de la Florida.

[1]Old [2]young people [3]arrives [4]becomes [5]century [6]French [7]works of art [8]lie [9]remains

1. For how many years has San Juan been the capital of Puerto Rico?
2. On which of his voyages did Christopher Columbus land on Puerto Rico?
3. Why did the Spaniards build El Morro?
4. What are two things you'll see when you visit the cathedral?

Lectura

Al centro comercial

Lee las actividades diferentes que puedes hacer en la semana del 11 al 17 de enero durante tu tiempo libre.

¡Vamos a la Plaza del Sol!

Aquí en la Plaza del Sol, ¡siempre hay algo que hacer!

Actividades para el 11 al 17 de enero

11 lunes
7.00 P.M.   Música andina

12 martes
7.00 P.M.   Clase de yoga

13 miércoles
8.00 P.M.   Noche de jazz

14 jueves
7.00 P.M.   Clase de repostería[1]

15 viernes
8.00 P.M.   Música andina

16 sábado
1.30 P.M.   Exposición de fotografía
2.00 P.M.   Show infantil
4.00 P.M.   Exhibición de yoga
8.00 P.M.   Sábado flamenco

17 domingo
1.30 P.M.   Exposición de fotografía
2.00 P.M.   Show infantil
4.00 P.M.   Exhibición de yoga
8.00 P.M.   Noche de tango

Música andina

El grupo Sol Andino toca música andina fusionada con bossa nova y jazz el lunes a las 8.00 P.M. Abierto[2] al público.

Clase de yoga

La práctica de yoga es todos los martes desde las 7.00 hasta las 9.00 P.M. La instructora Lucía Gómez Paloma enseña los secretos de esta disciplina. Inscríbase[3] al teléfono 224-24-16. Vacantes limitadas.

[1]pastry making   [2]Open   [3]Register

Sábado flamenco

El Sábado flamenco es el programa más popular de la semana. María del Carmen Ramachi baila acompañada por el guitarrista Ernesto Hermoza el sábado a las 8.00 P.M. Es una noche emocionante y sensacional de música y danza. Abierto al público.

Clase de repostería

Inscríbase gratis[4] en la clase de repostería programada para el jueves a las 7.00 P.M. Preparamos unos pasteles deliciosos gracias a la Repostería Ideal y al maestro Rudolfo Torres. Inscríbase al teléfono 224-24-16. Vacantes limitadas.

[4] free

¿Comprendes?

1. You will be in town from January 9 through February 2. Will you be able to take part in these activities? In which ones?

2. Which events require you to sign up in advance? Which do not?

3. You have to baby-sit your six-year-old sister. Which day(s) would be best to go with her?

4. Según los intereses de estos chicos, ¿a qué eventos van ellos?

   Raquel: Me gusta mucho hacer ejercicio.

   Roberto: Me encantan los pasteles.

   Teresa: Estudio baile. Tomo lecciones todos los jueves.

   Alejandro: Me gusta escuchar música; toda clase de música.

5. ¿Qué actividad es más interesante para ti?

Más práctica

- **Guided** Reading Support pp. 130–131
- **Communication** Writing pp. 77–78, Test Prep pp. 263–264
- *Real.* **para hispanohablantes** pp. 142–143

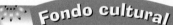
realidades.com

- Internet Activity
- Leveled Workbook
- Web Code: jcd-0405

Fondo cultural

Bolivia • Chile Ecuador • Perú

Andean music has become popular worldwide. This haunting style of music originated in the Andes mountains of Peru, Ecuador, Bolivia, and Chile. Performers sometimes wear typical Andean attire. Instruments commonly used in Andean music include the *quena* flute, *siku* panpipes, and a small guitar called a *charango*.

- The Andean sound is created using a particular set of instruments. What instruments define the music you enjoy?

La cultura en vivo

Rimas infantiles

Can you remember the chants and songs you learned as a child? Or do you remember the rhymes you or your friends recited while jumping rope?

Here are some chants and songs that children in the Spanish-speaking world use when they play. The first one is a Spanish-language equivalent to "Eenie, meenie, minie, moe . . ." It is a nonsense rhyme used to select the person who will be "It" in various games.

Niños saltando a la cuerda

Tin Marín de dopingüé
cucaramanga titirifuera
yo no fui,
fue Teté.
pégale, pégale,
que ella fue.

Here's a chant for jumping rope:

Niños jugando en San Sebastián, España

Salta, salta la perdiz	**The partridge jumps and jumps**
por los campos de maíz.	**Through the cornfields.**
¡Ten cuidado, por favor,	**Be careful, please!**
porque viene el cazador!	**Here comes the hunter!**
	(The jump rope then turns faster.)

Try it out! Here's a traditional game that combines Spanish, math, and hopping over a board. Place a long, narrow board on the floor. Take turns hopping with both feet from one side of the board to the other. Go forward as you hop. When you get to the end of the board, jump and turn in the air, facing the direction you came from. Continue hopping from side to side back to the other end. Be very careful! Try this in an area where you won't hurt yourself. As you are hopping, sing this song:

Brinca la tablita	**Jump over the board**
que yo la brinqué.	**That I already jumped.**
Bríncala tú ahora	**Now you jump**
que yo me cansé.	**Since I'm tired.**
Dos y dos son cuatro,	**Two and two are four,**
cuatro y dos son seis.	**Four and two are six.**
Seis y dos son ocho,	**Six and two are eight,**
y ocho dieciséis,	**And eight are sixteen,**
y ocho veinticuatro,	**And eight are twenty-four,**
y ocho treinta y dos.	**And eight are thirty two.**
Y diez que le sumo	**And ten that I add**
son cuarenta y dos.	**Equals forty-two.**

Think about it! What rhymes and songs do you know? What purpose do they serve in play?

Presentación oral
Un estudiante nuevo

Task
This is a new student's first day at school. You and a partner will play the roles of a new student and a student who has been at the school for a while. Find out information about the new student.

① Prepare You will need to prepare for both roles.

Experienced student: Make a list of at least four questions. Find out where the new student is from, activities he or she likes to do and on what days of the week, and where he or she goes and with whom. Plan to greet the new student and introduce yourself.

New student: Look at the questions the experienced student will ask you and jot down answers.

② Practice Work in groups of four, with two experienced students and two new students. Practice different questions and responses. Be sure you are comfortable in both roles. Go through your presentation several times. You can use your notes in practice, but not during the role play. Try to:

- obtain or provide information
- keep the conversation going
- speak clearly

③ Present Your teacher will tell you which role to play. The experienced student begins the conversation by greeting the new student. Listen to your partner's questions or responses and keep the conversation going.

④ Evaluation Your teacher may give you a rubric for how the presentation will be graded. You probably will be graded on:

- completion of task
- ability to keep the conversation going
- how well you were understood

Strategy
Using models
It helps to go back and review models that prepare you for a task like this role play. Reread *A primera vista* (pp. 172–175). Pay attention to the different questions and answers that will help you with this task.

realidades.com ✓
- Speak & Record

Estados Unidos

Histórico

The oldest permanent European settlement in the United States, St. Augustine, Florida, was established by Spain in 1565—55 years before the Pilgrims landed at Plymouth Rock. For more than two centuries after that, the Spanish controlled a large territory in North America that included what is now Mexico, parts of the southern United States, the states of Texas, New Mexico, Arizona, California, Nevada, and parts of Colorado and Utah.

Constructed as a mission in 1718, the Alamo (in San Antonio, Texas) today is best known as a key battleground in the secession of Texas from Mexico in 1836. The defeat of the Texians at the Alamo became a rallying cry for Texas independence, and Texas gained its freedom from Mexico two months later. ▶

¿Sabes que . . . ?

The language of the Nahua peoples of central Mexico, which included the Aztecs, is related to the languages of the Shoshone, Comanche, and Hopi tribes in the United States. When Spaniards pushed north from the newly conquered central Mexico, they often followed ancient Native American trade routes and used Nahua people as guides.

Canadá

Estados Unidos

OCÉANO PACÍFICO

México

Alaska Canadá

OCÉANO PACÍFICO

Hawaii

OCÉANO ATLÁNTICO

Golfo de México

Para pensar

You can find many Spanish names of cities, counties, and states in the United States. Work with a partner and write a list of at least ten places with Spanish names and then try to guess what they mean in English.

realidades.com

• Online Atlas
• Web Code: jce-0002

The French Quarter in New Orleans was named after the French who first settled here. In spite of its name, most of the buildings date to when Spain ruled Louisiana (1763–1803). Fires ravaged the area in 1788 and 1794, so when the rebuilding was done, the architectural style was Spanish. This can be seen in the landscaped patios and iron grillwork on balconies. Despite the destruction caused by Hurricane Katrina, the French Quarter remains.

A network of Spanish Catholic missions once extended throughout the Americas. Many cities in the southwestern United States, including San Francisco, San Diego, and Santa Fe, were originally built around Catholic missions, which in turn were often located at Native American villages or religious sites. The Mission San Xavier del Bac, in Arizona, combines the name of a Catholic saint (San Xavier) with the name of the Papago village where it was built (Bac, which means "where the water emerges"). Constructed in the early 1700s, the mission is still used by the Papago people and is considered one of the world's architectural treasures. ▼

Spain built the Castillo de San Marcos to protect both St. Augustine (Florida) and the sea routes for ships returning to Spain from enemy attacks. This fort was started in 1672 and took 23 years to build. When Spain sold Florida to the United States in 1821, the fort was renamed Fort Marion. The Castillo has been a National Monument since 1924.

Repaso del capítulo

Vocabulario y gramática

jcd-0489

to talk about leisure activities

ir de compras	to go shopping
ver una película	to see a movie
la lección de piano	piano lesson (class)
Me quedo en casa.	I stay at home.

to talk about places

la biblioteca	library
el café	café
el campo	countryside
la casa	home, house
en casa	at home
el centro comercial	mall
el cine	movie theater
el gimnasio	gym
la iglesia	church
la mezquita	mosque
las montañas	mountains
el parque	park
la piscina	swimming pool
la playa	beach
el restaurante	restaurant
la sinagoga	synagogue
el templo	temple, Protestant church
el trabajo	work, job

to tell where you go

a	to (prep.)
a la, al (a + el)	to the
¿Adónde?	(To) Where?
a casa	(to) home

to tell with whom you go

¿Con quién?	With whom?
con mis / tus amigos	with my / your friends
solo, -a	alone

to talk about when things are done

¿Cuándo?	When?
después	afterwards
después (de)	after
los fines de semana	on weekends
los lunes, los martes . . .	on Mondays, on Tuesdays . . .
tiempo libre	free time

to talk about where someone is from

¿De dónde eres?	Where are you from?
de	from, of

to indicate how often

generalmente	generally

other useful words and expressions

¡No me digas!	You don't say!
para + infinitive	in order to + infinitive

ir *to go*

voy	vamos
vas	vais
va	van

For *Vocabulario adicional*, see pp. 472–473.

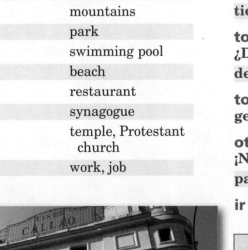

Más práctica

- **Core** Puzzle p. 74, Organizer p. 75
- **Communication** Practice Test pp. 266–268, Integrated Performance Assessment p. 265

realidades.com

- Tutorial
- Flashcards
- Puzzles
- Self-test
- Web Code: jcd-0406

Preparación para el examen

On the exam you will be asked to . . .	Here are practice tasks similar to those you will find on the exam . . .	If you need review . . .

Interpretive

jcd-0489

1 Escuchar Listen and understand as people ask questions about weekend events

Two friends are trying to make plans for the weekend. Based on their dialogue, what do they finally agree on? a) Who is going? b) Where are they going? c) When are they going?

pp. 172–175 *Vocabulario en contexto*
p. 186 Actividad 17

Interpersonal

2 Hablar Talk about places to go and things to do on the weekend

Your parents want to know what you're doing this weekend. Mention at least three places you plan to go or things you plan to do. For example, you might say *Voy de compras con mis amigos.*

pp. 172–175 *Vocabulario en contexto*
p. 177 Actividad 6
p. 178 Actividad 8
p. 181 Actividad 13
p. 182 Actividad 14
p. 186 Actividad 17

Interpretive

3 Leer Read about what a person does on particular days of the week

Someone has left his or her planner at your house. Read the schedule for two days to try to figure out what type of person owns it. Indicate whether you agree or disagree with the statements about the person.

MARTES: 6:00 Desayuno 4:00 Lección de piano
5:00 Trabajo 8:30 Clase aeróbica

JUEVES: 3:30 Gimnasio 4:30 Piscina
6:00 Trabajo 8:00 Biblioteca

¿Estás de acuerdo o no? a) Es muy perezoso(a); b) Es atlético(a); c) Le gusta ir de compras.

pp. 172–175 *Vocabulario en contexto*
p. 176 Actividad 4
p. 180 Actividad 11
pp. 188–189 *Lectura*

Presentational

4 Escribir Write a short note to a friend to let him or her know where you are going after school

Your friend is taking a make-up test after school, so you need to write her a short note to tell her what you are doing after school today. In the note, tell her where you are going and then at what time you are going home.

p. 176 Actividad 4
p. 179 Actividad 10
p. 181 Actividad 13
p. 182 Actividad 14
p. 186 Actividad 18

Cultures • Comparisons

5 Pensar Demonstrate an understanding of rhymes, songs, and games from Spanish-speaking cultures

Think about your favorite childhood game. How does it compare to the children's games you learned about in this chapter? Describe a traditional game from a Spanish-speaking country.

p. 190 *La cultura en vivo*

Paralympic Games Starting with the first Paralympic Games in Rome in 1960, the International Paralympics Committee has organized summer and winter games that follow the regular Olympic Games and are hosted by the same city. Athletes with all types of disabilities compete in the Paralympics. More than 160 nations participate in this nonprofit organization, with over 6,000 participants worldwide.

• How do you think athletes with disabilities benefit from competing in the Paralympics or in similar local events?

¿Quieres ir conmigo?

Chapter Objectives

- Talk about activities outside of school
- Extend, accept, and decline invitations
- Tell when an event happens
- Understand cultural perspectives on after-school activities

Video Highlights

Videocultura: *Los pasatiempos*

A primera vista: *¡A jugar!*

GramActiva Videos: *ir + a + infinitive;* the verb *jugar*

Country Connection

As you learn about after-school activities, you will make connections to these countries and places:

Texas
España
Nueva York
Florida
México
Chile

Más práctica

- *Real.* para hispanohablantes pp. 150–151

realidades.com ✔

- Fondo cultural Activity
- Video Activities
- Online Atlas
- Web Code: jce-0002

juegos paralímpicos
anta, Georgia

Vocabulario en contexto

jcd-0497

Read, listen to, and understand information about
- activities outside of school

Club Deportivo León

Parque de la Independencia

¿Te gustan los deportes? ¡**Puedes** practicar con uno de nuestros expertos! ¿**Juegas** bien o juegas mal? ¡No importa! Hay un deporte para ti.

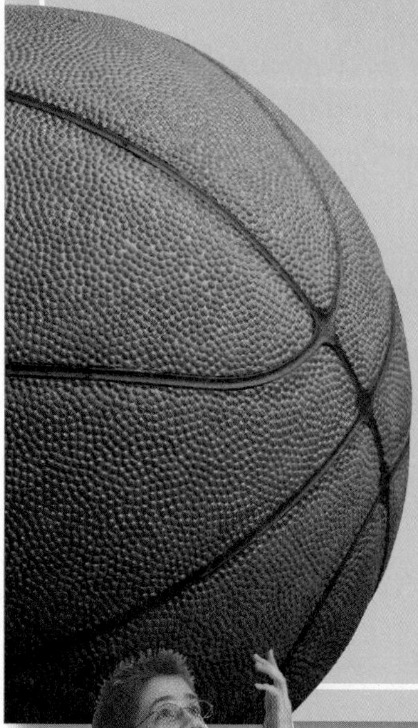

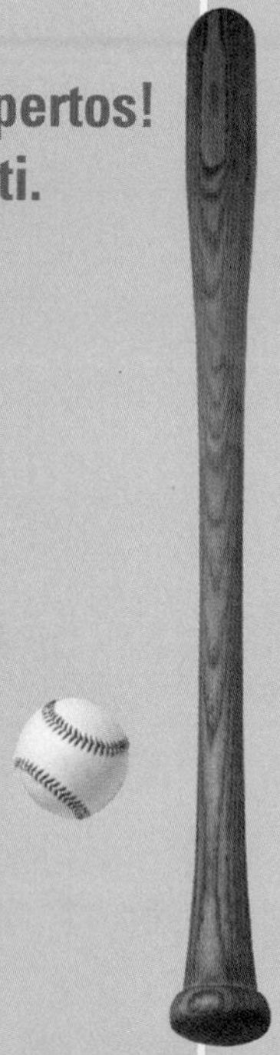

8.00	el fútbol
8.00	el vóleibol
10.00	el golf
10.00	el tenis
13.00	el béisbol
13.00	el básquetbol
16.00	el fútbol americano

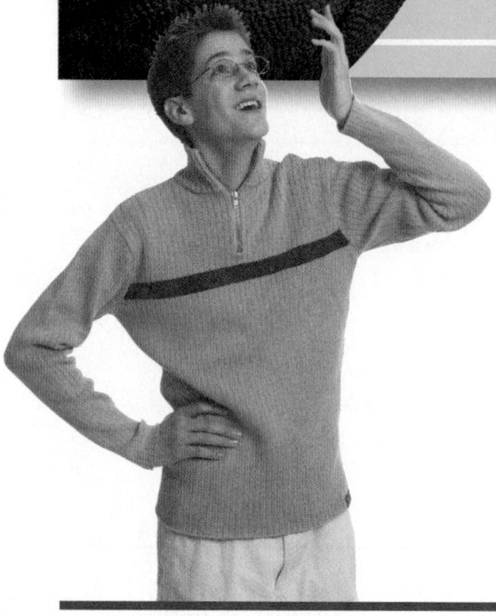

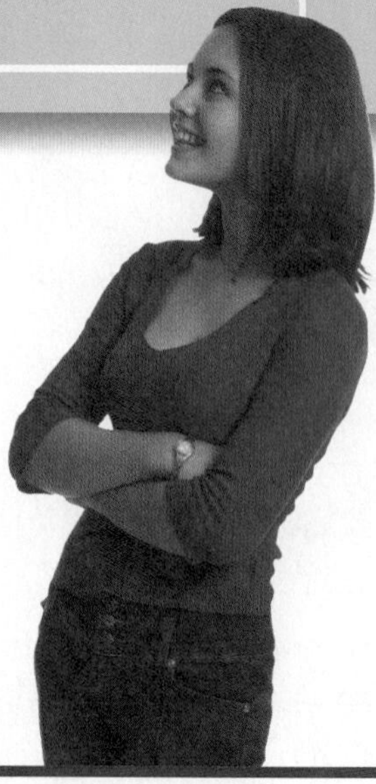

—¿Qué **quieres** hacer **a las ocho de la mañana, jugar al** fútbol o al vóleibol?

—A ver . . . No **quiero** jugar al fútbol. **Juego** muy **mal.** Prefiero jugar al vóleibol. Necesito practicar más. ¿Y qué **te gustaría** hacer a las cuatro **esta tarde?**

—**Me gustaría** jugar al fútbol americano.

el concierto   **la fiesta**   **el baile**   **el partido**

—¡Hola! ¡Soy Rosa! ¿Quieres hacer algo **conmigo este fin de semana?** Hay un concierto en el parque.

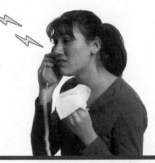

—**Lo siento,** pero no **puedo.** Estoy **demasiado ocupado** y tengo mucha tarea.

—No puedo porque **tengo que** trabajar. Trabajo **esta noche** a las siete y mañana trabajo **a la una de la tarde. Voy a estar** un poco **cansada.** ¡Ay! ¡Qué pena!

—¡Qué **triste!** No, no puedo ir **contigo.** Estoy **un poco enferma.**

ir de cámping   **ir de pesca**

—¡Qué buena idea! Pero no me gustan los conciertos. Prefiero ir de cámping. Siempre estoy muy **contenta** cuando voy de cámping. . . . **¿A qué hora?** ¿Mañana a las cinco de la tarde? **Entonces,** nos vemos.

1 ¡Deportemanía! 🔊

jcd-0497

Escuchar
Marcela is a sports fanatic! As she lists the days on which she will play the various sports, touch the picture of each sport.

2 ¿Cómo estás? 🔊

jcd-0497

Escuchar
You will hear how five people are feeling. Act out the adjectives that you hear.

Más práctica

- **Guided** Vocab. Flash Cards pp. 133–138
- **Core** Vocab. Practice pp. 76–77
- **Communication** Writing p. 84
- *Real.* **para hispanohablantes** p. 152

realidades.com ✔

- Audio Activities
- Leveled Workbook
- Flashcards
- Web Code: jcd-0411

¡A jugar!

Ignacio, Javier, Ana y Elena
están en el Parque del Retiro
en Madrid. ¿Qué van a jugar
y hacer? ¿De qué hablan?
Lee la historia.

Strategy

Looking to find key questions
Before you read the story, skim to
find where the characters are asking
questions. The answers may point to
important information in the story.

• Look at the questions. Which
characters are offering invitations?
What do you think they will do?

España

Javier

Ana

Elena

Ignacio

1 *Hoy es sábado y hace buen
tiempo. Ignacio, Javier, Ana
y Elena están en el parque
para jugar al fútbol.*

5 **Ignacio:** Oye, hay una
fiesta esta noche. Ana, tú y
Elena vais, ¿verdad?

Ana: ¡Claro!

Ignacio : Javier, ¿quieres ir
con nosotros a la fiesta?

Elena: ¡Qué buena idea!

6 **Javier:** ¿A qué hora es la
fiesta?

Ana: A las nueve **de la
noche.** En la escuela.

7 **Javier:** ¿Tengo que bailar?

Ana: Pues, sí. Puedes bailar
conmigo y con Elena.

Javier: No **sé** bailar muy
bien.

Ana: ¡Vamos, Javier!

Javier: Bien, voy.

2 Ignacio: ¡Oye, Javier! ¡Sabes jugar muy bien al fútbol!

Javier: Y tú también . . . Pero necesito practicar más. Ana, ¿quieres jugar?

Ana: ¡Por supuesto! Vamos a jugar.

3 Elena: Estoy demasiado cansada y tengo sed. ¿Por qué no tomamos un refresco?

Ignacio: ¡Genial! Yo también estoy un poco cansado.

4 Ana: ¿Juegas al vóleibol esta tarde?

Elena: Sí, a las seis.

8 Javier: Hasta las nueve, entonces.

Ignacio: ¡Genial! Hasta más tarde.

3 ¿Comprendes?

Escribir • Hablar

¿Quién habla: Ana, Elena, Ignacio o Javier?

1. No sé bailar bien.

2. Necesito practicar más.

3. Necesito beber algo después de jugar al fútbol.

4. Juego al vóleibol a las seis.

5. Voy a la fiesta a las nueve.

6. Estoy cansado.

Más práctica

- **Guided** Vocab. Check pp. 139–142
- **Core** Vocab. Practice pp. 78–79
- **Communication** Video pp. 79–80
- *Real.* para hispanohablantes p. 153

realidades.com ✔

- Audio Activities
- Video Activities
- Leveled Workbook
- Flashcards
- Web Code: jcd-0412

Vocabulario en uso

 Me gustaría ir . . .

Hablar

Say whether or not you would like to do these things this weekend.

> **Modelo**
>
> *Me gustaría ir a <u>una fiesta</u> este fin de semana.*
> o: *No me gustaría ir a <u>una fiesta</u> este fin de semana.*

1.

2.

3.

4.

5.

5 No sé jugar . . .

Escribir • Hablar

Indica si sabes o no sabes jugar estos deportes.

> **Modelo**
> *Sé jugar al <u>béisbol</u> muy bien.*
> o: *No sé jugar al <u>béisbol</u>.*

1.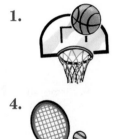

2.

3.

4.

5.

6.

6 ¿Qué deportes practicas?

Hablar

Using the information from Actividad 5, ask and tell about which sports you know, or don't know, how to play.

> **Modelo**
> A —*¿Sabes jugar al béisbol?*
> B —*¡Por supuesto! Sé jugar al béisbol muy bien.*
> o: —*No, no sé jugar al béisbol.*

7 ¿Cómo estás?

Leer · Escribir

You've asked your friends how they are. Now read each friend's reply and write the correct form of the missing word from the list.

cansado, -a	contento, -a
enfermo, -a	mal
ocupado, -a	triste

Tú: ¿Cómo estás?

Felipe: Muy __1.__ . Voy a un concierto esta noche con mis amigos.

Miguel: ¡ __2.__ ! Mi clase de ciencias es muy aburrida y no me gusta nada el profesor.

Marta: Estoy __3.__ . Me duele la cabeza. Hoy no puedo jugar al tenis ni patinar.

Carlos: Estoy __4.__ . Todos mis amigos van a la playa el sábado pero tengo que trabajar.

Gabriela: Un poco __5.__ . Todas las noches trabajo en el centro comercial.

Dolores: Demasiado __6.__ . Juego al básquetbol después de las clases, tomo lecciones de piano y practico cada día y tengo un trabajo también.

8 Lo siento

Hablar

Ask your partner if he or she wants to do these activities with you. Your partner can't go, and will offer excuses to explain why.

> **Modelo**
>
> A —¡Oye! ¿Quieres *patinar* conmigo esta tarde?
> B —*Lo siento. Hoy no puedo. Estoy demasiado enfermo(a).*

Estudiante A

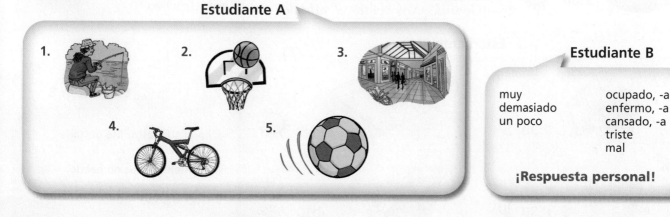

1. 2. 3.

4. 5.

Estudiante B

muy	ocupado, -a
demasiado	enfermo, -a
un poco	cansado, -a
	triste
	mal

¡Respuesta personal!

jcd-0498

9 Escucha y escribe 🔊

Escuchar · Escribir

You will hear three invitations to events and the responses given. On a sheet of paper, write the numbers 1–3. As you listen, write down what each invitation is for and whether the person accepted it (write *sí)* or turned it down (write *no).*

10 ¿A qué hora?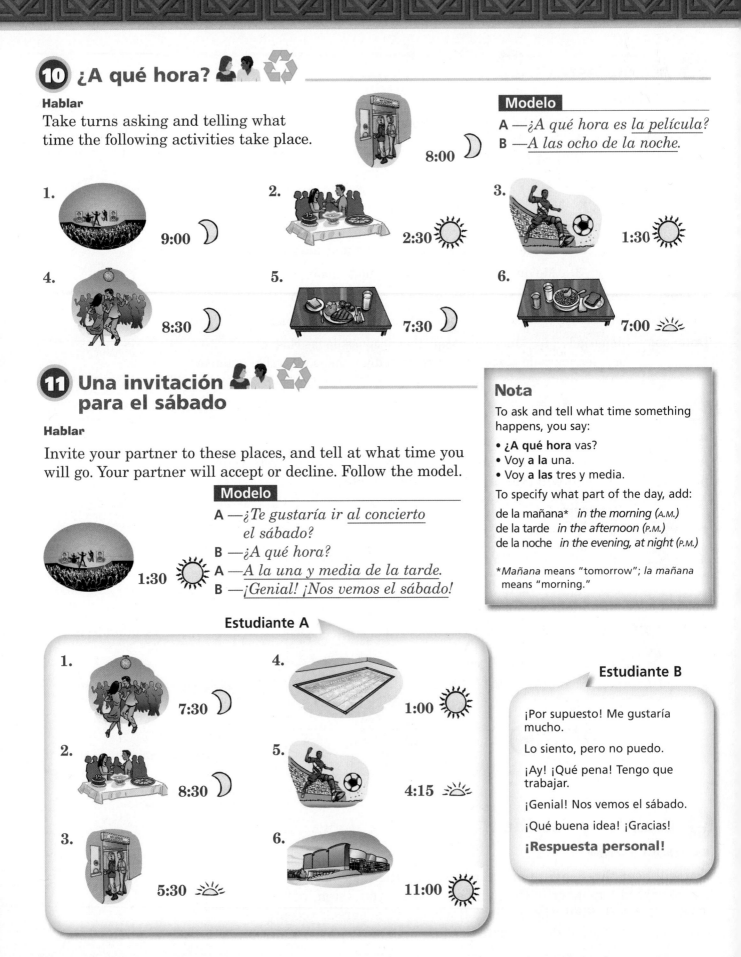

Hablar

Take turns asking and telling what time the following activities take place.

8:00

Modelo
A —¿A qué hora es *la película*?
B —*A las ocho de la noche.*

1. 9:00

2. 2:30

3. 1:30

4. 8:30

5. 7:30

6. 7:00

11 Una invitación para el sábado

Hablar

Invite your partner to these places, and tell at what time you will go. Your partner will accept or decline. Follow the model.

Modelo
A —¿Te gustaría ir *al concierto* el sábado?
B —¿A qué hora?
A —*A la una y media de la tarde.*
B —*¡Genial! ¡Nos vemos el sábado!*

1:30

Nota

To ask and tell what time something happens, you say:

- **¿A qué hora** vas?
- Voy **a la** una.
- Voy **a las** tres y media.

To specify what part of the day, add:

de la mañana* *in the morning* (A.M.)
de la tarde *in the afternoon* (P.M.)
de la noche *in the evening, at night* (P.M.)

*Mañana means "tomorrow"; la mañana means "morning."

Estudiante A

1. 7:30

4. 1:00

2. 8:30

5. 4:15

3. 5:30

6. 11:00

Estudiante B

¡Por supuesto! Me gustaría mucho.

Lo siento, pero no puedo.

¡Ay! ¡Qué pena! Tengo que trabajar.

¡Genial! Nos vemos el sábado.

¡Qué buena idea! ¡Gracias!

¡Respuesta personal!

Exploración del lenguaje

Spanish words borrowed from English

Languages often borrow words from one another. For example, "rodeo" and "patio" are Spanish words that have found their way into English. There are also many examples of English words that have entered Spanish. By recognizing these familiar words, you can increase your vocabulary in Spanish.

Try it out! Read the sentences and identify the "borrowed words." Don't forget to pronounce the words correctly in Spanish.

Quiero hacer videos.
¿Quieres jugar al básquetbol conmigo?
Practico el rugby y el ráquetbol.
Juego al fútbol en el cámping.
¡Me encantan los sándwiches!

Radio Taxi

447 52 83
447 23 23
24 horas a su servicio

12 Y tú, ¿qué dices?

Escribir · Hablar

1. ¿A qué hora te gusta ir al cine?
2. ¿Estás más contento(a) cuando practicas un deporte o cuando ves la televisión?
3. ¿Qué deportes te gustan más?
4. ¿Este fin de semana tienes que trabajar o puedes pasar tiempo con amigos?

Fondo cultural
México

La Noche de los Rábanos is just one of the many kinds of *fiestas* in the Spanish-speaking world. On the evening of December 23, people set up booths around the *zócalo* (town square) of Oaxaca, Mexico, to display and sell radishes *(los rábanos)* sculpted into a fantastic array of shapes. *Oaxaqueños* and visitors alike crowd the square to view the amazing creations.

• Do you know communities or regions in the United States that are known for particular crafts or products?

Rábanos esculpidos *(sculpted)*, Oaxaca, México

Gramática

Ir + a + infinitive

Just as you use "going" + an infinitive in English to say what you are going to do, in Spanish you use a form of the verb **ir + a + an infinitive** to express the same thing:

Voy a jugar al tenis hoy.
I'm going to play tennis today.

¿Tú **vas a jugar** al golf esta tarde?
Are you going to play golf this afternoon?

Mis amigas **van a ir de cámping** mañana.
My friends are going camping tomorrow.

Javier: ¿**Van a jugar** conmigo, o no?
Ana: Sí, **vamos a jugar** contigo.

GramActiva VIDEO

Want more help with *ir + a* + infinitive? Watch the **GramActiva** video.

Voy a comer.

---

jcd-0498

13 Escucha y escribe 🔊

Escuchar · Escribir

Rosario and Pablo have left messages on your answering machine telling you what they are going to do and inviting you to join them. On a sheet of paper, write their names and, under each one, the numbers 1–3. As you listen to each message, write down information to answer these three questions:

1. ¿Adónde quiere ir?   **2.** ¿Qué va a hacer?   **3.** ¿A qué hora va a ir?

14 Este fin de semana vamos a . . . ♻

Escribir · Hablar

¿Qué va a hacer la familia Ríos este fin de semana?

Modelo

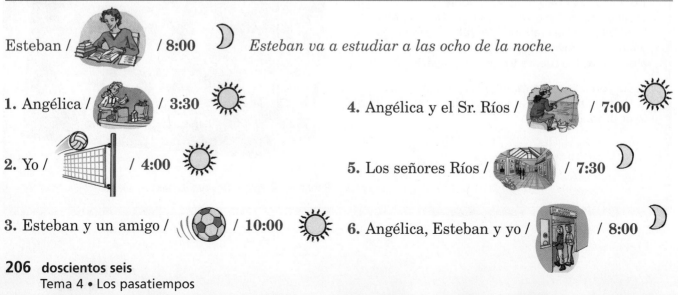

Esteban / [estudiar] / 8:00 🌙 *Esteban va a estudiar a las ocho de la noche.*

1. Angélica / [ ] / 3:30 ☀

2. Yo / [ ] / 4:00 ☀

3. Esteban y un amigo / ⚽ / 10:00 ☀

4. Angélica y el Sr. Ríos / [ ] / 7:00 ☀

5. Los señores Ríos / [ ] / 7:30 🌙

6. Angélica, Esteban y yo / [ ] / 8:00 🌙

15 **¿Qué vas a hacer?**

Escribir • Hablar

1 Make a chart like this one to describe five things you're going to do, when you're going to do them, and with whom. Use the following words to say when you're going to do these things: *esta tarde, esta noche, mañana, el jueves, el fin de semana.*

Modelo		
¿Qué?	¿Cuándo?	¿Con quién?
tocar la guitarra	esta tarde	mis amigos

2 Ask your partner what his or her plans are.

Modelo

A —¿Qué vas a hacer esta tarde?

B —Esta tarde mis amigos y yo vamos a tocar la guitarra.

Mañana voy a tocar la guitarra.

16 **El teléfono celular**

Leer • Escribir • Hablar

Lee el anuncio para el teléfono celular y contesta las preguntas.

1. ¿Por qué es bueno tener un teléfono celular?

2. ¿Te gusta hablar por teléfono celular? ¿Con quién?

3. ¿Crees que es bueno o malo usar un teléfono celular en un restaurante? ¿Por qué?

17 **¿Quieres ir conmigo?**

Hablar

Pretending to use a cell phone, greet a partner and invite him or her to do something with you. Your partner can't go and should tell you why.

Modelo

A —*Hola, Sara. Soy Rosa. ¿Quieres jugar al tenis conmigo esta tarde?*

B —*Lo siento, hoy no puedo. Voy a estudiar para la clase de inglés.*

A —*¡Ay! ¡Qué pena!*

¿Te gustaría . . .

pasar más tiempo con tus amigos?

ir de compras?

ir al cine?

escribir un mensaje?

escuchar música?

jugar un juego?

¡Por supuesto!

¡Con un teléfono celular puedes hacer planes para hacerlo todo!

Más práctica

- **Guided** Gram. Practice pp. 143–144
- **Core** Gram. Practice pp. 80–81
- **Communication** Writing p. 85
- *Real.* **para hispanohablantes** pp. 154–157

realidades.com ✔

- Audio Activities
- Video Activities
- Speak & Record
- Canción de hip hop
- Tutorial
- Leveled Workbook
- Web Code: jcd-0413

Gramática

The verb *jugar*

Use the verb *jugar* to talk about playing a sport or a game. Even though *jugar* uses the same endings as the other *-ar* verbs, it has a different stem in some forms. For those forms, the *-u-* becomes *-ue-*. This kind of verb is called a "stem-changing verb." Here are the present-tense forms:

(yo)	juego	(nosotros) (nosotras)	jugamos
(tú)	juegas	(vosotros) (vosotras)	jugáis
Ud. (él) (ella)	juega	Uds. (ellos) (ellas)	juegan

Nota

Many Spanish speakers always use *jugar a* and the name of the sport or game:

• ¿Juegas **al** vóleibol?

Others do not use the *a:*

• ¿Juegas vóleibol?

GramActiva VIDEO

Use the **GramActiva** video to help you learn more about the verb *jugar*.

 18 ¿A qué juegan?

Escribir

Escribe frases para decir qué deportes practican estas personas.

Albert Pujols

Modelo

Albert Pujols juega al béisbol.

1.

Sergio García

2.

Rebecca Lobo   y   Eduardo Nájera

3.

Carlos Valderrama

4.

Hanley Ramirez   y   Edgardo Alfonzo

5. Y tus amigos y tú, ¿a qué juegan Uds.?

También se dice . . .

el básquetbol = el baloncesto
　　　　　　(*muchos países*)

el fútbol = el balompié (*muchos países*)

el vóleibol = el balonvolea (*España*)

19 Juego

Dibujar · Escribir · Hablar · GramActiva

❶ On each of two index cards, draw a picture that represents a sport or game and write *muy bien, bien,* or *mal* to show how well you play that sport or game. Don't let your classmates see your cards.

❷ Get together with five other students. Put all the cards face down in the center of your group. Choose a card and try to identify who drew it by asking the others how well they play what is pictured. Keep track of what you learn about your classmates.

Modelo
A —*Enrique, ¿juegas bien al tenis?*
B —*No, juego muy mal al tenis.*

❸ Write six sentences about the sports and games the students in your group play.

Modelo
Óscar y Nacho juegan muy bien al fútbol. Teresa y yo jugamos bien al golf.

20 La ciudad deportiva

Leer · Escribir · Hablar

Lee sobre el sueño *(dream)* de Iván Zamorano y contesta las preguntas.

Mi sueño[1]

Quiero una ciudad[2] dedicada al deporte, a la familia y los niños.[3] Quiero servicios de calidad internacional, con profesores de excelencia. En mi sueño, los niños y jóvenes juegan y practican deportes para ser mejores.[4] Este sueño ya es realidad y quiero compartirlo contigo. El lugar[5] para hacer deporte en familia.

Escuelas de Fútbol, Tenis, Hockey

Inicio de inscripción[6]: 23 de marzo, a las 8
Inicio de actividades: 1 de abril, a las 14 horas

Avenida Pedro Hurtado 2650, Las Condes, Santiago, Chile
Teléfono: 212 2711

1. ¿Qué es el sueño de Iván Zamorano?
2. ¿Qué deportes juegan en la Ciudad Deportiva de Iván?
3. ¿Qué día empieza *(begins)* la inscripción para las escuelas? ¿A qué hora?
4. ¿A qué hora empiezan las actividades?
5. ¿Te gustaría ir a la Ciudad Deportiva de Iván Zamorano? ¿Por qué?

Más práctica

- **Guided** Gram. Practice pp. 145–146
- **Core** Gram. Practice p. 82
- **Communication** Writing p. 86, Test Prep p. 269
- *Real.* **para hispanohablantes** pp. 158–161

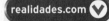 realidades.com

- Audio Activities
- Video Activities
- Speak & Record
- Animated Verbs
- Leveled Workbook
- Web Code: jcd-0414

¹dream
²city
³children
⁴better
⁵place
⁶registration

The letter *d*   jcd-0498

In Spanish, the pronunciation of the letter *d* is determined by its location in a word. When *d* is at the beginning of a word, or when it comes after *l* or *n*, it sounds similar to the *d* in "dog." Listen, then say these words:

diccionario	doce	donde
domingo	desayuno	día
deportes	calendario	bandera

When *d* comes between vowels and after any consonant except *l* or *n*, it sounds similar to the *th* of "the." Listen, then say these words:

cansado	ocupado	puedes
idea	sábado	partido
tarde	ensalada	atrevido

Try it out! Here is a tongue twister to give you practice in pronouncing the *d*, but also to give you something to think about!

**Porque puedo, puedes,
porque puedes, puedo;
Pero si no puedes,
yo tampoco puedo.**

Una voluntaria en un hospital

El español en el mundo del trabajo

There are many opportunities to use Spanish in the healthcare field—in hospitals, emergency rooms, and neighborhood clinics. This young woman volunteers in a California hospital. Since many of the patients come from Spanish-speaking homes, she is able to speak with them and their families in Spanish. *"Para mí, trabajar como voluntaria es una de mis actividades favoritas. Creo que mi trabajo es importante."*

• What opportunities are there in your community to do volunteer work where speaking Spanish is helpful?

21 ¡Vamos de cámping!

Leer • Pensar • Escribir

Tourism is an important industry in Spain. Many tourists prefer to go camping rather than stay in hotels. Read the following brochure about a campground and then answer the questions.

Conexiones | Las matemáticas

Camping Las Palmas

Miramar
Teléfono: 962 41 42 73   Fax: 962 01 55 05

85 kilómetros al sur de Valencia
110 kilómetros al norte de Alicante

• Un camping ideal

• Muchas actividades para todos

• Una buena opción para sus vacaciones

Con bellas palmas que dan[1] mucha sombra,[2] directamente sobre una bella playa. Ideal para toda la familia. Un sitio excelente para pescar.

¹give   ²shade

1. ¿Qué distancia en millas[3] hay entre[4] Valencia y el Camping Las Palmas?

2. ¿Qué distancia hay entre Alicante y el Camping Las Palmas?

Para convertir kilómetros en millas, es necesario dividir el número de kilómetros por 1.6.

³miles   ⁴between

Para decir más . . .

200 = doscientos

22 Y tú, ¿qué dices?

Escribir • Hablar

1. ¿Con quién te gustaría ir a una fiesta? ¿Por qué?

2. ¿Qué prefieres, ir de pesca o ir a un baile?

3. ¿Qué vas a hacer mañana a las ocho de la noche?

4. ¿Qué vas a hacer este fin de semana?

5. ¿Te gustaría ver un partido de fútbol o ir a un concierto?

Lectura

Sergio y Lorena: El futuro del golf

Lee dos artículos de una revista deportiva. Vas a conocer a[1] Sergio García y a Lorena Ochoa Reyes, dos atletas famosos.

Objectives

- Read about and compare the lives of two famous golfers
- Recognize specialized sports vocabulary
- Understand cultural perspectives regarding extracurricular activities
- Write an invitation to an event
- Learn facts about the contemporary United States

Strategy

Cognates
Use the cognates in the following article to help you understand what is being said about the golfers.

Sergio García

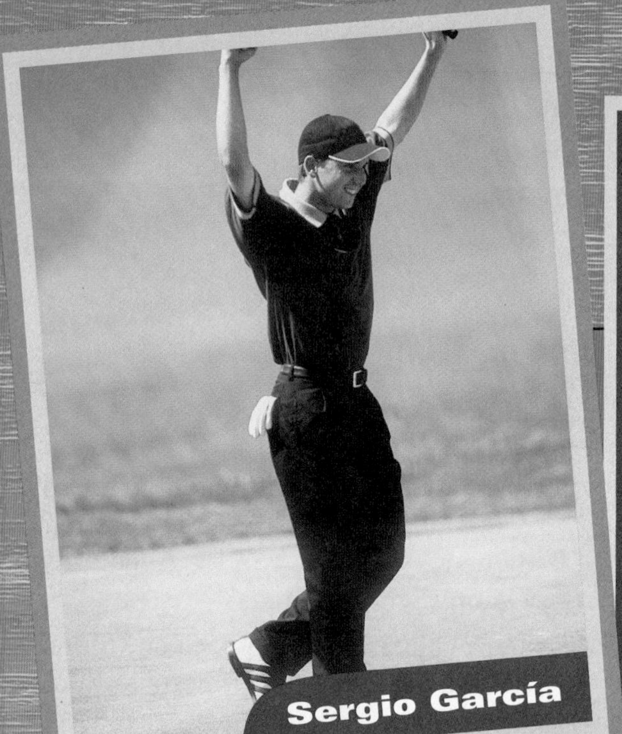

Nombre: Sergio García
Fecha de nacimiento: 9/1/80
Lugar de nacimiento: Borriol, Castellón (España)
Club: Club de Campo del Mediterráneo
Su objetivo: Ser el mejor del mundo
Profesional: Desde abril del 99
Aficiones[2]: Real Madrid, tenis, fútbol, videojuegos

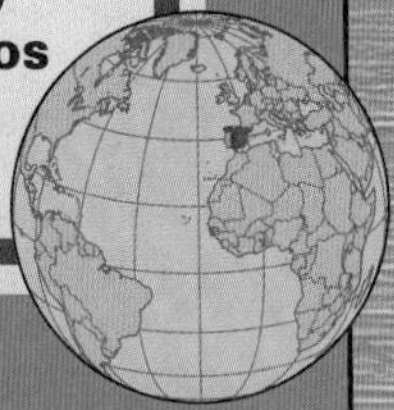

Sergio García es uno de los golfistas más populares en el mundo del golf profesional.

Sergio juega para el Club de Campo del Mediterráneo en Borriol, Castellón, donde su padre Víctor es golfista profesional. Juega al golf desde la edad[3] de tres años y a los 12 años es campeón[4] del Club de Campo. Es el golfista más joven en competir en el campeonato PGA desde Gene Sarazen en 1921 y gana[5] el segundo lugar.[6] Tiene el nombre "El niño." A los 15 años, juega en un torneo del circuito europeo de profesionales. Y a la edad de 17 años gana su primer torneo de profesionales.

Es evidente que este español tiene el talento para realizar su objetivo.

[1]You will meet [2]Interests [3]age [4]champion [5]he wins [6]second place

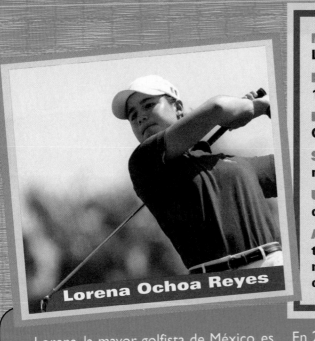

Lorena Ochoa Reyes

Nombre:
Lorena Ochoa Reyes

Fecha de nacimiento:
15/11/81

Lugar de nacimiento:
Guadalajara, México

Su objetivo: Ser la golfista número uno del mundo

Universidad: Universidad de Arizona

Aficiones: Básquetbol, tenis, bicicleta de montaña, correr, nadar, comida italiana

Lorena, la mayor golfista de México, es un ícono nacional. Juega al golf desde los cinco años de edad. A los 21 años, gana su primer torneo de profesionales. Ella dice que es necesario entrenar[9] y practicar golf todos los días. Desde 2004 al presente, Lorena gana muchos torneos importantes.

En 2008 ocupa el primer lugar del ranking mundial de golf femenino.

[9]to train

¿Comprendes?

Copy this Venn diagram on a sheet of paper. Make a list in English of at least eight facts that you learned about Sergio and Lorena. Write the facts on your Venn diagram. Include information about Sergio in the left oval, information about Lorena in the right oval, and any fact that applies to both of them in the overlapping oval.

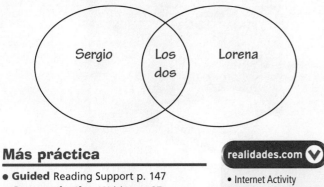

Sergio   Los dos   Lorena

Más práctica

- **Guided** Reading Support p. 147
- **Communication** Writing p. 87, Test Prep p. 270
- *Real.* **para hispanohablantes** pp. 162–163

realidades.com ✔
- Internet Activity
- Leveled Workbook
- Web Code: jcd-0415

Fondo cultural

Estados Unidos

Una jugadora profesional Rebecca Lobo, professional basketball player, won a gold medal in the 1996 Olympics. She became one of the WNBA's original players. Rebecca wrote a book called *The Home Team,* which tells about her life and her mother's struggle against breast cancer. In 2001, she established a college scholarship fund for minority students who plan to enter the healthcare field. Today, Rebecca is an announcer for the WNBA.

- Rebecca Lobo is a popular motivational speaker. What message do you think she gives to her audiences?

Perspectivas del mundo hispano

¿Qué haces en tu tiempo libre?

In many Spanish-speaking countries, extracurricular activities traditionally play a much smaller role in school life than in the United States. Students usually participate in activities such as music and athletics at clubs and institutions outside of school.

Jugando al hockey en Buenos Aires, Argentina

Although some schools have teams, many students who are interested in sports attend clubs such as el Club Deportivo General San Martín. At these clubs teens practice and compete on teams. They also participate in individual sports such as tennis. The competition between clubs is sometimes more intense than the competition between schools.

Students with artistic talents often go to a private institute to take music, dance, or art lessons. They might attend el Instituto de Música Clásica or el Instituto de Danza Julio Bocca.

¿Te gusta jugar al ajedrez?

Many students spend their time outside of classes studying a foreign language. They might learn English at la Cultura Inglesa or French at la Alianza Francesa.

In general, students do not hold jobs. They spend their time studying, being with family and friends, and participating in different activities.

Check it out! Take a survey of your friends to find out what they do after school. Do they work a part-time job? Do they participate in a sport with a school team or in extracurricular activities at school? Do they belong to a club or organization outside of school?

Think about it! How do the practices in your community compare with what you have learned about young people's after-school activities in Spanish-speaking countries?

Trabajando después de las clases

Presentación escrita
Una invitación

Task
A special event is coming up on the calendar and you want to invite a friend to go with you.

1 Prewrite Think about an event that you'd invite a friend to attend, such as a concert, sporting event, or party. Write an invitation that includes:

- the name of the event
- when, where, and at what time the event is taking place
- who is going

2 Draft Use the information from Step 1 to write a first draft of your invitation. Begin your invitation with *¡Hola . . . !* and close with *Tu amigo(a)* and your name.

3 Revise Read your note and check for correct spelling and verb forms. Share your invitation with a partner. Your partner should check the following:

- Did you give all the necessary information?
- Is there anything you should add or change?
- Are there any errors?

4 Publish Write a final copy of your invitation, making any necessary changes. You may want to give it to your friend or include it in your portfolio.

5 Evaluation Your teacher may give you a rubric for how your invitation will be graded. You probably will be graded on:

- how complete the information was
- use of vocabulary expressions
- accuracy of sentence structures

Strategy

Organizing information
Thinking about the correct format and necessary information beforehand will help you create a better invitation.

El mundo hispano

Estados Unidos

Contemporáneo

According to the 2000 census, 32,800,000 people (about 12 percent of the total population of the United States) classified themselves as being of Spanish or Hispanic descent. Out of that number, 30,700,800 indicated that they were of either Mexican, Puerto Rican, or Cuban descent. The remaining 2,099,200 people checked "Other Spanish/Hispanic" on their census questionnaires. This broad category included people who came from or who had ancestral ties to other Spanish-speaking countries in the Caribbean, Central and South America, or Spain.

Born in Costa Rica, Dr. Franklin Chang-Díaz (left) was the first Hispanic astronaut to fly in space. He was selected by NASA in 1980 and is a veteran of seven space flights. In 1990, Californian Dr. Ellen Ochoa (right) became the first Hispanic female astronaut. Since then she has logged more than 978 hours in space. Her dream is to help build a space station, which she considers "critical . . . to human exploration in space." Both Dr. Ochoa and Dr. Chang-Díaz are the recipients of many honors for their technical contributions and their scholarship. ▶

¿Sabes que . . . ?

The influence of Spanish-speaking cultures is evident throughout the United States. Musical artists such as Enrique Iglesias, Shakira, and Marc Anthony sell millions of CDs. Actors such as Salma Hayek, Jennifer López, Cameron Díaz, and Martin Sheen earn great acclaim for their work. And in politics, Spanish-speaking Americans serve in Congress and top-level Cabinet posts.

Para pensar

Work with a partner and interview a classmate, friend, or acquaintance who is Spanish-speaking or who has ties to a Spanish-speaking country. What is the person's name? Where did the family come from, and when? Why did the family move to your community? If this person had one thing to say to you and your classmates about the immigrant experience and cultural differences, what might that be? Write a short account of the interview and present it to your class or to a small group.

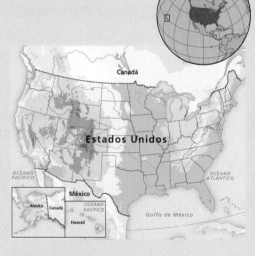

realidades.com
• Online Atlas
• Web Code: jce-0002

The music and poetry of New York City's Puerto Rican community are a creative blend of English and Spanish. *Nuyoricans* of the *Loisaida* (Lower East Side) rub shoulders with people of diverse ethnic backgrounds creating sounds and rhythms unlike any other in the world. The Nuyorican Poets Café has become an institution on the *Loisaida,* where poets, writers, performance artists, musicians, and visual artists of all nationalities can find an outlet for their work.

More than half of Miami's population is of Spanish-speaking descent. Calle Ocho is the heart of Little Havana, the largest Cuban American community in the United States. The Calle Ocho Festival, which takes place at the end of Carnaval Miami, is a great time to sample Cuban food and dance to some of the world's greatest salsa artists.

More Mexicans visit the border town of Laredo, Texas, than any other city in the United States; and more United States citizens visit the Mexican border town of Tijuana than any other foreign city. Most of the visitors come from nearby areas and stay for only a few hours to visit or shop.

Repaso del capítulo

Vocabulario y gramática

jcd-0499

Chapter Review

To prepare for the test, check to see if you . . .

- **know the new vocabulary and grammar**
- **can perform the tasks on p. 219**

to talk about leisure activities

el baile	dance
el concierto	concert
la fiesta	party
ir + a + *infinitive*	to be going to + *verb*
ir de cámping	to go camping
ir de pesca	to go fishing
jugar al básquetbol	to play basketball
jugar al béisbol	to play baseball
jugar al fútbol	to play soccer
jugar al fútbol americano	to play football
jugar al golf	to play golf
jugar al tenis	to play tennis
jugar al vóleibol	to play volleyball
el partido	game, match
(yo) sé	I know (how)
(tú) sabes	you know (how)

to describe how someone feels

cansado, -a	tired
contento, -a	happy
enfermo, -a	sick
mal	bad, badly
ocupado, -a	busy
triste	sad

to tell what time something happens

¿A qué hora?	(At) what time?
a la una	at one (o'clock)
a las ocho	at eight (o'clock)
de la mañana	in the morning
de la noche	in the evening, at night
de la tarde	in the afternoon
esta noche	this evening
esta tarde	this afternoon
este fin de semana	this weekend

to extend, accept, or decline invitations

conmigo	with me
contigo	with you
(yo) puedo	I can
(tú) puedes	you can
¡Ay! ¡Qué pena!	Oh! What a shame!
¡Genial!	Great!
lo siento	I'm sorry
¡Oye!	Hey!
¡Qué buena idea!	What a good / nice idea!
(yo) quiero	I want
(tú) quieres	you want
¿Te gustaría?	Would you like?
Me gustaría	I would like
Tengo que ___.	I have to ___.

other useful words and expressions

demasiado	too
entonces	then
un poco (de)	a little

jugar (a) *to play (games, sports)*

juego	jugamos
juegas	jugáis
juega	juegan

For *Vocabulario adicional,* see pp. 472–473.

Más práctica

● **Core** Puzzle p. 83, Organizer p. 84
● **Communication** Practice Test
   pp. 272–274, Integrated Performance
   Assessment p. 271

realidades.com ✓

• Tutorial
• Flashcards
• Puzzles
• Self-test
• Web Code: jcd-0416

Preparación para el examen

On the exam you will be asked to . . .	Here are practice tasks similar to those you will find on the exam . . .	If you need review . . .

Interpretive

jcd-0499

🔊

1 Escuchar Listen to and understand messages that give information about when and where to meet someone

On your answering machine, you hear your friend asking if you can go somewhere with her this weekend. Based on her message, try to tell: a) where she is going; b) what she is going to do; and c) what time she wants to go.

pp. 198–201 *Vocabulario en contexto*
p. 203 Actividad 9
p. 206 Actividad 13

Interpersonal

2 Hablar Make excuses for not accepting an invitation

You and a friend have planned a camping trip this weekend, but another friend now wants you to do something with him. With a partner, take turns rehearsing excuses for declining his invitation.

p. 202 Actividad 4
p. 203 Actividad 8
p. 204 Actividad 11
p. 207 Actividad 17

Interpretive

3 Leer Read and understand short messages about accepting or declining invitations

You find notes under your desk that were written to the person who was sitting there before you. Read them to see why people declined an invitation to a party:

pp. 198–201 *Vocabulario en contexto*
p. 203 Actividad 7
pp. 212–213 *Lectura*

a) Me gustaría, pero no puedo. Tengo que estudiar para un examen.

b) ¡Genial! ¡Una fiesta! Ay, pero no puedo. Voy de cámping.

c) ¿A las siete? No puedo. Juego un partido de vóleibol a las siete y media. Lo siento.

Presentational

✎

4 Escribir Write a short note telling what you are going to do during the week

As a counselor for an after-school program for children, you must write a note to the parents telling them at least three things their children are going to do during the week. (Hint: Start your note with *¡Hola! Esta semana . . .*)

pp. 198–201 *Vocabulario en contexto*
p. 206 *ir + a +* infinitive; Actividad 14
p. 207 Actividad 15
p. 215 *Presentación escrita*

Cultures • Comparisons

🌐

5 Pensar Demonstrate an understanding of cultural differences regarding extra-curricular activities

Think about what you and your friends typically do after school. Are your activities usually school-related? How would you compare what you do to what some Hispanic teens do in their after-school time?

p. 214 *Perspectivas del mundo hispano*

Tema 5 • Fiesta en familia

Capítulo 5A

Una fiesta de cumpleaños

Chapter Objectives

- Describe families
- Talk about celebrations and parties
- Ask and tell ages
- Express possession
- Understand cultural perspectives on family and celebrations

Video Highlights

Videocultura: *Fiesta en familia*

A primera vista: ¡Feliz cumpleaños!

GramActiva Videos: the verb *tener;* possessive adjectives

Videomisterio: *¿Eres tú, María?*, Episodio 1

Country Connection

As you learn about family celebrations and parties, you will make connections to these countries and places:

España

Texas

California

México

República Dominicana

Más práctica

- *Real.* para hispanohablantes pp. 170–171

realidades.com ✔

- Fondo cultural Activity
- Video Activities
- Online Atlas
- Web Code: jce-0002

familia mexicana
brando un cumpleaños

Vocabulario en contexto

jcd-0587 🔊

Objectives

Read, listen to, and understand information about
- families
- parties and celebrations

mis abuelos

Ricardo
mi **abuelo**, 68

Ana María
mi **abuela**, 61

Más vocabulario
el **padrastro** stepfather
la **madrastra** stepmother
el **hermanastro** stepbrother
la **hermanastra** stepsister

mis padres

María
mi **madre**, 39

José Antonio
mi **padre**, 42

Josefina
mi **tía**, 38

Andrés
mi **tío**, 42

mis **tíos**

Capitán
mi **perro**

Michi
mi **gato**

mis hermanos

Angélica
mi **hermana**, 16

Esteban
mi **hermano**, 15

Cristina
yo, 13

Carolina
mi **prima**, 17

Gabriel
mi **primo**, 13

mis **primos**

66 ¡Hola! Me llamo Cristina. Hoy es mi **cumpleaños.** Toda mi familia va a **preparar** una fiesta para **celebrar.** ¡Va a ser muy divertido! 99

66 Aquí está mi familia. Tengo dos hermanos: mi hermana **mayor,** Angélica, **que tiene 16 años,** y mi hermano, Esteban, que tiene 15 años. Y aquí están mis primos: Carolina tiene 17 años. **Su** hermano **menor,** Gabriel, tiene **sólo** 13 años 99.

66 Mira a **las personas** de **las fotos.** Es la familia de mi tía Josefina. Mi tío Andrés es **el esposo** de Josefina. Ellos tienen dos **hijos: su hijo** Gabriel y su **hija** Carolina 99.

el regalo

la cámara

❝Hoy es el cumpleaños de Cristina. Tengo un regalo para ella. Es una cámara. A Cristina **le encanta sacar fotos**❞.

Fiestamanía
¡Tenemos todo para tu fiesta de cumpleaños!

las luces

la piñata

la luz

el papel picado

la flor

los globos

las flores

el pastel

los dulces

calle Bolívar, 23
Tel. 455-23-19
Abierto de
10h a 20h

jcd-0587

1 La familia de Cristina

Escuchar

Listen as Cristina describes her family. If her statement is true, give a "thumbs-up" sign. If it is false, give a "thumbs-down" sign.

Más práctica

- **Guided** Vocab. Flash Cards pp. 149–154
- **Core** Vocab. Practice pp. 85–86
- **Communication** Writing p. 95
- **Real.** para hispanohablantes p. 172

realidades.com ✔

- Audio Activities
- Leveled Workbook
- Flashcards
- Web Code: jcd-0501

jcd-0587

2 Preparamos la fiesta

Escuchar

Now listen as Cristina and her mother prepare for the birthday party. Look at the items in the party shop ad on this page and touch each item they mention.

jcd-0587

¡Feliz cumpleaños!

¿Qué pasa en la fiesta de Cristina? Lee la historia.

Texas

Strategy

Using visuals
Look at the pictures as you read to help you get the details of the story.

Carolina

Esteban

Cristina

Gabriel

Angélica

1 **Esteban:** Vamos a **hacer un video.** Uno . . . dos . . . tres . . . ¡Acción!

Angélica: Hola, me llamo Angélica. Hoy es el cumpleaños de **nuestra** hermana, Cristina. Todos están aquí para celebrar.

5 **Angélica:** Aquí está mi madre. A **mamá** le gustan **las decoraciones.**

Madre: Sí. A mí me encanta **decorar** con papel picado.

6 **Angélica:** Y aquí está Cristina. Hoy es su cumpleaños. **¡Feliz cumpleaños!**

Cristina: ¿Cuándo puedo **abrir** mis regalos?

Angélica: Ahora no. Primero, la piñata.

7 **Padre:** ¡Vamos, Gabriel! ¿Puedes **romper** la piñata?

Gabriel: ¡Por supuesto!

Todos: *Dale, dale, dale, no pierdas el tino, porque si lo pierdes, pierdes el camino.* (¡Crac! *Gabriel rompe la piñata y . . .*)

2 Angélica: Aquí están mis abuelos. ¿Y **cuántos años tienen Uds.?**

Abuelo: Pues, yo tengo sesenta y ocho años y tu abuela . . .

Abuela: Por favor, Ricardo. Angélica, ¡qué pregunta!

3 Angélica: Aquí está Gabriel, mi primo menor. Le gusta mucho el fútbol. Y aquí está mi prima. ¿Cómo te llamas?

Carolina: Pero, Angélica, tú sabes mi nombre.

Angélica: Sí, pero es para el video. Por favor . . .

4 Angélica: Él es **nuestro** padre. ¿Qué haces, **papá?**

Padre: Voy a preparar unas hamburguesas y después voy a sacar fotos de la fiesta.

8 Madre: ¡Gabriel! ¡La piñata! ¡El pastel! ¡Ay, no!

3 ¿Comprendes?

Escribir · Hablar

1. ¿Quién va a hacer el video, Gabriel o Esteban?
2. ¿Quién tiene sesenta y ocho años, el abuelo o la abuela?
3. ¿A quién le gusta jugar al fútbol, a Esteban o a Gabriel?
4. ¿Qué va a hacer el padre, decorar o preparar hamburguesas?
5. ¿Con qué decora la madre, con globos o con papel picado?
6. ¿Quién rompe la piñata, Cristina o Gabriel?

Más práctica

- **Guided** Vocab. Check pp. 155–158
- **Core** Vocab. Practice pp. 87–88
- **Communication** Video pp. 88–90
- *Real.* **para hispanohablantes** p. 173

realidades.com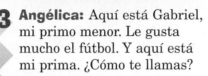

- Audio Activities
- Video Activities
- Leveled Workbook
- Flashcards
- Web Code: jcd-0502

Objectives

- **Communicate about families and parties**
- **Ask and tell what people have**
- **Ask and tell people's ages**
- **Tell to whom something belongs**
- **Learn to use the verb *tener* and possessive adjectives**

Vocabulario en uso

4 ¿Quién es?

Leer · Escribir · Hablar

Completa cada frase con la palabra apropiada.

Modelo

La madre de mi madre es mi <u>abuela</u>.

1. La esposa de mi tío es mi ___.
2. El padre de mi padre es mi ___.
3. El hijo de mi madrastra es mi ___.
4. Paco y Ana son mis tíos. Sus hijos son mis ___.

5. El hermano de mi madre es mi ___.
6. Los padres de mi padre son mis ___.
7. La hija de mi padrastro es mi ___.
8. El hermano de mi prima es mi ___.

5 En la fiesta de cumpleaños

Leer · Escribir · Hablar

Escribe la palabra apropiada para completar cada frase.

Hoy __1.__ *(celebramos / sacamos)* la fiesta de cumpleaños de mi hermana menor, Cristina. ¿Cuántos años __2.__ *(es / tiene)* ella? Trece.

A nuestra madre __3.__ *(le / me)* encantan las fiestas. Mamá y mi hermana __4.__ *(decoran / rompen)* el patio con __5.__ *(luces / pasteles)* y __6.__ *(fiestas / flores)*.

A __7.__ *(nuestro / nuestra)* hermano le gusta hacer un __8.__ *(regalo / video)* o __9.__ *(abrir / sacar)* fotos de la fiesta. Siempre hay una piñata que nosotros __10.__ *(abrimos / rompemos)*. En la piñata hay __11.__ *(dulces / flores)* sabrosos. Ahora Cristina va a __12.__ *(romper / abrir)* sus regalos.

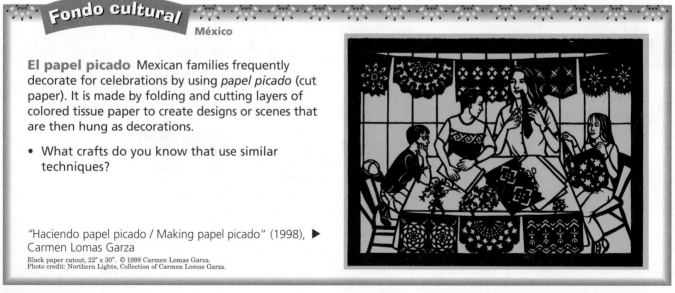

Fondo cultural

México

El papel picado Mexican families frequently decorate for celebrations by using *papel picado* (cut paper). It is made by folding and cutting layers of colored tissue paper to create designs or scenes that are then hung as decorations.

- What crafts do you know that use similar techniques?

"Haciendo papel picado / Making papel picado" (1998), ▶ Carmen Lomas Garza

Black paper cutout, 22" x 30". © 1998 Carmen Lomas Garza.
Photo credit: Northern Lights, Collection of Carmen Lomas Garza.

República Dominicana

6 Mi familia

Hablar

Habla de los miembros de tu familia o de otra familia.

Modelo

hermanos
A —¿Tienes _hermanos_?
B —_Sí, tengo un hermano y una hermana._
o: _No, no tengo hermanos._
A —¿Cómo se llaman?
B —_Mi hermano se llama David y mi hermana
se llama Abby._

Dos hermanos de la República Dominicana

Para decir más . . .
el (la) hijo(a) único(a) only child

Estudiante A

1. tíos
2. primos
3. un abuelo
4. una hermana mayor
5. hermanos menores
6. una tía favorita
7. una abuela
8. un gato o un perro

Estudiante B

¡Respuesta personal!

7 A mi familia le gusta . . .

Hablar

Habla de las actividades favoritas de los
miembros de tu familia o de otra familia.

Modelo

primo
A —¿Qué le gusta hacer a tu _primo_?
B —_Le gusta sacar fotos._

Estudiante A

1. padre
2. madre
3. abuelo
4. hermana
5. prima o primo favorito(a)
6. tía o tío favorito(a)
7. perro o gato

Estudiante B

¡Respuesta personal!

8 Y tú, ¿qué dices?

Escribir · Hablar

1. Describe a una persona de tu familia o de otra familia. ¿Cómo se llama?
¿Cuántos años tiene? ¿Cómo es? ¿Qué le gusta hacer?

2. ¿Tienes un perro o un gato? ¿Cómo se llama? ¿Cuántos años tiene?

3. ¿Qué te gusta hacer durante (during) una fiesta de cumpleaños?

Gramática

The verb *tener*

The verb *tener* is used to show relationship or possession.

Tengo un hermano mayor.   *I have an older brother.*
Tenemos un regalo para Tere.   *We have a gift for Tere.*

Some expressions in Spanish use *tener* where English uses "to be."

Mi primo **tiene** dieciséis años.   *My cousin is sixteen years old.*
Tengo hambre y sed.   *I am hungry and thirsty.*

Here are all the present-tense forms of *tener*:

(yo)	tengo	(nosotros) (nosotras)	tenemos
(tú)	tienes	(vosotros) (vosotras)	tenéis
Ud. (él) (ella)	tiene	Uds. (ellos) (ellas)	tienen

¿Recuerdas?

You have been using the verb *tener* for several chapters.

• **¿Tienes** una bicicleta?

• **Tengo** que hacer ejercicio.

GramActiva VIDEO

Want more help with the verb *tener*? Watch the **GramActiva** video.

tienen

---

9 **Rompecabezas**

Leer • Escribir • Pensar

Escribe la forma apropiada del verbo *tener* para cada frase.
Luego *(Then)* resuelve el problema.

El total de las edades *(ages)* de los hijos de nuestra familia es cien. Marta __1.__ 19 años. Paco y yo __2.__ dos años menos que Marta.

Laura y Eva __3.__ cinco años menos que Paco y yo. ¿Cuántos años __4.__ nuestro hermano mayor, Enrique?

---

10 **¿Qué hay para la fiesta?**

Hablar

Pregunta a otro(a) estudiante qué tienen estas personas para la fiesta.

Ana

Modelo
A — *¿Qué tiene Ana?*
B — *Ana tiene la piñata.*

1. David

2. Yolanda

3. tu abuela

4. tú

5. Uds.

6. Juan y Marcos

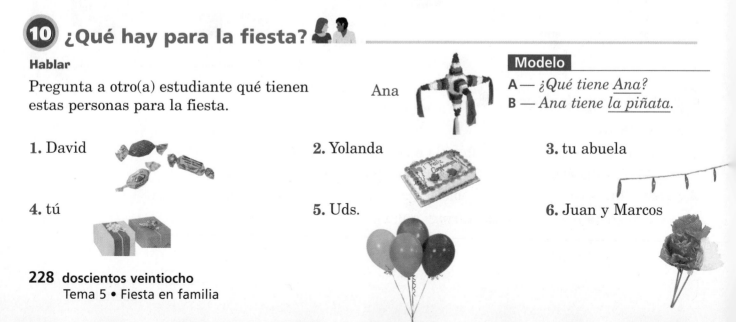

11 Entrevista

Hablar • Escribir

Interview a partner. Find out the answers to the following questions. Your partner may answer based on his or her own family or on a TV family. Write your partner's answers so that you can report your interview to the class.

1. ¿Cómo te llamas y cuántos años tienes? ¿Qué te gusta hacer?

2. ¿Cuántos hermanos mayores o menores tienes?

3. ¿Cómo se llaman tus hermanos(as) y cuántos años tienen?

4. ¿Cómo son tus hermanos(as)?

5. ¿Qué le gusta hacer a uno(a) de tus hermanos(as)?

6. ¿Tienes perros o gatos? ¿Cómo se llama(n)?

Nota

To say that a person likes or loves something, you use *le gusta(n)* or *le encanta(n)*. When you include the name of the person or the pronoun, be sure to add *a:*

• **A Pedro le** gustan los dulces.

• **A ella le** encanta sacar fotos.

12 ¡Reportaje!

Escribir • Hablar

Based on your notes from Actividad 11, write a report of your interview. Your teacher may ask you to read your report to the class.

Modelo

Anita tiene 13 años y le encanta escuchar música. Anita tiene tres hermanos: un hermano mayor y dos hermanos menores. Su hermano mayor, Peter, tiene 16 años. Sus hermanos menores se llaman Lisa y Kevin. Ellos tienen sólo once y ocho años. Son simpáticos y deportistas. A Kevin le gusta jugar al básquetbol. Anita no tiene ni perros ni gatos.

13 Preparar una fiesta de cumpleaños

Escribir • Hablar

Contesta las preguntas.

Cuando tu familia celebra un cumpleaños, ¿quién tiene que . . .

1. . . . decorar la casa? ¿Con qué?

2. . . . preparar la comida y las bebidas?

3. . . . comprar los regalos?

4. . . . hacer el pastel?

5. . . . hacer el video o sacar fotos?

¿Recuerdas?

Remember that *tener que* + infinitive means "to have to" (do something).

• Sofía **tiene que** decorar el pastel.

Celebrando un cumpleaños con una piñata

14 La familia de Sofía

Leer · Escribir

Look carefully at the photograph of Sofía's family, the royal family of Spain, as they celebrate her special day. As Sofía describes this family photo, complete the story with the appropriate forms of the verb *tener*.

Me llamo Sofía de Borbón y Ortiz. Mi cumpleaños es el 29 de abril. Nosotros __1.__ muchas fiestas en mi familia. En la foto celebramos un día muy especial para mí. Es el día de mi bautizo. (Yo) __2.__ una hermana mayor que se llama Leonor. Ella __3.__ dos años. También (yo) __4.__ seis primos; dos chicas y cuatro chicos: Victoria Federica que __5.__ siete años y su hermano Felipe. Felipe __6.__ nueve años. Victoria y Felipe son los hijos de mis tíos, la infanta[1] Elena y su esposo, Jaime. Ellos están a la izquierda, en el fondo[2] de la foto. A la derecha, en el fondo, están mis tíos Cristina e Iñaki con su hija Irene que __7.__ sólo cuatro meses más que mi hermana. Yo estoy en los brazos de mi mamá, la princesa Letizia. Mi padre, el príncipe Felipe, está al lado de ella con mi hermana. Mis abuelos, el rey Juan Carlos I y la reina Sofía, __8.__ 69 años. Ellos están a los dos lados de mis padres. Ellos son los reyes[3] de España. ¿ __9.__ tú tíos y primos? Me encanta tener una familia grande.

[1] In the Spanish royal family, *una infanta* is a princess (*una princesa*) who is not heir to the throne.
[2] background
[3] Note that *el rey + la reina = los reyes*

La familia de Juan Carlos I, rey de España

Más práctica

• **Guided** Gram. Practice pp. 159–160
• **Core** Gram. Practice p. 89
• **Communication** Writing p. 96
• *Real.* para hispanohablantes pp. 174–177, p. 181

realidades.com

• Audio Activities
• Video Activities
• Speak & Record
• Animated Verbs
• Tutorial
• Leveled Workbook
• Web Code: jcd-0504

15 ¿Quiénes son los miembros de la Familia Real?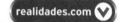

Leer · Hablar · Pensar

Work with a partner to identify the members of the royal family. Use the photograph and answers from Actividad 14 to help.

Modelo

A —*Creo que el número uno es el abuelo de Sofía. Se llama Juan Carlos I.*

B —*Estoy de acuerdo.*

o:—*No estoy de acuerdo.*

16 La familia de Carlos IV

Leer

Before the age of photography, painted portraits were used to capture the images of people. Look carefully at the painting "La familia de Carlos IV" by Francisco de Goya and then read about the family.

Conexiones El arte

La familia real tiene mucha importancia en la historia de España. Es el año 1800: Carlos IV *(Cuarto)* no es un rey popular y muchas personas creen que es demasiado indeciso[1]. En este cuadro[2] del pintor Francisco de Goya, puedes ver a la familia del rey Carlos IV. Carlos IV reinó[3] de 1788 a 1808.

• El pintor también está en el cuadro. ¿Puedes ver a Goya? ¿Dónde está?

◀ "La familia de Carlos IV" (1800), Francisco de Goya
Oil on canvas, 110 1/4" x 132 1/4 " (280 x 336 cm). Museo Nacional del Prado, Madrid.
Photo credit: Scala / Art Resource, NY.

[1] indecisive   [2] painting   [3] reigned

17 Carlos IV y su familia

Pensar • Hablar

Work with a partner. Point to different people in Goya's painting of the royal family and ask your partner who he or she thinks they are.

Modelo

A —¿Quién es?
B —Creo que es el hijo menor.

Fondo cultural
España

Dos familias reales The family photo of the Spanish royal family on the preceding page was taken in the year 2007, 207 years after Goya painted the portrait of Juan Carlos I's ancestor and his family. Study the two pictures as you answer these questions.

• In what ways are the two pictures similar?
• How are they different?
• How would you compare them to your own family portraits?

"Autorretrato" (ca. 1815)
Oil on canvas. Academia de San Fernando, Madrid, Spain. Courtesy The Bridgeman Art Library International Ltd.

Francisco de Goya (1746–1828) was one of the greatest Spanish painters and is considered by many to be the "Father of Modern Art." He was known for a wide range of art themes, including portraits of the royal family and other members of the nobility.

doscientos treinta y uno 231
Capítulo 5A

Gramática

Possessive adjectives

You use possessive adjectives to tell what belongs to someone or to show relationships. In English, the possessive adjectives are *my, your, his, her, its, our,* and *their.*

Here are the possessive adjectives in Spanish:

mi(s)	nuestro(s) nuestra(s)
tu(s)	vuestro(s) vuestra(s)
su(s)	su(s)

Javier y yo con **nuestra** abuela

Mis padres con **su** regalo

Like other adjectives, possessive adjectives agree in number with the nouns that follow them. Only *nuestro* and *vuestro* have different masculine and feminine endings.

mi cámara   mis cámaras

nuestro abuelo   nuestros abuelos

nuestra hija   nuestras hijas

Su and *sus* can have many different meanings: *his, her, its, your,* or *their.* To be more specific, you can use *de* + noun or pronoun.

sus flores = las flores **de ella**

sus regalos = los regalos **de Javier y Carlos**

GramActiva VIDEO

Want to learn more about possessive adjectives? Watch the **GramActiva** video.

18 La Cenicienta y su familia

Leer • Escribir

Escribe la palabra o los adjetivos posesivos apropiados para completar la historia de la Cenicienta.
La Cenicienta es un personaje de un cuento muy famoso. ¿Quién es?

Cenicienta tiene una madrastra y dos hermanastras muy perezosas. __1.__ *(Sus / Tus)* hermanastras se llaman Griselda y Anastasia. __2.__ *(Nuestra / Su)* madrastra y __3.__ *(su / sus)* hermanastras siempre dicen: "¡Cenicienta! Tenemos hambre. ¿Dónde está __4.__ *(mi / nuestra)* comida?" Cada mañana Griselda le dice:

"Quiero __5.__ *(mi / su)* desayuno. ¿Dónde está?" Una noche Cenicienta va al baile del príncipe. Él le pregunta a Cenicienta: "¿Cómo te llamas? ¿Quiénes son __6.__ *(tu / tus)* padres?" Las hermanastras __7.__ *(de / su)* Cenicienta ven al príncipe cuando baila con Cenicienta. Ellas dicen: "¡ __8.__ *(Nuestra / Su)* hermanastra baila con el príncipe! ¡Qué ridículo!".

19 **¿Quién es tu héroe o heroína?**

Leer • Escribir • Hablar

Lee el anuncio y contesta las preguntas.

No es sólo
mi padre.
También es
mi héroe.

**Y es nuestro
héroe también.**

Gracias.

Patrocinado por la Cámara de Comercio

1. En este anuncio, ¿quién es el héroe? ¿De quiénes es el héroe?

2. Trabaja con otro(a) estudiante. Pregunta quién es su héroe o heroína.

> **Modelo**
>
> **A** —*¿Quién es tu héroe o heroína? ¿Cómo es?*
> **B** —*Mi heroína es mi madre. Es muy inteligente.*

20 **¿Dónde está o dónde están?**

Leer • Pensar

Un grupo de estudiantes busca *(is looking for)* sus decoraciones para una fiesta en la escuela. Empareja *(Match)* cada pregunta con la respuesta más apropiada.

1. ¿Dónde están tus flores?

2. ¿Dónde está el papel picado de Clara?

3. ¿Dónde está mi papel picado?

4. ¿Dónde están los globos de Marta y Tere?

5. ¿Dónde están las flores de Teodoro?

6. ¿Dónde están mis globos?

a. Tu papel picado está allí.

b. Sus flores están allí.

c. Mis globos están allí.

d. Mis flores están detrás del escritorio.

e. Tus globos están debajo de la mesa.

f. Su papel picado está debajo de la carpeta.

g. Sus globos están al lado de la computadora.

21 Juego

Hablar · GramActiva

1 Working with a partner, make a set of two cubes using the template your teacher will give you.

- **Cube 1** Write a different subject pronoun on each side.

- **Cube 2** Write a different classroom object on each side. Make three of them singular and three of them plural.

- **Both cubes** Write a different point value from 1 to 6 on each side.

2 You and your partner will play against another pair of students. Team 1 rolls both of your cubes and says a sentence using the correct form of the verb *tener*, the appropriate possessive adjective, and the classroom object. If the sentence is correct, Team 1 receives the total points shown on the cubes. Team 2 then rolls the other cubes. Continue until a team reaches 100 points or time is called.

Modelo
Uds. tienen su calculadora.

22 ¿Qué tienen y para qué clase?

Hablar

¿Qué tienen tus compañeros hoy?

1 Escribe cinco cosas *(things)* que usas en la escuela y para qué clases son.

2 Pide *(Ask for)* las respuestas a tres compañeros y escríbelas en una hoja de papel.

Modelo
A —*¿Qué tienes para tus clases hoy?* **B** —*Tengo mi calculadora para la clase de matemáticas y mi carpeta para la clase de inglés.*

3 Escribe cinco frases para describir las cosas que tienen los estudiantes para las clases de hoy.

Modelo
Ana tiene su carpeta para la clase de inglés. *Paco y yo tenemos nuestros lápices para la clase de arte.*

¿Recuerdas?

You have been using vocabulary for classroom supplies for several chapters.

Más práctica

- **Guided** Gram. Practice pp. 161–162
- **Core** Gram. Practice pp. 90–91
- **Communication** Writing p. 97, Test Prep p. 275
- *Real.* **para hispanohablantes** pp. 178–181

realidades.com ✔

- Audio Activities
- Video Activities
- Speak & Record
- Canción de hip hop
- Tutorial
- Leveled Workbook
- Web Code: jcd-0505

Exploración del lenguaje

Diminutives

In Spanish you can add the suffix -*ito(a)* to a word to give it the meaning of "small" or "little." It can also be used to show affection. Words with this suffix are called diminutives (*diminutivos*).

abuelo → abue**lito**

perros → per**ritos**

hermana → herman**ita**

Now that you know what the suffix -*ito(a)* means, can you figure out the meanings of these words?

abuelita	gatito	Miguelito	hijita

Some very popular names are diminutives. What do you think the diminutives of these names are?

Ana	Juana	Eva	Lola

23 ¡Feliz cumpleaños!

Leer · Pensar

Read the birthday card. Who is it for? Find the diminutives. What words in the poem do you understand? How many objects in the picture can you name in Spanish?

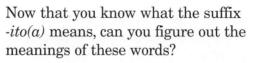

Escuchar

En una hoja de papel, escribe los números del 1 al 6. Mira la tarjeta *(card)* de cumpleaños y escucha las frases. Si la frase es cierta, escribe *C*. Si es falsa, escribe *F*.

Hay luces, y flores, dos globitos, un pastelito sabroso, y muchos regalitos,

y una piñata, y seis perritos que cantan y bailan, muy contentitos,

porque hoy cumples... ¡6 añitos!

Felipe

The letters *p, t,* and *q*

jcd-0588

In English the consonants *p, t, q,* and the hard *c* sound are pronounced with a little puff of air.

Hold a tissue loosely in front of your mouth as you say these English words. You will notice that the tissue moves.

pan	papa	too	tea
comb	case	park	take

Now say these Spanish words with the tissue in front of your mouth. Try to say the consonants so that there is no puff of air and the tissue does not move.

pan	papá	tú	tía
cómo	queso	parque	taco

Try it out! Listen to this nursery rhyme. Listen particularly for the *p, t,* and *q* sounds. Then repeat the rhyme.

**Tortillitas para mamá,
tortillitas para papá.
Las quemaditas,¹ para mamá,
las bonitas,² para papá.**

¹ The burned ones ² The pretty ones

Haciendo tortillas en Chiapas, México

Diego Rivera (1886–1957) This painting by Mexican muralist Diego Rivera shows a woman grinding maize on a *metate,* a utensil used for grinding grain. This is one of many paintings in which Rivera portrays the daily life of the indigenous peoples of Mexico.

• Through paintings, an artist conveys feelings to the viewer. What do you think Rivera wants you to feel about this woman and her task?

"La molendera" (1926), Diego Rivera

Oil on canvas, 35 7/16 X 46 1/16 inches. Museo Nacional de Arte Moderno, Instituto Nacional de Bellas Artes, Mexico City, D.F., Mexico. © 2009 Banco de México Diego Rivera & Frida Kahlo Museums Trust, México, D.F. / Artists Rights Society (ARS), New York.

El español en la comunidad

The five most common last names in the United States, in order, are Smith, Johnson, Williams, Jones, and Brown. The five most common last names in the United States for people of Spanish-speaking heritage, in order, are García, Martínez, Rodríguez, Hernández, and López.

• Look up these names in your local phone book. Count the number of entries for each. Do the numbers in your community match the statement made above? Can you identify two other Hispanic last names that are common in your community or that you are familiar with?

25 Un cumpleaños divertido

Hablar • Escribir

Find out from your classmates what they consider to be a great birthday. Make a chart like the one below on a sheet of paper and complete the first row about yourself. Then survey four classmates to find out what their preferences are and record the information in the chart.

Modelo

¿En qué mes es tu cumpleaños?
¿Cuál es tu actividad y lugar (place) favorito?
¿Cuáles son tus comidas favoritas?

	Mes del cumpleaños	Actividad y lugar favorito	Comidas favoritas
yo	julio	comer–un restaurante	pastel y helado
Miguel	enero	abrir regalos–en casa	pizza y ensalada
Anita	julio	bailar–un baile	hamburguesas y helado

26 ¿Quién es esta persona?

Escuchar • Hablar • Escribir • Leer

1 Use your completed chart from Actividad 25 and describe a classmate to the class. Do not give that person's name. The class will try to guess whom you are describing.

Modelo

Su cumpleaños es en enero. Para su cumpleaños le gusta abrir regalos en casa. Sus comidas favoritas en su cumpleaños son pizza y ensalada. ¿Quién es?

2 Write a paragraph describing the person you interviewed whose idea of a great birthday celebration is most like your own. Describe the similarities, but also mention differences.

Un chico con su mejor amigo

Modelo

Nuestro cumpleaños es en julio. Nuestra comida favorita es el helado. El lugar favorito para mi cumpleaños es un restaurante porque me gusta comer. Su lugar favorito es un baile porque le gusta bailar. A ella le gustan las hamburguesas pero a mí me gusta el pastel. ¿Quién es la persona? Es Anita.

Lectura

Mis padres te invitan a mi fiesta de quince años

Para muchas jóvenes hispanas, el día de sus quince años es una ocasión muy especial. Toda la familia y muchos amigos van a misa en la iglesia y después celebran con una fiesta. Es una tradición especialmente importante en México, América Central y los países hispanos del Caribe. También es importante entre muchos hispanohablantes en los Estados Unidos.

Aquí está la invitación a la fiesta de quince años de María Teresa Rivera Treviño.

Strategy

Scanning
What information would you expect to find on an invitation? Read quickly through this invitation and find the names of María Teresa's parents and the date and times of the two events to which you are invited.

Felipe Rivera López y
Guadalupe Treviño Ibarra
esperan el honor de su asistencia
el sábado, 15 de mayo de 2004
para celebrar los quince años de su hija,
María Teresa Rivera Treviño

Misa
a las cuatro de la tarde
Iglesia de Nuestra Señora de Guadalupe
2374 Avenida Linda Vista
San Diego, California

Recepción y cena-baile
a las seis de la tarde
Restaurante Luna
7373 Calle Florida
San Diego, California

❝Toda mi familia, mis amigos y yo vamos a la iglesia en la tarde. Después vamos a la recepción en un restaurante muy elegante donde comemos y bailamos. Bailo primero con mi padre y después con mis amigos❞.

66 Aquí estoy yo en el día de mis quince años. Es un día muy especial y toda la familia está conmigo para celebrar. Todo está perfecto para mi fiesta —la comida, las decoraciones, la música— ¡todo! 99

¿Comprendes?

1. ¿Cuál es la fecha de los quince años de María Teresa?

2. Necesitas una hora para ir de tu casa a la Iglesia de Nuestra Señora de Guadalupe. ¿A qué hora tienes que salir *(leave)* de casa?

3. ¿Dónde y a qué hora es la recepción? Según la invitación, ¿qué van a hacer en la recepción?

4. ¿Qué actividad de la fiesta de quince años te gusta más?

¡Vamos a comparar!

The special celebration of a girl's fifteenth birthday is called *la quinceañera, los quince,* or *los quince años.* Think about an event in the lives of your friends that has the importance of a *quince años* celebration. How are the events similar or different?

Fondo cultural
El mundo hispano

El nombre completo A person's full name *(nombre completo)* consists of a first name *(nombre),* which often consists of two names, plus two surnames—the father's family name *(apellido paterno),* followed by the mother's family name *(apellido materno).*

For example, look at the *nombres completos* of María Teresa's parents:

*Felipe Rivera López y
Guadalupe Treviño Ibarra*

• What is Felipe's *apellido paterno*?
• What is Guadalupe's *apellido materno*?
• Can you explain how María Teresa's name is formed?

María Teresa will most often use her first name and her father's family name. If she marries, she may add *de* and her husband's last name to her own name: María Teresa Rivera de García.

• Use the Spanish system to write your *nombre completo.* What advantages or disadvantages do you see to having a name formed this way?

Más práctica

● **Guided** Reading Support p. 163
● **Communication** Writing p. 98, Test Prep p. 276
● *Real.* **para hispanohablantes** pp. 182–183

realidades.com
• Internet Activity
• Leveled Workbook
• Web Code: jcd-0506

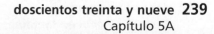

La cultura en vivo
El papel picado

As you've seen in this chapter, *el papel picado* (cut paper) is a well-known Mexican craft. Colored tissue paper is cut into small patterns similar to making paper snowflakes. The cut paper is then hung on string to make a banner to use as decoration at many different celebrations. Here's how to make *papel picado* to decorate your classroom.

Una fiesta con música de mariachi

Materials

- colored tissue paper cut into 12" x 18" sheets
- scissors
- stapler
- string

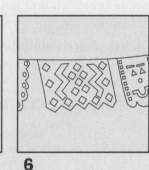

Directions

1 Spread the tissue paper flat. Fold down 1" on the 18" side for making a hanging flap.

2 Fold the paper in half on the 12" side and crease on the fold to make a sharp line.

3 Fold the paper twice, diagonally.

4 Cut out designs along the folded edge. Experiment with snowflake or other geometric designs.

5 Cut a scalloped design on the outside edge.

6 Open the cutout and staple to a string to hang across a room to decorate for a *fiesta*.

Presentación oral
Mi familia

Task
You are on an exchange program in Chile and your host family wants to know about your family back home. Show them photographs of three family members and talk about the people shown.

❶ **Prepare** Bring in three family photos or "create" a family using pictures from a magazine. Use a chart like this one to think through what you want to say about each person.

Strategy
Using graphic organizers
Simple charts can help you organize your thoughts for a presentation.

Nombre	Es mi ...	Edad	Actividad favorita
Isabel	hermana menor	9 años	le gusta cantar

❷ **Practice** Go through your presentation several times. You can use your notes in practice, but not when you present. Try to:

- provide all the information on each family member
- use complete sentences
- speak clearly

Modelo

Se llama Isabel. Ella es mi hermana menor y tiene 9 años. A Isabel le gusta cantar. Es muy artística.

❸ **Present** Show your pictures and give the information about each person.

❹ **Evaluation** Your teacher may give you a rubric for how the presentation will be graded. You probably will be graded on:

- how complete your preparation is
- how much information you communicate
- how easy it is to understand you

- Speak & Record

¿Eres tú, María?

Episodio 1

Madrid, España

Antes de ver el video

Personajes importantes

Doña Lupe, portera

DETECTIVES PRIVADOS

Lola Lago, detective

Nota cultural In many apartment buildings in Spain, you will find a *portero* or *portera*. In exchange for a small salary and free apartment (in Spain, an apartment is called *un piso*), this person watches over the building and its residents, doing small chores such as taking messages and receiving packages. Because the *portero* or *portera* knows everyone in the building, he or she is often a good source of information about the residents.

Resumen del episodio

Estamos en el piso de Lola Lago, una detective que trabaja en Madrid, la capital de España. Es la una de la mañana. Desde[1] su balcón, ella ve a dos personas hablando enfrente de un edificio[2]. ¿Qué pasa? Más tarde, Lola encuentra[3] algo muy importante en la calle[4]. Al día siguiente[5], doña Lupe, la portera del edificio, entra en el piso de doña Gracia y . . .

[1]From [2]building [3]finds [4]street [5]The next day

Palabras para comprender

investigar	to investigate
las llaves	keys
el periódico	newspaper
el piso	apartment; floor *(of a building)*

"¿Qué es esto?
Mañana voy a investigar".

"A ver. Unas llaves . . ."

"¡Ay de mí! Necesito
una ambulancia. Plaza
del Alamillo. Número 8.
Tercer piso. ¡Rápido!"

Después de ver el video

¿Comprendes?

Lee las frases y decide si son ciertas o falsas.
Si una frase es falsa, escríbela con la
información correcta.

1. Es la una de la tarde cuando Lola entra en
su piso.

2. Ella está sola en su piso.

3. Lola ve a dos hombres hablando
en la calle.

4. Las dos personas están muy contentas.

5. Lola encuentra un llavero con las iniciales
"J.R.D.".

6. Lola compra *(buys)* una revista en la
mañana.

7. Doña Lupe entra en el piso de Lola
con el periódico.

- Web Code: jcd-0507

Repaso del capítulo

Vocabulario y gramática 🔊

jcd-0589

to talk about family members

los abuelos	grandparents
el abuelo	grandfather
la abuela	grandmother
el esposo, la esposa	husband, wife
los hermanos	brothers; brother(s) and sister(s)
el hermano	brother
la hermana	sister
el hermanastro	stepbrother
la hermanastra	stepsister
los hijos	children; sons
el hijo	son
la hija	daughter
los padres (papás)	parents
el padre (papá)	father
la madre (mamá)	mother
el padrastro	stepfather
la madrastra	stepmother
los primos	cousins
el primo	(male) cousin
la prima	(female) cousin
los tíos	uncles; aunt(s) and uncle(s)
el tío	uncle
la tía	aunt

to discuss and compare ages

¿Cuántos años tiene(n) ——?	How old is / are ——?
Tiene(n) —— años.	He / She is / They are —— (years old).
mayor *pl.* mayores	older
menor *pl.* menores	younger

to talk about people

la persona	person

to name animals

el gato	cat
el perro	dog

to discuss what someone likes

(a + *person*) **le gusta(n)** / **le encanta(n)**	he / she likes / loves

For *Vocabulario adicional,* see pp. 472–473.

to describe activities at parties

abrir	to open
celebrar	to celebrate
decorar	to decorate
las decoraciones	decorations
hacer un video	to videotape
el video	video
preparar	to prepare
romper	to break
sacar fotos	to take photos
la foto	photo
la cámara	camera

to discuss celebrations

el cumpleaños	birthday
¡Feliz cumpleaños!	Happy birthday!
los dulces	candy
la flor *pl.* las flores	flower
el globo	balloon
la luz *pl.* las luces	light
el papel picado	cut-paper decorations
el pastel	cake
la piñata	piñata
el regalo	gift, present

other useful words

que	who, that
sólo	only

to indicate possession or relationship

tener *to have*

tengo	tenemos
tienes	tenéis
tiene	tienen

possessive adjectives

mi(s) my	**nuestro(s), -a(s)** our
tu(s) your	**vuestro(s), -a(s)** your *(pl.)*
su(s) your *(formal),* his, her, its	**su(s)** your *(pl.),* their

Más práctica

- **Core** Puzzle p. 92, Organizer p. 93
- **Communication** Practice Test pp. 278–281, Integrated Performance Assessment p. 277

realidades.com

- Tutorial
- Flashcards
- Puzzles
- Self-test
- Web Code: jcd-0508

Preparación para el examen

On the exam you will be asked to . . .	Here are practice tasks similar to those you will find on the exam . . .	If you need review . . .
Interpretive		
jcd-0589 **① Escuchar** Listen to and understand someone's description of a family member	At a friend's party, a woman is telling you stories about her brother, Jorge. a) How old is her brother? b) Who is older, the woman or her brother? c) What does her brother like to do?	**pp. 222–225** *Vocabulario en contexto* **p. 226** Actividad 4 **p. 227** Actividades 7–8 **p. 229** Actividad 11
Interpersonal		
② Hablar Describe some members of your family and what they like to do	At your first Spanish Club meeting, your teacher requests that all of you try to talk to each other in Spanish. Since you just learned how to talk about your family, you feel confident that you can talk about some of your family members. Tell about: a) how they are related to you; b) their ages; c) what they like to do; d) their personalities.	**pp. 222–225** *Vocabulario en contexto* **p. 226** Actividad 4 **p. 227** Actividad 7 **p. 229** Actividad 12 **p. 232** *Gramática: Possessive adjectives* **p. 237** Actividad 26
Interpretive		
③ Leer Read and understand someone's description of a problem he or she is having with a family member	Read this letter to an advice columnist. Can you describe in English what Ana's problem is? *Querida Dolores:* *Yo soy la hija menor de una familia de seis personas. Uno de mis hermanos mayores, Nacho, siempre habla de mí con mis padres. A él le encanta hablar de mis amigos y de mis actividades. Tenemos una familia muy simpática, pero ¡Nacho me vuelve loca!* *Ana*	**pp. 222–225** *Vocabulario en contexto* **p. 226** Actividades 4–5 **p. 232** Actividad 18
Presentational		
④ Escribir Write a brief note telling at least two facts about a friend or family member	The party planner at a local restaurant is helping you plan a birthday party for your cousin. Write a brief note telling her your cousin's name, age, two things he or she likes to do at a party, the kinds of decorations he or she likes, and one thing he or she loves to eat.	**p. 226** Actividad 5 **p. 227** Actividad 8 **p. 229** Actividad 12 **p. 237** Actividad 26
Cultures • Comparisons		
⑤ Pensar Demonstrate an understanding of some ways that Spanish-speaking families celebrate special occasions	Think about what you would consider your most important birthday. Based on what you know about important family traditions, describe why a fifteenth birthday is important for a young Spanish-speaking girl and what you would expect to see at her celebration.	**pp. 222–225** *Vocabulario en contexto* **p. 226** *Fondo cultural* **pp. 238–239** *Lectura* **p. 240** *La cultura en vivo*

Fondo cultural

El mundo hispano

Extended families tend to be close-knit in Spanish-speaking cultures. Parents, children, grandparents, aunts, uncles, and cousins get together often for meals or just to spend time together, and not just on special occasions. In fact, it is not uncommon for three generations to live under one roof or in the same neighborhood.

• How does the idea of extended families in Spanish-speaking cultures compare with what happens with you and your friends?

"Orgullo de familia" (1997), Simón Silva ▶
Courtesy of Simón Silva.

Una noche en
Sevilla, España

Capítulo 5B

¡Vamos a un restaurante!

Chapter Objectives

- Talk about family celebrations
- Describe family members and friends
- Ask politely to have something brought to you
- Order a meal in a restaurant
- Understand cultural perspectives on family celebrations

Video Highlights

Videocultura: *Fiesta en familia*

A primera vista: *En el restaurante Casa Río*

GramActiva Videos: the verb *venir;* the verbs *ser* and *estar*

Videomisterio: *¿Eres tú, María?,* Episodio 2

Country Connection

As you learn about family celebrations, describing family members, and restaurants, you will make connections to these countries and places:

España
Nuevo México
Texas
México
Colombia
Costa Rica
Paraguay
Argentina

Más práctica

- *Real.* para hispanohablantes pp. 190–191

realidades.com

- Fondo cultural Activity
- Video Activities
- Online Atlas
- Web Code: jce-0002

Vocabulario en contexto

jcd-0597

—Abuelito, ¿quiénes son las personas en la foto?

—La mujer es tu abuela y el hombre, soy yo. Y aquí está tu papá. Tiene sólo seis años.

el hombre

la mujer

el pelo castaño

alto

baja

pelirroja

el pelo largo

el pelo negro

el pelo corto

el pelo rubio

viejo

joven

el pelo canoso

—¿Quién es **el joven** alto y **guapo?**

—Es tu primo Rafael.

—¿Y **la joven** baja al lado del primo Rafael?

—Es su amiga, Sara. Y estas **otras** personas son amigos también.

el menú

la cuenta

el camarero

la sal

la pimienta

el azúcar

el tenedor

la servilleta

el cuchillo

la camarera

la taza

el plato

el vaso

la cuchara

—Abuela, ¿qué celebramos esta noche?

—Es el cumpleaños de tu abuelo.

—¿Quiénes **vienen** a la fiesta?

—Toda la familia **viene**.

 1 **¿Quiénes vienen?**  jcd-0597

Escuchar

Paquito is showing the family album to a friend. Point to the different pictures as he describes the people in the photographs.

Más práctica

- **Guided** Vocab. Flash Cards
  pp. 165–170
- **Core** Vocab. Practice pp. 94–95
- **Communication** Writing p. 105
- *Real.* para hispanohablantes
  pp. 192

realidades.com ✓

- Audio Activities
- Leveled Workbook
- Flashcards
- Web Code: jcd-0511

2 **¿Qué necesitas para . . . ?** jcd-0597

Escuchar

You will hear seven statements about the table setting. If a statement is correct, indicate *cierto* by raising one hand. If a statement is incorrect, indicate *falso* by raising two hands.

En el restaurante Casa Río

La familia de Angélica come la cena en este restaurante.
Lee lo que pasa durante la comida.

Texas

Strategy

Scanning
Think about what a waiter might say to you when you order in a restaurant. Look through the dialogue and find three expressions that the waiter uses.

Esteban   Cristina

Mamá   Papá

Angélica   Luis

1 **Luis:** Bienvenidos al restaurante Casa Río. Soy Luis, su mesero. Hoy es mi primer día de trabajo. Estoy un poco nervioso. El menú está en la mesa.

También se dice . . .

el (la) camarero(a) =
el (la) mesero(a) *(México, Puerto Rico)*; el (la) mozo(a) *(Argentina, Puerto Rico, Bolivia)*

5 **Esteban:** Señor, **me faltan** un cuchillo y un tenedor.

Luis: ¡Ah, sí! En un momento **le traigo** un cuchillo y un tenedor.

6 **Luis:** ¿Y para quién son las enchiladas?

Angélica: Creo que son para el señor de pelo castaño.

Luis: ¡Oh! ¡Gracias!

Angélica: De nada.

7 **Luis:** ¿Necesitan **algo más**? ¿Y cómo está la comida?

Mamá: La comida aquí es **deliciosa. ¡Qué rica!**

2 **Luis:** ¿Qué va a **pedir** Ud. de bebida?

Papá: ¡Uy! **Tengo calor.** Para mí, un té helado.

Mamá: Y yo **tengo frío.** Para mí, café.

3 **Luis:** Y ahora . . . , ¿qué **desean** Uds. **de plato principal?**

Angélica: Quisiera el arroz con pollo.

Esteban: Para mí, una hamburguesa con papas fritas.

4 **Luis:** ¿Y qué desea Ud.?

Cristina: ¿**Me trae** las fajitas de pollo, por favor?

Luis: ¡Muy bien!

8 **Luis:** Ahora, ¿desean **postre?**

Mamá: Pues, sí. Y **otro** café, por favor.

Papá: Para mí, nada. Pero quisiera un café, yo también. Ahora **tengo sueño.**

3 **¿Comprendes?**

Escribir • Hablar

1. ¿Cómo se llama el restaurante? ¿Cómo se llama el camarero?

2. ¿Por qué está nervioso Luis?

3. ¿Qué va a beber el padre? ¿Por qué?

4. ¿Quién come las fajitas? ¿La hamburguesa?

5. ¿Quién desea las enchiladas?

6. Según la mamá, ¿cómo es la comida?

Más práctica

- **Guided** Vocab. Check pp. 171–174
- **Core** Vocab. Practice pp. 96–97
- **Communication** Video pp. 99–101
- *Real.* **para hispanohablantes** p. 193

realidades.com

- Audio Activities
- Video Activities
- Leveled Workbook
- Flashcards
- Web Code: jcd-0512

Vocabulario en uso

4 **¿Quiénes son?** jcd-0598

Escuchar

Vas a escuchar descripciones de las personas en el dibujo. En una hoja de papel, escribe los números del 1 al 5. Al lado de cada número escribe el nombre de la persona que describen.

> **También se dice . . .**
>
> **pelirrojo(a)** = colorado(a) *(Argentina);* colorín, colorina *(Chile)*
>
> **el pelo** = el cabello *(muchos países)*
>
> **rubio(a)** = güero(a) *(México)*

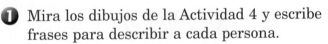

| Eduardo, 15 | Rosalía, 14 | Lucía, 18 | Alejandro, 20 | María Elena, 60 | Jorge, 65 |

5 **¿Quién es?**

Escribir • Hablar

1 Mira los dibujos de la Actividad 4 y escribe frases para describir a cada persona.

> **¿Recuerdas?**
>
> Adjectives agree in number and gender with the nouns they describe.

Modelo

El joven muy alto es Eduardo. Tiene 15 años. Tiene el pelo castaño. Le gusta jugar al tenis.

2 Describe a uno(a) de tus amigos(as).

6 Las analogías ♻

Leer • Pensar • Escribir

Many exams test your vocabulary by asking about the logical relationships, or analogies, between words. In analogies, the symbol ":" is used to mean "is to" (*es a*) and the symbol "::" is used to mean "as" (*como*). For example:

la madre : la hija :: el padre : el hijo

You would read this as "*La madre es a la hija como el padre es al hijo.*" Complete these analogies.

Modelo

trabajador : perezoso :: alto : bajo

1. aburrido : interesante :: largo : _____

2. comida : plato :: bebida : _____

3. escuela : profesora :: restaurante : _____

4. chico : joven :: abuelo : _____

5. bistec : plato principal :: pastel : _____

6. amigo : amiga :: hombre : _____

7. ensalada : tenedor :: sopa : _____

7 ¿Qué te gusta pedir? ♻

Escribir

Escribe frases para decir lo que te gusta pedir cuando tienes . . .

Modelo

Cuando tengo hambre, me gusta pedir pizza en un restaurante.

1.

2.

3.

4.

5.

Fondo cultural

Costa Rica • Colombia

Getting a server's attention at a restaurant in a Spanish-speaking country sometimes differs from how it is done in other cultures. For example, in Costa Rica people often make a *pfft* sound to get a server's attention, while in Colombia people may raise or clap their hands. Be very careful in using this sort of attention-getting device—it may seem rude when done by someone from outside the culture!

• How do you get a server's attention in a restaurant here in the United States? Compare this to what is acceptable in some Spanish-speaking countries.

En un restaurante en Cali, Colombia

8 En el restaurante

Leer • Hablar

Con otro(a) estudiante, lee la conversación entre un camarero y dos jóvenes. Empareja *(Match)* lo que dice el camarero con lo que contestan *(answer)* los jóvenes para crear *(create)* la conversación.

Un restaurante en la Argentina

El camarero

1. Buenas noches. ¿Qué desean de bebida?
2. ¿Qué desea pedir de plato principal?
3. ¡Ay, señor! Le falta el cuchillo, ¿no?
4. ¿Le gusta la sopa?
5. Señorita, ¿qué desea Ud. de postre?
6. Señor, ¿le traigo otra bebida?
7. ¿Desean Uds. algo más?
8. Gracias por venir a nuestro restaurante.

Los jóvenes

a. Sí, está deliciosa. Umm. ¡Qué rica!
b. No, sólo la cuenta, por favor.
c. Quisiera el arroz con pollo, por favor.
d. De nada. Hasta luego.
e. Un helado, por favor.
f. Sí. ¿Me trae uno, por favor?
g. Para mí, un refresco y, para la señorita, un té helado.
h. Sí, por favor. Tengo mucha sed.

9 Juego

Hablar

❶ Work in groups of three or four. Your teacher will give you copies of pictures of various table items. Cut or tear the pictures apart to make cards.

❷ Arrange the pictures in a table setting on a desk. While the other players have their backs turned, hide one or more of the cards. Then ask: *¿Qué me falta?* The first player to say correctly *Te falta(n)* . . . and name the missing item(s) receives a point.

❸ Put the hidden items back on the desk and continue playing until all players have had a chance to hide items. The player with the most points is the winner.

Nota

When one item is missing, use *me / te falta*. When more than one item is missing, use *me / te faltan*.

Exploración del lenguaje

Adjectives ending in *-ísimo*

Muy + an adjective can be expressed in another way by adding the correct form of *-ísimo* to the adjective. The *-ísimo* ending conveys the idea of "extremely."

> un chico muy guapo = un chico guapísimo
> una clase muy difícil = una clase dificilísima

Adjectives that end in *-co* or *-ca* have a spelling change to *-qu-*. The *-o* or *-a* is dropped.

> unos pasteles muy ricos = unos pasteles riquísimos

Try it out! Rework the following phrases using the correct *-ísimo* form.

un perro muy perezoso = ¿ ?   una clase muy aburrida = ¿ ?

dos libros muy interesantes = ¿ ?   unas chicas muy simpáticas = ¿ ?

⑩ El Café Buen Libro ♻

Leer • Pensar • Escribir • Hablar

Lee la crítica del café y lo que dicen estas *(these)* personas.
¿A quiénes recomiendas el café? ¿A quiénes no?

Café Buen Libro
Nuevo León, 28

✓✓ ++ $ ☺☺

Es un café tranquilo con un ambiente* intelectual donde puedes pasar el tiempo en la compañía de un buen amigo o un buen libro. Los precios son muy razonables. Puedes comer un sándwich, una ensalada, un postre riquísimo o simplemente beber un café. También tienen lo último en libros, videos y música. Un "plus" es la presentación de grupos musicales los fines de semana.

Ambiente
aburrido ✓
tranquilo ✓✓
fantástico ✓✓✓

Comida y bebida
regular +
buena ++
excelente +++

Precios
barato $
medio $$
caro $$$

Servicio
regular ☺
bueno ☺☺
superior ☺☺☺

* atmosphere

1. **Carmen:** "Quisiera comer un bistec sabroso".

2. **Marta:** "Me encanta escuchar música".

3. **Diego:** "Tengo muchísima hambre y poco tiempo".

4. **Lupe:** "Me gusta pasar tiempo con otras personas interesantes y graciosas".

5. **Ana:** "No tengo mucho dinero *(money)* ahora".

6. Y a ti, ¿te gustaría ir al Café Buen Libro? ¿Por qué?

Gramática

The verb *venir*

You use *venir* to say that someone is coming to a place or an event.

¿A qué hora **vienes** a mi casa?
*When **are you coming** to my house?*

Siempre **vengo** a esta playa.
*I **always come** to this beach.*

Here are all the present-tense forms:

(yo)	**vengo**	(nosotros) (nosotras)	**venimos**
(tú)	**vienes**	(vosotros) (vosotras)	**venís**
Ud. (él) (ella)	**viene**	Uds. (ellos) (ellas)	**vienen**

GramActiva VIDEO

Want more help with *venir*? Watch the **GramActiva** video.

vienen

---

11 **¿Cómo vienen?**

Leer • Escribir

Tu amigo Antonio invita a tu familia a su casa en el campo. Escribes una nota para explicar cómo y cuándo todos Uds. vienen. Completa la nota con las formas apropiadas del verbo *venir*.

Antonio:

¡Gracias por tu invitación! Yo __1.__ en bicicleta con mi amiga, Marta. Nosotros __2.__ a las dos porque Marta trabaja hasta la una. Mi abuela __3.__ en tren[1] con mis padres. Ellos __4.__ a las once para ayudar[2] con la cena. Mis hermanitos también __5.__ en tren con mis padres. Mi hermana mayor, Cecilia, __6.__ en monopatín. No sé a qué hora va a venir.

¡Nos vemos el sábado!

[1]train [2]to help

12 **Escucha, escribe y dibuja** jcd-0598

Escuchar • Escribir

Roberto, otro amigo de Antonio, también va a la fiesta con su familia. Vas a escuchar la descripción de su familia. Escribe las cuatro descripciones y después dibuja a la familia. Compara tu dibujo con el dibujo de otro(a) estudiante.

Una fiesta en familia

13 **¿Qué traen a tu casa?**

Hablar

Estás en casa de un(a) amigo(a). Habla de lo que traen las personas a la casa.

Modelo

A —*Cuando tus tíos vienen a tu casa, ¿traen algo?*
B —*Sí, generalmente traen el postre.*
o:—*No, generalmente no traen nada.*

Nota

Traer, "to bring," follows the pattern of *-er* verbs except for the irregular *yo* form: *traigo.*

• Mañana **traigo** pasteles para todos.

• Y tú, ¿**traes** bebidas?

Estudiante A

1. tu(s) abuelo(s)
2. tu mejor amigo(a)
3. tus amigos
4. tus tíos
5. tus primos
6. los amigos de tus padres

Estudiante B

el plato principal	el postre
un regalo	flores
nada	**¡Respuesta personal!**

Pronunciación

jcd-0598

The letters *b* and *v* 🔊

In Spanish, *b* and *v* are pronounced the same. At the beginning of a word or phrase, *b* and *v* sound like the *b* in "boy." Listen to and say these words:

voy bolígrafo vienen bien viejo video

In most other positions *b* and *v* have a softer "b" sound. The lips barely touch as the *b* or *v* sound is pronounced. Listen to and say these words:

abuelo divertido joven huevos globo Alberto

Try it out! Listen to and say this *trabalenguas:*

**Cabral clava un clavo.
¿Qué clavo clava Cabral?**

14 **¿Quiénes vienen?** ♻

Hablar

Estás en una fiesta en la escuela y hablas con los otros estudiantes.

1. ¿Quiénes vienen a la fiesta? ¿A qué hora vienen?

2. ¿Vienen todos los profesores a la fiesta? ¿Qué traen ellos?

3. ¿Traen los estudiantes pizza o sándwiches? ¿Frutas o pasteles?

4. ¿Quién trae las decoraciones? ¿Qué traes tú?

Más práctica

• **Guided** Gram. Practice pp. 175–176
• **Core** Gram. Practice p. 98
• **Communication** Writing p. 106
• *Real.* **para hispanohablantes** pp. 194–197

realidades.com ✔

• Audio Activities
• Video Activities
• Speak & Record
• Animated Grammar
• Leveled Workbook
• Web Code: jcd-0513

Gramática

The verbs *ser* and *estar*

You know that both *ser* and *estar* mean "to be." Their uses, however, are different.

(yo)	soy	(nosotros) (nosotras)	somos
(tú)	eres	(vosotros) (vosotras)	sois
Ud. (él) (ella)	es	Uds. (ellos) (ellas)	son

(yo)	estoy	(nosotros) (nosotras)	estamos
(tú)	estás	(vosotros) (vosotras)	estáis
Ud. (él) (ella)	está	Uds. (ellos) (ellas)	están

Use *ser* to talk about characteristics that generally do not change. *Ser* is used for descriptions that are not about conditions or location. For example:

- who a person is or what a person is like
- what something is or what something is like
- where a person or thing is from

Teresa **es** mi prima. **Es** muy graciosa.
Los tacos **son** mi comida favorita. **Son** riquísimos.
Mis tíos **son** de México. **Son** muy simpáticos.

Use *estar* to talk about conditions that tend to change. For example:

- how a person feels
- where a person or thing is

¿Dónde **está** Mariana? No **está** aquí.
No puede venir hoy porque **está** muy enferma.

GramActiva VIDEO

Want more help with *ser* and *estar*? Watch the **GramActiva** video.

---

15 **¿Dónde están las otras personas?**

Hablar

Estás en un café con un(a) amigo(a) y preguntas dónde están los otros amigos. Tu amigo(a) explica dónde están y cómo están.

Strategy

Using rhymes
To remember the uses of *estar*, memorize this rhyme:

For how you feel
And where you are,
Always use the verb *estar*.

Modelo

Marcos y Graciela **A** —¿Dónde están <u>Marcos y Graciela</u>?
 B —Están en <u>la biblioteca</u>. Están muy <u>ocupados</u>.

Estudiante A

1. Yolanda
2. Miguel y Fernando
3. Isabel y Raquel
4. Ana María
5. Federico
6. Enrique

Estudiante B

la escuela	ocupado, -a
casa	enfermo, -a
el trabajo	cansado, -a
la lección de . . .	triste
la biblioteca	mal
	contento, -a

¡Respuesta personal!

16 Entrevista con una chef ♻

Leer • Escribir

Lee la entrevista con la chef Ortiz y completa la conversación
con la forma apropiada del verbo *estar* o *ser*.

— Bienvenida, Chef Ortiz. ¿Cómo __1.__ Ud. hoy?
— __2.__ muy bien, gracias.
— Ud. trabaja aquí en Asunción ahora pero, ¿de dónde __3.__ Ud. originalmente?
— Mi familia y yo __4.__ del campo.
— ¿Y cuál __5.__ su trabajo aquí?
— Yo __6.__ directora de los chefs en el famoso restaurante La Capital.
— La Capital __7.__ un restaurante muy popular aquí. ¿Dónde __8.__ el restaurante?
— Al lado de la catedral.
— Los platos en su restaurante __9.__ muy típicos de Paraguay, ¿no?
— Sí, y según los clientes, la comida en nuestro restaurante __10.__ deliciosa.
— Y los postres __11.__ muy populares también, ¿no?
— Sí, tenemos pasteles ricos, helados simples con frutas exóticas, un poco de todo.
— ¡Muchas gracias, Chef Ortiz!
— De nada. Siempre __12.__ muy contenta de estar aquí con Uds.

¡Qué rico!

Paraguay

17 Un postre delicioso

Leer • Pensar

Your grandmother has given you her recipe for *arroz con leche* and you
want to try it out. But the ingredients are given in *gramos* and *litros* and
you don't know what the customary measure equivalents are. Study the
conversion chart, convert the measurements given in the recipe, and
answer the question.

ARROZ CON LECHE
Para 8

300 gramos de arroz   un poco de vainilla

3 litros de leche   canela[1]

400 gramos de azúcar

Pon el arroz en remojo[2] con la leche una hora y
media. Luego cocina a fuego lento[3] una hora más o
menos. Añade[4] el azúcar y la vainilla y cocina unos
5 minutos más. Pon el arroz en el refrigerador y
esparce[5] un poco de canela encima.

[1]cinnamon   [2]soak   [3]cook slowly   [4]Add   [5]sprinkle   [6]measure

Conexiones | Las matemáticas

> 1 kilo (k) = 2,2 libras *(pounds)*
> 1 gramo (g) = 0,035 onzas *(ounces)*
> 1 litro (l) = 1,057 cuartos *(quarts)*

Multiplica los kilos, gramos o litros por
su medida[6] correspondiente en el sistema
que usas.

Calcula las onzas o los cuartos que hay
en 300 gramos de arroz, tres litros de
leche y 400 gramos de azúcar.

• ¿Cuántas libras hay en dos kilos
de arroz?

18 ¡Es buenísimo para la salud!

Escribir · Hablar

Habla con otro(a) estudiante sobre cómo son las comidas en general.

❶ Escribe una lista de diez comidas y bebidas.

❷ Usa tu lista y pregunta a un(a) compañero(a) si come lo que le preguntas. Tu compañero(a) va a contestar y decirte por qué come o no come cada una de estas comidas.

> **Modelo**
>
> A —¿Comes muchas verduras?
> B —¡Por supuesto! Las verduras son muy buenas para la salud.
> o: —No. ¡Qué asco! Las verduras son horribles.

Nota
To describe what a food item is like in general, use *ser*. To describe how a food item tastes at a particular time, use *estar*.

bueno (para la salud)	sabroso
malo (para la salud)	delicioso
rico	horrible
riquísimo	

19 ¡La sopa está riquísima!

Hablar

Estás en un restaurante y el (la) camarero(a) te pregunta cómo está todo. Mira el menú para contestar.

> **Modelo**
>
> A —Señor(ita), ¿cómo está el arroz con pollo?
> B —Está muy sabroso. Me encanta.
> o: —Lo siento. Está malo. ¿Me trae otro plato principal?

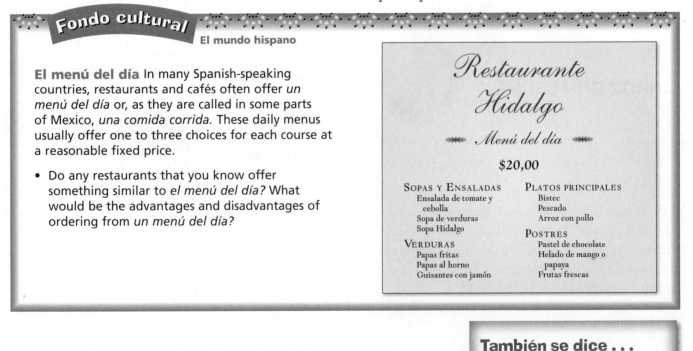

Fondo cultural

El mundo hispano

El menú del día In many Spanish-speaking countries, restaurants and cafés often offer *un menú del día* or, as they are called in some parts of Mexico, *una comida corrida*. These daily menus usually offer one to three choices for each course at a reasonable fixed price.

• Do any restaurants that you know offer something similar to *el menú del día*? What would be the advantages and disadvantages of ordering from *un menú del día*?

Restaurante
Hidalgo
❋ *Menú del día* ❋

$20,00

SOPAS Y ENSALADAS
 Ensalada de tomate y
  cebolla
 Sopa de verduras
 Sopa Hidalgo

VERDURAS
 Papas fritas
 Papas al horno
 Guisantes con jamón

PLATOS PRINCIPALES
 Bistec
 Pescado
 Arroz con pollo

POSTRES
 Pastel de chocolate
 Helado de mango o
  papaya
 Frutas frescas

También se dice . . .

el menú = la carta *(México, España)*

20 El menú del día

Escribir · Hablar

With a classmate, prepare to play the roles of a server and client *(cliente)* at the Restaurante Hidalgo, which is in San Juan, Puerto Rico. Write five questions that each one could ask. Use the menu in Actividad 19 to help you decide what to ask. Don't forget to use the formal *Ud.* form in your questions and answers.

Puerto Rico

Modelo

el (la) camarero(a)	el (la) cliente
¿Qué desea pedir de plato principal?	¿Cómo está el bistec?

21 En el restaurante

Hablar

Usa las preguntas y frases de la Actividad 20 para tener una conversación completa. En tu conversación habla de las sopas y ensaladas, verduras, platos principales y postres.

Modelo

A —¿Qué desea pedir de plato principal?
B —No sé. ¿Cómo está el bistec?
A —Está muy sabroso.
B —¡Genial! Quisiera el bistec, por favor.

El español en el mundo del trabajo

How can you combine an interest in nutrition and health with skills in Spanish? Here's one example. As you know, the U.S. Department of Agriculture provides the public with a wide range of nutritional information through print materials and Web sites. Much of this information is available in Spanish. There is a need for federal employees who are knowledgeable to translate and work with the Spanish-speaking community on issues related to nutrition.

• What other opportunities can you think of that would combine communication skills with a knowledge of nutrition?

Más práctica

• **Guided** Gram. Practice pp. 177–178
• **Core** Gram. Practice pp. 99–100
• **Communication** Writing p. 107, Test Prep p. 282
• *Real.* **para hispanohablantes** pp. 198–201

realidades.com

• Audio Activities
• Video Activities
• Speak & Record
• Tutorial
• Leveled Workbook
• Web Code: jcd-0514

Lectura

Una visita a Santa Fe

Lee esta carta que escriben Alicia y Pedro. Ellos hablan de una visita que van a hacer sus primos a Santa Fe. ¿Qué cosas interesantes van a hacer? ¿Qué van a visitar?

Nuevo México

Queridos Rosario y Luis:

¡Esperamos[1] su visita en agosto! Aquí en Santa Fe vamos a hacer muchas cosas. ¿Saben que es una ciudad[2] con más de 400 años de historia y cultura? Vamos a visitar museos y tiendas, y vamos a comer comida típica. ¡Los cinco días van a pasar rápidamente![3]

Tenemos planes para pasar una noche muy especial en honor de su visita. Vamos a comer en un "restaurante" histórico que se llama Rancho de las Golondrinas[4]. Está a diez millas de nuestra casa, al sur de Santa Fe. El Rancho, en realidad, no es un restaurante; es una casa española.

Durante los días de su visita, el Rancho va a celebrar "un fandango", un baile histórico y típico, con una cena tradicional. Toda la comida es riquísima, pero nuestro plato favorito es el chile con carne y queso. Después de comer, vamos a bailar. ¡No sabemos bailar pero va a ser muy divertido! Mandamos[5] el menú con la carta.

¡Nos vemos en agosto!

Sus primos de Nuevo México,

Alicia y Pedro

Un paraje[6] en El Camino Real[7] desde la Ciudad de México hasta Santa Fe, es del año 1710. Ahora es un museo.

[1] We're looking forward to [2] city [3] quickly [4] Swallows
[5] We're sending [6] stopping place [7] the Royal Highway

❧ Menú del Fandango ☙

Sopas
Sopa de arroz

Garbanzos con chile

Plato principal
Pollo relleno[8]

Chile con carne y queso

Postre
Bizcochitos[9]

Pudín de arroz con leche

Bebidas
Chocolate mexicano

Ponche

Café

[8]Stuffed chicken   [9]Cookies

La Capilla de San Miguel, la iglesia más vieja de Santa Fe, del año 1626

El Palacio de los Gobernadores, construído en 1610, es el edificio (building) público más viejo de los Estados Unidos que todavía se usa. Ahora es un museo de historia.

¿Comprendes?

1. ¿Cuáles son cuatro actividades que los primos van a hacer durante la visita? ¿Cuál te gustaría hacer en Santa Fe?

2. ¿Por qué es importante Santa Fe?

3. ¿Por qué quieren ir Alicia y Pedro al Rancho de las Golondrinas?

4. Si no te gusta nada la comida picante (spicy), ¿qué debes pedir del menú?

5. ¿Por qué es importante La Capilla de San Miguel?

Más práctica

- **Guided** Reading Support p. 179
- **Communication** Writing p. 108, Test Prep p. 283
- **Real. para hispanohablantes** pp. 202–203

realidades.com ✔
- Internet Activity
- Leveled Workbook
- Web Code: jcd-0515

Fondo cultural
Los Estados Unidos

¡A pensar! Santa Fe was established thirteen years before Plymouth Colony was settled by the Mayflower Pilgrims. It has been a seat of government for Spain, Mexico, and the Confederacy.

- Find out when the oldest building in your community was built. How does it differ in age from the Palacio de los Gobernadores in Santa Fe?

Perspectivas del mundo hispano

A la hora de comer

Imagine that you had two hours for lunch every day. Or imagine that every time you ate a meal, you sat down at a table with a friend or family member and had a lengthy conversation. Now imagine that you didn't jump up from dinner as soon as you finished eating. What do these situations have in common?

Una familia en Escazú, Costa Rica

In many Spanish-speaking cultures, even ordinary mealtimes are considered social events, a time to spend enjoying food and company. People often take time after a meal to relax, to sit around the table and enjoy a good conversation or just to have a laugh. This custom, called the *sobremesa,* is more important in many cultures than getting to the next appointment or saving time and money by buying a quick meal.

Not surprisingly, most Spanish-speaking countries have very few drive-through restaurants. Since people rarely take food "to go," they might be surprised if you suggested grabbing a sandwich to eat in the car. In fact, many cars don't have cup-holders.

A los jóvenes de muchos países hispanos les gusta hacer la sobremesa con amigos o con la familia. Los jóvenes en la foto pasan el tiempo en la Plaza Mayor de Madrid, España.

Check it out! Figure out how much time you and your family spend at breakfast, lunch, and dinner on days when you're not in school or at work. Compare your results with those of your classmates. Then complete the following statements about practices among families in your community.

| Modelo |

En mi comunidad, es común *(common)* comer el desayuno en <u>quince minutos</u>.

1. En mi comunidad, es común comer el desayuno en _____ .
2. En mi comunidad, es común comer el almuerzo en _____ .
3. En mi comunidad, es común comer la cena en _____ .

Think about it! What does your research say about the importance of relaxing and enjoying a leisurely meal with friends and family? How does it compare to what happens during meals in Spanish-speaking countries? Consider the two different attitudes towards mealtime. What benefits might each one have?

Presentación escrita
Un restaurante muy bueno

Strategy

Persuasion
Give specific information and concrete examples to persuade your readers to try a restaurant.

Task
Your school is developing a community guide for Spanish-speaking residents. Your class is in charge of writing about restaurants. Write a review of your favorite restaurant.

❶ **Prewrite** Think about the restaurant you and your family like best. Copy the word web. Write the name of the restaurant you are reviewing in the middle circle. Write words and expressions associated with each category inside the appropriate circles.

❷ **Draft** Write your review of the restaurant using information from the word web. Try to include any information that might persuade others to try the restaurant.

❸ **Revise** Read through your review and check for agreement, verb forms, and spelling. Share your review with a partner. Your partner should check the following:

• Did you provide information about all categories?

• Did you use the correct forms of the verbs?

• Do you have any errors in spelling or agreement?

• Is the review persuasive?

❹ **Publish** Write a final copy of your review and make any necessary changes or additions. You may want to add illustrations and include your review in a booklet with your classmates' reviews or in your portfolio.

❺ **Evaluation** Your teacher may give you a rubric for grading your review. You may be evaluated on:

• how complete the task was

• how you used new and previously learned vocabulary

• how accurate the agreement, verb forms, and spelling are

• correct use of verbs

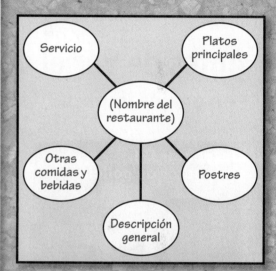

¿Eres tú, María?

Episodio 2

Antes de ver el video

Personajes importantes

Inspector Gil,
inspector de policía

Inspector Peña,
inspector de policía

Doña Gracia Salazar,
la víctima del crimen

Resumen del episodio

En este episodio, la ambulancia llega¹ y lleva²
a doña Gracia Salazar al hospital. También
llegan dos inspectores de policía. Le hablan a
doña Lupe, la portera, sobre el incidente en el
piso de doña Gracia. Lola se presenta³ a los dos
hombres y les dice⁴ lo que sabe del incidente.

¹arrives ²takes away ³introduces herself ⁴tells them

Nota cultural In the cities and towns of Spain
and many Spanish-speaking countries, you will
find *plazas*, open squares that are surrounded by
buildings. The *plazas* are the social center of the
community or neighborhood. They may contain
benches, trees and flowers, statues, and fountains.
In the evening, neighbors will spend time in the
plaza sharing details about families, daily events,
politics, and many other topics.

Palabras para comprender

vive *(vivir)*	she lives *(to live)*
la sobrina	niece
esperar	to wait
anoche	last night
vi *(ver)*	I saw *(to see)*
una barba	beard
¿Quién era?	Who was she?
ayudar	to help
saber	to know

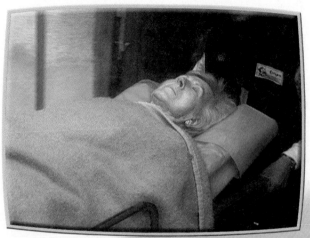

"Es doña Gracia Salazar. Vive en el tercer piso con su sobrina, María".

"Anoche a la una de la mañana, vi a un hombre y a una mujer".

—¿Ud. es detective pero no tiene una descripción exacta ni del hombre ni de la mujer?

—A la una de la mañana es imposible ver mucho, ¿no?

Después de ver el video

¿Comprendes?

A. ¿Quién . . . ?

1. ¿Quién es la víctima?

2. ¿Quiénes viven en el tercer piso?

3. ¿Quién es la sobrina?

4. ¿Quién es doña Lupe?

5. ¿Quiénes llegan para investigar el crimen?

6. ¿Quién espera en la plaza?

7. ¿Quién dice que es imposible ver mucho a la una de la mañana?

8. ¿Quién quiere ayudar a los inspectores?

B. Escoge una de las fotos de esta página y escribe tres frases para describir la foto.

• Web Code: jcd-0507

Repaso del capítulo

Vocabulario y gramática

jcd-0599 🔊

Chapter Review

To prepare for the test, check to see if you . . .
- **know the new vocabulary and grammar**
- **can perform the tasks on p. 269**

to talk about people

el hombre	man
la mujer	woman
el joven	young man
la joven	young woman

to describe people and things

alto, -a	tall
bajo, -a	short (stature)
corto, -a	short (length)
guapo, -a	good-looking
joven	young
largo, -a	long
viejo, -a	old
el pelo	hair
canoso	gray
castaño	brown (chestnut)
negro	black
rubio	blond
pelirrojo, -a	red-haired

to describe how someone is feeling

tener calor	to be warm
tener frío	to be cold
tener sueño	to be sleepy

to talk about food

delicioso, -a	delicious
desear	to want
pedir (e → i)	to order
el plato principal	main dish
de plato principal	as a main dish
el postre	dessert
de postre	for dessert
rico, -a	rich, tasty

For *Vocabulario adicional*, see pp. 472–473.

to describe table settings

el azúcar	sugar
la cuchara	spoon
el cuchillo	knife
la pimienta	pepper
el plato	plate, dish
la sal	salt
la servilleta	napkin
la taza	cup
el tenedor	fork
el vaso	glass

to talk about eating out

el camarero, la camarera	waiter, waitress
la cuenta	bill
el menú	menu

to express needs

Me falta(n) . . .	I need . . .
Quisiera	I would like
traer	to bring
Le traigo . . .	I will bring you . . .
¿Me trae . . . ?	Will you bring me . . . ?
yo traigo	I bring

other useful words

ahora	now
¿Algo más?	Anything else?
De nada.	You're welcome.
otro, -a	other, another
¡Qué + adjective!	How . . . !

venir *to come*

vengo	venimos
vienes	venís
viene	vienen

Más práctica

- **Core** Puzzle p. 101, Organizer p. 102
- **Communication** Practice Test pp. 285–287, Integrated Performance Assessment p. 284

realidades.com ⊙

- Tutorial
- Flashcards
- Puzzles
- Self-test
- Web Code: jcd-0516

Preparación para el examen

On the exam you will be asked to . . .	Here are practice tasks similar to those you will find on the exam . . .	If you need review . . .

Interpretive

jcd-0599

1 Escuchar Listen and understand as people complain to room service that something is missing from their order

As you listen to complaints about room service, see if you can tell if there is: a) missing silverware; b) missing food; c) missing condiments; d) all of the above.

pp. 248–251 *Vocabulario en contexto,* Actividad 2
p. 254 Actividades 8–9
p. 260 Actividades 18–19

Interpersonal

2 Hablar Describe physical characteristics of family members to another person

Your aunt and uncle are going to celebrate their anniversary with you in a restaurant, but they're late. You describe them to the waiter so that he can recognize them when they arrive. Mention at least two physical characteristics about each person, such as hair color, height, or age.

pp. 248–251 *Vocabulario en contexto*
p. 252 Actividades 4–5
p. 256 Actividad 12

Interpretive

3 Leer Read and understand a letter about an upcoming visit with a relative

As you read part of a letter about an upcoming trip to Santa Fe, can you determine what the writers are most looking forward to in the trip? What questions do they have about it?

Queridos Alicia y Pedro:
Nosotros también esperamos impacientemente nuestra visita a Santa Fe en el verano. Me encanta la idea de visitar una ciudad con mucha historia. Nuestra ciudad también es muy histórica. ¿Qué es una comida típica del Rancho de las Golondrinas?

p. 255 Actividad 10
p. 262 *Lectura*

Presentational

4 Escribir Write a short report telling whether people are coming to an event and what they are bringing with them

You and your classmates decide to bring either a main dish, dessert, eating utensils, glassware, plates, or condiments for the Spanish Club party. Write a note to the club president indicating who is coming and what they are bringing. For example: *Ryan viene y trae las servilletas.*

p. 256 Actividad 11
p. 257 Actividades 13–14
p. 265 *Presentación escrita*

Comparisons

5 Pensar Demonstrate an understanding of cultural perspectives regarding meals

Think about how you spend lunch or dinner time during the school week. What would be at least three things that would be different at mealtime if you were an exchange student in a Spanish-speaking country? What is a *sobremesa*?

p. 253 *Fondo cultural*
p. 260 *Fondo cultural*
p. 264 *Perspectivas del mundo hispano*

Fondo cultural

España

Salvador Dalí (1904–1989) was a painter born in Figueras, Spain. This is one of his most famous paintings, made when he was only 20. Here he has painted his sister, who appears only from the back.

• Why do you think that Dalí painted her looking out the window rather than facing the viewer?

"Muchacha en la ventana" (1925), Salvador Dalí ▶

© 2009 Salvador Dalí, Gala-Salvador Dalí Foundation/Artists Rights Society (ARS), New York.
Photo: Museo Español de Arte Contemporáneo, Madrid, Spain/ The Bridgeman Art Library.

Capítulo 6A

Calle Caminito, en Buenos Aires, Argentina

En mi dormitorio

Chapter Objectives

- Talk about your bedroom
- Describe bedroom items and electronic equipment
- Make comparisons
- Understand cultural perspectives on homes

Video Highlights

Videocultura: *La casa*

A primera vista: *El cuarto de Ignacio*

GramActiva Videos: making comparisons; the superlative; stem-changing verbs: *poder* and *dormir*

Videomisterio: *¿Eres tú, María?,* Episodio 3

Country Connection

As you learn how to describe your bedroom, you will make connections to these countries and places:

- España
- Estados Unidos
- México
- Colombia
- Argentina
- Uruguay

Más práctica

- *Real.* para hispanohablantes pp. 210–211

realidades.com

- Fondo cultural Activity
- Video Activities
- Online Atlas
- Web Code: jce-0002

Vocabulario en contexto

jcd-0687

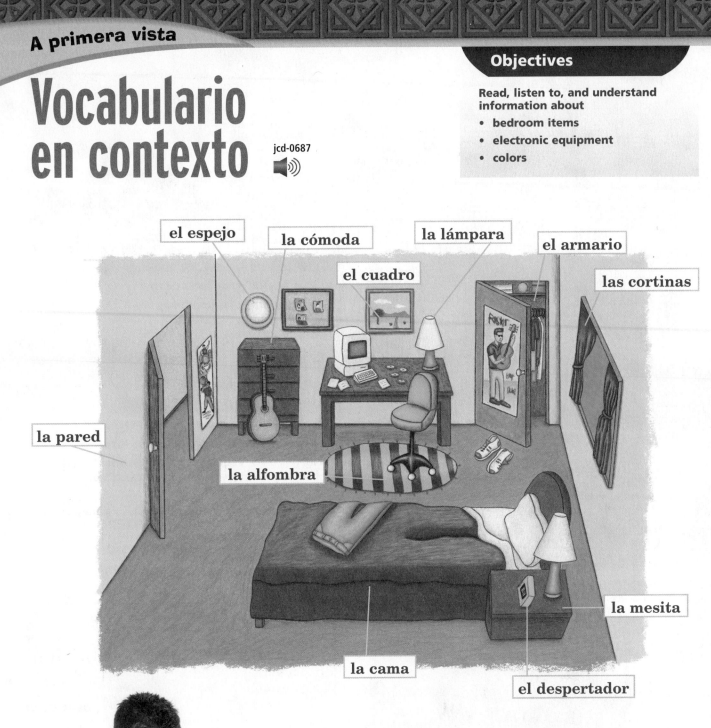

el espejo

la cómoda

la lámpara

el armario

el cuadro

las cortinas

la pared

la alfombra

la mesita

la cama

el despertador

" Tengo **un dormitorio pequeño.** Las paredes son azules. Tengo carteles de mis grupos musicales favoritos en las paredes. Generalmente mi dormitorio está muy desordenado, pero hoy está ordenado. No comparto el dormitorio con otra persona—es mi **propio** dormitorio.

En mi dormitorio tengo todas mis **posesiones más importantes:** mi guitarra, mis discos compactos, mis fotos, mi computadora. ¿Por qué me gusta mucho mi dormitorio? ¡Está encima del garaje! ¡Es **el mejor** dormitorio para tocar y escuchar música! **"**

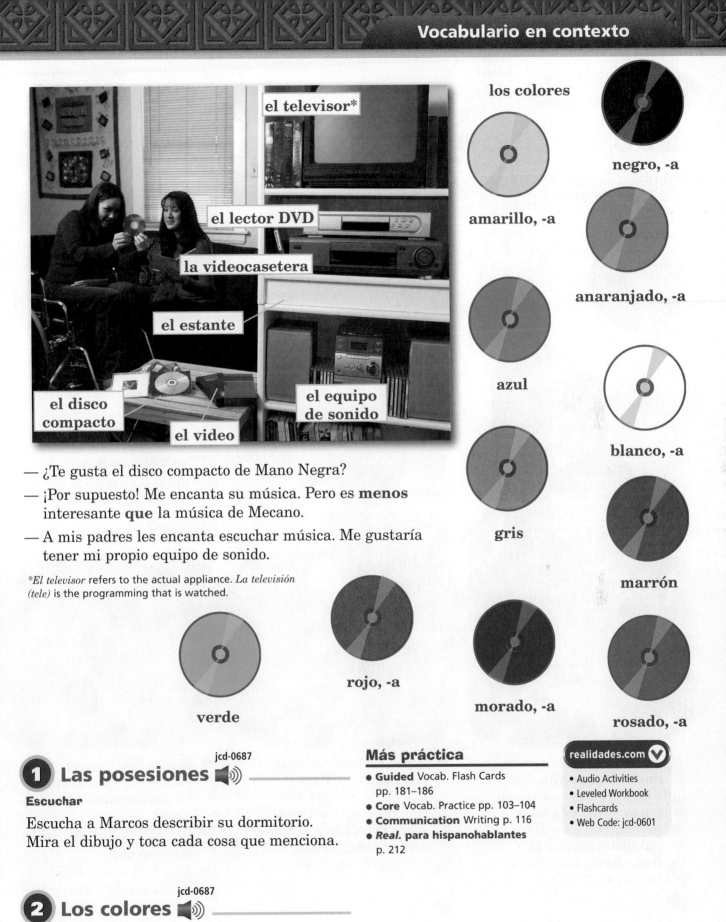

el televisor*

el lector DVD

la videocasetera

el estante

el disco
compacto

el video

el equipo
de sonido

los colores

negro, -a

amarillo, -a

anaranjado, -a

azul

blanco, -a

gris

marrón

rojo, -a

morado, -a

verde

rosado, -a

— ¿Te gusta el disco compacto de Mano Negra?

— ¡Por supuesto! Me encanta su música. Pero es **menos** interesante **que** la música de Mecano.

— A mis padres les encanta escuchar música. Me gustaría tener mi propio equipo de sonido.

El televisor refers to the actual appliance. *La televisión (tele)* is the programming that is watched.

---

jcd-0687

1 Las posesiones 🔊 ——————————

Escuchar

Escucha a Marcos describir su dormitorio. Mira el dibujo y toca cada cosa que menciona.

jcd-0687

2 Los colores 🔊 ——————————

Escuchar

Cuando escuches el nombre de un color, señala algo en estas páginas que es de ese color.

Más práctica

- **Guided** Vocab. Flash Cards pp. 181–186
- **Core** Vocab. Practice pp. 103–104
- **Communication** Writing p. 116
- *Real.* **para hispanohablantes** p. 212

realidades.com ✓

- Audio Activities
- Leveled Workbook
- Flashcards
- Web Code: jcd-0601

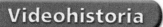

jcd-0687 🔊

El cuarto de Ignacio

¡El cuarto de Ignacio está muy desordenado!

España

Strategy

Using prior experience
Have you ever had someone go in and change things around in your room? How did you feel? Look at the photos and guess how Ignacio and his mother feel.

Ignacio

Mamá

1 **Mamá:** Mira este cuarto . . . ¡qué **feo!** ¡Está muy desordenado! Ignacio, ¿cómo puedes hacer esto?

También se dice . . .

el **dormitorio** = el *cuarto*
(España)

5 **Mamá:** Tu cuarto está mucho más **bonito.** Los libros **grandes** están aquí, y **a la izquierda** están las revistas. Y los discos compactos están **a la derecha de** los libros. Es mejor, ¿no crees?

6 **Ignacio:** Mamá, no es el **mismo** cuarto. **Para ti,** está **mejor que** antes, pero **para mí,** está **peor.** Tengo todas mis posesiones más importantes aquí y ahora no sé dónde están.

7 **Mamá:** Pero Ignacio, ¿cómo puedes **dormir** con todas las cosas encima de la cama?

Ignacio: Mamá, siempre **duermo** bien.

Mamá: ¡Ay! Está bien. Nunca más voy a organizar tu cuarto.

2 **Mamá:** ¿**De qué color** es esta camiseta? ¿Gris? ¿Blanca? Y esta camiseta de muchos colores, ¿qué es? ¡Ay, tengo que trabajar mucho en este cuarto!

3 **Mamá:** ¿Qué **podemos** hacer con este cuarto? El cuadro va en la pared y la lámpara va en la mesita. ¡Ay, ay, ay!

4 **Ignacio:** ¡Mamá! ¡Mi cuarto! ¡Mis **cosas**! ¿Dónde están?

8 **Ignacio:** ¡Eres la mejor mamá! Muchas gracias.
Mamá: De nada, Ignacio.

3 **¿Cierto o falso?** _____

Leer • Escribir

Lee las frases y decide si son ciertas o falsas. Si una frase es falsa, escríbela con la información correcta.

1. El cuarto de Ignacio siempre está muy ordenado.

2. La madre de Ignacio no está contenta.

3. La madre de Ignacio trabaja en el cuarto de Ignacio.

4. Ignacio no puede dormir bien en su cama.

5. Ahora Ignacio sabe dónde están todas sus posesiones.

6. A Ignacio no le gusta el trabajo de su madre.

7. Mañana la madre de Ignacio va a organizar el cuarto de Ignacio.

Más práctica

- **Guided** Vocab. Check pp. 187–190
- **Core** Vocab. Practice pp. 105–106
- **Communication** Video pp. 109–111
- *Real.* **para hispanohablantes** p. 213

realidades.com ✔

- Audio Activities
- Video Activities
- Leveled Workbook
- Flashcards
- Web Code: jcd-0602

Vocabulario en uso

4 Las palabras opuestas _____

Escribir

Escribe las palabras de la lista y su opuesto *(opposite)*.

Strategy

Making word associations
Learning vocabulary as opposites helps you make quick associations to other words.

Modelo

día   *noche*

1. bonito   3. derecha   5. alto   7. ordenado
2. grande   4. peor   6. negro   8. joven

5 Escucha, dibuja 🔊 jcd-0688 y escribe

Escuchar • Escribir

Copia el dibujo en una hoja de papel. Vas a escuchar a Celia describir su dormitorio. Dibuja las cosas que ella menciona en los lugares *(places)* correctos y escribe las palabras en español para cada cosa.

Tocando la guitarra, en México

También se dice . . .

el dormitorio = la habitación, la alcoba *(España);* la pieza *(Argentina, Chile);* la recámara *(México)*

bonito = lindo, chulo *(México);* mono *(España)*

marrón = de color café, castaño, de color chocolate *(México, América del Sur)*

la cómoda = el gavetero, el buró *(México, muchos países)*

el armario = el guardarropa, el ropero *(México, muchos países)*

pequeño = chico *(México, otros países)*

6 Tu propio dormitorio

Dibujar · Escribir

1 Dibuja tu propio dormitorio. Escribe el nombre de ocho cosas en el dibujo.

2 Escribe siete frases para describir o *(either)* tu dormitorio o el dormitorio de Celia de la Actividad 5.

Modelo

El espejo está al lado de la cama.
Las cortinas en el dormitorio son largas.

¿Recuerdas?

Use *estar* to tell the location of items.

Use *ser* to tell what items are like.

---

7 ¿Qué dormitorio es?

Escuchar · Hablar

Trabaja con otro(a) estudiante. Muestra *(Show)* los dibujos de tu dormitorio y del dormitorio de Celia a tu compañero(a). Lee una de las frases que escribiste *(that you wrote)* en la Actividad 6. Tu compañero(a) tiene que identificar qué dormitorio describes.

Modelo

A —*El espejo está al lado de la cama.*
B —*Es tu propio dormitorio.*
o: —*Es el dormitorio de Celia.*

Strategy

Labeling
Put Spanish labels on the items in your bedroom so that you will see them every day. This will help you learn new words quickly.

---

8 Juego

Escuchar · Hablar

Trabajen en grupos de tres personas. Necesitan una moneda *(coin)* y uno de los dibujos de la Actividad 6. Una persona describe dónde está la moneda en el dormitorio. Los otros dos tratan de colocar *(try to place)* la moneda en el cuarto correctamente. La primera persona que coloca la moneda correctamente recibe un punto.

Modelo

La moneda está debajo de la cama.

9 ¿Quién soy yo?

Leer · Pensar · Hablar

Aquí tienes una adivinanza *(riddle)* popular en las escuelas primarias en México. Trabaja con otro(a) estudiante para resolver la adivinanza.

**Cine no soy,
radio tampoco.
Tengo pantalla
y me creen poco.
¿Quién soy yo?**

Gramática

Making comparisons

Just as you can use *más . . . que* to compare two things, you can also use **menos . . . que** (*less . . . than*).

> El disco compacto de Los Toros es **menos** popular **que** el disco compacto de Los Lobos.
>
> *The CD by Los Toros is **less** popular **than** the CD by Los Lobos.*

The adjectives *bueno(a), malo(a), viejo(a),* and *joven* and the adverbs *bien* and *mal* have their own comparative forms. *Más* and *menos* are not used with these comparative adjectives and adverbs.

Adjective	Adverb	Comparative	
bueno, -a	bien	mejor (que)	*better than*
malo, -a	mal	peor (que)	*worse than*
viejo, -a		mayor (que)	*older than*
joven		menor (que)	*younger than*

Mejor, peor, mayor, and *menor* have plural forms that end in *-es.*

> Los discos compactos son **mejores que** los casetes.

¿Recuerdas?

You have learned to use *más . . . que* to compare two things.

- La clase de inglés es **más** interesante **que** la clase de matemáticas.

GramActiva VIDEO

Want more help with comparisons? Watch the **GramActiva** video.

más . . . que
menos . . . que

---

jcd-0688

🔟 Dos dormitorios 🔊

Escuchar • Escribir

En una hoja de papel, escribe los números del 1 al 6. Escucha las seis comparaciones de los dormitorios de Paco y de Kiko. Escribe *C* si la frase es cierta o *F* si es falsa.

El dormitorio de Paco

El dormitorio de Kiko

11 ¡Viva la música!

Escribir • Hablar

1 Escribe cinco frases con comparaciones de los varios tipos de música que ves aquí. Usa estos (these) adjetivos en la forma correcta con *más . . . que* o *menos . . . que.*

aburrido, -a	interesante
bonito, -a	popular
divertido, -a	serio, -a
feo, -a	triste
importante	

Modelo
Para mí, la salsa es más divertida que la música rap.

2 Lee tus comparaciones a otro(a) estudiante para ver si Uds. están de acuerdo.

Modelo
A —*Para mí, la salsa es más divertida que la música rap.*

B —*Sí, estoy de acuerdo, pero la salsa es menos popular que la música rap.*

12 ¿Cómo se comparan los dos?

Escribir • Hablar

Con otro(a) estudiante, escoge dos cosas o personas de cada categoría de la lista. En una hoja de papel, escribe una comparación de las dos. Después, túrnate (take turns) con tu compañero(a) para leer tus comparaciones y dar (give) tus opiniones.

Modelo
actividades

A —*Para mí, ir al cine es mejor que ver un video.*

B —*Estoy de acuerdo. Ver un video es menos divertido que ir al cine.*

1. actividades
2. deportes
3. comidas
4. clases
5. libros o revistas
6. personas famosas

Para decir más . . .

los blues	la música rap
la música reggae	el jazz
la música clásica	la música rock
la música folklórica	la salsa
la música hip-hop	

Fondo cultural
El mundo hispano

Latin Grammy awards recognize the talent of Spanish and Portuguese speaking artists every year. In 2005, Juanes won three Grammys for best rock song, music video, and rock solo vocalist.

• Who are some Latin recording artists you enjoy and what is their music like?

El cantante Juanes, de Colombia

Más práctica
- **Guided** Gram. Practice p. 191
- **Core** Gram. Practice p. 107
- **Communication** Writing p. 117
- ***Real.* para hispanohablantes** pp. 214–216

realidades.com
- Audio Activities
- Video Activities
- Speak & Record
- Tutorial
- Leveled Workbook
- Web Code: jcd-0603

Gramática

The superlative

To say that someone or something is the "most" or "least," use:

> definite article (**el, la, los, las**) + noun + **más / menos** + adjective

La foto de mi familia es **la posesión más importante** para mí.

To say that someone or something is the "best" or the "worst," use:

> definite article + **mejor(es) / peor(es)** + noun

Rojo y azul son **los mejores colores** para mi dormitorio.

GramActiva VIDEO

Want more help with the superlative? Watch the **GramActiva** video.

el mejor

13 Las casas de los ricos y famosos

Hablar

Un grupo de personas del programa de televisión "Las casas de los ricos y famosos" está en tu casa. Habla con el grupo sobre las cosas especiales en tu casa. Pregunta y contesta según el modelo.

1. posesión / importante
2. disco compacto / popular
3. video / gracioso
4. foto / bonita
5. videojuego / divertido
6. libro / interesante

Modelo
cuadro/bonito
A —*Para ti, ¿cuál es el cuadro más bonito?*
B —*Para mí, el cuadro más bonito es el cuadro de las flores rojas y amarillas.*

14 Los premios Héctor

Hablar · Escribir

① En grupos de cuatro estudiantes, pregunta y contesta sobre las mejores y peores cosas del año. Decide el (la) mejor y el (la) peor de cada categoría de la lista y escribe una frase para cada una.

Modelo
el mes

A —*Para ti, ¿cuál es el mejor mes del año?*
B —*Para mí, el mejor mes del año es junio.*
A —*¿Y cuál es el peor mes del año?*
B —*El peor mes del año es enero.*

1. el programa de televisión
2. el video
3. el grupo musical
4. la película
5. el disco compacto

② Prepara una presentación para la clase para dar un premio (*give a prize*) Héctor para las categorías indicadas.

Modelo
Nuestro grupo da el premio Héctor para el mejor mes del año a junio.
Nuestro grupo da el premio Héctor para el peor mes del año a enero.

HÉCTOR

15 Tus propias cosas

Hablar · Escribir

❶ Habla con otro(a) estudiante sobre las cosas que tienes en tu dormitorio. Pregunta y contesta según el modelo. Escribe las respuestas en una hoja de papel.

> **Modelo**
> A —*¿Tienes tu propia videocasetera?*
> B —*Sí, tengo mi propia videocasetera. ¿Y tú?*
> A —*No, pero puedo usar la videocasetera de mi familia.*

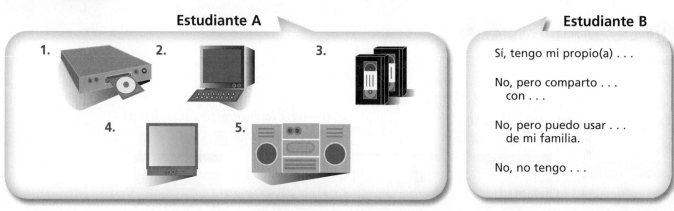

Estudiante A

1. 2. 3.

4. 5.

Estudiante B

Sí, tengo mi propio(a) . . .

No, pero comparto . . . con . . .

No, pero puedo usar . . . de mi familia.

No, no tengo . . .

❷ Trabajen con otra pareja. Sumen *(Add together)* los resultados del paso *(step)* 1. Escriban frases para presentar los resultados a la clase. Compartan los resultados del grupo de ustedes con los otros grupos y sumen los resultados de toda la clase.

> **Modelo**
> *Cuatro estudiantes tienen computadoras en sus casas.*

❸ Determinen un porcentaje *(percentage)* para cada aparato *(appliance)* tecnológico y creen *(create)* una gráfica para demostrar los resultados.

16 Cataluña y la tecnología

Comparar · Escribir · Hablar

Estudia la gráfica y contesta las preguntas.

1. ¿Cuáles son los aparatos más populares en las casas en la región de Cataluña, en España?

2. Haz una encuesta en tu clase. Escribe frases para comparar los resultados de tu clase y la información de la gráfica.

> **Modelo**
> *Nosotros tenemos más lectores DVD que . . .*

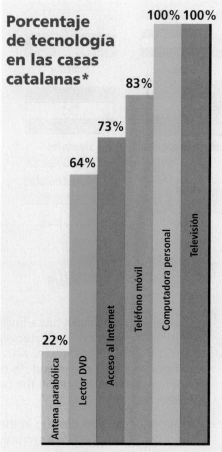

Porcentaje de tecnología en las casas catalanas*

100% 100%

83%

73%

64%

22%

Antena parabólica

Lector DVD

Acceso al Internet

Teléfono móvil

Computadora personal

Televisión

*Datos de 2005

17 ¿De qué color es tu día?

Pensar · Escribir · Hablar

¿Cuáles son los colores que asocias con estas palabras? Escribe los colores.

Modelo

regular   *gris*

1. contento
2. calor
3. artístico
4. horrible
5. reservado
6. triste
7. frío
8. sociable
9. gracioso
10. aburrido

Y para ti, ¿cuál es el color de tu personalidad?

18 Las banderas

Hablar

Identifica los colores de las banderas de los países *(countries)* o lugares de habla hispana. Trabaja con otro(a) estudiante.

Modelo

A —*La bandera tiene los colores rojo, amarillo y verde.*
B —*¿Es la bandera de Bolivia?*
A —*Sí.*

Argentina   Bolivia   Chile   Colombia   Costa Rica

Cuba   Ecuador   El Salvador   España   Guatemala

Guinea Ecuatorial   Honduras   Nicaragua   Panamá   Paraguay

Perú   Puerto Rico   República Dominicana   Uruguay   Venezuela

Fondo cultural
México

La bandera mexicana has a fascinating history. According to tradition, the Aztecs were to build their capital city, Tenochtitlán, where they found an eagle perched on a cactus and devouring a serpent. This image is what you see in the center of the Mexican flag today.

• What flags can you identify in the United States that also contain a symbol with historical significance?

19 ¿Qué significan los colores?

Leer • Pensar • Escribir

En la psicología, hay un estudio de los significados *(meanings)* de diferentes colores en diferentes culturas. Lee las descripciones aquí para contestar las preguntas.

Conexiones Las ciencias sociales

En muchas culturas, el verde significa buena salud, la primavera, las plantas y tranquilidad. Es un color de la paz.[1]

El blanco, en las culturas de las Américas, significa generalmente inocencia y paz. En ciertas culturas asiáticas, el blanco significa la muerte.[2]

El color que expresa energía, pasión y acción en muchas culturas diferentes es el rojo.

En muchas culturas, el amarillo significa atención, precaución, el sol y energía. Es muy fácil ver el amarillo y se usa mucho para los taxis.

Un color que expresa protección, autoridad, confianza[3] y armonía es el azul. Vemos este color mucho en los uniformes de la policía y los militares.

[1]peace [2]death [3]confidence

Find words or expressions in the reading to explain the following uses of color:
- yellow traffic light
- green recycling symbol
- blue police uniform
- red roses for Valentine's Day

20 Una bandera para ti

Escribir • Hablar

Imagina que vas a diseñar *(design)* una bandera para una organización, un club o un equipo *(team)*. ¿Qué colores vas a usar? ¿Por qué?

21 Y tú, ¿qué dices?

Escribir • Hablar

1. ¿Cuáles son tus colores favoritos? ¿Qué posesiones tienes en tu dormitorio de estos colores?

2. Escribe una lista de cinco cosas que están en tu dormitorio y el color de cada cosa. Por ejemplo: *Tengo una lámpara anaranjada.*

3. ¿De qué colores son los libros y las carpetas que tienes para tus clases?

Más práctica

- **Guided** Gram. Practice p. 191
- **Core** Gram. Practice p. 108
- **Communication** Writing p. 118
- ***Real.* para hispanohablantes** p. 217, p. 219, p. 221

realidades.com V
- Audio Activities
- Video Activities
- Speak & Record
- Tutorial
- Leveled Workbook
- Web Code: jcd-0604

Gramática

Stem-changing verbs: *poder* and *dormir*

Like *jugar, poder* and *dormir* are stem-changing verbs.
They have a change from *o → ue* in all forms except
nosotros and *vosotros*. Here are the present-tense forms:

(yo)	**pued**o	(nosotros) (nosotras)	**pod**emos
(tú)	**pued**es	(vosotros) (vosotras)	**pod**éis
Ud. (él) (ella)	**pued**e	Uds. (ellos) (ellas)	**pued**en

(yo)	**duerm**o	(nosotros) (nosotras)	**dorm**imos
(tú)	**duerm**es	(vosotros) (vosotras)	**dorm**ís
Ud. (él) (ella)	**duerm**e	Uds. (ellos) (ellas)	**duerm**en

GramActiva VIDEO

Want more help
with these
stem-changing verbs?
Watch the
GramActiva video.

Él duerme.

22 Rompecabezas

Leer • Escribir • Pensar

¿Cuántas horas duermen las personas en esta familia?
Escribe la forma apropiada del verbo *dormir* para cada
frase. Después contesta la pregunta.

¡Mis hermanos y yo __1.__ 50 horas al día! Es mucho, ¿no? Tomás, mi
hermano mayor, __2.__ menos, seis horas al día. Catalina __3.__ más
horas que todos—cuatro horas más que Tomás. Guillermo y yo __4.__
el mismo número de horas. Juntos *(Together)* nosotros __5.__ el mismo
número de horas que Tomás y Catalina. Paco y Laura __6.__ el mismo
número de horas. ¿Cuántas horas duerme cada persona (Tomás,
Catalina, Guillermo, Paco, Laura y yo)?

Nota

When the forms of *poder* are
followed by another verb, the
second verb is in the infinitive form.

• Ana no **puede hablar** español.

jcd-0688

23 El campamento Nadadivertido ◀))

Escuchar • Escribir • Hablar

Es el primer día en el campamento de verano Nadadivertido. Tu amigo(a) nunca escucha nada.
Escucha las reglas *(rules)* del campamento y después contesta las preguntas de tu amigo(a).

1. ¿Podemos usar el equipo de sonido en la
   tarde?

2. ¿Quiénes no pueden ir a los dormitorios de
   los chicos?

3. ¿Podemos ver videos en los dormitorios?

4. ¿Cuándo podemos escuchar discos compactos?

5. ¿Podemos beber refrescos en la cama?

6. ¿Podemos dormir hasta *(until)* las nueve?

24 Las reglas

Escribir • Hablar

Tienes que cuidar *(baby-sit)* a dos niños y no sabes las reglas de su casa. Primero escribe cinco preguntas para ellos. Después pregunta y contesta según el modelo. Aquí está una lista de verbos que puedes usar:

beber	escuchar	jugar
comer	ir	ver

Modelo

A —*¿Uds. pueden comer helado después de las siete?*

B —*No, nunca podemos comer helado después de las siete.*

o: —*¡Por supuesto! Siempre podemos comer helado después de las siete.*

25 ¡Podemos hacer muchas cosas!

Hablar

Trabaja con otro(a) estudiante para decir qué pueden hacer diferentes personas con las posesiones que tienen.

Modelo

Marcos / sacar fotos

A —*¿Marcos puede sacar fotos?*

B —*¡Por supuesto! Tiene una cámara muy buena.*

o: —*No. No tiene una cámara.*

Estudiante A

1. Uds. / ver películas en casa
2. Raquel / hacer la tarea de álgebra
3. tu papá (o tu mamá) / usar el Internet
4. tú / escuchar discos compactos
5. Guillo y Patricio / jugar videojuegos

Estudiante B

Pronunciación

jcd-0688

The letters *r* and *rr* 🔊

Except at the beginning of a word or after *l* or *n*, the sound of the letter *r* is similar to the *dd* in the English word *ladder*. Listen to and say these words:

derecha	quiero	amarillo	bandera
pero	puerta	alfombra	morado

The sound of *rr* is similar to saying "batter, batter, batter" over and over again very quickly. Listen to and say these words:

perro	correr	guitarra	marrón
aburrido	arroz	pelirrojo	horrible

When *r* is the first letter of a word or comes after *l* or *n*, it is pronounced like the *rr*.

Roberto	Rita	Ricardo	rojo	regalo
rubio	radio	reloj	romper	Enrique

Try it out! Listen to and say this *trabalenguas:*

**Erre con erre cigarro,
erre con erre barril.
Rápido corren los carros,
cargados de azúcar del
ferrocarril.**

26 ¿Duermes bien?

Leer • Escribir • Hablar

Lee este artículo de una revista y contesta las preguntas.

1. Según el artículo, ¿cuál es el problema?

2. ¿Qué porcentaje de las personas duerme menos de ocho horas diarias durante la semana?

3. ¿El artículo presenta estas ideas? Contesta *sí* o *no*.

 Las personas que duermen poco . . .
   . . . generalmente están más cansadas.
   . . . trabajan mejor.
   . . . juegan mucho y hacen ejercicio.
   . . . son menos sociables.

4. Y tú, durante los fines de semana, ¿cuántas horas duermes en la noche?

Exploración del lenguaje

Using root words

You can build your vocabulary, both in Spanish and in English, if you recognize the root of a word and know its meaning.

For example, because you know the root of one word, **com**er, you can more easily learn another word, *la* **comida**.

Try it out! Because you know the root of **beb**er, you can easily remember *la* __?__ . And since you know *ver la* **televisión**, you can easily recognize *el* __?__ .

Once you learn another language, your mastery of your own language can increase. This is because you begin to use words from your second language to help you understand words in English that are new to you.

Try it out! Since you know *verde, azul,* and *gris,* what do you think these words mean?

   verdant fields   *azure* sky   a *grizzled* old man

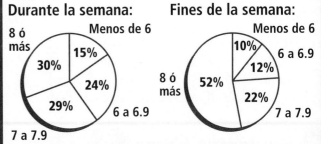

¿Cuántas horas duermes por noche?

Un nuevo estudio indica que muchos adultos no duermen ni[1] seis horas por noche, y afecta mucho a su calidad de vida.[2]

Durante la semana:

8 ó más

Menos de 6

30%   15%

24%

29%   6 a 6.9

7 a 7.9

Fines de la semana:

Menos de 6

10%   6 a 6.9

12%

8 ó más   52%   22%

7 a 7.9

Las personas que duermen menos de seis horas por noche:

■ Tienen más estrés y fatiga.

■ Están más tristes y menos alertas.

■ Hacen peor su trabajo.

■ Sufren más lesiones[3].

■ Tienen más problemas de relaciones interpersonales.

■ Comen más de lo usual.

■ Tienen menos energía.

[1]not even   [2]quality of life   [3]injuries

27 Juego

Escribir • Hablar

Con otro(a) estudiante, describe tres cosas y escribe las descripciones. Lee las frases a otra pareja para ver si ellos pueden identificar las cosas.

> **Strategy**
>
> **Circumlocution**
> When you don't know or can't remember the word for something, you can describe it. You can tell what it is used for, what size it is, what color it is, where it is often found, and so on.

Modelo

A —*Es una cosa que toca música. Puede ser grande o pequeño. Está en muchas casas. ¿Qué es?*
B —*Es un equipo de sonido.*

28 Y tú, ¿qué preguntas?

Escribir • Hablar • Dibujar

❶ Escribe cinco preguntas que puedes hacer *(ask)* a otra persona. Puedes preguntar sobre las actividades que le gustan, cómo es, sus colores favoritos, sus intereses en música y deportes.

❷ Haz tus preguntas a otro(a) estudiante. Escribe sus respuestas.

❸ Dibuja un dormitorio especial para el (la) estudiante según sus respuestas a tus preguntas. Usa lápices de color. Presenta tu dibujo a tu compañero(a) y explica por qué el dormitorio es especial para él o ella.

Modelo

El dormitorio es especial para ti porque tus colores favoritos son azul y rojo. Hay una foto de Lleyton Hewitt en la cómoda porque te gusta mucho el tenis. Hay muchas fotos en las paredes porque sacas fotos de tus amigos también. Tú eres muy gracioso y desordenado. Hay muchos videos y revistas en la cama. Te gusta escuchar la música hip-hop. Aquí, en el estante, están tus discos compactos.

El español en la comunidad

In many communities in the United States, you can see the influence of Spanish-style architecture. Spanish-style buildings often have tile roofs, stucco exteriors, and interior courtyards or patios.

• Identify houses, buildings, or neighborhoods in your community that feature this style. Draw or take a picture of one example.

Más práctica

● **Guided** Gram. Practice pp. 193–194
● **Core** Gram. Practice p. 109
● **Communication** Writing p. 119, Test Prep p. 288
● *Real.* **para hispanohablantes** p. 218, p. 220

realidades.com

• Audio Activities
• Video Activities
• Speak & Record
• Animated Verbs
• Canción de hip hop
• Tutorial
• Leveled Workbook
• Web Code: jcd-0605

Lectura

El desastre en mi dormitorio

Lee esta carta *(letter)* a Querida Magdalena.
Ella da soluciones a los problemas de los jóvenes
en una revista.

Strategy

Using cognates
As you read the letter and response, look for cognates to help you better understand Rosario's problem. Try to guess the meaning of some of the cognates: *el desorden, la situación, recomendar, considerar.*

¿Qué debo hacer?

Con tu amiga Magdalena

66 Querida Magdalena:

Mi problema tiene un nombre; es mi hermana Marta. Compartimos el mismo dormitorio y estoy desesperada. Todo en mi lado del dormitorio está en orden. Pero su lado es un desastre. Ella es la reina del desorden. Le encanta comer en el dormitorio. Hay pizza debajo de la cama. Hay botellas de agua en la mesita. Hay postre en el escritorio. Es horrible. Siempre deja[1] ropa,[2] videos y todas sus posesiones en el suelo,[3] en la mesita, en la cama. ¡No hay ni un libro en el estante!

Y ella no escucha sus propios discos compactos—¡no! Escucha mis discos compactos y sin pedir[4] permiso. Y escucha música a toda hora (y a un volumen muy alto) y ¡yo no puedo dormir!

Las paredes en su lado del dormitorio son negras. Es el peor color y es feísimo. Mi color favorito es el amarillo, claro. Es más bonito que el negro, ¿no?

Estoy cansada de compartir el dormitorio con ella y su desorden.
¿Qué debo hacer? 99

Rosario Molino
Montevideo, Uruguay

Mi problema tiene un nombre; es mi hermana, Marta.

[1]leaves [2]clothing [3]floor [4]asking for

¿Qué debo hacer?

¡Es difícil compartir un dormitorio con otra persona!

Querida Rosario:

¡Qué problema! Es difícil compartir un dormitorio con otra persona, especialmente si la persona es tu hermana. Uds. son muy diferentes, ¿no? Tú eres más ordenada que ella. Ella cree que el color negro es el más bonito.

Necesitas hablar con tu hermana delante de tus padres. Tienes que explicar[5] la situación y recomendar unas soluciones. Es necesario encontrar[6] un punto intermedio.[7] Si la situación no es mejor después de unas semanas, tienes que considerar la posibilidad de separar el dormitorio con una cortina. ¡Pero no debe ser una cortina ni negra ni amarilla!

Tu amiga,
Magdalena

[5]explain [6]find [7]middle ground

¿Comprendes?

Lee las frases y decide quién dice *(says)* la frase. ¿Es Rosario, Marta o su madre?

1. "Pero me gusta comer en la cama y escuchar música".

2. "Soy una persona muy simpática y el color amarillo representa mi personalidad".

3. "Estoy muy ocupada y no tengo tiempo para 'un dormitorio perfecto'".

4. "Uds. tienen que respetar las posesiones de la otra".

5. "Mi color favorito es el negro. No me gustan los colores amarillo, anaranjado o azul".

6. "Ella debe pedir permiso para escuchar mis discos compactos".

7. "Tu hermana no es ordenada como tú. Tienes que ser más paciente".

Y tú, ¿qué dices?

¿Eres desordenado(a) como *(like)* Marta o eres ordenado(a) como Rosario? ¿En qué? Incluye dos ejemplos en tu respuesta.

Fondo cultural
El mundo hispano

Los aparatos electrónicos Throughout the Spanish-speaking world you will find the latest electronic devices: DVRs, mp3 players, cell phones, computers, etc. In all countries, there is a demand for movies, music, and instant communication.

• What are some advantages and disadvantages of the new global community brought about by these technological innovations?

Más práctica

• **Guided** Reading Support p. 195
• **Communication** Test Prep p. 289
• *Real.* para hispanohablantes pp. 222–223

realidades.com

• Internet Activity
• Leveled Workbook
• Web Code: jcd-0606

La cultura en vivo
Las luminarias

To celebrate Christmas in Mexico and the southwest United States, countless bags, tons of sand, and candles are transformed into flickering outdoor lanterns called *luminarias.* They are lined up along window ledges, walkways, and roofs and are lit to welcome visitors.

En Santa Fe, Nuevo México

This tradition dates back more than 300 years, when villagers along the Río Grande built bonfires to light and warm their way to church on Christmas Eve. The luminarias used today go back to the 1820s, when traders introduced brown paper into the region and candles were set in sand in the bottom of the paper bags.

Try it out! Here's how you can make your own luminarias.

Materials

- 12" paper lunch bags
- sand
- small flashlights
- scissors

Figure 1

Figure 2

Figure 3

Directions

1. Trace a pattern on the side of the bag, leaving at least 4 inches at the top and 3 inches at the bottom. You may want to use the pattern in Fig. 1 or create your own.

2. Cut out the design, cutting through both sides of the bag. *(Fig. 1)*

3. Open the bag and fold down a 2" cuff around the top. *(Fig. 2)*

4. Fill the bag $\frac{1}{4}$ full of sand.

5. Place a flashlight in the sand. *(Fig. 3)*

6. Place the completed luminarias along your walkway, turn on the small flashlights, and enjoy these symbols of hope and joy for any special occasion.

Variations

1. Use white or brightly colored bags.

2. Paste or glue white or pastel tissue paper behind the cut-out design.

3. Cut a scalloped edge along the top of the bag instead of folding down the cuff.

4. Instead of sand, use soil, cat litter, or gravel to hold the flashlight in place.

Think about it! What kind of decorations do you use for special events? How is light used in different cultures to celebrate events?

Presentación oral
La personalidad de un dormitorio

Task
You are doing a study on how a bedroom can reflect the personality of its owner(s). Use a photograph or drawing of a bedroom and talk about what its contents and colors tell about the personality of the owner.

1 Prepare Bring in a picture of a bedroom. It can be a photo you took, one cut out from a magazine, or a picture that you drew. Use this word web to think through what you want to say about the room and the personality of the person who decorated it. Then answer the questions.

- En tu opinion, ¿cómo es la persona que vive *(lives)* en el dormitorio? ¿Qué le gusta hacer?

Strategy
Using graphic organizers
A word web can help you organize your thoughts for a presentation.

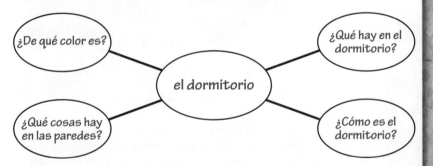

¿De qué color es?

¿Qué hay en el dormitorio?

el dormitorio

¿Qué cosas hay en las paredes?

¿Cómo es el dormitorio?

2 Practice Go through your presentation several times. You can use your notes in practice, but not when you present. Try to:

- support your statements with examples
- use complete sentences
- speak clearly

3 Present Show your picture and give the information about the bedroom and the personality behind it. Don't forget to stand up straight and project your voice!

4 Evaluation Your teacher may give you a rubric for how your presentation will be graded. You probably will be graded on:

- how complete your presentation is
- how much information you communicate
- how easy it is to understand you

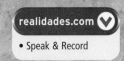

realidades.com
- Speak & Record

¿Eres tú, María?

Episodio 3

Antes de ver el video

Personajes importantes

Margarita, la secretaria de la oficina

Paco, quien trabaja en la oficina de Lola y la ayuda con las investigaciones

Nota cultural *El País* is probably Spain's most widely read and influential newspaper. You can consult an electronic version of *El País* on the Internet.

Resumen del episodio

Este episodio es muy importante. Lola le explica a Paco lo que pasó[1] en el incidente del domingo pasado.[2] En otra escena, Lola habla con doña Lupe quien le describe el incidente en el piso de doña Gracia. También doña Lupe le explica a Lola la historia de la familia de doña Gracia. ¿Por qué cree que María va a recibir toda la fortuna de doña Gracia?

[1] what happened   [2] last Sunday

Palabras para comprender

dinero money
periodista newspaper reporter
¿Qué pasó . . .? What happened . . .?
No ve casi nada. She can hardly see anything.
abro I open
muerta dead
busco I'm looking for
¿Robaron . . .? Did they steal . . .?
las joyas jewels
accidente de coche car accident
Pasó antes de venir a vivir con doña Gracia.
  It happened before she came to live
  with doña Gracia.
Pasó tres meses . . . She spent three months . . .
el nieto grandson
No viene aquí nunca. He never comes here.
No conoce a su abuela.
  He doesn't know his grandmother.

La familia Requena

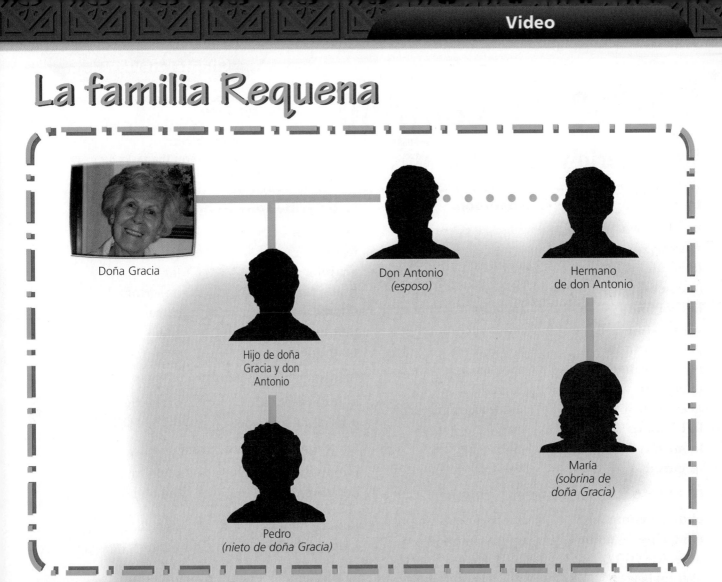

Doña Gracia

Don Antonio
(esposo)

Hermano
de don Antonio

Hijo de doña
Gracia y don
Antonio

María
*(sobrina de
doña Gracia)*

Pedro
(nieto de doña Gracia)

Después de ver el video

¿Comprendes?

Completa cada frase con la palabra apropiada
del recuadro.

periodista	hija
fortuna	accidente de coche
joyas	conoce
dinero	sobrina

1. Según Paco, si no hay cliente, si no hay _____,
entonces no hay nada.

2. Lola dice que trabaja para *El País,* un periódico
importante en España, y es _____.

3. María es la _____ de Lorenzo Requena y la _____ de
doña Gracia.

4. Doña Gracia es muy rica. Tiene una fortuna en dinero,
_____ y arte.

5. Antes de venir a vivir con doña Gracia, a María le pasó un
grave _____.

6. Pedro, el nieto de doña Gracia, vive en Italia y su abuela
no lo _____

7. Según doña Lupe, María va a recibir la _____ de doña Gracia.

realidades.com

• Web Code: jcd-0507

Repaso del capítulo

Vocabulario y gramática

jcd-0689

Chapter Review

To prepare for the test, check to see if you . . .
- know the new vocabulary and grammar
- can perform the tasks on p. 295

to talk about things in a bedroom

la alfombra	rug
el armario	closet
la cama	bed
la cómoda	dresser
las cortinas	curtains
el cuadro	painting
el despertador	alarm clock
el dormitorio	bedroom
el espejo	mirror
el estante	shelf, bookshelf
la lámpara	lamp
la mesita	night table
la pared	wall

to talk about electronic equipment

el disco compacto	compact disc
el equipo de sonido	sound (stereo) system
el lector DVD	DVD player
el televisor	television set
el video	videocassette
la videocasetera	VCR

to talk about colors

¿De qué color . . . ?	What color . . . ?
los colores	colors
amarillo, -a	yellow
anaranjado, -a	orange
azul	blue
blanco, -a	white
gris	gray
marrón	brown
morado, -a	purple
negro, -a	black
rojo, -a	red
rosado, -a	pink
verde	green

For *Vocabulario adicional,* see pp. 472–473.

to describe something

bonito, -a	pretty
feo, -a	ugly
grande	large
importante	important
mismo, -a	same
pequeño, -a	small
propio, -a	own

to indicate location

a la derecha (de)	to the right (of)
a la izquierda (de)	to the left (of)

to compare and contrast

mejor(es) que	better than
el / la mejor; los / las mejores	the best
menos . . . que	less, fewer . . . than
peor(es) que	worse than
el / la peor; los / las peores	the worst

other useful words

la cosa	thing
para mí	in my opinion, for me
para ti	in your opinion, for you
la posesión	possession

stem-changing verbs: *dormir* and *poder*

duermo	dormimos
duermes	dormís
duerme	duermen

puedo	podemos
puedes	podéis
puede	pueden

Más práctica

- **Core** Puzzle p. 110, Organizer p. 111
- **Communication** Practice Test pp. 291–293, Integrated Performance Assessment p. 290

realidades.com ✓
- Tutorial
- Flashcards
- Puzzles
- Self-test
- Web Code: jcd-0607

Preparación para el examen

On the exam you will be asked to . . .	Here are practice tasks similar to those you will find on the exam . . .	If you need review . . .

Interpretive

1 Escuchar Listen to and understand descriptions of bedrooms

jcd-0689 🔊

You will be spending a month in a Spanish immersion camp. You go to the camp Web site and click on the audio descriptions of the student rooms. Which items are provided? Which items do you have to bring?

pp. 272–275 *Vocabulario en contexto*
p. 276 Actividad 5
p. 277 Actividad 7
p. 281 Actividad 15

Interpersonal

2 Hablar Ask and answer questions about your bedroom and that of a classmate

You are asked to survey several classmates about their bedrooms to describe the "typical" teenage room for a class project. Ask a partner at least three questions including: a) information about the color of his or her room; b) whether or not there is a TV or sound system; c) whether he or she is able to study well in the room; d) what is on the walls.

pp. 272–275 *Vocabulario en contexto*
p. 277 Actividad 7
p. 281 Actividad 15

Interpretive

3 Leer Read and understand descriptions of bedroom colors that are associated with particular personality types

Decorators say that the colors of a room's walls should match the personality of the person living in it. Based on the descriptions of a "yellow personality" and a "blue personality," what kind of room best suits you? Why or why not?

A las personas más sociables les gustan los dormitorios amarillos. Es el color más popular para los jóvenes a quienes les gusta hablar y hablar por teléfono. ¡Ellos son los mejores amigos!
Al contrario, a las personas más serias les gustan los dormitorios azules. Ellos son los mejores estudiantes y los peores cómicos.

p. 282 Actividad 17
p. 283 Actividad 19
pp. 288-289 *Lectura*

Presentational

4 Escribir Write a short paragraph comparing your bedroom to a friend's bedroom

After surveying classmates, you are asked to write a comparison of your room to that of one of the people you surveyed. Use the information from Task 2 to practice. You might compare: a) the colors; b) the sizes; c) the types of furniture; d) the number of different things on the walls.

p. 277 Actividad 6
p. 278 Actividad 10
p. 291 *Presentación oral*

Cultures

5 Pensar Demonstrate an understanding of cultural perspectives regarding a celebration

Explain the historical significance of *las luminarias*. What is the history of other decorations used in the celebrations of different cultures?

p. 290 *La cultura en vivo*

Fondo cultural

Chile

La arpillera is a popular textile folk art of rough patchwork appliqués created by women in Chile. Done in brilliant colors, the themes show the story of daily life, traditions, and values in the country.

• What other types of crafts have you seen that portray life in a region or country?

Arpillera de Chile

Capítulo 6B

¿Cómo es tu casa?

Chapter Objectives

- Identify rooms in a house
- Name household chores
- Tell where you live
- Understand cultural perspectives on different types of housing

Video Highlights

Videocultura: *La casa*

A primera vista: *Los quehaceres de Elena*

GramActiva Videos: affirmative *tú* commands; the present progressive tense

Videomisterio: *¿Eres tú, María?*, Episodio 4

Country Connection

As you learn about rooms in a house and household chores, you will make connections to these countries and places:

España

México

Puerto Rico

Venezuela

Chile

Más práctica

- *Real.* para hispanohablantes pp. 230–231

realidades.com

- Fondo cultural Activity
- Online Atlas
- Video Activities
- Web Code: jce-0002

Vocabulario
en contexto

jcd-0697

- la escalera
- el segundo piso
- el primer piso
- la planta baja*
- el despacho
- el baño
- el comedor
- la cocina
- la sala
- el garaje
- el sótano
- el patio

*In most countries, Spanish speakers call the ground floor in a multi-story building *la planta baja,* the second floor *el primer piso,* the third floor *el segundo piso,* the fourth floor *el tercer piso,* and so on.

Se vende.
Casa particular de dos pisos y sótano. Sala grande, cocina moderna, comedor, despacho, 2 baños, 3 dormitorios, garaje.
Llama al 555-37-89.

—Me gustaría ver esta casa. Es grande y bonita.

—Sí, tiene tres dormitorios y un despacho. También tiene una cocina moderna, **si** te gusta cocinar.

SE VENDE
555-37-89

Más vocabulario

el apartamento — apartment
cerca (de) — close (to), near
lejos (de) — far (from)
bastante — enough, rather

lavar los platos sucios

poner la mesa

Hijos —
¡Tienen que hacer
los quehaceres
esta mañana!
Anita | Juanito

cortar el césped

lavar el coche

pasar la aspiradora

dar de comer al perro

lavar la ropa

sacar la basura

cocinar

hacer la cama

—¡Ay! ¡Mira todos los quehaceres!
Mamá sabe que tengo que ir de
compras con Cristina.
No puedo . . .

—Yo voy a jugar
al fútbol a la
una. Y tengo
más quehaceres
que tú.

quitar el polvo

arreglar el cuarto

limpiar el baño

---

1 **La casa de Elena** 🔊 *jcd-0697*

Escuchar

Escucha a Elena describir su casa. Señala cada cuarto
que describe.

2 **¿Es lógico o no?** 🔊 *jcd-0697*

Escuchar

Escucha cada frase. Si es lógica, haz el gesto del pulgar
hacia arriba *("thumbs-up" sign)*. Si no es lógica, haz el
gesto del pulgar hacia abajo *("thumbs-down" sign).*

Más práctica

- **Guided** Vocab. Flash Cards pp. 197–202
- **Core** Vocab. Practice pp. 112–113
- **Communication** Writing p. 126
- *Real.* para hispanohablantes p. 232

realidades.com ▼

- Audio Activities
- Leveled Workbook
- Flashcards
- Web Code: jcd-0611

Los quehaceres de Elena

Elena no quiere hacer sus quehaceres. ¿Qué hace ella?

España

Papá

Mamá

Elena

Jorgito

Strategy

Using language knowledge
You've just learned the infinitives for various household chores. Using what you know, what are the four activities that Elena tells Jorgito to do in Panel 5?

1 **Elena:** ¡Hola! Bienvenidos a mi casa. **Vivo** en el número 12 de la calle Apodaca. Vamos a entrar. Mi casa es su casa.

5 **Jorgito:** ¿**Cuáles** son los quehaceres que necesito hacer?

Elena: **Pon** la mesa, lava los platos sucios en la cocina, **haz** la cama en mi dormitorio y da de comer al perro.

6 **Mamá:** Elena, ¡qué trabajadora eres!

Papá: ¡Cómo ayudas en casa! Das de comer al perro, lavas los platos, **pones** la mesa . . .

Elena: Ah, . . . ¿**Recibo** mi dinero?

Mamá: **Un momento.** ¿Tu dormitorio está **limpio?**

7 **Mamá:** ¡Jorgito! ¡Qué perezoso eres! **¿Qué estás haciendo?**

Jorgito: Pero, . . . pero, . . .

Papá: Ni pero ni nada. ¡Jorgito, a tu dormitorio! Vamos a ver . . .

2 Elena: ¡Ay, no! Veo que tengo más quehaceres. Siempre lavo los platos sucios y **pongo** la mesa para la cena. ¡Y ahora necesito hacer más trabajo!

3 Elena: ¿Me **ayudas** con los quehaceres?

Jorgito: Quiero **dinero.**

Elena: No te **doy** dinero, pero puedes escuchar discos compactos en mi dormitorio.

4 Jorgito: A ver. Si hago unos de los quehaceres, me **das** los discos y escucho música por una hora.

Elena: Media hora.

Jorgito: Cuarenta y cinco minutos.

Elena: Está bien.

8 Mamá: Elena, tu dinero.

Elena: Gracias, mamá.

Papá: Jorgito, ¿cómo puedes vivir así? Tienes que arreglar tu cuarto, hijo: haz la cama, quita el polvo, pasa la aspiradora . . .

Jorgito: Pero, Elena . . .

Elena: ¡Adiós! ¡Voy al cine!

③ ¿Comprendes?

Escribir · Hablar

Lee las frases y escribe *cierta* si la frase es correcta o *falsa* si es incorrecta. Si la frase es incorrecta, escribe una frase nueva con la información correcta.

1. Elena siempre pone la mesa en su casa.

2. Jorgito está contento de escuchar los discos compactos.

3. Si hace unos de los quehaceres, Jorgito puede escuchar una hora de música.

4. Según los padres, Elena es muy trabajadora.

5. Según los padres, Jorgito es trabajador también.

6. Ahora Jorgito tiene mucho que hacer en su dormitorio.

Más práctica

- **Guided** Vocab. Check pp. 203–206
- **Core** Vocab. Practice pp. 114–115
- **Communication** Video pp. 120–122
- *Real.* **para hispanohablantes** p. 233

realidades.com ⓥ

- Audio Activities
- Video Activities
- Leveled Workbook
- Flashcards
- Web Code: jcd-0612

Vocabulario en uso

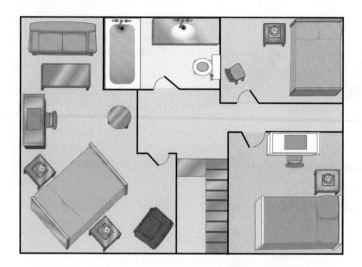

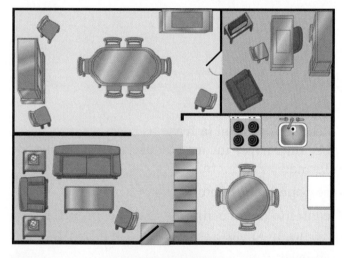

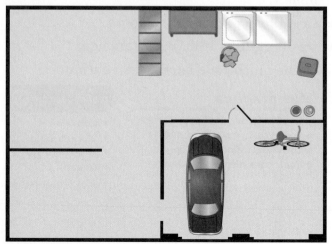

4 **La casa de los Ramírez** jcd-0698

Escuchar • Escribir

Los Ramírez van a comprar la casa que ves aquí. En una hoja de papel escribe los números del 1 al 8 y escribe el nombre de cada cuarto que describen.

> ### Nota
>
> *Primero(a)* and *tercero(a)* become *primer* and *tercer* before a masculine singular noun.
>
> - Mi dormitorio está en el **primer** piso.
> - Su apartamento está en el **tercer** piso.

5 **¿Cierto o falso?**

Escribir • Escuchar • Hablar

Escribe cinco frases para indicar dónde están los cuartos en la casa de los Ramírez. Las frases pueden ser ciertas o falsas. Lee tus frases a otro(a) estudiante, quien va a indicar si son ciertas o falsas. Si son falsas, tiene que dar la información correcta.

Modelo

A —*La sala está en el primer piso.*
B —*Falso. La sala está en la planta baja.*

> ### También se dice . . .
>
> **la sala** = el salón *(muchos países),* el living *(España)*
>
> **el despacho** = la oficina *(muchos países)*
>
> **el piso** = la planta *(muchos países)*
>
> **el apartamento** = el piso *(España),* el departamento *(muchos países)*

6 ¿Dónde pongo la silla?

Hablar

Ayudas a la familia Ramírez a mudarse *(move)* a su nueva casa pero no sabes dónde poner sus cosas. Otro(a) estudiante te va a explicar dónde tienes que poner todo.

Modelo

A —¿Dónde pongo *la silla*?
B —Vamos a poner *la silla* en *el comedor*.

> **Nota**
>
> *Poner*, "to put," is also used in the expression *poner la mesa*, "to set the table." It has an irregular *yo* form: *pongo*.
>
> • En la mañana **pongo** la mesa.

Estudiante A

Estudiante B

¡Respuesta personal!

7 ¿En qué cuarto?

Escribir

Ahora los Ramírez están muy contentos en su casa. ¿En qué cuarto hacen los Ramírez estos quehaceres? Escribe las frases.

Modelo
Sacan la basura en el garaje.

1.  2.  3.  4. 5. 6.

Fondo cultural

España

El patio in an apartment building in a large Spanish city is usually just an open area in the center of the building. In southern Spain, however, houses are often built around *patios*, which may have gardens as well as a fountain. The Moors brought this architectural style to Spain, and the Spaniards then carried it over to the Americas.

• How does the Spanish *patio* differ from what a patio is in your community? How is it similar?

Un patio típico en Córdoba, España

8 ¿Cómo ayudas en casa?

Hablar

¿Ayudas mucho en casa? Habla de tus quehaceres con otro(a) estudiante.

Nota

Dar means "to give" and is used in the expression *dar de comer,* "to feed." It has an irregular *yo* form: *doy.*

• En mi casa **doy** de comer al perro.

Modelo

A —¿Tienes que lavar el coche?
B —Sí, lavo el coche todos los sábados.

Estudiante A

Estudiante B

1.　2.　3.

4.　5.　6.

a veces
mucho
todos los días
todos los (sábados)
en el (verano)
los fines de semana
nunca

9 ¿Dónde vives?

Escribir • Hablar

Escribe una lista de cinco lugares en tu comunidad, como la escuela, el centro comercial, la biblioteca, etc. Pregunta a otro(a) estudiante si vive cerca o lejos de estos lugares.

Modelo

El cine Rex

A —¿Vives cerca del cine Rex?
B —Sí, vivo bastante cerca del cine.
o:—No, vivo muy lejos.

También se dice . . .

cocinar = guisar *(España)*

cortar el césped = cortar la hierba, cortar el pasto *(muchos países),* cortar el zacate *(México)*

lavar los platos = fregar los platos *(España)*

quitar el polvo = sacudir los muebles *(México)* desempolvar *(Bolivia)*

10 Y tú, ¿qué dices?

Escribir • Hablar

1. ¿Ayudas mucho o poco en casa? ¿Cuáles son tus quehaceres?

2. ¿Generalmente tu cuarto está sucio o limpio?

3. En tu casa, ¿quién pasa la aspiradora? ¿Quién saca la basura?

4. Para ti, ¿cuáles son los tres peores quehaceres? ¿Y los mejores?

5. Imagina que eres padre o madre. ¿Cuánto dinero recibe tu hijo(a) si hace sus quehaceres?

6. ¿Vives cerca o lejos de tu escuela?

Gramática

Affirmative *tú* commands

When you tell friends, family members, or young people to do something, you use an affirmative *tú* command. To give these commands, use the same present-tense forms that you use for *Ud., él, ella.*

INFINITIVE	UD. / ÉL / ELLA	AFFIRMATIVE *TÚ* COMMANDS
hablar	habla	¡Habla!
leer	lee	¡Lee!
escribir	escribe	¡Escribe!

- Certain verbs, like *poner* and *hacer,* have irregular command forms.

  Jorgito, ¡pon la mesa!   Jorgito, ¡haz tu cama!

¿Recuerdas?

In the direction lines of many activities, you have already seen many affirmative commands.

- **Habla** con otra persona.
- **Lee** las frases.
- **Escribe** la palabra apropiada.

GramActiva VIDEO

Want more help with the affirmative *tú* commands? Watch the **GramActiva** video.

Pon la mesa.

---

11 "Simón dice . . . "

Escuchar • GramActiva

Escucha y sigue *(follow)* las instrucciones de tu profesor(a) o de otro(a) estudiante. Si no dicen *"Simón dice,"* no debes hacer la acción.

---

12 ¡Habla bien!

Escribir

Un(a) amigo(a) quiere hablar bien el español. ¿Qué recomiendas? Escribe el mandato *(command)* de los siguientes verbos.

Modelo

usar: *usa*
Usa un buen diccionario.

1. estudiar
2. ver
3. escuchar
4. escribir
5. hacer
6. hablar con
7. leer
8. practicar

13 ¿Qué debo hacer? ♻

Leer • Escribir

Tu amiga Carmen tiene un problema
y te escribe una carta. Lee su carta y
escribe tus recomendaciones en otra
carta, usando los verbos de la lista.

Modelo

Mi querida Carmen,
Aquí están mis recomendaciones:
Come menos dulces, . . .

beber	dormir	jugar
comer	hacer ejercicio	¡Respuesta
correr	levantar pesas	personal!

¡Hola!

Tengo un problema grande. Quisiera estar
mejor de salud. No estoy muy enferma pero
tampoco estoy en buena forma. Siempre
tengo mucho sueño y poca energía. Si
camino a la escuela, estoy muy cansada.
Si hago muchos quehaceres por la casa,
también estoy cansada. ¡Y no quiero estar
cansada! ¿Qué debo hacer?

Tu amiga desesperada,

Carmen

14 Muchos quehaceres ♻

Hablar

Debes hacer muchos quehaceres en casa, pero no quieres. ¡A ver
si tu hermanito(a) puede hacer todo! Primero di *(say)* lo que está
sucio (o lo que no está limpio). Luego di lo que tiene que hacer.

Modelo

Los platos no están limpios. Lava los platos, por favor.

¿Recuerdas?

Adjectives agree in number
and gender with the nouns
they modify.
• **La** casa está suci**a**.
• **Los** plat**os** están limpi**os**.

1.   2.   3.

4.   5.   6.

Un patio español

15 ¿Quién hace los quehaceres? ♻

Leer · Escribir · Hablar

Un artículo de la revista española *Muy interesante* explica quién hace la mayoría de *(most of)* los quehaceres de la casa. Estudia las gráficas a la derecha y haz comparaciones entre *(between)* las mujeres y los hombres españoles. Después, explica si las mujeres hacen los siguientes quehaceres mucho más, un poco más o menos que los hombres.

Modelo

lavar los platos
Las mujeres lavan los platos mucho más que los hombres.

1. comprar cosas para la familia cada día
2. preparar la comida y la cena
3. cuidar *(take care of)* el coche
4. cuidar a las personas enfermas de la familia
5. lavar y planchar *(iron)* la ropa
6. ir al banco
7. limpiar la casa

¿Quién hace los quehaceres?

Lavar y planchar la ropa — 88% Mujeres, 4% Hombres, 8% Juntos*
Comprar la comida — 73% Mujeres, 8% Hombres, 19% Juntos
Preparar comidas — 68% Mujeres, 13% Hombres, 19% Juntos
Cuidar el coche — 14% Mujeres, 78% Hombres, 8% Juntos
Limpiar la casa — 60% Mujeres, 13% Hombres, 19% Juntos
Ir al banco — 37% Mujeres, 26% Hombres, 36% Juntos
Lavar los platos — 67% Mujeres, 10% Hombres, 23% Juntos
Cuidar a los enfermos — 31% Mujeres, 10% Hombres, 30% Juntos

*Together

Exploración del lenguaje

The endings *-dor* and *-dora*

Every day you use appliances and devices: a calculator, a computer, a stapler, a copier, a dryer, and so on. Many of these words in English add the ending *-er* or *-or* to the verb that tells what the appliance is for. Spanish follows a similar pattern. Look at these words you already know and identify the pattern: **despertador, computadora, calculadora, aspiradora.** Can you guess what the corresponding verbs are and what they mean?

Try it out! Read each statement on the left and decide which appliance is needed.

1. Tengo calor.
2. ¿Dónde está el pan tostado?
3. Mi ropa está sucia.
4. Necesito leche para el cereal.

a. Está en la tostadora.
b. Ponla en la lavadora.
c. Está en el refrigerador.
d. Necesitas el ventilador.

Más práctica

- **Guided** Gram. Practice pp. 207–208
- **Core** Gram. Practice p. 116
- **Communication** Writing p. 127
- *Real.* **para hispanohablantes** pp. 234–237

realidades.com ✔

- Audio Activities
- Video Activities
- Speak & Record
- Leveled Workbook
- Web Code: jcd-0613

Gramática

The present progressive tense

When you want to emphasize that an action is happening *right now*, you use the present progressive tense.

Paco **está lavando** los platos.   *Paco is washing dishes (now).*
Estoy haciendo la cama.   *I'm making the bed (right now).*

To form the present progressive tense, use the present-tense forms of *estar* + the present participle. The present participle is formed by dropping the ending of the infinitive and adding *-ando* for *-ar* verbs or *-iendo* for *-er* and *-ir* verbs.

(yo)	estoy	lavando comiendo escribiendo	(nosotros) (nosotras)	estamos	lavando comiendo escribiendo
(tú)	estás	lavando comiendo escribiendo	(vosotros) (vosotras)	estáis	lavando comiendo escribiendo
Ud. (él) (ella)	está	lavando comiendo escribiendo	Uds. (ellos) (ellas)	están	lavando comiendo escribiendo

Leer has an irregular spelling in the present participle: *leyendo.*

GramActiva VIDEO

Want more help with the present progressive? Watch the **GramActiva** video.

estoy jugando

---

16 **¿Qué están haciendo ahora?** ♻

Escribir

Escribe cinco frases para explicar lo que están haciendo varias personas en tu sala de clases.

Modelo
La profesora está escribiendo algo.

---

17 Escucha y escribe 🔊 ♻   jcd-0698

Escuchar · Escribir

Estos hermanos tienen muchos quehaceres. Escucha y escribe la pregunta de la madre y las excusas de los hijos.

18 Un momento, por favor

Hablar • Escribir

A veces no podemos hacer los quehaceres porque estamos haciendo otras cosas. Trabaja con otro(a) estudiante para dar un mandato y una excusa.

Modelo

A —*Por favor, da de comer al perro.*
B —*No puedo. Estoy estudiando para un examen.*

Estudiante A

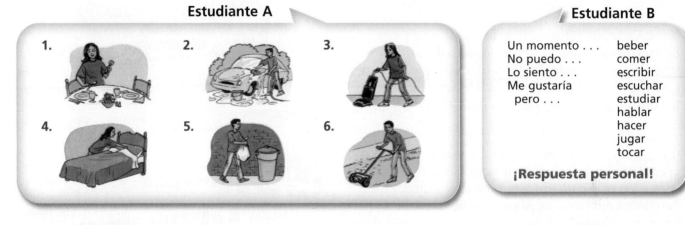

1. 2. 3.
4. 5. 6.

Estudiante B

Un momento . . .	beber
No puedo . . .	comer
Lo siento . . .	escribir
Me gustaría	escuchar
pero . . .	estudiar
	hablar
	hacer
	jugar
	tocar

¡Respuesta personal!

19 Juego

Escribir • Hablar • GramActiva

❶ En una hoja de papel (*sheet of paper*), escribe una frase para explicar lo que está haciendo una persona (usa la forma *tú*). En otra hoja de papel, escribe una frase para explicar lo que están haciendo dos personas (usa la forma *Uds.*).

Modelo

Estás levantando pesas.
Uds. están esquiando.

❷ Todas las frases van boca abajo (*face down*) encima de una mesa. Toma una frase. Si la frase usa la forma *tú*, haz la acción solo(a). Si la frase usa la forma *Uds.*, haz la acción con otro(a) estudiante. Los compañeros tienen que adivinar (*guess*) lo que estás (están) haciendo.

20 ¿Qué están haciendo todos?

Escribir • Hablar • GramActiva

Haz un dibujo de tres personas que están haciendo diferentes actividades. En otra hoja de papel, escribe dos preguntas sobre lo que está haciendo cada persona. Trabaja en un grupo de tres. Da tu dibujo a los otros estudiantes y lee tus preguntas. Tus compañeros tienen que contestar.

Modelo

A —*¿Qué está haciendo la chica?*
B/C —*Está lavando los platos sucios.*

Más práctica

- **Guided** Gram. Practice pp. 209–210
- **Core** Gram. Practice pp. 117–118
- **Communication** Writing p. 128, Test Prep p. 294
- *Real.* **para hispanohablantes** pp. 238–239

realidades.com
- Audio Activities
- Video Activities
- Speak & Record
- Animated Verbs
- Canción de hip hop
- Tutorial
- Leveled Workbook
- Web Code: jcd-0614

21 ¿Qué casa están _____ buscando?

Leer • Pensar

En Santiago, Chile, tres personas están buscando *(looking for)* una nueva casa y leen el anuncio a la derecha. ¿Quién crees que va a comprar *(buy)* la casa?

José Guzmán: "Quiero vivir bastante cerca de mi trabajo. Para mi esposa es importante tener una cocina equipada. Prefiero una casa con sólo un piso porque mis padres van a vivir con nosotros y las escaleras son muy difíciles para ellos".

Alejandro Lara: "Mis padres y yo vivimos en un apartamento ahora. Quiero una casa con tres dormitorios porque mis primos vienen a nuestra casa a veces. No quiero una casa muy grande porque no me gusta ni pasar la aspiradora ni limpiar los baños".

Dora Peña: "Mi familia y yo estamos buscando una casa nueva. Tenemos dos hijas y mi mamá vive con nosotros. Quiero una casa con un dormitorio un poco separado para mi mamá. Prefiero tener alfombra en los dormitorios porque nuestras hijas juegan mucho allí".

Chile

LAS MEJORES CASAS
EN LA AVENIDA LA FLORIDA

CASA VENECIA: 310 m² 3 PISOS
DESDE CHP¹ 40.000.000

Planta baja: Amplia sala • Comedor separado • Cocina y baño de visitas

Primer piso: Dormitorio principal, más 2 dormitorios y otro baño

Segundo piso: Amplio dormitorio con baño completo y una gran sala de estar

«VISITE NUESTRA OFICINA Y COMPRE HOY MISMO»

- Cerámica en el primer piso
- Alfombra en dormitorios
- Cocina equipada
- Papel vinílico en paredes
- Armarios terminados
- Ventanas de aluminio
- Amplio jardín

CASAS ROJAS
MAGALLANES 3400

¡Llame hoy! 232 9980

¹ Peso chileno

Pronunciación

jcd-0698

The letters *n* and *ñ* 🔊

In Spanish, the letter *n* sounds like the *n* in "no." Listen to and say these words:

anaranjado	nieva	nadar	joven	desayuno
necesito	encantado	número	nombre	donde

However, the sound changes when there is a tilde (~) over the *n*. The *ñ* then sounds like the *-ny-* of the English word *canyon*. Listen to and say these words:

señor	otoño	español	enseñar	año
montañas	niña	mañana	piñata	cumpleaños

Try it out! Listen to this *trabalenguas* and then try to say it.

El señor Yáñez come ñames¹ en las mañanas con el niño.

¹yam

22 ¿Dónde viven?

Leer • Pensar

En la capital de Venezuela, Caracas, analizaron *(they analyzed)* dónde viven unos 4.3 millones de habitantes. Según los estudios, ¿viven más personas en casas o en apartamentos? ¿Viven en casas y apartamentos grandes o pequeños? Estudia las gráficas y luego contesta las preguntas.

Venezuela

Nota

Do you see the pattern in the following numbers?

100,000 = cien mil
200,000 = doscientos mil
300,000 = trescientos mil

But watch out for 500,000:

542,656 = quinientos cuarenta y dos mil seiscientos cincuenta y seis

1,000,000 = un millón

Conexiones | **Las matemáticas**

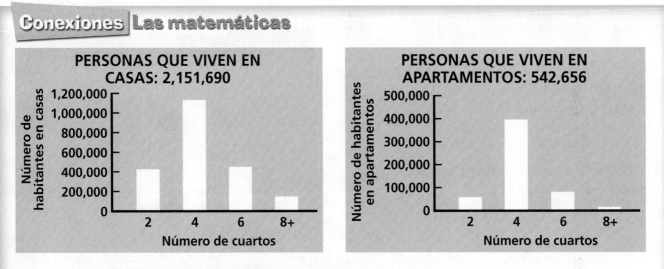

1. ¿Cuántas personas viven en una casa con dos cuartos? ¿Cuántas viven en un apartamento con dos cuartos?

2. ¿Cuántas personas viven en una casa con ocho o más cuartos? ¿Cuántas viven en un apartamento con ocho o más cuartos?

3. Calcula el porcentaje de personas que viven en una casa con cuatro cuartos. Calcula el porcentaje de personas que viven en un apartamento con cuatro cuartos.

El español en el mundo del trabajo

Across the country, "For Sale" signs in Spanish are appearing on lawns, in front of apartment buildings, and in office complexes.

• Look for ads in Spanish in the real estate section of your local newspaper.

La Casa J. Knox Corbett en el distrito histórico de Tucson, Arizona

Lectura

Objectives

- Read a version of "Cinderella"
- Learn about houses in the Spanish-speaking world
- Create a flyer to sell a house or apartment
- Watch *¿Eres tú, María?*, Episodio 4

Cantaclara

Lee esta historia sobre una joven que se llama Cantaclara.

Strategy

Skimming
This reading is based on the story of Cinderella. Quickly skim the story and find characters and dialogue that remind you of Cinderella.

Hay una muchacha que se llama Cantaclara. Ella vive con su madrastra y sus dos hermanastras, Griselda y Hortencia. Las cuatro viven en una casa grande y Cantaclara hace todos los quehaceres. Sus dos hermanastras y su madrastra no hacen nada.

—Cantaclara, saca la basura. Y después, pon la mesa —dice la madrastra.

—Cantaclara, haz mi cama y limpia el baño —dice Griselda.

—Haz mi cama también —dice Hortencia.

—Un momento. Estoy lavando los platos ahora mismo —dice Cantaclara.

¡Pobre[1] Cantaclara! Hace todos los quehaceres y cuando trabaja, ella canta. Tiene una voz[2] muy clara y le encanta cantar.

Un día, Cantaclara entra en el dormitorio de Griselda para hacer la cama. Ve en la televisión un anuncio[3] para un programa muy popular que se llama *La estrella[4] del futuro*. En la televisión hay un señor que dice: "¡Hola, amigos! ¿Tienen talento? ¿Cantan bien? ¿Por qué no cantan para nosotros? ¡Pueden tener un futuro fantástico y recibir muchísimo dinero!"

Cantaclara está muy contenta. Ella puede cantar. Ella quiere un futuro fantástico. En este momento, ella decide cantar para el programa *La estrella del futuro*.

[1]Poor [2]voice [3]ad [4]star

Es la noche del programa. Después de hacer todos los quehaceres, Cantaclara está saliendo[5] de casa cuando su madrastra le habla.

—Cantaclara, ¿adónde vas?

—Quiero salir por unas horas, madrastra. ¿Está bien?

—Ahora no. Tienes que limpiar la cocina —contesta la madrastra. —Está muy sucia.

—Pero, madrastra, tengo que . . .

—¡No importa, Cantaclara! ¡Limpia la cocina!

Cantaclara mira su reloj. Sólo tiene una hora. Va a la cocina y limpia todo. Trabaja muy rápidamente. Después de cuarenta y cinco minutos, termina el trabajo.

Cantaclara llega[6] al programa y canta su canción favorita. ¡Por supuesto ella canta mejor que todos![7] Ella va a tener un futuro fantástico y va a recibir muchísimo dinero.

Son las ocho de la noche. La madrastra y las dos hermanastras están en la sala y ven su programa favorito. Pero, ¿qué es esto? ¡Ven a Cantaclara en la pantalla!

—Mira, mamá. ¡Es Cantaclara! —dice Hortencia.

—¡Oh, no! Si Cantaclara es la nueva estrella del futuro, ¿quién va a hacer los quehaceres? —pregunta Griselda.

[5]is leaving   [6]arrives   [7]anyone else

¿Comprendes?

Pon las frases en orden según la historia.

1. Ella decide cantar en el programa *La estrella del futuro*.

2. Cantaclara es la persona que canta mejor en el programa.

3. Ella está lavando los platos.

4. Ella tiene que limpiar la cocina.

5. Ve el anuncio para *La estrella del futuro*.

6. Griselda no sabe quién va a hacer los quehaceres.

7. Cantaclara vive en una casa grande con su madrastra y sus dos hermanastras.

8. Son las ocho de la noche y la madrastra y las hermanastras están viendo la tele.

Fondo cultural
El mundo hispano

La Cenicienta The story of Cinderella is perhaps the best-known fairy tale in the world. Almost every culture seems to have its own version and there may be over 1,500 variations. The tale appears to date back to a Chinese story from the ninth century, "Yeh-Shen."

• What aspects of the story might change from culture to culture?

Más práctica

● **Guided** Reading Support p. 211
● **Communication** Writing p. 129, Test Prep p. 295
● *Real.* **para hispanohablantes** pp. 240–243

 realidades.com

• Internet Activity
• Leveled Workbook
• Web Code: jcd-0615

Perspectivas del mundo hispano

¿Cómo son las casas en el mundo hispano?

El patio de una casa en Córdoba, España

In many Spanish-speaking countries the architectural features of houses are very different from those in the United States. Houses tend to be separated from the outside by a barrier such as a tall wall or fence. The owner would open a gate to enter the property where there may be a carport or small outside area. In many communities, the outside wall of the house is located directly on the sidewalk and the front windows may contain bars or *rejas*. The doors may be large wooden or metal doors. A plain walled exterior gives no hints about what may be a beautiful, comfortable interior.

Inside, a home will often have an open space in the middle called the *patio*. Many rooms of the house open onto the *patio*, and it is a place for the family to meet, eat meals, talk, and spend time together. Privacy is valued, and the home and family activities are shielded from view from the outside.

Homes in Spanish-speaking countries are used for the family and to entertain very close relatives and friends. It is unusual to invite non-family members such as coworkers or casual friends into the home. Parties often take place in restaurants or small reception halls.

Una calle en una zona residencial de San Juan, Puerto Rico

Check it out! Look around your neighborhood. How does the architecture of houses compare with the design of houses in the Spanish-speaking world?

Think about it! If architectural features of houses in Spanish-speaking countries imply a desire for privacy, what do the architectural features of houses in the United States imply? How does the concept of a *patio* compare in these cultures?

Una casa en Caracas, Venezuela

Presentación escrita
Se vende casa o apartamento

Task

You have been asked to create a flyer in Spanish to promote the sale of your family's house or apartment. Create an attractive and inviting flyer that will make your home (or your dream house, if you prefer) appealing to a potential buyer.

Una casa en México, D.F.

1 Prewrite Think about the information you want to include in your flyer. Read these questions and jot down what you'd like to say about the house or apartment.

- En general, ¿cómo es la casa o el apartamento?

- ¿Cuántos cuartos hay? ¿Cuáles son? ¿Cómo son? ¿De qué colores son?

- ¿Hay algo especial en la casa (piscina, cuarto especial)?

- Incluye *(Include)* otra información importante como la dirección *(address)* y el precio *(price)*.

2 Draft Look at the ad on p. 310 to help you design your flyer. Use the answers to the Prewrite questions. Include an illustration and other features to make it attractive. Begin with the phrase *Se vende casa* or *Se vende apartamento.*

3 Revise Read through your ad to see that you have included all the information that a potential buyer might want. Make sure the words are spelled correctly. Share your flyer with a partner, who will check the following:

- Is the flyer neat and attractive? Does it include a visual?

- Is the key information provided?

- Does it make you want to look at the property?

4 Publish Write a final copy of your flyer, making any necessary changes. You may want to include it with your classmates' flyers in a collection called *Se venden casas y apartamentos* or in your portfolio.

5 Evaluation Your teacher may give you a rubric for grading your flyer. You probably will be graded on:

- neatness and attractiveness

- use of vocabulary

- amount of information provided

Strategy

Using key questions
Answering key questions can help you think of ideas for writing.

Casa Milá, en Barcelona, España

¿Eres tú, María? Episodio 4

Antes de ver el video

Personajes importantes

Pedro Requena, el nieto de doña Gracia. Está en Madrid para visitar a su abuela en el hospital.

Carmela, una buena amiga de Lola

Nota cultural *Tapas* are popular appetizers in Spain. *Tapas* come in small servings called *raciones,* and can be almost anything: olives, fish, meat, cheese, vegetables, shellfish, or any dish the chef cares to prepare. Eating *tapas* is a social event. Friends eat, drink, and relax as they talk. When you are done, you are charged according to how many platefuls of *tapas* you ate.

Resumen del episodio

Doña Gracia está mucho mejor y puede ir a casa en unos días. Pero no recuerda mucho del incidente. Lola llama por teléfono a su buena amiga, Carmela. Las dos van a un café para hablar y Carmela le dice a Lola que una de sus amigas, Rosalinda, trabaja en el hospital San Carlos. Es el hospital donde está doña Gracia. Deciden ir al hospital para hablar con Rosalinda y ver a doña Gracia. A la mañana siguiente, Lola habla con Pedro Requena.

Palabras para comprender

fui a visitarla I went to visit her
¿Habló del incidente?
    Did she talk about the incident?
¿Sabe . . .? Does she know . . .?
Lo único que recuerda . . .
    The only thing she remembers . . .
un golpe hit, blow
ahora mismo right away
preguntar por to ask about
los churros fried dough pastries
No estoy pensando en . . . I'm not planning to . . .
Voy a pensarlo. I'll think about it.

"Lo único que recuerda es un golpe aquí, en la cabeza. ¿La verdad? No sabe nada".

"Soy Pedro Requena. Exacto, el nieto de la Sra. Gracia Requena. Voy ahora mismo para el hospital".

—Si necesita más información, aquí tiene mi número de teléfono.
—Gracias, señorita. Voy a pensarlo.

Después de ver el video

¿Comprendes?

A. Lee las frases y ponlas *(put them)* en orden cronológico.

1. Pedro no sabe si quiere contratar a una detective.
2. Lola y Carmela van al café a comer unas tapas.
3. Lola habla con Pedro y le da su número de teléfono.
4. Paco y Lola hablan en la oficina.
5. Pedro Requena habla por teléfono con el Dr. Sánchez Mata.
6. Doña Lupe dice que fue al hospital y habló con doña Gracia.
7. Carmela dice que su amiga, Rosalinda, trabaja en el hospital San Carlos.

B. Lee las frases y escribe el nombre de la persona que dice cada frase: Pedro, Carmela, Lola, doña Lupe o Paco.

1. No podemos trabajar si no hay cliente y no hay dinero.
2. Buenas noticias. Doña Gracia está mejor.
3. ¿Quieres tomar un café conmigo?
4. Mi amiga trabaja allí. Puedes hablar con doña Gracia.
5. No estoy pensando en contratar a un detective.

• Web Code: jcd-0507

Repaso del capítulo

Vocabulario y gramática 🔊

jcd-0699

Chapter Review

To prepare for the test, check to see if you . . .

- **know the new vocabulary and grammar**
- **can perform the tasks on p. 319**

to talk about where someone lives

cerca (de)	close (to), near
lejos (de)	far (from)
vivir	to live

to talk about houses or apartments

el apartamento	apartment
el baño	bathroom
la cocina	kitchen
el comedor	dining room
el cuarto	room
el despacho	home office
la escalera	stairs, stairway
el garaje	garage
el piso	story, floor
la planta baja	ground floor
el primer piso	second floor
la sala	living room
el segundo piso	third floor
el sótano	basement

to name household chores

arreglar el cuarto	to straighten up the room
ayudar	to help
cocinar	to cook
cortar el césped	to cut the lawn
dar (yo doy, tú das)	to give
dar de comer al perro	to feed the dog
hacer la cama	to make the bed
lavar (el coche, los platos, la ropa)	to wash (the car, the dishes, the clothes)
limpiar el baño	to clean the bathroom
pasar la aspiradora	to vacuum
poner (yo pongo, tú pones)	to put, place
poner la mesa	to set the table
los quehaceres	chores
quitar el polvo	to dust
sacar la basura	to take out the trash

to describe household items

limpio, -a	clean
sucio, -a	dirty

other useful words

bastante	enough; rather
¿Cuáles?	which (ones)
el dinero	money
un momento	a moment
¿Qué estás haciendo?	What are you doing?
recibir	to receive
si	if, whether

affirmative *tú* commands

For regular verbs, use the *Ud. / él / ella* form:

-*ar*:	habla
-*er*:	lee
-*ir*:	escribe

For *hacer* and *poner*:

hacer	haz
poner	pon

present progressive tense

Use the present-tense forms of *estar* + the present participle to say that you are doing something right now.

present participles:

-*ar*:	stem + -ando → lavando
-*er*:	stem + -iendo → comiendo
-*ir*:	stem + -iendo → escribiendo

For *Vocabulario adicional,* see pp. 472–473.

Más práctica
- **Core** Puzzle p. 119, Organizer p. 120
- **Communication** Practice Test pp. 297–299, Integrated Performance Assessment p. 296

realidades.com ✓
- Tutorial
- Flashcards
- Puzzles
- Self-test
- Web Code: jcd-0616

Preparación para el examen

On the exam you will be asked to . . .	Here are practice tasks similar to those you will find on the exam . . .	If you need review . . .

Interpretive

jcd-0699

1 Escuchar Listen to and understand teenagers' excuses for not doing a particular chore at the moment they are asked to do it

As you listen to a teenager explain to his mother why he can't do a particular chore at the moment, identify: a) what the mother wants the teenager to do; b) what the teenager says he is busy doing.

pp. 298–301 *Vocabulario en contexto*
p. 303 Actividad 7
p. 304 Actividad 8
p. 308 Actividad 17
p. 309 Actividad 18

Interpersonal

2 Hablar Give advice to someone about how to be successful in school

Your school counselors have asked you to participate in an orientation for new Spanish-speaking students. Offer each student in the group a piece of advice. For example, you might say *Escucha bien en clase* or *Haz la tarea.*

p. 305 Actividad 12
p. 306 Actividad 13

Interpretive

3 Leer Read and understand ads for apartments that you might find in the classified section of a Spanish-language newspaper

A friend is moving to Spain and asks you to help find an apartment. He wants a two-bedroom, two-bath apartment with a small kitchen. He wants to live near a gym and a library. Read this ad and answer the following: a) Is this a good apartment for him? b) How many of his requested features does it have? c) What other features that are mentioned might he like?

pp. 298–301 *Vocabulario en contexto*
p. 302 Actividades 4–5
p. 310 Actividad 21
p. 315 *Presentación escrita*

> Este maravilloso apartamento tiene todo. Está cerca de un parque y un gimnasio moderno. Tiene una cocina pequeña, pero totalmente equipada. Tiene dos dormitorios con estantes y un baño muy grande. También tiene televisión por satélite y un garaje privado. No se permiten animales.

Presentational

4 Escribir Write a list of household chores that you are willing to do

You and your classmates are offering to do chores to earn money for your Spanish club. Make a list of at least eight chores that you would be willing to do.

pp. 298–301 *Vocabulario en contexto*
p. 303 Actividades 6–7
p. 304 Actividad 8
p. 306 Actividad 14
p. 307 Actividad 15

Cultures • Comparisons

5 Pensar Demonstrate an understanding of cultural perspectives regarding houses

Explain how the architectural features of many homes in the Spanish-speaking world reflect the importance the owners place on privacy. How do these features compare to those in homes in the United States?

p. 303 *Fondo cultural*
p. 314 *Perspectivas del mundo hispano*

Fondo cultural

España

Joan Miró (1893–1983) was born near Barcelona, Spain. He painted this self-portrait in 1919, when he was 26 years old. Here he portrays himself wearing a *garibaldina*, or cardigan, a collarless sweater or jacket that buttons in the front. *Garibaldinas* were popular at the time, and they were usually red, a color that makes this portrait even more intense.

• How do fashions change across time, or from culture to culture? Give three examples.

"El joven de la garibaldina roja" (autorretrato) ▶
(1919), Joan Miró

En Las Ramblas,
Barcelona, España

¿Cuánto cuesta?

Chapter Objectives

- Talk about clothes, shopping, and prices
- Describe your plans
- Talk about what you want and what you prefer
- Point out specific items
- Understand cultural perspectives on shopping

Video Highlights

Videocultura: *De compras*

A primera vista: *Una noche especial*

GramActiva Videos: stem-changing verbs *pensar, querer,* and *preferir;* demonstrative adjectives

Videomisterio: *¿Eres tú, María?*, Episodio 5

Country Connection

As you learn about clothing and shopping, you will make connections to these countries and places:

España
Puerto Rico
México
Venezuela
Costa Rica
Panamá
Colombia
Perú
Bolivia
Uruguay

Más práctica

- *Real.* para hispanohablantes pp. 250–251

realidades.com ✓

- Fondo cultural Activity
- Online Atlas
- Video Activities
- Web Code: jce-0002

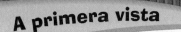

Vocabulario en contexto

jcd-0787

Objectives

Read, listen to, and understand information about
- shopping for clothes
- plans, desires, and preferences

Tienda de ropa La Preferida

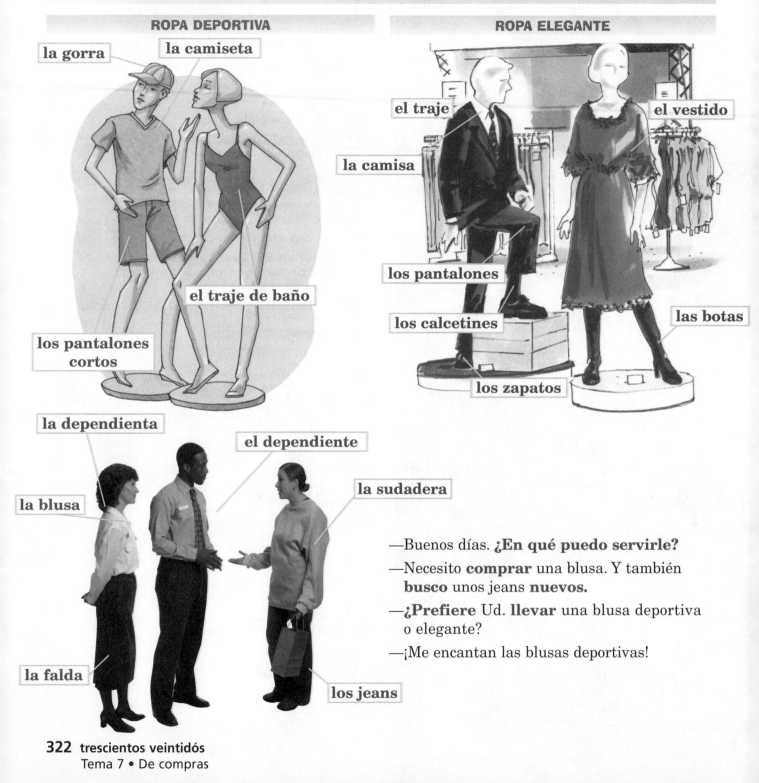

ROPA DEPORTIVA

- la gorra
- la camiseta
- el traje de baño
- los pantalones cortos

ROPA ELEGANTE

- el traje
- el vestido
- la camisa
- los pantalones
- los calcetines
- las botas
- los zapatos

- la dependienta
- el dependiente
- la sudadera
- la blusa
- la falda
- los jeans

—Buenos días. **¿En qué puedo servirle?**

—Necesito **comprar** una blusa. Y también **busco** unos jeans **nuevos.**

—**¿Prefiere** Ud. **llevar** una blusa deportiva o elegante?

—¡Me encantan las blusas deportivas!

el abrigo

el suéter   la chaqueta

—¿Qué **piensas** comprar hoy?

—Necesito comprar un abrigo. Me gusta **ese** abrigo. **¿Entramos** en **la tienda?**

—¡Uf! **Me queda mal.**

—**Tienes razón.** Es demasiado grande.

—**¿Cómo me queda** este abrigo?

—**Te queda bien.** Me gusta. ¿Qué piensas?

—Me gusta también. **¿Cúanto cuesta?**

—A ver . . . Cuesta ochocientos pesos. Es un buen **precio,** ¿no?

 **200**
doscientos **pesos**

 **300**
trescientos **pesos**

 **400**
cuatrocientos **pesos**

 **500**
quinientos **pesos**

 **600**
seiscientos **pesos**

 **700**
setecientos **pesos**

 **800**
ochocientos **pesos**

 **900**
novecientos **pesos**

1000
mil **pesos**

1 **¿Qué ropa llevan?** 🔊 ____ jcd-0787

Escuchar

Escucha qué ropa llevan hoy diferentes personas. Señala en la foto o en los dibujos cada artículo de ropa que escuchas.

Más práctica

- **Guided** Vocab. Flash Cards pp. 213–218
- **Core** Vocab. Practice pp. 121–122
- **Communication** Writing p. 136
- *Real.* para hispanohablantes p. 252

realidades.com
- Audio Activities
- Leveled Workbook
- Flashcards
- Web Code: jcd-0701

2 **¿Verano o invierno?** 🔊 ____ jcd-0787

Escuchar

On a sheet of paper, draw a snowman on one side and the sun on the other. If a statement you hear is most logical for winter, hold up the snowman. If it is most logical for summer, hold up the sun.

Una noche especial

¿Por qué necesita ir de compras Teresa? Lee la historia.

México

1 **Teresa:** **Esta** falda no me queda bien y **este** vestido no me gusta. No sé qué llevar para la fiesta.

Claudia: Pues, puedes comprar ropa nueva. Hay una tienda de ropa aquí cerca y tienen ropa muy bonita.

Teresa: Sí, **quizás** una falda nueva . . . **¡Vamos!**

Ramón · Teresa · Berta · Claudia · Manolo

5 **Manolo:** Ramón, son las ocho. La fiesta es a las nueve, ¿recuerdas?

Ramón: Sí, sí, tienes razón. Vamos.

6 **Berta:** Ramón, ¿tú piensas llevar esa ropa a la fiesta de Teresa? **¡Esos** jeans y esa camiseta y . . . esa gorra! No, no puedes.

Ramón: ¿Y por qué no?

Berta: Umm . . . Pues, aquí en México no llevamos esa ropa a las fiestas.

7 **Ramón:** ¡Yo quiero llevar mi gorra favorita, y me gustan **estos** jeans!

Manolo y Berta: Te ayudamos.

2 **Claudia:** ¡Mira esta tienda!

Teresa: Mmmm . . . No sé. No tengo mucho dinero y **esa** ropa es muy cara.

Claudia: ¡Vamos! **¡Queremos** ver qué tienen!

3 **Teresa: Perdón,** ¿señora?

Dependienta: ¿Sí? ¿En qué puedo servirle, señorita?

Teresa: Busco ropa para llevar a una fiesta. Me gustaría comprar esta falda y esta blusa.

Claudia: A ver . . . ¿Cuánto **cuestan?**

Teresa: ¡Seiscientos pesos! Pero, ¡es mucho dinero!

4 **Dependienta:** Bueno, aquí hay ropa que no cuesta **tanto.**

Claudia: Mira, Teresa. Esta falda cuesta trescientos pesos. ¿Qué piensas?

Teresa: ¡Genial! Y este suéter cuesta doscientos pesos. **Los dos** no cuestan tanto.

8 **Teresa:** ¡Hola! Buenas noches. Pero, ¿dónde está la gorra?

3 **¿Comprendes?**

Hablar · Escribir

1. ¿Por qué no está contenta Teresa? ¿Adónde va ella?
2. Según Claudia, ¿qué puede hacer Teresa?
3. ¿Adónde van las dos?
4. ¿Tiene Teresa mucho o poco dinero?
5. ¿Por qué no compra Teresa la primera falda y blusa?
6. ¿Cuánto cuestan la segunda falda y blusa?
7. ¿Qué quiere llevar Ramón a la fiesta?
8. Cuando Ramón entra en la casa de Teresa, ¿qué lleva?

Más práctica

- **Guided** Vocab. Check pp. 219–222
- **Core** Vocab. Practice pp. 123–124
- **Communication** Video pp. 130–132
- *Real.* **para hispanohablantes** p. 253

realidades.com

- Audio Activities
- Video Activities
- Leveled Workbook
- Flashcards
- Web Code: jcd-0702

Vocabulario en uso

Objectives

- Talk about shopping for clothes
- Discuss how clothes fit and how much they cost
- Ask and tell what you or others plan to do
- Ask and tell what you or others want and prefer
- Point things out using demonstrative adjectives

4 ¿Qué piensas llevar?

Escribir

¡Es importante llevar ropa diferente en diferentes ocasiones! ¿Qué ropa piensas llevar a estos lugares o actividades? Escribe las frases.

Modelo

la casa de un amigo
Pienso llevar unos jeans y una camiseta.

1. la playa
2. un baile elegante
3. un concierto
4. las montañas
5. un partido de béisbol

5 Escucha y escribe  jcd-0788

Escuchar · Escribir

Trabajas en una tienda de ropa y escuchas los comentarios de diferentes personas que buscan ropa. Escribe los números del 1 al 6 en una hoja de papel y escribe las frases que escuchas. Después indica con (+) o (-) si piensas que las personas van a comprar la ropa.

También se dice . . .

la camiseta = la playera *(México)*; la polera *(Chile)*; la remera *(Argentina)*

la chaqueta = la chamarra *(México, Bolivia)*; la campera *(Argentina, Chile, Paraguay, Uruguay)*

los jeans = los mahones *(el Caribe)*; las mezclillas *(México)*; los vaqueros *(Argentina, España)*; el pantalón vaquero *(España)*

el suéter = el jersey *(España)*; la chompa *(Bolivia, Ecuador, Paraguay, Perú, Uruguay)*

6 **¿En qué puedo servirle?**

Hablar

Tú y tu compañero(a) van de compras. Pregunta y contesta según el modelo. Escoge cinco cosas.

Modelo

A —*¿En qué puedo servirle, señor (señorita)?*
B —*Me gustaría comprar una camisa nueva.*
A —*¿De qué color?*
B —*Estoy buscando una camisa blanca.*

7 **Juego**

Escribir • Hablar

1 Escribe una descripción de la ropa de una persona en tu clase. Incluye dos o más cosas que lleva y los colores de la ropa.

2 Juega con otro(a) estudiante. Lee tu descripción. Tu compañero(a) tiene que identificar a la persona que describes. Antes de decir *(Before saying)* su nombre, él o ella tiene que hacer tres preguntas para saber más cosas. Por ejemplo: *¿Lleva una sudadera azul? ¿Tiene zapatos negros? ¿Sus calcetines son blancos? ¿Es Mateo?*

8 **¿Qué ropa llevan en el cuadro?**

Escribir

Escribe cuatro o más frases que describen la ropa que lleva la familia en este cuadro de Fernando Botero.

Modelo

La madre lleva . . .

9 En la tienda 🚶🧑‍🤝‍🧑 ♻

Pensar • Leer • Hablar

Con otro(a) estudiante lee la conversación entre un(a) dependiente(a) y un(a) joven. Empareja lo que dice el (la) dependiente(a) con lo que contesta el (la) joven.

el (la) dependiente(a)

1. Buenas tardes. ¿En qué puedo servirle?
2. ¿Qué color prefiere Ud.?
3. Pues, estos pantalones son muy populares.
4. Sólo 50 dólares.
5. Pues, hay otros pantalones que no cuestan tanto.
6. Creo que le quedan muy bien.

el (la) joven

a. Perdón . . . ese precio es demasiado para mí.
b. Entonces voy a comprar estos pantalones.
c. Quiero comprar unos pantalones nuevos.
d. Son bonitos. A ver si me quedan bien.
e. No sé—quizás negro.
f. Me gustan. ¿Cuánto cuestan?

10 ¿Cuánto cuesta en Montevideo? 🔊

jcd-0788

Escuchar • Escribir

Estás comprando ropa en Montevideo, Uruguay. Escucha los precios en pesos uruguayos. Escribe en tu hoja de papel el precio que escuchas.

Uruguay

Modelo

los zapatos
Escuchas: *Los zapatos cuestan mil ochocientos veinte pesos.*
Escribes: *1820 pesos*

1. la camiseta
2. la blusa
3. el traje de baño
4. el suéter
5. el vestido
6. la chaqueta

Fondo cultural

Bolivia • Costa Rica • Perú

The currencies of Bolivia, Peru, and Costa Rica are all different. Latin American countries have special names for their national currency and use different symbols as abbreviations. In Bolivia, the official currency is the *boliviano* (abbreviated *BOB*). The *nuevo sol* (abbreviated *s/*) is the official currency of Peru. Costa Rica's money is called the *colón*, and its symbol is a ₡ placed in front of the amount, as in ₡100 (meaning 100 *colones*). Cents are either *céntimos* or *centavos* in most Latin American countries. The images on the printed money honor each country's history and culture.

• How do the images on these currencies compare to those on bills and coins in the United States?

11 ¿Cómo me queda?

Hablar

Estás en una tienda de ropa. Te pruebas *(You're trying on)* la ropa y necesitas la opinión honesta de tu amigo(a). Tu amigo(a) siempre te hace *(gives you)* comentarios. Escoge dos artículos de ropa.

> **Nota**
>
> *Me / te queda(n)* follows the same pattern as *me / te gusta(n)*.
>
> • La camisa **me** queda bien pero los jeans **me** quedan mal.

Modelo

A —¿*Me queda* bien *el traje*? ¿Qué piensas?
B —*Te queda bien*. *¡Qué guapo estás!*

Estudiante A

Estudiante B

> Te queda(n) bien / mal.
>
> Es / son muy / bastante / demasiado . . .
>
> ¡Qué guapo / bonita estás!
>
> (No) me gusta(n) mucho.

Pronunciación

The letter *z* jcd-0788

In most Spanish-speaking countries, the letter *z* sounds like the *s* in *see*. Listen to and say these words:

zapato	arroz	almuerzo	cabeza	izquierda
haz	razón	nariz	azul	quizás

In many parts of Spain, however, the letter *z* is pronounced like the *th* in *think*. Listen to the words as a Spaniard says them and practice saying them as if you were in Spain.

Try it out! Listen to *"En la puerta del cielo"* ("At Heaven's Gate"), a traditional poem from Puerto Rico. Then say the poem aloud.

**En la puerta del cielo,
venden zapatos
para los angelitos
que andan descalzos.**

12 Y tú, ¿qué dices?

Escribir · Hablar

1. ¿Qué ropa llevas en el verano? ¿Y en el invierno? Incluye tres artículos de ropa para cada estación.

2. ¿Cuáles son tres artículos de ropa que te gustaría comprar? ¿Cuánto cuesta cada uno? ¿Cuál es el total?

3. Describe alguna ropa nueva que tienes.

Gramática

Stem-changing verbs:
pensar, querer, and *preferir*

Verbs like *pensar* ("to think," "to plan"), *querer* ("to want"), and *preferir* ("to prefer") are *e→ie* stem-changing verbs. The *-e-* of the stem changes to *-ie-* in all forms except *nosotros* and *vosotros*. Here are the forms:

(yo)	pienso quiero prefiero	(nosotros) (nosotras)	pensamos queremos preferimos
(tú)	piensas quieres prefieres	(vosotros) (vosotras)	pensáis queréis preferís
Ud. (él) (ella)	piensa quiere prefiere	Uds. (ellos) (ellas)	piensan quieren prefieren

¿Recuerdas?

You have used *quiero / quieres* and *prefiero / prefieres* to say what you want or prefer.

Use the infinitive for any verb that follows *pensar, querer,* or *preferir*.

¿Piensas comprar esa blusa?
***Do you plan to buy** that blouse?*

GramActiva VIDEO

Want more help with stem-changing verbs? Watch the **GramActiva** video.

pienso

---

13 ¿Qué prefieren llevar? ♻ 🔊
jcd-0788

Escuchar • Escribir

❶ En una hoja de papel escribe los números del 1 al 6. Escucha lo que quieren o piensan hacer diferentes personas y escribe las frases.

❷ Escribe otra frase para decir qué piensan llevar las personas para sus actividades.

Modelo

Mis primas quieren ir a un baile el viernes.
Piensan llevar una falda y una blusa.

14 ¿Qué piensas hacer? ♻

Hablar

Habla con otro(a) estudiante sobre qué piensas hacer tú y qué piensan hacer otras personas.

Modelo

tu amigo(a) / después de las clases
A —¿Qué *piensa* hacer tu amigo después de las clases?
B —*Mi amigo David piensa montar en monopatín.*

Estudiante A

1. tus amigos(as) / mañana
2. tu familia / este fin de semana
3. tus amigos y tú / esta tarde
4. tú / el domingo
5. tu amigo(a) / esta noche

Estudiante B

¡Respuesta personal!

15 ¿Qué quieren comprar?

Escribir

Después de dos semanas de trabajo, todos los jóvenes tienen dinero y quieren ir de compras. Escribe frases para decir qué prefieren comprar y cuándo piensan ir de compras.

Modelo

Catalina quiere ir de compras. Prefiere comprar unos pantalones cortos. Piensa ir a la tienda de ropa el sábado.

Catalina / el sábado

1. Isidoro y Lorenzo / esta tarde

2. Julia y yo / mañana

3. Javier / este fin de semana

4. yo / ¿ ?

16 ¿Qué piensan hacer Uds.?

Escribir • Hablar

❶ Copia la gráfica en una hoja de papel y escribe los nombres de tres personas con quienes vas a salir. ¿Adónde quieren ir Uds. y qué piensan hacer?

¿CON QUIÉN?	¿ADÓNDE?	¿QUÉ?
Pepe	el gimnasio	levantar pesas

Pensamos comprar algo en el mercado.

❷ Dile *(Tell)* a otro(a) estudiante adónde quieren ir tú y la otra persona. Tu compañero(a) va a adivinar *(guess)* qué piensan hacer Uds. Puede continuar adivinando hasta *(until)* decir la actividad correcta.

Modelo

A —*Pepe y yo queremos ir al gimnasio.*
B —*¿Uds. piensan jugar al básquetbol?*
A —*No, no pensamos jugar al básquetbol.*
B —*¿Uds. piensan levantar pesas?*
A —*Sí, tienes razón. Pensamos levantar pesas.*

Más práctica

• **Guided** Gram. Practice pp. 223–224
• **Core** Gram. Practice p. 125
• **Communication** Writing p. 137, Test Prep p. 300
• *Real.* **para hispanohablantes** pp. 254–257

realidades.com

• Audio Activities
• Video Activities
• Speak & Record
• Animated Verbs
• Leveled Workbook
• Web Code: jcd-0703

Gramática

Demonstrative adjectives

You use demonstrative adjectives to point out nouns: **this** cap, **these** socks, **that** shirt, **those** shoes. Notice that "this" and "these" refer to things that are close to you, while "that" and "those" refer to things that are at some distance from you.

Here are the corresponding demonstrative adjectives in Spanish. Like other adjectives, demonstrative adjectives agree in gender and number with the nouns that follow them.

	"this," "these"	"that," "those"
SINGULAR	este suéter esta falda	ese vestido esa chaqueta
PLURAL	estos suéteres estas faldas	esos vestidos esas chaquetas

Strategy

Using rhymes to remember meaning

To remember the difference between these demonstrative adjectives that are spelled very similarly, memorize this rhyme:

"This" and "these" both have *t's*, "that" and "those" don't.

GramActiva VIDEO

Want more help with demonstrative adjectives? Watch the **GramActiva** video.

¿Esta manzana?

---

17 En la tienda de ropa

Leer • Escribir

Carmen está en una tienda y habla con su amiga sobre la ropa que se están probando *(trying on)*. Escribe la forma correcta de *este(a)* o *estos(as)* para cada número.

Carmen: __1.__ botas son bonitas, ¿no?

Mariel: Sí, pero creo que __2.__ zapatos son bastante feos.

Carmen: ¿Qué piensas de __3.__ blusa? A mí me gusta mucho.

Mariel: A mí también. __4.__ suéter es demasiado grande, ¿no?

Carmen: Tienes razón. Y pienso que __5.__ falda es muy larga también.

Mariel: Quizás. __6.__ jeans no cuestan mucho. ¡Qué bueno!

18 **¡Un día con tu hermanito!**

Hablar

Tienes que cuidar *(take care of)* a tu hermanito. Tus padres tienen toda la ropa para él encima de la cama, pero ¡tu hermanito tiene sus propias ideas!

| Modelo |

A (tú)—*Tienes que llevar esta ropa.*
B (tu hermanito)—*¡No! No quiero llevar esa ropa. Prefiero esta ropa que está en el armario.*

19 **Juego**

Escribir · Hablar

¿Quién en tu clase sabe mejor cuánto cuestan diferentes cosas?

1 Trabaja con otro(a) estudiante. Escojan un objeto o una foto de un objeto. Puede ser ropa, algo de la casa, algo de la escuela, etc. Escriban una descripción de ese objeto y determinen cuánto cuesta.

| Modelo |

Este suéter azul y amarillo es . . . . Puedes llevar este suéter a . . . . Puedes comprar este suéter en . . . . ¿Cuánto cuesta este suéter? (Cuesta 55 dólares.)

2 Ahora, trabajen en grupos de cuatro parejas (ocho estudiantes). Lean la descripción de su objeto sin decir cuánto cuesta. La pareja que da el precio más aproximado *(closest)* sin exceder *(without exceeding)* el precio, gana.

| Modelo |

—*Pensamos que el suéter cuesta 50 dólares.*
—*Daniel y Eva, Uds. ganan. El suéter cuesta 55 dólares.*

Exploración del lenguaje

Nonverbal language

You've learned about the gesture *¡Ojo!*, which means "be careful." Another common gesture used by Spanish speakers conveys the meaning of "a lot of money." This gesture is made by holding the hand palm-up and rubbing the fingertips together. It is often accompanied by expressions such as *¡Cuesta muchísimo!* or *Es mucho dinero.* It can even be used when you're describing someone who is rich.

20 ¡Muchos regalos!

Leer • Hablar

Muchas personas en tu familia y unos amigos tienen cumpleaños este mes y tienes que comprar regalos. Tú y un(a) compañero(a) miran este anuncio de una tienda de ropa. Habla con tu compañero(a) sobre qué necesitas comprar.

Modelo

tu tía o tío

A —*Necesito un regalo para <u>mi tía</u>. Voy a buscar <u>un suéter</u> para <u>ella</u>.*

B —*Buena idea. ¿Te gusta <u>este suéter rosado</u>? Sólo cuesta 32 dólares.*

A —*Sí. Vamos a la tienda a buscar <u>este suéter</u>.*

1. tu hermano o amigo
2. tu hermana o amiga
3. tu abuelo o abuela
4. tu mamá o papá

 21 En la tienda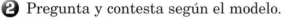

Pensar • Hablar

La tienda de ropa Perfección

¡Sólo 1 día!

$35 orig. $50

$25 orig. $38

$18 orig. $30

$19 orig. $28

$11 orig. $18

$32 orig. $45

$16 orig. $24

$8 orig. $14

Conexiones | Las matemáticas

Estás ahora en la tienda de ropa Perfección de la Actividad 20. Hablas con un(a) dependiente(a) sobre los descuentos que hay en la ropa hoy.

❶ Calcula el porcentaje de descuento de la ropa en el anuncio.

❷ Pregunta y contesta según el modelo.

Modelo

A —*Perdón, señor (señorita). ¿Cuánto cuesta <u>ese suéter rosado</u>?*

B —*Hoy <u>este suéter</u> cuesta sólo <u>32</u> dólares. Es un descuento del <u>29</u> por ciento.*

A —*¡Genial! Quiero comprar <u>el suéter</u>. ¡Qué buen precio!*

22 Un desfile de modas

Escribir · Hablar

Trabajen en grupos de tres. Una persona de los tres va a ser el (la) modelo en un desfile de modas *(fashion show)*. Decidan qué va a llevar el (la) modelo. En una hoja de papel, describan tres o más cosas que lleva el (la) modelo. Pueden incluir los colores, cuánto cuesta, dónde pueden comprar la ropa y en qué ocasión o estación pueden llevar la ropa.

Su modelo va a participar con los otros modelos de la clase en el desfile de modas. Los otros dos leen la descripción de la ropa.

Para decir más . . .	
cómodo, -a	comfortable
elegante	elegant
de algodón	cotton
de lana	wool
de seda	silk

Modelo

El (La) modelo que entra en este momento lleva . . .

Fondo cultural

Venezuela

Carolina Herrera is one of the world's leading fashion designers. This Venezuelan designer makes clothes, perfume, and accessories for women and cologne for men. She is one of many creative Spanish-speaking designers who are making their mark in the fashion world.

• Think of the names of some fashion designers from the United States. In what ways do you think they influence everyday culture?

BOUTIQUE GUADALAJARA

Vestidos y accesorios para toda ocasión

Ropa sport y vaquera; sombreros, botas

♦ *Invitaciones y regalos*

♦ *Libros y revistas*

♦ *Envío de dinero y tarjetas telefónicas*

1819 First Street Sonora, Arizona

El español en la comunidad

Locate a store in your community or on the Internet that sells products from Spanish-speaking countries. Visit the store or Web site and list the types of items you find there. Are they similar to the items listed in the ad? Bring your list to class and compare it with other students' lists. What are the most common types of items found in these stores?

Más práctica

- **Guided** Gram. Practice pp. 225–226
- **Core** Gram. Practice pp. 126–127
- **Communication** Writing p. 138
- ***Real.* para hispanohablantes** pp. 258–261

realidades.com

- Audio Activities
- Video Activities
- Speak & Record
- Canción de hip hop
- Tutorial
- Leveled Workbook
- Web Code: jcd-0704

Lectura

Tradiciones de la ropa panameña

Panamá

Mar Caribe

ISLAS DE SAN BLAS

COSTA RICA

Canal de Panamá

Ciudad de Panamá

Golfo de Panamá

PANAMÁ

Las Tablas

LOS SANTOS

OCÉANO PACÍFICO

COLOMBIA

Una tradición panameña de mucho orgullo[1] es llevar el vestido típico de las mujeres, "la pollera". Hay dos tipos de pollera, la pollera montuna[2] y la pollera de gala, que se lleva en los festivales. La pollera de gala se hace a mano y cuesta muchísimo por la cantidad de joyas[3] que adornan el vestido. ¿Cuánto cuesta una pollera de gala? Puede costar unos 1.850 dólares americanos, y requiere aproximadamente siete meses de trabajo. La pollera es tan importante que en la ciudad de Las Tablas celebran el Día Nacional de La Pollera el 22 de julio.

Si quieres celebrar con los panameños, puedes visitar la ciudad de Las Tablas en la provincia de Los Santos. Las Tablas es famosa por ser el mejor lugar para celebrar los carnavales. Durante el carnaval y en otros festivales, puedes admirar los vestidos y los bailes tradicionales.

El canal de Panamá conecta el océano Pacífico con el mar Caribe y el océano Atlántico.

El istmo de Panamá es la conexión entre dos continentes, y tiene costas sobre el océano Pacífico y el mar Caribe. Es famoso por el canal en el que navegan barcos[4] de todo el mundo. El folklore panameño es muy variado. La música, los bailes y los vestidos son importantes en la vida[5] social, especialmente en las provincias del centro del país.

¹pride   ²from the mountains   ³jewels   ⁴ships   ⁵life

Molas de colores brillantes
con formas de animales

Otro tipo de ropa auténtica de Panamá viene de los indios Kuna, un grupo de indígenas que viven en las islas de San Blas. Las mujeres llevan una blusa hecha[6] de molas. Las molas son paneles decorativos que forman la parte de adelante y de atrás de las blusas. Las mujeres demuestran[7] su talento y expresión personal con los diseños[8] originales de las molas. Los diseños representan formas humanas y animales. Hoy día, puedes ver y admirar molas como objetos de arte en muchos museos y colecciones.

[6]made   [7]demonstrate   [8]designs

¿Comprendes?

1. ¿Por qué es importante Panamá en el comercio global?

2. ¿Cuáles son las dos formas de ropa auténtica de Panamá en el artículo?

3. ¿Qué puedes celebrar si visitas Las Tablas?

4. ¿Cuánto puede costar una pollera de gala? En tu opinión, ¿es mucho o poco dinero?

5. ¿Cómo se llama el grupo de indígenas que viven en las islas de San Blas?

6. ¿Quiénes llevan las molas, los hombres o las mujeres?

7. ¿Por qué es diferente cada mola?

Más práctica

- **Guided** Reading Support p. 227
- **Communication** Writing p. 139, Test Prep p. 301
- *Real.* **para hispanohablantes** pp. 262–263

realidades.com
- Internet Activity
- Leveled Workbook
- Web Code: jcd-0705

Fondo cultural

El mundo hispano

Carnaval is a traditional celebration in many Latin American countries. It takes place in the weeks before the season of Lent. *Carnaval* normally includes the coronation of a beauty queen, parades, elaborate costumes, street music, and dancing. The *Carnaval* in Las Tablas, a town near the Pacific coast in Panama, is very popular and attracts thousands of visitors every year.

- What traditional parades or celebrations take place in your community? How do they compare to the celebration of *carnaval*?

La cultura en vivo
Las molas

Molas are the bright fabric artwork created by the Kuna Indians of the San Blas Islands, a group of islands off the Panama coast in the Caribbean Sea. *Mola* is a Kuna word meaning "blouse." This art form was originally used to make clothing, but today the term *mola* refers to any piece of fabric made using this method.

Kuna women cut out a cloth pattern and sew it onto layers of cloth that have been sewn together. Pieces of the upper layers are cut away to expose the underlying colors and create a design. Later, the women embroider details. Many designs on *molas* represent nature or animals. Each *mola* may take many weeks to complete.

Try it out! Here's how you can make *molas* out of paper.

Materials

- 2 pencils
- rubber bands
- construction paper
- paste or glue
- scissors

Figure 1

Directions

1 Your teacher will provide a pattern to trace on a piece of construction paper. You may prefer to trace around a cookie cutter or draw a simple design found in nature (for example, a leaf, flower, or fir tree). *(Fig. 1)*

2 Double all the lines by drawing with two pencils fastened together with rubber bands. *(Fig. 2)*

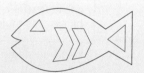

Figure 2

3 Cut out all spaces that do NOT fall between the double lines. *(Fig. 3)*

4 Paste or glue the cutout figure onto construction paper of a contrasting color.

5 Cut around the pasted or glued figure, leaving a border of the second color. *(Fig. 4)*

Figure 3

6 Paste or glue this cutout figure onto another piece of construction paper and cut around it, leaving a border of the new color. Paste the entire piece on a contrasting background.

Think about it! Do you or anyone in your family practice a traditional handicraft? Do you have any clothes or outfits that you have made or customized to express your interests or personality?

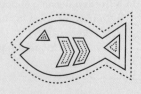

Figure 4

Presentación oral

¿En qué puedo servirle?

Task

You and a partner will play the roles of a customer and a salesclerk in a clothing store. You will ask and answer questions about the articles of clothing sold in the store. The customer will then decide whether or not to buy the articles.

❶ Prepare Work with a partner to prepare the skit. One of you will play the role of the salesperson, and the other will be the shopper. Be prepared to play both roles. Decide the type of clothing the store will sell and bring to class articles of clothing or pictures from a magazine. Give the store a name.

> **Cliente:** Make a list of expressions and questions you can use to ask about, describe, and say whether you will buy an article of clothing.

> **Dependiente(a):** Make a list of expressions and questions you can use to help your client, answer his or her questions, and show him or her the clothing.

❷ Practice Work with your partner and practice both roles. You might want to review *A primera vista,* the *Videohistoria,* and Actividad 9 for ideas. You can use your written notes when you practice, but not during the actual role play.

❸ Present Your teacher will assign the roles. The clerk will begin the conversation. Keep talking until the customer has made a decision to buy or not to buy the article of clothing.

❹ Evaluation Your teacher may give you a rubric for how your presentation will be graded. You probably will be graded on:

- how well you sustain a conversation
- how complete your preparation is
- how well you use new and previously learned vocabulary

- Speak & Record

Strategy

Seeking feedback
As you practice with a partner, seek his or her feedback to correct errors you have made and to improve your overall performance.

¿Eres tú, María?

Episodio 5

Antes de ver el video

Personaje importante

Rosalinda, una amiga de Carmela, trabaja en el hospital San Carlos

Resumen del episodio

Lola y Carmela van al hospital para hablar con Rosalinda sobre doña Gracia y María. Aprenden más sobre el accidente de coche de María. Ocurrió entre María y otra joven, Julia. Las dos fueron llevadas[1] al Hospital San Carlos. Desafortunadamente,[2] Julia murió. Rosalinda va a los archivos para buscar los historiales clínicos de Julia y María. Pero hay un problema. . . .

[1] were brought [2] unfortunately

Palabras para comprender

Estuvo aquí . . . She was here . . .

¿Te acuerdas de ella? Do you remember her?

Sí, me acuerdo de María. Yes, I remember María.

Dos coches chocaron . . . Two cars crashed . . .

la carretera highway

murió died

Les ayudó a las dos. He helped the two of them.

No viene a trabajar.
 He hasn't been coming to work.

el archivo records

los historiales clínicos medical records

los visitantes visitors

"Primero, quiero hablar de una paciente que se llama María Requena. Estuvo aquí, en el hospital".

"Pues, no está su historial clínico. Ni un papel. Nada, absolutamente nada sobre María Requena".

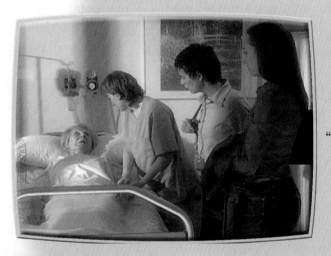

"¿Eres tú, María?"

Después de ver el video

¿Comprendes?

Lee las frases. Decide a quién(es) describe cada frase: Lola, Rosalinda, Carmela, doña Gracia, Julia, María o Luis Antonio.

1. Dos coches y dos chicas. Fue muy triste.
2. Ella murió en el accidente.
3. Hay un enfermero que ayudó a las dos.
4. Es muy simpática tu amiga.
5. No hay nada sobre ellas en los archivos.
6. Está bastante mal.
7. Las amigas de Carmela son amigas mías.

Nota gramatical Rosalinda uses two *vosotros* commands when she is talking with Carmela and Lola: *esperad* ("wait") and *venid* ("come"). You will hear this verb form often if you go to Spain.

realidades.com

• Web Code: jcd-0507

Repaso del capítulo

Vocabulario y gramática 🔊

jcd-0789

Chapter Review

To prepare for the test, check to see if you . . .

- **know the new vocabulary and grammar**
- **can perform the tasks on p. 343**

to talk about shopping

buscar	to look for
comprar	to buy
el dependiente, la dependienta	salesperson
¿En qué puedo servirle?	How can I help you?
entrar	to enter
la tienda	store
la tienda de ropa	clothing store

to talk about clothing

el abrigo	coat
la blusa	blouse
las botas	boots
los calcetines	socks
la camisa	shirt
la camiseta	T-shirt
la chaqueta	jacket
la falda	skirt
la gorra	cap
los jeans	jeans
los pantalones	pants
los pantalones cortos	shorts
la sudadera	sweatshirt
el suéter	sweater
el traje	suit
el traje de baño	swimsuit
el vestido	dress
los zapatos	shoes
¿Cómo me / te queda(n)?	How does it (do they) fit (me / you)?
Me / te queda(n) bien / mal.	It fits (They fit) me / you well / poorly.
llevar	to wear
nuevo, -a	new

other useful words

quizás	maybe
Perdón.	Excuse me.
¡Vamos!	Let's go!

to talk about prices

¿Cuánto cuesta(n) . . . ?	How much does (do) . . . cost?
costar (o → ue)	to cost
el precio	price
tanto	so much
doscientos, -as	two hundred
trescientos, -as	three hundred
cuatrocientos, -as	four hundred
quinientos, -as	five hundred
seiscientos, -as	six hundred
setecientos, -as	seven hundred
ochocientos, -as	eight hundred
novecientos, -as	nine hundred
mil	a thousand

to indicate if someone is correct

tener razón	to be correct

to indicate specific items

los / las dos	both
este, esta	this
estos, estas	these
ese, esa	that
esos, esas	those

pensar *to think, to plan*

pienso	pensamos
piensas	pensáis
piensa	piensan

preferir *to prefer*

prefiero	preferimos
prefieres	preferís
prefiere	prefieren

querer *to want*

quiero	queremos
quieres	queréis
quiere	quieren

For *Vocabulario adicional,* see pp. 472–473.

Más práctica

- **Core** Puzzle p. 128, Organizer p. 129
- **Communication** Practice Test pp. 303–305, Integrated Performance Assessment p. 302

realidades.com

- Tutorial
- Flashcards
- Puzzles
- Self-test
- Web Code: jcd-0706

Preparación para el examen

On the exam you will be asked to . . .	Here are practice tasks similar to those you will find on the exam . . .	If you need review . . .

Interpretive

jcd-0789

1 Escuchar Listen and understand why people are returning clothing items

Listen as people explain to the clerk in a department store why they are returning or exchanging clothing they received as gifts. Try to decide if the reason is: a) it doesn't fit well; b) it's the wrong color or style; c) it's too expensive; d) they just didn't like it.

pp. 322–325 *Vocabulario en contexto*
p. 326 Actividad 5
p. 328 Actividad 10
p. 329 Actividad 11
p. 332 Actividad 17

Interpersonal

2 Hablar Describe what you are planning to buy with gift certificates from your favorite clothing store

You got gift certificates from your favorite clothing store for your birthday. Describe at least four items you would like to buy. You could say something like: *Me gustaría comprar un suéter rojo. Prefiero esos suéteres que me quedan grandes.*

pp. 322–325 *Vocabulario en contexto*
p. 327 Actividad 6
p. 328 Actividad 9
p. 329 Actividad 12
p. 330 Actividad 13
p. 331 Actividad 15
p. 334 Actividad 20
p. 339 *Presentación oral*

Interpretive

3 Leer Read and understand an online order form for a popular department store

You want to apply for a job at a department store. They need someone who understands Spanish to interpret the online orders that come in. Read the entries to see if you can tell them: a) the description of the item ordered; b) the color; c) the price.

pp. 322–325 *Vocabulario en contexto*
p. 328 Actividad 10
p. 334 Actividad 20

	Artículo	Color	Precio
A.	sudadera	rojo/azul	355 pesos
B.	abrigo	negro	801 pesos
C.	falda	blanco/marrón/verde	506 pesos

Presentational

4 Escribir Fill in an order form for specific clothing items you might purchase as gifts

Order the following items using the online order form: a) black boots for your sister, who is very little; b) a blue-and-white baseball cap for your brother, who would need a small size; c) three pairs of gray socks for your dad, who has VERY big feet!

pp. 322–325 *Vocabulario en contexto*
p. 327 Actividades 7–8
p. 329 Actividad 12
p. 331 Actividad 15

Artículo	Color	Tamaño

Cultures

5 Pensar Demonstrate an understanding of cultural perspectives on crafts and clothing

Think about something you would consider to be American folk art that has been passed on from one generation to another. How would it be similar to or different from the *molas* made by the Kuna Indians?

pp. 336–337 *Lectura*
p. 338 *La cultura en vivo*

trescientos cuarenta y tres 343
Capítulo 7A

Fondo cultural

Paraguay

Ñandutí, which means "spider web" in the Guaraní language, refers to the fine lace weavings from the small South American country of Paraguay. Wall hangings and table linens are just a few of the intricately woven and multicolored items made from this fabric. *Ñandutí* looms are routinely found outside the doorways of houses in Itauguá, a small town where much of the country's *ñandutí* is made.

• Handmade items are usually more expensive than mass-produced ones. Why do you think some people are willing to pay more for these items?

Capítulo 7B

¡Qué regalo!

Chapter Objectives

- Talk about buying gifts
- Tell what happened in the past
- Use direct object pronouns
- Understand cultural perspectives on gift-giving

Video Highlights

Videocultura: *De compras*

A primera vista: *Un regalo especial*

GramActiva Videos: the preterite of *-ar* verbs; the preterite of verbs ending in *-car* and *-gar*; direct object pronouns

Videomisterio: *¿Eres tú, María?*, Episodio 6

Country Connection

As you learn about shopping and buying gifts, you will make connections to these countries and places:

Texas · Nueva York · Illinois · España · Florida · California · Puerto Rico · México · República Dominicana · Cuba · Panamá · Colombia · Paraguay · Chile · Argentina

Más práctica

- *Real.* para hispanohablantes pp. 270–271

realidades.com

- Fondo cultural Activity
- Video Activities
- Online Atlas
- Web Code: jce-0002

El centro comercial Perisur,
Ciudad de México, México

trescientos cuarenta y cinco **345**
Capítulo 7B

Vocabulario en contexto

jcd-0797 🔊

Objectives

Read, listen to, and understand information about

- stores
- shopping for gifts and accessories
- things done in the past

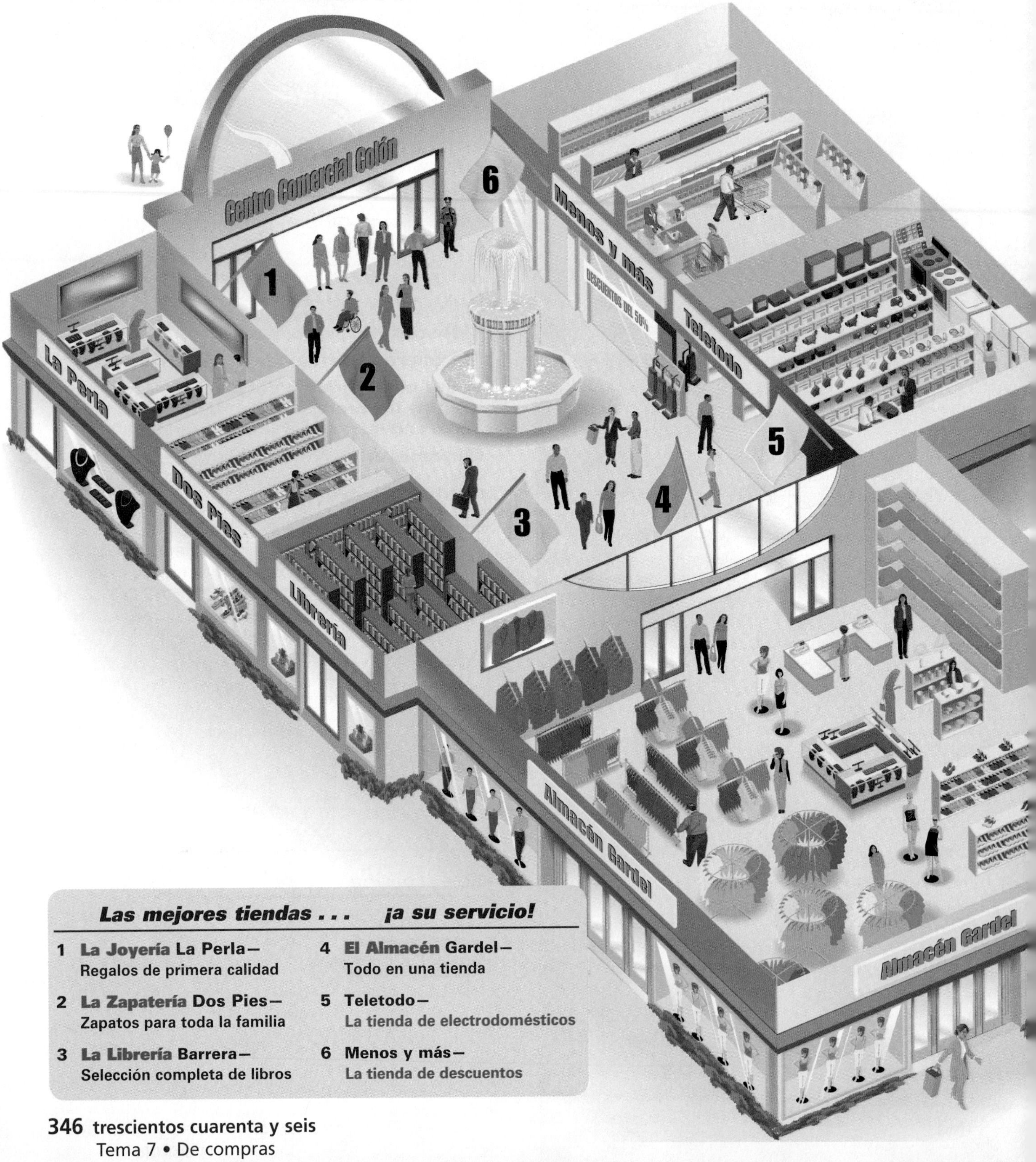

Centro Comercial Colón

La Perla

Dos Pies

Librería

Menos y más

Teletodo

DESCUENTOS DEL 50%

Almacén Gardel

Almacén Gardel

Las mejores tiendas . . .   ¡a su servicio!

1 **La Joyería La Perla**— Regalos de primera calidad

2 **La Zapatería Dos Pies**— Zapatos para toda la familia

3 **La Librería Barrera**— Selección completa de libros

4 **El Almacén Gardel**— Todo en una tienda

5 **Teletodo**— La tienda de electrodomésticos

6 **Menos y más**— La tienda de descuentos

346 trescientos cuarenta y seis
Tema 7 • De compras

—¡**Mira!** Todo cuesta menos aquí. ¡Qué **barato!**

—¡No puede ser! Yo **compré** esta cartera en el Almacén Gardel **hace una semana** y **pagué** mucho más. **¡Uf!**

la cartera   la corbata

MENOS Y MÁS

los anteojos de sol

el llavero

los guantes

el bolso   el perfume

la cadena   el reloj pulsera

el collar

la pulsera

los aretes   el anillo

—Mi **novio** necesita un reloj pulsera.

—¿Por qué no **lo** compras? Cuesta 30 dólares. No es muy **caro.**

—¡Buena idea! Vamos a entrar.

1 ¿Qué vas a hacer? 🔊)) jcd-0797

Escuchar

Estás de compras con tu hermana en un centro comercial. Tu hermana te está diciendo todo lo que quiere hacer, o lo que necesita en el centro comercial. Para cada cosa que dice, señala dónde en el centro comercial tiene que ir.

2 ¿Dónde lo llevas? 🔊)) jcd-0797

Escuchar

Escucha cada una de estas frases. Señala la parte del cuerpo en la que una persona lleva cada artículo que se menciona.

Más práctica

- **Guided** Vocab. Flash Cards pp. 229–232
- **Core** Vocab. Practice pp. 130–131
- **Communication** Writing p. 146
- **Real.** para hispanohablantes p. 272

realidades.com ⌄

- Audio Activities
- Leveled Workbook
- Flashcards
- Web Code: jcd-0711

Un regalo especial

¿Qué pasó cuando Manolo compró un regalo para su tía? Lee la historia.

México

la tía de Manolo

Claudia

Manolo

1 **Manolo:** Necesito comprar un regalo para mi tía. Mañana es su cumpleaños.

Claudia: ¿Qué compraste **el año pasado?**

Manolo: Compré un libro. Quizás otro libro.

Claudia: ¡Qué aburrido! Vamos al centro comercial . . .

5 *Claudia y Manolo están esperando el autobús. Tienen el regalo para la tía. A su derecha hay otra chica con un perro y otro regalo también.*

6 **Manolo:** ¡Vamos, Claudia! Aquí viene el autobús.

Claudia: Bueno . . . bueno.

7 **Manolo:** ¡Feliz cumpleaños, tía! Te compré este regalo **ayer.**

Tía: ¿Para mí? Ah, es muy bonito, pero . . . sabes que no tenemos perro.

Manolo: ¡No entiendo . . . !

2 **Manolo:** Aquí **venden** guantes, corbatas . . .

Claudia: ¿Corbatas para tu tía? ¿No tienes otra idea? Mira, aquí hay otras cosas . . .

3 **Manolo:** ¡Ah! Tengo una idea. **Anoche** compré un videojuego **en la Red** con mi computadora. ¿Quizás podemos comprar **software?**

Claudia: Para un amigo, sí, pero para tu tía, ¡no!

4 **Claudia:** Yo prefiero la joyería: una pulsera, un collar, un anillo. A ver. Señorita, ¿cuánto cuesta ese collar?

Dependienta: Cuesta 200 pesos con el descuento.

Claudia: ¡Qué barato! **La semana pasada** yo **pagué** 300 pesos **por** un collar.

8 **Perro:** ¡Me gusta mucho este collar nuevo! Me queda bien, ¿no crees?

3 **¿Comprendes?**

Escribir • Hablar

1. ¿Por qué van de compras Manolo y Claudia?
2. ¿Qué compró Manolo para su tía el año pasado?
3. ¿Qué piensa Claudia de comprar otro libro?
4. A Claudia, ¿qué regalos le gustan más?
5. ¿Qué regalo compran y cuánto pagan?
6. ¿A la tía le gusta el collar? ¿Por qué?
7. Al fin *(At the end)*, ¿quién tiene el mejor collar?

Más práctica

- **Guided** Vocab. Check pp. 233–236
- **Core** Vocab. Practice pp. 132–133
- **Communication** Video pp. 140–142
- **Real.** para hispanohablantes p. 273

realidades.com

- Audio Activities
- Video Activities
- Leveled Workbook
- Flashcards
- Web Code: jcd-0712

Vocabulario en uso

Objectives

- Talk about stores and where they are located
- Ask and tell about shopping and buying
- Talk about the past
- Learn to use the preterite of *-ar* verbs and verbs that end in *-car* and *-gar*
- Use the direct object pronouns *lo, la, los,* and *las*

jcd-0798

4 Escucha y escribe

Escuchar • Escribir

① Vas a escuchar lo que unos jóvenes dicen de algunas tiendas. En una hoja de papel escribe los números del 1 al 6. Escribe lo que escuchas.

② Escribe frases para describir lo que crees que van a comprar los jóvenes en cada tienda.

Modelo

Creo que él (ella) va a comprar . . .

5 En tu comunidad ♻

Escribir • Hablar

① Para cada tienda de la lista, piensa en una que está en tu comunidad. Escribe una frase para describir dos o más cosas que venden allí.

Modelo

una tienda de ropa
En la tienda de ropa Moda, venden camisas, pantalones y corbatas.

1. una librería
2. una tienda de descuentos
3. una tienda de electrodomésticos
4. una joyería
5. un almacén
6. una zapatería

② Trabaja con otro(a) estudiante. Lee lo que venden en cada tienda sin decir qué tipo de tienda es. Tu compañero(a) debe identificar qué tipo de tienda es.

Modelo

A —*Venden camisas, pantalones y corbatas allí.*
B —*¿Es una tienda de ropa?*

Fondo cultural

El mundo hispano

Los centros comerciales and *grandes almacenes* are popular in Spanish-speaking countries, but many people still shop in traditional specialty stores. These stores are often owned and operated by families, and customer loyalty is built over generations.

- Why do you think small specialty stores continue to survive when large, one-stop superstores and malls are very popular? Where do you prefer to shop? Why?

Tienda en España

6 **¿Dónde está el almacén _____ La Galería?**

Dibujar · Escribir · Hablar

Habla con otro(a) estudiante sobre dónde están las tiendas en un centro comercial.

1 Haz un dibujo de un centro comercial. En el dibujo incluye *(include)*:

una zapatería	una tienda de descuentos	una tienda de
un almacén	una tienda de regalos	electrodomésticos
un restaurante	una tienda de ropa	**¡Respuesta personal!**
una librería		

2 Inventa un nombre para cada tienda y el restaurante. Escribe los nombres en tu dibujo.

3 Muestra *(Show)* tu dibujo a otro(a) estudiante. Haz seis preguntas sobre el centro comercial. Tu compañero(a) debe contestar.

> **Modelo**
>
> **A** —*¿Dónde está el restaurante La Mariposa?*
> **B** —*Está detrás de la zapatería y la librería.*
> **A** —*¿Por qué quieres ir allí?*
> **B** —*Quiero comer con mi amigo.*

¿Recuerdas?

To tell the location of something, use *está* . . . :

a la derecha de	delante de
a la izquierda de	detrás de
al lado de	lejos de
cerca de	

Para decir más . . .

entre	between
enfrente de	across from

vas / voy a . . .	comer . . .
quieres / quiero . . .	buscar . . .
necesitas / necesito . . .	comprar . . .
te / me gustaría . . .	mirar . . .
piensas / pienso . . .	

7 **Un buen regalo** _____

Hablar

Habla con otro(a) estudiante sobre los buenos regalos para diferentes personas.

> **Modelo**
>
> un señor que trabaja en una oficina
>
> **A** —*¿Cuál es un buen* regalo para un señor que trabaja en una oficina?*
> **B** —*Creo que una corbata es el mejor regalo para él.*
> **A** —*¿Sabes dónde venden corbatas?*
> **B** —*Por supuesto. En la tienda de ropa.*

Estudiante A

1. un(a) joven que no es puntual
2. un(a) joven que trabaja en un almacén
3. tu hermano(a) mayor (menor)
4. tu mejor amigo(a)
5. tu novio(a)
6. tu abuelo(a)

Estudiante B

¡Respuesta personal!

*Buen is used in front of a masculine singular noun.

8 ¡Qué barato! ¡Qué caro!

Hablar

El fin de semana pasado compraste muchas cosas. Ahora un(a) amigo(a) quiere saber dónde compraste todas las cosas y cuánto pagaste.

Modelo

A —¿Dónde compraste tu suéter nuevo?
B —Lo compré en la tienda de ropa.
A —¿Cuánto pagaste?
B —Pagué 25 dólares.
A —¡Qué barato!
o: ¡Uf! ¡Qué caro!

Estudiante A

1.
2.
3.
4.
5.
6.

Estudiante B

¡Respuesta personal!

9 Vamos a la joyería

Leer · Escribir · Hablar

Lee el anuncio de una joyería en Tegucigalpa, Honduras, y luego contesta las preguntas.

1. ¿Qué venden en la tienda?

2. Según el anuncio, ¿las cosas que venden en la tienda cuestan mucho o poco?

3. Además de (In addition to) vender, ¿qué otros servicios hay en la joyería?

4. Pregunta a dos personas diferentes:
   • ¿Qué te gustaría comprar en una joyería?
   • ¿Qué joyas tienes?

Strategy

Using cognates and context clues

Try to figure out the meanings of unknown words by looking for cognates or by seeing how other words are used in the sentence.

• Can you guess the meanings of *bajos, diamantes, piedras preciosas, baterías,* and *arreglos* in this ad?

JOYERÍA HERMANOS SILVA

Vendemos relojes variados y todo tipo de joyas para toda ocasión

¡Precios bajos todos los días!

• Anillos y collares de diamantes y otras piedras preciosas

• Baterías de reloj, incluyendo instalación

• Hacemos reparaciones y joyas nuevas de su oro* viejo

• Reparación de cadenas y arreglos de pulseras

MENCIONE ESTE ANUNCIO Y RECIBA UN DESCUENTO DEL 10%

Abierto lunes a sábado de 10:00 hs. a 18:00 hs.

---

*gold

Exploración del lenguaje

Nouns that end in -ería

The Spanish word ending, or suffix, -ería usually indicates a place where something is sold, made, or repaired. This suffix is added to a form of the word that names the specialty item. For example, if you know that *una joya* is a piece of jewelry, you understand that you can buy jewelry at *la joyería*.

Try it out! You will often see these signs over stores. Tell what each one sells.

heladería	librería	pastelería
papelería	panadería	zapatería

Modelo

joyería
En la joyería venden joyas como anillos, pulseras y collares.

Venden flores para todas las ocasiones en esta florería en Argentina.

Esta joyería vende pulseras, anillos y collares.

Muchos españoles compran su pan cada día en una panadería.

Muchos mexicanos compran tortillas frescas en una tortillería cerca de su casa.

10 Y tú, ¿qué dices?

Escribir · Hablar

1. A qué tiendas vas de compras? ¿Qué te gusta comprar?
2. ¿Para quiénes compras regalos? ¿Qué tipo de regalos compras?
3. ¿Qué regalo compraste recientemente? ¿Cuándo y dónde compraste el regalo? ¿Pagaste mucho o poco dinero?

Gramática

The preterite of -ar verbs

To talk about actions that were completed in the past, you use the preterite tense. To form the preterite tense of a regular -ar verb, add the preterite endings to the stem of the verb. Here are the preterite forms of *comprar*:

(yo)	compré	(nosotros) (nosotras)	compramos
(tú)	compraste	(vosotros) (vosotras)	comprasteis
Ud. (él) (ella)	compró	Uds. (ellos) (ellas)	compraron

Notice the accent marks on the endings -é and -ó.

The *nosotros* form is the same in the present and preterite tenses. You will need to look for other context clues to tell which tense is intended.

¿Recuerdas?

In Spanish, the endings of verbs identify both who is performing the action (the subject) and when it is being performed (the tense).

GramActiva VIDEO

Need more help with the preterite of -ar verbs? Watch the **GramActiva** video.

hablé

---

jcd-0798

11 ¿El presente o el pasado?

Escuchar

En una hoja de papel escribe los números del 1 al 8. Vas a escuchar ocho frases que describen los quehaceres de una familia. ¿Ocurren los quehaceres en el presente o el pasado (*past*)? Escribe *presente* o *pasado*.

12 El dinero es un buen regalo

Escribir • Hablar

Tus abuelos les regalaron (*gave*) a todos dinero y cada uno compró algo. Explica lo que compraron todos y cuándo compraron las cosas.

Modelo

Mi hermano _____ hace una semana.
Mi hermano compró un reloj pulsera hace una semana.

1. Mi madre _____ ayer.

2. Mis primos _____ anoche.

3. Mi papá _____ el año pasado.

4. Tú _____ hace tres días.

5. Mis tíos _____ hace un mes.

6. Mi hermana y yo _____ ayer.

13 Juego

Hablar • GramActiva

❶ Tu profesor(a) va a enseñar a todos cómo deben señalar *(point to)* a diferentes personas *ella, nosotros, tú, ellos,* etc. Practica con tu profesor(a).

❷ Trabaja en un grupo de cuatro. Una persona es líder y dice un infinitivo de la lista y un sujeto *(subject)*. Por ejemplo: *cantar/ella.* Los otros tienen que señalar a la persona, o a las personas, y decir el verbo en el pretérito: *ella cantó.* Continúa así con tres sujetos más y el mismo verbo. Después, cambia de *(change)* líderes.

¿Recuerdas?

arreglar	hablar
bailar	lavar
caminar	levantar
cantar	limpiar
cocinar	montar
cortar	nadar
dibujar	pasar
escuchar	patinar
esquiar	trabajar
estudiar	usar

14 Hace una semana

Escribir • Hablar

Usa el pretérito para escribir y hablar de tus actividades.

❶ Copia la tabla en una hoja de papel. Usa los verbos de la lista de la Actividad 13 para escribir seis actividades que hiciste *(you did)* en el pasado. Indica cuándo hiciste cada actividad.

¿Qué?	¿Cuándo?
patiné	la semana pasada

❷ Usa la información de la tabla para escribir frases sobre tus actividades. Incluye información para contestar *¿dónde?* y *¿con quién?* Después, lee tus frases a otro(a) estudiante y pregunta: *¿Y tú?* Tu compañero(a) debe contestar. Escribe la respuesta de tu compañero(a).

Modelo

A —*Patiné en el parque con mis amigos la semana pasada. ¿Y tú?*

B —*Monté en monopatín con mi hermana la semana pasada.*

❸ Escribe tres frases con la información del paso 2.

Modelo

Patiné en el parque con mis amigos la semana pasada, pero Luisa montó en monopatín con su hermana.

Nota

To say when something happened, use *hace* + a time expression. It's like saying "ago."

• Compré la pulsera **hace un año.**
  *I bought the bracelet **a year ago.***

Más práctica

• **Guided** Gram. Practice pp. 237–238
• **Core** Gram. Practice p. 134
• **Communication** Writing p. 147
• ***Real.* para hispanohablantes** pp. 274–277

 realidades.com

• Audio Activities
• Video Activities
• Speak & Record
• Animated Verbs
• Tutorial
• Leveled Workbook
• Web Code: jcd-0713

Gramática

The preterite of verbs ending in *-car* and *-gar*

Verbs that end in *-car* and *-gar* have a spelling change in the *yo* form of the preterite.

> **buscar: *c → qu***   yo bus**qué**
>
> Silvia y Rosa bus**caron** aretes pero yo bus**qué** un collar.
>
> **pagar: *g → gu***   yo pa**gué**
>
> ¿Cuánto pa**gaste** por tu cadena? Pa**gué** 13 dólares.

Verbs such as *jugar* that have a stem change in the present tense do not have a stem change in the preterite.

> El sábado pasado **jugué** al tenis.
> Mis hermanos **jugaron** al básquetbol.

¿Recuerdas?

You know these verbs that end in *-car* and *-gar*:

buscar   practicar
jugar   sacar
pagar   tocar

GramActiva VIDEO

Need more help with the preterite of verbs ending in *-car* and *-gar*? Watch the **GramActiva** video.

pagar, jugar . . .

---

15 El viernes pasado ♻

Escribir · Leer

El viernes pasado Juan invitó a unos amigos a su casa. Completa la descripción de sus actividades con la forma apropiada del pretérito de los verbos *jugar, pagar, sacar* y *tocar*.

El viernes pasado mis amigos pasaron tiempo conmigo en mi casa. Tomás y Fernando **1.** videojuegos en mi dormitorio pero yo no **2.** con ellos. Yo **3.** la guitarra en la sala y todos cantamos. Jorge **4.** el piano un poco también. Después de cantar, nosotros **5.** al vóleibol. Mi amiga Ana **6.** fotos de nosotros. ¡Qué graciosas son las fotos! A las nueve fuimos por pizza y ¡mis padres **7.** la cuenta! ¡Qué bueno porque nunca tengo mucho dinero! Yo **8.** fotos de todos mis amigos en la pizzería. ¡Qué bien lo pasamos nosotros!

Fondo cultural

Colombia

El Museo del Oro in Bogotá, Colombia, houses over 33,000 objects of gold, emeralds, and other precious stones made by pre-Columbian cultures—cultures that existed long before the arrival of Columbus in the Americas. These ancient civilizations viewed gold as life-giving energy from the sun.

• What kinds of specialized museums have you visited in your community or in other locations? What did you learn from the types of objects that were included there?

El Museo del Oro en Bogotá, Colombia

356 trescientos cincuenta y seis
Tema 7 • De compras

Pronunciación

The letter combinations *gue*, *gui*, *que*, and *qui* jcd-0798

You know that when the letter *g* appears before the letters *a, o,* or *u,* it is pronounced like the *g* in "go," and that *g* before *e* and *i* is pronounced like the *h* in "he."

To keep the sound of the *g* in "go" before *e* and *i,* add the letter *u: gue, gui.* Don't pronounce the *u.* Listen to and say these words:

Guillermo	guitarra	espaguetis
guisantes	hamburguesa	Miguel

You also know that the letter *c* before *a, o,* or *u* is pronounced like the *c* in "cat," while the *c* before *e* and *i* is usually pronounced like the *s* in "Sally."

To keep the sound of the *c* in "cat" before *e* and *i,* words are spelled with *qu: que, qui.* The *u* is not pronounced. Listen to and say these words:

queso	quince	quieres	riquísimo
quehacer	quinientos	quisiera	querer

Try it out! Listen to the first verse of this traditional song from Puerto Rico entitled *"El coquí." El coquí* is a little tree frog found in Puerto Rico, named for the *coquí, coquí* sound that it makes at night. Say the verse.

> **El coquí, el coquí siempre canta.**
> **Es muy suave el cantar del coquí.**
> **Por las noches a veces me duermo**
> **con el dulce cantar del coquí.**
> **Coquí, coquí, coquí, quí, quí, quí,**
> **coquí, coquí, coquí, quí, quí, quí.**

16 Juego

Escribir • Escuchar • Hablar • GramActiva

❶ Escribe en una hoja de papel una o dos frases para indicar qué regalo compraste, para quién es, dónde lo compraste y cuánto pagaste.

Modelo

Compré un collar para mi novia en la Red. Pagué 45 dólares.

❷ Trabaja con un grupo de cuatro. Pon tu hoja de papel en una bolsa *(bag)* con las otras hojas del grupo. Cada uno toma una hoja, que debe ser de otro(a) estudiante del grupo. Cambia una parte de la frase y lee la nueva frase al grupo. ¿Quién puede identificar el cambio?

Modelo

A —*Esta persona compró un collar <u>para su madre</u> en la Red. Pagó 45 dólares.*

B —*No es cierto. Compré un collar <u>para mi novia.</u>*

17 Una lección de historia

Leer • Pensar • Escribir • Hablar

Estudia la línea cronológica *(timeline)*, los eventos y el mapa. Luego usa el pretérito para emparejar estos eventos históricos con las personas en la línea cronológica.

Nota

Here is how you say dates:

- **1500** mil quinientos
- **1898** mil ochocientos noventa y ocho
- **2005** dos mil cinco

Modelo

1. *En 1492, Cristóbal Colón llegó* (arrived) *a la República Dominicana.*

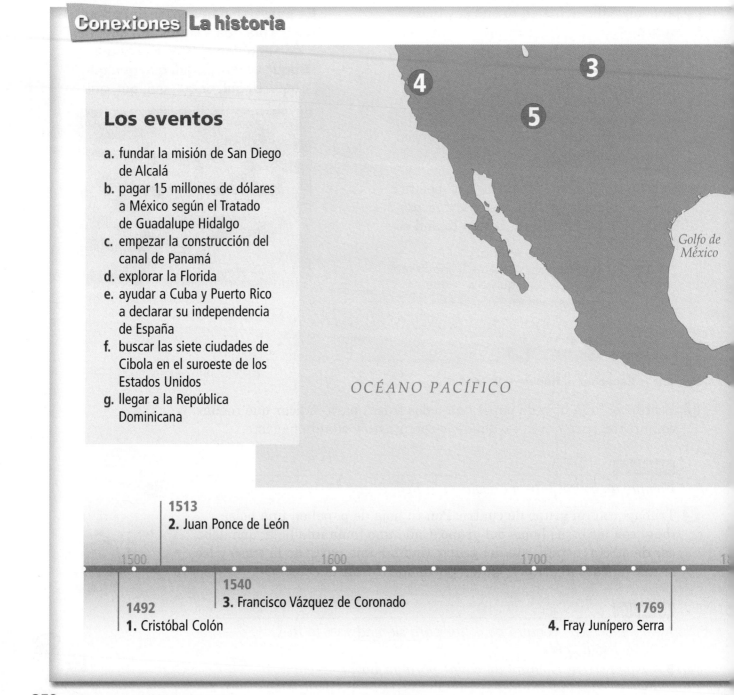

Conexiones La historia

Los eventos

a. fundar la misión de San Diego de Alcalá

b. pagar 15 millones de dólares a México según el Tratado de Guadalupe Hidalgo

c. empezar la construcción del canal de Panamá

d. explorar la Florida

e. ayudar a Cuba y Puerto Rico a declarar su independencia de España

f. buscar las siete ciudades de Cibola en el suroeste de los Estados Unidos

g. llegar a la República Dominicana

Golfo de México

OCÉANO PACÍFICO

1513
2. Juan Ponce de León

1500   1600   1700   1

1540
3. Francisco Vázquez de Coronado

1492
1. Cristóbal Colón

1769
4. Fray Junípero Serra

El edificio más antiguo de los Estados Unidos está en San Agustín, en la Florida.

La misión de San Diego de Alcalá, en California, fue fundada en 1769.

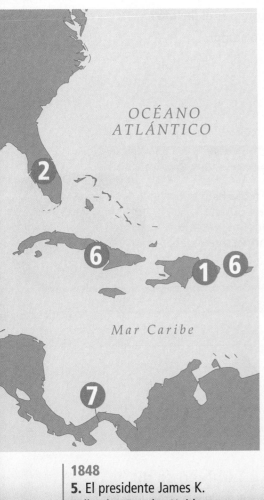

OCÉANO ATLÁNTICO

Mar Caribe

1848
5. El presidente James K. Polk y los Estados Unidos

1900

1898
6. El presidente William McKinley y los Estados Unidos

1904
7. El presidente Theodore Roosevelt y los Estados Unidos

Fray Junípero Serra

18 Y tú, ¿qué dices?

Escribir • Hablar

1. ¿Qué deportes practicaste el año pasado?

2. ¿Jugaste algún partido de tenis o de fútbol el mes pasado? ¿Cómo jugaste?

3. ¿Tocaste un instrumento musical ayer? ¿Cuál? Si no, ¿te gustaría saber tocar algún instrumento? ¿Cuál?

4. ¿Sacaste fotos durante tus vacaciones? Si no, ¿quién las sacó? ¿De qué?

5. Para el cumpleaños de tu mejor amigo(a), ¿qué compraste? ¿Cuánto pagaste?

Más práctica

- **Guided** Gram. Practice p. 239
- **Core** Gram. Practice p. 135
- **Communication** Writing p. 148, Test Prep p. 306
- *Real.* **para hispanohablantes** p. 278

realidades.com ▼

- Audio Activities
- Video Activities
- Speak & Record
- Canción de hip hop
- Tutorial
- Leveled Workbook
- Web Code: jcd-0714

Gramática

Direct object pronouns

A direct object tells who or what receives the action of the verb.

> Busco **una cadena**.

> Compré **unos guantes**.

To avoid repeating a direct object noun, you can replace it with a direct object pronoun.

> ¿Dónde compraste **tus aretes**?
> *Where did you buy **your earrings**?*

> **Los** compré en la joyería Sánchez.
> *I bought **them** at Sánchez Jewelry.*

Direct object pronouns agree in gender and number with the nouns they replace.

> ¿Tienes **mi pulsera**? No, no **la** tengo.

> ¿Tienes **mis anillos**? No, no **los** tengo.

A direct object noun *follows* the conjugated verb. A direct object pronoun comes *before* the conjugated verb.

When an infinitive follows a conjugated verb, the direct object pronoun can either be placed before the conjugated verb or be attached to the infinitive.

> ¿Quieres comprar **el llavero**?

> Sí, **lo** quiero comprar.

> o: Sí, quiero comprar**lo**.

	SINGULAR		PLURAL	
M.	**lo**	*it*	**los**	*them*
F.	**la**	*it*	**las**	*them*

GramActiva VIDEO

For more help with direct object pronouns watch the **GramActiva** video.

Las compré.

19 ¡No compraron nada!

Escribir

Ayer muchas personas fueron *(went)* al centro comercial y miraron muchas cosas pero ¡no compraron nada! Escribe lo que no compraron.

Modelo

Carlos

Ayer Carlos miró unas carteras pero no las compró.

1. Juanita

2. los novios

3. tú

4. nosotros

5. el señor Miró

6. yo

También se dice . . .

el anillo = la sortija *(muchos países)*

los aretes = los pendientes *(España);* los aros *(Argentina, Uruguay)*

la pulsera = el brazalete *(muchos países)*

el bolso = la cartera *(Argentina, Bolivia);* la bolsa *(Chile, México)*

los anteojos de sol = las gafas de sol *(Argentina, España)*

la cartera = la billetera *(Argentina, Uruguay, Bolivia)*

20 ¿Quién compró qué?

Leer • Pensar • Escribir

¿Te gusta ser detective? ¡Vamos a ver si puedes descubrir lo que compraron las personas, dónde compraron las cosas y cuánto costó cada cosa!

1 Lee las pistas *(clues)*. Luego copia la tabla en una hoja de papel y completa la tabla.

Las pistas

1. José gastó *(spent)* $35 en la joyería.
2. El software costó $45.
3. Paco no compró la novela.
4. Isabel fue *(went)* de compras a la tienda de electrodomésticos.
5. Luisa gastó $20 en la librería.
6. Los guantes costaron $25.
7. Paco fue de compras al almacén, pero no compró el collar.

Nombre	¿Qué compró?	¿Dónde lo compró?	¿Cuánto costó?

2 Usa la información de la tabla y escribe tus frases completas.

> **Modelo**
> *José compró . . . . Los (Las / Lo / La) compró en . . . . Costaron (Costó) . . . .*

21 ¡Demasiadas preguntas!

Hablar

Tu hermanito te hace muchas preguntas. Trabaja con otro(a) estudiante y contesta todas sus preguntas con mucha paciencia.

1. ¿Vas a comprar perritos calientes?
2. ¿Quieres leer este libro?
3. ¿Tienes que hacer la tarea?
4. ¿Quieres jugar videojuegos conmigo?
5. ¿Puedo comer este pastel?
6. ¿Vas a hacer mi cama?

> **Modelo**
> **A** —*¿Necesito llevar mis botas en el invierno?*
> **B** —*Sí, necesitas llevarlas.*
> **o:** —*No, no necesitas llevarlas.*

22 ¿Cuándo los compró?

Escribir • Hablar

1 Escribe cuatro frases para indicar lo que compró una persona y cuándo lo compró.

Modelo

Mi padre compró unos guantes la semana pasada.

2 Lee tus frases a otro(a) estudiante sin decir cuándo la persona compró el artículo. Tu compañero(a) va a preguntar cuándo lo compró.

Modelo

A —*Mi padre compró unos guantes.*
B —*¿Cuándo los compró?*
A —*Los compró la semana pasada.*

23 Juego

Hablar • GramActiva

Play this game in groups of five.

1 Each student in a group of five puts an object in the center of the group. The objects must be items for which you have learned the name in Spanish. One student turns around while another hides one of the objects.

2 The student who turned around now guesses who has the object. Correct first guesses are worth five points; correct second guesses are worth three. If the second guess is wrong, the student who has the object must say that he or she has it. All take turns being the "guesser."

Modelo

A —*Marta, ¿tienes el llavero?*
B —*No, no lo tengo.*
A —*Carlos, ¿tienes el llavero?*
C —*No, no lo tengo.*
A —*¿Quién tiene el llavero?*
D —*¡Yo lo tengo!*

Fondo cultural

México

The Zapotecs and other indigenous groups in the Mexican state of Oaxaca have their own languages and cultures. However, every July they all gather to celebrate the *Guelaguetza*, a Zapotec word that means "offering" or "gift." The *Guelaguetza* was first celebrated more than 3,000 years ago with music, dance, and food products. Today the festivities last two weeks and celebrate regional dances, music, costumes, and foods.

• What celebration in your culture is similar?

La fiesta de la Guelaguetza en Oaxaca, México ▶

24 Pero mamá, necesito . . .

Hablar

Quieres ir de compras, pero primero debes hablar con tu madre o padre. Explica lo que necesitas y ¡pide *(ask for)* dinero! Tu madre o padre va a explicar por qué no necesitas comprar nada. Tu profesor(a) te dará el papel *(will assign the role)* que vas a hacer.

1 **Hijo(a):** Piensa en lo que quieres comprar y cómo vas a convencer *(convince)* a tu padre o madre.

Padre (Madre): Tienes que decir a tu hijo(a) que no necesita lo que pide. Piensa en razones *(reasons)* para convencerle de esto.

2 Practica el drama con otro(a) estudiante.

3 Presenta el drama a tus compañeros. Ellos van a decidir quién tiene las mejores razones: los padres o los hijos.

Fondo cultural

España

Madrid's *El Rastro* is said to be the world's largest flea market. Located in one of the oldest sections of the city, *El Rastro* attracts thousands of visitors every Sunday of the year. Vendors line the streets with their stalls and offer everything from blue jeans to fine art. Bargain hunters as well as serious antique collectors bargain for the best prices.

• Have you ever gone to a flea market in your community or state? What kinds of things did you find there? How do you think they would differ from the things found in Madrid's *El Rastro?*

El Rastro, en Madrid, España

El español en el mundo del trabajo

Large stores and mail-order companies employ buyers who search the world over for goods to offer their customers. Buyers often need to rely on their language skills when looking for products in places where English may not be spoken, and when negotiating prices.

• What stores in your community might employ buyers who travel the world (or the Internet) in search of products from Spanish-speaking countries?

Más práctica

• **Guided** Gram. Practice p. 240
• **Core** Gram. Practice p. 136
• *Real.* **para hispanohablantes** pp. 279–281

realidades.com

• Audio Activities
• Video Activities
• Speak & Record
• Leveled Workbook
• Web Code: jcd-0715

Lectura

¡De compras!

Lee este artículo de una revista. A Luisa le encanta ir de compras. ¿Qué puede comprar en cada ciudad?

De COMPRA$
con Luisa, la compradora

¡Me encanta ir de compras! Hay muchos lugares donde me gusta ir de compras en los vecindarios[1] hispanos. Siempre es una experiencia divertida. Hay cosas que uno puede comprar que son muy baratas y que no hay en otros lugares. Voy a hablar de mis aventuras por las comunidades hispanas de Nueva York, Miami, Los Ángeles y San Antonio.

En el Barrio de Nueva York, en la calle[2] 116, venden ropa, comida típica del Caribe, discos compactos, libros y mucho más. Allí compré una camiseta con la bandera de Puerto Rico. En junio siempre hay una celebración grande que se llama el Festival de la calle 116. ¡Me encanta Nueva York!

La Pequeña Habana y la calle Ocho son el corazón[3] de la comunidad cubana en Miami. Hay bodegas[4] que venden productos típicos cubanos: frijoles[5] negros y frutas tropicales como el maguey y la papaya. Allí compré pasta de guayaba, un dulce delicioso que los cubanos comen con queso blanco. ¡Qué rico!

[1]neighborhoods   [2]street   [3]heart
[4]grocery stores   [5]beans

La calle 116, en Nueva York

Tienda en la Pequeña Habana, Miami

Pasta de guayaba

De compras en la calle Olvera, Los Ángeles

El Mercado en San Antonio, Texas

La calle Olvera es la calle más antigua[6] de la ciudad de Los Ángeles y allí uno puede ver la cultura mexicana. Hay muchos restaurantes y muchos lugares para comprar artesanías.[7] Me encanta ir de compras en las joyerías porque las joyas me fascinan. En las joyerías de la calle Olvera, venden joyas de plata:[8] aretes, collares, anillos y mucho más. En una joyería de allí compré una pulsera muy bonita a un precio muy bajo.

¡Ahora vamos a hablar de San Antonio! ¡Qué compras! En esta ciudad bonita de Texas, hay tiendas de artesanías mexicanas que son fabulosas. Mis favoritas están en el Mercado o como dicen en inglés, *Market Square*. Allí compré una piñata para mi hermano, una blusa bordada[9] para mi madre, una cartera para mi padre y un sarape[10] para decorar mi dormitorio...¡y no pagué mucho!

[6]oldest   [7]handicrafts   [8]silver   [9]embroidered   [10]shawl; blanket

¿Comprendes?

1. De los cuatro lugares en *¡De compras!*, ¿adónde debe ir cada persona?

   Ana: Me gustaría comprar algo de Puerto Rico.

   Lorenzo: A mí me fascinan las artesanías mexicanas.

   Miguel: ¿Mi almuerzo favorito? El sándwich cubano.

2. ¿Qué compró Luisa en cada lugar?

Más práctica

- **Guided** Reading Support p. 241
- **Communication** Writing p. 149, Test Prep p. 307
- *Real. para hispanohablantes* pp. 282–283

realidades.com ▶

- Internet Activity
- Leveled Workbook
- Web Code: jcd-0716

Fondo cultural
El mundo hispano

Las artesanías Handicrafts from Puerto Rico, Mexico, and other Spanish-speaking countries have been popular for years among tourists looking for gift ideas. Now these handicrafts are receiving recognition as museum quality artwork. At the Mexican Fine Arts Center Museum in the Pilsen neighborhood of Chicago, visitors can see permanent collections of paintings, weavings, sculpture, pottery, and silver jewelry from all over Mexico. Other types of handmade items are for sale in the museum's gift shop.

- Do you think that handicrafts should be displayed in museums along with fine art? Why or why not?

Una caja pintada de El Salvador

Perspectivas del mundo hispano
¿Por qué vas al centro comercial?

Why do people go to the mall? Note the differences between consumers in Chile and the United States.

In the United States many people go to the mall to see what merchandise is available and to spend time. In Chile, many people go to the mall because they want to make a specific purchase. They decide where to go according to the merchandise they need to buy.

For many in the United States, going to the mall is more than going shopping. The mall offers an opportunity to eat and to spend time with friends. For 50% of United States consumers the atmosphere of a mall is very important. Only 13% of Chilean consumers think that atmosphere is important.

Although their motivation for going to the mall is different, 80% of both Chilean and United States consumers make a purchase once they are in the stores.

Check it out! Interview at least three people your age and at least three adults that you know and find out what their main reasons for going to a mall are, how they decide which mall to go to, and if they usually make a purchase while at the mall. Compare what you find out with the results above for shoppers in the United States and Chile.

Think about it! Why might shoppers in the United States consider the mall atmosphere an important factor in their decision about where to shop? Given what you have read about the reasons Chileans go shopping, what do you think a store clerk in a mall in Chile might expect you to do if you entered his or her store? How might a Chilean exchange student feel if he or she went to the mall with you and your friends?

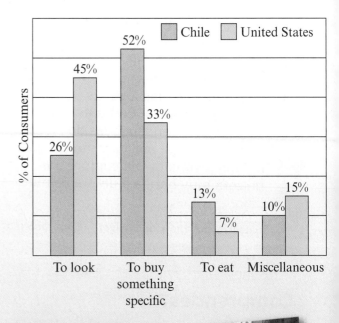

Chart: % of Consumers (Chile / United States)
- To look: 26% (Chile), 45% (United States)
- To buy something specific: 52% (Chile), 33% (United States)
- To eat: 13% (Chile), 7% (United States)
- Miscellaneous: 10% (Chile), 15% (United States)

En el centro comercial Galerías Pacífico, en Buenos Aires, Argentina

Presentación escrita
Un regalo para mi . . .

Task
You recently bought a gift for a member of your family. Write a letter to a cousin or other relative about the gift so that he or she will not buy the same item.

1 Prewrite A member of your family is celebrating a special birthday. Think about the gift you bought. Answer the following questions to help organize your thoughts.

- ¿Para quién es el regalo?
- ¿Qué compraste?
- ¿Dónde compraste el regalo?
- ¿Por qué compraste ese regalo?
- ¿Cuánto pagaste por el regalo?
- ¿Cuándo es la fiesta de cumpleaños?

2 Draft Use the answers to the questions in Step 1 to help you write a first draft of your letter. You may want to begin your letter with *Querido(a) . . .* or *Hola . . .*, and close it with *Tu primo(a) . . .* or *Saludos,* or *Hasta pronto.*

3 Revise Read the letter and check spelling, vocabulary choice, verb forms, and agreement. Share the letter with your partner, who will check the following:

- Is the letter easy to read and understand?
- Does it provide all the necessary information?
- Did you use appropriate letter form?
- Are there any errors?

4 Publish Rewrite the letter, making any necessary changes or additions. Share your letter with your teacher. You may also want to add it to your portfolio.

5 Evaluation Your teacher may give you a rubric that will be used to grade the letter. You may be evaluated on:

- how easy the letter is to understand
- how much information is included about the gift
- how appropriate the greeting and closing are
- the accuracy of the use of the preterite

Strategy

Organizing information
Thinking about the correct format and necessary information beforehand will help you write a better letter.

Querido Mauricio:

Compré un reloj pulsera para el abuelito. Lo compré en el almacén Génova que está en el centro comercial Plaza del Río. No pagué mucho por él. Creo que al abuelito le va a gustar. Voy a ver a toda la familia el dos de octubre para la fiesta de cumpleaños del abuelito.

Tu primo,

Luis

¿Eres tú, María?

Episodio 6

Antes de ver el video

Resumen del episodio

Lola llega a su oficina y hay un recado de Pedro Requena. Él viene a hablar con ella sobre su abuela, doña Gracia. Necesita un detective privado y quiere la ayuda de Lola y Paco. Pedro explica que su abuela es una mujer muy rica y que tiene joyas preciosas. Pero hay un problema. Las joyas de doña Gracia no están en el piso. Pedro cree que un ladrón robó las joyas. Pero, ¿cómo sabe el ladrón que hay joyas en el piso de doña Gracia?

"Por favor, ¿por qué no me tuteas?"

Nota cultural Lola quotes Pedro a price for her agency's services in euros. The euro is the currency in Spain and many other countries in Europe that are part of the European Union.

Nota cultural In Spain, it is customary for adults to speak to new acquaintances using the formal *Ud.* In most cases, the other person will then invite you to address them informally using the *tú* form. This is called *tutear*. In this scene, Pedro invites Lola to speak to him informally. When you visit Spain, you should address new adult acquaintances in the *Ud.* form and wait to be invited to *tutear*.

Palabras para comprender

un recado a message

una cita an appointment

Acabo de venir del hospital.
I just came from the hospital.

Vi a su abuela. I saw your grandmother.

necesito saber . . . I need to know . . .

el ladrón robó the burglar stole

nosotros cobramos we charge

"Mi abuela es una mujer rica. Tiene dinero y joyas de valor. Son de la familia".

"María va a recibir todo el dinero, todas las joyas, todo de mi abuela".

"Pedro, vamos a buscar las joyas".

Después de ver el video

¿Comprendes?

Termina las frases con la palabra más apropiada del recuadro.

fotos	recado
joyas	dinero
sobrina	abuela
teléfono	nieto

1. Lola, hay un _____ para ti de un tal Pedro Reteña, Resqueña o Retena. Algo así.

2. El _____ de doña Gracia viene a la una y media.

3. ¡Qué bueno! Un cliente con _____ .

4. Acabo de venir del hospital. Vi a su _____ .

5. Aquí tengo unas _____ de ella.

6. Mira, las _____ no están en el piso.

7. Aquí está el número de _____ : 318 18 02.

realidades.com

• Web Code: jcd-0507

Repaso del capítulo

Vocabulario y gramática

jcd-0799 🔊

to talk about places where you shop

el almacén	department store
pl. los almacenes	
en la Red	online
la joyería	jewelry store
la librería	bookstore
la tienda de descuentos	discount store
la tienda de electrodomésticos	household appliance store
la zapatería	shoe store

to talk about gifts you might buy

el anillo	ring
los anteojos de sol	sunglasses
los aretes	earrings
el bolso	purse
la cadena	chain
la cartera	wallet
el collar	necklace
la corbata	tie
los guantes	gloves
el llavero	key chain
el perfume	perfume
la pulsera	bracelet
el reloj pulsera	watch
el software	software

to talk about who might receive a gift

el novio	boyfriend
la novia	girlfriend

For *Vocabulario adicional,* see pp. 472–473.

to talk about buying or selling

barato, -a	inexpensive, cheap
caro, -a	expensive
mirar	to look (at)
pagar (por)	to pay (for)
vender	to sell

to talk about time in the past

anoche	last night
el año pasado	last year
ayer	yesterday
hace + *time expression*	ago
la semana pasada	last week

other useful expressions

¡Uf!	Ugh! Yuck!

preterite of regular *-ar* verbs

compré	compramos
compraste	comprasteis
compró	compraron

preterite of *-car* and *-gar* verbs

These verbs have a spelling change in the *yo* form of the preterite.

buscar *c → qu*	yo busqué
pagar *g → gu*	yo pagué
jugar *g → gu*	yo jugué

direct object pronouns

	SINGULAR	PLURAL
M.	**lo** *it*	**los** *them*
F.	**la** *it*	**las** *them*

Más práctica

- **Core** Puzzle p. 137, Organizer p. 138
- **Communication** Practice Test pp. 309–311, Integrated Performance Assessment p. 308

realidades.com
- Tutorial
- Flashcards
- Puzzles
- Self-test
- Web Code: jcd-0717

Preparación para el examen

On the exam you will be asked to . . .	Here are practice tasks similar to those you will find on the exam . . .	If you need review . . .

Interpretive

jcd-0799

1 Escuchar Listen as someone describes what she bought as a gift and where she bought it

As a teenager tells what she bought for her friend's *quinceañera,* see if you can tell: a) what she bought; b) where she bought it; c) how much she paid for it.

pp. 346–349 *Vocabulario en contexto*
p. 347 Actividad 1
p. 350 Actividad 4

Interpersonal

2 Hablar Exchange opinions about whether certain items are expensive or inexpensive

Think about a gift you've bought. Tell your partner what you bought, for whom you bought it, and how much you paid. Then ask your partner whether he or she thinks the gift was expensive or inexpensive. Your partner will then share the same information and ask the same questions about a gift that he or she bought.

p. 350 Actividad 5
p. 351 Actividades 6–7
p. 352 Actividad 8
p. 354 Actividad 12

Interpretive

3 Leer Read and understand an online advertisement for a store you might find on the Internet

While shopping online, you find a Web site for a discount store in Mexico City. Can you list at least two advantages for customers who shop here?

pp. 346–349 *Vocabulario en contexto*
p. 352 Actividad 9

Tienda virtual de descuentos

Todos nuestros clientes reciben un descuento del 10%. Tenemos de todo —perfume para su novia, bolsos para su mamá, videojuegos para su hermano y software para Ud. Tenemos los mejores precios y descuentos en la Red. Si paga por algo en la Tienda virtual, va a recibir "ePesos". Puede usarlos en su próxima visita.

Presentational

4 Escribir Write a short explanation about some items that you have bought this school year with your own money

As an entry for your class journal, explain how you spent your money last month. Describe: a) at least two new clothing items or accessories you bought; b) where you bought the items; c) how much you paid for them.

p. 354 Actividad 12
p. 357 Actividad 16
p. 360 Actividad 19
p. 361 Actividad 20
p. 362 Actividad 22
p. 367 *Presentación escrita*

Cultures

5 Pensar Demonstrate an understanding of cultural perspectives regarding shopping

Think about what you do when you go to a shopping mall. Based on what you've learned in this chapter, would these be the same things that Chileans do? What similarities and differences would you expect to see in shopping malls and in attitudes of shoppers in both countries?

p. 366 *Perspectivas del mundo hispano*

Tema 8 • Experiencias

Fondo cultural

España

View of Toledo is one of the most famous paintings by El Greco (the Greek). Born Doménikos Theotokópoulos in 1541 on the island of Crete, El Greco moved to Spain and settled in Toledo, a city south of Madrid. His *"View of Toledo"*, painted around 1597, was considered radical for its time because of its use of green, blue, and purple hues and its bold style. Instead of being realistic, the painting highlights the city's landmarks and its grandeur. El Greco's style has greatly influenced other painters.

• What would you highlight if you were painting your town or city?

"Vista de Toledo" (1597), El Greco ▶

Oil on canvas.†Metropolitan Museum of Art, New York/Index/
Bridgeman Art Library, London/New York.

Capítulo 8A

De vacaciones

Chapter Objectives

- Talk about things to do on vacation
- Describe places to visit while on vacation
- Talk about events in the past
- Understand cultural perspectives on travel and vacations

Video Highlights

Videocultura: *Experiencias*

A primera vista: *¿Qué te pasó?*

GramActiva Videos: the preterite of *-er* and *-ir* verbs; the preterite of *ir*; the personal *a*

Videomisterio: *¿Eres tú, María?*, Episodio 7

Country Connection

As you learn about travel and vacations, you will make connections to these countries and places:

España
México
República Dominicana
Nicaragua
Costa Rica
Puerto Rico
Ecuador
Perú
Chile
Argentina

Más práctica

- *Real.* para hispanohablantes pp. 290–291

realidades.com ✔

- Fondo cultural Activity
- Video Activities
- Online Atlas
- Web Code: jce-0002

El Museo Guggenheim en Bilbao, España

Vocabulario en contexto

jcd-0887

el parque de diversiones

el teatro

la obra de teatro

el lago

pasear en bote

el monumento

el museo

PICASSO

el oso

el mono

el zoológico

—**Dime,** ¿adónde **fuiste** el mes pasado?

—**Fui de vacaciones** con mis padres a **un lugar fantástico.**

—¿Qué lugar **visitaste?**

—Fui a Barcelona. Me gusta mucho **viajar** a otros **países como** México, España, Guatemala . . .

el estadio

—**¿Qué hiciste?**

—Pues, fui al zoológico con mi familia.

—**¿Te gustó?** ¿Qué **viste?**

—**Fue** fantástico. **Vi** muchos **animales** como osos y monos y también muchas otras **atracciones.** También compré **unos recuerdos:** una camiseta, unos aretes y un llavero.

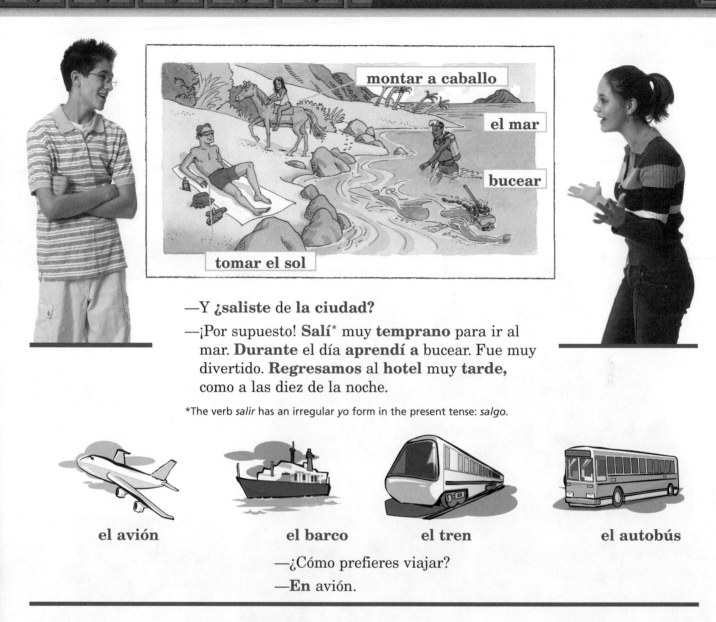

montar a caballo

el mar

bucear

tomar el sol

—Y ¿**saliste** de **la ciudad?**

—¡Por supuesto! **Salí*** muy **temprano** para ir al mar. **Durante** el día **aprendí a** bucear. Fue muy divertido. **Regresamos** al **hotel** muy **tarde,** como a las diez de la noche.

*The verb *salir* has an irregular *yo* form in the present tense: *salgo.*

el avión

el barco

el tren

el autobús

—¿Cómo prefieres viajar?

—**En** avión.

1 El viaje de María Luisa 🔊 — jcd-0887

Escuchar

Vas a escuchar a María Luisa describir su viaje. Señala en tu libro cada lugar que ella menciona.

Más práctica

- **Guided** Vocab. Flash Cards pp. 243–248
- **Core** Vocab. Practice pp. 139–140
- **Communication** Writing p. 156
- *Real.* **para hispanohablantes** p. 292

realidades.com 🅥

- Audio Activities
- Leveled Workbook
- Flashcards
- Web Code: jcd-0801

2 ¿Qué piensas? 🔊 jcd-0887 ¿Sí o no?

Escuchar

Vas a escuchar diez frases. Si la frase es lógica, haz el gesto del pulgar hacia arriba *("thumbs-up" sign).* Si es ilógica, haz el gesto del pulgar hacia abajo *("thumbs-down" sign).*

¿Qué te pasó?

¿Qué le pasó a Tomás durante su visita al parque nacional Sarapiquí en Costa Rica?

Strategy

Using visuals to make predictions
Before you read the story, look at the pictures to try to predict what will happen. After you finish reading, see how your predictions compared with what you read.

Costa Rica

Raúl   Gloria   Tomás

1 **Raúl:** Aquí están **los boletos** para el autobús.

Tomás: ¿Cuánto dura **el viaje?**

Gloria: El parque está a 82 kilómetros de San José. Es un viaje de hora y media.

5 **Gloria:** Va a ser una foto fantástica, Tomás. Un momento . . . un poco más a la izquierda.

Tomás: ¿Aquí?

Gloria: No, un poco más. Uno, dos . . .

Tomás: ¡Ay!

Raúl: Tomás, ¿dónde estás? ¿Estás bien?

6 **Gloria:** Lo siento, Tomás. ¿Quieres regresar a casa?

Raúl: ¿Quieres **descansar** un poco?

Tomás: No. Estoy bien. ¡Vamos a la catarata* La Paz!

*waterfall

7 **Tomás:** Quiero una foto de la catarata. ¡Es **tremenda, impresionante!** Uno puede estar muy cerca de ella.

Raúl: No, creo que estar un poco lejos de ella es mejor. Voy a ayudarte, Tomás.

Gloria: Un poco más hacia atrás* y a la derecha . . .

*towards the back

2 Gloria: Mira este mapa del **parque nacional.** Es mi parque favorito y lo llamamos "bosque lluvioso".* No hace ni frío ni calor, pero llueve mucho.

Tomás: Aquí hay un libro sobre los animales del parque.

*rain forest

3 Gloria: ¿Lo viste? Allí en el árbol.

Tomás: No, no lo vi. ¿Qué es?

Gloria: Es **un pájaro.** Es un tucán. Hay más de cuatrocientas especies de pájaros en el parque.

4 Raúl: Tomás, ¿qué te pasó?

Tomás: ¡Hay agua en las palmas! Eh . . . ¡no es nada divertido!

Raúl: Pero, Tomás, es un bosque lluvioso y llueve todo el tiempo. Siempre hay agua en las palmas. Pero sólo es un poco de agua.

Gloria: Estás aprendiendo muchas cosas, ¿verdad?

8 Mamá: ¡Tomás! ¿Cómo lo pasaste? ¿Qué te pasó?

Gloria: Pobre* Tomás . . . **fue un desastre.**

Tomás: No fue tan malo. Me gustó. Aprendí mucho y vi muchas cosas nuevas. ¡Pero hay mucha agua en el bosque lluvioso y en la catarata!

*Poor

③ ¿Comprendes?

Leer • Escribir

1. Haz una lista de cinco cosas que aprendiste sobre el bosque lluvioso Sarapiquí.

2. ¿A quién se refiere cada frase: a Tomás, a Gloria o a Raúl?

   a. Compró los boletos para el autobús.

   b. Sacó fotos de los otros.

   c. No vio el pájaro.

   d. Sarapiquí es su parque favorito.

   e. Ayudó a Tomás delante de la catarata La Paz.

   f. Vio un libro sobre los animales del parque.

   g. Decidió no descansar.

   h. Cree que el viaje a Sarapiquí fue un desastre.

Más práctica

- **Guided** Vocab. Check pp. 249–252
- **Core** Vocab. Practice pp. 141–142
- **Communication** Video pp. 150–152
- *Real.* **para hispanohablantes** p. 293

realidades.com ▼

- Audio Activities
- Video Activities
- Leveled Workbook
- Flashcards
- Web Code: jcd-0802

Vocabulario en uso

4 Una lista de actividades

Escribir • Hablar

1 ¿Qué actividades te gusta hacer cuando vas de vacaciones? ¿Qué actividades no te gusta hacer? En una hoja de papel, haz tres columnas y escribe *me gusta mucho, me gusta* y *no me gusta nada*. Debajo de cada expresión, escribe estas actividades en la columna apropiada.

ver . . .

visitar . . .

sacar fotos de . . .

ir a . . .

ir a . . .

comprar . . .

2 Usa tu lista de actividades y habla con otro(a) estudiante. Pregunta y contesta según el modelo. Haz por lo menos (*at least*) cuatro preguntas.

Modelo

A —*Cuando vas de vacaciones, ¿qué te gusta más: ver una obra de teatro o ir al zoológico?*
B —*Me gusta más ir al zoológico.*

jcd-0888
5 Escucha y escribe 🔊

Escuchar • Escribir

Vas a escuchar a una persona describir su viaje a Puerto Rico. Uno de los lugares que visitó es El Yunque. En una hoja de papel escribe los números del 1 al 6 y escribe las frases que escuchas.

El Yunque, un parque nacional de Puerto Rico

6 ¿Qué te gustaría hacer?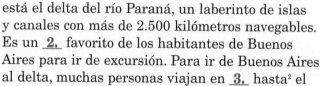

Hablar

Habla con otro(a) estudiante sobre adónde les gustaría ir de vacaciones.

Modelo

A —*Dime, ¿te gustaría ir de vacaciones a una ciudad?*

B —*Sí, porque en una ciudad puedes ir de compras y comer en restaurantes fantásticos.*

o: —*No. Me gustaría más ir a un parque nacional porque puedes ir de cámping.*

Estudiante A

1. una ciudad
2. un parque nacional
3. un lago
4. el mar

Estudiante B

¡Respuesta personal!

7 El delta del río[1] Paraná

Leer • Escribir

Lee la descripción del delta del río Paraná, a 30 kilómetros de Buenos Aires, y completa las frases con las palabras correctas de los recuadros. Después contesta las preguntas.

| tren | ciudad | país | lugar |

Al norte de la **1.** de Buenos Aires, Argentina, está el delta del río Paraná, un laberinto de islas y canales con más de 2.500 kilómetros navegables. Es un **2.** favorito de los habitantes de Buenos Aires para ir de excursión. Para ir de Buenos Aires al delta, muchas personas viajan en **3.** hasta[2] el Tigre, un pueblo[3] pequeño.

| descansar | regresar | pasear | montar |

Aquí las personas pueden **4.** en bote por los canales, **5.** y tomar el sol en la orilla[4], **6.** a caballo o practicar el esquí acuático.

| recuerdos | lagos | pájaros | árboles |

Argentina

El delta del río Paraná, en la Argentina

También pueden comprar comida y **7.** turísticos en los mercados[5]. Las personas siempre tienen sus cámaras en las excursiones al delta porque hay muchos tipos de animales y **8.** que viven en los **9.** muy altos.

- Para ti, ¿es el delta del río Paraná un buen lugar para ir de vacaciones? ¿Por qué?

- ¿Qué actividades te gustaría hacer en este lugar?

[1]river [2]as far as [3]town [4]riverbank [5]markets

8 Cómo puedes viajar

Hablar

Mira los mapas al principio del libro. Dile a tu compañero(a) que te gustaría viajar de un lugar o país a otro. Tu compañero(a) debe decir cómo puedes viajar entre los dos lugares.

También se dice . . .

el autobús =
   el camión (México);
   el colectivo, el ómnibus (Argentina, Bolivia); la guagua (Puerto Rico, Cuba); el micro (Perú, Chile)

Modelo

A —*Me gustaría viajar de la República Dominicana a Puerto Rico.*

B —*Pues, entonces, puedes viajar en barco o en avión.*

Estudiante A

¡Respuesta personal!

Estudiante B

Pronunciación

Diphthongs jcd-0888

In Spanish, there are two groups of vowels: "strong" (*a, e* and *o*) and "weak" (*i* and *u*).

When a weak vowel is combined with any other vowel, the individual vowel sounds become blended to form a single sound called a diphthong (*un diptongo*). Listen to and say these words:

limpiar	*baile*	*siete*	*seis*	*estadio*	*ciudad*
fuimos	*cuarto*	*juego*	*aire*	*piensas*	*autobús*

When two strong vowels are together, each vowel is pronounced as a separate sound. Listen to and say these words:

teatro	*museo*	*pasear*	*bucear*
cereal	*video*	*leer*	*zoológico*
traer	*idea*	*tarea*	*cumpleaños*

If there is an accent mark over a weak vowel, it causes that letter to be pronounced as though it were a strong vowel. Listen to and say these words:

día	*frío*	*tíos*	*zapatería*
joyería	*país*	*esquío*	*gustaría*

Try it out! Listen to some of the lines of "*Cielito lindo,*" a song from Mexico that is very popular with mariachi bands. Can you identify the diphthongs in the lyrics? Try saying the words and then singing the song.

De la sierra morena,
cielito lindo, vienen bajando
un par de ojitos negros,
cielito lindo, de contrabando.
¡Ay, ay, ay, ay!
Canta y no llores,
porque cantando se alegran,
cielito lindo, los corazones.

9 ¿Quieres aprender a bucear?

Leer • Escribir • Hablar

Lee el anuncio y contesta las preguntas.

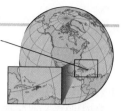

República Dominicana

Escuela de buceo "Flor del mar"

Puerto Plata, República Dominicana

Cursos de buceo "Flor del mar"
¡Aprende a bucear en sólo tres cursos!
Ve peces impresionantes y otros animales del mar.
Practica un deporte interesante y divertido.
Pasa tiempo con amigos en un lugar fantástico.

Señales de buceo

Hay un lenguaje especial que permite a los buzos comunicarse en el agua con señales. En los cursos de buceo, puedes aprender estas señales. Así no vas a tener ningún problema practicando este deporte. Algunas de las señales más importantes son:

Si quieres información sobre un curso de buceo en la República Dominicana, comunícate al 555-19-19 con la Dra. María Elena Santos o al 555-02-28 con Marcos Morelos.

| Alto | Ir hacia arriba | Ir hacia abajo | Preguntar si estás bien | Contestar OK o sí | Hay un problema | ¡Peligro! |

1. ¿Por qué debes estudiar cursos de buceo en la escuela "Flor del mar"?
2. Practica las señales con otro(a) estudiante. ¿Qué puedes comunicar?

10 ¿Dónde aprendiste a bucear?

Hablar

Habla con otro(a) estudiante sobre dónde aprendió a hacer las actividades de la lista.

1. bucear
2. montar a caballo
3. esquiar
4. montar en bicicleta
5. patinar
6. tocar la guitarra

Modelo

nadar

A —¿Dónde aprendiste a _nadar_?
B —Aprendí a _nadar_ en _California_.
o:—No aprendí a _nadar_ nunca pero me gustaría aprender.
o:—No aprendí a _nadar_ nunca y no quiero aprender.

11 ¿Adónde fuiste?

Hablar

La primavera pasada fuiste de vacaciones a la Ciudad de México. Ahora tienes tus fotos y hablas con otro(a) estudiante. En la Ciudad de México viste estas cosas:

El Paseo de la Reforma con el monumento del Ángel de la Independencia ¡Impresionante!

un partido de fútbol
muchas atracciones
una obra de teatro
el monumento del Ángel de la Independencia
animales como osos y monos
muchos cuadros interesantes

Modelo

A —¿Adónde fuiste?
B —Fui al Paseo de la Reforma.
A —¿Qué viste?
B —Vi el monumento del Ángel de la Independencia.
A —¿Cómo lo pasaste allí? ¿Te gustó?
B —Fue impresionante. Me gustó mucho.

1.

Museo de arte de Frida Kahlo
¡Fantástico!

2.

El Zoológico del Parque Chapultepec
¡Tremendo!

3.

El parque de diversiones en el
Parque Chapultepec
¡Muy divertido!

4.

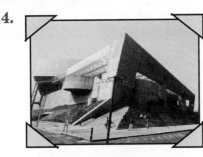

El Teatro del Auditorio
¡Fenomenal!

5.

El Estadio Azteca
¡Genial!

12 Y tú, ¿qué dices?

Escribir · Hablar

1. ¿Adónde te gustaría ir de vacaciones en los Estados Unidos? ¿Cómo quieres viajar? ¿Qué te gustaría hacer?

2. ¿Qué ciudades te gustaría visitar? ¿Qué lugares en esas ciudades quieres ver?

3. Cuando viajas, ¿prefieres salir temprano o tarde?

4. Durante un viaje, ¿descansas mucho o regresas a casa muy cansado(a)?

Manos a la obra

Gramática

The preterite of *-er* and *-ir* verbs

Regular *-er* and *-ir* verbs are similar to one another in the preterite. Here are the preterite forms of *aprender* and *salir*. Notice the accent marks on the endings *-í* and *-ió*:

(yo)	**aprendí**	(nosotros) (nosotras)	**aprendimos**
(tú)	**aprendiste**	(vosotros) (vosotras)	**aprendisteis**
Ud. (él) (ella)	**aprendió**	Uds. (ellos) (ellas)	**aprendieron**

(yo)	**salí**	(nosotros) (nosotras)	**salimos**
(tú)	**saliste**	(vosotros) (vosotras)	**salisteis**
Ud. (él) (ella)	**salió**	Uds. (ellos) (ellas)	**salieron**

The verb *ver* is regular in the preterite but does not have accent marks in any of its forms:

vi   viste   vio   vimos   visteis   vieron

GramActiva VIDEO

Want more help with the preterite of *-er* and *-ir* verbs? Watch the **GramActiva** video.

comí, salí
-er -ir

13 Ricitos de Oro y los tres osos ♻

Leer • Escribir

Escribe los verbos apropiados en el pretérito para completar cada frase del cuento de *Ricitos de Oro y los tres osos*.

Un día los tres osos __1.__ *(salir / beber)* temprano de su casa para caminar. Ricitos de Oro, una chica muy bonita, __2.__ *(comer / ver)* la casa de los tres osos y __3.__ *(recibir / abrir)* la puerta. Ella no __4.__ *(ver / comprender)* que era[1] la casa de los tres osos y __5.__ *(comer / aprender)* toda la comida del oso chiquito. Luego ella __6.__ *(beber / decidir)* dormir un poco. Poco después, los tres osos regresaron a su casa, __7.__ *(abrir / salir)* la puerta y __8.__ *(deber / ver)* a Ricitos de Oro en la cama del osito. Cuando Ricitos de Oro __9.__ *(viajar / ver)* a los osos, __10.__ *(abrir / salir)* de la casa rápidamente. __11.__ *(Comer / Correr)* hasta llegar[2] a su propia casa.

[1]it was   [2]until she arrived

Fondo cultural

México

Mexico City's *Metro* is one of the most advanced subway systems in the world. It is fast, modern, and very inexpensive. In addition, an extensive bus service crosses the whole city. Smaller green and gray minibuses, called *peseros,* also serve passengers along major routes.

• Why do you think Mexico City has such an advanced and varied public transportation system?

14 Durante las vacaciones

Escribir

Escribe seis frases para decir qué hicieron *(did)* estas
personas durante sus vacaciones. Usa las palabras de la lista.

| comer en . . . |
| compartir una casa en . . . |
| escribir . . . |
| correr en . . . |
| aprender a . . . |
| ver . . . |
| salir de casa temprano para . . . |
| salir con . . . |

Modelo

*Durante las vacaciones, mi hermana y yo corrimos en la
playa de Santa Mónica.*

1. mi familia y yo   **3.** yo   **5.** mi hermano(a)

2. mis amigos   **4.** mis padres   **6.** mi amigo(a) *(nombre)*

15 Tú y yo

Escribir • Hablar

1 Trabaja con otro(a) estudiante. Lee una
frase de la Actividad 14. Tu compañero(a)
va a contestar si tiene una idea similar
en su hoja de papel.

Modelo

A—*Mi hermana y yo corrimos en la playa
de Santa Mónica.*

B—*Mi amigo y yo también corrimos, pero
nosotros corrimos en un estadio.*

o: —*Yo no corrí en las vacaciones. Escribí
cuentos todos los días.*

2 Escribe seis frases para comparar lo que
hicieron tú y tu compañero(a) durante las
vacaciones.

Modelo

*Adela y yo corrimos durante las vacaciones.
Ella corrió en un estadio con su amigo.
Yo corrí en la playa con mi hermana.*

Más práctica

- **Guided** Gram. Practice pp. 253–254
- **Core** Gram. Practice p. 143
- **Communication** Writing p. 157,
  Test Prep p. 312
- *Real.* **para hispanohablantes**
  pp. 294–297

realidades.com
- Audio Activities
- Video Activities
- Speak & Record
- Animated Verbs
- Tutorial
- Leveled Workbook
- Web Code: jcd-0803

Fondo cultural

Argentina • Chile

La Patagonia is a vast, windy region of diverse
climates and terrains at the southern tip of South
America. It lies east of the Andes and spans
parts of Chile and nearly a quarter of Argentina.
A sparsely populated area, it is home to many
species, including a large colony (325,000 breeding
pairs) of Magellanic penguins, whose breeding
grounds are the eastern and western coasts of
Chile and Argentina, as well as offshore islands.

- What regions of the United States can be
  compared to Patagonia? What types of animals
  live in those regions?

Pingüinos de la Patagonia

Gramática

The preterite of *ir*

Ir is irregular in the preterite. Notice that the preterite forms of *ir* do not have accent marks:

(yo)	**fui**	(nosotros) (nosotras)	**fuimos**
(tú)	**fuiste**	(vosotros) (vosotras)	**fuisteis**
Ud. (él) (ella)	**fue**	Uds. (ellos) (ellas)	**fueron**

The preterite of *ir* is the same as the preterite of *ser*. The context makes the meaning clear.

José **fue** a Barcelona.   *José* **went** *to Barcelona.*
El viaje **fue** un desastre.   *The trip* **was** *a disaster.*

Strategy

Using memory devices
Here's a memory tip to help you remember the subjects of *fui* and *fue:*

The "I" form ends in *-i (fui).*

The "he" and "she" form ends in *-e (fue).*

GramActiva VIDEO

Want more help with the preterite of *ir?* Watch the **GramActiva** video.

¿Adónde fuiste?

16 ¿Adónde fueron?

Hablar

Con otro(a) estudiante, di adónde y cómo fueron estas personas a estos lugares.

Óscar y Lourdes

Modelo

A —*¿Adónde fueron Óscar y Lourdes?*
B —*Fueron al teatro.*
A —*¿Cómo fueron?*
B —*Fueron en coche.*

1.

los Sánchez

2.

tus amigos y tú

3.

Liliana

4.

Uds.

5.

Gregorio

6.

¡Respuesta personal!

tú

17 Juego

Escribir • Hablar • GramActiva

❶ Play in groups of four. Each person cuts a sheet of paper to form a perfect square. Fold that square into four smaller squares. Unfold the paper and label the squares *a, b, c,* and *d.* Follow Step a below for the *a* square. Fold the corner of that little square so it covers what you have written. Pass the paper to the person on your left. Follow Step b for the *b* square on the paper you receive from the person on your right, fold down the corner, and pass it to your left. Continue until all the squares have been filled. Do not look at what is written on the paper you receive. Write all of your answers in Spanish.

a. Write a subject plus the correct preterite form of *ir.*

b. Write a destination or place *(a / al / a la . . .).*

c. Write a mode of transportation.

d. Write a reason *(para + infinitive)* for going somewhere.

❷ When you get your original paper back, unfold each square and read the complete sentence to your group. Let the group decide, *¿Cuál es la frase más tonta* (silly)? Read your silliest sentence to the class. Then make changes to the sentence so it makes sense.

a.	b.
Mis amigos fuéron	al estadio
en barco	para ver una obra de teatro
c.	d.

18 Tus vacaciones pasadas

Escribir • Hablar

❶ Piensa en un lugar donde fuiste de vacaciones. Copia la tabla y escribe el lugar, dos o más actividades que hiciste y una descripción del viaje.

¿Adónde fuiste?	¿Qué hiciste?	¿Cómo fue?
San Diego	Visité el zoológico, vi muchos animales, compré recuerdos	fantástico

❷ Habla con dos estudiantes sobre sus vacaciones.

❸ Escribe una descripción de los viajes de los dos estudiantes con quienes hablaste.

Modelo

A —¿*Adónde fuiste de vacaciones?*
B —*Fui a San Diego.*
A —¿*Qué hiciste allí?*
B —*Visité el zoológico y vi muchos animales. Compré recuerdos también.*
A —¿*Cómo lo pasaste? ¿Te gustó?*
B —*Fue fantástico.*

Modelo

Pedro fue a San Diego. Visitó el zoológico. Vio muchos animales y compró recuerdos. Su viaje fue fantástico. Miguel fue a . . .

Más práctica

- **Guided** Gram. Practice p. 255
- **Core** Gram. Practice p. 144
- **Communication** Writing p. 158
- ***Real.* para hispanohablantes** p. 298

realidades.com ✔

- Audio Activities
- Video Activities
- Speak & Record
- Animated Verbs
- Canción de hip hop
- Tutorial
- Leveled Workbook
- Web Code: jcd-0804

Gramática

The personal *a*

You know that the direct object is the person or thing that receives the action of a verb. When the direct object is a person or group of people, you usually use the word *a* before the object. This is called the "personal *a*."

Visité **a mi abuela**.   *I visited **my grandmother**.*

Vimos **a Juan y Gloria**.   *We saw **Juan and Gloria**.*

You can also use the personal *a* when the direct object is a pet.

Busco **a mi perro**, Capitán.

To ask who receives the action of a verb, use
¿*A quién?*

¿A quién visitaron Uds.?

GramActiva VIDEO

Watch the **GramActiva** video for more help with the personal *a*.

Vi a mi abuela.

---

19 Don Pepito y don José

Leer • Escribir • Hablar

❶ Lee esta rima tradicional.

—Hola, don Pepito.
—Hola, don José.
—¿Pasó* Ud. por mi casa?
—Por su casa no pasé.
—¿Vio Ud. a mi abuela?
—A su abuela no la vi.
—Adiós, don Pepito.
—Adiós, don José.

* Did (you) stop by

Nota

You have learned the direct object pronouns *lo*, *la*, *los*, and *las*. These direct object pronouns can refer to people as well as to things. Note that the direct object pronouns do not take the personal *a*.

—¿Viste **a tus primos** durante tus vacaciones?

—Sí, **los** vi.

❷ Ahora escribe las líneas *¿Vio Ud. a mi abuela?* y *A su abuela no la vi* y sustituye estos miembros de la familia por "abuela". Usa el pronombre *(pronoun)* apropiado.

1. tíos   **2.** hermano   **3.** primas   **4.** hermanita

❸ Con otro(a) estudiante, lee la rima. Un(a) estudiante va a ser don Pepito y el (la) otro(a), don José. Lean la rima cuatro veces, cada vez con un miembro diferente de la familia.

En Barcelona, España

20 De visita

Hablar

Pregunta a otro(a) estudiante si visitó a diferentes personas o diferentes lugares durante las vacaciones.

Modelo

tus tíos

A —¿*Visitaste a tus tíos durante las vacaciones?*
B —*Sí, los visité.*
o: —*No, no los visité.*

Estudiante A

1. tus abuelos
2. un(a) amigo(a) que no vive aquí
3. un parque de diversiones
4. tus primos
5. otra ciudad
6. el museo de arte

Estudiante B

¡Respuesta personal!

21 Juego de geografía: Las Américas

Leer • Pensar

¿Conoces[1] bien los países de las Américas? Empareja las descripciones con los países apropiados.

Conexiones La geografía

1. Este país es el más grande de América Central. En el suroeste hay un lago muy grande que tiene el mismo nombre que el país. El lago está muy cerca de la frontera[2] con Costa Rica. En el este del país está el mar Caribe donde el clima es tropical y llueve mucho.

2. Este país pequeño tiene dos regiones tropicales, en el este y en el oeste, con montañas en el centro. Un cuarto de las personas en el país son de origen indígena y hablan quechua, el idioma[3] de los incas. Su nombre viene de la línea imaginaria que cruza el país.

3. Las ciudades más grandes de este país, como la capital, están en el centro del país donde hay montañas y volcanes. En el norte hay desiertos extensos y en el sur hay selvas[4] tropicales. Este país comparte una frontera con los Estados Unidos.

4. Este país es el más grande de América del Sur, con el río más grande del mundo[5]. Una gran parte del país es selva tropical con miles de especies de plantas, árboles y animales como monos, jaguares y tucanes. No hablan español aquí; hablan portugués.

5. Es el único[6] país de América del Sur que tiene playas en el mar Caribe y el océano Pacífico. Es un país famoso por su café, que viene de los valles fértiles.

México
El Salvador
Nicaragua
Colombia
Brasil
Uruguay
Chile
Bolivia
Ecuador
Cuba

norte

oeste — este

sur

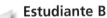

[1] Do you know   [2] border   [3] language   [4] forests   [5] world   [6] only

Exploración del lenguaje

Nouns that end in -io and -eo

Latin words for buildings and places have carried into many modern languages, including Spanish. In many place names, the Latin ending -um (which remains in a number of words in English today) changed to an -io or -eo in Spanish. You know some of these words: *el estadio, el museo, el gimnasio.*

Try it out! Based on your knowledge of English and what you have learned about Spanish place names from Latin, match the definitions with the Spanish words in the list.

El Acuario de Madrid, España

1. where you stand to deliver a speech
2. usually found in a cemetery
3. where you can see all kinds of sea life
4. where you sit when you see school plays or concerts
5. where you go to learn about stars and planets
6. where the ancient Romans went to see sporting events

a. el auditorio
b. el podio
c. el acuario
d. el planetario
e. el coliseo
f. el mausoleo

22 Y tú, ¿qué dices?

Escribir • Hablar

1. ¿Qué puedes visitar en tu comunidad? ¿Hay museos, parques de diversiones o monumentos? ¿Cuál prefieres visitar?

2. El año pasado, ¿fuiste a ver una obra de teatro en tu comunidad o en tu escuela? ¿Te gustó? ¿Por qué? ¿Cuestan mucho los boletos de teatro?

3. El año pasado, ¿visitaste un museo o un zoológico en tu comunidad? ¿Cómo lo pasaste?

4. ¿Prefieres viajar a otros países o ciudades, o prefieres visitar lugares en tu comunidad?

Más práctica

- **Guided** Gram. Practice p. 256
- **Core** Gram. Practice p. 145
- *Real.* para hispanohablantes pp. 299–301

realidades.com

- Audio Activities
- Video Activities
- Speak & Record
- Tutorial
- Leveled Workbook
- Web Code: jcd-0805

El español en la comunidad

Your community may have some of the tourist destinations you learned about in this chapter, such as *un museo, un teatro, un zoológico,* or *un parque de diversiones.* Think of different opportunities to use your Spanish at each of the locations. As you learn more Spanish, perhaps you could provide tours to visitors who speak Spanish. You could help write brochures and maps in Spanish to assist Spanish-speaking visitors. Can you think of other opportunities?

- Visit one of these locations in person or online and see what written resources are available in Spanish. Bring these materials to class to share with other students.

Lectura

Perú

Álbum de mi viaje al Perú

Por Sofía Porrúa

domingo, 25 de julio

Estoy en el Perú con mis amigos Beto y Carmen. Vamos en autobús al Cuzco, antigua capital del imperio inca. Hoy día es una ciudad pequeña y una atracción turística. Beto está sacando muchas fotos con su cámara digital. Carmen está dibujando todo lo que ve. Las montañas son fantásticas.

OCÉANO
PACÍFICO

PERÚ

Lima

Machu
Picchu

Cuzco

Nazca

Lago
Titicaca

miércoles, 28 de julio

Hoy es el Día de la Independencia peruana. En esta fecha en 1821, José de San Martín proclamó la independencia del Perú. En Lima, gran ciudad moderna y capital del país, hay grandes celebraciones.

jueves, 29 de julio

Hoy estamos en Machu Picchu, ruinas impresionantes de una ciudad antigua de los incas. A más de 2.000 metros de altura en los Andes, los incas construyeron calles, casas, acueductos, palacios, templos y terrazas para cultivar. Hiram Bingham, un arqueólogo de la Universidad de Yale, descubrió[1] Machu Picchu en 1911.

390 trescientos noventa
Tema 8 • Experiencias

[1]discovered

sábado, 31 de julio

Estamos paseando en bote por el lago Titicaca, en la frontera del Perú y Bolivia. Es el lago más grande de estos países y el más alto del mundo.[2] ¡Estamos a más de 3.800 metros sobre el nivel del mar!

miércoles, 4 de agosto

Ahora estamos en un avión pequeño. Sobre la tierra[3] podemos ver algo muy misterioso: hay un desierto donde vemos enormes dibujos de animales y figuras geométricas. Estos dibujos se llaman las Líneas de Nazca. Miden[4] más de 300 metros y tienen más de dos mil años. ¿Quiénes los dibujaron, y por qué? Es necesario estar en un avión para verlos. ¿Cómo dibujaron los artistas algo tan[5] grande sin poder verlo?

Mañana regresamos al Cuzco y el domingo salimos de Perú. ¡Un viaje muy interesante! Beto tiene sus fotos y Carmen, sus dibujos. Yo no soy ni fotógrafa ni artista, por eso voy a comprar tarjetas postales como recuerdos.

[2]world   [3]ground   [4]They measure   [5]so

¿Comprendes?

1. ¿Cómo va a recordar Sofía su viaje al Perú? ¿Y Beto y Carmen?

2. Pizarro y los españoles descubrieron muchas de las ciudades de los incas. ¿Por qué piensas que no descubrieron Machu Picchu? ¿Quién la descubrió?

3. Para muchos turistas que visitan el lago Titicaca es difícil caminar y respirar *(breathe)*. ¿Por qué piensas que tienen estos problemas?

4. ¿Cuáles son los misterios de las Líneas de Nazca?

5. Copia la tabla en una hoja de papel. Usa la información de la lectura para comparar Perú con los Estados Unidos.

		Perú	Estados Unidos
a.	Dos lugares históricos y turísticos		
b.	Día de la Independencia		
c.	Año de la proclamación de la independencia		
d.	Capital del país hoy		
e.	Héroe nacional		

Más práctica

- **Guided** Reading Support p. 257
- **Communication** Writing p. 159, Test Prep p. 313
- *Real.* para hispanohablantes pp. 302–303

realidades.com

- Internet Activity
- Leveled Workbook
- Web Code: jcd-0806

La cultura en vivo
El ojo de Dios

Traveling in the Spanish-speaking world you will encounter a marvelous variety of artwork and crafts, many of which have their origins in the time before the Spaniards came to the Americas. One form of art that is popular among visitors to parts of Mexico is the *ojo de Dios*.

Mujer tarahumara en San Rafael, México

The *ojo de Dios* is a diamond-shaped weaving. As a gift, it symbolizes good wishes from one person to another. *Ojos de Dios* may have originated in Peru about 300 B.C. The people best known for making these today are the Indians of Mexico's Sierra Madre region. The Cora, Huichol, Tarahumara, and Tepehuane all make and use these weavings in their daily lives.

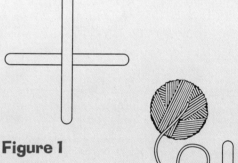

How to make an ojo de Dios

Materials
- yarn
- scissors
- two sticks of the same size
- optional: feathers, beads, or tassels for finishing touches

Figure 1

Directions

1 Tie the sticks together to form a cross. *(Fig. 1)*

2 Tie the end of the yarn to the center of the cross.

3 Weave the yarn over and around each stick, keeping the yarn pulled tight. *(Fig. 2)* To change color, knot together two ends of different-colored yarn. The knot should fall on the back side. Continue wrapping until the sticks are covered with yarn. Tie a small knot at the back and leave enough yarn to make a loop for hanging.

4 You may want to add feathers, beads, or tassels to the ends of the sticks. Hang your decorative piece for everyone to enjoy.

Figure 2

Think about it! What are some of the traditional handicrafts in the United States? What is the ethnic heritage of these crafts?

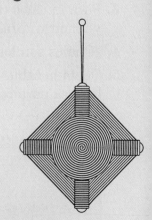

Figure 3

Presentación oral
Mi viaje

Task
Tell a friend about a trip you took. It could be a vacation or a trip to visit family members, or you can make up a trip. Use photographs or drawings to make your talk more interesting.

1 Prepare Use the word web to help you think about what you did on your trip. Think of information and events to include in each circle. Bring in photos from the trip or draw pictures to illustrate each part of the trip represented on the word web. Design the illustration of your trip so it looks appealing.

Strategy

Using graphic organizers
Using a graphic organizer such as a word web will help you think through what you want to say in your presentation.

¿Qué lugares visitaste? ¿A quiénes viste? Mi viaje a ... ¿Qué hiciste? ¿Qué compraste?

2 Practice Work with a partner and use the information in your word web to tell about your trip. Go through your story several times using the photographs or illustrations. You can use your notes in practice, but not when you present. End your presentation by saying how you felt about the trip.

Modelo

En marzo, fui a la Florida para visitar a mi abuelita y a mis primos. Tomamos el sol en la playa y nadamos mucho. Aprendí a bucear y vi animales muy interesantes en el mar. Me gusta mucho la Florida. Es un lugar fantástico. El viaje fue muy divertido.

3 Present Talk about your trip to a small group or the whole class. Use your photos or drawings to help you present.

4 Evaluation Your teacher may give you a rubric for how your presentation will be graded. You may be evaluated on:

- how much information you provide
- how well you use photographs or visuals to illustrate your story
- how well you are understood

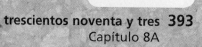

realidades.com

• Speak & Record

¿Eres tú, María?

Episodio 7

Antes de ver el video

Resumen del episodio

Lola y Pedro visitan el piso elegante de doña Gracia. Entran en la habitación[1] de María. Hay ropa, libros, unas fotos y una tarjeta postal. Lola y Pedro leen algo muy interesante en la tarjeta postal. Después, van al piso de Julia. Allí vive un hombre que no conoce a Julia. Pero antes vivía[2] una chica en el piso. Todavía hay unas cosas de esa chica: ropa, unas cartas y unos papeles. ¿Y qué más?

[1] bedroom   [2] used to live

Nota cultural Addresses in Spain are written differently than in the United States. For example, the name of Julia's street is Calle Norte. The building number is 23. The 1° *(primero)* indicates the apartment is on the first floor (not the ground floor, but what we would call the second floor), and Julia lives in apartment D.

Palabras para comprender

¡Suerte! Good luck!

No la conozco. I don't know her.

tenía un secretario had a secretary

tuvo problemas con él
had problems with him

¡Qué casualidad! What a coincidence!

"Lola, te llamo porque tengo información sobre la otra chica en el accidente. Tengo la dirección de su piso. Es Calle Norte, 23, 1°, D".

"¿A quién buscáis? Antes aquí vivía una chica . . .".

"Mira esta tarjeta postal. Interesante, ¿no?"

"¿Sabes, Pedro? En mi profesión la casualidad no existe".

Después de ver el video

¿Comprendes?

Pon las frases en orden según el episodio.

1. Pedro recuerda el nombre de Luis Antonio Llamas, un secretario de su papá.

2. Leen la tarjeta postal de Luis Antonio.

3. Pedro llama a Lola para invitarla a visitar el piso de su abuela.

4. El joven en el piso de Julia no está nada contento.

5. Rosalinda llama a Lola para darle la dirección de Julia.

6. Quieren ver la habitación de María.

7. Deciden visitar el piso de Julia.

> **Nota gramatical** In this episode you will hear a few more examples of the *vosotros* form: *queréis, sois, podéis, buscáis*. Remember that in Spain you use *vosotros* or *vosotras* when talking to more than one person whom you would address individually as *tú*.

realidades.com

• Web Code: jcd-0507

Repaso del capítulo

Vocabulario y gramática 🔊

jcd-0889

to talk about places to visit on vacation

la ciudad	city
el estadio	stadium
el lago	lake
el lugar	place
el mar	sea
el monumento	monument
el museo	museum
el país	country
el parque de diversiones	amusement park
el parque nacional	national park
el teatro	theater
la obra de teatro	play
el zoológico	zoo

to talk about things to see on vacation

el animal	animal
el árbol	tree
la atracción pl. las atracciones	attraction(s)
el mono	monkey
el oso	bear
el pájaro	bird

to talk about things to do on vacation

aprender (a)	to learn
bucear	to scuba dive / snorkel
(comprar) recuerdos	(to buy) souvenirs
descansar	to rest, to relax
montar a caballo	to ride horseback
pasear en bote	to go boating
tomar el sol	to sunbathe
visitar	to visit

to talk about ways to travel

en	by
el autobús	bus
el avión	airplane
el barco	boat, ship
el tren	train

to talk about your vacation

el boleto	ticket
como	like, such as
¿Cómo lo pasaste?	How was it (for you)?
dime	tell me
fantástico, -a	fantastic
Fue un desastre.	It was a disaster.
el hotel	hotel
impresionante	impressive
ir de vacaciones	to go on vacation
Me gustó.	I liked it.
¿Qué hiciste?	What did you do?
¿Qué te pasó?	What happened to you?
regresar	to return
salir	to leave, to go out
¿Te gustó?	Did you like it?
tremendo, -a	tremendous
vi	I saw
¿viste . . . ?	Did you see . . . ?
viajar	to travel
el viaje	trip

to express time

durante	during
tarde	late
temprano	early

preterite of -er and -ir verbs

aprendí salí	aprendimos salimos
aprendiste saliste	aprendisteis salisteis
aprendió salió	aprendieron salieron

preterite of ir

fui	fuimos
fuiste	fuisteis
fue	fueron

For *Vocabulario adicional*, see pp. 472–473.

Más práctica

- **Core** Puzzle p. 146, Organizer p. 147
- **Communication** Practice Test
  pp. 315–318, Integrated Performance
  Assessment p. 314

realidades.com

- Tutorial
- Flashcards
- Puzzles
- Self-test
- Web Code: jcd-0807

Preparación para el examen

On the exam you will be asked to . . .	Here are practice tasks similar to those you will find on the exam . . .	If you need review . . .

Interpretive

jcd-0889

1 Escuchar Listen to and understand what someone says he did and where he went during his last vacation

As part of a presentation in Spanish class, a student talked about his last vacation. As you listen, see if you can determine: a) where he went; b) one thing he did; c) one thing he saw.

pp. 374–377 *Vocabulario en contexto*
p. 375 Actividad 1
p. 378 Actividades 4–5

Interpersonal

2 Hablar Tell about your best trip or vacation

Find out where your partner went on his or her best vacation, and what he or she did and saw. As you listen, make a drawing that includes details of the trip. Then your partner will ask you to describe your best vacation. Do your drawings match the descriptions?

p. 379 Actividad 6
p. 380 Actividad 8
p. 382 Actividad 11
p. 385 Actividad 16
p. 386 Actividad 18
p. 393 *Presentación oral*

Interpretive

3 Leer Read and understand a vacation postcard

Read the postcard Javier sent to his friend last summer during his family vacation. Which things does he say he liked? Was there anything he didn't like?

p. 379 Actividad 7
p. 381 Actividad 9
p. 388 Actividad 21
pp. 390–391 *Lectura*

¡Hola! Salí de vacaciones la semana pasada y ahora estamos aquí en Puerto Rico. Visitamos a nuestra tía en San Juan. Ayer fuimos al Viejo San Juan, donde vi muchos monumentos. También vi El Morro, un lugar muy famoso. ¡Fue fabuloso! Hoy fui a la playa de Luquillo y tomé el sol. Los otros bucearon por tres horas, pero a mí no me gusta el mar. Después, comimos arroz con pollo en un restaurante. ¡Uf! ¡Siempre arroz con pollo aquí! Regreso el sábado. ¡Hasta luego! Javier

Presentational

4 Escribir Write a brief narrative about an imaginary character's trip

You have been asked by a first-grade teacher to write a story in Spanish for her students. She has a stuffed bear in her room, *el Oso Teo,* so you decide to write the story about him and his trip. Tell where he went, what he did, what he saw, and what he ate. Begin with something like, *"El Oso Teo fue de viaje a su parque favorito . . ."*

p. 378 Actividad 4
p. 384 Actividades 14–15
p. 386 Actividad 18
p. 389 Actividad 22
pp. 390–391 *Lectura*

Cultures • Comparisons

5 Pensar Demonstrate an understanding of cultural perspectives regarding artwork and crafts

Think about a gift you might give someone to symbolize good luck and good fortune in our culture. Compare it to a traditional craft from Mexico that is given for the same reason. Describe its significance and history in the Spanish-speaking world.

p. 392 *La cultura en vivo*

Fondo cultural

Guatemala

The United States Peace Corps has programs in countries throughout the world. The volunteer in this photo is working on a project in Guatemala, where more than 4,000 United States volunteers have served since the establishment of the Peace Corps program. Since 1963, Peace Corps volunteers in Guatemala have been helping rural communities through projects in agriculture, the environment, health, and business development.

• How do you think your language skills could help you serve other people? What types of projects might you want to work on if you were a Peace Corps volunteer?

Un proyecto del Cuerpo de Paz, en Guatemala

Ayudando en la comunidad

Chapter Objectives

- Discuss volunteer work and ways to protect the environment
- Talk about what people say
- Talk about what people did for others
- Understand cultural perspectives on volunteer work

Video Highlights

Videocultura: *Experiencias*

A primera vista: *Cómo ayudamos a los demás*

GramActiva Videos: the present tense of *decir;* indirect object pronouns; the preterite of *hacer* and *dar*

Videomisterio: *¿Eres tú, María?*, Episodio 8

Country Connection

As you learn about volunteer work and ways to protect the environment, you will make connections to these countries and places:

Más práctica

- *Real.* para hispanohablantes pp. 310–311

realidades.com ✔

- Fondo cultural Activity
- Video Activities
- Online Atlas
- Web Code: jce-0002

Vocabulario en contexto

jcd-0897

Objectives

Read, listen to, and understand information about
• volunteer work
• community-service tasks
• what people did to help others

¿Quieres ayudar a los demás?

¡Trabaja como voluntario en tu comunidad!

¡Habla con los Amigos del barrio hoy! ¡Tú puedes ser la diferencia!

ayudar en un jardín de verduras

trabajar en un proyecto de construcción

hacer trabajo voluntario en una escuela primaria

trabajar en un campamento de deportes

—Mira el cartel. Hay **problemas*** en nuestra comunidad. Debemos trabajar como voluntarios.

—Tienes razón. ¿Cómo puedes **decidir** qué hacer? Es la primera **vez** que trabajo como voluntario.

—Quiero enseñar**les** a **los niños** a leer. **Es necesario** poder leer, ¿no crees?

*Even though *problema* ends in *-a*, it is a masculine noun: *Tengo **un problema.***

recoger la basura de la calle

al lado del río

Centro de reciclaje

los periódicos

las latas

las botellas

el plástico

el vidrio

las cajas

las bolsas

el cartón

 1 El trabajo voluntario 🔊   jcd-0897

Escuchar

Gloria investiga *(is researching)* los trabajos voluntarios en la comunidad. Señala cada lugar que ella menciona.

—¿Me ayudas a **reciclar** la basura del río y de las calles? Son cosas que se pueden usar **otra vez. Dicen** que tenemos que **separar**las.

—Bueno, te ayudo. ¿Adónde vamos a **llevar**las?

—Al centro de reciclaje en la calle Bolívar.

jcd-0897

2 ¿Qué puedes reciclar? 🔊

Escuchar

Estás separando unos artículos en dos cajas: una es para el papel y la otra es para todos los demás artículos. Levanta una mano si debes poner el artículo en la caja para papel. Levanta dos manos si debes ponerlo en la otra caja.

Más práctica

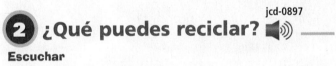

- **Guided** Vocab. Flash Cards pp. 259–264
- **Core** Vocab. Practice pp. 148–149
- **Communication** Writing p. 166
- *Real.* **para hispanohablantes** p. 312

realidades.com ✓

- Audio Activities
- Leveled Workbook
- Flashcards
- Web Code: jcd-0811

Cómo ayudamos a los demás

Gloria, Raúl y Tomás hacen trabajo voluntario. ¿Por qué les gusta ser voluntarios?

Costa Rica

Strategy

Activating prior knowledge
Before you read this selection, think about what you know about the topic of volunteer work. In what ways can one volunteer in your community?

Raúl   Gloria   Tomás

1 Gloria: Raúl y yo trabajamos como voluntarios en **el Hospital** Nacional de Niños. ¿Quieres venir con nosotros?

Tomás: Sí. Me encanta el trabajo voluntario. Es **increíble** la satisfacción que **nos** da cuando ayudamos a los demás.

5 Raúl: El año pasado yo trabajé en un centro para **ancianos.** Pasé mucho tiempo con ellos.

6 Tomás: Soy miembro de un club que se llama "Casa Latina". El año pasado recogimos ropa **usada.** ¿Sabes que **hay que** separar la ropa y después lavarla?

Gloria: ¿Qué más **hicieron** Uds.?

Tomás: Luego le **dimos** la ropa a **la gente pobre.**

7 Raúl: Aquí podemos reciclar el papel y las botellas.

Gloria: Mira, para el plástico, el papel y el vidrio.

Tomás: En mi comunidad también reciclamos.

2 Papá: Un momento. ¿Pueden Uds. reciclar este papel y estas botellas?

Tomás: ¡Por supuesto! Dame la bolsa de plástico.

3 Tomás: ¿Y qué hacen Uds. en el hospital?

Gloria: Ayudamos con los niños. Leemos libros y cantamos y jugamos con ellos. **A menudo** les traemos **juguetes.**

4 Gloria: A veces es difícil porque los niños están muy enfermos. Pero es **una experiencia inolvidable.**

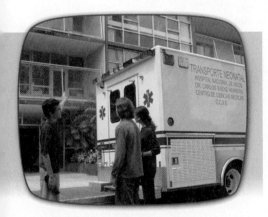

8 Raúl: Mira. Aquí está el hospital. ¿Entramos?

③ ¿Comprendes? _____

Leer • Hablar

¿A quién describe cada frase: a Gloria, a Tomás o a Raúl? ¡Ojo! Una frase puede describir a más de una persona.

1. "Me gusta mucho el trabajo voluntario".

2. "Trabajo en un hospital para niños".

3. "Ayudar a los demás me da mucha satisfacción".

4. "Trabajo con los niños y les traigo juguetes".

5. "Me gusta pasar tiempo con los ancianos. Les leo el periódico y hablo con ellos".

6. "Recojo· la ropa usada".

7. "Es importante reciclar las botellas y latas".

*Recoger is a regular -er verb with a spelling change in the yo form of the present tense: recojo.

Más práctica

- **Guided** Vocab. Check pp. 265–268
- **Core** Vocab. Practice pp. 150–151
- **Communication** Video pp. 160–162
- *Real.* **para hispanohablantes** p. 313

realidades.com ✔

- Audio Activities
- Video Activities
- Leveled Workbook
- Flashcards
- Web Code: jcd-0812

Vocabulario en uso

4 Escucha y escribe 🔊

jcd-0898

Escuchar · Escribir

En la región de Cataluña en España, hay un sistema para reciclar que usan muchas personas.

España

También se dice . . .

la lata = el bote *(España, Puerto Rico)*

1 En una hoja de papel, escribe los números del 1 al 6. Escucha la descripción de este sistema y escribe las frases.

2 Escribe tres frases para describir el sistema de reciclaje que usan, o que deben usar, en tu comunidad o barrio. Si quieres, usa las frases sobre Cataluña como modelo.

En Cataluña, España

5 El reciclaje

Hablar

Habla con otro(a) estudiante sobre el reciclaje.

¿Recuerdas?

The direct object pronouns *lo, la, los,* and *las* replace nouns. They have the same gender and number as the nouns they replace.

Modelo

A —*En nuestra comunidad, ¿hay que reciclar el papel?*

B —*¡Por supuesto! Lo separamos y lo ponemos en la caja azul.*

o:—*No sé. Nosotros no lo reciclamos.*

1.

2.

3.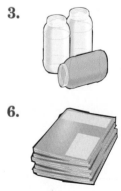

4.

5.

6.

6 **El trabajo voluntario**

Leer · Pensar · Escribir · Hablar

Según las preferencias de los jóvenes de las fotos, explica dónde debe trabajar cada uno de ellos.

Modelo

Samuel debe trabajar en un hospital.

Teresa: Prefiero los trabajos al aire libre* como un proyecto de construcción. Me encanta trabajar con las manos.

*outdoors

Rafael: Mi trabajo voluntario favorito es estar con niños en un campamento o una escuela primaria. Para mí es una experiencia inolvidable ver cómo aprenden tanto.

Samuel: Me gusta mucho ayudar a la gente pobre o a las víctimas de los desastres. Sus problemas son muy importantes para mí.

Bárbara: Me gusta mucho pasar tiempo con los ancianos. Son muy interesantes y simpáticos y me enseñan muchas cosas.

1.

2.

3.

4.

5.

6.

Fondo cultural

España

El reciclaje Spain is one of the leading European countries in recycling. Spain's glass recycling program is called *Ecovidrio,* from the Spanish words for ecology *(ecología)* and glass *(vidrio). Ecovidrio* started in the 1990s and has been very successful. Glass recycling is an excellent way of reducing waste and protecting the environment.

• How do efforts in your community compare to glass recycling in Spain? What other efforts are available in your community?

Reciclaje en Cataluña, España

Nouns that end in *-dad*, *-tad*, *-ción*, and *-sión*

You know that *actividad* means "activity" and that *comunidad* means "community." In Spanish, nouns that end in *-dad* or *-tad* usually correspond to nouns in English that end in *-ty*. Nouns that end in *-dad* or *-tad* are feminine.

In a similar way, nouns in Spanish that end in *-ción* or *-sión* frequently correspond to nouns in English that end in *-tion* or *-sion*. These nouns are also feminine. You know that *construcción* means "construction" and that *posesión* means "possession."

Try it out! Figure out the meanings of these Spanish words.

la generosidad	la comunicación
la responsabilidad	la comisión
la variedad	la vegetación
la tranquilidad	la información
la libertad	la organización
la universidad	la presentación

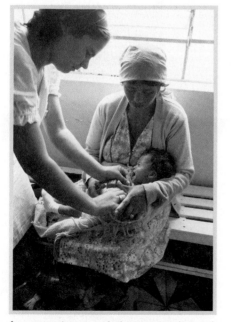

Una enfermera asiste a un bebé en una clínica de salud en Honduras.

Fondo cultural

México

El arte de vidrio Mexico is known for its production of beautiful glassware. Many of these works of art—including a wonderful variety of drinking glasses, bowls, and vases—are made from recycled bottles or car windshields. The glass is melted and hand-blown into new forms. Artisans also make trays and decorative windows by cutting different pieces of colored glass into a collage, then melting them together into a single piece. Each recycled glass artwork is unique.

- What everyday items or art objects are you familiar with that are made from recycled materials?

Arte de vidrio de México

7 Y tú, ¿qué dices?

Escribir • Hablar

1. ¿Qué cosas reciclas en casa? ¿Y en la escuela? ¿Qué más podemos reciclar?

2. ¿Qué puede hacer la gente para tener un barrio más limpio?

3. ¿Qué tipo de trabajo voluntario te gustaría hacer?

4. Escribe dos recomendaciones sobre cómo debemos ayudar a los demás.

5. ¿Qué organizaciones en tu comunidad reciben ropa usada o juguetes como donación? ¿Qué más podemos darles a las personas que necesitan ayuda?

8 La protección de las áreas naturales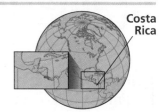

Leer • Hablar • Escribir

Costa Rica es un país increíble con mucha vegetación y una gran variedad de animales. La conservación de estas áreas naturales del país es muy importante. Por eso hay muchas áreas protegidas[1] en el país.

Costa Rica

Conexiones | Las matemáticas

1. Mira el mapa de Costa Rica. Las áreas protegidas (como parques nacionales y reservas) están indicadas en verde. Estima qué porcentaje del área total del país es el área protegida.

2. Mira la tabla que compara las áreas protegidas con el área total del país. Trabaja con otro(a) estudiante para:
   - calcular qué porcentaje del área total es el área protegida.
   - comparar la respuesta con las estimaciones que hicieron Uds.

Áreas protegidas	Área total
4.656 millas cuadradas	19.730 millas cuadradas

3. Averigua[2] cuántas millas cuadradas tiene los Estados Unidos y cuántas de estas millas son parques nacionales o estatales y, por lo tanto[3], áreas protegidas. Busca la información en una enciclopedia o en el Internet.

4. Calcula qué porcentaje del área total de los Estados Unidos son estos parques. Preparen un informe sobre los resultados.

Modelo

El área total de los Estados Unidos es de ___ millas cuadradas.
___ millas cuadradas son parques nacionales o estatales.
Estos parques representan el ___ por ciento del país.

[1] protected [2] Figure out [3] therefore

Fondo cultural
Costa Rica

La Asociación Conservacionista de Monteverde in Costa Rica helps protect the rain forest in the Monteverde Cloud Forest Preserve. Young people from around the world come to help preserve the natural forest. Volunteers maintain trails and help in preservation projects.

- What programs in your community or state are similar to the program in Costa Rica?

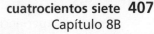

Gramática

The present tense of *decir*

The verb *decir* means "to say" or "to tell." Here are all its present-tense forms:

(yo)	**digo**	(nosotros) (nosotras)	**decimos**
(tú)	**dices**	(vosotros) (vosotras)	**decís**
Ud. (él) (ella)	**dice**	Uds. (ellos) (ellas)	**dicen**

The *yo* form is irregular: ***digo.***

Notice that the *e* of *decir* changes to *i* in all forms except *nosotros* and *vosotros.*

¿Recuerdas?

You have used forms of *decir* in the questions *¿Cómo se dice?* and *Y tú, ¿qué dices?*

GramActiva VIDEO

Need more help with the verb *decir*? Watch the **GramActiva** video.

digo

---

9 Hay que reciclar

Escribir

Escribe las formas apropiadas del verbo *decir* para completar las opiniones de diferentes personas sobre cómo tener una comunidad limpia.

1. Mis padres _____ que es necesario recoger la basura en las calles.

2. La gente _____ que es importante llevar los periódicos a un centro de reciclaje.

3. Las personas en mi comunidad _____ que tenemos que separar la basura.

4. Mi profesor de biología _____ que es necesario reciclar el vidrio y el plástico.

5. Nosotros _____ que debemos limpiar nuestro barrio y comunidad.

6. Yo _____ que el reciclaje es muy importante.

7. ¿Qué _____ tú?

Nota

Use the *él/ella* form of the verb with *la gente.*

To tell *what* people say, use *que* after *decir.*

• La gente **dice que** . . .

---

10 ¿Qué dices tú?

Leer • Escribir

Lee las frases del 1 al 5 de la Actividad 9. Escribe otras para decir si haces estas mismas actividades a menudo, a veces o nunca.

Más práctica

- **Guided** Gram. Practice p. 269
- **Core** Gram. Practice p. 152
- **Communication** Writing p. 167
- ***Real.* para hispanohablantes** pp. 314–316

realidades.com

- Audio Activities
- Video Activities
- Speak & Record
- Animated Verbs
- Tutorial
- Leveled Workbook
- Web Code: jcd-0813

11 **¿Cómo debemos participar más?**

Escribir · Hablar

❶ Forma un grupo con cuatro estudiantes. Comparen las frases que escribieron para la Actividad 10 y digan con qué frecuencia *(how often)* todos hacen las cosas. Cada grupo va a presentar sus frases a la clase.

❷ Cada estudiante debe anotar las respuestas de todos los grupos.

| Modelo |

En nuestro grupo, una persona dice que recoge la basura en las calles a menudo. Tres personas dicen que no la recogen nunca.

❸ Después de escuchar y anotar las frases de todos los grupos, calcula el porcentaje de estudiantes que hacen estas actividades a menudo, a veces o nunca. Escribe frases sobre los resultados.

| Modelo |

En esta clase, el 10 por ciento de las personas dicen que recogen la basura en las calles a menudo; el 70 por ciento dicen que la recogen a veces; y el 20 por ciento dicen que no la recogen nunca.

12 **Las 3 Rs**

Leer · Hablar · Escribir

Lee el anuncio que está abajo *(below)*. Habla de Puerto Rico y la importancia de la conservación. Luego contesta las preguntas.

Puerto Rico

¡Tú puedes ser parte de la solución del problema de la basura en nuestra isla!

Recuerda esta guía práctica de las 3Rs

Reduce: Cuando vas de compras, decide no comprar cosas que no son necesarias.

Reusa: Usa un producto, objeto o material varias veces[1]. No debes tirar[2] a la basura las cosas que puedes usar otra vez.

Recicla: Usa los mismos materiales otra vez o usa un proceso natural o industrial para hacer el mismo o nuevos productos.

Lo que compras, comes, cultivas o tiras puede ser la diferencia entre un buen futuro o un futuro de destrucción para Puerto Rico.

Reduce
Reusa
Recicla

Vidrio
Aluminio
Papel y periódicos
Cartón
Plástico
Materia orgánica

[1]several times   [2]throw away

1. ¿Cómo puedes "reducir"? ¿Qué cosas compras o usas a veces que no son necesarias?

2. ¿Cómo puedes reciclar o reusar cosas en casa o en la escuela?

3. Según las frases que escribiste para la Actividad 11, escribe tres recomendaciones para cuidar *(take care of)* más tu comunidad.

Gramática

Indirect object pronouns

An indirect object tells *to whom* or *for whom* an action is performed. Indirect object pronouns are used to replace an indirect object noun.

Les doy dinero.	*I give money to them.*
Te llevo el vidrio y las latas.	*I'll bring you the glass and the cans.*
¿**Nos** reciclas estas botellas, por favor?	*Will you please recycle these bottles for us?*

The indirect object pronoun comes right before the conjugated verb. Here are the different indirect object pronouns:

SINGULAR		PLURAL	
me	(to / for) me	nos	(to / for) us
te	(to / for) you	os	(to / for) you
le	(to / for) him, her; you (*formal*)	les	(to / for) them; you (*formal*)

When an infinitive follows a conjugated verb, the indirect object pronoun can be attached to the infinitive or be placed before the conjugated verb.

Quiero **darle** un juguete al niño.

o: Le quiero **dar** un juguete al niño.

Because *le* and *les* have more than one meaning, you can make the meaning clear, or show emphasis, by adding *a* + the corresponding name, noun, or pronoun.

Les damos lecciones **a Miguel y a Felipe.**

Les damos lecciones **a los niños.**

Les damos lecciones **a ellos.**

GramActiva VIDEO

Need more help with indirect object pronouns? Watch the **GramActiva** video.

13 Las Olimpíadas Especiales

Leer • Escribir

Unos jóvenes ayudan con las Olimpíadas Especiales. Escribe *me, te, le, nos* o *les* para completar cada frase.

Modelo

___ llevan comida a los padres de los niños.
Les llevan comida a los padres de los niños.

1. ___ dan naranjas y jugo a los participantes.
2. ___ hacen una donación a la señora que organizó el evento.
3. ___ traen agua a mis compañeros porque tienen sed.
4. ___ dan lecciones de varios deportes a los participantes.
5. ___ dicen a nosotros que debemos preparar los concursos (*contests*).
6. ___ traen a mí un sándwich porque tengo hambre.
7. ___ dicen a nosotros que necesitan más ayuda.

Lanzador de bala (*shotputter*)

14 Juego

Hablar • GramActiva

1 Tu profesor(a) va a dividir a los estudiantes en grupos de cinco. Cada grupo forma una fila *(line)*. Las primeras personas de cada fila van al frente de la clase y el (la) profesor(a) les dice una frase.

2 Las personas regresan a sus grupos y le dicen a la primera persona en la fila, *"Me dice que . . . "* y repite la frase del (de la) profesor(a). Luego la primera persona repite la frase a la segunda persona de la fila.

3 Cada grupo continúa hasta decir la frase a la última *(last)* persona. Esta persona escribe la frase que escucha en una hoja de papel. El grupo más rápido y que dice la frase más correcta gana *(wins)* el juego.

15 ¿Cómo ayuda la gente a los demás?

Escribir

Escribe frases para decir cómo la gente ayuda a los demás. Usa las palabras de las listas y *a menudo, a veces* o *nunca*.

dar	dinero	ropa usada	los pobres
enseñar	flores	juguetes	los niños
comprar	cuentos	periódicos	las personas
llevar	comida	revistas	enfermas
leer		una lección de . . .	los ancianos

Modelo

A veces la gente les lleva comida a los ancianos.

16 Regalos

Escribir • Hablar

1 En una hoja de papel, haz dos listas. En la primera, escribe los nombres de cinco personas. En la segunda, escribe un regalo para cada una de estas personas.

2 Habla con otro(a) estudiante sobre los regalos que vas a comprar.

Modelo

A —*¿A quién vas a comprar un regalo?*
B —*Le voy a comprar un regalo a mi abuela.*
A —*¿Qué le vas a comprar?*
B —*Le voy a comprar flores.*

Más práctica

- **Guided** Gram. Practice pp. 270–271
- **Core** Gram. Practice p. 153
- **Communication** Writing p. 168
- *Real.* **para hispanohablantes** pp. 317–318

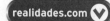 **realidades.com**

- Audio Activities
- Video Activities
- Speak & Record
- Canción de hip hop
- Tutorial
- Leveled Workbook
- Web Code: jcd-0815

Gramática

Hacer and *dar* are irregular verbs in the preterite. Notice that these verbs do not have any accent marks in the preterite.

- The preterite stem for *hacer* is *hic-*. In the *Ud./él/ella* form, the *-c-* changes to a *-z-* so that it keeps the "s" sound: *hizo*.

- The preterite stem for *dar* is *di-*. The same stem is used for all the preterite forms.

¿Recuerdas?

You used the preterite *tú* form of *hacer* when you asked, *¿Qué hiciste?*

(yo)	hice	(nosotros) (nosotras)	hicimos
(tú)	hiciste	(vosotros) (vosotras)	hicisteis
Ud. (él) (ella)	hizo	Uds. (ellos) (ellas)	hicieron

(yo)	di	(nosotros) (nosotras)	dimos
(tú)	diste	(vosotros) (vosotras)	disteis
Ud. (él) (ella)	dio	Uds. (ellos) (ellas)	dieron

GramActiva VIDEO

Watch the **GramActiva** video to learn more about the preterite of *hacer* and *dar*.

17 En un hospital ♻ _____

Leer • Escribir

Una joven habla de su experiencia como voluntaria en un hospital. Escribe los verbos en el pretérito para completar las frases.

Mis amigos y yo **1.** *(dar/decidir)* hacer un trabajo voluntario en un hospital. Nosotros **2.** *(ir/hacer)* dibujos para los ancianos en el hospital. La semana pasada una amiga y yo **3.** *(llevar/hablar)* los dibujos al hospital. La enfermera[1] nos **4.** *(dar/decidir)* permiso para entrar en los cuartos de varios ancianos. Nosotros **5.** *(llevar/visitar)* a los ancianos y les **6.** *(decidir/dar)* los dibujos. Los ancianos nos **7.** *(hablar/llevar)* de sus familias y nos **8.** *(decidir/dar)* abrazos.[2] Ésta fue la primera vez que yo **9.** *(hacer/llevar)* un trabajo voluntario. Fue una experiencia inolvidable para nosotros. Vamos a regresar al hospital otra vez.

[1] nurse [2] hugs

Fondo cultural
España

El Hospital de la Caridad, a hospice in Seville, Spain, was founded in the 1600s by the monks of *la Hermandad de la Caridad* (Charity Brotherhood). Today, the brothers still look after people who are old or poor, as part of a long tradition of caring for the needy.

- What programs in your community provide support for people in need?

El Hospital de la Caridad en Sevilla, España

18 Las donaciones  jcd-0898

Escuchar • Escribir

Vas a escuchar cómo varias personas y organizaciones,
como la Cruz Roja, ayudaron a las víctimas de un
desastre en El Salvador. En una hoja de papel, escribe
los números del 1 al 6. Escribe las frases que escuchas.

La Cruz Roja ayuda en El Salvador.

19 ¿Qué hicieron el sábado pasado?

Escribir • Hablar

1 Escribe lo que hicieron estas personas el fin
de semana pasado.

tu mejor amigo(a)	tu madre (padre)
tú y tus amigos	tu profesor(a) de . . .
tus amigos(as)	tú

2 Habla con otro(a) estudiante sobre lo que
hicieron las personas.

Modelo

tus amigos

A —¿Qué *hicieron* tus amigos el fin de semana
   pasado?

B —*Mis amigos fueron al río. Y tus amigos, ¿qué
   hicieron ellos?*

A —*Vieron una película en el cine.*

o:—*No sé qué hicieron ellos.*

Un grupo de amigos juegan al básquetbol en
Managua, Nicaragua.

20 Y tú, ¿qué dices?

Escribir • Hablar

1. ¿Qué hiciste el viernes pasado? ¿Qué hicieron
   tus amigos?

2. ¿Qué hizo tu familia el verano pasado?

3. ¿Qué les diste a tus hermanos o a tus amigos para su
   cumpleaños? ¿Qué te dieron a ti?

4. ¿Qué hizo la gente de tu comunidad el año pasado para
   ayudar a los pobres o a las víctimas de un desastre?

5. ¿Hizo tu barrio algo para ayudar a los ancianos o
   a los niños? ¿Qué?

Más práctica

- **Guided** Gram. Practice p. 272
- **Core** Gram. Practice p. 154
- **Communication,** Test Prep p. 319
- **Real.** para hispanohablantes
  pp. 319–321

 realidades.com

- Audio Activities
- Video Activities
- Speak & Record
- Animated Verbs
- Tutorial
- Leveled Workbook
- Web Code: jcd-0814

21 Juego

Escribir • Hablar

1 En grupos de cuatro, deben pensar en diferentes premios *(prizes)* que reciben las personas: por ejemplo, el premio Nobel, el Heisman, el Óscar, el Emmy, el Golden Globe o el Grammy. Cada uno escribe una pregunta que tu grupo va a hacerle a otro grupo sobre los premios que dieron el año pasado.

2 Tu grupo debe leer una de las preguntas a otro grupo, que tiene 30 segundos para contestarla. Si el grupo contesta bien la primera vez, recibe tres puntos. Si contesta bien la segunda vez, recibe un punto. Si contesta mal, tu grupo debe decirles la respuesta.

Modelo

A —¿A quién le dieron el Óscar por ser la mejor actriz el año pasado?

B —Le dieron el premio a . . .

Para decir más . . .	
la actriz	actress
el actor	actor
el / la cantante	singer
el / la atleta	athlete

Al autor colombiano Gabriel García Márquez le dieron el premio Nobel de Literatura.

Pronunciación

The letter *x*

jcd-0898

The letter *x* is pronounced several ways. When it is between vowels or at the end of a word, it is pronounced /ks/. Listen to and say these words:

examen	taxi	aproximadamente
exactamente	dúplex	éxito

When the *x* is at the beginning of a word, it is usually pronounced /s/. At the end of a syllable, the *x* can be pronounced /s/, /ks/, or /gs/. Listen to and say these words:

xilófono	explicar	experiencia
exploración	experimento	experto

Try it out! Work with a partner to ask and answer these questions, paying special attention to how you pronounce the letter *x*.

1. ¿En qué clase son más difíciles los exámenes?

2. ¿Qué clase tienes durante la sexta hora?

3. ¿En qué clase haces experimentos? ¿Qué tipo de experimentos haces?

4. ¿En qué clase hablas o escribes mucho de tus experiencias personales?

In the 1500s, the *x* represented the "h" sound of the Spanish letter *j*. That is why you see some words, like México, Oaxaca, and Texas written with *x*, even though the *x* is pronounced like the letter *j*. In words from indigenous languages of Mexico and Central America, the *x* has the /sh/ sound, as with the Mayan cities of Xel-há and Uxmal.

Una familia en Xochimilco, México

22 Las tortugas tinglar

Leer • Escribir • Hablar

Lee esta información sobre las tortugas tinglar. Luego contesta las preguntas.

¡La tortuga tinglar es enorme! Es la tortuga marina más grande del mundo[1]. Los tinglares adultos pueden ser de hasta siete pies de largo y pesar[2] hasta 1.400 libras[3]. Cada año, entre febrero y julio, esta tortuga sale del mar en la noche y pone sus huevos en playas tropicales, como las de la República Dominicana, Costa Rica o de la isla de Culebra cerca de Puerto Rico. Después regresa a aguas frías.

Desde 1970 el tinglar está en peligro[4] de extinción. Por eso, en la primavera voluntarios de diferentes países van a las playas como las de la isla de Culebra. Llevan trajes de baño, jeans, sudaderas, camisetas, cámaras, binoculares, linternas[5], repelente contra mosquitos y muchas ganas de[6] ayudar a las tortugas. Patrullan[7] las playas buscando las tortugas.

Después que las tortugas ponen los huevos, los voluntarios los llevan a un nido artificial. Aproximadamente 60 días después, las tortuguitas salen de los huevos. Los voluntarios llevan a las tortuguitas al mar donde nadan contínuamente por unas 28 horas. Estos voluntarios son muy importantes para la preservación de la tortuga tinglar.

[1]in the world   [2]weigh   [3]pounds   [4]danger   [5]flashlights   [6]the desire   [7]They patrol

1. Para ti, ¿cuáles son los hechos *(facts)* más increíbles sobre la tortuga tinglar?

2. Escribe una lista, en orden, del trabajo que hacen los voluntarios en la playa.

3. ¿Te gustaría trabajar como voluntario en una de las playas donde están las tortugas tinglar? ¿Por qué?

El español en el mundo del trabajo

There may be community service organizations in your neighborhood where knowing Spanish is helpful. These organizations include medical clinics, food kitchens, senior centers, career counseling and job training, and after-school programs. Volunteering your skills for these agencies is the first step to finding out if you would be interested in pursuing work in the nonprofit sector.

• Check with local agencies to find out which ones offer services in Spanish (or in other languages). Develop a class list of volunteer opportunities in your community in which you could use your Spanish skills.

Protegiendo a las tortugas en las Islas Cayman

¡Adelante!

Lectura

Lee este artículo sobre una organización que hace proyectos de construcción en muchos países del mundo.

Objectives

- **Read about an international volunteer organization**
- **Learn about volunteer work in Spanish-speaking countries**
- **Create a poster announcing a community-service project**
- **Watch ¿Eres tú, María?, Episodio 8**

Strategy

Recognizing cognates
Recognizing cognates in the following article can help improve your understanding of the reading.

Hábitat para la Humanidad Internacional

Un proyecto de Hábitat para la Humanidad Internacional

Hábitat es una organización internacional que ayuda a la gente pobre a tener casa. Su objetivo es construir casas seguras[1] que no cuestan mucho para las personas que no tienen mucho dinero. Hábitat trabaja con las familias pobres, con los grupos de voluntarios y con las personas que les dan dinero. Esta organización tiene más de 2.500 proyectos en muchas comunidades de los Estados Unidos y otros 1.600 proyectos en más de 83 países diferentes. Hábitat ha construido[2] unas 250.000 casas en todo el mundo.

Guatemala tiene quince afiliados de Hábitat. Cada afiliado tiene su propio dinero y hace su plan de construcción y sus proyectos. Los afiliados de Guatemala tienen mucho éxito[3]. Han construido más de 10.000 casas y tienen planes para construir 15.000 más en los años que vienen. Según Hábitat, las personas pobres tienen que ayudar a construir sus casas. Es una manera positiva de ayudar a los demás. Hábitat les da los materiales de construcción y los trabajadores voluntarios. Cuando la casa está construida, el nuevo propietario[4] paga una pequeña hipoteca[5] cada mes. Después, los nuevos propietarios tienen que ayudar a otros futuros propietarios a construir sus casas.

[1] safe [2] has built [3] success [4] owner [5] mortgage

Para todos, es una experiencia increíble.

Trabajadores de Hábitat para la Humanidad Internacional

—Ayer fue mi cumpleaños y recibí el mejor regalo de mi vida, mi propia casa —dijo una señora de la comunidad de Baja Verapaz.

La mayoría[6] del dinero viene de donaciones privadas y del trabajo voluntario de muchísimas personas.

¿Sabes que el ex-presidente Jimmy Carter y su esposa Rosalynn son dos de los primeros miembros voluntarios de Hábitat? Los grupos de voluntarios son una parte fundamental del éxito de la organización.

—Es una experiencia inolvidable para ayudar a los demás —dijo un voluntario en Guatemala.

[6] the majority

¿Comprendes?

1. ¿Qué hace Hábitat?
2. ¿Con quiénes trabaja Hábitat?
3. ¿En cuántos países está Hábitat?
4. ¿Cuántas casas construyeron los afiliados de Guatemala?
5. ¿Qué tienen que pagar los nuevos propietarios?
6. ¿Qué tienen que hacer los nuevos propietarios?
7. ¿De dónde viene el dinero para construir las casas?
8. Y a ti, ¿te gustaría trabajar con Hábitat? ¿Por qué?

Más práctica

- **Guided** Reading Support p. 273
- **Communication** Writing p. 169, Test Prep p. 320
- *Real.* **para hispanohablantes** pp. 322–323

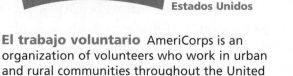

realidades.com
- Internet Activity
- Leveled Workbook
- Web Code: jcd-0816

Fondo cultural
Estados Unidos

El trabajo voluntario AmeriCorps is an organization of volunteers who work in urban and rural communities throughout the United States. They teach children to read, assist victims of natural disasters, and participate in other activities that benefit needy people.

One of the advantages of serving as an AmeriCorps volunteer is learning skills that can be used later in the workplace.

- What are some of the skills a volunteer might learn? Why are they important?

Doctores de las Naciones Unidas en Santa Cruz, Perú

Perspectivas del mundo hispano
¿Trabajas como voluntario?

Throughout the Spanish-speaking world students are involved in volunteer activities and organizations. In many private schools students are encouraged to serve their community for two to three hours per week to help them learn responsibilities that will make them good citizens. Community service also provides a good occasion to explore different professions such as education, medicine, or social work. For example, many young people work with local branches of the *Cruz Roja* (Red Cross) and learn how to respond in times of emergency. Courses are offered by the organization, and some students even study for a degree in health services.

In many Spanish-speaking countries, students are involved in causes dealing with the environment. In these countries, the natural beauty of the land is not only a source of national pride, it is also an economic resource and important to the well-being of the country. Students work at recycling centers collecting paper, glass, and plastic and collect trash along roadsides and in parks.

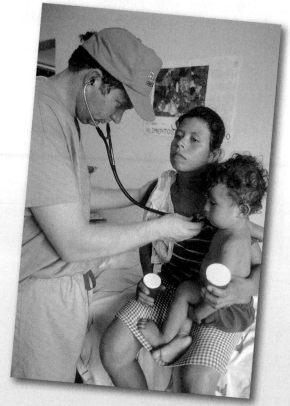

En una clínica en Trinidad, Honduras

Check it out! Survey the students in your class. Who does volunteer work? What kind of work do they do? How often are they involved in community service activities?

Think about it! How does the involvement in volunteerism among teenagers in many Spanish-speaking countries compare with the involvement of teenagers in your community?

En la Reserva Ecológica El Ángel, en el Ecuador

Presentación escrita

¿Puedes ayudarnos?

Task

Your school sponsors community-service projects every year, so you want to organize a clean-up campaign for a park, recreation center, school playground, or other place in your community. Make a poster announcing the project and inviting students to participate.

1 **Prewrite** Answer the following questions about your project:

- ¿Qué van a limpiar?
- ¿Qué tienen que hacer?
- ¿Dónde está el lugar?
- ¿Cuándo van a trabajar?
- ¿Cuántas horas van a trabajar?
- ¿Quién(es) puede(n) participar?

2 **Draft** Prepare a first draft using the answers to the questions. Organize the information in a clear and logical manner. Remember that you want students to stop and read the poster.

3 **Revise** Check your poster idea for spelling, accent marks, punctuation, and vocabulary usage. Share your work with a partner, who will check the following:

- Is the information presented clearly and easy to understand?
- Is it arranged logically?
- Is there anything that you should add or change?
- Are there any errors?

4 **Publish** Prepare a final version of the poster making any necessary changes. Add visuals to make the poster appealing. Display it in the classroom, cafeteria, or school library, or add it to your portfolio.

5 **Evaluation** Your teacher may give you a rubric for grading the poster. You may be evaluated on:

- how complete the information is
- the accuracy of the language in the poster
- the visual presentation

Strategy

Using key questions
Answering key questions can help you think of ideas for writing.

¿Eres tú, María?

Episodio 8

Antes de ver el video

"A ver. Esta foto. Yo conozco a este hombre. Pero no sé de qué. ¡Qué problema!"

Resumen del episodio

Después de visitar el piso de Julia, Lola y Pedro van a un café a tomar unos refrescos. Hablan de las cosas de Julia que el joven acaba de darles:[1] la ropa, las fotos, los papeles. Cuando Lola llega a su piso en la noche, ve que una mujer entra en el edificio número 8. Lola cree que es María. Sale rápidamente de su piso y espera[2] enfrente. Una mujer sale del edificio y Lola le pregunta, "¿Eres tú, María?"

[1] just gave them   [2] waits

Palabras para comprender

María tenía las llaves.
  María had the keys.

Ella las perdió. She lost them.

¡No me sigas! Don't follow me!

Acabo de ver . . . I just saw . . .

Acabo de hablar con . . .
  I just spoke with . . .

—¿Eres María Requena?
—¿Por qué quieres saberlo?

—Acabo de hablar con María Requena
delante del piso de doña Gracia.

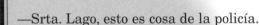

—Srta. Lago, esto es cosa de la policía.

Después de ver el video

¿Comprendes?

A. ¿Quién lo dice: Lola, Carmela, Pedro, el Inspector Gil, la camarera o María?

1. ¿Qué desean Uds.?

2. Y yo, un agua mineral.

3. ¿Cómo es que tienes las llaves del piso de Julia?

4. ¿Sabes algo más sobre el caso de doña Gracia?

5. Las diez y media. ¡Por fin!

6. ¿Qué quieres? ¿Quién eres?

7. ¡No me sigas! ¡No me sigas!

8. Acabo de ver a María Requena.

9. Ahora trabajo para Pedro Requena, el nieto de doña Gracia.

10. Hay que decirlo todo a la policía.

B. Escribe dos frases que describan cada foto de esta página.

realidades.com

• Web Code: jcd-0507

Repaso del capítulo

Vocabulario y gramática

jcd-0899

Chapter Review

To prepare for the test, check to see if you . . .
- **know the new vocabulary and grammar**
- **can perform the tasks on p. 423**

to talk about recycling

la bolsa	bag, sack
la botella	bottle
la caja	box
el cartón	cardboard
el centro de reciclaje	recycling center
la lata	can
llevar	to take; to carry
el periódico	newspaper
el plástico	plastic
reciclar	to recycle
recoger	to collect; to gather
separar	to separate
usado, -a	used
el vidrio	glass

to talk about places in a community

el barrio	neighborhood
la calle	street, road
la comunidad	community
el jardín	garden, yard
el río	river

to discuss possibilities for volunteer work

los ancianos	older people
el anciano	older man
la anciana	older woman
el campamento	camp
los demás	others
la escuela primaria	primary school
la gente	people
el hospital	hospital
el juguete	toy
los niños	children
el niño	young boy
la niña	young girl
pobre	poor
el problema	problem

el proyecto de construcción	construction project
el trabajo voluntario	volunteer work
el voluntario, la voluntaria	volunteer

other useful expressions

a menudo	often
decidir	to decide
Es necesario.	It's necessary.
la experiencia	experience
Hay que . . .	One must . . .
increíble	incredible
inolvidable	unforgetable
¿Qué más?	What else?
la vez *pl.* las veces	time
otra vez	again

decir *to say, to tell*

digo	decimos
dices	decís
dice	dicen

indirect object pronouns

SINGULAR	PLURAL
me (to / for) me	**nos** (to / for) us
te (to / for) you	**os** (to / for) you
le (to / for) him, her; you *(formal)*	**les** (to / for) them; you *(formal)*

preterite of *dar*

di	dimos
diste	disteis
dio	dieron

preterite of *hacer*

hice	hicimos
hiciste	hicisteis
hizo	hicieron

For *Vocabulario adicional,* see pp. 472–473.

Más práctica

- **Core** Puzzle p. 155, Organizer p. 156
- **Communication** Practice Test pp. 322–324, Integrated Performance Assessment p. 321

realidades.com
- Tutorial
- Flashcards
- Puzzles
- Self-test
- Web Code: jcd-0817

Preparación para el examen

On the exam you will be asked to . . .	Here are practice tasks similar to those you will find on the exam . . .	If you need review . . .

Interpretive

jcd-0899

1 Escuchar Listen and understand as someone describes what he did in his community

A radio station is sponsoring a contest to encourage people to help in the community. Listen as a teen tells the announcer what he did. Identify whether he: a) helped older people; b) worked on a recycling project; c) contributed money; d) volunteered in a hospital or school.

pp. 400–403 *Vocabulario en contexto*
p. 401 Actividades 1–2
p. 404 Actividad 4
p. 413 Actividad 18

Interpersonal

2 Hablar Ask and answer questions about what you or someone you know did to help others in the past few months

Many organizations offer scholarships to students who help others. With a partner, practice asking and answering the following questions for the scholarship interviews with a local agency that works in the Spanish-speaking community: a) What did you do to help others? b) Why did you decide to do volunteer work?

p. 404 Actividad 5
p. 405 Actividad 6
p. 406 Actividad 7

Interpretive

3 Leer Read and understand what people gave as donations to various people or groups

The Spanish Club treasurer's report about charitable contributions is ready for the members. Read one line item from the report. Indicate whether the member(s) donated: a) cash; b) lessons for an individual or group; c) clothing; d) furniture. For example, you might read: *Scott y Jamie le dieron una cama y una cómoda a una familia pobre.*

p. 412 Actividad 17
p. 415 Actividad 22
pp. 416–417 *Lectura*

Presentational

4 Escribir Write a list of things teenagers can do to help in your community

To encourage your classmates to participate in *La semana de la comunidad,* make a poster for your classroom with at least five suggestions for activities. For example: *Recicla las botellas. Ayuda a los niños de la escuela primaria.*

p. 408 Actividades 9–10
p. 409 Actividad 12
p. 410 Actividad 13
p. 411 Actividad 15
p. 412 Actividad 17
p. 419 *Presentación escrita*

Cultures

5 Pensar Demonstrate an understanding of cultural perspectives regarding volunteer work

Think about the volunteer activities in which you and your friends participate. Based on what you've learned in this chapter, compare these to the type of work teenage volunteers do in Spanish-speaking countries.

pp. 400–403 *Vocabulario en contexto*
p. 407 *Fondo cultural*
p. 416–417 *Lectura*
p. 417 *Fondo cultural*
p. 418 *Perspectivas del mundo hispano*

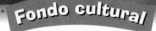

España

Portrait of Luis Buñuel Luis Buñuel (1900–1983) was a Spanish-born film director. He made films in Spain, the United States, Mexico, and France. His films were often controversial because of their strong imagery and difficult topics. Buñuel made two surrealist films with artist Salvador Dalí (1904–1989), Spain's most famous surrealist painter. The films mixed reality and dreams. This portrait of Buñuel was painted by Dalí in 1924 when the painter was 20 years old and Buñuel was 24.

• Who are some young film directors today whose films are considered to be "cutting edge"?

"Retrato de Luis Buñuel" (1924), Salvador Dalí ▶

Oil on canvas, .70 x .60 m. Coll. Luis Buñuel, Mexico City, D.F., Mexico. © 2009
Salvador Dalí, Gala-Salvador Dalí Foundation/Artists Rights Society (ARS),
New York. Photo: Bridgeman-Giraudon / Art Resource, NY.

Capítulo 9A

El cine y la televisión

Chapter Objectives

- Describe movies and television programs
- Express opinions about media entertainment
- Talk about things you have done recently
- Understand cultural perspectives on common gestures

Video Highlights

Videocultura: *Medios de comunicación*

A primera vista: *¿Qué dan en la tele?*

GramActiva Videos: *acabar de* + infinitive; *gustar* and similar verbs

Videomisterio: *¿Eres tú, María?*, Episodio 9

Country Connection

As you learn about movies and television programs, you will make connections to these countries and places:

- España
- Florida
- Venezuela
- México
- Chile
- Argentina

Más práctica

- *Real.* para hispanohablantes pp. 330–331

realidades.com

- Fondo cultural Activity
- Video Activities
- Online Atlas
- Web Code: jce-0002

Vocabulario en contexto

jcd-0987 🔊

Objectives

Read, listen to, and understand information about
- movies and television programs
- opinions on media entertainment

¡LE DAMOS EL MUNDO EN EL CANAL 9!

¿Qué le interesa? Un programa...

¿...de entrevistas?

Entre tú y yo
Pablo Ramírez habla con personas fascinantes.

¿...educativo?

Nuestro planeta
Explora el mundo de los animales.

¿...de concursos?

¡Una fortuna para ti!
¡Los participantes pueden recibir mucho dinero!

¿...de noticias?

Las noticias de hoy
Presentamos todo lo que necesita saber del mundo en 30 minutos.

¿...deportivo?

Fútbol hoy
Hay fútbol, fútbol y mas fútbol.

¿...una telenovela?

Secretos de amor
¿Qué va a pasar con Rosario y Felipe en este programa **emocionante**?

¿...musical?

Ritmos latinos
Le presenta música de **más de** 20 países diferentes.

¿...de dibujos animados?

Patito y Paquito
Una presentación **cómica** para todos los niños.

—¿Qué quieres ver en la tele?

—¿La verdad? **Me aburre** la televisión. No me interesan nada los programas que **dan.**

—No estoy de acuerdo. Pienso que la televisión presenta muchos programas interesantes y divertidos.

CINE FLORIDA

una película policíaca
El crimen perfecto
15:15 17:50 20:25 23:00

una comedia
MI TÍO TONTO
16:40 18:50 21:00 23:10

un drama
La tragedia de Laura
11:20 13:50 16:20 18:50 21:20

una película de ciencia ficción
¡Los extraterrestres atacan!
14:00 16:00 18:00 20:00

una película romántica
Antonio y Ana
15:10 16:30 17:50 19:10

una película de horror
EL TERROR EN EL CASTILLO
13:45 16:15 18:45 21:15

—¿Qué dan en el Cine Florida?

—Hay seis películas. Mis amigos dicen que esta película policíaca es muy **violenta.** No quiero verla. Me interesan más las películas románticas como *Antonio y Ana.*

—Yo también quiero verla. ¿A qué hora va a **empezar?**

—**Empieza** a las cuatro y media, y **termina antes de** las seis. **Dura menos de** una hora y **media.**

—¿**De veras?** Son **casi** las cuatro. ¡Vamos ahora!

Más práctica

- **Guided** Vocab. Flash Cards pp. 275–280
- **Core** Vocab. Practice pp. 157–158
- **Communication** Writing p. 176
- *Real.* **para hispanohablantes** p. 332

realidades.com

- Audio Activities
- Leveled Workbook
- Flashcards
- Web Code: jcd-0901

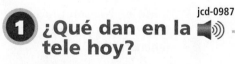

jcd-0987

1 ¿Qué dan en la tele hoy? 🔊

Escuchar

Vas a escuchar información sobre ocho programas del Canal 9. Señala cada tipo de programa en tu libro.

jcd-0987

2 ¿Qué película vamos a ver? 🔊

Escuchar

Vas a escuchar siete frases sobre las películas que dan en el Cine Florida. Si una frase es lógica, haz el gesto del pulgar hacia arriba. Si no es lógica, haz el gesto del pulgar hacia abajo.

¿Qué dan en la tele?

¿Qué programa de
televisión van a ver los
chicos? Lee la historia.

España

Strategy

Scanning
Looking for details prior to reading
can help with comprehension. Scan
the reading and look for instances
in which one or more people
disagree about something. What do
they disagree about and what are
some expressions used?

1 Ignacio: ¿Qué dan en la
televisión? Elena, ¿dónde
está el mando a distancia?*

Elena: Está encima de
la mesita, al lado de la
lámpara.

Ignacio: ¡Ah, sí! Lo veo.
Vamos a ver lo que hay . . .

*remote control

Ignacio   Javier   Jorgito   Elena   Ana

5 Ignacio: No me gustan
estos programas **infantiles.**
¿Qué más hay?

Elena: Un momento
. . . este programa de
entrevistas es mi favorito.
Hablan de todo. Ohhh,
¡acaban de hablar con mi
actor favorito!

Ignacio: Sí, y ya
terminaron. **Por eso** no
tenemos que verlo.

6 Ignacio: Podemos ver un
programa de concursos.

Javier: ¿O un programa
educativo? ¿O las noticias?

Todos: ¡Nooo!

Ignacio: ¡Tantos canales y
no hay nada que ver!

Ana: ¿Por qué no vamos
al cine?

7 Ana: Quiero ver una
comedia.

Elena: Yo prefiero ver una
película romántica.

Ignacio: No, son tontas.
¿Qué tal una película de
ciencia ficción?

Todos: ¡Nooo!

Javier: Dan un drama
nuevo en el Cine Capitol.

Todos: ¡Nooo!

2 Ana: ¡Fabuloso! Mi telenovela favorita.

Elena: Sí, me encanta. Es muy emocionante. **El actor** y **la actriz** principales son muy guapos.

Ignacio: ¡No! Me aburren las telenovelas. Vamos a ver otro canal.

Ana y Elena: Ignacio, ¡nuestra telenovela, por favor!

3 Elena: ¿Qué más hay? Mmmm. **¿Qué clase de** programa es éste?

Ana: Es **un programa de la vida real.** Es muy **realista.**

Ignacio: No son realistas. Pienso que son **tontos.** ¿Verdad, Javier?

Javier: Pues, no sé mucho **sobre** esta clase de programas.

4 Jorgito: Elena, quiero ver dibujos animados. **Ya** son las cuatro.

Elena: Jorgito, ¿no ves que estoy con mis amigos? Tú puedes ver la tele más tarde. Mira, puedes escuchar música en mi dormitorio.

Jorgito: Está bien, pero sólo hoy.

Todos: Adiós, Jorgito.

8 Jorgito: Ahora puedo ver los dibujos animados, **especialmente** mi favorito, *Rin, ran, run.* ¡Qué bien!

3 ¿Comprendes?

Escribir · Hablar

¿A quién(es) se refiere *(refers)* cada frase: Ana, Elena, Ignacio, Javier o Jorgito? Una frase puede referirse a más de una persona.

1. No me interesan nada las telenovelas.

2. No veo mucho los programas de la vida real.

3. Me encanta este programa. Hablan con actores.

4. Me encantan las telenovelas.

5. Voy a escuchar música.

6. Yo prefiero ver una película romántica.

7. Ahora no hay nadie aquí. Puedo ver mi programa favorito.

Más práctica

- **Guided** Vocab. Check pp. 281–284
- **Core** Vocab. Practice pp. 159–160
- **Communication** Video pp. 170–172
- *Real.* **para hispanohablantes** p. 333

realidades.com ✔

- Audio Activities
- Video Activities
- Leveled Workbook
- Flashcards
- Web Code: jcd-0902

Vocabulario en uso

Objectives

- Talk about different kinds of movies and television programs
- Express opinions and preferences about entertainment
- Use *acabar de* + infinitive to talk about things you have just done
- Tell why you don't do something
- Learn to use *gustar* and similar verbs

4 Muchas opiniones

jcd-0988

Escuchar · Escribir · Hablar

Un programa de radio les pregunta a sus oyentes *(listeners)* qué piensan de los diferentes programas de televisión.

1 En una hoja de papel copia la tabla y escribe los números del 1 al 6. Vas a escuchar las opiniones de unas personas. Escribe la clase de programa en la primera columna y la descripción en la segunda columna. Luego escribe frases para expresar tu opinión.

Programa de televisión	Descripción
1. las comedias	muy cómicas

Modelo

Me encantan las comedias porque son muy cómicas.

2 Habla con otro(a) estudiante. Di si estás de acuerdo con sus opiniones.

Modelo

Estoy de acuerdo. Las comedias son muy cómicas.
o:—*No estoy de acuerdo. Las comedias son muy tontas.*

5 Buenos ejemplos

Escribir

Escoge seis de los siguientes programas de televisión. Luego escribe frases para dar un buen ejemplo de los diferentes programas.

Modelo

Two and a Half Men *es una comedia.*

6 ¿Te gustaría ver . . . ?

Hablar

Usa la información que escribiste en la Actividad 5 y habla con otro(a) estudiante sobre qué clase de programas le gustaría ver. Él o ella puede usar las siguientes palabras.

me aburren	tontos, -as	fascinantes
me gustan	emocionantes	cómicos, -as
me interesan	violentos, -as	infantiles
me encantan	realistas	**¡Respuesta personal!**

Modelo

A —¿Te gustaría ver *una comedia* como Two and a Half Men?
B —¡Uf! *Me aburren las comedias. Son tontas.*
o: —¡Por supuesto! *Me encantan las comedias. Son cómicas.*

jcd-0988

7 Escucha y escribe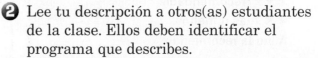

Escuchar · Escribir

Escucha y luego escribe en una hoja de papel lo que dice un joven sobre un programa de televisión que ve.

8 ¿Qué programa ves tú?

Escribir · Hablar

❶ Usa la descripción del programa de televisión de la Actividad 7 como modelo y escribe sobre un programa que tú ves. No debes nombrar el programa en la descripción.

❷ Lee tu descripción a otros(as) estudiantes de la clase. Ellos deben identificar el programa que describes.

Fondo cultural

Argentina • España • México • Venezuela

Las telenovelas Venezuela, Mexico, Argentina, and Spain produce many soap operas that are popular with people of all ages. Unlike soap operas in the United States that continue for years with the same characters, the *telenovelas* frequently last only a matter of months. They are then replaced with new shows and different characters.

• What are the advantages of stories that continue for years versus stories that are new every several months? Which would you prefer?

Los actores practican para la telenovela *Cuidado con el ángel.*

Leer • Hablar

Lee el artículo abajo que escribieron los críticos Guillo y
Nadia. Luego trabaja con otro(a) estudiante para decidir qué
película van a ver. Contesta las preguntas en el recuadro.

Nota

Use *más* / *menos de* with
numbers.

• más **de** tres horas

• menos **de** diez personas

Modelo

A —*Acabo de leer un artículo sobre la película . . .*
   ¿Te gustaría verla?

B —*¿Qué clase de película es?*

¿Qué clase de película es?	¿Cuánto tiempo dura?
¿De veras? ¿Cómo es?	¿Quiénes son los actores principales?
¿Sí? ¿Qué pasa en la película?	Pues, ¿quieres verla?

En nuestra opinión

¿Piensas ir al cine este fin de
semana? Nadia y Guillo te dan
sus impresiones de tres nuevas
películas . . .

Guillo **Nadia**

★★★ recomendable

★★ más o menos

★ no la recomiendo

Cuando el amor llega Con Cristina Campos y
Rafael Montenegro. Una película romántica
sobre un joven rico enamorado de una chica
pobre. Ante la oposición de sus padres, el
amor de los jóvenes es imposible. Esta
película, de dos horas y media, es similar a
las viejas fórmulas de las telenovelas—un
poco tonta y aburrida. Los protagonistas son
buenos, pero los actores secundarios son
demasiado dramáticos. Recomendable para
personas que no tienen nada que hacer.(★)

Mis padres son de otro planeta Unos chicos
descubren que sus padres son originarios
de otra galaxia y que están en este planeta
para explorar y planear una invasión. Una
producción para toda la familia que combina
elementos de comedia y ciencia ficción. Es

tan fascinante y cómica que no puedes
creer que estás en el cine por más de tres
horas. Los actores principales, Javier
Zaragoza y Miguel Vilar, son fantásticos.
(★★★)

Mi perro es mi héroe Un drama para toda
la familia—no es violenta y es bastante
realista. Un poco infantil, pero con mucha
acción y emoción. El mejor amigo del
hombre, el perro, con inteligencia y valor, le
salva la vida* a toda la familia. La película
es divertida pero un poco corta (menos de
dos horas). Tiene muy buenos actores, como
Ana Jiménez y Antonio Barrera. Es una
buena película. (★★★)

*saves the life

10 ¿Cuántas horas de tele?

Pensar · Hablar · Escribir

Vas a calcular el promedio *(average)* de horas que tus compañeros ven la tele.

Conexiones | Las matemáticas

❶ Escribe el número de horas que viste la tele cada día de la semana pasada. Suma *(Add up)* estas horas. Calcula el promedio de horas para cada día.

_____ *(total de horas)* dividido por 7

❷ Trabaja con un grupo de cuatro personas. Pregunta a tus compañeros(as) el tiempo promedio que vieron la televisión cada día. Escribe la información que recibes de tu grupo.

Modelo

A —*Como promedio, ¿cuántas horas viste la tele cada día?*

B —*La vi casi dos horas cada día.*

❸ Calcula el promedio de horas que tu grupo vio la tele cada día la semana pasada. Escribe una frase para presentar la información a la clase.

---

11 La tele en tu vida

Pensar · Leer · Hablar

En un estudio reciente, se dio a conocer que, como promedio, las personas de los Estados Unidos ven ocho horas de tele al día. ¡La suma de estas horas equivale a casi cuatro meses al año frente a la televisión!

❶ Usa el promedio de horas de tu grupo de la Actividad 10 y calcula el número total de horas que vieron la tele en un año.

• 365 días al año por *(promedio de horas)* son *(total de horas)* al año

❷ Usa el total de horas al año para contestar estas preguntas. *(Nota: Hay aproximadamente 720 horas en un mes.)*

1. ¿Tu grupo ve la tele más de un mes al año o menos?

2. ¿La ven Uds. más que el promedio de personas en los Estados Unidos o menos? ¿Y de las personas en los otros países de la gráfica?

3. ¿Crees que las personas en los países de la gráfica ven demasiada tele? ¿Por qué?

Los cinco países que ven más televisión al día

Source: Organisation for Economic Co-Operation and Development

Gramática

Acabar de + infinitive

When you want to say that something just happened,
use the present tense of *acabar de* + infinitive.

Acabo de ver un programa musical. *I just saw a music program.*

Mis padres **acaban de ir** al cine. *My parents just went to the movies.*

Acabamos de hablar de esa película. *We just talked about that movie.*

Although the action took place in the past, the
present-tense forms of *acabar* are used.

GramActiva VIDEO

Want more help with
acabar de + infinitive?
Watch the
GramActiva video.

acabo de

12 **¡Acaban de hacer ♻ muchas cosas!**

Escribir

La familia Martínez acaba de hacer muchas
cosas esta mañana antes de ir a estudiar y
trabajar. Lee la lista de quehaceres y escribe
quién acaba de hacer qué cosa.

Modelo

mamá / preparar el desayuno de sus hijos
*Mamá acaba de preparar el desayuno de
sus hijos.*

Quehaceres . . .

1. mamá / preparar el desayuno de sus hijos ✓
2. Carlitos / comer el desayuno ✓
3. Mariel / limpiar su dormitorio ✓
4. Ezequiel / sacar la basura ✓
5. Ezequiel, Carlitos y Mariel / terminar su tarea ✓
6. papá / pasar la aspiradora en la sala ✓
7. Elena / dar de comer al gato ✓
8. todos / buscar sus abrigos ✓

Fondo cultural

El mundo hispano

Sábado gigante is one of the longest running
shows in television history. Its popular host, Don
Francisco, started this unique variety program in
his native Chile in 1962. It now airs from Miami
every Saturday night and brings comedy, celebrity
guests, musical performances, games, and contests
to its more than 100 million viewers in 42 countries.
In June, 2005, the program celebrated its 1000th
episode on the Miami-based Univisión network.

• What television shows do you know that have
enjoyed continued success over the years?

El famosísimo Don Francisco ▲

13 Acabo de ver . . .

Escribir • Hablar

1 Copia la gráfica en una hoja de papel. Escribe tres clases de programas de televisión, obras de teatro o películas que acabas de ver. Da el nombre y haz una descripción.

Acabo de ver . . .	Nombre	Descripción
Una película romántica	¡No puedo vivir sin ti!	demasiado triste

¿Recuerdas?

Some adverbs you can use in descriptions are:

bastante   muy

demasiado   un poco

2 Trabaja con otro(a) estudiante para hablar sobre lo que acaban de ver.

Modelo

A —*Acabo de ver <u>una película romántica</u>.*
B —*¿De veras? ¿Cómo se llama?*
A —*¡No puedo vivir sin ti!*
B —*¿Te gustó?*
A —*No, <u>no me gustó</u> porque es <u>demasiado triste</u>.*

Más práctica

- **Guided** Gram. Practice pp. 285–286
- **Core** Gram. Practice p. 161
- **Communication** Writing p. 177, Test Prep p. 325
- ***Real.* para hispanohablantes** pp. 334–337

realidades.com

- Audio Activities
- Video Activities
- Speak & Record
- Tutorial
- Leveled Workbook
- Web Code: jcd-0903

Exploración del lenguaje

Words of Greek and Arabic origin

Languages change when regions and nations interact with, or are conquered or colonized by, people who speak a different language. Long before the Romans brought Latin to Spain, certain Greek words had entered the Latin language. Words like *el problema, el programa,* and *el drama* originally were masculine nouns in Greek. When they came into Latin and then Spanish, they kept their masculine gender even though they end in *a*.

Try it out! Which of these new words would you use in the following sentences?

el clima   el sistema   el poema

1. No comprendo _____ de clasificación de películas en ese país.

2. Me gustaría visitar Panamá porque _____ allí es tropical.

3. Me gusta _____ que acabo de leer.

Arabic also had a large influence on Spanish. Around A.D. 700 the Arabic-speaking Moors invaded Spain from northern Africa. They ruled for 800 years and played a major role in the development of the Spanish language and culture. Words that came from Arabic often begin with the letters *al-*. Many words in Spanish that have a *z* or a *j* in them are also of Arabic origin. You know these words that came from Arabic: *alfombra, azúcar, naranja.*

Try it out! You also know these words that are from Arabic. Fill in the missing letters.

a_ul   _macén   _anahoria

Gramática

Gustar and similar verbs

Even though we usually translate the verb *gustar* as "to like," it literally means "to please." So when you say, *Me gustan los programas deportivos,* you're actually saying, "Sports programs are pleasing to me." *Programas deportivos* is the subject of the sentence, and *me* is the indirect object. Here's the pattern:

indirect object + form of *gustar* + subject

The subject in a sentence with *gustar* usually follows the verb. You need to know if the subject is singular or plural to know which form of *gustar* to use. If the subject is singular, use *gusta.* If it's plural, use *gustan.* If it's an infinitive, use *gusta.*

Me gusta **el actor** en la telenovela pero no me gusta**n las actrices.**

A mis amigos les gusta **ver** películas.

To emphasize or clarify *who* is pleased, you can use an additional *a* + pronoun:

A mí me gustan los dibujos animados, pero **a él** no le gustan.

Here are the other verbs you know that are similar to *gustar:*

aburrir	A mí **me aburren** las películas románticas.
doler *(o→ue)*	A Fernando **le duelen** los pies.
encantar	A mis padres **les encanta** el teatro.
faltar	**Me faltan** un cuchillo y un tenedor.
interesar	**Nos interesan** mucho los programas musicales.
quedar	¿No **te queda** bien el vestido?

¿Recuerdas?

You have used *me gusta(n), te gusta(n),* and *le gusta(n)* to talk about what a person likes.

- A mí **me gusta** el cine pero a mi hermano **le gusta** más la televisión.

GramActiva VIDEO

Want more help with *gustar* and other similar verbs? Watch the **GramActiva** video.

---

jcd-0988

14 Escucha y escribe

Escuchar • Escribir

Escucha las opiniones de la familia Linares sobre los programas que dan en la televisión. En una hoja de papel, escribe los números del 1 al 6 y escribe las frases que escuchas.

Mirando la tele en familia.

15 A mí y a ti

Escribir • Hablar

❶ Trabaja con otro(a) estudiante. Copia el diagrama Venn en una hoja de papel. Escribe el nombre de tu compañero(a) encima del óvalo a la derecha. En el óvalo indicado con *A mí* escribe cinco clases de películas o programas de televisión que te gustan.

❷ Pregunta a tu compañero(a) si le gustan las clases de programas y películas que tú escribiste. Si a él o a ella le gusta la clase de programa o película, escribe el nombre en el óvalo de la derecha. (Vas a usar el diagrama Venn en la Actividad 16.)

Modelo

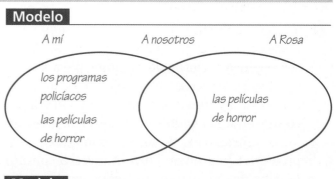

Modelo

A —*¿Te gustan los programas policíacos?*
B —*A ver . . . no, no me gustan mucho.*
A —*Pues, ¿te gustan las películas de horror?*
B —*Sí, me gustan mucho.*

16 A nosotros nos gusta . . .

Escribir

Compara los dos lados de tu diagrama. Escribe las clases de programas y películas que a los dos les gustan en el centro de ese diagrama. Escribe al menos cinco frases completas para describir qué les gusta a Uds.

Modelo

Modelo

A nosotros nos gustan las películas de horror. A mí me gustan los programas policíacos pero a Rosa no le gustan.

Fondo cultural

El mundo hispano

Cable television The cable and satellite television industry in Latin America has grown tremendously. Hundreds of channels are available to viewers. Some cable channels specialize in news or sports, and offer their programming to other countries as well. Among the sports, soccer is the one that attracts the most viewers. The World Cup is enormously popular in Latin America and around the world.

• What Latin American programs can you find in your local cable or satellite listings? Watch some of them to find out where these programs are produced.

17 Juego

Escribir · Hablar · GramActiva

1 Trabaja en grupos de cuatro personas. Necesitas 20 tarjetas de tres colores. Debes tener cinco tarjetas de un color para la columna 1, cinco de otro color para la columna 2 y diez del tercer color para la columna 3. En cada tarjeta, escribe una de las palabras o expresiones de las dos primeras columnas. Para la tercera columna, escribe dos palabras para cada categoría (por ejemplo, para "cuerpo" puedes escribir *el brazo* en una tarjeta, y *la pierna* en otra).

a mí	encanta(n)	cuerpo
a mi amigo(a)	duele(n)	películas
a nosotros	interesa(n)	clases
a mis amigos	aburre(n)	ropa
a Uds.	queda(n) bien	comidas

2 Baraja *(Shuffle)* las tarjetas de cada columna y ponlas boca abajo *(face down)* en sus tres grupos. Toma una tarjeta de cada grupo, forma una frase completa y di la frase. *Importante:* Para las palabras del primer grupo, vas a tener que escoger una de estas palabras: *me, te, le, nos, les.* Si tu grupo decide que la gramática de tu frase es correcta, recibes 1 punto. Recibes otro punto si la frase es lógica. Si puedes cambiar la frase para hacerla lógica, recibes 2 puntos.

Modelo

A mi amigo le duele el pescado. (1 punto)
A mi amigo le duele la pierna. (2 puntos)

Pronunciación

Linking words

In Spanish just as in English, you don't pronounce a sentence as completely separate words. Instead, the words flow together in phrases. That is why it often seems that phrases or sentences sound as if they are one long word.

How the words flow together depends on the last sound of a word and the beginning sound of the following word. The flow of sounds is usually created by two of the same vowels, two different vowels, or a consonant followed by a vowel. Listen to and say these word combinations:

| me‿encanta | de‿entrevistas | le‿aburre |
| nos‿interesa | dibujos‿animados | de‿horror |

Try it out! Listen to and say these sentences. Be careful not to break the flow of sound where you see "‿".

Me‿interesa‿ese programa de‿entrevistas.

A‿Ana le‿aburre‿ese programa‿educativo.

La película de‿horror dura‿una‿hora‿y media.

Vamos‿a ver lo que‿hay‿en la tele.

Me‿encanta‿el‿actor y la‿actriz de‿esa telenovela.

18 ¿Qué hay en la tele?

Escribir • Hablar

A veces decimos, "¡Hay tantos canales y programas en la tele pero no hay nada interesante!". Ahora tienes la oportunidad de planear seis horas de televisión para el sábado, desde las 17.00 horas hasta las 23.00 horas, para un concurso que se llama "Tus propias seis horas en la tele".

1 Trabaja en un grupo de tres. Escriban una lista de programas o películas que les gustaría incluir *(include)* en las seis horas. Den esta información para cada programa o película:

- la clase de programa
- el nombre
- cómo es

- cuánto tiempo dura
- para quiénes es recomendable
- por qué le va a interesar al público

2 Preparen una presentación para la clase. Pueden hacer algo visual para acompañar su presentación.

3 Después de escuchar a los diferentes grupos, cada grupo va a votar por la mejor presentación. ¡No pueden votar por la suya *(your own)*! Los grupos tienen que escribir cuatro frases para explicar su decisión. El grupo que recibe más votos gana el concurso.

> **Modelo**
>
> *Nosotros votamos por la presentación del grupo de Ana, David y Kathy. Tienen muchos programas que nos interesan a nosotros.*

El español en la comunidad

While many television networks are losing viewers, the number of viewers watching Spanish-language networks is growing. Look in your newspaper's TV guide and find listings for a Spanish-language network. Find the name of a program for each kind of show on p. 426. Watch a few minutes of one of the programs. Although you might find it difficult to understand, tune in from time to time. You'll be amazed at how much you'll learn!

- How are the listings similar to or different from those for the networks you usually watch? Write your impressions of the television show you watched.

Más práctica

- **Guided** Gram. Practice pp. 287–288
- **Core** Gram. Practice pp. 162–163
- **Communication** Writing p. 178
- *Real.* **para hispanohablantes** pp. 338–341

realidades.com ⊙

- Audio Activities
- Video Activities
- Speak & Record
- Canción de hip hop
- Tutorial
- Leveled Workbook
- Web Code: jcd-0904

Lectura

Una semana sin televisión

Strategy

Reading for comprehension
Read without stopping at unknown words. Then go back, decide if the words are important, and see if you can guess their meanings.

¿Sabes que los niños estadounidenses pasan más horas al año pegados a la pantalla de su televisión que haciendo cualquier otra cosa, a excepción de dormir?

Hay estudios que dicen que ver demasiado la televisión puede causar malos hábitos de comida, falta de ejercicio y obesidad. En cuatro horas de dibujos animados el sábado por la mañana los niños pueden ver 202 anuncios sobre refrescos, dulces y cereales azucarados. Esta comida combinada con las horas frente a la pantalla resulta en que uno de cada seis niños estadounidenses tenga exceso de peso.

También hay estudios que dan nuevas pruebas de la relación entre la televisión y la violencia. Uno de estos estudios indica que niños que ven más de una hora de televisión al día tienen más probabilidad de ser violentos y agresivos de adultos.

Used with permission from TIME FOR KIDS magazine.

¿Quieres participar en una solución? Durante el mes de abril millones de personas en más de treinta países apagan la tele por una semana. En vez de ver la tele los participantes van con sus familias o con amigos al campo, o a caminar, montar en bicicleta o visitar un parque.

¿Y qué pasa después de unos días sin televisión? Una niña de diez años dice: —¿Para qué necesito la tele? Hay muchas cosas más interesantes que puedo hacer.

¿Comprendes?

Prepara información para un debate sobre la cuestión: ¿Es bueno o malo ver la televisión?

1. Escribe una lista de cuatro razones (reasons) en favor de no ver la tele. Usa información que leíste en el artículo.

2. Escribe una lista de cuatro razones en favor de ver la tele.

Y tú, ¿qué dices?

1. Usa la información en tu lista para expresar tu opinión: ¿Es bueno o malo ver la televisión? ¿Por qué?

2. Para ti, ¿va a ser fácil o difícil pasar una semana sin ver la televisión? ¿Por qué?

3. En Chile, a una persona que ve mucha televisión se le llama "un(a) tevito(a)". ¿Qué puedes decirle a un(a) tevito(a) para persuadirlo(a) a hacer otras cosas que son mejores para la salud?

Más práctica

- **Guided** Reading Support p. 289
- **Communication** Writing p. 179, Test Prep p. 326
- **Real. para hispanohablantes** pp. 342–343

- Internet Activity
- Leveled Workbook
- Web Code: jcd-0905

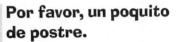

La cultura en vivo
Comunicación sin palabras

Every culture has gestures that communicate a message. You've already seen gestures for *¡ojo!* and *más o menos*. Here are a few more gestures used in many Spanish-speaking countries to communicate a message.

mucha gente

¡Hay mucha gente en la fiesta!

(Place your fingertips together, then open your hand. Repeat this motion in a rhythmic gesture.)

un poco

Por favor, un poquito de postre.

¡a comer!

¡Vamos a comer!

(With your fingertips bunched, bring your hand up close to your mouth, then extend it forward, bending your arm at the elbow. Repeat the motion two or three times.)

¡qué rico!

¡Este plato está muy rico!

(Kiss the bunched fingertips of one hand, then quickly pull your hand away, extending your fingers.)

no sé

No sé dónde está el libro.

nada

No tengo nada.

Try it out! Work with a partner and create a short skit in which you use one of these gestures. Present it for the class.

Think about it! What gestures do you use most often? Do you ever use gestures that are the same as or similar to the ones shown on this page? Do you think you would understand some of the gestures on this page even without an explanation?

Presentación oral
¿Qué dan esta semana?

Task
You are reviewing a movie or television show you have just seen for your school's closed-circuit TV system. Prepare a summary of the movie or show.

① Prepare Choose a movie or TV show to talk about. Cut out ads or photos about it from a newspaper or TV guide or download them from the Internet. Copy the chart below on a sheet of paper and provide the information for the movie or show you have chosen.

Nombre	
Clase de película o programa	
Actor / actores	
Actriz / actrices	
Cómo es	
Cuánto tiempo dura	
Para quiénes es	
Tus impresiones	

Strategy

Using charts
Create a chart to help you think through the key information you will want to talk about. This will help you speak more effectively.

② Practice Use your notes from the chart for your presentation. Create a poster with the visuals you have collected. Go through your presentation several times. You may use your notes in practice, but not when you present. Try to:

- provide all key information about the film or show
- use complete sentences in your presentation
- speak clearly

③ Present Present your chosen movie or television show to a small group or the class. Use your poster to help guide you through the presentation.

④ Evaluation Your teacher may give you a rubric for how your presentation will be graded. You probably will be graded on:

- how complete your presentation is
- how much information you communicate
- how easy it is to understand you

¿Eres tú, María?

Episodio 9

Antes de ver el video

"Paco, te digo que te necesito ahora mismo.
Por favor, rápido. Y a Margarita, también".

Nota gramatical What's a good mystery without an expression like "Follow her!"? In this episode you'll hear several uses of the verb to follow: *seguir.*

sigo	seguimos
sigues	seguís
sigue	siguen

Resumen del episodio

Al día siguiente Lola va a su trabajo, cuando ve a María. ¡Qué suerte! Lola la sigue y llama a Paco y a Margarita. Ella necesita a los dos ahora mismo para ayudarla. Vigilan¹ a María y a un hombre en el café, y Margarita muestra² sus talentos de detective. Es evidente que María y el hombre no están nada contentos. Pero, ¿quién es este hombre misterioso y por qué quiere irse de Madrid?

¹They watch   ²shows

Palabras para comprender

¡Venid! Come!

ve a sentarte go sit

aparece appears

quiere irse wants to go away

vengan en seguida come right away

sigue vigilando continue watching

—¡Ay de mí!
—Cálmate, Lola.

"Lola, ¿quién es ese hombre? ¿De qué están hablando?"

Madrid • **Barcelona**

"Ahora lo comprendo todo. Voy a llamar al Inspector Gil".

Después de ver el video

¿Comprendes?

A. Contesta las preguntas.

1. ¿Quiénes ayudan a Lola con la investigación?

2. ¿Quién va al café para escuchar a María y al hombre?

3. ¿Está Lola tranquila o nerviosa? ¿Por qué?

4. Según Lola, ¿quién es el hombre en el café?

5. Según Margarita, ¿quién es la chica en el café?

6. Según Margarita, ¿el hombre quiere quedarse *(stay)* en Madrid o quiere irse?

B. Lola dice, "Ahora lo comprendo todo". En tu opinión, ¿qué comprende Lola? ¿Cuál es la solución del misterio?

realidades.com

• Web Code: jcd-0507

Repaso del capítulo

Vocabulario y gramática

jcd-0989 🔊

Chapter Review

To prepare for the test, check to see if you . . .
- **know the new vocabulary and grammar**
- **can perform the tasks on p. 447**

to talk about television shows

el canal	channel
el programa de concursos	game show
el programa deportivo	sports show
el programa de dibujos animados	cartoon show
el programa de entrevistas	interview program
el programa de la vida real	reality program
el programa de noticias	news program
el programa educativo	educational program
el programa musical	musical program
la telenovela	soap opera

to talk about movies

la comedia	comedy
el drama	drama
la película de ciencia ficción	science fiction movie
la película de horror	horror movie
la película policíaca	crime movie, mystery
la película romántica	romantic movie

to give your opinion of a movie or program

cómico, -a	funny
emocionante	touching
fascinante	fascinating
infantil	for children; childish
realista	realistic
tonto, -a	silly, stupid
violento, -a	violent
me aburre(n)	it bores me (they bore me)
me interesa(n)	it interests me (they interest me)

For *Vocabulario adicional*, see pp. 472–473.

to ask and tell about movies or programs

el actor	actor
la actriz	actress
dar	to show
durar	to last
empezar *(e → ie)*	to begin
terminar	to end
más / menos de	more / less than
medio, -a	half
¿Qué clase de . . . ?	What kind of . . . ?

to talk about what has just happened

acabar de + *infinitive*	to have just . . .

verbs similar to *gustar*

aburrir	to bore
doler *(o → ue)*	to hurt, to ache
encantar	to please very much, to love
faltar	to be missing
interesar	to interest
quedar	to fit

other useful expressions

antes de	before
casi	almost
¿De veras?	Really?
especialmente	especially
por eso	therefore, for that reason
sobre	about
ya	already

Más práctica

- **Core** Puzzle p. 164, Organizer p. 165
- **Communication** Practice Test pp. 328–330, Integrated Performance Assessment p. 327

realidades.com ✓

- Tutorial
- Flashcards
- Puzzles
- Self-test
- Web Code: jcd-0906

Preparación para el examen

On the exam you will be asked to . . .	Here are practice tasks similar to those you will find on the exam . . .	If you need review . . .

Interpretive

jcd-0989 🔊

1 Escuchar Listen and understand as people express opinions about movies and TV programs

Listen as you hear a phone pollster ask people about TV programs they have watched on the new Spanish-language cable station. For each viewer, decide if the shows were: a) boring; b) interesting; c) too violent; d) too childish or silly.

pp. 426-429 *Vocabulario en contexto*
p. 430 Actividad 4
p. 431 Actividades 6–7
p. 435 Actividad 13

Interpersonal

2 Hablar Ask and answer questions about the types of movies and TV programs people prefer

Tell your partner about a movie or TV program you just saw and express your opinion about it. Ask if your partner saw the same thing and what he or she thought of it. If your partner didn't see it, ask him or her to tell about something he or she just saw. You might say: *Acabo de ver una película fantástica con Tom Cruise . . .*

pp. 426-429 *Vocabulario en contexto*
p. 430 Actividad 4
p. 431 Actividad 6
p. 432 Actividad 9
p. 435 Actividad 13
p. 437 Actividad 15
p. 443 Presentación oral

Interpretive

3 Leer Read and understand what an entertainment critic writes about a new TV program

Before class begins, you grab a Spanish-language magazine and turn to the entertainment section. After reading part of the entertainment critic's review, see if you can determine his opinion of a new soap opera series, *Mi secreto*. Does he like it? Why or why not?

*En el primer episodio de **Mi secreto**, nos aburren con una historia infantil y con actores sin talento que quieren ser emocionantes pero no pueden. ¡Pienso que este programa es para las personas que no tienen nada que hacer!*

pp. 426-429 *Vocabulario en contexto*
p. 432 Actividad 9

Presentational

4 Escribir Write about a movie you recently saw

You are keeping a journal to practice writing in Spanish. Today you are going to write about a movie you saw recently. Mention the name of the movie, the type of movie it is, and what you liked or disliked about it.

p. 431 Actividad 8
p. 435 Actividad 13
p. 437 Actividades 15–16
p. 443 *Presentación oral*

Cultures • Comparisons

5 Pensar Demonstrate an understanding of common gestures

You have learned that almost all cultures can communicate without words. With a partner, see if you can demonstrate the six gestures you have learned in this chapter from the Spanish-speaking world. Are these gestures similar to those in our culture?

p. 442 *La cultura en vivo*

Fondo cultural

España

"Reading the Letter" is from painter Pablo Picasso's Neo-Classical period, when he was influenced by ancient Roman sculpture. He used simplified color and heavy lines. The thickness of the hand over the man's shoulder on the right can remind you of weighty, unmoving, ancient statuary.

• What other characteristics of statuary do you see in the painting?

"Reading the Letter" (1921), Pablo Picasso ▶

Oil on canvas, 184 X 105 cm. © 2009 Estate of Pablo Picasso/ Artists Rights Society (ARS), New York.
Photo: Réunion des Musées Nationaux/ Art Resource, NY.

Edificio de Correos, Madrid, España

La tecnología

Chapter Objectives

- Talk about computers and the Internet
- Learn to ask for something and to tell what something is used for
- Talk about knowing people or knowing how to do things
- Understand cultural perspectives on using technology

Video Highlights

Videocultura: *Medios de comunicación*

A primera vista: *¿Cómo se comunica?*

GramActiva Videos: the present tense of *pedir* and *servir; saber* and *conocer*

Videomisterio: *¿Eres tú, María?, Episodio 10*

Country Connection

As you learn about different means of communication and how technology changes people's lives, you will make connections to these countries and places:

México España Texas

Más práctica

- *Real.* para hispanohablantes pp. 350–351

realidades.com ✔

- Fondo cultural Activity
- Video Activities
- Online Atlas
- Web Code: jce-0002

cuatrocientos cuarenta y nueve 449
Capítulo 9B

Vocabulario en contexto

jcd-0997

> En el laboratorio en nuestra escuela, los estudiantes saben usar las computadoras para hacer muchas cosas. A muchos estudiantes les gusta . . .

. . . **crear documentos** o escribir **una composición,**

. . . hacer **gráficos,**

la diapositiva **la computadora portátil**

. . . y preparar **presentaciones** con diapositivas.

Otros estudiantes **están en línea** para **navegar en la Red.** Pueden **buscar un sitio Web** o **bajar información** para **un informe.**

una canción

Para bailar la bamba

A otros les interesa **grabar un disco compacto.** Esta chica graba canciones "

—Nunca **me comunico** con **el correo electrónico.** ¿Es **complicado?** ¿Debo **tomar un curso** para aprender?

—No, abuelito, puedes aprender fácilmente. No debes **tener miedo de** usar la computadora. Y siempre me puedes **pedir** ayuda. ¿Cómo **te comunicas** con tus amigos que no viven cerca?

—Prefiero **enviarles** una carta o una tarjeta o puedo visitarlos para hablar cara a cara. Es mucho más personal.

la carta

Querida amiga,

la tarjeta

Feliz cumpleaños

hablar cara a cara

---

1 ¿Sí o no? 🔊 jcd-0997

Escuchar

Vas a escuchar siete frases. Si una frase es cierta, haz el gesto del pulgar hacia arriba. Si una frase es falsa, haz el gesto del pulgar hacia abajo.

Más práctica

- **Guided** Vocab. Flash Cards pp. 291–294
- **Core** Vocab. Practice pp. 166–167
- **Communication** Writing p. 185
- *Real.* **para hispanohablantes** p. 352

realidades.com ✓
- Audio Activities
- Leveled Workbook
- Flashcards
- Web Code: jcd-0911

2 ¿Es lógico? 🔊 jcd-0997

Escuchar

Primero lee las respuestas. Luego escucha cada conversación y escoge el comentario más lógico.

1. a. Al papá le gusta usar la Red.
   b. El papá no sabe usar la Red.
2. a. El estudiante quiere grabar un disco compacto.
   b. El estudiante quiere bajar información.
3. a. Va a enviarle una carta.
   b. Va a enviarle una tarjeta.

¿Cómo se comunica?

Ana sabe usar una cámara digital y una computadora. Ella puede navegar en la Red y tiene su propia página Web. ¿Qué le va a enseñar a Javier?

Strategy

Recognizing cognates
Recognizing cognates in the following dialogue can help improve your understanding. Skim the reading and make a list of the cognates.

España

Javier   Ana

1 **Javier:** Hola, Ana. ¿Cómo estás?

Ana: Muy bien, ¿y tú? Mira. Acabo de comprar esta **cámara digital.** Es fascinante. ¿La **conoces?**

Javier: A ver. No **conozco** ese tipo de cámara. ¡Qué interesante!

5 **Ana:** Aquí puedes navegar en la Red o **visitar salones de chat.** Mira, mi **página Web.** Yo la hice.

Javier: ¿Tú la hiciste? ¡Qué bien! Pero . . . **¿para qué sirve?**

Ana: El Internet **sirve para** mucho. Puedes **escribir por** correo electrónico, buscar información, jugar juegos . . .

6 **Ana:** Tengo una idea. Tu amigo Esteban tiene **dirección electrónica,** ¿no?

Javier: Creo que sí. ¡Ah! Aquí está en su carta.

7 **Javier:** Hola, Esteban. Saludos desde un cibercafé en Madrid . . .

Ana: ¡Eso es! Tú vas a escribirle por correo electrónico. Y le vamos a enviar esta foto de nosotros.

2 **Ana:** ¿Adónde vas?

Javier: Voy a enviar una tarjeta a Esteban, mi amigo en San Antonio. Mira, tengo una foto de él.

Ana: Mmmm. Es muy simpático, ¿no? Si quieres, te acompaño.

3 **Ana:** Vamos, Javier. Uno, dos, tres. Y mira, aquí estás. **¿Qué te parece?**

Javier: Muy bien. Sacaste las fotos muy **rápidamente.** Veo que no es complicado.

4 **Javier:** Un momento, voy a enviar mi tarjeta.

Ana: ¿Por qué no te comunicas con Esteban por correo electrónico?

Javier: Porque no tengo ordenador.

Ana: No importa. En Madrid hay muchos cibercafés. Vamos a uno.

8 **Javier:** . . . y aquí estoy con mi buena amiga, Ana. ¿Qué tal la familia? Y el cumpleaños de Cristina, ¿cómo lo pasaste?

Esteban: Es evidente que Javier está muy contento en Madrid.

También se dice . . .

la **computadora** = el **ordenador**
(España)

3 **¿Comprendes?**

Leer · Escribir

En cada frase hay un error. Lee la frase y después escribe la frase con la información correcta.

1. Ana acaba de comprar una computadora portátil.
2. Javier quiere enviarle a Esteban una carta.
3. Javier no le escribe por correo electrónico porque no le gusta usar las computadoras.
4. Javier saca las fotos con la cámara digital.
5. Según Ana, la Red no sirve para mucho.
6. Ana le escribe a Esteban por correo electrónico.
7. Javier le pregunta a Esteban sobre el cumpleaños de Angélica.

Más práctica

- **Guided** Vocab. Check pp. 295–298
- **Core** Vocab. Practice pp. 168–169
- **Communication** Video pp. 180–182
- *Real.* **para hispanohablantes** p. 353

realidades.com ✔

- Audio Activities
- Video Activities
- Leveled Workbook
- Flashcards
- Web Code: jcd-0912

Vocabulario en uso

4 La computadora y tú

Leer • Pensar • Hablar

1 Toma esta prueba *(test)* sobre cómo usas la computadora. Determina tu evaluación y lee la recomendación del Centro de Computación.

2 Pregunta a otro(a) estudiante qué curso debe tomar según los resultados de la prueba. Tiene que darte tres razones *(reasons)* para justificar el curso.

Modelo

A —¿Qué curso debes tomar?

B —Debo tomar un curso avanzado.

A —¿Por qué?

B —Porque ya navego en la Red y busco sitios Web. Sé crear un sitio Web.

Fondo cultural

España

Las cuevas de Altamira Long before people were able to write, they drew pictures on cave walls. These are the first records we have of communication. Spectacular paintings of bison, deer, horses, and wild boars were discovered in 1879 in the caves of Altamira in northern Spain. These drawings are more than 14,000 years old.

- Why do you think the cave dwellers drew pictures of animals? What would you draw?

Un bisonte en la cueva de Altamira

La computadora y tú

1. ¿Cómo te comunicas más con otras personas?
   a. Les hablo cara a cara.
   b. Les envío cartas o tarjetas.
   c. Les escribo por correo electrónico.
   d. Visito salones de chat.

2. ¿Cómo buscas información cuando escribes informes?
   a. Voy a la biblioteca por un libro.
   b. Les pido ayuda a mis amigos.
   c. Navego en la Red y busco sitios Web.
   d. Bajo documentos que me sirven mucho.

3. ¿Qué sabes hacer en la computadora?
   a. Sé encender* la computadora.
   b. Sé escribir una composición.
   c. Sé crear una presentación usando diapositivas.
   d. Sé crear un sitio Web.

4. ¿Para qué te sirve la computadora?
   a. No me sirve para nada.
   b. Me sirve para jugar juegos.
   c. Me sirve para navegar en la Red.
   d. Me sirve para buscar y bajar información.

5. ¿Cuál es tu opinión de las computadoras?
   a. Tengo miedo de las computadoras.
   b. Las computadoras son demasiado complicadas.
   c. Las computadoras me ayudan a hacer cosas más rápidamente.
   d. Las computadoras son necesarias para la comunicación.

Evaluación
Cada a = 1 punto
Cada b = 3 puntos
Cada c = 4 puntos
Cada d = 6 puntos

El Centro de Computación tiene cursos ideales para ti. Según el resultado de la prueba, debes tomar uno de estos cursos:

Puntos	Tu curso ideal
de 5 a 10	Básico 1
de 11 a 16	Básico 2
de 17 a 23	Intermedio
de 24 a 30	Avanzado

*to turn on

5 Opiniones diferentes 🔊 ——————

jcd-0998

Escuchar · Escribir

❶ Vas a escuchar las opiniones de cuatro personas sobre cómo prefieren comunicarse. En una hoja de papel, escribe los números del 1 al 4 y escribe lo que escuchas.

❷ Después de escuchar sus opiniones, indica si crees que las personas que tienen estas opiniones están en la sala o en el laboratorio de computadoras.

6 Definiciones ————————————————————

Leer · Escribir

Lee las definiciones y escribe la palabra correspondiente.

Modelo

Es cómo puedes enviar una carta por computadora.
el correo electrónico

1. Es una foto que podemos proyectar durante una presentación.

2. Es una composición musical que podemos cantar.

3. Es una forma de comunicación que usa bolígrafo y papel. *(Hay dos posibilidades.)*

4. Es un lugar en la Red que da información sobre una organización o una persona.

5. Es una computadora pequeña que puedes llevar a diferentes lugares.

6. Es un lugar en la escuela donde hay muchas computadoras que los estudiantes pueden usar.

7. Es una forma de comunicación bonita o cómica que le envías* a una persona para su cumpleaños.

8. Es algo visual que puedes crear o ver en la computadora.

9. Es algo que escribes sobre un tema para una clase. *(Hay dos posibilidades.)*

*Enviar has an accent mark on the i in all present-tense forms except nosotros and vosotros.

Fondo cultural

España

La Real Academia Española was founded in Spain in 1713 with a mission to preserve the quality, elegance, and purity of the Spanish language. There are now *Academias* in all the Spanish-speaking countries, including the Philippines and the United States. Today the *Academias* ensure that changes in Spanish reflect the needs of its more than 360 million native speakers. La Real Academia Española publishes the most complete, authoritative dictionary of the Spanish language.

• Why do you think that it's important to preserve the quality and purity of a language?

La Real Academia Española en Madrid

7 **¿Cómo te comunicas?**

Escribir • Hablar

1 Mira cada dibujo y escribe qué forma de comunicación es. Luego escribe por qué se usa esta forma de comunicación.

Modelo

hablar por teléfono
Casi todos tienen teléfonos. Es fácil.

1. **2.**

2 Trabaja con un grupo de cinco personas y pregunta a tus compañeros cómo se comunican con otras personas y por qué. Escriban sus respuestas.

3 Una persona de cada grupo va a escribir en la pizarra la forma preferida de comunicación de su grupo. Según esta información, ¿cuál es la forma de comunicación preferida de la clase?

3. **4.**

Modelo

A —*¿Cómo te comunicas con otras personas?*
B —*Les hablo por teléfono.*
A —*¿Por qué?*
B —*Porque casi todos tienen teléfonos y es fácil.*

8 **¿Quiénes están en línea?** _____

Leer • Escribir • Hablar

Lee el anuncio y luego contesta estas preguntas.

1. ¿Quiénes usan más el Internet: los estadounidenses o los españoles? ¿Los estadounidenses o los groenlandeses?

2. ¿Usas tú el Internet a menudo, a veces o nunca?

3. Entre *(Among)* las personas que conoces, ¿quién usa más el Internet? ¿Para qué lo usa?

¡A sus teclados¹, listos . . . a navegar!

¿Usas el Internet? En el mundo hay más de mil millones de internautas. El récord lo tienen los groenlandeses:² nueve de cada diez personas usan la Red. En los Estados Unidos, siete de cada diez estadounidenses³ la usan. En España la gente está lejos de esa cifra.⁴ Sólo seis de cada diez españoles están conectados al Internet.

¹keyboards ²Greenlanders ³Americans ⁴figure

9 Y tú, ¿que dices?

Escribir · Hablar

1. ¿Tienes tú, o tiene tu familia o un(a) amigo(a), una computadora portátil? ¿Qué te parece?

2. ¿A veces tienes miedo de las computadoras? ¿Por qué?

3. ¿Tienes tu propia dirección electrónica? Crea una nueva dirección electrónica "inolvidable" para las personas que nunca recuerdan *(remember)* tu dirección.

4. ¿Qué sabes crear en la computadora?

5. ¿Qué sitio Web conoces mejor? ¿Qué te parece?

Exploración del lenguaje

Using *-mente* to form an adverb

Adverbs are words that describe verbs. They often tell *how* an action is performed. Many adverbs in English end in the letters *-ly: slowly, frequently, happily,* and so on. To form similar adverbs in Spanish, add the ending *-mente* to the feminine singular form of an adjective. This *-mente* ending is equivalent to the *-ly* ending in English.

rápida → rápidamente   fácil → fácilmente   general → generalmente

práctica → prácticamente   feliz → felizmente   especial → especialmente

Note that if the adjective has a written accent, as with *rápida, fácil,* and *práctica,* the accent appears in the same place in the adverb form.

Try it out! Give the adverb for each of the adjectives in the list. Then use each adverb in one of the sentences. Some sentences have more than one possible answer.

normal   total   completo   frecuente   reciente

1. El laboratorio de nuestra escuela es ___ nuevo.

2. ___ les escribo a mis amigos por correo electrónico pero hoy les envío una carta.

3. ___ mis padres nos compraron una nueva computadora.

4. Mi hermano está ___ contento cuando está usando la computadora.

5. ___ grabamos canciones en un disco compacto.

Gramática

The present tense of *pedir* and *servir*

Pedir and *servir* are stem-changing verbs in which the *e* in the stem of the infinitive changes to *i* in all forms except *nosotros* and *vosotros*.

Here are the present-tense forms of *pedir* and *servir*:

(yo)	pido	(nosotros) (nosotras)	pedimos
(tú)	pides	(vosotros) (vosotras)	pedís
Ud. (él) (ella)	pide	Uds. (ellos) (ellas)	piden

(yo)	sirvo	(nosotros) (nosotras)	servimos
(tú)	sirves	(vosotros) (vosotras)	servís
Ud. (él) (ella)	sirve	Uds. (ellos) (ellas)	sirven

Pedir means "to ask for."

Juan **pide** la dirección electrónica.

Pedimos más información sobre la Red.

Servir means "to serve" or "to be useful for."

Servimos refrescos después de la clase.

Las computadoras **sirven** para mucho.

GramActiva VIDEO

Need more help with *pedir* and *servir*? Watch the **GramActiva** video.

pido, sirvo

10 En la clase de tecnología

Escribir

En la clase de tecnología hay muchas cosas que los estudiantes no pueden hacer. Por eso le piden ayuda al profesor. Escribe las frases.

Modelo

Fernando (no poder / bajar los gráficos)
Fernando le pide ayuda al profesor porque no puede bajar los gráficos.

1. Mario (no saber / grabar un disco compacto)
2. nosotros (no comprender / por qué hay un error)
3. tú (querer / crear una canción)
4. Marisol y Elena (no poder / abrir el documento)
5. yo (desear / enviar una foto por correo electrónico)
6. Vicente y yo (no poder / crear nuestro sitio Web)

Nota

In English you say that you ask *for* help. In Spanish, "for" is implied in the meaning of *pedir* and a separate word is *not* used.

11 **¿Pides muchas cosas?**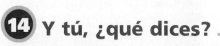

Hablar

Habla con otro(a) estudiante sobre las cosas que les pides a diferentes personas.

Modelo

dinero

A —¿A quién le pides <u>dinero</u>?
B —<u>Le pido dinero a mi mejor amiga, Luisa.</u>
o: —<u>Les pido dinero a mis padres.</u>

> **¿Recuerdas?**
> The indirect object pronouns *le* and *les* mean "to him, her, you *(pl.)*, them." With *pedir*, they refer to the person whom you ask for something.

1. ropa nueva
2. tiempo libre sin tarea
3. ayuda con . . .
4. tu propio(a) . . .
5. tiempo libre sin quehaceres
6. **¡Respuesta personal!**

12 **Los mejores restaurantes**

Hablar • Escribir

❶ Piensa en los restaurantes que conoces. ¿Qué sirven allí que te gusta? Con otro(a) estudiante, habla sobre los restaurantes y la comida que sirven.

Modelo

A —*¿En qué restaurante comes?*
B —*Como en el restaurante . . . . A menudo pido . . . allí. Es muy . . . . Lo sirven con . . . .*

❷ Ahora hablen con otra pareja de los restaurantes donde Uds. comen, lo que piden y con qué sirven las comidas. Preparen tres o más recomendaciones de restaurantes para presentar a la clase.

Modelo

Si Uds. quieren comer bien, recomendamos el restaurante Las Palmeras. Siempre pedimos el pescado . . . ¡es delicioso! Lo sirven con arroz. . . .

13 **Juego**

Escribir • Hablar

Con otro(a) estudiante, escriban descripciones de tres cosas y expliquen para qué sirven. Lean las frases a otra pareja para ver si ellos pueden identificar las cosas.

Modelo

A —*Es una cosa bastante pequeña. Puede estar en tu mochila o pupitre. No cuesta mucho dinero.*
B —*¿Para qué sirve?*
A —*Sirve para escribir cartas o composiciones.*
B —*Es un bolígrafo.*

14 **Y tú, ¿qué dices?**

Escribir • Hablar

1. ¿A quién le pides ayuda con la computadora? ¿Le pides ayuda a menudo o sólo a veces?

2. ¿Qué haces cuando tus amigos te piden ayuda con la computadora? ¿Para qué cosas te piden ayuda?

Más práctica

- **Guided** Gram. Practice pp. 299–300
- **Core** Gram. Practice p. 170
- **Communication** Writing p. 186, Test Prep p. 331
- *Real.* **para hispanohablantes** pp. 354–357

realidades.com ✓

- Audio Activities
- Video Activities
- Speak & Record
- Animated Verbs
- Tutorial
- Leveled Workbook

Gramática

GramActiva VIDEO

Watch the
GramActiva video to
learn more about
using the verbs *saber*
and *conocer.*

Sé bailar.

15 Lo que sabemos hacer

Hablar

Habla con otro(a) estudiante sobre quiénes saben
hacer las diferentes actividades en los dibujos.

Modelo

A —¿*Quién sabe esquiar?*
B —*Mario sabe esquiar.*
  Lo hace a menudo.

1.

2.

3.

4.

5.

6.

16 ¿Qué lugares conoces?  ¿Y a qué personas?

Escribir · Hablar

Si una persona visita tu comunidad y tu escuela, ¿puedes ayudarla a conocer a diferentes personas y lugares? Escribe frases completas con las formas apropiadas del verbo *conocer* y la información necesaria. Después lee tus frases a otro(a) estudiante. ¿Conocen Uds. a las mismas personas y los mismos lugares?

1. (Yo) _____ a muchos de los estudiantes en la clase de . . .

2. Mis amigos y yo (no) _____ a la secretaria de la escuela. Es la Sra. . . .

3. Mi hermano(a) / amigo(a) _____ bastante bien al (a la) profesor(a) de . . .

4. Mis amigos _____ bien el parque de diversiones . . .

5. (Yo) _____ la tienda . . . donde me gusta comprar . . .

6. Mi madre (padre) _____ bien *(un lugar en tu ciudad)* . . .

7. Si la persona necesita usar la computadora, nosotros _____ el programa de software . . .

¿Conoces la Plaza de España en Sevilla?

España

17 ¿Saber o conocer?

Hablar

Trabaja con otro(a) estudiante para ver lo que sabe y conoce.

Modelo

la persona que trabaja en la biblioteca de la escuela
A —¿Conoces a la persona que trabaja en la biblioteca de la escuela?
B —Sí, la conozco. Es la Sra. Wilton. Es muy simpática.
o: —No, no la conozco.

bailar salsa
A —¿Sabes bailar salsa?
B —Sí, sé bailar salsa. Me encanta.
o: —No, no sé bailar salsa.

1. la hermana de . . .
2. bajar información de la Red
3. el nombre de una canción en español
4. las cámaras digitales

5. España o México
6. la dirección electrónica de . . .
7. un sitio Web interesante
8. enviar fotos por la Red

Dividing words into syllables

jcd-0998

Knowing how to divide words into syllables will help you sound out a new word. Just as in English, all syllables in Spanish include a vowel. When there is a consonant between two vowels, you divide the word into syllables before the consonant. The letter combinations *ch, ll,* and *rr* are never divided in Spanish.

Listen to and say these words:

ju-gar	pá-gi-na	la-bo-ra-to-rio	na-ve-gar
ca-lle	no-ti-cias	co-mu-ni-dad	a-bu-rri-do

When there are two consonants between vowels, you divide the word between the consonants. Exceptions are the blends *pr, pl, br, bl, fr, fl, tr, dr, cr, cl, gr,* and *gl.* These blends are never divided and go with the following vowel: *pro-ble-ma.* Listen to and say these words:

car-ta	in-fan-til	con-cur-sos	jar-dín
par-que	a-bri-go	des-can-sar	pa-dres

When there are three or more consonants between vowel sounds, the first two go with the vowel that precedes them and the third goes with the vowel that follows them: *trans-por-te.* When the second and third consonants form a blend, however, the first consonant goes with the vowel before it and the other consonants go with the vowel that follows them: *en-tre.*

Listen to and say these words:

es-cri-to-rio	com-pli-ca-do
en-tre-vis-tas	com-pras-te

Try it out! See if you can separate the following words into the correct syllables.

1. emocionante
2. rápidamente
3. computadora
4. problema
5. electrónico
6. comunicamos

---

18 Los tres cerditos

Leer • Escribir

Lee el anuncio y contesta las preguntas.

1. ¿Conocen los cerditos a la "persona" que está en la ventana? ¿Saben ellos lo que quiere?

2. ¿Tiene tu familia un servicio de identificación de llamadas en su teléfono? ¿Te gusta este servicio, o te gustaría tener este servicio? ¿Por qué?

3. ¿Te parece bien saber quién llama por teléfono? ¿Por qué?

4. ¿Te gusta hablar por teléfono? ¿Con quién te gusta hablar más?

¿Sabes quién es?

Pide el servicio de identificación de llamadas.
Si eres cliente de Teléfonos Caribe, es completamente gratis.

Así, siempre vas a saber quién está llamando.
¡Pídelo hoy! Llama al teléfono 20-05-617.

19 ¿Qué inventos conoces?

Leer • Pensar • Escribir • Dibujar

Mucho antes de la invención de la computadora personal, había *(there were)* otros inventos que nos ayudaron a comunicar y que seguimos *(keep)* usando. Mira la línea cronológica y lee la lista de inventos. Luego contesta las preguntas.

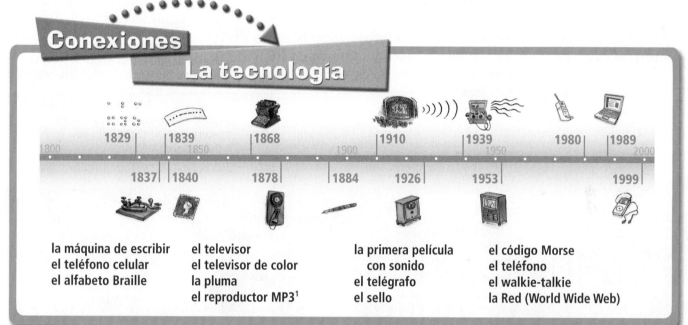

Conexiones

La tecnología

la máquina de escribir	el televisor
el teléfono celular	el televisor de color
el alfabeto Braille	la pluma
	el reproductor MP3[1]

la primera película	el código Morse
con sonido	el teléfono
el telégrafo	el walkie-talkie
el sello	la Red (World Wide Web)

[1]compressed audio tracks

1. Identifica cada invento según el año en que se inventó y explica qué impacto tiene sobre la comunicación.

2. Busca información en la Red o en la biblioteca para identificar los inventores de cada invento de la lista.

3. ¿Cuál de estos inventos te parece el más importante? ¿Por qué?

4. Piensa en un invento que quieres hacer. ¿Para qué sirve? Escribe un párrafo y haz un dibujo para explicar tu invento.

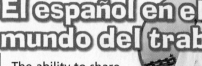

El español en el mundo del trabajo

The ability to share information is crucial in the 21st century. Innovations from medicine, science, technology, engineering, manufacturing, and social services need to be communicated across the globe. With a partner, make a list of six ways in which information can be spread. For each, tell how knowing Spanish would be beneficial. Share your ideas with the class.

Más práctica

- **Guided** Gram. Practice pp. 301–302
- **Core** Gram. Practice pp. 171–172
- **Communication** Writing p. 187
- *Real.* **para hispanohablantes** pp. 358–361

realidades.com ✔

- Audio Activities
- Video Activities
- Speak & Record
- Animated Verbs
- Canción de hip hop
- Tutorial
- Leveled Workbook
- Web Code: jcd-0914

Lectura

La invasión del ciberspanglish

Lee este artículo sobre el Internet. El Internet sirve para muchas cosas aquí en los Estados Unidos y también en los otros países donde hablan español. Pero no es siempre fácil traducir[1] los términos técnicos.

La invasión del ciberspanglish

¿Te gusta usar el Internet? Actualmente[2] hay gente en todos los países del mundo que usa el Internet. Sirve para muchas cosas: para hacer compras, divertirse, educarse, trabajar, buscar información, hacer planes para un viaje y mucho más. Hoy en día uno no puede pensar en una vida sin computadoras o el Internet.

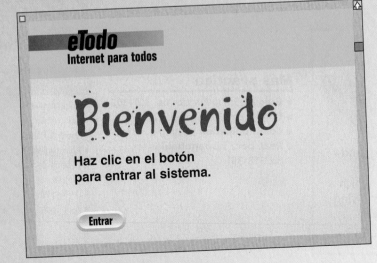

eTodo
Internet para todos

Bienvenido

Haz clic en el botón para entrar al sistema.

Entrar

Si quieres explorar el Internet en español, hay una explosión de portales (sitios que sirven como puerta al Internet) en los Estados Unidos, España y América Latina. Como puedes imaginar, hay una rivalidad[3] grande entre estos portales para atraer[4] a los hispanohablantes. Algunos portales dan la misma información en inglés y español; sólo tienes que hacer clic para cambiarla.

[1]to translate   [2]Nowadays
[3]rivalry   [4]to attract

Juntos,[5] el inglés y el español en el Internet dieron origen al "ciberspanglish". A algunas personas no les gusta nada este nuevo "idioma"[6]. Piensan que el español es suficientemente rico para poder traducir los términos del inglés. Hay otros que dicen que no hay problema con mezclar[7] los idiomas para comunicarse mejor. Piensan que el "ciberspanglish" es más fácil y lógico porque los términos técnicos vienen del inglés y expresarlos en español es bastante complicado.

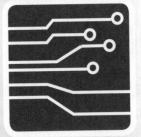

Éste es un debate que va a durar[8] mucho tiempo, y no presenta grises.

Términos de ciberspanglish	Términos en español
emailear	mandar por correo electrónico
espam	un bombardeo de grandes cantidades de correo electrónico
chatear	conversar
hacer clic	picar con el ratón
hacer doble clic	picar dos veces con el ratón
rebootear	rearrancar
linkear	enlazar con una página en Internet
crashear	quebrar o chocar
formatear	hacer un formato
programar	escribir un programa
escanear	rastrear o digitalizar
surfear	explorar o navegar
hacer un upgrade	actualizar o subir un grado
el clipart	dibujos artísticos
hacer un exit	salir
printear	imprimir

[5]Together   [6]language   [7]mixing   [8]to last

¿Comprendes?

1. Look at the list you created for the Strategy "Using prior knowledge." Place a check mark next to any pieces of information mentioned in the article.

2. According to the article, how could the Internet help you learn more Spanish?

3. Summarize briefly the two sides of the argument related to *ciberspanglish*.

4. You have already learned that Spanish borrowed words from languages such as Greek and Arabic. Is *ciberspanglish* different? Why or why not?

5. What do you think the statement *Éste es un debate que . . . no presenta grises* means? Why is it appropriate as the closing statement for this article?

Más práctica

- **Guided** Reading Support p. 303
- **Communication** Writing p. 188, Test Prep p. 332
- *Real.* **para hispanohablantes** pp. 362–363

realidades.com ⌄

- Internet Activity
- Leveled Workbook
- Web Code: jcd-0915

Perspectivas del mundo hispano
¿Para qué usas una computadora?

In many Spanish-speaking countries, the use of computers and access to the Internet are often not as widespread as in the United States. Some homes don't have telephones, computers cost more money, and in some cases, the Internet is not as accessible. Schools and libraries may not have computers or the same access to the Internet as they often do in most communities in the United States. For these reasons, many cybercafés have opened. Cybercafés are nice places for students to meet after school and work on assignments, do research, or e-mail friends. They offer very inexpensive access to the Internet.

Usando computadoras para estudiar en Quito, Ecuador

In recent years, the number of *portales* (portals) that serve as access points to the Internet has increased and many of these are offered in Spanish as well as English. The number of *buscadores* (search engines) has also increased, making it easier for Spanish speakers to search for information or just surf the Internet.

Check it out! Survey your friends. Over the course of one week, how much time do they spend using a computer and for what reasons?

Think about it! Name three ways that you think Spanish-language Internet sites could help you learn more Spanish and understand the perspectives of Spanish speakers.

Haciendo la tarea en la computadora

Presentación escrita
La computadora en mi vida

Task
Your parents think that you are spending too much time on the computer and you disagree. Send an e-mail message (of course!) to your best friend in Mexico explaining your position and how you plan to defend your computer use to your parents.

❶ Prewrite Create a chart. In the first column, list at least three ways you use the computer. In the second column, write the benefit *(la ventaja)* to you.

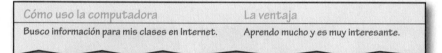

Cómo uso la computadora	La ventaja
Busco información para mis clases en Internet.	Aprendo mucho y es muy interesante.

❷ Draft Use the information from the chart to write the first draft of your e-mail. Here are some expressions you might include:

pienso que . . .   tengo que . . .
creo que . . .   primero (segundo, tercero), . . .

Strategy

Using supporting examples
When preparing a persuasive argument, you should first clearly state your position and then provide examples to support it. Making a list of your arguments will help you make a strong statement.

❸ Revise Check for spelling, accent marks, verb forms, pronouns, and vocabulary use. Share the e-mail with a partner. Your partner should check the following:

- Is the paragraph easy to read and understand?
- Does it provide good reasons and support for your position?
- Is there anything that you could add to give more information or change to make it clearer?
- Are there any errors?

❹ Publish Rewrite the e-mail, making necessary changes. Make a copy for your teacher and add it to your portfolio.

❺ Evaluation Your teacher may give you a rubric for grading the paragraph. You may be evaluated on:

- the amount of information provided
- how well you presented each reason and its benefit
- use of vocabulary and accuracy of spelling and grammar

¿Eres tú, María?

Episodio 10

Antes de ver el video

   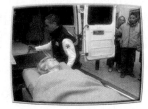

Resumen del episodio

Es el último episodio y Lola y el Inspector Gil van a solucionarlo todo. En realidad, ¿quién es María? ¿Qué importancia tiene Luis Antonio? ¿Quién tiene las joyas? ¿Cómo y por qué ocurrió el crimen? ¿Quién va a la cárcel? ¿Quién va a necesitar un buen abogado? ¿Qué pasa cuando Pedro ve a su abuela por primera vez?

Palabras para comprender

Deténgala. Arrest her.

No quería. I didn't want to.

las reconoció recognized them

los novios boyfriend and girlfriend

tomó took

mucha suerte a lot of luck

robarlas to steal them

no quería esperar didn't want to wait

Parece que . . . It seems like . . .

la cárcel jail

un abogado lawyer

Y tú, ¿qué piensas?

¿Sabes lo que va a pasar en este episodio?
Escribe tus respuestas a las preguntas en el
Resumen del episodio. Ahora, mira el episodio
y compara tus respuestas con lo que pasó.
¿Tenías razón?

Después de ver el video

¿Comprendes?

A. ¿A quién(es) describe cada frase: Lola,
María, Julia, Luis Antonio, Pedro o doña
Gracia?

1. Pues, señorita, es evidente que Ud. sabe
   mucho.

2. Las reconoció en el hospital.

3. Es evidente en la foto que son novios.

4. Murió en el hospital.

5. No puede ver muy bien.

6. Viene a Madrid para vivir con ella.

7. Tiene ochenta y cinco años y está en
   buena salud.

8. Entra en el piso y ataca a la señora.

9. Ud. no va a París, señor. Ud. va a la cárcel.

10. La mejor detective de Madrid.

B. Con un grupo de tres o cuatro estudiantes,
escoge una escena del video. Tu profesor(a)
les va a dar el guión *(script)* de la escena.
Representen la escena para la clase. Hay
que aprender de memoria el papel *(the part)*,
llevar la ropa del personaje y representar la
escena de una manera bien profesional.

• Web Code: jcd-0507

Repaso del capítulo

Vocabulario y gramática 🔊

jcd-0999

Chapter Review

To prepare for the test, check to
see if you . . .
- **know the new vocabulary
  and grammar**
- **can perform the tasks on p. 471**

to talk about communication

cara a cara	face-to-face
la carta	letter
comunicarse	to communicate
(yo) me comunico	(with)
(tú) te comunicas	
enviar	to send
la tarjeta	card

to talk about computer-related activities

bajar	to download
buscar	to search (for)
la cámara digital	digital camera
la canción,	song
pl. las canciones	
la composición,	composition
pl. las composiciones	
la computadora portátil	laptop computer
crear	to create
el curso	course
tomar un curso	to take a course
la diapositiva	slide
la dirección electrónica	e-mail address
el documento	document
escribir por correo	to send an e-mail
electrónico	message
estar en línea	to be online
grabar un disco	to burn a CD
compacto	
los gráficos	graphics
la información	information
el informe	report
el laboratorio	laboratory
navegar en la Red	to surf the Web
la página Web	Web page
la presentación,	presentation
pl. las presentaciones	
el sitio Web	Web site
visitar salones de chat	to visit chat rooms

For *Vocabulario adicional,* see pp. 472–473.

other useful expressions

complicado, -a	complicated
¿Para qué sirve?	What's it (used) for?
¿Qué te parece?	What do you think?
rápidamente	quickly
Sirve para . . .	It's used for . . .
tener miedo (de)	to be afraid (of)

pedir (e → i) *to ask for*

pido	pedimos
pides	pedís
pide	piden

servir (e → i) *to serve, to be useful for*

sirvo	servimos
sirves	servís
sirve	sirven

saber *to know (how)*

sé	sabemos
sabes	sabéis
sabe	saben

conocer *to know, to be acquainted with*

conozco	conocemos
conoces	conocéis
conoce	conocen

Más práctica

- **Core** Puzzle p. 173, Organizer p. 174
- **Communication** Practice Test pp. 334–336, Integrated Performance Assessment p. 333

realidades.com ⓥ

- Tutorial
- Flashcards
- Puzzles
- Self-test
- Web Code: jcd-0916

Preparación para el examen

On the exam you will be asked to . . .	Here are practice tasks similar to those you will find on the exam . . .	If you need review . . .

Interpretive

jcd-0999
🔊

1 Escuchar Listen and understand as people talk about how they use computers

You overhear some people expressing their opinions about computers. Tell whether each person likes or dislikes using computers.

pp. 450–454 *Vocabulario en contexto*
p. 451 Actividades 1–2
p. 455 Actividad 5

Interpersonal

2 Hablar Ask and answer questions about what you know about computers and the Internet

A local Internet company wants to interview you to work as a telephone tech support assistant. To prepare, you and your partner take turns interviewing each other. Ask if your partner: a) knows how to surf the Web; b) is familiar with Web sites for teens; c) knows how to use the computer to create music; d) knows how to make graphics. Then switch roles.

pp. 450–454 *Vocabulario en contexto*
p. 454 Actividad 4
p. 457 Actividad 9
p. 459 Actividad 14
p. 460 Actividad 15
p. 461 Actividad 17

Interpretive

3 Leer Read and understand part of an online conversation in a chat room

A teen in the chat room *Mis padres y yo* is upset. According to the teenager, what do his parents not understand? What is his parents' opinion?

¡Yo soy muy impaciente! Para hacer la tarea, me gusta tener la información que necesito rápidamente. Mis padres dicen que puedo ir a la biblioteca y buscar libros allí para hacer mi tarea, pero me gustaría tener mi propia computadora. Ellos piensan que las computadoras sólo sirven para jugar videojuegos. ¿Qué hago?

pp. 450–454 *Vocabulario en contexto*
p. 454 Actividad 4
p. 455 Actividad 6
p. 456 Actividad 8
pp. 464–465 *Lectura*

Presentational

4 Escribir Write your personal profile *(perfil)* for a Web survey

You are completing a Web survey online for *MundoChat*. Provide answers to the following questions: a) what you like to do; b) your favorite Web site; c) how often you visit chat rooms; d) how much time you spend online each day.

p. 458 Actividad 10
p. 459 Actividad 14
p. 461 Actividad 16
p. 467 *Presentación escrita*

Cultures • Comparisons

5 Pensar Demonstrate an understanding of cultural perspectives regarding technology

Explain why cybercafés are so popular in many Spanish-speaking countries. Compare how you use computers to the way in which teenagers might use them in these countries. If you were to live in one of these countries, how might you approach homework differently?

p. 466 *Perspectivas del mundo hispano*

Vocabulario adicional

Las actividades

coleccionar sellos / monedas to collect stamps / coins

jugar al ajedrez to play chess

patinar sobre hielo to ice-skate

practicar artes marciales *(f.)* to practice martial arts

tocar to play *(an instrument)*

    el bajo bass

    la batería drums

    el clarinete clarinet

    el oboe oboe

    el saxofón *pl.* **los saxofones** saxophone

    el sintetizador synthesizer

    el trombón *pl.* **los trombones** trombone

    la trompeta trumpet

    la tuba tuba

    el violín *pl.* **los violines** violin

Las clases

el alemán German

el álgebra *(f.)* algebra

el anuario yearbook

la banda band

la biología biology

el cálculo calculus

el drama drama

la fotografía photography

el francés French

la geografía geography

la geometría geometry

el latín Latin

la química chemistry

la trigonometría trigonometry

Las cosas para la clase

la grapadora stapler

las grapas staples

el sacapuntas *pl.* **los sacapuntas** pencil sharpener

el sujetapapeles *pl.* **los sujetapapeles** paper clip

las tijeras scissors

Las comidas

Las frutas

el aguacate avocado

la cereza cherry

la ciruela plum

el coco coconut

el durazno peach

la frambuesa raspberry

el limón *pl.* **los limones** lemon

el melón *pl.* **los melones** melon

la pera pear

la sandía watermelon

la toronja grapefruit

Las verduras

el apio celery

el brócoli broccoli

la calabaza pumpkin

el champiñón *pl.* **los champiñones** mushroom

la col cabbage

la coliflor cauliflower

los espárragos asparagus

las espinacas spinach

el pepino cucumber

La carne

la chuleta de cerdo pork chop

el cordero lamb

la ternera veal

Los condimentos

la mayonesa mayonnaise

la mostaza mustard

la salsa de tomate ketchup

Otro tipo de comidas

los fideos noodles

Los lugares y actividades

el banco bank

el club club

el equipo de . . . ___ team

la farmacia pharmacy

la oficina office

la práctica de . . . ___ practice

la reunión *pl.* **las reuniones de . . .** ___ meeting

el supermercado supermarket

Los animales

el conejillo de Indias guinea pig

el conejo rabbit

el gerbo gerbil

el hámster *pl.* **los hámsters** hamster

el hurón *pl.* **los hurones** ferret

el loro parrot

el pez *pl.* **los peces** fish

la serpiente snake

la tortuga turtle

Los miembros de la familia

el bisabuelo, la bisabuela great-grandfather, great-grandmother

el nieto, la nieta grandson, granddaughter

el sobrino, la sobrina nephew, niece

Las descripciones de personas

llevar anteojos to wear glasses
ser
    calvo, -a bald
    delgado, -a thin
    gordo, -a fat
tener
    la barba beard
    el bigote moustache
    las pecas freckles
    el pelo lacio straight hair
    el pelo rizado curly hair
    las trenzas braids

Las partes de la casa y cosas en la casa

el balcón *pl.* **los balcones** balcony
la estufa stove
el jardín *pl.* **los jardines** garden
el lavadero laundry room
la lavadora washing machine
el lavaplatos *pl.* **los lavaplatos** dishwasher
el microondas *pl.* **los microondas** microwave oven
los muebles furniture
el patio patio
el refrigerador refrigerator
la secadora clothes dryer
el sillón *pl.* **los sillones** armchair
el sofá sofa
el tocador dressing table

Los quehaceres

quitar
    la nieve con la pala to shovel snow
    los platos de la mesa to clear the table

rastrillar las hojas to rake leaves

Los colores

(azul) claro light (blue)
(azul) marino navy (blue)
(azul) oscuro dark (blue)

Las expresiones para las compras

ahorrar to save
el dinero en efectivo cash
gastar to spend
la(s) rebaja(s) sale(s)
regatear to bargain
se vende for sale

La ropa

la bata bathrobe
el chaleco vest
las pantimedias pantyhose
el paraguas *pl.* **los paraguas** umbrella
el pijama pajamas
la ropa interior underwear
el saco loose-fitting jacket
los tenis tennis shoes
las zapatillas slippers
los zapatos atléticos athletic shoes
los zapatos de tacón alto high-heeled shoes

Las expresiones para los viajes

el aeropuerto airport
la agencia de viajes travel agency
los cheques de viajero travelers' checks

el equipaje luggage
hacer una reservación to make a reservation
el lugar de interés place of interest
el pasaporte passport
volar *(o → ue)* to fly

Los animales del zoológico

el ave *(f.) pl.* **las aves** bird
el canguro kangaroo
la cebra zebra
el cocodrilo crocodile
el delfín *pl.* **los delfines** dolphin
el elefante elephant
la foca seal
el gorila gorilla
el hipopótamo hippopotamus
la jirafa giraffe
el león *pl.* **los leones** lion
el oso bear
el oso blanco polar bear
el pingüino penguin
el tigre tiger

Las expresiones para las computadoras

la búsqueda search
comenzar *(e → ie)* **la sesión** to log on
el disco duro hard disk
la impresora printer
imprimir to print
el marcapáginas *pl.* **los marcapáginas** bookmark
multimedia multimedia
la página inicial home page
la tecla de borrar delete key
la tecla de intro enter key

Resumen de gramática

Grammar Terms

Adjectives describe nouns: *a **red** car.*

Adverbs usually describe verbs; they tell when, where, or how an action happens: *He read it **quickly**.* Adverbs can also describe adjectives or other adverbs: ***very** tall, **quite** well.*

Articles are words in Spanish that can tell you whether a noun is masculine, feminine, singular, or plural. In English, the articles are ***the, a,*** and ***an.***

Commands are verb forms that tell people to do something: ***Study!, Work!***

Comparatives compare people or things.

Conjugations are verb forms that add endings to the stem in order to tell who the subject is and what tense is being used: *escrib**o**, escrib**iste**.*

Conjunctions join words or groups of words. The most common ones are ***and, but,*** and ***or.***

Direct objects are nouns or pronouns that receive the action of a verb: *I read the **book**. I read **it**.*

Gender in Spanish tells you whether a noun, pronoun, or article is masculine or feminine.

Indirect objects are nouns or pronouns that tell you to whom / what or for whom / what something is done: *I gave **him** the book.*

Infinitives are the basic forms of verbs. In English, infinitives have the word "to" in front of them: ***to walk.***

Interrogatives are words that ask questions: ***What** is that? **Who** are you?*

Nouns name people, places, or things: ***students, Mexico City, books.***

Number tells you if a noun, pronoun, article, or verb is singular or plural.

Prepositions show relationship between their objects and another word in the sentence: *He is **in** the classroom.*

Present tense is used to talk about actions that always take place, or that are happening now: *I always **take** the bus; I **study** Spanish.*

Present progressive tense is used to emphasize that an action is happening *right now: I **am doing** my homework; he **is finishing** dinner.*

Preterite tense is used to talk about actions that were completed in the past: *I **took** the train yesterday; I **studied** for the test.*

Pronouns are words that take the place of nouns: ***She** is my friend.*

Subjects are the nouns or pronouns that perform the action in a sentence: ***John** sings.*

Superlatives describe which things have the most or least of a given quality: *She is the **best** student.*

Verbs show action or link the subject with a word or words in the predicate (what the subject does or is): *Ana **writes**; Ana **is** my sister.*

Nouns, Number, and Gender

Nouns refer to people, animals, places, things, and ideas. Nouns are singular or plural. In Spanish, nouns have gender, which means that they are either masculine or feminine.

Singular Nouns	
Masculine	Feminine
libro	carpeta
pupitre	casa
profesor	noche
lápiz	ciudad

Plural Nouns	
Masculine	Feminine
libros	carpetas
pupitres	casas
profesores	noches
lápices	ciudades

Definite Articles

El, *la*, *los*, and *las* are definite articles and are the equivalent of "the" in English. *El* is used with masculine singular nouns; *los* with masculine plural nouns. *La* is used with feminine singular nouns; *las* with feminine plural nouns. When you use the words *a* or *de* before *el*, you form the contractions *al* and *del*: *Voy al centro; Es el libro del profesor.*

Masculine		Feminine	
Singular	Plural	Singular	Plural
el libro	los libros	la carpeta	las carpetas
el pupitre	los pupitres	la casa	las casas
el profesor	los profesores	la noche	las noches
el lápiz	los lápices	la ciudad	las ciudades

Indefinite Articles

Un and *una* are indefinite articles and are the equivalent of "a" and "an" in English. *Un* is used with singular masculine nouns; *una* is used with singular feminine nouns. The plural indefinite articles are *unos* and *unas*.

Masculine		Feminine	
Singular	Plural	Singular	Plural
un libro	unos libros	una revista	unas revistas
un escritorio	unos escritorios	una mochila	unas mochilas
un baile	unos bailes	una bandera	unas banderas

Pronouns

Subject pronouns tell who is doing the action. They replace nouns or names in a sentence. Subject pronouns are often used for emphasis or clarification: *Gregorio escucha música. Él escucha música.*

A direct object tells who or what receives the action of the verb. To avoid repeating a direct object noun, you can replace it with a *direct object pronoun.* Direct object pronouns have the same gender and number as the nouns they replace: *¿Cuándo compraste el libro? Lo compré ayer.*

An indirect object tells to whom or for whom an action is performed. *Indirect object pronouns* are used to replace an indirect object noun: *Les doy dinero. (I give money to them.)* Because *le* and *les* have more than one meaning, you can make the meaning clear, or show emphasis, by adding *a* + the corresponding name, noun, or pronoun: *Les doy el dinero a ellos.*

After most prepositions, you use *mí* and *ti* for "me" and "you." The forms change with the preposition *con*: *conmigo, contigo.* For all other persons, you use subject pronouns after prepositions.

The personal a

When the direct object is a person, a group of people, or a pet, use the word *a* before the object. This is called the "personal *a*": *Visité a mi abuela. Busco a mi perro, Capitán.*

Subject Pronouns		Direct Object Pronouns		Indirect Object Pronouns		Objects of Prepositions	
Singular	Plural	Singular	Plural	Singular	Plural	Singular	Plural
yo	nosotros, nosotras	me	nos	me	nos	(para) mí, conmigo	nosotros, nosotras
tú	vosotros, vosotras	te	os	te	os	(para) ti, contigo	vosotros, vosotras
usted (Ud.)	ustedes (Uds.)	lo, la	los, las	le	les	Ud.	Uds.
él, ella	ellos, ellas					él, ella	ellos, ellas

Adjectives

Words that describe people and things are called adjectives. In Spanish, most adjectives have both masculine and feminine forms, as well as singular and plural forms. Adjectives must agree with the noun they describe in both gender and number. When an adjective describes a group including both masculine and feminine nouns, use the masculine plural form.

Masculine	
Singular	**Plural**
alto	altos
inteligente	inteligentes
trabajador	trabajadores
fácil	fáciles

Feminine	
Singular	**Plural**
alta	altas
inteligente	inteligentes
trabajadora	trabajadoras
fácil	fáciles

Shortened Forms of Adjectives

When placed before masculine singular nouns, some adjectives change into a shortened form.

bueno	buen chico
malo	mal día
primero	primer trabajo
tercero	tercer plato
grande	gran señor

One adjective, **grande,** changes to a shortened form before any singular noun: *una* **gran** *señora, un* **gran** *libro.*

Possessive Adjectives

Possessive adjectives are used to tell what belongs to someone or to show relationships. Like other adjectives, possessive adjectives agree in number with the nouns that follow them.

Only *nuestro* and *vuestro* have different masculine and feminine endings. *Su* and *sus* can have many different meanings: *his, her, its, your,* or *their.*

Singular	**Plural**
mi	mis
tu	tus
su	sus
nuestro, -a	nuestros, -as
vuestro, -a	vuestros, -as
su	sus

Demonstrative Adjectives

Like other adjectives, demonstrative adjectives agree in gender and number with the nouns that follow them. Use *este, esta, estos, estas* ("this" / "these") before nouns that name people or things that are close to you. Use *ese, esa, esos, esas* ("that" / "those") before nouns that name people or things that are at some distance from you.

Singular	**Plural**
este libro	estos libros
esta casa	estas casas

Singular	**Plural**
ese niño	esos niños
esa manzana	esas manzanas

Interrogative Words

You use interrogative words to ask questions. When you ask a question with an interrogative word, you put the verb before the subject. All interrogative words have a written accent mark.

¿Adónde?	¿Cuándo?	¿Dónde?
¿Cómo?	¿Cuánto, -a?	¿Por qué?
¿Con quién?	¿Cuántos, -as?	¿Qué?
¿Cuál?	¿De dónde?	¿Quién?

Comparatives and Superlatives

Comparatives Use *más . . . que* or *menos . . . que* to compare people or things: *más interesante que . . . , menos alta que . . .*

When talking about number, use *de* instead of *que: Tengo* **más de** *cien monedas en mi colección.*

Superlatives Use this pattern to express the idea of "most" or "least."

el
la   + noun + más / menos + adjective
los
las

Es la chica más seria de la clase.
Son los perritos más pequeños.

Several adjectives are irregular when used with comparatives and superlatives.

older	mayor
younger	menor
better	mejor
worse	peor

Affirmative and Negative Words

To make a sentence negative in Spanish, *no* usually goes in front of the verb or expression. To show that you do not like either of two choices, use *ni . . . ni.*

Alguno, alguna, algunos, algunas and *ninguno, ninguna* match the number and gender of the noun to which they refer. *Ningunos* and *ningunas* are rarely used. When *alguno* and *ninguno* come before a masculine singular noun, they change to *algún* and *ningún.*

Affirmative	Negative
algo	nada
alguien	nadie
algún	ningún
alguno, -a, -os, -as	ninguno, -a, -os, -as
siempre	nunca
también	tampoco

Adverbs

To form an adverb in Spanish, *-mente* is added to the feminine singular form of an adjective. This *-mente* ending is equivalent to the "-ly" ending in English. If the adjective has a written accent, such as *rápida, fácil,* and *práctica,* the accent appears in the same place in the adverb form.

general	→ generalmente
especial	→ especialmente
fácil	→ fácilmente
feliz	→ felizmente
rápida	→ rápidamente
práctica	→ prácticamente

Verbos

Regular Present and Preterite Tenses

Here are the conjugations for regular *-ar*, *-er,* and *-ir* verbs in the present and preterite tense.

Infinitive	Present		Preterite	
estudiar	estudio	estudiamos	estudié	estudiamos
	estudias	estudiáis	estudiaste	estudiasteis
	estudia	estudian	estudió	estudiaron
correr	corro	corremos	corrí	corrimos
	corres	corréis	corriste	corristeis
	corre	corren	corrió	corrieron
escribir	escribo	escribimos	escribí	escribimos
	escribes	escribís	escribiste	escribisteis
	escribe	escriben	escribió	escribieron

Present Progressive

When you want to emphasize that an action is happening *right now,* you use the present progressive tense.

estudiar	estoy	estudiando	estamos	estudiando
	estás	estudiando	estáis	estudiando
	está	estudiando	están	estudiando
correr	estoy	corriendo	estamos	corriendo
	estás	corriendo	estáis	corriendo
	está	corriendo	están	corriendo
escribir	estoy	escribiendo	estamos	escribiendo
	estás	escribiendo	estáis	escribiendo
	está	escribiendo	están	escribiendo

Affirmative tú Commands

When telling a friend, a family member, or a young person to do something, use an affirmative *tú* command. To give these commands for most verbs, use the same present-tense forms that are used for *Ud., él, ella.* Some verbs have an irregular affirmative *tú* command.

Regular	Irregular	
¡Estudia!	decir	di
¡Corre!	hacer	haz
¡Escribe!	ir	ve
	poner	pon
	salir	sal
	ser	sé
	tener	ten
	venir	ven

Stem-changing Verbs

Here is an alphabetical list of the
stem-changing verbs. Next year, you
will learn the preterite verb forms
that are shown here in italic type.

Infinitive and Present Participle	Present		Preterite	
costar (o → ue) costando	cuesta	cuestan	costó	costaron
doler (o → ue) doliendo	duele	duelen	dolió	dolieron
dormir (o → ue) *durmiendo*	duermo duermes duerme	dormimos dormís duermen	dormí dormiste *durmió*	dormimos dormisteis *durmieron*
empezar (e → ie) empezando	empiezo empiezas empieza	empezamos empezáis empiezan	*empecé* empezaste empezó	empezamos empezasteis empezaron
jugar (u → ue) jugando	juego juegas juega	jugamos jugáis juegan	jugué jugaste jugó	jugamos jugasteis jugaron
llover (o → ue) lloviendo	llueve		llovió	
nevar (e → ie) nevando	nieva		nevó	
pedir (e → i) *pidiendo*	pido pides pide	pedimos pedís piden	pedí pediste *pidió*	pedimos pedisteis *pidieron*
pensar (e → ie) pensando	pienso piensas piensa	pensamos pensáis piensan	pensé pensaste pensó	pensamos pensasteis pensaron
preferir (e → ie) *prefiriendo*	prefiero prefieres prefiere	preferimos preferís prefieren	preferí preferiste *prefirió*	preferimos preferisteis *prefirieron*
sentir (e → ie) *sintiendo*	*See* **preferir**			
servir (e → i) *sirviendo*	*See* **pedir**			

Spelling-changing Verbs

These verbs have spelling changes in different tenses. The spelling changes are indicated in black.

Next year, you will learn the preterite verb forms that are shown here in italic type.

Infinitive and Present Participle	Present		Preterite	
buscar (c → qu) buscando	*See regular verbs*		**busqué** buscaste buscó	buscamos buscasteis buscaron
comunicarse (c → qu) *comunicándose*	*See reflexive verbs*		*See reflexive verbs and* **buscar**	
conocer (c → zc) conociendo	**conozco** conoces conoce	conocemos conocéis conocen	*See regular verbs*	
creer (i → y) *creyendo*	*See regular verbs*		creí creíste *creyó*	creímos creísteis *creyeron*
empezar (z → c) empezando	*See stem-changing verbs*		**empecé** empezaste empezó	empezamos empezasteis empezaron
enviar (i → í) enviando	**envío** **envías** **envía**	enviamos enviáis **envían**	*See regular verbs*	
esquiar (i → í) esquiando	*See* **enviar**		*See regular verbs*	
jugar (g → gu) jugando	*See stem-changing verbs*		**jugué** jugaste jugó	jugamos jugasteis jugaron
leer (i → y) leyendo	*See regular verbs*		*See* **creer**	
pagar (g → gu) pagando	*See regular verbs*		*See* **jugar**	
parecer (c → zc) pareciendo	*See* **conocer**		*See regular verbs*	
practicar (c → qu) practicando	*See regular verbs*		*See* **buscar**	
recoger (g → j) recogiendo	**recojo** recoges recoge	recogemos recogéis recogen	*See regular verbs*	
sacar (c → qu) sacando	*See regular verbs*		*See* **buscar**	
tocar (c → qu) tocando	*See regular verbs*		*See* **buscar**	

Irregular Verbs

These verbs have irregular patterns.
Next year, you will learn the preterite verb
forms that are shown here in italic type.

Infinitive and Present Participle	Present		Preterite	
dar dando	doy das da	damos dais dan	*di* *diste* *dio*	*dimos* *disteis* *dieron*
decir *diciendo*	digo dices dice	decimos decís dicen	*dije* *dijiste* *dijo*	*dijimos* *dijisteis* *dijeron*
estar estando	estoy estás está	estamos estáis están	*estuve* *estuviste* *estuvo*	*estuvimos* *estuvisteis* *estuvieron*
hacer haciendo	hago haces hace	hacemos hacéis hacen	hice hiciste hizo	hicimos hicisteis hicieron
ir *yendo*	voy vas va	vamos vais van	fui fuiste fue	fuimos fuisteis fueron
poder *pudiendo*	puedo puedes puede	podemos podéis pueden	*pude* *pudiste* *pudo*	*pudimos* *pudisteis* *pudieron*
poner poniendo	pongo pones pone	ponemos ponéis ponen	*puse* *pusiste* *puso*	*pusimos* *pusisteis* *pusieron*
querer queriendo	quiero quieres quiere	queremos queréis quieren	*quise* *quisiste* *quiso*	*quisimos* *quisisteis* *quisieron*
saber sabiendo	sé sabes sabe	sabemos sabéis saben	*supe* *supiste* *supo*	*supimos* *supisteis* *supieron*
salir saliendo	salgo sales sale	salimos salís salen	salí saliste salió	salimos salisteis salieron
ser siendo	soy eres es	somos sois son	fui fuiste fue	fuimos fuisteis fueron
tener teniendo	tengo tienes tiene	tenemos tenéis tienen	*tuve* *tuviste* *tuvo*	*tuvimos* *tuvisteis* *tuvieron*

Irregular Verbs (continued)

Next year, you will learn the preterite verb forms that are shown here in italic type.

Infinitive and Present Participle	Present		Preterite	
traer *trayendo*	traigo traes trae	traemos traéis traen	*traje trajiste trajo*	*trajimos trajisteis trajeron*
venir *viniendo*	vengo vienes viene	venimos venís vienen	*vine viniste vino*	*vinimos vinisteis vinieron*
ver viendo	veo ves ve	vemos veis ven	vi viste vio	vimos visteis vieron

Reflexive Verbs

Next year, you will learn the preterite verb forms that are shown here in italic type.

Infinitive and Present Participle	Present	
comunicarse *comunicándose*	me comunico te comunicas *se comunica*	nos comunicamos *os comunicáis* se comunican
Affirmative Familiar (*tú*) Command	Preterite	
comunícate	me comuniqué te comunicaste *se comunicó*	nos comunicamos os comunicasteis se comunicaron

Expresiones útiles para conversar

The following are expressions that you can use when you find yourself in a specific situation and need help to begin, continue, or end a conversation.

Greeting Someone

Buenos días. Good morning.

Buenas tardes. Good afternoon.

Buenas noches. Good evening. Good night.

Making Introductions

Me llamo . . . My name is . . .

Soy . . . I'm . . .

¿Cómo te llamas? What's your name?

Éste es mi amigo *m.* **. . .** This is my friend . . .

Ésta es mi amiga *f.* **. . .** This is my friend . . .

Se llama . . . His / Her name is . . .

¡Mucho gusto! It's a pleasure!

Encantado, -a. Delighted.

Igualmente. Likewise.

Asking How Someone Is

¿Cómo estás? How are you?

¿Cómo andas? How's it going?

¿Cómo te sientes? How do you feel?

¿Qué tal? How's it going?

Estoy bien, gracias. I'm fine, thank you.

Muy bien. ¿Y tú? Very well. And you?

Regular. Okay. Alright.

Más o menos. More or less.

(Muy) mal. (Very) bad.

¡Horrible! Awful!

¡Excelente! Great!

Talking on the Phone

Aló. Hello.

Diga. Hello.

Bueno. Hello.

¿Quién habla? Who's calling?

Habla . . . It's [name of person calling].

¿Está . . . , por favor? Is . . . there, please?

¿De parte de quién? Who is calling?

¿Puedo dejar un recado? May I leave a message?

Un momento. Just a moment.

Llamo más tarde. I'll call later.

¿Cómo? No le oigo. What? I can't hear you.

Making Plans

¿Adónde vas? Where are you going?

Voy a . . . I'm going to . . .

¿Estás listo, -a? Are you ready?

Tengo prisa. I'm in a hurry.

¡Date prisa! Hurry up!

Sí, ahora voy. OK, I'm coming.

Todavía necesito . . . I still need . . .

¿Te gustaría . . . ? Would you like to . . . ?

Sí, me gustaría . . . Yes, I'd like to . . .

¡Claro que sí (no)! Of course (not)!

¿Quieres . . . ? Do you want to . . . ?

Quiero . . . I want to . . .

¿Qué quieres hacer hoy? What do you want to do today?

¿Qué haces después de las clases? What do you do after school (class)?

¿Qué estás haciendo? What are you doing?

Te invito. It's my treat.

¿Qué tal si . . . ? What about . . . ?

Primero . . . First . . .

Después . . . Later . . .

Luego . . . Then . . .

Making an Excuse

Estoy ocupado, -a. I'm busy.

Lo siento, pero no puedo. I'm sorry, but I can't.

¡Qué lástima! What a shame!

Ya tengo planes. I already have plans.

Tal vez otro día. Maybe another day.

Being Polite

Con mucho gusto. With great pleasure.

De nada. You're welcome.

Disculpe. Excuse me.

Lo siento. I'm sorry.

Muchísimas gracias. Thank you very much.

Te (Se) lo agradezco mucho. I appreciate it a lot.

Muy amable. That's very kind of you.

Perdón. Pardon me.

¿Puede Ud. repetirlo? Can you repeat that?

¿Puede Ud. hablar más despacio? Can you speak more slowly?

Keeping a Conversation Going

¿De veras? Really?

¿Verdad? Isn't that so? Right?

¿En serio? Seriously?

¡No lo puedo creer! I don't believe it!

¡No me digas! You don't say!

Y entonces, ¿qué? And then what?

¿Qué hiciste? What did you do?

¿Qué dijiste? What did you say?

¿Crees que . . . ? Do you think that . . . ?

Me parece bien. It seems alright.

Perfecto. Perfect.

¡Qué buena idea! What a good idea!

¡Cómo no! Of course!

De acuerdo. Agreed.

Está bien. It's all right.

Giving a Description When You Don't Know the Name of Someone or Something

Se usa para . . . It's used to / for . . .

Es la palabra que significa . . . It's the word that means . . .

Es la persona que . . . It's the person who . . .

Ending a Conversation

Bueno, tengo que irme. Well, I have to go.

Chao. (Chau.) Bye.

Hasta pronto. See you soon.

Hasta mañana. See you tomorrow.

Vocabulario español-inglés

The *Vocabulario español–inglés* contains all active vocabulary from the text, including vocabulary presented in the grammar sections.

A dash (—) represents the main entry word. For example, **pasar la —** after **la aspiradora** means **pasar la aspiradora.**

The number following each entry indicates the chapter in which the word or expression is presented. The letter *P* following an entry refers to the *Para empezar* section.

The following abbreviations are used in this list: *adj.* (adjective), *dir. obj.* (direct object), *f.* (feminine), *fam.* (familiar), *ind. obj.* (indirect object), *inf.* (infinitive), *m.* (masculine), *pl.* (plural), *prep.* (preposition), *pron.* (pronoun), *sing.* (singular).

A

a to *(prep.)* (4A)

  — ...le gusta(n) he/she likes (5A)

  — ...le encanta(n) he/she loves (5A)

  — casa (to) home (4A)

  — la derecha (de) to the right (of) (6A)

  — la izquierda (de) to the left (of) (6A)

  — la una de la tarde at one (o'clock) in the afternoon (4B)

  — las ocho de la mañana at eight (o'clock) in the morning (4B)

  — las ocho de la noche at eight (o'clock) in the evening / at night (4B)

  — menudo often (8B)

  — mí también I do (like to) too (1A)

  — mí tampoco I don't (like to) either (1A)

  ¿— qué hora? (At) what time? (4B)

  — veces sometimes (1B)

  — ver Let's see (2A)

el abrigo coat (7A)

abril April (P)

abrir to open (5A)

la abuela, el abuelo grandmother, grandfather (5A)

los abuelos grandparents (5A)

aburrido, -a boring (2A)

me aburre(n) it bores me (they bore me) (9A)

aburrir to bore (9A)

acabar de + *inf.* to have just ...(9A)

el actor actor (9A)

la actriz *pl.* **las actrices** actress (9A)

acuerdo:

  Estoy de —. I agree. (3B)

  No estoy de —. I don't agree. (3B)

¡Adiós! Good-bye! (P)

¿Adónde? (To) where? (4A)

agosto August (P)

el agua *f.* water (3A)

ahora now (5B)

al *(a + el),* **a la,** to the (4A)

  al lado de next to (2B)

la alfombra rug (6A)

algo something (3B)

¿— más? Anything else? (5B)

allí there (2B)

el almacén *pl.* **los almacenes** department store (7B)

el almuerzo lunch (2A)

  en el — for lunch (3A)

alto, -a tall (5B)

amarillo, -a yellow (6A)

el amigo male friend (1B)

la amiga female friend (1B)

anaranjado, -a orange (6A)

la anciana, el anciano older woman, older man (8B)

los ancianos older people (8B)

el anillo ring (7B)

el animal animal (8A)

anoche last night (7B)

los anteojos de sol sunglasses (7B)

antes de before (9A)

el año year (P)

el — pasado last year (7B)

¿Cuántos años tiene(n) ...? How old is/are ...? (5A)

Tiene(n) ... años. He/She is / They are ... (years old). (5A)

el apartamento apartment (6B)

aprender (a) to learn (to) (8A)

aquí here (2B)

el árbol tree (8A)

los aretes earrings (7B)

el armario closet (6A)

arreglar el cuarto to straighten up the room (6B)

el arroz rice (3B)

el arte:

  la clase de — art class (2A)

artístico, -a artistic (1B)

asco:

  ¡Qué —! How awful! (3A)

la atracción *pl.* **las atracciones** attraction(s) (8A)

atrevido, -a daring (1B)

el autobús *pl.* **los autobuses** bus (8A)

el avión *pl.* **los aviones** airplane (8A)

¡Ay! ¡Qué pena! Oh! What a shame/pity! (4B)

ayer yesterday (7B)

ayudar to help (6B)

el azúcar sugar (5B)

azul blue (6A)

B

bailar to dance (1A)

el baile dance (4B)

bajar (información) to download (9B)

bajo, -a short (5B)

la bandera flag (2B)

el baño bathroom (6B)

  el traje de — swimsuit (7A)

barato, -a inexpensive, cheap (7B)

el barco boat, ship (8A)

el barrio neighborhood (8B)

el básquetbol: jugar al — to play basketball (4B)

bastante enough, rather (6B)

beber to drink (3A)

las bebidas beverages (3B)

béisbol: jugar al — to play baseball (4B)

la biblioteca library (4A)

bien well (P)

el bistec steak (3B)

blanco, -a white (6A)

la blusa blouse (7A)

la boca mouth (P)

el boleto ticket (8A)

el bolígrafo pen (P)

la bolsa bag, sack (8B)

el bolso purse (7B)

bonito, -a pretty (6A)

las botas boots (7A)

el bote: pasear en — to go boating (8A)

la botella bottle (8B)

el brazo arm (P)

bucear to scuba dive, to snorkel (8A)

bueno (buen), -a good (1B)

Buenas noches. Good evening. (P)

Buenas tardes. Good afternoon. (P)

Buenos días. Good morning. (P)

buscar to look for (7A); to search (for) (9B)

C

el caballo: montar a — to ride horseback (8A)

la cabeza head (P)

cada día every day (3B)

la cadena chain (7B)

el café coffee (3A); café (4A)

la caja box (8B)

los calcetines socks (7A)

la calculadora calculator (2A)

la calle street, road (8B)

calor:

Hace —. It's hot. (P)

tener — to be warm (5B)

la cama bed (6A)

hacer la — to make the bed (6B)

la cámara camera (5A)

la — digital digital camera (9A)

el camarero, la camarera waiter, waitress (5B)

caminar to walk (3B)

la camisa shirt (7A)

la camiseta T-shirt (7A)

el campamento camp (8B)

el campo countryside (4A)

el canal (TV) channel (9A)

la canción pl. **las canciones** song (9B)

canoso: pelo — gray hair (5B)

cansado, -a tired (4B)

cantar to sing (1A)

cara a cara face-to-face (9B)

la carne meat (3B)

caro, -a expensive (7B)

la carpeta folder (P)

la — de argollas three-ring binder (2A)

la carta letter (9B)

el cartel poster (2B)

la cartera wallet (7B)

el cartón cardboard (8B)

la casa home, house (4A)

a — (to) home (4A)

en — at home (4A)

casi almost (9A)

castaño: pelo — brown (chestnut) hair (5B)

catorce fourteen (P)

la cebolla onion (3B)

celebrar to celebrate (5A)

la cena dinner (3B)

el centro:

el — comercial mall (4A)

el — de reciclaje recycling center (8B)

cerca (de) close (to), near (6B)

el cereal cereal (3A)

los cereales grains (3B)

cero zero (P)

la chaqueta jacket (7A)

la chica girl (1B)

el chico boy (1B)

cien one hundred (P)

las ciencias:

la clase de — naturales science class (2A)

la clase de — sociales social studies class (2A)

cinco five (P)

cincuenta fifty (P)

el cine movie theater (4A)

la ciudad city (8A)

la clase class (2A)

la sala de clases classroom (P)

¿Qué — de...? What kind of ...? (9A)

el coche car (6B)

la cocina kitchen (6B)

cocinar to cook (6B)

el collar necklace (7B)

el color pl. **los colores** (6A)

¿De qué — ...? What color ... ? (6A)

la comedia comedy (9A)

el comedor dining room (6B)

comer to eat (3A)

cómico, -a funny, comical (9A)

la comida food, meal (3A)

como like, as (8A)

¿cómo?:

¿— eres? What are you like? (1B)

¿— es? What is he/she like? (1B)

¿— está Ud.? How are you? *formal* (P)

¿— estás? How are you? *fam.* (P)

¿— lo pasaste? How was it (for you)? (8A)

¿— se dice ...? How do you say ...? (P)

¿— se escribe ...? How is ... spelled? (P)

¿— se llama? What's his/her name? (1B)

¿— te llamas? What is your name? (P)

¿— te queda(n)? How does it (do they) fit you? (7A)

la cómoda dresser (6A)

compartir to share (3A)

complicado, -a complicated (9B)

la composición *pl.* **las composiciones** composition (9B)

comprar to buy (7A)

comprar recuerdos to buy souvenirs (8A)

comprender to understand (3A)

la computadora computer (2B)

la — portátil laptop computer (9B)

usar la — to use the computer (1A)

comunicarse to communicate (9B)

(tú) te comunicas you communicate (9B)

(yo) me comunico I communicate (9B)

la comunidad community (8B)

con with (3A)

— mis/tus amigos with my/your friends (4A)

¿— quién? With whom? (4A)

el concierto concert (4B)

conmigo with me (4B)

conocer to know, to be acquainted with (9B)

contento, -a happy (4B)

contigo with you (4B)

la corbata tie (7B)

correr to run (1A)

cortar el césped to cut/to mow the lawn (6B)

las cortinas curtains (6A)

corto, -a short (5B)

los pantalones cortos shorts (7A)

la cosa thing (6A)

costar (o → ue) to cost (7A)

¿Cuánto cuesta(n) ...? How much does (do) ... cost? (7A)

crear to create (9B)

creer to think (3B)

Creo que ... I think ... (3B)

Creo que no. I don't think so. (3B)

Creo que sí. I think so. (3B)

el cuaderno notebook (P)

el cuadro painting (6A)

¿Cuál? Which?, What? (3A)

¿— es la fecha? What is the date? (P)

¿Cuándo? When? (4A)

¿cuánto?: ¿— cuesta(n) ... ? How much does (do) ... cost? (7A)

¿cuántos, -as? how many? (P)

¿Cuántos años tiene(n) ...? How old is/are ...? (5A)

cuarenta forty (P)

el cuarto room (6B)

cuarto, -a fourth (2A)

y — *(time)* quarter past (P)

menos — *(time)* quarter to (P)

cuatro four (P)

cuatrocientos, -as four hundred (7A)

la cuchara spoon (5B)

el cuchillo knife (5B)

la cuenta bill (5B)

el cumpleaños birthday (5A)

¡Feliz —! Happy birthday! (5A)

el curso: tomar un curso to take a course (9B)

D ───────────

dar to give (6B)

— + *movie or TV program* to show (9A)

— de comer al perro to feed the dog (6B)

de of (2B); from (4A)

¿— dónde eres? Where are you from? (4A)

— la mañana/la tarde/la noche in the morning /afternoon / evening (4B)

— nada. You're welcome. (5B)

— plato principal as a main dish (5B)

— postre for dessert (5B)

¿— qué color ...? What color ...? (6A)

¿— veras? Really? (9A)

debajo de underneath (2B)

deber should, must (3B)

decidir to decide (8B)

décimo, -a tenth (2A)

decir to say, to tell (8B)

¿Cómo se dice ...? How do you say ...? (P)

dime tell me (8A)

¡No me digas! You don't say! (4A)

¿Qué quiere — ...? What does ... mean? (P)

Quiere — ... It means ... (P)

Se dice ... You say ... (P)

las decoraciones decorations (5A)

decorar to decorate (5A)

el dedo finger (P)

delante de in front of (2B)

delicioso, -a delicious (5B)

los demás, las demás others (8B)

demasiado too (4B)

el dependiente, la dependienta salesperson (7A)

deportista sports-minded (1B)

derecha: a la — (de) to the right (of) (6A)

el desayuno breakfast (3A)

en el — for breakfast (3A)

descansar to rest, to relax (8A)

los descuentos: la tienda de — discount store (7B)

desear to wish (5B)

¿Qué desean (Uds.)? What would you like? (5B)

desordenado, -a messy (1B)

el despacho office (home) (6B)

el despertador alarm clock (6A)

después afterwards (4A)

después (de) after (4A)

detrás de behind (2B)

el día day (P)

    Buenos —s . Good morning. (P)

    cada — every day (3B)

    ¿Qué — es hoy? What day is today? (P)

    todos los —s every day (3A)

la diapositiva slide (9B)

dibujar to draw (1A)

el diccionario dictionary (2A)

diciembre December (P)

diecinueve nineteen (P)

dieciocho eighteen (P)

dieciséis sixteen (P)

diecisiete seventeen (P)

diez ten (P)

difícil difficult (2A)

digital: la cámara — digital camera (9B)

dime tell me (8A)

el dinero money (6B)

la dirección electrónica e-mail address (9B)

el disco compacto compact disc (6A)

    grabar un disco compacto to burn a CD (9B)

el disquete diskette (2B)

divertido, -a amusing, fun (2A)

doce twelve (P)

el documento document (9B)

doler (o → ue) to hurt (9A)

domingo Sunday (P)

dónde:

    ¿—? Where? (2B)

    ¿De — eres? Where are you from? (4A)

dormir (o → ue) to sleep (6A)

el dormitorio bedroom (6A)

dos two (P)

    los/las dos both (7A)

doscientos, -as two hundred (7A)

el drama drama (9A)

los dulces candy (5A)

    durante during (8A)

    durar to last (9A)

E

la educación física: la clase de — physical education class (2A)

el ejercicio: hacer — to exercise (3B)

el the *m. sing.* (1B)

él he (1B)

los electrodomésticos: la tienda de — household appliance store (7B)

electrónico, -a: la dirección — e-mail address (9B)

ella she (1B)

ellas they *f. pl.* (2A)

ellos they *m. pl.* (2A)

emocionante touching (9A)

empezar (e → ie) to begin, to start (9A)

en in, on (2B)

    — + *vehicle* by, in, on (8A)

    — casa at home (4A)

    — la ... hora in the ... hour (class period) (2A)

    — la Red online (7B)

    ¿— qué puedo servirle? How can I help you? (7A)

encantado, -a delighted (P)

encantar to please very much, to love (9A)

    a él/ella le encanta(n) he/she loves (5A)

    me/te encanta(n) ... I/you love ... (3A)

encima de on top of (2B)

enero January (P)

enfermo, -a sick (4B)

la ensalada salad (3A)

la — de frutas fruit salad (3A)

enseñar to teach (2A)

entonces then (4B)

entrar to enter (7A)

enviar (i → í) to send (9B)

el equipo de sonido sound (stereo) system (6A)

    ¿Eres...? Are you ...? (1B)

    es is (P); (he/she/it) is (1B)

    — el *(number)* **de** *(month)* it is the ... of ... *(in telling the date)* (P)

    — el primero de *(month)*. It is the first of ... (P)

    — la una. It is one o'clock. (P)

    — necesario. It's necessary. (8B)

    — un(a) ... it's a ... (2B)

la escalera stairs, stairway (6B)

escribir:

    ¿Cómo se escribe ...? How is ... spelled? (P)

    — cuentos to write stories (1A)

    — por correo electrónico to write e-mail (9B)

    Se escribe ... It's spelled ... (P)

el escritorio desk (2B)

escuchar música to listen to music (1A)

la escuela primaria primary school (8B)

ese, esa that (7A)

eso: por — that's why, therefore (9A)

esos, esas those (7A)

los espaguetis spaghetti (3B)

el español: la clase de — Spanish class (2A)

especialmente especially (9A)

el espejo mirror (6A)

la esposa wife (5A)

el esposo husband (5A)

esquiar (i → í) to ski (1A)

la estación *pl.* **las estaciones** season (P)

el estadio stadium (8A)

el estante shelf, bookshelf (6A)

estar to be (2B)

    ¿Cómo está Ud.? How are you? *formal* (P)

    ¿Cómo estás? How are you? *fam.* (P)

— + *present participle to be +*
present participle (6B)

— **en línea** to be online (9B)

Estoy de acuerdo. I agree.
(3B)

No estoy de acuerdo. I don't
agree. (3B)

este, esta this (7A)

esta noche this evening (4B)

esta tarde this afternoon (4B)

este fin de semana this
weekend (4B)

el estómago stomach (P)

estos, estas these (7A)

Estoy de acuerdo. I agree. (3B)

el/la estudiante student (P)

estudiar to study (2A)

estudioso, -a studious (1B)

la experiencia experience (8B)

F

fácil easy (2A)

la falda skirt (7A)

faltar to be missing (9A)

la familia family (1B)

fantástico, -a fantastic (8A)

fascinante fascinating (9A)

favorito, -a favorite (2A)

febrero February (P)

la fecha: ¿Cuál es la —? What is
the date? (P)

¡Feliz cumpleaños! Happy
birthday! (5A)

feo, -a ugly (6A)

la fiesta party (4B)

el fin de semana:

este — this weekend (4B)

los fines de semana on
weekends (4A)

la flor *pl.* **las flores** flower (5A)

la foto photo (5A)

las fresas strawberries (3A)

frío:

Hace —. It's cold. (P)

tener — to be cold (5B)

fue it was (8A)

— **un desastre.** It was a
disaster. (8A)

el fútbol: jugar al — to play soccer
(4B)

el fútbol americano: jugar al —
to play football (4B)

G

la galleta cookie (3A)

el garaje garage (6B)

el gato cat (5A)

generalmente generally (4A)

¡Genial! Great! (4B)

la gente people (8B)

el gimnasio gym (4A)

el globo balloon (5A)

el golf: jugar al — to play golf (4B)

la gorra cap (7A)

grabar un disco compacto to
burn a CD (9B)

gracias thank you (P)

gracioso, -a funny (1B)

los gráficos computer graphics (9B)

grande large (6A)

las grasas fats (3B)

gris gray (6A)

los guantes gloves (7B)

guapo, -a good-looking (5B)

los guisantes peas (3B)

gustar:

a él/ella le gusta(n) he/she
likes (5A)

(A mí) me gusta … I like
to … (1A)

(A mí) me gusta más …
I like to … better (I prefer
to …) (1A)

(A mí) me gusta mucho …
I like to … a lot (1A)

(A mí) no me gusta … I don't
like to … (1A)

(A mí) no me gusta nada …
I don't like to … at all. (1A)

Le gusta … He/She likes …
(1B)

Me gusta … I like … (3A)

Me gustaría …
I would like … (4B)

Me gustó. I liked it. (8A)

No le gusta … He/She doesn't
like … (1B)

¿Qué te gusta hacer? What
do you like to do? (1A)

¿Qué te gusta hacer más?
What do you like better
(prefer) to do? (1A)

Te gusta … You like … (3A)

¿Te gusta …? Do you like
to …? (1A)

¿Te gustaría …? Would you
like … ? (4B)

¿Te gustó? Did you like it? (8A)

H

hablar to talk (2A)

— **por teléfono** to talk on the
phone (1A)

hacer to do (3B)

hace + *time expression* ago (7B)

Hace calor. It's hot. (P)

Hace frío. It's cold. (P)

Hace sol. It's sunny. (P)

— **ejercicio** to exercise (3B)

— **la cama** to make the bed
(6B)

— **un video** to videotape (5A)

haz *(command)* do, make (6B)

¿Qué hiciste? What did you
do? (8A)

¿Qué tiempo hace? What's
the weather like? (P)

(yo) hago I do (3B)

(tú) haces you do (3B)

hambre: Tengo —. I'm
hungry. (3B)

la hamburguesa hamburger (3A)

hasta:

— **luego.** See you later. (P)

— **mañana.** See you
tomorrow. (P)

Hay There is, There are (P, 2B)

— **que** one must (8B)

el helado ice cream (3B)

el hermano, la hermana brother, sister (5A)

el hermanastro, la hermanastra stepbrother, stepsister (5A)

los hermanos brothers; brother(s) and sister(s) (5A)

el hijo, la hija son, daughter (5A)

los hijos children; sons (5A)

la hoja de papel sheet of paper (P)

¡Hola! Hello! (P)

el hombre man (5B)

la hora:

en la ... — in the ... hour (class period) (2A)

¿A qué hora? At what time? (4B)

el horario schedule (2A)

horrible horrible (3B)

el horror: la película de — horror movie (9A)

el hospital hospital (8B)

el hotel hotel (8A)

hoy today (P)

los huevos eggs (3A)

I

la iglesia church (4A)

igualmente likewise (P)

impaciente impatient (1B)

importante important (6A)

impresionante impressive (8A)

increíble incredible (8B)

infantil childish (9A)

la información information (9B)

el informe report (9B)

el inglés: la clase de — English class (2A)

inolvidable unforgettable (8B)

inteligente intelligent (1B)

interesante interesting (2A)

interesar to interest (9A)

me interesa(n) it interests me (they interest me) (9A)

el invierno winter (P)

ir to go (4A)

— **a** + *inf.* to be going to + *verb* (4B)

— **a la escuela** to go to school (1A)

— **de cámping** to go camping (4B)

— **de compras** to go shopping (4A)

— **de pesca** to go fishing (4B)

— **de vacaciones** to go on vacation (8A)

¡Vamos! Let's go! (7A)

izquierda: a la — (de) to the left (of) (6A)

J

el jardín *pl.* **los jardines** garden, yard (8B)

los jeans jeans (7A)

el joven, la joven young man, young woman (5B)

joven *adj.* young (5B)

la joyería jewelry store (7B)

las judías verdes green beans (3B)

jueves Thursday (P)

jugar (a) (u → ue) to play (games, sports) (4B)

— **al básquetbol** to play basketball (4B)

— **al béisbol** to play baseball (4B)

— **al fútbol** to play soccer (4B)

— **al fútbol americano** to play football (4B)

— **al golf** to play golf (4B)

— **al tenis** to play tennis (4B)

— **al vóleibol** to play volleyball (4B)

— **videojuegos** to play video games (1A)

el jugo:

— **de manzana** apple juice (3A)

— **de naranja** orange juice (3A)

el juguete toy (8B)

julio July (P)

junio June (P)

L

la the *f. sing.* (1B); it, her *f. dir. obj. pron.* (7B)

el laboratorio laboratory (9B)

lado: al — de next to, beside (2B)

el lago lake (8A)

la lámpara lamp (6A)

el lápiz *pl.* **los lápices** pencil (P)

largo, -a long (5B)

las the *f. pl.* (2B); them *f. dir. obj. pron.* (7B)

— **dos, los dos** both (7A)

la lata can (8B)

lavar to wash (6B)

— **el coche** to wash the car (6B)

— **la ropa** to wash the clothes (6B)

— **los platos** to wash the dishes (6B)

le (to/for) him, her, *(formal)* you *sing. ind. obj. pron.* (8B)

— **gusta ...** He/She likes ... (1B)

— **traigo ...** I will bring you ... (5B)

No — gusta ... He/She doesn't like ... (1B)

la lección *pl.* **las lecciones de piano** piano lesson (class) (4A)

la leche milk (3A)

la lechuga lettuce (3B)

el lector DVD DVD player (6A)

leer revistas to read magazines (1A)

lejos (de) far (from) (6B)

les (to/for) them, *(formal)* you *pl. ind. obj. pron.* (8B)

levantar pesas to lift weights (3B)

la librería bookstore (7B)

el libro book (P)

la limonada lemonade (3A)

limpiar el baño to clean the bathroom (6B)

limpio, -a clean (6B)

línea: estar en — to be online (9B)

llamar:

¿Cómo se llama? What's his/her name? (1B)

¿Cómo te llamas? What is your name? (P)

Me llamo ... My name is ... (P)

el llavero key chain (7B)

llevar to wear (7A); to take, to carry, to bring (8B)

llover (o → ue): Llueve. It's raining. (P)

lo it, him *m. dir. obj. pron.* (7B)

— siento. I'm sorry. (4B)

los the *m. pl.* (2B); them *m. dir. obj. pron* (7B)

— dos, las dos both (7A)

— fines de semana on weekends (4A)

— lunes, los martes ... on Mondays, on Tuesdays ... (4A)

el lugar place (8A)

lunes Monday (P)

los lunes on Mondays (4A)

la luz *pl.* **las luces** light (5A)

M

la madrastra stepmother (5A)

la madre (mamá) mother (5A)

mal bad, badly (4B)

malo, -a bad (3B)

la mano hand (P)

mantener: para — la salud to maintain one's health (3B)

la mantequilla butter (3B)

la manzana apple (3A)

el jugo de — apple juice (3A)

mañana tomorrow (P)

la mañana:

a las ocho de la — at eight (o'clock) in the morning (4B)

de la — in the morning (4B)

el mar sea (8A)

marrón *pl.* **marrones** brown (6A)

martes Tuesday (P)

los martes on Tuesdays (4A)

marzo March (P)

más:

¿Qué —? What else? (8B)

— ... que more ... than (2A)

— de more than (9A)

— o menos more or less (3A)

las matemáticas: la clase de — mathematics class (2A)

mayo May (P)

mayor older (5A)

me (to/for) me *ind. obj. pron.* (8B)

— aburre(n) it/they bore(s) me (9A)

— falta(n) ... I need ... (5B)

— gustaría I would like (4B)

— gustó. I liked it. (8B)

— interesa(n) it/they interest(s) me (9A)

— llamo ... My name is ... (P)

— queda(n) bien/mal. It/They fit(s) me well/poorly. (7A)

— quedo en casa. I stay at home. (4A)

¿— trae ...? Will you bring me ...? (5B)

media, -o half (P)

y — thirty, half-past (P)

mejor:

el/la —, los/las —es the best (6A)

—(es) que better than (6A)

menor younger (5A)

menos:

más o — more or less (3A)

— ... que less/fewer ... than (6A)

— de less/fewer than (9A)

el menú menu (5B)

menudo: a — often (8B)

el mes month (P)

la mesa table (2B)

poner la — to set the table (6B)

la mesita night table (6A)

la mezquita mosque (4A)

mi, mis my (2B, 5A)

mí:

a — también I do (like to) too (1A)

a — tampoco I don't (like to) either (1A)

para — in my opinion, for me (6A)

miedo: tener — (de) to be scared (of), to be afraid (of) (9B)

miércoles Wednesday (P)

mil a thousand (7A)

mirar to look (at) (7B)

mismo, -a same (6A)

la mochila bookbag, backpack (2B)

el momento: un — a moment (6B)

el mono monkey (8A)

las montañas mountains (4A)

montar:

— a caballo to ride horseback (8A)

— en bicicleta to ride a bicycle (1A)

— en monopatín to skateboard (1A)

el monumento monument (8A)

morado, -a purple (6A)

mucho a lot (2A)

— gusto pleased to meet you (P)

muchos, -as many (3B)

la mujer woman (5B)

el museo museum (8A)

muy very (1B)

— bien very well (P)

N

nada nothing (P)

(A mí) no me gusta — ... I don't like to ... at all. (1A)

De —. You're welcome. (5B)

nadar to swim (1A)

la naranja: el jugo de — orange juice (3A)

la **nariz** *pl.* **las narices** nose (P)

navegar en la Red to surf the Web (9B)

necesario: Es —. It's necessary. (8B)

necesitar:

  (yo) necesito I need (2A)

  (tú) necesitas you need (2A)

negro, –a black (6A)

  el pelo — black hair (5B)

nevar (e → ie) Nieva. It's snowing. (P)

ni … ni neither … nor, not … or (1A)

el **niño, la niña** young boy, young girl (8B)

los **niños** children (8B)

No estoy de acuerdo. I don't agree. (3B)

¡No me digas! You don't say! (4A)

no soy I am not (1A)

noche:

  a las ocho de la — at eight (o'clock) in the evening, at night (4B)

  Buenas —s. Good evening. (P)

  de la — in the evening, at night (4B)

  esta — this evening (4B)

  nos (to/for) us *ind. obj. pron.* (8B)

  ¡— vemos! See you later! (P)

nosotros, -as we (2A)

novecientos, -as nine hundred (7A)

noveno, -a ninth (2A)

noventa ninety (P)

noviembre November (P)

el **novio, la novia** boyfriend, girlfriend (7B)

nuestro(s), -a(s) our (5A)

nueve nine (P)

nuevo, -a new (7A)

nunca never (3A)

o or (1A)

la **obra de teatro** play (8A)

ochenta eighty (P)

ocho eight (P)

ochocientos, -as eight hundred (7A)

octavo, -a eighth (2A)

octubre October (P)

ocupado, -a busy (4B)

el **ojo** eye (P)

once eleven (P)

ordenado, -a neat (1B)

os (to/for) you *pl. fam. ind. obj. pron.* (8B)

el **otoño** fall, autumn (P)

otro, -a other, another (5B)

  otra vez again (8B)

¡Oye! Hey! (4B)

P

paciente patient (1B)

el **padrastro** stepfather (5A)

el **padre (papá)** father (5A)

los **padres** parents (5A)

  pagar (por) to pay (for) (7B)

la **página Web** Web page (9B)

el **país** country (8A)

el **pájaro** bird (8A)

el **pan** bread (3A)

  el — tostado toast (3A)

la **pantalla** (computer) screen (2B)

los **pantalones** pants (7A)

  los — cortos shorts (7A)

las **papas** potatoes (3B)

  las — fritas French fries (3A)

el **papel picado** cut-paper decorations (5A)

la **papelera** wastepaper basket (2B)

  para for (2A)

  — + *inf.* in order to + *inf.* (4A)

  — la salud for one's health (3B)

  — mantener la salud to maintain one's health (3B)

  — mí in my opinion, for me (6A)

  ¿ — qué sirve? What's it (used) for? (9B)

  — ti in your opinion, for you (6A)

la **pared** wall (6A)

el **parque** park (4A)

  el — de diversiones amusement park (8A)

  el — nacional national park (8A)

el **partido** game, match (4B)

  pasar:

  ¿Cómo lo pasaste? How was it (for you)? (8A)

  — la aspiradora to vacuum (6B)

  — tiempo con amigos to spend time with friends (1A)

  ¿Qué pasa? What's happening? (P)

  ¿Qué te pasó? What happened to you? (8A)

  pasear en bote to go boating (8A)

el **pastel** cake (5A)

los **pasteles** pastries (3B)

  patinar to skate (1A)

  pedir (e → i) to order (5B); to ask for (9B)

la **película** film, movie (9A)

  la — de ciencia ficción science fiction movie (9A)

  la — de horror horror movie (9A)

  la — policíaca crime movie, mystery (9A)

  la — romántica romantic movie (9A)

  ver una — to see a movie (4A)

  pelirrojo, -a red-haired (5B)

el **pelo** hair (5B)

  el — canoso gray hair (5B)

  el — castaño brown (chestnut) hair (5B)

  el — negro black hair (5B)

  el — rubio blond hair (5B)

  pensar (e → ie) to plan, to think (7A)

  peor:

  el/la —, los/las —es the worst (6A)

—(es) que worse than (6A)

pequeño, -a small (6A)

Perdón. Excuse me. (7A)

perezoso, -a lazy (1B)

el perfume perfume (7B)

el periódico newspaper (8B)

pero but (1B)

el perrito caliente hot dog (3A)

el perro dog (5A)

la persona person (5A)

pesas: levantar — to lift weights (3B)

el pescado fish (3B)

el pie foot (P)

la pierna leg (P)

la pimienta pepper (5B)

la piñata piñata (5A)

la piscina pool (4A)

el piso story, floor (6B)

primer — second floor (6B)

segundo — third floor (6B)

la pizza pizza (3A)

la planta baja ground floor (6B)

el plástico plastic (8B)

el plátano banana (3A)

el plato plate, dish (5B)

de — principal as a main dish (5B)

el — principal main dish (5B)

la playa beach (4A)

pobre poor (8B)

poco: un — (de) a little (4B)

poder (o → ue) to be able (6A)

(yo) puedo I can (4B)

(tú) puedes you can (4B)

policíaca: la película — crime movie, mystery (9A)

el pollo chicken (3B)

poner to put, to place (6B)

pon (*command*) put, place (6B)

— la mesa to set the table (6B)

(yo) pongo I put (6B)

(tú) pones you put (6B)

por:

— eso that's why, therefore (9A)

— favor please (P)

¿— qué? Why? (3B)

— supuesto of course (3A)

porque because (3B)

la posesión *pl.* **las posesiones** possession (6A)

el postre dessert (5B)

de — for dessert (5B)

practicar deportes to play sports (1A)

práctico, -a practical (2A)

el precio price (7A)

preferir (e → ie) to prefer (7A)

(yo) prefiero I prefer (3B)

(tú) prefieres you prefer (3B)

preparar to prepare (5A)

la presentación *pl.* **las presentaciones** presentation (9B)

la primavera spring (P)

primer (primero), -a first (2A)

— piso second floor (6B)

el primo, la prima cousin (5A)

los primos cousins (5A)

el problema problem (8B)

el profesor, la profesora teacher (P)

el programa program, show (9A)

el — de concursos game show (9A)

el — de dibujos animados cartoon (9A)

el — de entrevistas interview program (9A)

el — de la vida real reality program (9A)

el — de noticias news program (9A)

el — deportivo sports program (9A)

el — educativo educational program (9A)

el — musical musical program (9A)

propio, -a own (6A)

el proyecto de construcción construction project (8B)

puedes: (tú) — you can (4B)

puedo: (yo) — I can (4B)

la puerta door (2B)

pues well (*to indicate pause*) (1A)

la pulsera bracelet (7B)

el reloj — watch (7B)

el pupitre student desk (P)

Q

que who, that (5A)

qué:

¿Para — sirve? What's it (used) for? (9B)

¡— + adj.! How …! (5B)

¡— asco! How awful! (3A)

¡— buena idea! What a good/nice idea! (4B)

¿— clase de …? What kind of … ? (9A)

¿— desean (Uds.)? What would you like? (5B)

¿— día es hoy? What day is today? (P)

¿— es esto? What is this? (2B)

¿— hiciste? What did you do? (8A)

¿— hora es? What time is it? (P)

¿— más? What else? (8B)

¿— pasa? What's happening? (P)

¡— pena! What a shame/pity! (4B)

¿— quiere decir … ? What does … mean? (P)

¿— tal? How are you? (P)

¿— te gusta hacer? What do you like to do? (1A)

¿— te gusta más? What do you like better (prefer) to do? (1A)

¿— te parece? What do you think (about it)? (9B)

¿— te pasó? What happened to you? (8A)

¿— **tiempo hace?** What's the weather like? (P)

quedar to fit (7A), to stay (4A)

¿Cómo me queda? How does it fit (me)? (7A)

Me / te queda bien. It fits me / you well. (7A)

Me quedo en casa. I stay home. (4A)

el **quehacer (de la casa)** (household) chore (6B)

querer (e → ie) to want (7A)

¿Qué quiere decir ...? What does ... mean? (P)

Quiere decir ... It means ... (P)

quisiera I would like (5B)

(yo) quiero I want (4B)

(tú) quieres you want (4B)

el **queso** cheese (3A)

¿Quién? Who? (2A)

quince fifteen (P)

quinientos, -as five hundred (7A)

quinto, -a fifth (2A)

quisiera I would like (5B)

quitar el polvo to dust (6B)

quizás maybe (7A)

R

rápidamente quickly (9B)

el **ratón** *pl.* **los ratones** (computer) mouse (2B)

razón: tener — to be correct (7A)

realista realistic (9A)

recibir to receive (6B)

reciclar to recycle (8B)

recoger (g → j) to collect, to gather (8B)

los **recuerdos** souvenirs (8A)

comprar recuerdos to buy souvenirs (8A)

la **Red:**

en la — online (7B)

navegar en la — to surf the Web (9B)

el **refresco** soft drink (3A)

el **regalo** gift, present (5A)

regresar to return (8A)

regular okay, so-so (P)

el **reloj** clock (2B)

el **— pulsera** watch (7B)

reservado, -a reserved, shy (1B)

el **restaurante** restaurant (4A)

rico, -a rich, tasty (5B)

el **río** river (8B)

rojo, -a red (6A)

romántico, -a: la película — romantic movie (9A)

romper to break (5A)

la **ropa: la tienda de —** clothing store (7B)

rosado, -a pink (6A)

rubio, -a blond (5B)

S

sábado Saturday (P)

saber to know (how) (9B)

(yo) sé I know (how to) (4B)

(tú) sabes you know (how to) (4B)

sabroso, -a tasty, flavorful (3B)

el **sacapuntas** pencil sharpener (2B)

sacar:

— fotos to take photos (5A)

— la basura to take out the trash (6B)

la **sal** salt (5B)

la **sala** living room (6B)

la **sala de clases** classroom (P)

la **salchicha** sausage (3A)

salir to leave, to go out (8A)

la **salud:**

para la — for one's health (3B)

para mantener la — to maintain one's health (3B)

el **sándwich de jamón y queso** ham and cheese sandwich (3A)

sé: (yo) — I know (how to) (1B)

sed: Tengo —. I'm thirsty. (3B)

según according to (1B)

— mi familia according to my family (1B)

segundo, -a second (2A)

— piso third floor (6B)

seis six (P)

seiscientos, -as six hundred (7A)

la **semana** week (P)

este fin de — this weekend (4B)

la — pasada last week (7B)

los fines de — on weekends (4A)

señor (Sr.) sir, Mr. (P)

señora (Sra.) madam, Mrs. (P)

señorita (Srta.) miss, Miss (P)

separar to separate (8B)

septiembre September (P)

séptimo, -a seventh (2A)

ser to be (3B)

¿Eres ...? Are you ...? (1B)

es he/she is (1B)

fue it was (8A)

no soy I am not (1B)

soy I am (1B)

serio, -a serious (1B)

la **servilleta** napkin (5B)

servir (e → i) to serve, to be useful (9B)

¿En qué puedo servirle? How can I help you? (7A)

¿Para qué sirve? What's it (used) for? (9B)

Sirve para ... It's used for ... (9B)

sesenta sixty (P)

setecientos, -as seven hundred (7A)

setenta seventy (P)

sexto, -a sixth (2A)

si if, whether (6B)

sí yes (1A)

siempre always (3A)

siento: lo — I'm sorry (4B)

siete seven (P)

la **silla** chair (2B)

simpático, -a nice, friendly (1B)

sin without (3A)

la sinagoga synagogue (4A)

el sitio Web Web site (9B)

sobre about (9A)

sociable sociable (1B)

el software software (7B)

el sol:

Hace —. It's sunny. (P)

los anteojos de — sunglasses (7B)

tomar el — to sunbathe (8A)

sólo only (5A)

solo, -a alone (4A)

Son las ... It's ... (time) (P)

la sopa de verduras vegetable soup (3A)

el sótano basement (6B)

soy I am (1B)

su, sus his, her, your formal, their (5A)

sucio, -a dirty (6B)

la sudadera sweatshirt (7A)

sueño: tener — to be sleepy (5B)

el suéter sweater (7A)

supuesto: por — of course (3A)

T

tal: ¿Qué — ? How are you? (P)

talentoso, -a talented (1B)

también also, too (1A)

a mí — I do (like to) too (1A)

tampoco: a mí — I don't (like to) either (1A)

tanto so much (7A)

tarde late (8A); afternoon (4B)

a la una de la — at one (o'clock) in the afternoon (4B)

Buenas —s. Good afternoon. (P)

de la tarde in the afternoon (4B)

esta — this afternoon (4B)

la tarea homework (2A)

la tarjeta card (9B)

la taza cup (5B)

te (to/for) you sing. ind. obj. pron. (8B)

¿— gusta ...? Do you like to ... ? (1A)

¿— gustaría ...? Would you like ...? (4B)

¿— gustó? Did you like it? (8A)

el té tea (3A)

el — helado iced tea (3A)

el teatro theater (8A)

el teclado (computer) keyboard (2B)

la tecnología technology/computers (2A)

la clase de — technology/ computer class (2A)

la telenovela soap opera (9A)

el televisor television set (6A)

el templo temple; Protestant church (4A)

temprano early (8A)

el tenedor fork (5B)

tener to have (5A)

(yo) tengo I have (2A)

(tú) tienes you have (2A)

¿Cuántos años tiene(n) ...? How old is/are ... ? (5A)

— calor to be warm (5B)

— frío to be cold (5B)

— miedo (de) to be scared (of), to be afraid (of) (9B)

— razón to be correct (7A)

— sueño to be sleepy (5B)

Tengo hambre. I'm hungry. (3B)

Tengo que ... I have to ... (4B)

Tengo sed. I'm thirsty. (3B)

Tiene(n) ... años. He/She is/ They are ... years old. (5A)

el tenis: jugar al — to play tennis (4B)

tercer (tercero), -a third (2A)

terminar to finish, to end (9A)

ti you fam. after prep.

¿Y a —? And you? (1A)

para — in your opinion, for you (6A)

el tiempo:

el — libre free time (4A)

pasar — con amigos to spend time with friends (1A)

¿Qué — hace? What's the weather like? (P)

la tienda store (7A)

la — de descuentos discount store (7B)

la — de electrodomésticos household appliance store (7B)

la — de ropa clothing store (7A)

Tiene(n) ... años. He/She is / They are ... (years old). (5A)

el tío, la tía uncle, aunt (5A)

los tíos uncles; aunt(s) and uncle(s) (5A)

tocar la guitarra to play the guitar (1A)

el tocino bacon (3A)

todos, -as all (3B)

— los días every day (3A)

tomar:

— el sol to sunbathe (8A)

— un curso to take a course (9B)

los tomates tomatoes (3B)

tonto, -a silly, stupid (9A)

trabajador, -a hardworking (1B)

trabajar to work (1A)

el trabajo work, job (4A)

el — voluntario volunteer work (8B)

traer:

Le traigo ... I will bring you ... (5B)

¿Me trae ...? Will you bring me ...? (5B)

el traje suit (7A)

el — de baño swimsuit (7A)

trece thirteen (P)

treinta thirty (P)

treinta y uno thirty-one (P)

tremendo, -a tremendous (8A)

el tren train (8A)

tres three (P)

trescientos, as three hundred (7A)

triste sad (4B)

tu, tus your (2B, 5A)

tú you *fam.* (2A)

U

Ud. (usted) you *formal sing.* (2A)

Uds. (ustedes) you *formal pl.* (2A)

¡Uf! Ugh!, Yuck! (7B)

un, una a, an (1B)

un poco (de) a little (4B)

la una: a la — at one o'clock (4B)

uno one (P)

unos, -as some (2B)

usado, -a used (8B)

usar la computadora to use the computer (1A)

usted (Ud.) you *formal sing.* (2A)

ustedes (Uds.) you *formal pl.* (2A)

las uvas grapes (3B)

V

las vacaciones: ir de — to go on vacation (8A)

¡Vamos! Let's go! (7A)

el vaso glass (5B)

veinte twenty (P)

veintiuno (veintiún) twenty-one (P)

vender to sell (7B)

venir to come (5B)

la ventana window (2B)

ver to see (8A)

a — ... Let's see (2A)

¡Nos vemos! See you later! (P)

— la tele to watch television (1A)

— una película to see a movie (4A)

el verano summer (P)

veras: ¿De —? Right? (9A)

¿Verdad? Right? (3A)

verde green (6A)

el vestido dress (7A)

la vez, *pl.* **las veces** time (8B)

a veces sometimes (1B)

otra — again (8B)

vi I saw (8A)

viajar to travel (8A)

el viaje trip (8A)

el video videocassette (6A)

la videocasetera VCR (6A)

los videojuegos: jugar — to play video games (1A)

el vidrio glass (8B)

viejo, -a old (5B)

viernes Friday (P)

violento, -a violent (9A)

visitar to visit (8A)

— salones de chat to visit chat rooms (9B)

¿Viste? Did you see? (8A)

vivir to live (6B)

el vóleibol: jugar al — to play volleyball (4B)

el voluntario, la voluntaria volunteer (8B)

vosotros, -as you *pl.* (2A)

vuestro(s), -a(s) your (5A)

Y

y and (1A)

¿— a ti? And you? (1A)

— cuarto quarter past (P)

— media thirty, half-past (*in telling time*) (P)

¿— tú? And you? *fam.* (P)

¿— usted (Ud.)? And you? *formal* (P)

ya already (9A)

yo I (1B)

el yogur yogurt (3A)

Z

las zanahorias carrots (3B)

la zapatería shoe store (7B)

los zapatos shoes (7A)

el zoológico zoo (8A)

English-Spanish Vocabulary

The *English-Spanish Vocabulary* contains all active vocabulary from the text, including vocabulary presented in the grammar sections.

A dash (—) represents the main entry word. For example, **to play —** after **baseball** means **to play baseball.**

The number following each entry indicates the chapter in which the word or expression is presented. The letter *P* following an entry refers to the *Para empezar* section.

The following abbreviations are used in this list: *adj.* (adjective), *dir. obj.* (direct object), *f.* (feminine), *fam.*(familiar), *ind. obj.* (indirect object), *inf.* (infinitive), *m.* (masculine), *pl.* (plural), *prep.* (preposition), *pron.* (pronoun), *sing.* (singular).

A

a, an un, una (1B)

  a little un poco (de) (4B)

  a lot mucho, -a (2A)

  a thousand mil (7A)

able: to be — poder (o → ue) (6A)

about sobre (9A)

according to según (1B)

  — my family según mi familia (1B)

acquainted: to be —with conocer (9B)

actor el actor (9A)

actress la actriz *pl.* las actrices (9A)

address: e-mail — la dirección electrónica (9B)

afraid: to be — (of) tener miedo (de) (9B)

after después (de) (4A)

afternoon:

  at one (o'clock) in the afternoon a la una de la tarde (4B)

  Good —. Buenas tardes. (P)

  in the — de la tarde (4B)

  this — esta tarde (4B)

afterwards después (4A)

again otra vez (8B)

ago hace + *time expression* (7B)

agree:

  I —. Estoy de acuerdo. (3B)

  I don't —. No estoy de acuerdo. (3B)

airplane el avión *pl.* los aviones (8A)

alarm clock el despertador (6A)

all todos, -as (3B)

almost casi (9A)

alone solo, -a (4A)

already ya (9A)

also también (1A)

always siempre (3A)

am:

  I — (yo) soy (1B)

  I — not (yo) no soy (1B)

amusement park el parque de diversiones (8A)

amusing divertido, -a (2A)

and y (1A)

  ¿— you? ¿Y a ti? *fam.* (1A); ¿Y tú? *fam.* (P); ¿Y usted (Ud.)? *formal* (P)

animal el animal (8A)

another otro, -a (5B)

Anything else? ¿Algo más? (5B)

apartment el apartamento (6B)

apple la manzana (3A)

  — juice el jugo de manzana (3A)

April abril (P)

Are you … ? ¿Eres … ? (1B)

arm el brazo (P)

art class la clase de arte (2A)

artistic artístico, -a (1B)

as como (8A)

  — a main dish de plato principal (5B)

to ask for pedir (e → i) (9B)

at:

  — eight (o'clock) a las ocho (4B)

  — eight (o'clock) at night a las ocho de la noche (4B)

  — eight (o'clock) in the evening a las ocho de la noche (4B)

  — eight (o'clock) in the morning a las ocho de la mañana (4B)

  — home en casa (4A)

  — one (o'clock) a la una (4B)

  — one (o'clock) in the afternoon a la una de la tarde (4B)

  — what time? ¿A qué hora? (4B)

attraction(s) la atracción *pl.* las atracciones (8A)

August agosto (P)

aunt la tía (5A)

aunt(s) and uncle(s) los tíos (5A)

autumn el otoño (P)

B

backpack la mochila (2B)

bacon el tocino (3A)

bad malo, -a (3B); mal (4B)

badly mal (4B)

bag la bolsa (8B)

balloon el globo (5A)

banana el plátano (3A)

baseball: to play — jugar al béisbol (4B)

basement el sótano (6B)

basketball: to play — jugar al básquetbol (4B)

bathroom el baño (6B)

to be ser (3B); estar (2B)

  He/She is / They are … years old. Tiene(n) … años. (5A)

  How old is/are … ? ¿Cuántos años tiene(n) … ? (5A)

  to — + *present participle* estar + *present participle* (6B)

  to — able poder (o → ue) (6A)

  to — acquainted with conocer (9B)

  to — afraid (of) tener miedo (de) (9B)

  to — cold tener frío (5B)

  to — correct tener razón (7A)

  to — going to + *verb* ir a + *inf.* (4B)

  to — online estar en línea (9B)

to — **scared (of)** tener miedo (de) (9B)

to — **sleepy** tener sueño (5B)

to — **useful** servir (e → i) (9B)

to — **warm** tener calor (5B)

beach la playa (4A)

bear el oso (8A)

because porque (3B)

bed la cama (6A)

to make the — hacer la cama (6B)

bedroom el dormitorio (6A)

beefsteak el bistec (3B)

before antes de (9A)

to **begin** empezar (e → ie) (9A)

behind detrás de (2B)

best: the — el/la mejor, los/las mejores (6A)

better than mejor(es) que (6A)

beverages las bebidas (3B)

bicycle: to ride a — montar en bicicleta (1A)

bill la cuenta (5B)

binder: three-ring — la carpeta de argollas (2A)

bird el pájaro (8A)

birthday el cumpleaños (5A)

Happy —! ¡Feliz cumpleaños! (5A)

black negro (6A)

black hair el pelo negro (5B)

blond hair el pelo rubio (5B)

blouse la blusa (7A)

blue azul (6A)

boat el barco (8A)

boating: to go — pasear en bote (8A)

book el libro (P)

bookbag la mochila (2B)

bookshelf el estante (6A)

bookstore la librería (7B)

boots las botas (7A)

to **bore** aburrir (9A)

it/they —(s) me me aburre(n) (9A)

boring aburrido, -a (2A)

both los dos, las dos (7A)

bottle la botella (8B)

box la caja (8B)

boy el chico (1B)

—**friend** el novio (7B)

young — el niño (8B)

bracelet la pulsera (7B)

bread el pan (3A)

to **break** romper (5A)

breakfast el desayuno (3A)

for — en el desayuno (3A)

to **bring** traer (5B); llevar (8B)

I will — you ... Le traigo ... (5B)

Will you — me ...? ¿Me trae ...? (5B)

brother el hermano (5A)

brothers; brother(s) and sister(s) los hermanos (5A)

brown marrón *pl.* marrones (6A)

— (chestnut) hair el pelo castaño (5B)

to **burn a CD** grabar un disco compacto (9B)

bus el autobús *pl.* los autobuses (8A)

busy ocupado, -a (4B)

but pero (1B)

butter la mantequilla (3B)

to **buy** comprar (7A)

to — souvenirs comprar recuerdos (8A)

by + *vehicle* en + *vehicle* (8A)

C

café el café (4A)

cake el pastel (5A)

calculator la calculadora (2A)

camera la cámara (5A)

digital — la cámara digital (9B)

camp el campamento (8B)

can la lata (8B)

can:

I — (yo) puedo (4B)

you — (tú) puedes (4B)

candy los dulces (5A)

cap la gorra (7A)

car el coche (6B)

card la tarjeta (9B)

cardboard el cartón (8B)

carrots las zanahorias (3B)

to **carry** llevar (8B)

cartoon el programa de dibujos animados (9A)

cat el gato (5A)

CD: to burn a CD grabar un disco compacto (9B)

to **celebrate** celebrar (5A)

cereal el cereal (3A)

chain la cadena (7B)

chair la silla (2B)

channel (TV) el canal (9A)

cheap barato, -a (7B)

cheese el queso (3A)

chicken el pollo (3B)

childish infantil (9A)

children los hijos (5A); los niños (8B)

chore: household — el quehacer (de la casa) (6B)

church la iglesia (4A)

Protestant — el templo (4A)

city la ciudad (8A)

class la clase (2A)

classroom la sala de clases (P)

clean limpio, -a (6B)

to **clean the bathroom** limpiar el baño (6B)

clock el reloj (2B)

close (to) cerca (de) (6B)

closet el armario (6A)

clothing store la tienda de ropa (7A)

coat el abrigo (7A)

coffee el café (3A)

cold:

It's —. Hace frío. (P)

to be — tener frío (5B)

to **collect** recoger (g → j) (8B)

color:

    What — ...? ¿De qué color ...? (6A)

    —s los colores (6A)

to come venir (5B)

    comedy la comedia (9A)

    comical cómico, -a (9A)

to communicate comunicarse (9B)

    I — (yo) me comunico (9B)

    you — (tú) te comunicas (9B)

community la comunidad (8B)

compact disc el disco compacto (6A)

    to burn a — grabar un disco compacto (9B)

complicated complicado, -a (9B)

composition la composición *pl.* las composiciones (9B)

computer la computadora (2B)

    — graphics los gráficos (9B)

    — keyboard el teclado (2B)

    — mouse el ratón (2B)

    — screen la pantalla (2B)

    —s/technology la tecnología (2B)

    laptop — la computadora portátil (9B)

    to use the — usar la computadora (1A)

concert el concierto (4B)

construction project el proyecto de construcción (8B)

to cook cocinar (6B)

    cookie la galleta (3A)

    correct: to be — tener razón (7A)

to cost costar (o → ue) (7A)

    How much does (do) ... — ? ¿Cuánto cuesta(n)? (7A)

    country el país (8A)

    countryside el campo (4A)

    course: to take a course tomar un curso (9B)

    cousin el primo, la prima (5A)

    —s los primos (5A)

to create crear (9B)

    crime movie la película policíaca (9A)

    cup la taza (5B)

curtains las cortinas (6A)

to cut the lawn cortar el césped (6B)

    cut-paper decorations el papel picado (5A)

D ─────────────

dance el baile (4B)

to dance bailar (1A)

    daring atrevido, -a (1B)

    date: What is the —? ¿Cuál es la fecha? (P)

    daughter la hija (5A)

    day el día (P)

        every — todos los días (3A); cada día (3B)

        What — is today? ¿Qué día es hoy? (P)

December diciembre (P)

to decide decidir (8B)

to decorate decorar (5A)

    decorations las decoraciones (5A)

    delicious delicioso, -a (5B)

    delighted encantado, -a (P)

    department store el almacén *pl.* los almacenes (7B)

    desk el pupitre (P); el escritorio (2B)

    dessert el postre (5B)

        for — de postre (5B)

    dictionary el diccionario (2A)

    Did you like it? ¿Te gustó? (8A)

    difficult difícil (2A)

    digital camera la cámara digital (9B)

    dining room el comedor (6B)

    dinner la cena (3B)

    dirty sucio, -a (6B)

    disaster: It was a — . Fue un desastre. (8A)

    discount store la tienda de descuentos (7B)

    dish el plato (5B)

        as a main — de plato principal (5B)

        main — el plato principal (5B)

    diskette el disquete (2B)

to do hacer (3B)

— (command) haz (6B)

    — you like to ...? ¿Te gusta ...? (1A)

    I — (yo) hago (3B)

    What did you —? ¿Qué hiciste? (8A)

    you — (tú) haces (3B)

document el documento (9B)

dog el perro (5A)

    to feed the — dar de comer al perro (6B)

door la puerta (2B)

to download bajar (información) (9B)

drama el drama (9A)

to draw dibujar (1A)

    dress el vestido (7A)

    dresser la cómoda (6A)

to drink beber (3A)

    during durante (8A)

to dust quitar el polvo (6B)

    DVD player el lector DVD (6A)

E ─────────────

e-mail:

    — address la dirección electrónica (9B)

    to write an — message escribir por correo electrónico (9B)

early temprano (8A)

earrings los aretes (7B)

easy fácil (2A)

to eat comer (3A)

    educational program el programa educativo (9A)

    eggs los huevos (3A)

    eight ocho (P)

    eight hundred ochocientos, -as (7A)

    eighteen dieciocho (P)

    eighth octavo, -a (2A)

    eighty ochenta (P)

    either tampoco (1A)

        I don't (like to) — a mí tampoco (1A)

    eleven once (P)

else:

   Anything —? ¿Algo más? (5B)

      What —? ¿Qué más? (8B)

to end terminar (9A)

   English class la clase de inglés (2A)

   enough bastante (6B)

to enter entrar (7A)

   especially especialmente (9A)

   evening:

      Good —. Buenas noches. (P)

      in the — de la noche (4B)

      this — esta noche (4B)

   every day cada día (3B); todos los días (3A)

   Excuse me. Perdón. (7A)

to exercise hacer ejercicio (3B)

   expensive caro, -a (7B)

   experience la experiencia (8B)

   eye el ojo (P)

F

face-to-face cara a cara (9B)

fall el otoño (P)

family la familia (1B)

fantastic fantástico, -a (8A)

far (from) lejos (de) (6B)

fascinating fascinante (9A)

fast rápidamente (9B)

father el padre (papá) (5A)

fats las grasas (3B)

favorite favorito, -a (2A)

February febrero (P)

to feed the dog dar de comer al perro (6B)

fewer:

   — ... than menos ... que (6A)

   — than ... menos de ... (9A)

fifteen quince (P)

fifth quinto, -a (2A)

fifty cincuenta (P)

film la película (9A)

finger el dedo (P)

to finish terminar (9A)

   first primer (primero), -a (2A)

fish el pescado (3B)

   to go —ing ir de pesca (4B)

to fit:

   How does it (do they) fit me / you? ¿Cómo me / te queda(n)? (7A)

   It / They —(s) me well / poorly. Me queda(n) bien / mal. (7A)

five cinco (P)

five hundred quinientos, -as (7A)

flag la bandera (2B)

flavorful sabroso, -a (3B)

floor el piso (6B)

   ground — la planta baja (6B)

   second — el primer piso (6B)

   third — el segundo piso (6B)

flower la flor *pl.* las flores (5A)

folder la carpeta (P)

food la comida (3A)

foot el pie (P)

football: to play — jugar al fútbol americano (4B)

for para (2A)

   — breakfast en el desayuno (3A)

   — lunch en el almuerzo (3A)

   — me para mí (6A)

   — you para ti (6A)

fork el tenedor (5B)

forty cuarenta (P)

four cuatro (P)

four hundred cuatrocientos, -as (7A)

fourteen catorce (P)

fourth cuarto, -a (2A)

free time el tiempo libre (4A)

French fries las papas fritas (3A)

Friday viernes (P)

friendly simpático, -a (1B)

from de (4A)

   Where are you —? ¿De dónde eres? (4A)

fruit salad la ensalada de frutas (3A)

fun divertido, -a (2A)

funny gracioso, -a (1B); cómico, -a (9A)

G

game el partido (4B)

   — show el programa de concursos (9A)

garage el garaje (6B)

garden el jardín *pl.* los jardines (8B)

to gather recoger (g → j) (8B)

generally generalmente (4A)

gift el regalo (5A)

girl la chica (1B)

   —friend la novia (7B)

   young — la niña (8B)

to give dar (6B)

glass el vaso (5B); el vidrio (8B)

gloves los guantes (7B)

to go ir (4A)

   Let's —! ¡Vamos! (7A)

   to be —ing to + *verb* ir a + *inf.* (4B)

   to — boating pasear en bote (8A)

   to — camping ir de cámping (4B)

   to — fishing ir de pesca (4B)

   to — on vacation ir de vacaciones (8A)

   to — shopping ir de compras (4A)

   to — to school ir a la escuela (1A)

   to — out salir (8A)

golf: to play — jugar al golf (4B)

good bueno (buen), -a (1B)

   — afternoon. Buenas tardes. (P)

   — evening. Buenas noches. (P)

   — morning. Buenos días. (P)

Good-bye! ¡Adiós! (P)

good-looking guapo, -a (5B)

grains los cereales (3B)

grandfather el abuelo (5A)

grandmother la abuela (5A)

grandparents los abuelos (5A)

grapes las uvas (3B)

graphics los gráficos (9B)

gray gris (6A)

   — hair el pelo canoso (5B)

Great! ¡Genial! (4B)

green verde (6A)

   — **beans** las judías verdes (3B)

ground floor la planta baja (6B)

guitar: to play the — tocar la guitarra (1A)

gym el gimnasio (4A)

H

hair el pelo (5B)

   black — el pelo negro (5B)

   blond — el pelo rubio (5B)

   brown (chestnut) — el pelo castaño (5B)

   gray — el pelo canoso (5B)

half media, -o (P)

   — **-past** y media (P)

ham and cheese sandwich el sándwich de jamón y queso (3A)

hamburger la hamburguesa (3A)

hand la mano (P)

happy contento, -a (4B)

   — **birthday!** ¡Feliz cumpleaños! (5A)

hardworking trabajador, -a (1B)

to have tener (5A)

   to — just ... acabar de + *inf.* (9A)

   I — to ... tengo que + *inf.* (4B)

he él (1B)

he/she is es (1B)

   He/She is / They are ... years old. Tiene(n) ... años. (5A)

head la cabeza (P)

health:

   for one's — para la salud (3B)

   to maintain one's — para mantener la salud (3B)

Hello! ¡Hola! (P)

to help ayudar (6B)

   How can I — you? ¿En qué puedo servirle? (7A)

her su, sus *possessive adj.* (5A); la *dir. obj. pron.* (7B); le *ind. obj. pron.* (8B)

here aquí (2B)

Hey! ¡Oye! (4B)

him lo *dir. obj. pron.* (7B); le *ind. obj. pron.* (8B)

his su, sus (5A)

home la casa (4A)

   at — en casa (4A)

   — **office** el despacho (6B)

   (to) — a casa (4A)

homework la tarea (2A)

horrible horrible (3B)

horror movie la película de horror (9A)

horseback: to ride — montar a caballo (8A)

hospital el hospital (8B)

hot:

   — **dog** el perrito caliente (3A)

   It's —. Hace calor. (P)

hotel el hotel (8A)

hour: in the ... — en la ... hora (class period) (2A)

house la casa (4A)

household:

   — **chore** el quehacer (de la casa) (6B)

   — **appliance store** la tienda de electrodomésticos (7B)

how:

   — + *adj.*! ¡Qué + *adj.*! (5B)

   — **awful!** ¡Qué asco! (3A)

how? ¿cómo? (P)

   — **are you?** ¿Cómo está Ud.? *formal* (P); ¿Cómo estás? *fam.* (P); ¿Qué tal? *fam.* (P)

   — **can I help you?** ¿En qué puedo servirle? (7A)

   — **do you say ... ?** ¿Cómo se dice ...? (P)

   — **does it (do they) fit (you)?** ¿Cómo te queda(n)? (7A)

   — **is ... spelled?** ¿Cómo se escribe ...? (P)

   — **many?** ¿cuántos, -as? (P)

   — **much does (do) ... cost?** ¿Cuánto cuesta(n) ...? (7A)

   — **old is/are ...?** ¿Cuántos años tiene(n) ...? (5A)

   — **was it (for you)?** ¿Cómo lo pasaste? (8A)

hundred: one — cien (P)

hungry: I'm —. Tengo hambre. (3B)

to hurt doler (o → ue) (9A)

husband el esposo (5A)

I

I yo (1B)

   — **am** soy (1B)

   — **am not** no soy (1B)

   — **do too** a mí también (1A)

   — **don't either** a mí tampoco (1A)

   — **don't think so.** Creo que no. (3B)

   — **stay at home.** Me quedo en casa. (4A)

   — **think ...** Creo que ... (3B)

   — **think so.** Creo que sí. (3B)

   — **will bring you ...** Le traigo ... (5B)

   — **would like ...** Me gustaría (4B); quisiera (5B)

   —**'m hungry.** Tengo hambre. (3B)

   —**'m sorry.** Lo siento. (4B)

   —**'m thirsty.** Tengo sed. (3B)

ice cream el helado (3B)

iced tea el té helado (3A)

if si (6B)

impatient impaciente (1B)

important importante (6A)

impressive impresionante (8A)

in en (P, 2B)

   — **front of** delante de (2B)

   — **my opinion** para mí (6A)

   — **order to** para + *inf.* (4A)

   — **the ... hour** en la ... hora (class period) (2A)

   — **your opinion** para ti (6A)

incredible increíble (8B)

inexpensive barato, -a (7B)

information la información (9B)

intelligent inteligente (1B)

to interest interesar (9A)

   it/they interest(s) me me interesa(n) (9A)

interesting interesante (2A)

interview program el programa de entrevistas (9A)

is es (P)

he/she — es (1B)

it la, lo *dir. obj. pron.* (7B)

— **fits (they fit) me well/poorly.** Me queda(n) bien/mal. (7A)

— **is ...** Son las *(in telling time)* (P)

— **is one o'clock.** Es la una. (P)

— **is the ... of ...** Es el *(number)* de *(month) (in telling the date)* (P)

— **is the first of ...** Es el primero de *(month).* (P)

— **was** fue (8A)

— **was a disaster.** Fue un desastre. (8A)

—**'s a ...** es un/una ... (2B)

—**'s cold.** Hace frío. (P)

—**'s hot.** Hace calor. (P)

—**'s necessary.** Es necesario. (8B)

—**'s raining.** Llueve. (P)

—**'s snowing.** Nieva. (P)

—**'s sunny.** Hace sol. (P)

J

jacket la chaqueta (7A)

January enero (P)

jeans los jeans (7A)

jewelry store la joyería (7B)

job el trabajo (4A)

juice:

apple — el jugo de manzana (3A)

orange — el jugo de naranja (3A)

July julio (P)

June junio (P)

just: to have — (done something) acabar de + *inf.* (9A)

K

key chain el llavero (7B)

keyboard (computer) el teclado (2B)

kind: What — of ... ? ¿Qué clase de ...? (9A)

kitchen la cocina (6B)

knife el cuchillo (5B)

to know saber (4B, 9B); conocer (9B)

I — (yo) conozco (9B)

I — (how to) (yo) sé (4B)

you — (tú) conoces (9B)

you — (how to) (tú) sabes (4B)

L

laboratory el laboratorio (9B)

lake el lago (8A)

lamp la lámpara (6A)

laptop computer la computadora portátil (9B)

large grande (6A)

last:

— **night** anoche (7B)

— **week** la semana pasada (7B)

— **year** el año pasado (7B)

to last durar (9A)

late tarde (8A)

later: See you — ¡Hasta luego!, ¡Nos vemos! (P)

lazy perezoso, -a (1B)

to learn aprender (a) (8A)

to leave salir (8A)

left: to the — (of) a la izquierda (de) (6A)

leg la pierna (P)

lemonade la limonada (3A)

less:

less ... than menos ... que (6A)

less than menos de (9A)

Let's go! ¡Vamos! (7A)

Let's see A ver ... (2A)

letter la carta (9B)

lettuce la lechuga (3B)

library la biblioteca (4A)

to lift weights levantar pesas (3B)

light la luz *pl.* las luces (5A)

like como (8A)

to like:

Did you — it? ¿Te gustó? (8A)

Do you — to ...? ¿Te gusta ...? (1A)

He/She doesn't — ... No le

gusta ... (1B)

He/She —s ... Le gusta ... (1B); A él/ella le gusta(n) ... (5A)

I don't — to ... (A mí) no me gusta ... (1A)

I don't — to ... at all. (A mí) no me gusta nada ... (1A)

I — ... Me gusta ... (3A)

I — to ... (A mí) me gusta ... (1A)

I — to ... a lot (A mí) me gusta mucho ... (1A)

I — to ... better (A mí) me gusta más ... (1A)

I —d it. Me gustó. (8A)

I would — Me gustaría (4B); quisiera (5B)

What do you — better (prefer) to do? ¿Qué te gusta más? (1A)

What do you — to do? ¿Qué te gusta hacer? (1A)

What would you —? ¿Qué desean (Uds.)? (5B)

Would you —? ¿Te gustaría? (4B)

You — ... Te gusta ... (3A)

likewise igualmente (P)

to listen to music escuchar música (1A)

little: a — un poco (de) (4B)

to live vivir (6B)

living room la sala (6B)

long largo, -a (5B)

to look:

to — (at) mirar (7B)

to — for buscar (7A)

lot: a — mucho, -a (2A)

to love encantar (9A)

He/She —s ... A él/ella le encanta(n) ... (5A)

I/You — ... Me/Te encanta(n)... (3A)

lunch el almuerzo (2A)

for — en el almuerzo (3A)

M

madam (la) señora (Sra.) (P)

main dish el plato principal (5B)

as a — de plato principal (5B)

to maintain one's health para mantener la salud (3B)

make (*command*) haz (6B)

to make the bed hacer la cama (6B)

  mall el centro comercial (4A)

man el hombre (5B)

  older — el anciano (8B)

many muchos, -as (3B)

  how — ¿cuántos, -as? (P)

March marzo (P)

match el partido (4B)

mathematics class la clase de matemáticas (2A)

May mayo (P)

maybe quizás (7A)

me me *ind. obj. pron* (8B)

  for — para mí (6A), me (8B)

  — too a mí también (1A)

  to — me (8B)

  with — conmigo (4B)

meal la comida (3A)

to mean:

  It —s ... Quiere decir ... (P)

  What does ... — ? ¿Qué quiere decir ... ? (P)

meat la carne (3B)

menu el menú (5B)

messy desordenado, -a (1B)

milk la leche (3A)

mirror el espejo (6A)

miss, Miss (la) señorita (Srta.) (P)

missing: to be — faltar (9A)

moment: a — un momento (6B)

Monday lunes (P)

  on Mondays los lunes (4A)

money el dinero (6B)

monkey el mono (8A)

month el mes (P)

monument el monumento (8A)

more:

  — ... than más ... que (2A)

  — or less más o menos (3A)

  — than más de (9A)

morning:

Good —. Buenos días. (P)

  in the — de la mañana (4B)

mosque la mezquita (4A)

mother la madre (mamá) (5A)

mountains las montañas (4A)

mouse (computer) el ratón (2B)

mouth la boca (P)

movie la película (9A)

  to see a — ver una película (4A)

  — theater el cine (4A)

to mow the lawn cortar el césped (6B)

Mr. (el) señor (Sr.) (P)

Mrs. (la) señora (Sra.) (P)

much: so — tanto (7A)

museum el museo (8A)

music:

  to listen to — escuchar música (1A)

  —al program el programa musical (9A)

must deber (3B)

  one — hay que (8B)

my mi (2B); mis (5A)

  — name is ... Me llamo ... (P)

mystery la película policíaca (9A)

N ─────────────

name:

  My — is ... Me llamo ... (P)

  What is your —? ¿Cómo te llamas? (P)

  What's his/her —? ¿Cómo se llama? (1B)

napkin la servilleta (5B)

national park el parque nacional (8A)

near cerca (de) (6B)

neat ordenado, -a (1B)

necessary: It's —. Es necesario. (8B)

necklace el collar (7B)

to need

  I — necesito (2A)

  I — ... Me falta(n) ... (5B)

  you — necesitas (2A)

neighborhood el barrio (8B)

neither ... nor ni ... ni (1A)

never nunca (3A)

new nuevo, -a (7A)

news program el programa de noticias (9A)

newspaper el periódico (8B)

next to al lado de (2B)

nice simpático, -a (1B)

night:

  at — de la noche (4B)

  last — anoche (7B)

night table la mesita (6A)

nine nueve (P)

nine hundred novecientos, -as (7A)

nineteen diecinueve (P)

ninety noventa (P)

ninth noveno, -a (2A)

nose la nariz *pl.* las narices (P)

not ... or ni ... ni (1A)

notebook el cuaderno (P)

nothing nada (P)

November noviembre (P)

now ahora (5B)

O ─────────────

o'clock:

  at eight — a las ocho (4B)

  at one — a la una (4B)

  It's one —. Es la una. (P)

  It's ... — Son las ... (P)

October octubre (P)

of de (2B)

  — course por supuesto (3A)

office (home) el despacho (6B)

often a menudo (8B)

Oh! What a shame/pity! ¡Ay! ¡Qué pena! (4B)

okay regular (P)

old viejo, -a (5B)

  He/She is / They are ... years —. Tiene(n) ... años. (5A)

  How — is/are ... ? ¿Cuántos años tiene(n) ... ? (5A)

  —er mayor (5A)

  —er man el anciano (8B)

—er people los ancianos (8B)

—er woman la anciana (8B)

on en (2B)

— Mondays, on Tuesdays ... los lunes, los martes ... (4A)

— top of encima de (2B)

— weekends los fines de semana (4A)

one uno (un), -a (P)

at — (o'clock) a la una (4B)

one hundred cien (P)

one must hay que (8B)

onion la cebolla (3B)

online en la Red (7B)

to be — estar en línea (9B)

only sólo (5A)

to open abrir (5A)

opinion:

in my — para mí (6A)

in your — para tí (6A)

or o (1A)

orange anaranjado, -a (6A)

— juice el jugo de naranja (3A)

to order pedir (e → i) (5B)

other otro, -a (5B)

others los/las demás (8B)

our nuestro(s), -a(s) (5A)

own propio, -a (6A)

P

painting el cuadro (6A)

pants los pantalones (7A)

paper: sheet of — la hoja de papel (P)

parents los padres (5A)

park el parque (4A)

amusement — el parque de diversiones (8A)

national — el parque nacional (8A)

party la fiesta (4B)

pastries los pasteles (3B)

patient paciente (1B)

to pay (for) pagar (por) (7B)

peas los guisantes (3B)

pen el bolígrafo (P)

pencil el lápiz *pl.* los lápices (P)

— sharpener el sacapuntas (2B)

people la gente (8B)

older — los ancianos (8B)

pepper la pimienta (5B)

perfume el perfume (7B)

person la persona (5A)

phone: to talk on the — hablar por teléfono (1A)

photo la foto (5A)

to take —s sacar fotos (5A)

physical education class la clase de educación física (2A)

piano lesson (class) la lección *pl.* las lecciones de piano (4A)

pink rosado, -a (6A)

piñata la piñata (5A)

pizza la pizza (3A)

place el lugar (8A)

to place poner (6B)

plastic el plástico (8B)

plate el plato (5B)

play la obra de teatro (8A)

to play jugar (a) (u → ue) (4B); tocar (1A)

to — baseball jugar al béisbol (4B)

to — basketball jugar al básquetbol (4B)

to — football jugar al fútbol americano (4B)

to — golf jugar al golf (4B)

to — soccer jugar al fútbol (4B)

to — sports practicar deportes (1A)

to — tennis jugar al tenis (4B)

to — the guitar tocar la guitarra (1A)

to — video games jugar videojuegos (1A)

to — volleyball jugar al vóleibol (4B)

please por favor (P)

to please very much encantar (9A)

pleased to meet you mucho gusto (P)

pool la piscina (4A)

poor pobre (8B)

possession la posesión *pl.* las posesiones (6A)

poster el cartel (2B)

potatoes las papas (3B)

practical práctico, -a (2A)

to prefer preferir (e → ie) (7A)

I — (yo) prefiero (3B)

I — to ... (a mí) me gusta más ... (1A)

you — (tú) prefieres (3B)

to prepare preparar (5A)

present el regalo (5A)

presentation la presentación *pl.* las presentaciones (9B)

pretty bonito, -a (6A)

price el precio (7A)

primary school la escuela primaria (8B)

problem el problema (8B)

program el programa (9A)

purple morado, -a (6A)

purse el bolso (7B)

to put poner (6B)

I — (yo) pongo (6B)

— (command) pon (6B)

you — (tú) pones (6B)

Q

quarter past y cuarto (P)

quarter to menos cuarto

quickly rápidamente (9B)

R

rain: It's —ing. Llueve. (P)

rather bastante (6B)

to read magazines leer revistas (1A)

realistic realista (9A)

reality program el programa de la vida real (9A)

Really? ¿De veras? (9A)

to receive recibir (6B)

to recycle reciclar (8B)

recycling center el centro de reciclaje (8B)

red rojo, -a (6A)

    —-haired pelirrojo, -a (5B)

to relax descansar (8A)

    report el informe (9B)

    reserved reservado, -a (1B)

to rest descansar (8A)

    restaurant el restaurante (4A)

to return regresar (8A)

    rice el arroz (3B)

    rich rico, -a (5B)

to ride:

    to — a bicycle montar en bicicleta (1A)

    to — horseback montar a caballo (8A)

    right: to the — (of) a la derecha (de) (6A)

    Right? ¿Verdad? (3A)

    ring el anillo (7B)

    river el río (8B)

    road la calle (8B)

    romantic movie la película romántica (9A)

    room el cuarto (6B)

    to straighten up the — arreglar el cuarto (6B)

    rug la alfombra (6A)

to run correr (1A)

S

    sack la bolsa (8B)

    sad triste (4B)

    salad la ensalada (3A)

    fruit — la ensalada de frutas (3A)

    salesperson el dependiente, la dependienta (7A)

    salt la sal (5B)

    same mismo, -a (6A)

    sandwich: ham and cheese — el sándwich de jamón y queso (3A)

    Saturday sábado (P)

    sausage la salchicha (3A)

to say decir (8B)

    How do you —? ¿Cómo se dice? (P)

    You — ... Se dice ... (P)

    You don't —! ¡No me digas! (4A)

    scared: to be — (of) tener miedo (de) (9B)

    schedule el horario (2A)

    science:

    — class la clase de ciencias naturales (2A)

    — fiction movie la película de ciencia ficción (9A)

    screen: computer — la pantalla (2B)

to scuba dive bucear (8A)

    sea el mar (8A)

to search (for) buscar (9B)

    season la estación *pl.* las estaciones (P)

    second segundo, -a (2A)

    — floor el primer piso (6B)

to see ver (8A)

    Let's — A ver ... (2A)

    — you later! ¡Nos vemos!, Hasta luego. (P)

    — you tomorrow. Hasta mañana. (P)

    to — a movie ver una película (4A)

to sell vender (7B)

to send enviar (i → í) (9B)

to separate separar (8B)

    September septiembre (P)

    serious serio, -a (1B)

to serve servir (e → i) (9B)

to set the table poner la mesa (6B)

    seven siete (P)

    seven hundred setecientos, -as (7A)

    seventeen diecisiete (P)

    seventh séptimo, -a (2A)

    seventy setenta (P)

to share compartir (3A)

    she ella (1B)

    sheet of paper la hoja de papel (P)

    shelf el estante (6A)

    ship el barco (8A)

    shirt la camisa (7A)

    T- — la camiseta (7A)

    shoe store la zapatería (7B)

    shoes los zapatos (7A)

    short bajo, -a; corto, -a (5B)

    shorts los pantalones cortos (7A)

    should deber (3B)

    show el programa (9A)

to show + *movie or TV program* dar (9A)

    shy reservado, -a (1B)

    sick enfermo, -a (4B)

    silly tonto, -a (9A)

to sing cantar (1A)

    sir (el) señor (Sr.) (P)

    sister la hermana (5A)

    site: Web — el sitio Web (9B)

    six seis (P)

    six hundred seiscientos, -as (7A)

    sixteen dieciséis (P)

    sixth sexto, -a (2A)

    sixty sesenta (P)

to skate patinar (1A)

to skateboard montar en monopatín (1A)

to ski esquiar (i fi í) (1A)

    skirt la falda (7A)

to sleep dormir (o → ue) (6A)

    sleepy: to be — tener sueño (5B)

    slide la diapositiva (9B)

    small pequeño, -a (6A)

to snorkel bucear (8A)

    snow: It's —ing. Nieva. (P)

    so much tanto (7A)

    so-so regular (P)

    soap opera la telenovela (9A)

    soccer: to play — jugar al fútbol (4B)

    sociable sociable (1B)

    social studies class la clase de ciencias sociales (2A)

    socks los calcetines (7A)

    soft drink el refresco (3A)

    software el software (7B)

    some unos, -as (2B)

    something algo (3B)

sometimes a veces (1B)

son el hijo (5A)

  —s; —(s) and daughter(s) los hijos (5A)

song la canción *pl.* las canciones (9B)

sorry: I'm —. Lo siento. (4B)

sound (stereo) system el equipo de sonido (6A)

soup: vegetable — la sopa de verduras (3A)

souvenirs los recuerdos (8A)

  to buy — comprar recuerdos (8A)

spaghetti los espaguetis (3B)

Spanish class la clase de español (2A)

to spell:

  How is … spelled? ¿Cómo se escribe … ? (P)

  It's spelled … Se escribe … (P)

to spend time with friends pasar tiempo con amigos (1A)

  spoon la cuchara (5B)

  sports:

    to play — practicar deportes (1A)

    —-minded deportista (1B)

    — show el programa deportivo (9A)

spring la primavera (P)

stadium el estadio (8A)

stairs, stairway la escalera (6B)

to start empezar (e → ie) (9A)

to stay: I — at home. Me quedo en casa. (4A)

  stepbrother el hermanastro (5A)

  stepfather el padrastro (5A)

  stepmother la madrastra (5A)

  stepsister la hermanastra (5A)

  stereo system el equipo de sonido (6A)

stomach el estómago (P)

store la tienda (7A)

  book— la librería (7B)

  clothing — la tienda de ropa (7A)

  department — el almacén *pl.* los almacenes (7B)

discount — la tienda de descuentos (7B)

household appliance — la tienda de electrodomésticos (7B)

jewelry — la joyería (7B)

shoe — la zapatería (7B)

story el piso (6B)

stories: to write — escribir cuentos (1A)

to straighten up the room arreglar el cuarto (6B)

strawberries las fresas (3A)

street la calle (8B)

student el/la estudiante (P)

studious estudioso, -a (1B)

to study estudiar (2A)

  stupid tonto, -a (9A)

  sugar el azúcar (5B)

  suit el traje (7A)

  summer el verano (P)

to sunbathe tomar el sol (8A)

  Sunday domingo (P)

  sunglasses los anteojos de sol (7B)

  sunny: It's —. Hace sol. (P)

to surf the Web navegar en la Red (9B)

  sweater el suéter (7A)

  sweatshirt la sudadera (7A)

to swim nadar (1A)

  swimming pool la piscina (4A)

  swimsuit el traje de baño (7A)

  synagogue la sinagoga (4A)

T

T-shirt la camiseta (7A)

table la mesa (2B)

  to set the — poner la mesa (6B)

to take llevar (8B)

  to — a course tomar un curso (9B)

  to — out the trash sacar la basura (6B)

  to — photos sacar fotos (5A)

talented talentoso, -a (1B)

to talk hablar (2A)

to — on the phone hablar por teléfono (1A)

tall alto, -a (5B)

tasty sabroso, -a (3B); rico, -a (5B)

tea el té (3A)

  iced — el té helado (3A)

to teach enseñar (2A)

  teacher el profesor, la profesora (P)

  technology/computers la tecnología (2A)

  technology/computer class la clase de tecnología (2A)

  television: to watch — ver la tele (1A)

  television set el televisor (6A)

to tell decir (8B)

  — me dime (8A)

temple el templo (4A)

ten diez (P)

tennis: to play — jugar al tenis (4B)

tenth décimo, -a (2A)

thank you gracias (P)

that que (5A); ese, esa (7A)

  —'s why por eso (9A)

the el, la (1B); los, las (2B)

  — best el/la mejor, los/las mejores (6A)

  — worst el/la peor, los/las peores (6A)

theater el teatro (8A)

movie — el cine (4A)

their su, sus (5A)

them las, los *dir. obj. pron.* (7B); les *ind. obj. pron.* (8B)

then entonces (4B)

there allí (2B)

  — is/are hay (P, 2B)

therefore por eso (9A)

these estos, estas (7A)

they ellos, ellas (2A)

thing la cosa (6A)

to think creer (3B) pensar (e → ie) (7A)

  I don't — so. Creo que no. (3B)

  I — … Creo que … (3B)

I — so. Creo que sí. (3B)

What do you — (about it)? ¿Qué te parece? (9B)

third tercer (tercero), -a (2A)

third floor el segundo piso (6B)

thirsty: I'm —. Tengo sed. (3B)

thirteen trece (P)

thirty treinta (P); y media *(in telling time)* (P)

thirty-one treinta y uno (P)

this este, esta (7A)

   — afternoon esta tarde (4B)

   — evening esta noche (4B)

   — weekend este fin de semana (4B)

   What is — ? ¿Qué es esto? (2B)

those esos, esas (7A)

thousand: a — mil (7A)

three tres (P)

three hundred trescientos, -as (7A)

three-ring binder la carpeta de argollas (2A)

Thursday jueves (P)

ticket el boleto (8A)

tie la corbata (7B)

time la vez *pl.* las veces (8B)

   At what —? ¿A qué hora? (4B)

   free — el tiempo libre (4A)

   to spend — with friends pasar tiempo con amigos (1A)

   What — is it? ¿Qué hora es? (P)

tired cansado, -a (4B)

to a *(prep.)* (4A)

   in order — para + *inf.* (4A)

   — the a la, al (4A)

   — the left (of) a la izquierda (de) (6A)

   — the right (of) a la derecha (de) (6A)

toast el pan tostado (3A)

today hoy (P)

tomatoes los tomates (3B)

tomorrow mañana (P)

   See you —. Hasta mañana. (P)

too también (1A); demasiado (4B)

I do (like to) — a mí también (1A)

me — a mí también (1A)

top: on — of encima de (2B)

touching emocionante (9A)

toy el juguete (8B)

train el tren (8A)

to travel viajar (8A)

tree el árbol (8A)

tremendous tremendo, -a (8A)

trip el viaje (8A)

Tuesday martes (P)

   on —s los martes (4A)

TV channel el canal (9A)

twelve doce (P)

twenty veinte (P)

twenty-one veintiuno (veintiún) (P)

two dos (P)

two hundred doscientos, -as (7A)

U

Ugh! ¡Uf! (7B)

ugly feo, -a (6A)

uncle el tío (5A)

uncles; uncle(s) and aunt(s) los tíos (5A)

underneath debajo de (2B)

to understand comprender (3A)

unforgettable inolvidable (8B)

us: (to/for) — nos *ind. obj. pron.* (8B)

to use:

   to — the computer usar la computadora (1A)

   What's it —d for? ¿Para qué sirve? (9B)

used usado, -a (8B)

useful:

   to be — servir (9B)

   is — for sirve para (9B)

V

vacation: to go on — ir de vacaciones (8A)

to vacuum pasar la aspiradora (6B)

VCR la videocasetera (6A)

vegetable soup la sopa de verduras (3A)

very muy (1B)

   — well muy bien (P)

video games: to play — jugar videojuegos (1A)

videocassette el video (5A, 6A)

to videotape hacer un video (5A)

violent violento, -a (9A)

to visit visitar (8A)

to — chat rooms visitar salones de chat (9B)

volleyball: to play — jugar al vóleibol (4B)

volunteer el voluntario, la voluntaria (8B)

   — work el trabajo voluntario (8B)

W

waiter, waitress el camarero, la camarera (5B)

to walk caminar (3B)

wall la pared (6A)

wallet la cartera (7B)

to want querer (e → ie) (7A)

   I — (yo) quiero (4B)

   you — (tú) quieres (4B)

warm: to be — tener calor (5B)

was fue (8B)

to wash lavar (6B)

   to — the car lavar el coche (6B)

   to — the clothes lavar la ropa (6B)

   to — the dishes lavar los platos (6B)

wastepaper basket la papelera (2B)

watch el reloj pulsera (7B)

to watch television ver la tele (1A)

water el agua (*f.*) (3A)

we nosotros, -as (2A)

to wear llevar (7A)

weather: What's the — like? ¿Qué tiempo hace? (P)

Web:

   to surf the — navegar en la Red (9B)

   — page la página Web (9B)

   — site el sitio Web (9B)

Wednesday miércoles (P)

week la semana (P)

   last — la semana pasada (7B)

weekend:

   on —s los fines de semana (4A)

   this — este fin de semana (4B)

welcome: You're —. De nada. (5B)

well bien (P); pues … *(to indicate pause)* (1A)

   very — muy bien (P)

what? ¿cuál? (3A)

   — are you like? ¿Cómo eres? (1B)

   (At) — time? ¿A qué hora? (4B)

   — color … ? ¿De qué color … ? (6A)

   — day is today? ¿Qué día es hoy? (P)

   — did you do? ¿Qué hiciste? (8A)

   — do you like better (prefer) to do? ¿Qué te gusta hacer más? (1A)

   — do you like to do? ¿Qué te gusta hacer? (1A)

   — do you think (about it)? ¿Qué te parece? (9B)

   — does … mean? ¿Qué quiere decir … ? (P)

   — else? ¿Qué más? (8B)

   — happened to you? ¿Qué te pasó? (8A)

   — is she/he like? ¿Cómo es? (1B)

   — is the date? ¿Cuál es la fecha? (P)

   — is this? ¿Qué es esto? (2B)

   — is your name? ¿Cómo te llamas? (P)

   — kind of … ? ¿Qué clase de…? (9A)

   — time is it? ¿Qué hora es? (P)

   — would you like? ¿Qué desean (Uds.)? (5B)

   —'s happening? ¿Qué pasa? (P)

   —'s his/her name? ¿Cómo se llama? (1B)

   —'s it (used) for? ¿Para qué sirve? (9B)

   —'s the weather like? ¿Qué tiempo hace? (P)

what!:

   — a good/nice idea! ¡Qué buena idea! (4B)

   — a shame/pity! ¡Qué pena! (4B)

When? ¿Cuándo? (4A)

Where? ¿Dónde? (2B)

   — are you from? ¿De dónde eres? (4A)

   (To) —? ¿Adónde? (4A)

whether si (6B)

which? ¿cuál? (3A)

white blanco, -a (6A)

who que (5A)

Who? ¿Quién? (2A)

Why? ¿Por qué? (3B)

wife la esposa (5A)

Will you bring me … ? ¿Me trae … ? (5B)

window la ventana (2B)

winter el invierno (P)

with con (3A)

   — me conmigo (4B)

   — my/your friends con mis/tus amigos (4A)

   — whom? ¿Con quién? (4A)

   — you contigo (4B)

without sin (3A)

woman la mujer (5B)

   older woman la anciana (8B)

work el trabajo (4A)

volunteer — el trabajo voluntario (8B)

to work trabajar (1A)

worse than peor(es) que (6A)

worst: the — el/la peor, los/las peores (6A)

Would you like …? ¿Te gustaría …? (4B)

to write:

   to — e-mail escribir por correo electrónico (9B)

   to — stories escribir cuentos (1A)

Y

yard el jardín *pl.* los jardines (8B)

year el año (P)

   He/She is / They are … —s old. Tiene(n) … años. (5A)

   last — el año pasado (7B)

yellow amarillo, -a (6A)

yes sí (1A)

yesterday ayer (7B)

yogurt el yogur (3A)

you fam. *sing.* tú (2A); *formal sing.* usted (Ud.) (2A); *fam. pl.* vosotros, -as (2A); *formal pl.* ustedes (Uds.) (2A); *fam. after prep.* ti (1A); *sing. ind. obj. pron.* te (8B); *pl. fam. ind. obj. pron.* os (8B); *ind. obj. pron.* le, les (8B)

   And — ? ¿Y a ti? (1A)

   for — para ti (6A)

   to/for — *fam. pl.* os (8B)

   to/for — *fam. sing.* te (8B)

   with — contigo (4B)

   — don't say! ¡No me digas! (4A)

   — say … Se dice … (P)

You're welcome De nada (5B)

young joven (5B)

   — boy/girl el niño, la niña (8B)

   — man el joven (5B)

   — woman la joven (5B)

   —er menor (5A)

your *fam.* tu (2B); *fam.* tus, vuestro(s), -a(s) (5A); *formal* su, sus (5A)

Yuck! ¡Uf! (7B)

Z

zero cero (P)

zoo el zoológico (8A)

Grammar Index

Structures are most often presented first in *A primera vista*, where they are practiced lexically. They are then explained later in a *Gramática* section or a *Nota*. Light-face numbers refer to the pages where structures are initially presented or, after explanation, where student reminders occur. **Bold-face numbers** refer to pages where structures are explained or are otherwise highlighted.

a 26–29, 180
+ definite article 172–173, **177**
+ indirect object **410**
after **jugar** 200, **208**
in telling time 198
personal **387**
personal after **conocer 460**
with **ir** + infinitive 199, **206**
aburrir 426, **436**
acabar de 428, **434**
accent marks **13**, **183**
in interrogative words **184**
in preterite **356, 383**
over weak vowels **380**
adjectives:
agreement and formation 50–51, **55**, 70, **156**, 168, 252, 306
comparative 75, 272–273, **278**, 294
demonstrative 198–199, 324–325, **332**
ending in **-ísimo** 255
plural. *See* adjectives: agreement and formation
position of **62**
possessive 28, 100, 120, 224, **232**, 244
superlative 272, **280**, 294
adverbs:
Using **-mente** to form **457**
affirmative **tú** commands 300, **305**, 318
age 222, **228**, 244
alphabet 12

-ar verbs 32
present 75, 76–77, **84**, 96, 132
preterite 347, **354, 356**, 370
spelling-changing 347, 349, **356**, 370
articles:
definite **11**, **60**, 70, **110**, 120
definite, with **a** 172–173, **177**
definite, with days of the week 173, 178
definite, with titles of respect 78
indefinite **60**, 70, **110**, 120

-car and **-gar** verbs, preterite 347, 349, **356**, 370
cognates **34**, 57
commands (**tú**), affirmative 300, **305**, 318
comparison 75, 272–273, **278**, 294, **432**
compound subject **82**
conocer 452, **460**, 470

dar 301, **304**, 318
preterite 402, **412**, 422
dates 14–15, **358**
de:
in compound nouns **130**
in prepositional phrases 101, 105
possessive 101, **111**, **232**
decir 401, **408**, 422
derivation of words 81, 160, 178, 205, 389, 435
diminutives **235**
direct object pronouns **360**, 404 *See also* pronouns
with personal **a**, **387**
doler 9, **436**
dormir 274, **284**, 294

encantar 125, **135**, 229, **436**
-er verbs 32
present 124–125, **132**, 144
preterite 374, **383**, 396

estar 100–101, **107**, 120, 351
use of in present progressive 300, **308**, 318
vs. **ser 258**, **260**, 277
Exploración del lenguaje:
Adjectives ending in **-ísimo 255**
Cognates **34**
Cognates that begin with **es-** + consonant **57**
Connections between Latin, English, and Spanish **81**
Diminutives **235**
Language through gestures **106**
Nonverbal language **333**
Nouns that end in **-dad**, **-tad**, **-ción**, and **-sión 406**
Nouns that end in **-io** and **-eo 389**
Nouns that end in **-ería 353**
Origins of the Spanish days of the week **178**
Similar nouns **307**
Spanish words borrowed from English **205**
Tú vs. **usted** 4, **5,** 82
Using a noun to modify another noun **130**
Using **-mente** to form adverbs **457**
Using root words **286**
Where did it come from? **160**
Words of Greek and Arabic origin **435**

faltar 250, 254, **436**

gender **11**
of adjectives agreeing with nouns **55**, 70, **156**, 168, 232, 252, 306
of articles **60**, 70
of pronouns **82**
gustar 26, 50, **135**, 229, **436**

hace + time 347, **355**, 370

Acknowledgments

Maps Mapping Specialists

Technical Illustration/Additional Graphics Herman Adler Design; New England Typographic Services; Publicom; John Reece; Joseph Taylor; p. xxxi, XNR Productions: Map of Florida

Illustrations Wilkinson Studios Artists; Bob Brugger: pp. 136, 167, 210, 257, 285, 307, 329, 383; Donna Catanese: pp. 235; Dennis Dzielak: pp. 8, 67, 81, 96, 133, 136, 205, 323, 373, 380; George Hamblin: p. 382; Seitu Hayden: pp. 6, 12, 16, 27, 32, 36, 37, 77, 172, 173, 176, 199, 202, 203, 204, 276, 303, 306, 329, 331, 355, 430, 448; Reggie Holladay: pp. 18, 27, 37, 58, 86, 188, 189, 246, 256, 257; Tim Jones: pp. 18, 26, 31, 32, 54, 56, 58, 63, 74, 79, 199, 206, 252, 253, 278, 293, 299, 308, 310, 311, 322, 326, 327, 373, 376, 428, 456, 460; Victor Kennedy: pp. 39, 84, 254, 257, 409; Gary Krejca: pp. 27, 37; Miguel Luna: pp. 7, 12, 86, 155, 378; Jonathan Massie: pp. 102, 149, 298, 302, 346, 401, 404, 406, 457, 460; Tom McKee: pp. 2, 4, 15, 54, 58, 115, 154, 190, 209, 248, 249, 312, 313, 323, 332, 335, 352, 372, 392, 397, 427, 453; Donna Perrone: pp. 86, 128, 130, 131, 148, 153, 159, 272; Ted Smykal: 14, 100, 101, 183, 329, 426, 430; Jud Stead: pp. 3, 18, 60, 79, 105, 198, 204, 223, 273, 280, 282, 350, 352, 354, 359, 449; Nicole Wong: pp. 8, 172, 173, 176, 334, 347, 361, 383, 463

Photography **Front Cover:** (L) ©George Doyle/Getty Images, (TC) ©Jon Arnold Images/Danita Delimont, Agent, (C) ©Jochem D. Wijnands/Getty Images, (CC) © Jack Hollingsworth/Corbis, (C) ©Wayne Walton/Lonely Planet Images/Getty Images, (BC) ©Chris Clinton/Getty Images

vi, ©LWA-Stephen Welstead/CORBIS; vii, © Bo Zaunders/Corbis; xvi-xvii, ©José Fuste Raga/CORBIS; xvi inset, ©Danny Lehman/CORBIS, xvii inset, ©Phil Schermeister/CORBIS; xvii-xix, ©Danny Lehman/CORBIS; xx-xxi, ©David Zimmerman/ CORBIS; xx inset, ©Stuart Westmorland/CORBIS; xxii-xix, ©Jim Erickson/CORBIS; xxiv-xxv ©Galen Rowell/CORBIS; xxvi-xxvii ©Paul Hardy/CORBIS, xxvi inset, ©Mark L. Stephenson, xxvii br inset ©José Fuste Raga/CORBIS; xxvii inset, ©Strauss/Curtis/CORBIS; xxviii ©Craig Tuttle/CORBIS; xxviii, © Bob Daemmrich/ The Image Works, Inc.; xxix br inset, ©Ron Watts/CORBIS, xxix bl inset Royalty– Free/Corbis; xxx tl, Pablo Picasso (1881-1973) Don Quijote. © 2010 Estate of Pablo Picasso/ Artists Rights Society (ARS), New York/Photo: Erich Lessing/Art Resource, NY; xxx tr, ©Paul Barton/CORBIS; xxx bm, ©Jarno Gonzalez Zarraonandia/Shutterstock; xxxii ©Robert Frerck/Odyssey/Chicago; 1 t, ©Robert Frerck/Odyssey/Chicago; 1 b, H. Huntly Hersch/DDB; 3 (1), Bob Daemmrich/SB; 3 (2), Spencer Grant/SB; 3 (3), David Young-Wolff/PhotoEdit; 3 (4), M. Ferguson/PhotoEdit; 3 (5), Bachmann/SB; 3 (6), Mary Kate Denny/PhotoEdit; 5, Mary Kate Denny/PhotoEdit; 8, Dalí, Salvador (1904–1989). The Persistence of Memory. 1921. Oil on canvas, 9 ½ x 13 in. (24.1 x 33 cm). Given anonymously. ©2009 Salvador Dalí, Gala-Salvador Dalí Foundation/Artists Rights Society (ARS), New York/A.K.G., Berlin/SuperStock; 11, Michael Newman/PhotoEdit; 13, Bridgeman Art Library International, Ltd./Museo Nacional de Antropología, Mexico City, Mexico; 15, David Young-Wolff/PhotoEdit; 16, AFP/ Getty Images; 17, Peter Wilson/Dorling Kindersley Media Library ©CONACULTA-INAH-MEX. Authorized reproduction by the Instituto Nacional de Antropología e Historia; 18 (1-4), George Gold/SuperStock, Inc.; 19 (1), ©Gordon R. Gainer/CORBIS; 19 (2), ©Getty Images; 19 (3), Joseph Nettis/Photo Researchers, Inc.; 19 (4), ©Raymon Berk/Shutterstock; 20 tl, Spencer Swanger/Tom Stack & Associates, Inc.; 20 tr, Ann Duncan/Tom Stack & Associates, Inc.; 20 bl, J. Schulte/DDB; 20 br, Ricardo Carrasco/DDB; 20 m, ©ESA/ELI/CORBIS; 24-25, Latin Focus.com; 24 inset, Picasso, Pablo (1881–1973). Three musicians. 1921. Oil on canvas, 6' 7" X 7' 3 3/4". Mrs. Simon Guggenheim Fund, #55.1949. ©2009 Estate of Pablo Picasso/Artists Rights Society (ARS), New York. Photo: ©The Museum of Modern Art/Scala/Art Resource, NY.; 28 tm, Roberto M. Arakaki/ImageState/International Stock Photography Ltd.; 28 bm, ©Danny Lehman/CORBIS; 29 tm, SuperStock, Inc.; 29 bm, Buddy Mays/IS; 31 bl, Peter Menzel/ StockBoston; 34 m, Museo Bellapart; 35 tl, Bonnie Kamin/PhotoEdit; 35 tr, Blaine Harrington; 35, Jeff Greenberg/PhotoEdit; 35 bl, David Young-Wolff/PhotoEdit; 35 br, PictureQuest; 40 t, David Young-Wolff/PhotoEdit; 40 b, Marison Diaz/LF; 41, ©Robert Frerck/Odyssey/ Chicago; 41 t, Blaine Harrington; 41 b, Myrleen Ferguson Cate/PhotoEdit Inc.; 42, Danilo Boschung/eStock Photography LLC; 43 t, Bob Daemmrich Photography, Inc.; 43 b, Kathy Ferguson-Johnson/PhotoEdit; 44-45, ©Mark L. Stephenson/ CORBIS; 45, ©José Fuste Raga/CORBIS; 45, ©Owen Franken/CORBIS; 45, ©Adam Woolfitt/CORBIS; 46, ©Tom Carter/Alamy; 48 inset, Oil on masonite, 16 X 12 inches. Courtesy of Albright-Knox Art Gallery, Buffalo, NY. Bequest of A. Conger Goodyear, 1966. ©2009 Banco de México, Diego Rivera & Frida Kahlo Museums Trust, México, D.F./Artists Rights Society (ARS), New York.; 48, © Bob Daemmrich/The Image Works, Inc.; 51 br, Paul Mark Smith/Panos Pictures; 57, David Simson/SB; 58 b, The Bridgeman Art Library International, Ltd.; 59 b, David Sanger Photography; 60, b, © Richard Cummins/Corbis; 62,Gary Bogdon/ NewSport/Corbis; 65, ©Robert Frerck/OP; 66 tr, Huntly Hersch/D. Donne Bryant Stock Photography; 66 br, David Simson/SB; 66 tl, Tony Arruza/CORBIS; 66 bl, RFP; 68-69, ©Reinhard Eisele/CORBIS; 69 inset t, ©Richard Bickel/CORBIS; 69 inset m, ©Roger Ressmeyer/CORBIS; 69 inset b, ©Jan Butchofsky-Houser/CORBIS; 72-73, ©Robert Fried/Stock Boston; 72 inset, Botero, Fernando (1932–). Pedrito. 1997. Marlborough Gallery, Inc.; 80, Jeff Greenberg/PhotoEdit; 81, Dave Bartruff/SB; 83 (1) ©Tetra Images/GettyImages; 83 (8), ©Robert Frerck/OP; 83 (2,6), RFP; 83 (3), Charlie Marsden/Panos Pictures; 83 (4), Jeff Greenberg/ PhotoEdit; 83 (5), Owen Franken/SB; 83 (7), Richard Pasley/SB; 85, Carlos S. Pereyra/DDB; 86 lt, Ulrike Welsch/PhotoEdit; 86 lb, Paul Conklin/PhotoEdit; 88, Charlie Marsden/Panos Pictures; 89, br, © Larry Kolvoord/The Image Works, Inc.; 90, ©José Fuste Raga/CORBIS; 90 inset, Bob Daemmrich/SB; 91 t, ©2004 Ulrike Welsch/SB; 91 b, RFP; 92 t, RFP; 92 b, Joe Viesti/VC; 93 t, ©2004 Ulrike Welsch/SB; 93 b, Jeff Greenberg/PhotoEdit; 94-95, José Fuste Raga/CORBIS; 95 inset tr, ©Lindsay Hebberd/

314 m, Bob Krist/eStock Photography, LLC; 314 b, Rob Crandall/SB; 315 t, Kal Muller/WC; 315 b, RFP; 320-321, ©Robert Frerck/Odyssey/Chicago; 320 inset, Miró, Joan (1893–1983). Self-portrait, 1919. Oil on canvas. ©2009 Successió Miró/Artists Rights Society (ARS), New York/ADAGP, Paris. Photo: J. G. Berizzi. Musée Picasso, Paris, France. ©Réunion des Musées Nationaux/Art Resource, NY.; 326, Robert Frerck/Woodfin Camp & Associates; 327 inset, Botero, Fernando (1932–). En familia. 1983. Marlborough Gallery, Inc.; 328 money, Jimmy Dorantes/Latin Focus.com; 331,b, © David Young-Wolff/PhotoEdit; 335, ©Mitchell Gerber/CORBIS; 336 bl, t, Joe Viesti/VC; 336 m, IFA Bilderteam/eStock Photography LLC; 337 tl, IFA Bilderteam/eStock Photography; 337 b, Joe Viesti/VC; 338, Wolfgang Kaehler Photography; 339 t, ©Javier Larrea/AGE Fotostock; 339 b, Robert Frerck/WC; 344-345, Robert Frerck/WC; 344 inset, Englebert Photography, Inc.; 350, ©2004 Ulrike Welsch Photography; 353 tl and tr, RFP; 353 bl, Jeff Greenberg/Photo Edit; 353 br, Bonnie Kamin/PhotoEdit; 356, Robert Frerck/WC; 357, Thomas R. Fletcher/SB; 359 tl, SuperStock, Inc.; 359 tm, San Diego Historical Society; 359 tr, Richard Pasley/SB; 362, Joe Viesti/VC; 363, Robert Frerck/ Woodfin Camp & Associates; 363, ©Robert Frerck/OP; 364 t, Spencer Grant/PhotoEdit; 364 m, Leslye Borden/PhotoEdit; 365 tl, Richard Carroll/Ambient Images; 365 tr, Joe Viesti/VC; 366, Walter Bibikow/SB; 367, David Young-Wolff/PhotoEdit; 372-373, ©Robert Frerck/OP; 372 inset, El Greco, View of Toledo, Metropolitan Museum of Art, New York/Index/Bridgeman Art Library, London/New York; 377 bl, Michael Sewell/Peter Arnold; 378, ©Wolfgang Kaehler/CORBIS; 379, Robert Fried/DDB; 380 b, Suzanne Murphy Larronde/DDB; 381, Art Womack/IS; 382 t, ©Danny Lehman/CORBIS; 382 (1), Salatiel Barragan/LF; 382 (2), Ulrike Welsch/PhotoEdit; 382 (3), RFP; 382 (4), Salatiel Barragan/Latin Focus.com; 382 (5), Russell Gordon/Danita Delimont, Agent; 383, ©Nina Raingold/Getty Images; 384, Mireille Vautier/Woodfin Camp & Associates; 387, Steve Bly/Bly Photography; 389 t, Richard Cummins/Corbis; 389 b, Jimmy Dorantes/LF; 390 tl, Michele Burgess/SB; 390 m, Gisela Damm/eStock Photography, LCC; 390 bl, ©Robert Frerck/OP; 391 t, Gavin Hellier/Getty Images; 391 b, ©Robert Frerck/OP; 392 t, Steve Bly/Bly Photography; 393 t, ©Robert Frerck/OP; 393 b, ©Radius/SuperStock; 398-399, Courtesy of the Peace Corps; 404, AGE Fotosctock America, Inc.; 405 (1), David Young-Wolff/PhotoEdit; 405 (2, 3, 4,), Michael Newman/PhotoEdit; 405 b, ©2004 Ulrike Welsch Photography; 406 tr, Jimmy Dorantes/Latin Focus.com; 406 bl, ©Jenny Matthews /Alamy; 407, b, Comstock Images/Alamy; 409 br, Puerto Rican Foundation For Conservation; 410, Chris Hamilton/CORBIS; 412, ©Fernando Alda/CORBIS; 413 t, Steve Raymer/NGS Image Collection; 413 b, ©Jenny Matthews /Alamy; 414 t, Marcelo Salinas/LF; 414 b, SuperStock, Inc.; 415, bl, W. Lynn Seldon Jr./D. Donne Bryant Stock Photography; 415 t, Ro De La Harpe/Animals Animals/Earth Scenes; 415 br, Jeremy Horner/Panos Pictures; 416 b, Mary Kate Denny/PhotoEdit; 417 t, A. Ramey/PhotoEdit; 417 b, SuperStock, Inc.; 418 t, Bob Daemmrich/SB; 418 b, Bruce Farnsworth/Chuch Place Photography; 419 t, Jonathan Nourok/PhotoEdit; 419 b, ©Robert Fried/Digital Railroad; 424-425, Courtesy of Bizbirije/Primer Impacto;©Univisión Communications Inc. 2002, All rights reserved; 424 inset, Dalí, Salvador, Portrait of Luis Buñuel, 1924. Oil on canvas. .70 x .60 m. Coll. Luis Buñuel, Mexico City, D.F., Mexico. ©2009 Salvador Dalí, Gala-Salvador Dalí Foundation/Artists Rights Society (ARS), New York. Photo: Bridgeman-Giraudon/Art Resource, NY.; 430, Reuters NewMedia Inc./CORBIS; 431, ©Dario Lopez-Mills/AP Images; 432 l, David Young-Wolff/PhotoEdit; 432 r, Michael Newman/PhotoEdit; 434 b, ©Bob Daemrich/Stock Boston/Aurora Photos; 436 b, Steve Chenn/CORBIS; 437 b, David Young-Wolff/Photo Edit, b, Jeremy Horner/CORBIS; 439 b, Noticiero Univisión; 440 t, Scott Barrow/IS; 440 b, ©Michael Bussy/CORBIS; 441 l, Russell Gordon; 441 r, Joe Viesti/The Viesti Collection, Inc.; 443 t, ©Danita Delimont/Alamy; 443 m, David Young-Wolff/PhotoEdit; 443 b, ©David R. Frazier Photolibrary/Alamy; 448-449, ©Dallas & John Heaton/Stock Connection/Digital Railroad; 448 inset, Picasso, Pablo (1881-1973). Reading the Letter, 1921. Oil on canvas, 184 X 105 cm. ©2009 Estate of Pablo Picasso/Artists Rights Society (ARS), New York. Photo: Réunion des Musées Nationaux/Art Resource, NY.; 454 b, ©Robert Frerck/OP; 455 b, Candida Höfer/Biblioteca de la Real Academia de la Lengua Madrid IV; 456, Michael Newman/PhotoEdit; 461, t, © J. Griffis Smith/Texas Department of Transportation; 463 bl, Jeff Greenberg/IS; 463 br, ©Robert Frerck/OP; 463, ©John Vachon/CORBIS; 466 t, ©2004 Ulrike Welsch Photography; 466 b, Najlah Feanny/SB; 467 t, James Davis/IS; 467 b, ©Robert Frerck/OP.

Text Chapter 6B, p. 307: "¿Quién hace las tareas?" by Matilde de la Vara from *Muy Interesante* – Marzo 2002, No. 250. Published by G Y J España Ediciones, S.L., S. en C. Reprinted by permission. Chapter 8B, p. 409: "*Reduce-Reusa-Recicla*" from La Fundación Puertorriqueña de Conservación & Logo of Fundación Puertorriqueña de Conservación. Copyright © 2001. Reprinted by permission of Fundación Puertorriqueña de Conservación. Chapter 9A, p. 440: Adapted from "¡Apagala!" from *Time For Kids*. April 12, 2002, Vol. 7, No. 22. Copyright © 2002 TIME For Kids. Reprinted by permission. Chapter 9B, p. 456: Adapted from "A sus teclados, listos… ¡a navegar!" Text by Anne-Laure Fournier – Le Ray © Images Doc/Reportero Doc, Bayard Jeunesse, 2002. Reprinted by permission.

Video *¿Eres tú, María?* is based on the novel *¿Eres tú, María?* (from the "Lola Lago, Detective" series) by Lourdes Miguel and Neus Sans, Difusión Centro de Investigación y Publicaciones de Idiomas, S. L. Barcelona, Spain, 1989.

Key D. Donne Bryant Stock Photography = DDB: Image State/international Stock Photography, Ltd. = IS; Latin Focus Photo Agency = LF; Odyssey Productions, In. = OP; The Viesti Collection, Inc. = VC; Woodfin Camp & Associates = WC; Robert Fried Photography = RFP; Stock Boston = SB

Note: Every effort has been made to locate the copyright owner of material used in this textbook. Omissions brought to our attention will be corrected in subsequent editions.